BULLECOURT 1917
BREACHING THE HINDENBURG LINE

Dear Mrs Stewart

I expect that by now you are acquainted with the sad news of Jack's death in action. I know I shall be opening an old wound but felt that I could not let it pass without letting you know of the appreciation of his comrades. I was his intimate pal ... He had the respect of both officers and all the boys in our Coy. We went out together in the fight on April 11th and Jack won everyone's praise in jumping at a machine gun that was troubling us. He probably saved our lives and an officer's, who was himself killed afterwards and would have recommended him for bravery. Jack got the machine gun but unfortunately fell. He suffered no pain but his thoughts were of home.

I will not say any more but all that gets out of the fight in our company will remember him as a man who died as good as he lived, helping his pals. I am sorry it was impossible to get his belongings owing to a counter-attack by the Germans.

May God comfort you in your troubles and if in his mercy God sees fit for me to return I will visit you as I would like to see the people of a dear pal.

Letter from Private Bertram Harry Perry to the mother of Private Jack Stewart.

The author and the Jean and Denise Letaille Bullecourt Museum are always looking to gather further information about the battles of Bullecourt. If you are related to any of the participants of these battles and have photographs, personal testimonies, letters, diaries or any relevant information, please contact Paul Kendall at paul.kendall193@ btinternet.com.

This book is dedicated to Jean and Denise Letaille and the villagers of Bullecourt who have ensured that the soldiers from Australia and Britain who perished in the fight for Bullecourt are never forgotten, and to the memory of my great grandfather, Private William Kendall 44291 22nd Manchester Regiment, who was killed at Bullecourt on 13th May 1917.

Such was the first battle of Bullecourt – a glorious failure; glorious because the Australians were asked to do the apparently impossible and they did it. They penetrated the great Hindenburg line, and held it for hours. It was an ill conceived venture, and the lives of good Australians were sacrificed.

Lieutenant Colonel Raymond Leane, Commanding Officer 48th Battalion AIF.

BULLECOURT 1917

BREACHING THE HINDENBURG LINE

PAUL KENDALL

The
History
Press

Front of jacket: **Above, 2nd Lieutenant
Harold Clarkson's Tank 586; below, the
death of Major Black. (Australian War
Memorial: ART03558), see page 147.**

Title Page: **RFC photograph of the ruins of
Bullecourt, 24th April 1917.**

First published 2010 by Spellmount
This paperback edition first published 2017

The History Press
The Mill, Brimscombe Port
Stroud, Gloucestershire, GL5 2QG
www.thehistorypress.co.uk

British Library Cataloguing in Publication Data.
A catalogue record for this book is available from the British Library.

ISBN 978 0 7509 8178 1

Typesetting and origination by The History Press
Printed and bound by CPI Group (UK) Ltd

CONTENTS

PART 4   MEMORIALS AND CEMETERIES

ACKNOWLEDGEMENTS

This book on the battle of Bullecourt is the culmination of many years of research. I am indebted to many individuals without whose help producing such a work would be impossible. I would like to thank Yves Fohlen for his friendship and for sharing information regarding Bullecourt. Yves spent many months compiling the Bullecourt database which lists all British and Australian soldiers who were killed at Bullecourt during March to June 1917 and was generous in allowing me to use it for research and as a source for the appendices within this book. As archivist at the Jean and Denise Letaille Bullecourt Museum he has introduced me to descendants of the soldiers who fought for this village during 1917. I have spent numerous days walking the Bullecourt battlefield with him, which has helped and inspired me to write this volume. I would also like to extend my thanks to the late Jean Letaille, the owner of the Jean and Denise Letaille Bullecourt Museum who has always given my family and me a warm welcome when we have visited Bullecourt. He and his late wife Denise have done so much to preserve the memory of those soldiers who were killed at Bullecourt and I feel that it is appropriate for this work to be dedicated to them and the fellow villagers who promote remembrance and demonstrate that the French do appreciate those who travelled so far to fight for their freedom and liberty nearly a century ago.

I would like to thank the Trustees of the Imperial War Museum, London for permission to use material from the Department of Documents and Sound Collections, in particular Anthony Richards from the IWM Department of Documents and Margaret Brooks IWM Department of Sound for assisting me in contacting copyright holders. Every effort has been made to contact copyright holders and if anyone has been missed the Publishers apologise and will endeavour to correct the omission on reprint.

I would like to extend my thanks to Major-General Steve Gower, Director Australian War Memorial for his support and advice regarding copyright of AWM documents.

I am grateful to Nicholas Coney at the National Archives for advising me on copyright issues and Judy Noakes of the Office of Public Sector Information for confirming copyright status of London Gazette material. I also appreciate the guidance provided by Cara Downs relating to copyright status of service records held at the National Archives of Australia.

I also thank Bert Innes, from the Gordon Highlanders Museum, Stuart Wheeler, Tank Museum, Bovington, Anne Pedley, archivist at the Royal Welch Fusiliers Museum, Major C.M.J. Deedes (Retd), Rifles Secretary Yorkshire, Jeff Elson, Staffordshire Regiment Museum; Martin Starnes, Surrey History Centre, Justine Taylor, archivist at the Honourable Artillery Company, Helen Jones from the archives of the Keep Military Museum of Devonshire and Dorset, Barry Attoe and Rebecca Tomlinson from The Post Office Archives for providing information and photos. I am thankful to Richard Davies for granting me permission to quote from sources held at the Liddle Collection.

The reader will find short biographies of the soldiers who fought at Bullecourt throughout this book. While it is perfectly possible to follow the narrative without reference to these, it is hoped that they make the sacrifice more accessible, more real; and of course these brief notes are intended as their own kind of inadequate memorial.

I am indebted to all the following relatives who have kindly provided photos and information, as well as giving their time to review the relevant draft pieces. I thank them for their generosity and for allowing me to pay homage to their brave forebears:

PRIVATE WILLIAM ARTERY, 13th Battalion AIF: Wilma Artery (Great niece)
SERGEANT GEORGE BEARDSWORTH, 22nd Battalion Manchester Regiment: Shelagh Cheesman (Great niece)
CORPORAL REGINALD STARMER BILLINGHAM MM, 2nd Battalion Honourable Artillery Company: Judith Gardner (Niece) and Gill Maud (Niece)
2ND LIEUTENANT CUTHBERT BIRKETT, D Battalion: Julie Caspar (Daughter)
PRIVATE WILLIAM BIRTHISEL, 14th Battalion AIF: Shane Birthisel (Great nephew)
2ND LIEUTENANT WILLIAM BLASKETT, 48th Battalion AIF: Malcolm Blaskett (Nephew)
PRIVATE ERNEST BUSBY, 22nd Battalion AIF: Marcia Holdsworth (Great niece)
PRIVATE HERBERT CLARK, 46th Battalion AIF: Helen Turnball (Daughter)
LANCE SERGEANT HARRY CATTERSON, 14th Battalion AIF: Noeleen Ridgeway (Great niece)
PRIVATE WALTER CHATTERLEY, 2nd Battalion Royal Warwickshire Regiment: Kenneth Chatterley (Son)
LANCE CORPORAL WALTER DAKIN, 20th Battalion Manchester Regiment: Judith Wheatley (Granddaughter)

PRIVATE FRANCIS DARE, 18th Battalion AIF: Scott Wilson (Relative)

2ND LIEUTENANT HAROLD DAVIES: D Battalion Heavy Branch Machine Gun Company: Hugh Davies (Nephew) and Bryan Davies (Nephew)

PRIVATE ALBERT DAVIES, 46th Battalion AIF: Kevin Davies (Nephew)

GUNNER ANGUS DRUMMOND, D Battalion Heavy Branch Machine Gun Company: Carol Collins and Charles Drummond (Relatives)

CORPORAL JAMES DUFFUS, 2nd Battalion Gordon Highlanders: Retd Colonel Jim Duffus (Grandson)

CAPTAIN FRANK DUNN MC, 23rd Battalion AIF: Janet Hawkins (Great niece)

PRIVATE AMOS DYER, 13th Battalion AIF: Pat McGufficke (Relative)

LANCE CORPORAL ARTHUR FITZ-JOHN, 2nd/5th Battalion Duke of Wellington's Regiment: Rob Fitz-John (Grandson)

2ND LIEUTENANT SIMON FRASER, 58th Battalion AIF: Max and Maria Cameron (Great nephew)

PRIVATE DAVID FREEMAN, 22nd Battalion AIF: Jacque Stephens (Relative)

PRIVATE NORMAN GILL, 13th Battalion AIF: Jack Gill (Relative)

PRIVATE ARTHUR GRAHAM, 24th Battalion AIF: Elsie Graham (Daughter-in-law)

PRIVATE WILLIE GREAVES, 2nd/6th Battalion West Yorkshire Regiment: Mrs K.J. Lydon (Niece)

QUARTERMASTER SERGEANT ALFRED GUPPY, 14th Battalion AIF: Russell Williams (Grandson)

SAPPER ALEXANDER HAIR, 5th Field Company, Australian Engineers: Glenda and Ian Malcolm (Great nephew)

PRIVATE ALBERT HANNAH, 1st Battalion Royal Welsh Fusiliers: John Hannah (Great nephew)

PRIVATE FREDERICK HARNESS, D Battalion Machine Gun Corps Heavy Branch: Margaret Harness (Great niece)

PRIVATE CECIL HASLER, 2nd/4th Battalion London Regiment: Carole Ridley (Great granddaughter)

CORPORAL ERNIE HAYWARD DCM MM, D Battalion Machine Gun Corps Heavy Branch: Lyn and Grahame Pigney (Granddaughter)

PRIVATE THOMAS HIGSON, 22nd Battalion Manchester Regiment: Peter Higson (Grandson) and David Quarmby (Relative)

PRIVATE HUBERT HOBBS, 2nd/3rd Battalion London Regiment: Jack Hobbs (Son)

PRIVATE CHARLES HUNT, 2nd/4th Battalion London Regiment: David Lane (Great nephew)

LANCE CORPORAL WILLIAM IRISH, 8th Battalion Devonshire Regiment: Alan Quirk (Grandson)

PRIVATE ERNEST JOHNS, 9th Battalion Devonshire Regiment: Gerald Foggins (Relative)

PRIVATE ROBERT JOHNSTON, 22nd Battalion AIF: Christine Baker (Great niece) and Teresa Prince (Great niece)

LANCE SERGEANT CHARLES KAY, 22nd Battalion Manchester Regiment: Brian Kay (Son)

SERGEANT ALFRED KNIGHT VC, 2nd/8th Battalion London Regiment Post Office Rifles: Anne Walsh (Granddaughter)

LANCE CORPORAL JOSEPH KENNEDY, 23rd Battalion AIF: Ron Wilson (Great nephew)

PRIVATE W.T. KING, 2nd/2nd Battalion London Regiment: Annette Chesher (Great Niece)

PRIVATE JOSEPH LAMB, 22nd Manchester Regiment: Simon Lamb (Grandson)

LANCE CORPORAL WILLIAM LAYBURN, 22nd Battalion AIF: Wilf Layburn (Grandson)

PRIVATE NATHAN LEGGETT, 25th Battalion AIF: Ian Pinder (Grandson)

PRIVATE TOM LOXTON, 48th Battalion AIF: David Bomford (Grandson)

PRIVATE JOHN MACCORMICK, 2nd Battalion Gordon Highlanders: Donald MacCormick (Son)

CAPTAIN W.C.D. MAILE: Timothy Maile (Grandson)

PRIVATE CHARLES MALTHOUSE, West Yorkshire Regiment: Janet Coatman (Granddaughter)

PRIVATE OSWALD MCCLELLAND, 13th Battalion AIF: Aaron Pergram (Great grandson)

PRIVATE JAMES MODDREL, 2nd/5th Battalion London Regiment (London Rifle Brigade): James Moddrel (Son)

PRIVATE GEORGE MOPPET, 13th Battalion AIF: Alan Beattie (Relative)

PRIVATE FREDERICK MORLEY, 15th Battalion AIF: Kevin Morley (Great nephew)

PRIVATE FREDERICK MURRIN, 9th Battalion Devonshire Regiment: Neil Murrin (Relative)

SERGEANT CHARLES NEWNS, 2nd/6th Battalion Duke of Wellington Regiment: Michael Newns (Relative)

PRIVATE THOMAS OLDFIELD, 23rd Battalion AIF: Philip Whitehead (Second generation cousin)

RIFLEMAN LEON PAGEOT, 2nd/6th Battalion London Regiment: Marianne Pratt (Granddaughter) and Henri Pageot (Grandson)

PRIVATE CHRIS PARTLON, 16th Battalion AIF: Lesley Reid (Granddaughter)

PRIVATE LESLIE PEZET, 15th Battalion AIF: Ken Pezet (Grandson)

SERGEANT ALFRED PICKLES, 2nd/8th Battalion London Regiment (Post Office Rifles): Paul Baldock (Grandson).

PRIVATE GEORGE PURDIE, 48th Battalion AIF: Judi Eggers (Granddaughter)

PRIVATE WILLIAM PURDY, 20th Battalion Manchester Regiment: Dorothy Rowlands (Granddaughter)

COMPANY SERGEANT MAJOR WILLIAM RATHKE, 2nd/5th Battalion West Yorkshire Regiment: Peter Rathke (Son)

LANCE CORPORAL RAYMOND RICHARDS: Christine Parker (Granddaughter)

PRIVATE JAMES RILEY, 2nd/5th Kings Own Yorkshire Light Infantry: Christopher Preston (Grandson)

SERGEANT CHARLES ROONEY, 46th Battalion AIF: Gayleen Rooney (Relative)

PRIVATE GEORGE PURDIE, 48th Battalion AIF: Norma Rzeszkowski (Daughter)

LEONARD RZESZKOWSKI MM, 16th Battalion AIF: Norma Rzeszkowski (Second generation cousin)

CAPTAIN FRANK SATCHWELL, 2nd Battalion Honourable Artillery Company: Sigrid Duly (Granddaughter)

PRIVATE HORACE SHEPHERD, 48th Battalion AIF: Jillian Thomas (Great niece)

LIEUTENANT MONTAGUE SANDOE, 9th Battalion Devonshire Regiment: Roger Sandoe (Grandson)

PRIVATE ALBERT SHILLABEER, 48th Battalion AIF: Rose Shillabeer (Relative)

PRIVATE NORMAN SIVIOUR, 48th Battalion AIF: Maurice Siviour (Great nephew)

SERGEANT ROBERT SMITH, 21st Battalion Manchester Regiment: Paul Fitzgerald (Grandson)

CORPORAL BERT SMYTHE, 3rd Battalion AIF and Lieutenant Edward Smythe, 24th Battalion AIF: Jacqui Smythe, (Relative)

PRIVATE JACK STEWART, 14th Battalion AIF: Lesley Desborough (Great niece)

PRIVATE HERBERT THOMAS, 21st Battalion, Manchester Regiment: Simon Lamb (Grandson)

PRIVATE ARTHUR TOFT, 47th Battalion AIF: Lloyd Toft (Son)

CAPTAIN PERCY TOFT, 15th Battalion AIF: Lloyd Toft (Nephew)

LANCE CORPORAL GEORGE TWIVY, 2nd/6th West Yorkshire Regiment: Keith Twivy (Grandson)

LANCE CORPORAL STANLEY VINCE, 20th Battalion Manchester Regiment: Clive Mabbutt (Grandson)

LANCE CORPORAL SAMUAL WADESON, 16th Battalion AIF: John Wadeson (Relative)

PRIVATE STANLEY WATSON, 2nd Battalion Borders Regiment: Betty Dixon (Step daughter) and Lynn Dixon (Step Granddaughter)

COPORAL IVOR WILLIAMS, 21st Battalion AIF: Hugh Williams (Son)

PRIVATE JOHN (JOCK) WILLIAMSON, 16th Battalion AIF: John Williamson (Son)

PRIVATE HENRY WOOD, 6th Machine Gun Company, AIF: Dave Cooper and Eileen Ring (Great nephew and great niece)

PRIVATE IAN WOOD, 11th Battalion AIF: Wendy Johnson (Relative)

PRIVATE THOMAS WINTERSGILL, West Yorkshire Regiment: Richard Wintersgill (Grandson)

I am grateful to the following individuals. Neil Conduit for the photo and information relating to Private Albert Hill; John Moore for providing information about Lieutenant Montague Sandoe; and Andrew Pittaway for kindly providing copies of *Reveille*.

I extend my gratitude to Shaun Barrington and the team at Spellmount Publishers for their support and enthusiasm. I appreciate the support given by my friends and colleagues, Gary Shaw and Peter Metcalfe who have taken a keen interest in this project. I am thankful for the support given by Roy and Janet Johnston and enjoyed our trip to Bullecourt. I would also like to thank my parents David and Sylvia Kendall for their support and for the adventures experienced on the various pilgrimages to the World War One battlefields during the past decade. I would also like to thank my partner Tricia Newsome for her encouragement and support.

Please note that when referring to the men who took part in the battle of Bullecourt I have referred to the ranks that they held at the time of the battle.

Paul Kendall, London

2nd Lieutenant Cuthbert Birkett MC, Tank Officer D Battalion, Machine Gun Corps Heavy Branch.

'You need not worry in the slightest about me. I am going on top-hole, the broken foot is very comfy, the amputated one is getting on A1. I get a little pain at the dressings, every other day of the shrapnel wounds, but the doctors and nurses are the last word in kindness and thoughtfulness. The living here is tres bon. I've lived on chicken breasts and champagne etc.'

Letter from No.2 Red Cross Hospital, Rouen, to his father, 21st April 1917

INTRODUCTION

It was doubtful that the allied and German nations could continue to wage war effectively through 1917. Both sides had suffered terribly during 1916. The British and Australians had lost heavily on the Somme, the French Army fought with dogged determination to defend Verdun. The German Army was exhausted as a consequence of these offensives; 1917 would become a year of endurance for all nations. General Robert Nivelle had been appointed as French Commander-in-Chief as a replacement for General Joffre. Nivelle had plans to unleash an initiative in the Chemin-des-Dames during April 1917 with the purpose of breaking through the lines and defeating the German army. In order to assist Nivelle's offensive Haig was asked to launch a British offensive on the Arras front simultaneously, to tie down German reserves in the region and distract attention from Nivelle's campaign in Champagne. General Sir Henry Horne's First Army was ordered to capture Vimy Ridge, which would provide a defensive flank for Third Army commanded by General Sir Edmund Allenby to launch an offensive that would drive east from Arras towards Cambrai. Cambrai was an important communications hub for the occupying German Army. The Fifth Army commanded by General Sir Hubert de la Poer Gough launched a major offensive upon the Hindenburg Line at Bullecourt assisting Allenby's right flank. Bullecourt would consume the lives of approximately 10,000 Australian soldiers and 7,000 British soldiers. The divisions that fought a ferocious battle to capture the village were the British 7th, 58th and 62nd Divisions; together with the Australian 1st, 2nd, 4th and 5th Divisions. They encountered strong resistance from the German 27th Württemberg Division and 3rd Guard Division.

Expectations of a complete victory were high. Germany was fighting a war on the Western and Eastern Fronts. With the escalation of the submarine war upon merchant shipping and the prospect of antagonising American opinion through this strategy against merchant fleets, Germany was fearful of the US entering the war and sending millions of American troops to bolster the depleted ranks of the Allied armies; the weary German Army risked being outnumbered and their lines overwhelmed. The Somme campaign during 1916 had left a bulge in the German line, so in anticipation of an Allied attack on this salient in early 1917, the German Army withdrew to positions where they could prepare for the expected onslaught. General Ludendorff chose to withdraw his forces to a new defensive line he called the Siegfried Line. The British would refer to this new line of defence as the Hindenburg Line, and Ludendorff's strategy of withdrawal would release 10 German Infantry Divisions which would be used to secure their position on the Western Front. The village of Bullecourt was incorporated within the formidable fortifications of this defensive position, containing a network of trenches, concrete machine gun emplacements and dense fields of barbed wire entanglements of various heights.

During April–May 1917 the village of Bullecourt saw heavy fighting as General Sir Hubert Gough's Fifth Army attacked this sector of the Hindenburg Line in support of General Horne's First Army offensive at Vimy Ridge and General Allenby's Third Army thrust east from Arras towards Cambrai. The British assault in this sector of the Western Front was to assist General Nivelle's attack in the south near to Rheims and Soissons, by forcing the diversion of German reserves from the south to the north. Gough suggested the offensive at Bullecourt, but he was only able to launch an attack on a narrow front because he did not have the resources for a large-scale attack. Bullecourt was chosen as the point of this subsidiary attack because it was close to the German second line of defence, called the Drocourt–Quéant Switch, which ran north from the Hindenburg Line. If the British broke through at Arras, then the Germans would withdraw to this secondary defensive line. If Gough could simultaneously capture the junction of the Hindenburg Line and the Drocourt–Quéant Switch close to Bullecourt, then the German Army would be left in a very insecure situation. Switch lines were like swinging gates, where any Allied assault could find itself confined in a deadly salient, within each intersection of trenches they could be confronted by heavily fortified villages and woods. If Gough could capture Bullecourt the Fifth Army could sweep up the Drocourt–Quéant line and meet Horne and Allenby's First and Third Armies in the north.

The Battle at Bullecourt was fought in three stages, commencing with the first attack on 11th April involving 4th Australian Division (I Anzac Corps) and 62nd Division, both commanded by General Gough,

Fifth Army. These Divisions were present with the 2nd Australian Division during the German counter attack at Lagnicourt on 15th April. The Second battle of Bullecourt was fought 3rd–17th May. V Corps comprising the 7th, 58th and 62nd Divisions and I Anzac Corps, including the 1st, 2nd and 5th Australian Divisions, participated in this action. The battle for Bullecourt was one of attrition fought with violent savagery on both sides. After several weeks of terrible fighting, the village was eventually captured; but this was a flawed victory, achieved with the loss of thousands of British and Australian soldiers. The Australian 4th Division had lost 3,289 at the first Bullecourt battle on 11th April, including 1,170 prisoners of the war. This was the highest number of Australian prisoners captured in one place during the war. The second Bullecourt battle fought during May would consume approximately 7,000 Australian and 7,000 British casualties. The overall loss of approximately 17,000 soldiers to capture a village and nearby trenches is appalling. Was the slaughter of so many husbands, fathers and sons from Britain and Australia to capture this objective worth the sacrifice?

The action is associated with much controversy. The first Bullecourt battle came to be regarded as the worst Australian defeat of the Great War when Australian infantry assaulted the Hindenburg Line without artillery and tank support. They were badly let down by the unreliable tanks, but the British tank crews were let down in their turn by their own commanders, who put them in the forefront of the attack in Mark II training tanks, which were prone to malfunction and not armour plated.

The Australian Divisions included many experienced troops who had fought in previous battles during the first years of the war. They had fought Turkish forces on the Gallipoli peninsula during 1915 and fought on the Somme in 1916. The British 7th Division had also gained much experience from the beginning of the war. The experienced soldiers from these divisions would be able to use their initiative when things went wrong on the battlefield at Bullecourt. When they had sustained heavy casualties, losing officers and NCOs, such men from the ranks were able to carry on and try to achieve their objectives despite losing their commanders and despite confronting heavy German resistance. Flesh and blood would charge across No Man's Land at the wire and the German defenders without artillery and tank support. Remarkably large numbers fought their way into the German lines at Bullecourt. The Australians achieved the impossible and cemented their reputation as an effective, reliable and formidable force. Marshal Foch regarded the soldiers of the AIF as 'the finest shock troops in the world'.

Gough, however, committed the 58th and 62nd Divisions, who were untried. It was here that they would learn vital lessons as they experienced battle for the first time – if they survived. It was the experienced battalions from the 7th Division who would capture Bullecourt after a two-week struggle during May 1917. The British forces must be commended for their role in overcoming a strong German defence. They were given a daunting objective. Ordered to go into the ruins of the village fortified by snipers and machine gun emplacements amongst the rubble and against an enemy able to deploy reserves via a network of underground tunnels beneath the village, all three British divisions suffered heavily at Bullecourt but would play an important role in overwhelming the German defence.

The bloody sacrifices made by Australian and British soldiers notwithstanding, the fighting at Bullecourt resulted in the first breakthrough of the 'impregnable' Hindenburg Line. Captain W Maile from the 2/3rd Home Counties Field Ambulance who led stretcher bearers under German machine gun fire to recover British wounded, wrote:

> The battle of Bullecourt was one of the fiercest and bloodiest of the war. Bullecourt was a village of a few hundred inhabitants very strongly held and fortified by the Hun. The only trouble was it caused a nasty bulge in our fairly straight front line. The Higher Authorities strongly objected to this and so decided it must be taken! After weeks of fighting and the efforts of four Divisions with all the necessary guns, it still held out. Of course hundreds of men were killed, but things like that seemed to be of very little importance to the high command. It probably inflated their ego. It required five divisions, roughly 60,000 men, to take the village. We were the last division to have a go after four divisions had failed. Eventually we took it, but at a terrible cost in lives.[2]

The village was reduced to rubble. It was in British hands by the end of May, but the overall objective – to make a sufficient gap in the Hindenburg Line at Bullecourt to enable Gough's 4th Cavalry Divisions to break through the German lines and join Allenby's three cavalry divisions at Arras to deliver a decisive victory and win the war – had failed. The loss of 17,000 men was a disaster and Bullecourt would contain lessons for all military commanders in how not to conduct a battle.

Bullecourt caused much consternation because one nation's army was being commanded by another nation's generals. Bullecourt forced the Australian Government to request direct Australian command of its own men, which would result in the appointment of General John Monash commanding the Australian Corps. The Australian Imperial Force was a highly trained, experienced resource, which would raise its profile from being a colonial support force into a pivotal, dependable fighting machine, one that would help the allies defeat Germany. Lieutenant Colonel Raymond Leane, commander of the 48th Battalion recalled:

As the Australians commenced at Gallipoli on April 25, 1915, so they fought throughout the Great War – always brave and cheerful, and full of dash; frequently directed to do the seemingly impossible. Named storm troops by our enemy, and evidently assessed at that value by the High Command; for it cannot be denied that the Australians were exploited to their fullest extent.[3]

The acrimony between Australian and British command and the politicking amongst all commanders involved with this tragic story has been well documented. This book tackles the subject of Bullecourt from a different angle. Although it features the story of the battle at staff level and provides a narrative of the desperate battle for the village, it focuses on the personal experiences of the men who fought at Bullecourt, how it affected them, how their loss affected their families after the war, and how they are remembered.

My great-grandfather, Private William Kendall, was killed during the battle for the village on 13th May, while serving with 22nd Manchester Regiment. I knew very little about what he did during this terrible war. I was the first member of my family to visit the Arras

Memorial, in April 1999. Since he was listed as missing and has no known grave, his name is commemorated there. Soon after, my father and I made a pilgrimage to Arras and Bullecourt to follow in Private William Kendall's footsteps. Through the help of my friend, Yves Fohlen, the French author and military historian, I was able to discover more about what happened at Bullecourt and surmise what could have happened to my great-grandfather.

Yves' friendship has prompted me to make many pilgrimages to Bullecourt during the past decade. His knowledge is vast. I have been moved to see how the French inhabitants of the village and surrounding region pay homage to the soldiers who travelled from foreign lands to fight for their freedom, a century after the war ended. Their appreciation is displayed by the memorials that they have built. Their attendance and the prominent role they play at the annual ANZAC Day ceremonies in April demonstrate their heartfelt gratitude towards these brave men.

David & Paul Kendall (author) grandson and great-grandson of Private William Kendall, who was killed at Bullecourt on 13th May 1917. This pilgrimage to Bullecourt took place on 4th August 1999, 82 years after the battle. (Sylvia Kendall)

Personally I have experienced a warm welcome from the villagers of Bullecourt. In particular, my family and I remember the kind hospitality of the late Jean and Denise Letaille, who invited us into their home because our ancestor had been killed at Bullecourt so many years ago.

The ANZAC Day ceremony at Bullecourt shows that the war is firmly in the collective memory of Australians who travel so far to commemorate their courageous forebears. The Australian Government sends representatives from the Australian Embassy in Paris and from their armed services each year. Many Australian schools make the journey. Mike Goodwin, a teacher from Mackay School in Queensland, has brought his students on a sombre yet life enhancing experience to visit the World War One battlefields of Turkey, France and Belgium on several occasions. They too play a role in the ANZAC Day ceremony at Bullecourt, ensuring that the Australian soldiers who fought there will never be forgotten.

The British who fought at Bullecourt came from communities throughout Britain including London, Manchester, Yorkshire, Devonshire, Wales and Scotland. Several thousand British soldiers would make the ultimate sacrifice at Bullecourt. Many British men who had emigrated to Australia had also enlisted to join the Australian Imperial Force.

A significant proportion of soldiers killed at Bullecourt have no known grave; 2,249 Australian and 1,876 British soldiers were listed as missing. Among them were veterans of the Gallipoli and Somme campaigns. It is important to analyse the journeys of these men and to look at their experiences prior to Bullecourt. After suffering the ordeals of several battles these soldiers knew what they faced in their attempts to take the village. Those who survived would be affected by their experiences years after the war had ended. Many of the men who were wounded at Bullecourt would endure the discomfort of their wounds for the rest of their lives, while nearly all would carry with them the horrors of their experience, which would impinge on their future lives psychologically. For this reason many soldiers refused to recount their stories after the war and were keen to try to forget.

I hope that I have paid an adequate tribute to these men who fought against tremendous odds to secure a foothold in the formidable Hindenburg Line.

NOTES

1. *Reveille*: 1st January 1934.
2. IWM Department of Documents: IWM 7266/76/65/1: Captain W.C.D. Maile testimony.
3. *Reveille*: 1st April 1933: Lieutenant Colonel Raymond Leane, 48th Battalion testimony.

PART ONE

THE ROAD TO BULLECOURT

CHAPTER 1

THE BRITISH JOURNEY TO BULLECOURT

The 7th Division, 58th and 62nd British Divisions played a significant role in the capture of Bullecourt in 1917. The 7th Division was the first of these units to be deployed to join the British Expeditionary Force in 1914, which was sent to resist the German advance through Belgium. Its battalions would see a great deal of action during the early years of the war. Many of the 7th Division troops who fought at Bullecourt in 1917 had been fighting since August 1914. They had endured the deprivations of a squalid life amidst insanitary conditions. They had to survive in waterlogged, muddy trenches, sometimes in the cold and living off meagre rations. Their nerves were shattered; they were far from home and from their families. No one can really comprehend what these men had gone through. Fighting a determined enemy, they bonded with comrades as they depended on each other to get through each day. Many would see their mates die horrific deaths, which would further derange their shell-shattered sensibilities.

The 7th Division had been established with great haste from three regular battalions who remained in England after the British Expeditionary Force left for Belgium, and from nine battalions stationed overseas recalled to England when the war broke out. The 7th Division assembled at Lyndhurst in the New Forest from 31st August until 4th October 1914. The 2nd Border Regiment came from Pembroke Dock in Wales while the 2nd Royal Warwickshire's and the 1st Royal Welch Fusiliers were recalled from their station at Malta; the 2nd Gordon Highlanders were brought from their post in Egypt; the 2nd Queen's (Royal West Surrey) Regiment and the 1st South Staffordshire's were recalled from the Cape. On arrival in the New Forest they prepared themselves for war. By early October 1914 German

forces were descending upon the Belgian port of Antwerp. On 4th October 1914 the 7th Division received orders to mobilize and join the Royal Naval Division in an attempt to prevent Antwerp from falling into German hands.

The long journey of the 7th Division to Bullecourt in 1917 began at Southampton on 4th/5th October 1914 when it embarked aboard troopships destined for Antwerp. Within four hours of receiving the order to mobilize, the first units of the 7th Division were boarding troopships. The 22nd Brigade from the 7th Division were regular soldiers from the 1st Royal Welch Fusiliers, 2nd Queen's (Royal West Surrey) Regiment, 2nd Battalion Royal Warwickshire Regiment and the 1st South Staffordshire's. Sailing across the English Channel under the protection of the Royal Navy, these units disembarked at the Belgium port at Zeebrugge during 6th/7th October 1914. They were then sent to Bruges and then on to Ghent. They were too late to save Antwerp and were ordered to head for Ypres. At 9.00 pm on 10th October the 7th Division began to march towards Ypres. Reports of German Uhlan patrolling the vicinity were received and they were ordered to march in silence and if they came into contact with the enemy they were to engage them with the bayonet. Soldiers from the 1st Royal Welch Fusiliers had marched 30 miles in 24 hours. Arriving on 14th October exhausted and hungry, for they had not eaten, the 7th Division was ordered to establish a line of defence south east and east of Ypres between Zillebeke and Vormezeele. The battalion was heavily involved in the First Battle of Ypres and when the campaign concluded 37 officers and 1,024 men were lost. Replacements joined the battalion and they took part in the battles of 1915 and at the Somme during 1916.

As German forces advanced towards the Belgian town at Ypres the 7th Division was holding a line from Zandvoorde, south of Gheluvelt, which went northwards straight across the Menin Road towards Zonnebeke. The 2nd Queen's (Royal West Surrey), 1st Royal Welch Fusiliers and the 1st South Staffordshire's were holding the line at Zonnebeke while the Borders and the 2nd Gordon Highlanders were holding the line south of the Menin Road. These battalions held off the German thrust to the sea near Gheluvelt during October 1914. The 2nd Gordon Highlanders held the line near to Kruiseecke. On 23rd October 1914, they held off German attacks under enemy artillery and sniper fire. It was during this action that Drummer William Kenny from the battalion rescued five wounded comrades as shells poured down around him. For his courage he was awarded the Victoria Cross. Three years later he would tend the wounded at Bullecourt.

The 7th Division had played an important role in the defence of Ypres. If the German advance had pushed through their lines during October 1914 at Gheluvelt then they would have taken Ypres and captured the Channel ports, which would have dealt a decisive blow. The entire British Expeditionary Force would have been stranded in France and Paris would have been vulnerable. Arguably, the war would have ultimately been lost if it were not for the 7th Division making a stand at Gheluvelt. They paid a heavy price for holding the line against overwhelming German forces and the battalions suffered heavy casualties.

During the early months of 1915 the men of the 7th Division were given a period to rest, recover and reorganise themselves, before they entered operations again later that year.

During May 1915 the Division was commanded by General Hubert Gough. They were ordered to attack German fortified positions at Festubert, which were untouched by the preparatory artillery bombardment. The battalions from this division would find themselves in a similar position at Bullecourt, where they were ordered to attack the fortified Hindenburg Line despite the enemy defensive wire not being cut. During the Battle of Festubert on 16th May 1915 the 1st Royal Welch Fusiliers suffered heavy casualties as they advanced. Despite the strong resistance they overwhelmed the German defences and captured 100 prisoners, at a cost of losing 19 officers and 559 men.

The 22nd Brigade of the 7th Division would receive a mauling during 1915 at the Battle of Loos, 25th September–8th October. It was a significant moment in British military history because it was the first occasion that the British Army used poison gas. The Germans had used gas at Ypres during April 1915. The British response was a failure because a change of wind direction blew the poison back into the faces of the soldiers of the British battalions. The 1st Royal Welch Fusiliers were overcome by the gas before they left their trenches. As the 22nd Brigade advanced towards the German lines at Loos, they found that the artillery had not smashed the German wire. The German machine gun fire savaged the British units.

After sustaining massive casualties during 1915, the British Army had to reorganise and replace the losses with newly trained and inexperienced recruits. Before they reached Bullecourt in 1917, the 7th Division would suffer the ordeal of the Somme campaign during 1916. The 22nd Brigade was at the forefront of the opening assault on 1st July 1916. The 1st Royal Welch Fusiliers bombed their way along the sunken road trench towards Fricourt. They successfully captured five lines of strongly fortified trenches on a front of 800 yards. The battalion entered Fricourt on the morning of 2nd July 1916. The 22nd Brigade launched an attack on Mametz Wood during the early hours of 5th July. The 1st Royal Welch Fusiliers entered the wood, captured and consolidated the German trench system that defended the wood and fought off two German counter attacks.

The 22nd Manchesters and the 1st South Staffordshire's from the 91st Brigade, 7th Division played a prominent role in the capture of Mametz on 1st July 1916. 2nd Lieutenant Cecil Philcox, who was to later lose his life at Bullecourt, was one of the officers who led the South Staffordshire's in the assault on the village. The battalion advanced 200 yards across No Man's Land towards the German front-line trenches with minimal losses. As they continued the attack towards the German second line trenches they came under heavy German fire from machine gunners positioned at Danzig Alley and from within the village of Mametz. Within fifteen minutes of leaving their starting position they had advanced 700 yards into German lines. They had captured Cemetery Trench, which ran across the southern perimeter of Mametz. The 22nd Manchesters had captured Bucket Trench on their eastern flank. The South Staffordshire's proceeded to enter the ruins of Mametz, until a German counter attack from the north and north-west of the village forced them to pull back towards Cemetery Trench. Small parties from the South Staffordshire's held onto their positions in the rubble. At 9.30 am reinforcements from the 2nd Queen's (Royal West Surrey) Regiment and the 21st Manchester Regiment arrived to support the counter assault upon Mametz. Both these battalions also took part in the battle for Bullecourt in 1917. The 2nd Queen's went to Bucket Trench to support the 22nd Manchesters and the 21st Battalion supported the South Staffordshire's. At 1 pm the 2nd Queen's, supported by an artillery barrage, had captured Danzig Alley, which led north-eastwards from Mametz, The 1st South Staffordshire's simultaneously fought their way back into Mametz, reaching small pockets which had held on throughout the morning. They captured houses in the south sector of the village, and then drove their attack through the centre and up the north-eastern part of Danzig Alley, which had been captured by the 2nd Queen's.

When the 7th Division was relieved on 20th July, they had suffered 7,500 casualties during the first three weeks of the Somme campaign. The 7th Division was back in the line during September when on 3rd September the 1st Royal Welch Fusiliers attacked Guillemont, losing 50 per cent casualties after two days of fighting.

2nd Lieutenant Ralph Cooney, who would command Tank 795 at Bullecourt, had seen action during the Somme Campaign as an infantry officer while serving with the 2nd Royal Scots Fusiliers. On 12th October 1916 Cooney advanced with the battalion in an assault on the Butte de Warlencourt. He was in the rear waves and saw the majority of the attacking force in front of him mown down by German machine gun fire. The battalion made an advance of 150 yards and was forced to withdraw. Cooney later recalled the horror:

The attack we took part in was on 12th October near the Butte de Warlencourt, Ligny Thilloy and le Barque, three villages behind the line. ... we had to attack up a reverse slope where we were quite protected from the Bosch and then over the top of the hill the Bosch had his lines down there; and the Bosch had a very powerful machine gun barrage rigged up. The preliminary bombardment did not disturb it. The result was we attacked in four lines one after the other and as each one went over the top it got caught in this machine gun fire and was wiped out. I was in the last column and I found myself in all this peat. I got myself down into a hole and stayed there until it was dark. How I was not hit in that attack I never can remember. I had bullets through my hat, I had a belt with a pistol and a bullet had gone inside the belt and out through the buckle through my trousers.[1]

After several months of fighting on the Somme, battalions were severely decimated compelling the British Army to be reorganised. The 2nd HAC (Honourable Artillery Company), which would assault Bullecourt on 3rd May 1917, would form part of that reorganisation process. The fresh battalion replaced the 2nd Royal Irish of the 22nd Brigade, 7th Division, on 2nd October 1916. The 2nd HAC was a territorial unit which had been formed at the start of the war. It had remained in England during the first two years of the war and its sole purpose was to train and send replacement men to bolster the 1st HAC fighting in France.

Private William Parry-Morris had joined the 2nd HAC on his 18th birthday on 23rd April 1915. Parry-Morris was a law student studying at the University of Edmonton, Alberta, Canada, when war broke out. His father was a reservist and was recalled to England to serve in the British Army and brought his family with him. His father made William promise that he would not enlist until he was aged 18 and he honoured that promise. He chose to serve with the HAC because he met an officer from the regiment on the passage from Canada to England. He had to enlist at the headquarters at Armoury House, Finsbury Pavement in London. It was his first visit to London and he found it difficult to find his way around the capital. Before entering the headquarters to enlist he was accosted by a woman who presented him with a white feather. 'I said "you can have it back in half an hour"'.[2]

The enlistment process was swift. 'I was accepted as a volunteer straight away and given my uniform and everything within two hours.'[3] After completing basic training Parry-Morris and the 2nd HAC carried out guard duties at the Tower of London during 1915. Apart from guarding the Main Gate and Wharf Gate, they also took part in the Ceremony of the Keys, which took place each evening, as well as guarding the Bank of England and the Royal Mint.

The steady pace of daily sentry duty was tame for the young men of the battalion. Parry-Morris considered his experience at the Tower as 'boring'[4] and was keen to get to the Western Front and play an active role in the war.

Wounded soldiers from the 1st HAC brought home to recover from wounds sustained on the front would tell of the horrors of war to the inexperienced soldiers from the 2nd HAC. Despite being told how bad life was in the trenches, Parry-Morris wanted to get to the war in France as soon as possible.

During August 1916, the 2nd HAC received orders to mobilize. Lieutenant Colonel Albert Lambert-Ward was assigned as battalion commander towards the end of September 1916. Lambert-Ward had served with the HAC since 1893 and when he was appointed Commanding Officer of the 2nd Battalion he had been commanding Howe Battalion of the 63rd (Royal Naval) Division on the western front. They were given 10 days embarkation leave. The 2nd HAC marched from the Tower of London at 6 am on 1st October to Victoria Station. There was no fanfare, no ceremony, no Londoners lining the streets of the city of London to say farewell. They travelled by train to Southampton where they embarked aboard the paddle steamer *La Marguerite*. Nine hundred soldiers from the 2nd HAC arrived in Havre in October 1916. They were then sent by train to Steenwerck in Belgium. Here they were met by Brigadier General Steele, commanding officer of the 22nd Brigade, who was not pleased that the experienced 2nd Royal Irish were to be replaced by the 2nd HAC, a Territorial battalion with no experience. The battalion took over trenches at Ploegsteert Wood. They spent two weeks in the trenches there during October, 25 yards from the German trenches. Private William Parry-Morris recalled that in the first days the 2nd HAC spent the initial period in the line at Sanctuary Wood, despite the battalion unit history stating that they first deployed to Ploegsteert Wood. Parry-Morris described Sanctuary Wood: 'Very little of the wood left, honeycombed with trenches, but very few trees ... there was not much of the wood left, just a few tree stumps'.[5]

The 2nd HAC very soon would become aware of a particular hazard at Ploegsteert Wood: 'If a shell happened to hit a tree stump, you got some splinters'.[6] Parry-Morris described the intolerable conditions which these men endured while in the line. 'Trenches full of water ... very poor dug-outs, just a hole in the trench wall, nothing like the German dug-outs'.[7]

At Ploegsteert Wood the 2nd HAC sustained their first two casualties. 'One of our fellows, although he was warned not to do it, put his head above the top and was shot through the head straight away'.[8] German snipers were vigilant and the trenches were no place to behave impulsively. Parry-Morris:

> The wood was still standing, very thick wood and very heavily shelled all the time ... our trenches were on the edge of the wood ... plenty of shelling but no attack. The trenches were not very deep because around the Ypres salient, if you dug below 2 or 3 feet in the ground, you struck water at once, so you had to build it up with sandbags.[9]

The 2nd HAC was ordered to deploy to Beaumont Hamel on the Somme during November 1916. They had to march 25 km a day for several days in order to get there. The distance from the Ypres salient to the Somme was a hundred miles. On portable cookers pulled by horses, cooks would prepare food as the battalion marched. They first experienced life on the Somme at Bertrancourt, near Beaumont Hamel. At Beaumont Hamel the 2nd HAC took part in the Battle of Ancre. Parry-Morris remembered feeling 'apprehensive' prior to the attack. 'Remember going over the top, did not see any Germans at all, they retreated, but we took the German trenches and I had to dig in to make sure we could hold them, and we stayed there for two days and two nights'.[10]

'We were fired at ... they did not retreat until we attacked them ... machine gun fire and plenty of shells'.[11]

> On our right when we attacked at Beaumont Hamel, the 51st Highland Division went over on the right of

us and they had a lot of casualties and I can always remember talking about bayonets, seeing a dead Gordon Highlander and a dead German, each with a bayonet in each other lying in a shell hole. They killed each other with bayonets.[12]

The 2nd Battalion HAC had sustained 30 to 50 casualties during their baptism of fire. They had returned to Bertrancourt to their billets, but would go back to Beaumont Hamel where they held the line during the cold winter of 1916–17. 'Awful, the mud at Beaumont Hamel was terrible, waist deep in some places ... very miserable, very cold too'.[13]

Seven days in trenches then seven days out of the line were spent at Bertrancourt in huts. Sleep deprivation while in the trenches became a problem: 'Difficult to sleep, trenches were full of mud and our dug-outs were very poor'.[14]

Vermin were everywhere. Parry-Morris described how rats feasted upon the fallen: 'There were some German dug-outs on the slope behind the front line and I was wondering around them one night and there were three dead Germans lying in one of these dug-outs and the rats had been eating their faces'.[15]

> We called lice chats. We were absolutely alive with them. We had to take our shirts and vest off, turned it inside out and run a candle along the seams of the shirt to kill all the eggs. There were absolutely hundreds of them ... it is not an exaggeration to say that there were a couple of hundred on you.[16]

By April 1917 the 7th Division was commanded by Major General Thomas Shoubridge and all units, including the 2nd HAC who joined the Division in late 1916, had gained valuable experience during the short time that they had served on the Western Front.

The 62nd (West Riding) Division commanded by Major General Walter Braithwaite was formed in 1915. These men were recruited from Yorkshire. The 62nd Division arrived in France on 13th January 1917 and had entered the line on 15th February on the Ancre sector of the Somme. Although most of his men had not been tested in battle, Braithwaite had been Chief of Staff to General Ian Hamilton during the Gallipoli campaign and consequently had some knowledge of how not to fight a war. Held in contempt by some Australian commanders for his role in Gallipoli, it may have been politically insensitive to place Braithwaite close to I ANZAC Corps at Bullecourt. Though he had been personally affected by the war. His only son Valentine Braithwaite, serving with the 1st Somerset Light Infantry, was killed at Beaumont Hamel on 2nd July 1916, listed as missing. When the 62nd Division was holding the line on the Somme during February

1917 Braithwaite spent precious spare hours searching shell holes in vain for his son.

The 62nd Division did have some experienced soldiers within its ranks, amongst them William Watson. At Bullecourt he would die while commanding the 2nd/5th Battalion Kings Own Yorkshire and Lancashire Infantry on 3rd May 1917. During August 1914 he was serving with the Somerset Light Infantry in Belgium and took part in the retreat from Mons. He distinguished himself during this action and was twice mentioned in dispatches. With heavy losses sustained during the 1914 campaign he was able to climb through the ranks quickly. During early 1915 he was promoted to Brevet Major and when he was wounded near Ypres in June 1915 he was in command of his own battalion.

The 62nd Division would experience war for the first time in rearguard actions with German forces as they withdrew towards the Hindenburg Line during March and April 1917. The 58th Division, made up of inexperienced battalions from London, also arrived in France in January 1917 and would be thrown in at the deep end when they were ordered to take Bullecourt during May.

All three British Divisions, the 7th, 58th and 62nd, would suffer through the harsh winter of 1916/17. The freezing conditions made life almost unendurable. Continuous frosts hindered efforts to dig trenches. The food was frozen and difficult to eat. Respiratory diseases including bronchitis and influenza spread quickly throughout the ranks. Trench foot, caused by standing in cold and wet terrain, was common. When the frost thawed the soldiers would have to deal with mud swamps. Lieutenant Gordon Wills wrote of the harsh weather conditions that the 22nd Machine Gun Company endured during that winter:

> We were billeted in a French farmhouse with stone floors. We had five small stoves to warm the quarters, of which one was for the officers and four for the troops. It was infernally cold and there was no alternative means of getting warm except exercising, but one can't exercise and sleep at the same time. So we all sat around the one stove set aside for the officers. Often we invited a Sgt or two or other NCOs to sit with us. That frost lasted 28 days. It ended with snow and sleet and just to celebrate the occasion, we were ordered back to the front line to relieve one of the battalions that had reinforced us when we had come out. The line had broken under German counter attack. We had to go back and restore the line. There is nothing worse than melting mud, which of course happened as soon as it started to rain. After that incident and the break in the weather we had a quiet time for a few weeks. There were occasional scraps but nothing serious. I think both we and the Germans were fed up with the weather and the long cold winter.[17]

NOTES

1. IWM Department of Sound: IWM Ref: 494: 2nd Lieutenant Ralph Cooney.
2. IWM Department of Sound: IWM 9488: Private William Parry-Morris, 2nd Battalion Honourable Artillery Company.
3. Ibid.
4. Ibid.
5. Ibid.
6. Ibid.
7. Ibid.
8. Ibid.
9. Ibid.
10. Ibid.
11. Ibid.
12. Ibid.
13. Ibid.
14. Ibid.
15. Ibid.
16. Ibid.
17. *World War 1 Experiences of my Grandfather*, Gordon Wills, 2005.

CHAPTER 2

THE TANKS FROM CONCEPTION TO BULLECOURT

Tanks had first appeared on the battlefield six months prior to the attack on Bullecourt in April 1917. General Gough would have been aware of their deployment and had seen their potential as well as their vulnerabilities. After all, he had ordered their use during the attacks on Thiepval and Beaumont Hamel during 1916. The landships made their debut on 15th September 1916, during the latter stages of the Somme campaign and from then until 1917 their performance in battle had a mixed reception. A large number of tanks were either late arriving at their designated starting positions at Zero Hour or they completely broke down during the course of the battle. In the few instances when they did reach their objectives and captured enemy positions with minimum loss of life, they were highly regarded.

The failure of the tank at Bullecourt was a watershed in the early stages of tank warfare. It was the first time that they had been used on a small front en masse and the first time that infantry would attack a strongly fortified position supported by tanks alone, without artillery support. So much depended upon the tank at Bullecourt on 11th April. It is therefore important to look at the development of the tank and performance from its first appearance on the battlefield on the Somme through to that disastrous day at Bullecourt.

When trenches were dug from the Swiss border across the fields of France to the Belgian coast, towards the end of October 1914, the war of movement came to an end. Trenches defended by acres of belts of tangled barbed wire caused a stalemate preventing both Allied and German forces from making any advances impossible. The trench barrier would prove to be impassable to existing vehicles. Flesh and bone could not cross No-Man's Land. During early 1915, both sides sought ways of overcoming the obstacle of the unconquerable trenches and barbed wire. The German answer to breaking the stalemate was to use gas. During April 1915, in defiance of the Geneva Convention, German forces unleashed gas for the first time into the Canadian and French lines north-east of Ypres. Whilst prompting international condemnation, the Germans succeeded in making a breakthrough.

The British answer to overcoming the trench was the tank. In an initiative supported by Winston Churchill, the First Lord of the Admiralty, the British Government approved the experimental phase in 1915 and the Treasury provided funds to finance the venture. Lieutenant Colonel Ernest Swinton was one of the main protagonists in the conception of the tank as a new form of weapon. Swinton, from the Royal Engineers, had first suggested using armoured caterpillar tanks as a means to cross trenches in October 1914. In February 1915 Winston Churchill established the Landships Committee led by Eustace Tennyson d'Eyncourt, Director of Naval Construction, whose remit was to oversee the role, design and implementation of armoured vehicles.

The first tank, known as 'Little Willie', was soon built. Swinton produced a report dated 15th June 1915 that detailed the dimensions and specifications of this new armoured weapon. Little Willie did not fit the bill. The tank should be designed within the following criteria: that it should be armour plated in order to protect its occupants from armour piercing bullets; and it should be armed with a light gun or two machine guns for the purpose of destroying enemy strong points. The most important feature was that it should be able to traverse trenches, so it would be necessary for the vehicle to climb a 5-foot bank and cross a trench 5 ft wide. These specifications were sent to Lieutenant Walter Wilson, from the Royal Naval Air Service, and William Triton, who designed the tank. The result was a rhomboid motorized vehicle with a long track length and a low centre of gravity. This new prototype named 'Big Willie' or 'His Majesty's Ship Centipede' would become the prototype for the Mark I tanks. Once they had completed the design, Fosters, based in Lincoln, won the contract to build.

The first use of the word tank was in December 1915. Lieutenant Colonel Swinton wrote of how the name for these armoured vehicles came about:

> Why 'Tank'? Why should a fighting automobile have been so inappropriately named? The reply can be given in two words – for secrecy. In its experimental

stage the machine was known as a 'Land-cruiser' or 'Landship'. But it is a military platitude that the 'element of surprise' – as it is always called in the text-books – has immense value in war; and it was naturally realised that the greatest results to be expected from the employment of this new weapon would be attained if it could be launched unexpectedly, so that the enemy might be caught unprepared to meet it. And when it crystallized into a definite shape, and reached the stage of production, it became obvious that its original names were far too suggestive of the real thing. It was therefore decided to christen it by some non-committal word which would give no inkling of its nature to those not 'in the know', and would, at the same time, be sufficiently descriptive and short to be readily adopted by all legitimately concerned.[1]

Questions were asked by those who were associated with the construction of these machines about their purpose. There were various rumours and speculation circulating regarding their existence. A common rumour was that they were built to transport water across the deserts of Egypt and Mesopotamia to British soldiers who were either stationed or fighting in these regions. Another rumour suggested that they were destined to be sent to the Russian front to be employed as snow ploughs. The idea that these contraptions were designed for carrying water because they looked like a water tank helped in the provision of a cover story. Swinton described the purported role of the tank:

> They are powerfully-engined armed automobiles, enclosed in a bullet-proof casing for the protection of their crews. Propelled on the caterpillar principle, they possess considerable powers of travelling over rough ground, both in crossing trenches, craters, and other cavities, and climbing over raised obstacles such as parapets, can tear their way through wire entanglements, can uproot largish trees, and can throw down the walls of ordinary dwelling-houses. Nevertheless, in spite of their elemental strength and apparent clumsiness, in the hands of skilled drivers they are as docile as trained elephants under their own mahouts.[2]

The first tank ran on its tracks during early January 1916 and after completing trials lasting a month, the potential of the Mark I tank as a means of breaking through the trenches had won over those sceptics and an order for 100 was placed on 12th February 1916. This order was extended to 150 tanks. There were two different designs for the tank which were named 'Male' and 'Female' tanks. The Male Tank was armed with two 6 pounder guns with the purpose of destroying strongly

held machine gun positions. The Female tank was armed with four light machine guns. Swinton:

> The male is par excellence the machine-gun hunter and destroyer. He carries light, quick-firing guns capable of firing shell ... The female, which, in accordance with the laws of Nature, is the man-killer, carries nothing but machine-guns for employment against enemy personnel. Her special role is to keep down hostile rifle fire, to beat back counter-attacks and rushes of infantry.[3]

75 Male and 75 Female Mark I Tanks were constructed by Fosters. As the first batch of tanks was being constructed, Swinton set about recruiting crews. He found suitable recruits for the newly established tank force during March 1916 from within the British Army, from motorized units, the cycling corps, as well as from the Royal Navy.

Six companies were initially formed. Four of those companies were sent to France and took part in the final months of the Somme Campaign September–October 1916. C and D Companies had provided demonstrations to King George V and the Cabinet prior to leaving for France. When the tanks were introduced for the first time in the history of modern warfare in the fields of Picardy, the Somme campaign was three and half months old and in that time British and Commonwealth forces had penetrated four miles deep into German-occupied territory.

As the campaign continued and losses mounted, Field Marshal Sir Douglas Haig, Commander-in-Chief of the BEF, was anxious for a major breakthrough on the Somme before the summer ended. Thiepval and the trenches that formed part of the third German defence line had been objectives for the first day of the campaign and were still occupied by German forces during mid August. Haig was determined to push forward his advance towards Bapaume and capture this third line. In August 1916 Haig ordered Lieutenant General Sir Henry Rawlinson commanding the Fourth Army to make preparations for an offensive to capture the third line of trenches in the middle of September 1916. The plan would involve deploying all the available British Reserve Divisions into an attack north of the Albert-Bapaume Road, which would secure a defensive position on the ridge south of the Ancre valley. At the same time an attack would be driven south of the Albert-Bapaume Road to capture the German third line of trench systems between Le Sars and Morval. If this could be achieved, Haig would send in the cavalry and advance towards Bapaume. Haig was aware of the new weapon, the tank and was very keen to use it to crush enemy wire and enter German trenches.

How were commanders to use this new weapon? Fifty tanks were assigned for operations on the Somme. The first 15 of these tanks began to leave England from 15th August and were transported to France over the following three weeks. Tanks from C and D Company were in forward positions by 10th September and within days they were ordered to take part in an offensive that was to drive through German lines northwards along the Albert–Bapaume Road and pivot on the high ridges south of the River Ancre, to put Haig in a better position to secure Thiepval. At the same time, Haig would also push his front north-east between the villages of Morval and Le Sars, extending the British line. Most of the men from these Companies had not been to France and had not experienced combat.

A demonstration of the tank's manoeuvrability was given to General Joffre, Sir Douglas Haig and the Staff from General Headquarters. A conference was called on 13th September to plan tactics. When was the right time to deploy the tanks? It was essential that the timing was right. If the tanks started too soon then that would attract German artillery fire. If the tanks arrived too late and the infantry reached their objectives ahead of them, no benefit would be gained in using these secret weapons. After deliberation it was decided the tanks should advance so that when they reached the first objective, they would arrive five minutes ahead of the infantry. They would be deployed in groups of two or three and their role would be to engage and overwhelm enemy strong points.

Tank commanders were shown many aerial reconnaissance photos, which meant very little to them. They were however provided with maps with routes marked and compass bearings to be taken, which were useful. However, for every three tanks, only one set of orders and one map was supplied. This made it very difficult for the other two tank commanders to absorb and understand the content of the orders. Matters were further complicated when at 5.00 pm on 14th September, the orders for the drive towards Bapaume were cancelled and new ones were issued verbally. There were no written orders, so all tank commanders had to digest these orders and commit them to memory.

As they tried to digest what was expected of them, the crews were busy testing spare engine parts, adjusting guns and preparing to drive into battle for the first time. They were attracting the curious attention of British infantry units.

A total of 49 tanks were detailed to lead the drive into the German lines on 15th September 1916 in an attack which would become known as the Battle of Flers-Courcelette. Ten tanks were assigned to the Guards Division and seven were allocated to 6th and 56th Divisions. They carried the left flank and would advance from Delville Wood towards the villages of Ginchy and Flers. Eight tanks were to support the central components of the assault and they advanced

between High Wood and east of Martinpuich. 15 Corps was supported by a further 17 tanks as they advanced on the left flank upon trenches between Pozières and Martinpuich.

No one could foresee what the outcome would be. Lieutenant General Sir Henry Rawlinson expressed concern about not having using the tanks soon enough – if they were to prove successful; an odd case of being wise before the event. And if they were to fail in this first attack, then the secret of this new weapon of war would be out. He felt uncomfortable in placing too much reliance upon the tanks. If they were to fail, then the infantry would be vulnerable to heavy casualties. This situation would be echoed at Bullecourt six months later. Gough would place high expectations on the tanks to make a breakthrough, flattening the wire defences to enable the infantry to enter the trenches. Rawlinson was in fear of the tank malfunctioning and exposing his infantry to German machine gun positions. Rawlinson wrote of the dilemma he faced in using the tank in the Flers-Courcelette offensive:

> The presence of the fifty 'tanks' however raises entirely new, but at the same time somewhat problematical, possibilities. Should they prove successful we might lose valuable time and miss an opportunity by confining our operations only to the capture of system (a) [the Combles-Martinpuich line]. On the other hand we may, by expecting too much of the 'tanks', be tempted to undertake an operation which is beyond our power, and which might cause very heavy losses to the 'tanks' themselves and to the infantry engaged in their support. Moreover, if the attack failed, the secret of the 'tanks' would be given away once and for all. Setting aside the enormous value of first surprise the chief asset of the 'tanks' will be lost when they cease to be an unknown quantity. Till the enemy know exactly what they have to deal with they cannot arrange or prepare an antidote. We must therefore endeavour to keep them a mystery as long as possible.[4]

Zero Hour was 6.00 am on 15th September. Seventeen tanks broke down and failed to reach their designated starting points, as they drove in the dark across the mud and shell holes. One tank had to pass through a sunken road, where many dead German soldiers lay. It was a harrowing experience for the tank driver to grind over these bodies. The tank was claustrophobic. Lacking ventilation, temperatures reaching close to 50 degrees Celsius, the air was polluted by cordite fumes from the weapons and carbon monoxide and fuel vapours from the engine. Inhaling the toxic air caused nausea.

As the guns roared and shells fell on German lines, 32 tanks successfully reached their starting positions.

Nine tanks were unable to keep pace with the advancing infantry, but they did prove effective in clearing up enemy positions. Five other tanks were ditched and unable to move; a further nine tanks broke down. These 14 were utilized as rallying points for the infantry. Many of the crews who abandoned these tanks took up arms and joined the infantry on foot.

Nine tanks successfully advanced ahead of the infantry, drove into enemy trenches and caused destruction, but more importantly aroused fear amongst the German defenders as they saw these mechanical beasts for the first time.

Tank 765, commanded by Captain Harold Mortimore, is recorded as being one of the first tanks to enter the battlefield. Mortimore was ordered to support the 14th Division attack upon German trenches east of Delville Wood, then to clear German positions east of Flers. Private Henry Leat, a participant in the first battle at Bullecourt, belonged to the crew of Tank 765 on 15th September 1916.

Infantry from the 6th Battalion Kings Own Yorkshire Light Infantry followed this tank eastwards from Delville Wood and succeeded in reaching the objective and capturing many frightened German soldiers. Mortimore could see the faces of the terrified trench occupants as he opened fire upon them:

> I managed to get astride one of the German trenches in front of the wood and opened fire with the Hotchkiss machine-guns. There were some Germans in the dug-outs and I shall never forget the look on their faces when they emerged and saw my tank astride their trench![5]

Tank 765 was knocked out of the battle when a shell struck the starboard side killing two of the crewmen and disabling the starboard track. Leat was fortunate to have survived the first battle; but his luck would run out at Bullecourt.

Tank D 17, a D Company tank commanded by Second Lieutenant Stuart Hastie, also succeeded in advancing ahead of the infantry and engaging the enemy effectively. Hastie had named his tank 'Dinnaken'. He was ordered to assist the British 122nd Infantry Brigade in their attack upon the German lines near to the village of Flers. One tank from his company, D 14, commanded by Second Lieutenant Gordon Court, was wedged in a support trench when it collapsed beneath them. Second Lieutenant Victor Huffam in D 9 made an attempt to pull D 14 from the trench, but as Huffam brought his tank alongside, his sponsoon became entangled with the sponsoon aboard D 14 resulting in both tanks becoming locked together. It was left to Hastie in D 17 to advance towards Flers alone. The tank had to crash through barbed wire before entering the German Flers

Trench, a barricade in front of Flers. Before reaching the wire the steering gear of Tank D 17 had been hit. In order to steer the tank they had to apply the brake on each track alternatively to maintain direction along the Flers-Delville Wood Road. Encountering mechanical problems as well as drawing enemy fire, they were in a very precarious situation.

In the skies above the Somme, an observer aboard a reconnaissance aeroplane from the Royal Flying Corps reported a 'tank seen in main street Flers going on with large number of troops following it'. There was no infantry following Hastie and his crew in D 17; they were alone and isolated in an enemy-occupied village. Some elements of the 124th Brigade entered the village, but were forced to take cover from enemy shell fire and German machine gunners fortified within the village. With no infantry on hand and damaged steering gear, Hastie and his crew were vulnerable. The tank crew commanded by Lieutenant Skinner that entered the village at Bullecourt would face a similar situation.

The presence of the tank in Flers would did have a damaging affect upon the morale of the German occupiers. The British Press celebrated the prospect of 'a tank seen in the main street of Flers with the British Army cheering behind' and used it to give hope to the British public. Images of the tank would appear in newspapers and on postcards to celebrate the achievement and breakthrough. For the past two years, trench warfare had slaughtered thousands of British soldiers for very little gain. The vision of a tank breaking through the enemy lines and proceeding through a village occupied by the enemy demonstrated that Britain had found a weapon that could trample over barbed wire; which could enter enemy trenches despite German machine gun fire and could assist in the capture and consolidation of enemy positions.

Despite entering Flers and eventually meeting up with British infantry units, Hastie would experience more mechanical problems as he returned to camp. British infantry units were more concerned with consolidation of Flers Trench and without infantry support in Flers itself, Hastie decided to return to the British lines. As they went back the engine seized up, the tracks of the tank had been knocked out by shell fire and the Tank D 17 was immobilized.

Tanks were faltering on other sectors of the Flers-Courcelette battlefield during that day. The six tanks assigned to support the 2nd Canadian Division experienced difficulties. These were commanded by Captain Arthur Inglis from No.1 Section, C Company Heavy Section Machine Gun Corps and they were ordered to assist the Canadians in their assault upon the heavily fortified sugar factory at Courcelette. Inglis wrote a detailed report of his role in the operation and the role of the section. Inglis commanded Tank No 721 or C5, which he named 'Crème de Menthe'. From this report we can follow the movements of the first tank operation in the history of warfare. The Tanks from No.1 Section left their position in Albert at 7pm on 14th September, the night before the battle. Tank C5 was then taken by driver Sergeant G. B. Shepherd along the north eastwards along Albert–Bapaume Road leading the five other tanks in the section. It took over two hours to drive to a fuel dump located near to an advanced dressing station 300 yards south of Pozières at 9.20 pm. They replenished the tank with oil and petrol supplies at a dump and at midnight they proceeded to their starting positions at the Windmill situated north east of Pozières. Inglis and the seven crewmen aboard C5 had no sleep that night. The other crews also lacked sleep. As the tanks made their way through German shell fire to reach their starting position the stub axle broke off on Tank No.522 C2 commanded by Lieutenant F.W. Bluemal. This setback occurred in Pozières and had to be repaired.

Inglis arrived at the start position at 2 am on the morning of 15th September. (Today, the Tank Memorial stands near to the starting positions of No.1 Section C Company.) As they waited they endured a torrent of enemy shell fire. A shell destroyed one of the rear wheels of Inglis's tank. Shell fire damaged the steering wheel aboard Tank No.709, C1, commanded by Lieutenant A.J.C. Wheeler.

Most of the tanks of No. 1 section never reached the sugar factory. 2nd Lieutenant G.O.L. Campbell experienced difficulties when the left track on Tank No. 503 C4 became loose. Under shell fire two of his crew, Corporal C.N. Harrison and Private D.D Cronin, tightened both of the tracks to keep going. Despite the brave efforts of Harrison and Cronin the tank was unable to get to the starting point. Campbell ordered Harrison to take the crew back to base, while he joined Captain Inglis and accompanied him into battle.

Lieutenant Bluemal in Tank 522 C2 that broken a stub axle earlier that morning had further problems at Zero Hour. Bluemal later reported to Inglis:

> We had to adjust the tracks at Zero, before starting off and proceeded to move off (6.20 am); and at 6.50 got stuck at the point 35.a.3.9 owing to being unable to steer properly. The steering gear having been broken, and we had to steer on brakes which was difficult as the crump holes are so numerous and the tank slipped sideways into communication trench. We succeeded in digging ourselves out and started off again, but owing to the difficulty of steering we could not get away from the C.T.[6]

Bluemel and his crew were in a deadly situation as they were wedged tightly in a Communication Trench. Having got his crew out of the tank, they tried in vain to dislodge the vehicle. For an hour they showed great determination and tenacity in trying to free the tank. Under heavy shell fire they made a brave attempt to dig themselves out. They managed to get the tank moving but without the ability to steer they were unable to get it right out of the trench. Despite strenuous efforts to lever the tank with timber Bluemel had no choice but to abandon it and return to British lines. Bluemel later wrote:

> We succeeded in digging ourselves out and started off again, but owing to the difficulty of steering we could not get away from the C.T we then shoved the side up with timber and managed to get the tank on the ground. We were unable to carry on all the time as we were continuously under heavy shell fire. We eventually had to cease work at 8.00 pm owing to the shelling caused by our infantry reinforcements coming up. We removed our gunlocks, fastened up the tank and brought the crew back.[7]

Shell fire had also knocked out the steering gear aboard Tank No.701 C3 commanded by 2nd Lieutenant S.D.H. Clark. They could go no further when this tank was stuck in a large shell hole containing several broken tree trunks. Clark and his crew laboured for three and a half hours to try to dig out the tank while exposed to enemy fire.

Tank No. 709 C1 had its steering wheel damaged by shell fire en route to the starting position. Lieutenant A.J.C. Wheeler, commanding the tank would face further problems with a loose track that had to be tightened before Zero Hour. At 6.20 am they began the advance towards the sugar factory but never reached it; at 7.00 am Tank 709 C1 had bellied, which meant the tracks of the tank were turning round but the tank was unable to move. For nearly four hours the crew, assisted by three Canadian soldiers, tried to dig out the tank. By 10.45 am the German shelling became so intense that it was impossible to continue. Wheeler ordered his crew and the three Canadian soldiers to the rear.

Tank D17 commanded by Lieutenant Stuart Hastie entering Flers. (*The Great War*, Amalgamated Press 1917)

Only two tanks managed to reach the sugar factory at Courcelette. Tank No.504 C6 commanded by 2nd Lieutenant John Allen came through enemy shell fire and engaged the enemy on several occasions heading towards Courcelette. The tank then headed for the factory but found the position to have been captured by the Canadians who had been assisted by Captain Inglis in Tank 721 C5. On seeing that there was no further work for them, they returned to camp.

So Inglis's Tank 721 C5 was the only tank from No.1 Section to assist the Canadian infantry from the 21st (Eastern Ontario) Battalion in overwhelming the garrison at the factory at Courcelette and then capturing it. The Canadians were far ahead of Inglis and were pinned down in shell holes in front of deadly German machine gun fire coming from the factory. Inglis recounted his part in the first tank assault in an official report:

At Zero [6.20 am] we commenced our advance and made for the SUGAR FACTORY, which was my objective. Soon after crossing our front line trench, a group of about 50 Germans came up towards the tank to surrender. Our infantry was well in advance of the tank, and were in the SUGAR FACTORY by the time I arrived; but I was able to make use of my Hotchkiss Guns. I skirted the southern and eastern side of the factory and went up to the trench where our infantry were consolidating. Having found an officer who informed me that the position had been made good, I commenced my return journey, and laid out about 400 yards of telephone wire which I carried on the tail of the tank. In this I was assisted by an officer of the Signals. Before reaching the Windmill the wire drum was smashed in by a shell. I eventually reached a point on the Pozières-Albert Road 300 yards from the Camp, when the track came completely off. The successful way in which we reached our objective and eventually withdrew was due to the very fine driving of Sergt. Shepherd, A.S.C.[8]

Magnus McIntyre Hood was one of the Canadian soldiers from the 24th Battalion (Queen Victoria's Rifles) who had advanced to the sugar factory and bore witness to the first effective use of a tank in battle:

The attack had been held up at this point, and a party of us had to rush up with more ammunition, bullets and grenades, to the 21st Battalion, lying in shell holes in front of the refinery. As we reached them, we saw a 'landship', named the Crème de Menthe, pass ahead, and go right up to the walls of the refinery, its guns blazing. It seemed to lean against one of the walls which collapsed, and the monster roared into the fort, while we could see the Germans streaming out of it, offering an excellent target to the riflemen in shell holes.[9]

The startled Germans also described the tank as a monster. The German infantry holding the trenches were shocked and distressed when they first saw a tank approaching their lines. Although many of the tanks broke down that day, those that engaged with the enemy had a powerful effect upon the senses and morale of these men. They brought fear and terror to an enemy who had defended their trenches with dogged determination. Feldwebel Weinert, serving with the 211th Infantry Regiment wrote of the initial German perception of this new, fearsome weapon of war:

A man came running in from the left, shouting, 'There is a crocodile crawling into our lines!' The poor wretch was off his head. He had seen a tank for the first time and had imagined this giant of a machine, rearing up and dipping down as it came, to be a monster. It presented a fantastic picture, this Colossus in the dawn light. One moment its front section would disappear into a crater, with the rear section still protruding, the next its yawning mouth would rear up out of the crater, to roll slowly forward with terrifying assurance.[10]

German High Command did not alert the German public to the new weapon used by the British at Flers. The thought of the new tanks horrified German commanders for they could see the potential threat could alter the balance of the war.

The role of No.1 Section at Courcelette can be regarded as a partial success because the objective was achieved, however the malfunctioning of the majority of the tanks and damaged sustained to them by shell fire meant that most of the section had failed. Despite the failure, Inglis had shown the potential of the tank as an effective weapon.

Lieutenant-General Julian Byng who commanded the Canadian Corps wrote an assessment of the performance of the tanks during the assault on Courcelette. Overall he was pleased with their role in aiding his Canadian

Tank commanded by Captain Arthur Inglis on way to attack Sugar Factory at Courcelette on 15th September 1916. (Author)

troops in capturing the sugar factory: 'The tanks were very useful at the Sucrerie; they had a fairly good road to reach their objective, and consequently arrived very quickly.'11 Byng was referring to the two tanks which reached the sugar factory and in his report he did highlight the failings of the tank at Flers. These failings would be repeated six months later at Bullecourt.

Byng comments on the lack of synchronization of tank and infantry starting times and the lack of communication between them. He identified the limitations of the tank when travelling over uneven ground. 'It seems conclusively proved that the tanks cannot move over the shell-pitted ground except on rare occasions; but with a fairly good road or track they ought to reach their objective.'12 Byng also recognised their vulnerability to shell fire and mechanical fragility. 'They are very susceptible to injury from shell, and are liable to break down.'13

Despite these failings Byng could see the positive impact of the tank as a means to assist advancing infantry and as a weapon to terrorise the enemy:

> Sometimes the infantry will be far ahead (as in this case) when the tank can come up later and assist in mopping up, and sometimes the infantry may be hung up when the tank may break down the defence. Neither the infantry nor the tanks advance at a level pace. Without doubt, the tanks are a moral support to infantry so long as they are in action, and a good deal of the shrapnel is diverted from the infantry on to them.[14]

In conclusion Byng was certain that reliance should never be placed upon the tank in battle, but only to assist the infantry. 'No action of the infantry should ever be made subservient to that of the tanks. Tanks are a useful accessory to the infantry, but nothing more.'15 If Gough had studied Byng's report he may not have proceeded with the shambolic attack on the Hindenburg Line at Bullecourt in April 1917.

Major General R.E. Turner commanding the 2nd Canadian Division echoed those sentiments in his report on the action of the tanks from No.1 Section C Company, Heavy Section Machine Gun Corps. He strongly felt that the usefulness of the tank would be in assisting the process of consolidation of captured positions:

> From my experience it seemed that mopping up will, in future, be the chief role of these engines. Tanks suitably placed would release a large number of men, at present required for mopping up, as they would be able to deal promptly with any enemy attempting to resist after the leading waves had passed: it would probably be sufficient to leave a small party to clear dug-outs and round up prisoners. [16]

Turner concluded in his report by highlighting the weak areas of the tank. 'The tanks appear to be immune to everything but a direct hit by something larger than a field gun, except the steering gear and tail which are at present weak spots.'17

The Battle of Flers–Courcelette had demonstrated that the German trenches were no longer impregnable. Providing there were no mechanical breakdowns, or damaged sustained from direct hits by shell fire, the tank could enter German trenches and take out fortified positions. The most important feature of the tank was to invoke fear in the enemy.

The idea of sending men protected by armoured machines across No Man's Land to reaching enemy trenches with minimal casualties was a seductive proposition. Colonel E.D. Swinton later wrote of the necessity to exploit the concept of armoured vehicles:

> That Friday in September, 1916, marked a step forward. It was the beginning of an era in which dwindling manpower will force more and more into prominence the necessity for the conservation of life, and in which the power and insensibility of machinery will have to be as fully exploited upon the field of battle as they have been in history. [18]

The credibility of the tank as a means of breaking through was further enhanced 11 days later at Geudecourt on the Somme. On 26th September one tank, D 14, commanded by 2nd Lieutenant Charles Storey, advancing with infantry, attacked Gird Trench, located south east of the village of Geudecourt. When the infantry were held up by strong resistance in Gird Trench, D 14 was called upon to attack the trench in support of the infantry. With the aid of a low flying reconnaissance aeroplane they were able to enter the trench. This sole tank approached the enemy from the southern end of the trench. At the same time the aeroplane was flying above and firing its own machine gun. D 14 drove along Gird Trench attracting heavy enemy fire until the petrol was exhausted. German bullets penetrated inside the cabin of the tank and all but two of Storey's crew were wounded. The Germans were trapped within their own trench. By 8.30 am, after sustaining many casualties eight German officers with 362 men were waving white handkerchiefs. This trench and the 370 prisoners were captured at a loss of only five casualties. In recognition of the achievement of D 14, Storey was awarded the Distinguished Service Order.

On that same day at midday on 26th September General Gough launched an offensive to capture Thiepval Ridge. Soldiers from the Salford Pals had been wiped out by German machine gunners as they struggled towards this heavily fortified garrison on 1st July 1916. In this second attempt to remove the German occupiers, Gough used the element of surprise to evict them, together with eight tanks. No artillery barrage was fired so as not to alert the enemy. The tanks helped the infantry to enter the German trenches before the enemy machine gunners rose from the deep dug-outs to repel the attack.

The performance of these companies had impressed the British commanders to the extent that Haig ordered production of 1,000 tanks and that each of the six existing companies be expanded into a battalion. Volunteers to form these battalions were selected from motor machine-gun batteries and from other corps within the British Army. A, B, C and D Battalions would be formed in France, E and F in England. Each battalion would consist of three companies that would contain 12 tanks. Tanks had been assigned to the Machine Gun Corps as a cover and for pay and administration purposes.

As mentioned, Male tanks with 6-pounder naval guns on the port and starboard sides were to engage fortified positions. Female tanks carried two machine guns on the left and right turrets, with the purpose of chasing and hunting down enemy infantry units. Tanks would carry 25 rounds of 6-pounder ammunition for both left and right guns. Female tanks would carry a dozen boxes of machine gun ammunition for both sides with 1,000 rounds in belts or in drums for Lewis machine guns. According to Bullecourt veteran Corporal Ernie Hayward, aviation fuel was used in the tanks. Tanks could travel at 9 or 10 mph downhill and at 4 mph uphill.

D Company had been withdrawn from the Somme region on 27th November 1916 and sent to billets in the Blangy-sur-Ternoise area. With the expansion of the Heavy Section Machine Gun Corps and in order to incorporate new tanks and recruits into a branch that would evolve into the Tank Corps, it was decided that D Company would form the nucleus for the newly formed D Battalion. Brigadier General J. Hardress Lloyd DSO was appointed commander of D Battalion. He had previously commanded the 1st Inniskillen Fusiliers. The battalion would comprise three companies: Nos 10, 11 and 12, each company being organised into four sections. No. 11 Company, commanded by Captain H Mortimore, would take part in the first attack on Bullecourt. No.12 Company commanded by Major J.J. Joyce would take part in the second battle of Bullecourt. Reinforcements for D Battalion were drawn from infantry, MMG (Motorised Machine Gun Branch) and Cyclists Corps who were already based in France. These men would take part in the Battle of Bullecourt and some of them had already experienced combat. Lieutenant Hugh Swears had seen action in a tank. 2nd Lieutenant Ralph Cooney serving with the 2nd Royal Scots Fusiliers advanced on the Butte de Warlencourt on 12th October 1916 and witnessed the majority of the attacking force being wiped out by German machine gun fire. Cooney also experienced battle inside a tank when he commanded one during the assault in Vimy Ridge on 9th April 1917, three weeks before taking

Tank D 14 commanded by 2nd Lieutenant Charles Storey, capture of Gird Trench Geudecourt on 26th September 1916. (Author)

A British tank attacking German occupied trenches at Beaumont Hamel November 1918. (Author)

The potential of the tank in modern warfare was realised during the Somme campaign in 1916. Britain had found a way of crossing No Man's Land in defiance of barbed wire and machine guns. (Author)

part in the second Bullecourt battle. 2nd Lieutenant Harold Clarkson was another tank commander who had seen action before Bullecourt. Clarkson was an insurance clerk before the war. When war erupted he enlisted and served in the Royal Army Medical Corps as a Private prior to transferring to the Northumberland Fusiliers where he was commissioned as a 2nd Lieutenant.

Clarkson had been wounded on 1st July 1916 when the Northumberland Fusiliers advanced on La Boiselle on the first day of the Somme campaign. 2nd Lieutenant Herbert Chick is another example for he had served at Antwerp during 1914 and Gallipoli in 1915 as a rating with Hawke Battalion, Royal Naval Division. Chick would command a tank during the second Bullecourt battle.

These reinforcements arrived at Blangy-sur-Ternoise during December 1916. The officers and NCOs were sent on a maintenance and driving course at Bernicourt, which lasted a week. Further training was given to everyone in the battalion on the use of the 6-pounder naval gun and Lewis machine gun. They also developed infantry, reconnaissance and signalling skills as well as receiving instruction on Anti-gas measures and physical training.

During January 1917 tactical training involving dummy tanks took place. This was a very bizarre experience for the men who took part. Corporal Ernie Hayward remembered the primitive methods of training tank crews using mock-up tanks made of wooden frames and canvas:

> We could not get tanks so we had mock-up tanks, a wooden frame, with a canvas screen around it and go lumbering about over trenches and ditches and all sorts of things and imagine that we were in some sort of tank. It was not on wheels, but carried by the crews being trained.[19]

Hayward regarded these eccentric efforts with amusement and recalled that the crews regarded these mock up tanks as 'a latrine'. He remembered that a crew of seven would be involved and 'sometimes the right gunner would fall in a hole and he would have to be dug out'.[20] The purpose of this training was 'to enable the tank commander to get familiar with his crew and give tank movement orders'.[21]

2nd Lieutenant Ralph Cooney (commander of Tank 795 at second Bullecourt) also recalled how tank crews were trained during the early days of the Tank Corps:

> We had the weapons; they existed, not in the tanks but on mountings in the training area. We had not got the vehicles; they were all in workshops teed up for the next battle. We made up mock tanks out of hessian and wood, which we carried about and pretended that they were tanks. For our technical training we went across to Bernicourt where the headquarters was and where they had a stripped down tank in a marquee. It was a very cold winter and it was all frozen up.[22]

As tank crews were being trained fifty Mark II tanks were being built from December 1916 to January 1917. The Mark II Tank was never intended to be used in combat

British tanks support the Canadian Infantry assault upon Vimy Ridge on 9th April 1917. (Author)

and they were only built for training purposes. The Mark II was identical to its predecessor, the Mark 1 Tank except the tail had been removed and it was unarmoured, as the steel was not heat treated to resist bullets. A crew of eight would be used to drive it and it could travel at 3.7 miles per hour with a range of 23 miles.

On 28th March No.11 Company from D Battalion received 12 Mark IIs and was entrained for Achiet-le-Grand, from where they proceeded to their camp at Behagnies. No.12 Company received eight Mark II tanks and they were taken by train to Mont-St. Eloi before going to their camp at Bois de Moreil.

Eight tanks from No.12 Company would support the Canadian advance on Vimy Ridge on 9th April 1917. Zero Hour was 5.30 am. These tanks left their starting position at Elbe Trench behind advancing Canadian infantry. The tanks proceeded well until they reached the German front-line trench where they found that the intensive bombardment had created shell holes that made it impossible for the tanks to pass. Each of the tanks' commanders had to leave their cabins and lead their tanks on foot. As they went forward the tanks ditched between the 2nd and 3rd German lines and remained there until their crew dug them out in the days that followed. Lieutenant Ralph Cooney was a tank commander during the assault on Vimy Ridge:

> There were not any comforts, but there was a certain satisfaction being surrounded with armour which you had not got when you are on your feet outside and that operated until ... one suddenly became aware that all the petrol which was high octane was in big tanks on each side of you and if anything hit that, that was the end of you, but generally speaking the driver and the officer had a comfortable seat to sit on. The gunners had little bicycle seats on which they sat and the secondary gearsman sat on the cold steel.[23]

Cooney understood that the terrain impeded performance at Vimy.

It was snowing and it was 4 o'clock in the morning and quite dark and it was just as lousy as it could be ... When we went up to the line in April at Vimy Ridge ... the poor old tanks just could not make it. The place was just blasted to bits, after ten days bombardment ... you could not get a grip on anything, it was just a sludgy mess. We just got along and eventually we got stuck.

We chugged on and eventually the infantry caught us up, by this time everything was getting a bit disjointed, the barrage had practically finished and the German replies practically were finished and it was just a case of struggling onto the objective and we had gone down. Some of them got to the top of the ridge. They were bogged down when they got to the top where there were Cochshires, the German gunners but that was the end of it as far as we were concerned, I think of no value at all for the tanks. The conditions were hopeless. That was the tendency of the Higher Command was to use tanks in those conditions at Ypres and Passchendaele, hopeless conditions.[24]

The Tank Memorial at Pozières stands close to the position where the first tanks used in warfare went into action on 15th September 1916. (Author)

One of the four tank sculptures that adorn the Tank Memorial at Pozières. The ruins of the Windmill, which was captured by the Australians, can be seen in the background. (Author)

Two days later eight tanks from No.11 Company would be thrown into the Battle of Bullecourt. Within three weeks, Cooney would command Tank 580 into the second battle of Bullecourt.

NOTES

1. *The Tanks*, Colonel E.D. Swinton CB, DSO Royal Engineers, George H. Doran Company, New York 1918.
2. Ibid.
3. Ibid.
4. IWM Docs Fourth Army papers: proposals for attack on 15th September 1916.
5. *The Tanks at Flers*, T. Pidgeon, Fairline Books 1995: p148.
6. National Archives: WO 95/1047: Lieutenant F.W. Bluemel report.
7. Ibid.
8. National Archives: WO 95/1047 Captain A. Ingliss Report of Operations of the Tanks of No.1 Section 'C' Company' HSMGC.
9. IWM Department of Documents: IWM REF 7376 76/169/1: Magnus McIntyre Hood.
10. *The Tanks at Flers*, p132.
11. Ibid.
12. Ibid.
13. Ibid.
14. Ibid.
15. Ibid.
16. National Archives: WO 95/1047 Major General R.E. Turner's report on the actions of the tank on 15th September 1916.
17. Ibid.
18. *The Tanks*.
19. IWM Department of Sound: IWM Ref: 7029: Corporal Ernie Hayward DCM, MM, D Battalion Machine Gun Corps Heavy Branch.
20. Ibid.
21. Ibid.
22. IWM Department of Sound: IWM Ref: 494: 2nd Lieutenant Ralph Cooney.
23. Ibid.
24. Ibid.

CHAPTER 3

THE AUSTRALIANS' PATH TO BULLECOURT

For the Australians, the path to Bullecourt began 12,000 miles distant and would take them via Turkey to the Western Front in France and Belgium. The battles into which they would be propelled before reaching Bullecourt would help the Australians establish their esprit de corps and the soldiers of the Australian Imperial Force would develop into a professional army. Despite the perception that they lacked discipline they demonstrated their abilities as soldiers during the disastrous Gallipoli campaign of 1915, the shambles of Fromelles in 1916 and the bloody battle of Poizeres in August 1916. It was through these bitter battles that the digger spirit was developed, feelings of mateship and looking out for your cobber were the defining characteristics of the Australian soldier. Thrown into poorly planned campaigns, often by commanders who had no concept of how to fight a modern war, bonds were nurtured as they were compelled to stick together to ensure that they got through. By the time they were confronted with the formidable defences of the Hindenburg Line at Bullecourt, they had developed into a professional fighting force that could win through against all odds.

When the First World War broke out, Australia, as part of the British Empire, was obligated to fight. A contingent of 20,000 men, the 1st Division AIF (Australian Imperial Force) was raised to be sent as an expeditionary force to support Britain. Many of the soldiers who fought at Bullecourt had enlisted to join the AIF as volunteers in 1914. Some men were motivated by loyalty to King and Empire, while others saw it as an experience, an exciting adventure that would take them abroad and be over and done with before Christmas.

It is quite something to ask men living on the other side of the world to interrupt their lives, give up their jobs, say goodbye to their families and loved ones in order to join up and fight for freedom and liberty in a place which had no direct effect upon their own lives; but many men volunteered.

The battalions who fought at Bullecourt on 11th April contained volunteers from across Australia. The origins of the 4th Brigade battalions show this. The 13th

Battalion was created in the last week of September in New South Wales. The 14th Battalion was raised in Melbourne, Victoria, towards the end of September and recruited men from the city and its suburbs. The 15th Battalion was formed in Queensland and also took recruits from the island state of Tasmania. The 16th Battalion was established six weeks after the war had begun on 16th September 1914. 75% of soldiers recruited in September 1914 originated from Western Australia, while the remainder was drawn from the state of Southern Australia. The 13th, 14th, 15th and 16th Battalions would be joined together to create the 4th Brigade commanded by Colonel John Monash.

The 16th Battalion conducted basic training at Blackboy Hill. After completing basic training many soldiers who had enlisted in 1914 embarked on troopships bound for Egypt. The recruits expected to be sent to France but Turkey had entered the war.

The battalions from the 4th Brigade embarked on troopships on Boxing Day and began a six-week passage across the Indian Ocean. The destination was not disclosed. The 18,500 ton troopship HMAT *Ceramic* carried 72 officers and 2,632 ranks from the 15th and 16th Battalions. Percy Toft, a private from the 15th Battalion who would serve at Bullecourt wrote of his thoughts as he left Port Melbourne aboard HMAT *Ceramic*:

> With a steady pulse the boat moved westwards – whilst we gazed at the fast fading shores. Our hearts and minds were full, as, in a calm sea, we moved forward to the Great Unknown, and left our country, former days and youth.[1]

HMAT *Ceramic* first sailed for Albany, Western Australia which was the rendezvous point with 16 other troopships. The convoy would be protected by one Australian submarine, AE2. The soldiers were assigned positions onboard for the passage. The berths were very cramped. Toft lived in a tiny area which accommodated 20 men. Here they would eat and sleep. Every space onboard was utilised. 'On board together there were nearly three and a half thousand souls, and although our ship was huge, it would have been impossible to carry them all, had not the men slept in hammocks, clearing the mess tables.[2]

The food was poor, a daily diet of bread, jam and rabbit stew. There was plenty of time for training during the long passage. Harry Murray recalled training hard while aboard and becoming quite proficient with the bayonet. Though the men still had a lot of time on their hands. Many gambled on the lengthy voyage. Private Bert Smythe serving with the 3rd Battalion AIF had set off for the war on 20th October 1914. Smythe was destined to die at Bullecourt. He wrote home to his parents:

There is a lot of gambling done here by the men. Nearly everyone on board indulges in it. The other day four men were arrested for having money on them that they could not account for to the satisfaction of the police.[3]

It was only natural that arguments would erupt within these close confines. When tempers became inflamed, disagreements were settled in the boxing ring. Toft wrote of these boxing matches: 'All arguments were settled on deck with gloves after 5 pm, and what fights they were. Some of the men's efforts were of the highest standard. Some were extremely comical. The spectators may have numbered three thousand.'[4]

Once the troopships left the Australian coast, they headed directly for Aden in the Middle East, while a few others went via Colombo in Ceylon. As they sailed closer to Aden the temperature rose. After leaving Aden the troopships would cross the Red Sea and pass through the Suez Canal. It was here that Private Percy Toft recalled seeing trenches for the first time, guarded by the men from the 1st Australian Division. HMAT *Ceramic* arrived in Alexandria on 1st February 1915 and the following day Toft and the men from 15th Battalion travelled for seven hours by train to Cairo. They were marched from Cairo to camps at Heliopolis where they received further training. The 1st Australian Division would be joined by the New Zealand Infantry Brigade. They would be known as the Australian and New Zealand Army Corps (ANZAC). Lieutenant General Sir William Birdwood, an Indian Army officer, was appointed commander. Known as Birdie, he became a prominent figure during the war. Percy Toft recalled that the 15th Battalion was given a one-day holiday for them to get acclimatized to their new surroundings. After that day the training would commence. Toft: 'We soon realised that life would be different to that which we had before known. Now we were to be trained to fight. We were two months behind the first contingent in training and we were required to work hard. Life was now a serious matter.'[5]

On 4th February their training in Egypt began. They were woken early in the morning to the sound of the trumpets of the Light Horsemen. During the following months, the 4th Brigade were subjected to long route marches across the desert during the day and night which culminated in a simulated battle, to test their endurance, resolve and fighting ability when exhausted. Life was very uncomfortable in the intense desert heat, plagued by flies. Percy Toft:

Our brigade commanders were keen to know the exact limit of endurance. Brigadier General Monash, a civil engineer, was fascinated by strains and applied his measurements to his troops. We were kept at work from early morning to late in the evening. On field days we left the parade ground at 6.30 am and arrived back in camp at 8.30 pm. On the hardest day 35 miles were covered. Over the desert troops marched. Sometimes on hard sand, when men ricked their ankles through rolling on pebbles. Sometimes men trudged through loose sand which covered their boots. Up and down hillocks, battle formations were kept, whilst the sun scorched, the glare hurt the eyes, and dust, stirred by men's feet, hung like a pall. Men's parched throats demanded water.[6]

The intensive training left each soldier with very little time for himself. They would be granted Saturday and Sunday afternoons for leave, except for those men who were detailed to guard or fatigue duties. When they were granted leave Australian soldiers ventured into the chaotic bazaars of Cairo. Not only was there an immeasurable cultural divide between the Egyptians and the Australians, there was also a great divide between the Australian and British armies and there were numerous disciplinary problems when Australian soldiers refused to salute British officers.

The Australian battalions were then sent to Alexandria where they embarked on troopships which would take them to the Greek island of Lemnos, in the Aegean Sea, where they would train for the impending Gallipoli campaign. The terrain at Lemnos was similar to the rugged and steep cliffs they would encounter at Anzac Cove and Cape Helles in Gallipoli. Here they would receive rigorous training in how to disembark off the side of troopships using rope ladders and then climb into small rowing boats. They would practise rowing ashore and climbing steep hills and cliff faces. This training was carried out on a daily basis.

The strike at Gallipoli was driven by the desire to capture Constantinople and knock Turkey out of the war. If the allies controlled the Dardanelles Straits, then they would be able to reach Black Sea ports and send vital aid to Russia. The plan was devised by Winston Churchill, First Lord of the Admiralty, who was frustrated by the stalemate of trench warfare on the Western Front. Poor planning, ignorance of the rugged terrain and under-estimation of the Turkish forces' ability to defend their homeland were key factors in the disastrous campaign.

The 3rd Australian Brigade landed at Anzac Cove at 5.30 am on 25th April 1915. The second assault wave comprising the 1st Brigade followed at 8.00 am. The 1st Brigade would take part in the second Bullecourt battle during May 1917. Private Bert Smythe of the 3rd Battalion, who would later be killed at the second Bullecourt, gave a graphic account of his first horrific experience of war:

> The landing was commenced very early in the morning of Sunday 25/4/15, the 3rd BDE going first and that BDE had the most landing casualties. The Turks were right on the beach, despite the fact that the warships had shelled the place very thoroughly and the first few boat loads of our boys lost heavily but as soon as they got ashore they dug them out with the bayonet. During the whole of the landing the Turks were giving our boys shrapnel a treat and one boat was sunk by a shell exploding on her water line ...
>
> We landed in a bad place, and it's just as well. The Turks were expecting us at another place, and had we gone there we would never have got ashore. They had guns and machine guns, splendid trenches, obstacles, and even barbed wire entanglements and mines in the water to welcome us with. Where we actually did land was not very strongly guarded and we sort of surprised them, and we had got ashore and established ourselves before they could bring sufficient troops to prevent us. Once we got ashore it was just a matter of holding on ... Finally we got on top of a hill with a pretty good trench in it. The fact that it was a Turkish trench didn't worry our consciences in the least. We just took possession of it and inwardly thanked the Turks for saving us the trouble of digging one ... Every few seconds a

shell burst, sometimes near us and sometimes a bit off, and they kept our nerves on edge all the time. Shrapnel looks very pretty. The shell bursts up in the air and makes a pretty cloud of white smoke, and when several burst near each other at the same time the effect is very striking. But when the shooting is good it is very nerve wracking. The shell can be heard some distance off coming with half a scream and half a hiss, culminating in a deafening report as the charge in the shell explodes, and drives 300 bullets in a steep angle to the ground with great velocity.[7]

Although the 3rd Battalion held the cliff top ridges, the Turkish snipers and artillery dominated their position denying them free movement. This was their homeland. They knew the terrain and they would use the features of the gullies and the undergrowth to position their snipers and machine gunners. They held the high ground and dominated the region. The Australians were pinned down during that day. Private Bert Smythe:

> There are only two things that ought to be barred in war and they are artillery and machine guns, they are both fiendish. They shelled us all that day and searched all over the ground with their machine guns and we couldn't do a thing. The whole country is covered with short scrub about three feet high and it's almost impossible to see a man lying down at 20 yds. Of course that style of country just suits the Turks and their snipers and machine guns can work without any fear of being discovered.[8]

While the 3rd Brigade were fighting their way up the cliffs and along the gullies under Turkish fire, men from the 4th Australian Brigade were on the island of Lemnos preparing to join their comrades. Some of the men who were to find themselves fighting through the dense wire at Bullecourt and into the German trenches experienced the trauma of battle on the beaches at Gallipoli that

Australian landing beach at Anzac Cove, 25th April 1915. Many of the soldiers who fought at Bullecourt first saw action on this beach. (Author)

Another view of Anzac Cove, Gallipoli; 600 metres and eight months of misery. The Cove was always under the Turkish guns at Gaba Tepe to the south. (Author)

day. The soldiers that would three years later attack Bullecourt were from the 4th Australian Brigade. Lance Corporal Hugh Orr from the 16th Battalion, 4th Brigade, was a Gallipoli veteran who would fight at Bullecourt. At midday Lance Corporal Orr recalled attending church parade before they set out. The padre giving the service was very blunt, but truthful in his sermon as he prepared these brave men for the worst. 'I remember the chaplain getting up and he said, well boys. I know you are going into action today and some of you will never see another sunrise. That was what he told us.'[9]

The journey to Gallipoli was a short passage and the sounds of the gunfire could be heard soon after leaving Lemnos. The first waves that had landed at dawn were fiercely holding on to their positions as support battalions approached. Orr and the 16th Battalion could observe the battle taking place on the British landing beaches at Cape Helles as they sailed northwards to their own designated landing beach at Anzac Cove. To hear the sound of guns and shell fire and to see it from a distance must have had an effect upon the senses of these men, making them more tense, more anxious about what was about to hit them. Orr:

So at 12 o'clock we had dinner and all that and then started to move out of Lemnos. Shortly after we went out of Lemnos, may be about half an hour or so we were hearing gunfire and we thought we are coming close to it now. The next thing we see is the shape of the land there and seeing little puffs of smoke going up which was the shell fire and that was down at Cape Helles, was the first place we saw. Well, we watched the battle there. You could see the battle but you couldn't distinguish which was which, it was too far out like and we kept going on and going on. We thought this is funny; we are passing by this lot here at Cape Helles. This seems to be where the fighting is but shortly after we see another patch further up. This was up at Anzac. So, we just got up there opposite Anzac. Our signaller was standing not far from where we were and they were signalling from the shore and we said to the signaller what is this then? He said, they want Infantry ashore at once.[10]

Before they reached the beach they had to disembark from their troopships down rope ladders onto smaller vessels which would take them closer to the shore, then they would have to transfer to small boats and under heavy Turkish gunfire row to the beach. The 16th Battalion landed at Anzac Cove at 5.30 pm. Once on the beach they had to dash across the blood-soaked sands to find cover in the cliffs:

So we got orders then to get ready in our fighting orders and get ready to disembark. Well, up comes a

little destroyer called Ribble and there were about 60, I suppose anything up to 60 rope ladders down the side of the ship and this destroyer came up and just came alongside the ship. Never stopped. Just kept moving slowly along and we were climbing down the rope ladders and had to get on the destroyer. Well, we got onto the destroyer and she went in as far as she could until she got into her depth and up came a little pinnace with about eight or nine lifeboats behind it and we got into the lifeboats and off we went to the shore with the pinnace. Well, the pinnace went in as far as it could. Luckily I was on the first lifeboat and when it went in we were up to our knees in water. That was the grounding position for the pinnace. Now, the pinnace came in and cut off and let the boats drift in and our boat being the first boat went into about knee deep in water but I don't know how the others got on. They had to go up to their waist in water but of course, you didn't have time to look. We hopped out of the boat and got on the shore and ran into the foot of the hill as quick as we could.[11]

4th Brigade were landed in the wrong position and organisation on the beach was in disarray with battalions intermingled with other battalions:

Well, we were mixed up a bit because you couldn't help that. There were different regiments on the beach and you just fell in and you marched up. Sometimes there were some of them missing for three or four days from the Battalion. They were supposed to be missing and that and yet they belonged to another unit. Then when they got a chance to get away to that other unit and go relieved from it they came back to their Battalion.[12]

The 16th Battalion was also mixed in with the 26th Indian Mountain Battery, who landed at the same time and were heading inland to reinforce the beach head before night drew in. It was important to move off the beach as soon as possible because the sights of the Turkish guns were trained on the beach. The 16th Battalion ventured up the muddy passage known as Monash Gully in the dark. The fragile beach head secured that morning was constantly being threatened throughout the day by counter attacks from Turkish forces determined to push the Australians into the sea. Orr:

We got up on to a place which was known as Pope's Hill. Just as we got up on to the top of Pope's Hill a New Zealander came by and he said, you better stop here and now and dig in because the Turks are coming down. Well, we stopped there and we got behind the hill and got all ready for the Turks coming and three Turks came down and the New

Zealander, he was an interpreter and he could speak Hindustani and he got on to the three of them. He told us, we were lying just behind him in the trench, now look if these men move don't let them get away because I will give you the word whether they are Turks or not.[13]

Some Indian units had landed during that day with the Australian and New Zealand battalions so it was important to ascertain whether they were friend or foe. Orr continued: 'So he questioned them in Hindustani and they couldn't answer him. So then they admitted that they belonged to the Ottoman Army and with that of course, that started the war as far as we were concerned.'[14]

Pope's Hill was named after Lieutenant Colonel Harold Pope, the 16th Battalion's commanding officer. Orr and men from the 16th Battalion spent the first three days holding onto their positions on Pope's Hill. Between their position and the sea was another hill called Russell's Top, occupied by Turkish snipers.

The 15th Battalion had secured a holding on 15th Battalion on Russell's top Private Percy Toft wrote of these snipers:

> The spur we occupied appeared to run North and South. It formed a right angle with the ridge that extended from Quinn's Post to Courtney's Ridge. At the junction there was a high ridge named 'No Man's Ridge', difficult for either side to hold, owing to nearby enfilade from Pope's Hill and Quinn's Post, and the opposing enemy positions. Enemy snipers made posts there, which permitted them by day to snipe men moving past certain spots in Monash Gully and the bottom of Quinn's Post.[15]

During that first night on Gallipoli the Turks held the advantage. They knew where the Australians were and could direct effective sniper, machine gun and artillery fire upon their positions. All the Australians could do as they clung to the cliffs was to fire in the direction of any light. Private Bert Smythe wrote: 'All night both sides kept up a heavy rifle fire – the Turks firing where they knew our trenches were and our boys firing wherever they saw flame.'[16]

On Sunday 2nd May the 4th Brigade took part in its first assault on the Gallipoli Peninsula. The objective was to secure the ridge adjacent to Quinn's Post, known as the 'Bloody Angle' and was led by the 16th Battalion and supported by the 13th and 15th Battalions. At 7.15 pm the 16th Battalion had begun to climb a ridge that connected Quinn's Post and another position known as 'the Chessboard'. They ascended this steep slope without the enemy firing upon them. It was not until they reached the top of the ridge that they attracted heavy enemy fire from Turkish positions known as the Nek and the Chessboard. They tried to dig trenches as they fought through the night. It was a dangerous task for runners to carry boxes of ammunition to those men holding the top of the ridge and many men were killed. Lance Corporal Percy Black held his position resolutely and kept on firing despite being wounded twice earlier that week. He tenaciously fought off Turkish counter attacks until all his ammunition had been expended.

The following morning the 16th Battalion was compelled to withdraw. The Battalion had landed at Anzac Cove with strength of approximately 1,000 men. Within a month they had been reduced to 300 men.

The 15th Battalion entered the attack with 500 men, but suffered many casualties during that same attack. It was a scale of loss which some within the battalion would experience two years later on the fields of Bullecourt. Private Toft:

> The whole business was sickening ... No noise could swell the volume of the din. Our heads would soon be above the level of the trench where machine guns and rifles had for an hour or more sent dirt, sparks and pebbles flying ... We climbed into the inferno of rifle and machine gun fire ... I moved straight ahead wondering why I wasn't hit. Forward we went to the depression. No-Man's Land appeared to be empty, save for forms that would never move again. Lying down within thirty yards of the enemy's blazing line, I was aware of some of our men. 'Pass the word along, Sergeant Corrigan in command.' I heard this Sergeant's order. 'Prepare to charge!' I rose hurriedly to find only five of us attacking. Five hundred had climbed out of our trench. Sergeant Corrigan seeing the position yelled out RETIRE!'[17]

'What a sorry business it had been? What indescribable stupidity to imagine a surprise could take place? Where were the Staff Officers? Why was not the attack abandoned when it was seen surprise was not possible?'[18] This was Gallipoli 1915, but these were questions which would be asked at Bullecourt in 1917.

On 19th May Lance Corporal Hugh Orr was in action again when the 16th Battalion held Quinn's Post and defended the position against a major Turkish initiative to capture the position:

> I was in Quinn's Post at the time ... You could stand up and just open fire. They came in quite close I suppose. I should say 50 yards. They were running into it at the time. Some of them were firing as they ran. Naturally you are pulling the trigger as you go but they stopped about 50 yards off the trench when they gave it up, stopped coming in. Our fire was pretty heavy I don't mind telling you because

Anzac trenches,
Gallipoli.
(Author)

we were all up there and we were letting them have it as quick as we could. The excitement of battle I think hunted the fear out of you altogether. The excitement of the battle was the thing. You just got up there and fired away as quick as you could pull the trigger and you were letting it go.[19]

Private Percy Toft witnessed the Turkish attack from the position held by the 15th Battalion:

In the afternoon a big Turkish attack launched in front of Quinn's and Courtney's was defeated. We had a fine view of the charge from our parados, but could do nothing to help. The Turks were in swarms ... The battle raged for three hours, the Turkish attack failing badly, with enormous loss of life.[20]

At Quinn's Post, Australian and Turkish trenches were extremely close to each other. The risk of attack was always in the thoughts of the soldiers as they defended their ground. They were within range of Turkish bombs that could be lobbed from their trenches. The men from the 16th Battalion would find themselves in a similar situation when they were holding sections of OG 1 and OG 2 Trenches at Bullecourt three years later. The major difference was that if they faltered and their line collapsed, Turkish forces would push them into the sea. Another contrast to Bullecourt was that on 11th April 1917, veterans from Gallipoli would be fighting in the snow. During 1915, Australian soldiers were fighting a campaign in terrible heat, which would help spread disease and encourage smells from decaying corpses to fill the air. Orr remembered:

It was beginning to get a bit awkward and a nasty smell and all that kicking around the place if you happened to be near them. In some parts of the trench at Quinn's Post you were only about six yards apart and with the attack there and the bombs going in there were a lot of dead men lying all around all over the place. The stench was pretty bad there for a while.[21]

During 6th August 1915 the 4th Brigade AIF in conjunction with the 29th Indian Brigade launched an assault on Hill 971, which was the highest summit in the Sari Bair range. Control of this range would mean control of the Gallipoli Peninsula. They set off during the night in complete darkness four miles north of Anzac Cove and then turned right into the ravines and began the arduous ascent up Sari Bair Range. The operation was a disaster, they entered the wrong gully and their path was obstructed by steep precipices. Turkish machine gunners dominated the region and cut them down. After losing many casualties for this objective Turkish counter attacks forced the Australians from the summit:

We went out from a gully towards the Sphinx. We went out from there towards Suvla Bay and we had to join up, we were supposed to join up with the troops that landed at Suvla Bay but we went out and we had to meet the Gurkhas at a gully just in front of Achi Baba and we got out there and met the Ghurkas at just about daybreak and we had to charge then up this Hill 971. We were after 971 and when we started to drop the Turks were just clearing out. We were just too late to get the gun. They just got out and you could see them round the corner galloping away. Anyhow, we got up on to 971. The Ghurkas were a bit ahead of us. They were a bit smarter than we were and our Navy started firing on them because they didn't know that they were up so high. They were too quick and they fired on them just as they got near the top. Well, we were stopped there and we couldn't go any further. Anyhow, we came back then owing to the failure of the Suvla Bay landing, they didn't get up. We had to come back and connect the line. Save the left flank and that was where the Ghurkas and men out of the 16th Battalion, there were about 60 of them. They were mixed up with the Ghurkas. Well, we held that position for four or five days before we were relieved. Right in the left of the line. That was on top of the Apex and after that they relieved us there. ... we went back down to what they called Hill 60.[22]

The 4th Brigade reorganised on 7th August and launched a further attack at 3.00 am that morning. The men were fatigued and lost direction. At sunrise they found that they were exposed to Turkish machine guns. Bitter close quarter combat took placed that morning. The 4th Brigade lost casualties amounting to 750 men and had no option but to withdraw. The 13th and 14th Battalion, with only 500 men, were thrown into another assault on 21st August. They captured the front-line Turkish trenches but the attack soon faltered.

The 18th AIF Battalion was another unit that would assault Bullecourt in 1917 who took part in the attack on Hill 60 in August 1915. Days after landing at Anzac Cove, they were ordered to capture Hill 60. The battalion entered the battle with 750 men and suffered 383 casualties, half of that number killed.

By December 1915 the allied forces on Gallipoli were exhausted, suffering from disease and feeling dejected at the failure of the campaign to secure Gallipoli. Winter was about to descend and there was no motivation for Allied commanders to continue the campaign. The respected Australian journalist Keith Murdoch wrote a report highlighting the poor conditions that the Australian forces were living under and the low morale of the soldiers. He condemned the command of Sir Ian Hamilton. This report was sent to the Australian Prime Minister Andrew Fisher. He also expressed his opinions to members of the British Cabinet. As a consequence, Hamilton was dismissed as commander of allied forces on Gallipoli. Lord Kitchener visited Gallipoli on 9th November and could see that it was impossible to persist with the campaign. Plans were being made for evacuation.

After eight months of bitter fighting the Australian units began withdrawing from their lines on 18th December and proceeded during the night of 19th and 20th December. There was great relief amongst those leaving Gallipoli; mingled with grief at leaving the 8,141 Australian comrades who died during the campaign. As they quietly made their way down the gullies towards Anzac Cove, they passed the crosses marking the graves of their dead cobbers. Feelings of bitterness that they had died in a futile campaign tainted with failure were strongly felt. It is ironic that the only success on Gallipoli was the evacuation.

After the evacuation from Gallipoli the AIF expanded and reorganised itself. Two new divisions were created in Egypt. When the 4th Brigade arrived in Egypt after the Gallipoli ordeal, half of the remnants from the 13th, 14th, 15th and 16th Battalions were assigned to form the 12th Brigade. For example, the 13th and 14th Battalions were split into two; half of each of the battalions used to form new battalions, so that inexperienced reinforcements would be absorbed into battalions comprised of hardened soldiers who had experienced the Gallipoli campaign. Soldiers from the 14th Battalion were taken to form the 46th Battalion, which would fight at the first Bullecourt battle. Men from the 13th Battalion formed the nucleus of the 45th Battalion, which was held in reserve during the first Bullecourt battle. This measure proved unpopular amongst the Gallipoli veterans who were attached to their battalions, but it was necessary to ensure that each of the new battalions comprised 50% of men with combat experience.

The 4th Brigade arrived in Marseille in June 1916 and would spend two days travelling by train to Bailleul in northern France. They arrived in Bailleul on 10th June and were soon deployed in trenches in a quiet sector of the Western Front at Bois Grenier, near Armentières. The 14th Battalion was the first unit to engage with German forces on 2nd July when a company was sent to raid an enemy trench. They succeeded in capturing a section of the trench but they were forced to retreat when all participants became casualties.

The 54th Battalion, which would play an important role in defending the line at Bullecourt on 15th May, would also see action on the Western Front during July 1916. The battalion was raised from Gallipoli veterans who served with the 2nd Battalion during February 1916 The battalion absorbed new recruits from Australia. They were sent to France in June 1916 and on 19th July this battalion lost 65% casualties during the disastrous diversionary attack at Fromelles, 10 miles west of Lille. Lieutenant General Sir Richard Haking commanding XI Corps ordered the 5th Australian Division and 61st British Division to attack German trenches at Fromelles, which were occupied by experienced soldiers from the 6th Bavarian Reserve Division, Corporal Adolf Hitler amongst them. The purpose of the assault on Fromelles was to divert German battalions from the Somme campaign that was raging in the south. This was another poorly planned assault where Australian troops, together with British infantry from the 61st Division, were ordered to capture trenches that did not exist. They were sent across No Man's Land in broad daylight exposed to heavy German machine gun fire. It was similar to the Bullecourt fiasco. The 54th Battalion succeeded in capturing the first line of German trenches and was expected to advance further to capture a second line of support trenches. These trenches were waterlogged ditches. By 4.30 am on 20th July, the Australians barely held onto their positions in the German lines, as the casualties increased and the supplies of ammunition depleted. Later that morning they had no choice but to retire back across machine-gun-swept No Man's Land to their original lines.

Captain Alfred Morris, 54th Battalion, who endured heavy German shelling at Bullecourt, distinguished himself at Fromelles as a scout officer. His recommendation for the Military Cross:

> He had gone forward with the first wave, but took charge of a platoon as so many officers were casualties. He worked with Lt. Harris in holding the left front. His coolness and resource were very marked indeed. When the left Brigade retired and our left flank was exposed, and the Germans came in, Lieut. Morris took his men through the enemy and although wounded it is stated that he shot two of them with his revolver.[23]

Company Sergeant Major Patrick Mealey was another soldier from the 54th Battalion who distinguished himself at Fromelles, a year before he was killed at

Bullecourt. Mealey won the MM for repelling German counter attacks with grenades.

The 58th Battalion was another Australian unit who fought at Fromelles before seeing action at Bullecourt. 2nd Lieutenant Simon Fraser who was killed at Bullecourt had distinguished himself at Fromelles by going out into No Man's Land on numerous occasions to rescue wounded comrades while exposed to enemy machine-gun fire.

Meanwhile, battalions from the 1st, 2nd and 4th Australian Divisions were assembling on the Somme, destined to take part in the desperate battle for Pozières towards the end of July 1916. They were assigned to General Hubert Gough's Reserve Army, which would later become the Fifth Army. These battalions would fight at Bullecourt in 1917. The first day of the Somme campaign in 1st July 1916 was a complete disaster for the British Army who lost 20,000 men killed. Haig was anxious to capture the German second defensive line on the Somme which ran along Pozières Ridge. It afforded clear observation of the Somme Valley towards Albert and by capturing Pozières, Haig would be in a position to capture Thiepval, still occupied by German forces.

The engagement at Pozières is a precursor to the Bullecourt battle in that the Australians were ordered to attack a strongly defended German position commanding high ground, a German defensive system comprising two trenches. 23,000 casualties were sustained by the 1st, 2nd and 4th Australian Divisions ordered to take Pozières during from 21st July to 30th August. The second German defensive line consisted of two trenches that crossed the Albert–Bapaume Road north of Pozières. The Australians would name the front line OG 1 and the secondary support line, which ran close to the windmill, as OG 2, OG meaning Old German. Australian commanders would name the two German lines in the Hindenburg Line OG 1 and OG 2 at Bullecourt, after the trenches at Pozières.

The most important link is that General Gough, Fifth Army commander, was overseeing this offensive. Haig had ordered Gough to capture the ridge at Pozières without delay on 18th July. The impulsive Gough took Haig's command literally and immediately ordered Major General Harold Walker to send the 1st Australian Division to capture Pozières during the night of the following day. Walker was dismayed by Gough's orders, considering his Division was not on the line and there was not sufficient time to reconnoitre the area. There was no time to plan or prepare the troops. Gough demonstrated the same rash and impetuous side to his character at Pozières as did at Bullecourt. Walker protested to Gough with these arguments and was granted a day to prepare. Further protestations from Lieutenant General Sir William Birdwood, commander of I ANZAC Corps, together with his Chief of Staff Major

General Cyril Brudenell White, persuaded Gough to delay the attack upon Pozières one more day.

After the debacle at Fromelles Haig told Gough on 20th July to pay attention to detail. This was the 1st AIF Division's first action on the Western Front and he did not want another failure. The attack on Pozières was therefore scheduled to take place on 23rd July. This delay allowed the soldiers from the 1st Division AIF to prepare. Jump off positions were entrenched into No Man's Land to reduce the distance to the enemy trenches, reconnaissance patrols were sent out in order to get familiar with the terrain. The attack was launched upon the village from the south at 12.30 am on 23rd July. The 8th Battalion fought a tough, desperate action to capture the village the following day.

From 23rd July for three days, German artillery pulverised the ground at Pozières and inflicted casualties of 5,285 upon the exhausted 1st Australian Division. The 2nd Australian Division, which would play an important role at the second Bullecourt battle, was sent to relieve them.

All British and Australian units heading for Pozières would pass through the town of Albert. Soldiers from the 2nd Australian Division recorded in their diaries the utter devastation of Albert and the derelict terrain. Every soldier would march along the Roman road that dissected the town and pass one of the iconic images of the First World War. Private Oswald Blows, serving with the 28th Battalion, described it as he passed through the town on 27th July 1916:

> Albert is shelled daily – since this morning, a shell has fallen every five minutes, one or two of them rather close to us. I can see the Church of Albert has been badly knocked about, a statue of the Holy Virgin holding out the baby Jesus for the world, standing erect on the top of the steeple is now pointing downwards over the side – a heavy base keeps it from dropping quite over. There is a good sentiment amongst the French people, that if it is knocked completely down by a Hun shell, the German crown will fall with it, or if it falls on its own, then the war will end.[24]

German artillery did not shoot down the statue; British shells eventually did. The statue represented the determined resolution to stand against an oppressive enemy and must have captured the imagination of the Diggers and the Tommies who passed through the town square beneath it.

When the battalions from the 2nd Australian Division reached Pozières, they could see only the remnants of a village, the buildings had been reduced to rubble. Corporal Ivor Williams from the 21st Battalion recalled in his diary the desolation:

Two photos of the ruins of the basilica at Albert. The statue of the Holy Virgin holding the baby Jesus became an iconic image of the First World War. All soldiers who passed through Albert to the frontline during the Somme campaign in 1916 en route to Bullecourt in 1917 would have passed this symbol. (Author)

There is, on the road up, the remains of Contalmaison and woods, now a few scattered bricks and splintered logs and stumps. There is not one spot where one can find one square foot of earth not dug up by shells. Next we come to the remains of Pozières. Here it is something awful. There is not the slightest trace of a house or woods left. In most places even the bricks and tree stumps are missing, having been pounded to dust.

The ground is just honeycombed with shell holes and the whole aspect and contour of the ground is changed. All the old German dug-outs which have been some fine places; are now all practically destroyed and are full of corpses in all stages of decomposition. Some of these are 40 feet below the ground.

The saps, or the remains of same and the ground is just covered with corpses, some terribly mangled and all in an advanced state of decomposition, the stench is something awful.

These are bodies of the Huns, Tommies and Australians killed in the last advance. This is the most awful sight I have ever seen. The shells that pass from side to side are enormous and many. One cannot bear the row at times. During the afternoon I was hit on the back of the head with a log of wood, but luckily, my steel helmet saved me, so now have a fine old lump and a headache.

I never in all my life thought things could be in such a state of desolation and ruin. Even from pictures you cannot imagine the time we are having.

My word it has made a different man of me. There are hundreds of dead and decaying dead lying everywhere. There are arms, legs, pieces of bodies, armless, legless, and headless. They are the most gruesome sights I have ever seen in all my life.

Even after they are dead they could not rest in peace as the shells would land on top of them and blow them to pieces. The casualties are very heavy and we cannot keep pace with the wounded who are lying everywhere and who are being wounded over and over again and being killed in dozens. I think I had better shut up or you will be getting the blues.[25]

The 23rd Battalion was among the Bullecourt units which took part in the battle to capture Pozières. Private Joseph Kennedy from the 23rd Battalion reported in his diary 'The village of Pozières has not got a solid brick left and what was once green woods are now dead and fallen trees. Every yard of ground has been ploughed up by shells. The cemetery close to the village has not an erect tombstone left.'[26]

During 29th July, the 28th Battalion launched an assault to take OG 1 and OG 2 Trenches from the Albert–Bapaume Road to the Ovillers–Courcelette track, together with the 25th and 26th Battalions. The 26th, 25th and 28th Battalions from the inexperienced 7th Brigade were exposed as they assembled along Tramway Trench. They were to capture OG 1 and OG 2 Trenches and so all their assault waves were assembled in great depth along the start line that stretched north from the Albert–Bapaume Road. The Germans shelled along this road regularly. The 28th Battalion was positioned next to this road and was vulnerable to German artillery fire. Private Oswald Blows:

As far as I could judge the Huns were in a sharp angled salient. Our firing line – a captured battered trench – was about 400 yards from the Huns, our hopping-off trench in front in No-Man's Land. The Hun's trenches were in the ridge almost, of a gentle rising slope. We were at this time between the wholly ruined Pozières village, the ridge, our sector taking the road from Albert to Bapaume. The stench was bad from the dead; we'd passed many on our way.[27]

The 28th Battalion was ordered to rush the first trench, while allied artillery bombarded the second German trench line. After six minutes the barrage would lift and the battalion would advance onto the second trench. It was planned to establish an outpost by the ruins of the windmill east of Pozières. Private Oswald Blows wrote in his diary, 'To me this ground is the holiest on earth.'[28]

Under enemy machine gun fire and the light from flares the battalions from the 7th Brigade advanced upon the OG trench system. Men from the 28th Battalion became entangled in the barbed wire. A stretch of uncut wire obstructed their path towards OG 1. Private Blows:

When our line went forward to the wire they were mown down by enemy machine guns, when the wire was reached, it was almost intact. Our guns opened up more at 12.15 and then some played on the barbed wire and amongst our own men, and what with the enemies' artillery (from front and from each side), bombs and machine guns, men dropped in dozens, many on the wire. It was impossible to get through, the barbed barrier was thick, and the enemy being in the know, he put up a living hell. Shell holes were filled with dead, dying and wounded men, and others, and so it was till daybreak, no one retiring until ordered to do so. The boy's all fought gamely, up against certain death whenever they stood up, and the whole ground was swept with shrapnel.[29]

Desperate to force a path through the wire some men used their bare hands to clear the way. German and British shells were falling at the same time in the area. Machine gun crews concentrated their fire upon these men trying to break through the wire:

We knew that under the conditions things were a complete failure, and when orders came, all that remained of us had to retire – to crawl along to an old trench much battered, and many dead there, both ours and the Huns. We would not put our wounded in from No-man's land owing to the intense fire. We pushed our way down this long trench helping the walking wounded and over the top when the trench was levelled. The trench was so full of wounded that any man unwounded who wished to get along had to go along the parapet.[30]

On entering another trench he described it as 'much broken and containing many dead — some most gruesome sights, bodies being in all positions and some awfully mangled, and the stench was awful.'[31]

Supporting waves reached the wire to find their comrades dead, including most of the company commanders. Many Australian officers and men were killed at the wire. The 28th Battalion suffered 400 casualties including their commander Lieutenant Colonel Herbert Collett who was wounded. Private Blows recorded that 695 men were wounded, missing or killed out of 1,000 men from the 28th Battalion. He wrote of his 'thankful deliverance from a living hell.'[32]

The 'living hell' would continue. At dawn on 5th August soldiers from the 22nd and 26th Battalions who were occupying OG 2 and machine gunners and men from the 27th in OG 1 near the Windmill observed German reinforcements coming over the crest of the ridge. All the Australian units fired upon this German party and dispersed them into the shelter of shell holes. Blows saw the German waves advancing towards the line being occupied by the 27th Battalion. His diary extract states that these Germans were forced to advance at gunpoint by their superiors:

The Germans attacked on the front of the 27th Battalion, who were reinforced by us. The Huns advanced in a mob, and an officer behind with a revolver. The enemy wavered before our machine guns and rifle fire, but dared not turn back on all of their officers. The officer was immediately sniped by one of our fellows, when he fell; the Germans threw down their rifles, putting their hands up ran to our trenches shouting 'mercy comrade!' Their own artillery caught many of them, but about 200 came in one trench, and many other smaller parties. One was a Sergeant Major with an Iron Cross – he said he was the only Sergeant Major left amongst the mob (167th Prussian Reserve) and only had the cross presented to him the day before he was captured.[33]

Undaunted by Australian firepower some German units managed to get near to OG 1, more precisely near to machine guns commanded by Lieutenant Percy Cherry positioned between the 25th and 27th Battalions. Only one machine gun crew with two men from the 27th Battalion was there to oppose this German attack.

Captain Cecil Foss from the 28th Battalion was ordered to reinforce this gap in the line between the 25th and 27th Battalions. Remnants of this thwarted German attack were taking refuge in shell holes. Australian snipers and trench mortar shells trapped them. Cherry found himself in a personal duel with a German officer in a nearby shell hole. At one point both officers stood up from their shell holes to fire at each other. The German officer fired a bullet that struck Cherry's helmet. Cherry fired a shot that delivered a mortal wound. Cherry approached the German officer as he lay dying. He could speak fluent English and as Cherry knelt beside him the German asked he could post some personal letter once he had passed them through the censor. Cherry agreed and posted the letters.

OG 2 Trench near to the Windmill was still occupied by German forces. Foss organised an attack with men from the 27th and 28th Battalions. As they attacked from OG 1 many Germans surrendered. As they were sent back to Australian lines as prisoners, they were killed. There is a dispute as to how this happened. It is thought they may have been killed by German shell fire, while other witnesses say that they were killed by Australians bringing up the rear who had mistaken their movements as another German counter attack.

Foss managed to secure OG 2 Trench near the Windmill and set up a machine gun position here. Pozières Ridge was steeped in blood from both sides:

> The living hell was said to be now as bad or worse as any at Verdun. Stretcher bearers did marvellous work ... Casualties were very heavy – saps were levelled for yards together, and I saw such sights as I never wish to see again, dead lying at every turn, men seriously and slightly wounded, strong men crying and shaking from shell shock filled the saps the whole time and we with dispatches had hard times on our journeys. Smelling bad, the ground on which the battered bodies of our missing and dead men ... some of the bodies blown to pieces ... Why should men slaughter one another like this?[34]

The 2nd Division had captured Pozières Ridge. From there they could see the village of Courcelette and the green landscape untouched by shells that stretched towards Bapaume. The only German presence seen from the ridge was stretcher bearers recovering their wounded up the slope. The Australians allowed them to continue their work without interference.

During the ten days that the 2nd Australian Division was on the Pozières front they lost 6,848 soldiers. Many of those casualties were suffering from shell shock. They were relieved by the 4th Australian Division, who would advance upon the Hindenburg Line at Bullecourt and

2nd Australian Division is commemorated on the ruins of the Windmill Memorial, Pozières. The Windmill was heavily contested during the battle of Pozières and was captured by battalions from the 2nd Division. Captain Albert Jacka launched a decisive counter attack north of the windmill during August 1916, to the right of this picture. (Author)

had played a significant role in the defence of the Ridge during 1916.

On 7th August the 4th Australian Division resisted a strong German initiative to recapture Pozières. German forces overwhelmed the Australian lines and the initial phase of the offensive looked successful as they bombed Australian dug-outs and swept over trenches. Many Australians were captured. However, their success was temporary. Lieutenant Albert Jacka VC was in one of the dug-outs with his platoon. Several members of his platoon were wounded by hand grenades thrown into the confined space. A German sentry was ordered to guard the entrance to this dug-out as the main wave advanced towards Pozières. Jacka was undaunted and led eight men up the stairs, shot the German sentry and launched a counter attack from behind the German assault. Jacka's action was seen by other Australians who had become dispersed and disorganised. Inspired by Jacka's fighting spirit they joined in the counter attack from the rear. Jacka's onslaught resulted in the killing and capture of many German soldiers, the rescuing of Australian prisoners and the recovery of lost ground. Jacka had swayed the battle through his initiative, courage and determination.

The last German attempt to recapture Pozières Ridge had failed. Despite delivering a devastating artillery barrage that decimated Australian battalions, the Germans could not regain control.

Once Pozières had been secured, it was necessary to continue the drive to create a salient behind Thiepval, in an effort to isolate this heavily fortified position and cut off the Germans defending the garrison. The 4th Australian Brigade was designated to drive the line northwards to Mouquet Farm. On 8th August the 15th Battalion entered the communication trench close to Mouquet Farm, but was forced to withdraw because the 7th Suffolk's supporting on their left flank had faltered leaving them exposed. The Australian Divisions continued to fight for Mouquet Farm throughout August.

Sergeant Peter Kibble was an original member of the 13th Battalion. He was wounded at Gallipoli on 3rd May 1915 and a year later he demonstrated his courage at Mouquet Farm on 29th August 1916. Kibble was awarded the Distinguished Conduct Medal for his bravery. His recommendation stated:

> During the charge on night 29th August he became separated from his Company; he took charge of a number of men who were leaderless, rallied them, and led them, under heavy machine gun fire, to an enemy trench which was strongly held. At the head of his men he charged and dislodged them, and, after consolidating, he held the trench for over an hour, repelling one counter-attack before he was forced to withdraw in the face of a superior force.[35]

Kibble was wounded at Bullecourt and was killed at a dressing station in the sunken road by a shell.

The Australians had launch 19 successive attacks in their effort to capture Pozières and Mouquet Farm during July and August at a cost of 23,000 men. Pozières, like the Gallipoli campaign, was an arduous conflict that required the soldiers to be mentally and physically resilient in order to endure, carry out their job and survive to fight the next day. It is important to highlight the fact that many of the Australians who fought at Bullecourt during 1917 were veterans of Pozières and Gallipoli. Nearly every soldier who fought at Pozières was affected by shell shock in some way; such was the intensity of the artillery bombardments. Post Combat Stress was not heard of during World War One, there was no treatment or counselling for the thousands of men who suffered from what was described as shell shock in those terrible days. Those Australian veterans who endured Gallipoli and Pozières would assault the Hindenburg Line with their bodies exhausted, their minds haunted by visions of horror and their nerves shattered by shell fire.

NOTES

1. 'Playing a Man's Game': Article in the *Queensland Digger* by Captain Percy Toft MC: 2nd December 1935: Courtesy Lloyd Toft.
2. Ibid.
3. Corporal Bert Smythe Papers: Letter to parents: 25th October 1914: Courtesy Jacqui Kennedy.
4. 'Playing a Man's Game'
5. Ibid.
6. Ibid.
7. Corporal Bert Smythe Papers, Letter to parents: 9th May 1915: Courtesy Jacqui Kennedy.
8. Ibid.
9. Liddle Collection: Lance Corporal Hugh Orr interview: Reference Tape 239.
10. Ibid.
11. Ibid.
12. Ibid.
13. Ibid.
14. Ibid.
15. 'Playing a Man's Game'
16. Corporal Bert Smythe Papers: Letter to parents: 9th May 1915: Courtesy Jacqui Kennedy.
17. 'Playing a Man's Game'
18. Ibid.
19. Liddle Collection: Lance Corporal Hugh Orr interview: Reference Tape 239.
20. 'Playing a Man's Game'
21. Liddle Collection: Lance Corporal Hugh Orr interview: Reference Tape 239.
22. Ibid.
23. Australian War Memorial: AWM 28/1/255P1/0030: Recommendation Military Cross: Captain Alfred Morris.
24. Imperial War Museum: Department of Documents: Private Oswald Blows IWM Con Shelf.
25. Corporal Ivor William's diary: Courtesy Hugh Williams.
26. Private Joseph Kennedy's diary: 5th August 1916. Courtesy Ron Wilson.
27. Imperial War Museum: Department of Documents: Private Oswald Blows IWM Con Shelf.
28. Ibid.
29. Ibid.
30. Ibid.
31. Ibid.
32. Ibid.
33. Ibid.
34. Ibid.
35. Australian War Memorial: AWM 28/1/183P1/0014: Sergeant Peter Kibble DCM Recommendation.

CHAPTER 4

THE CREATION OF THE HINDENBURG LINE

By the end of 1916, Allied forces had taken five months to penetrate a few miles to achieve objectives planned for the first day of the Somme campaign. Haig persisted in pushing forward and wearing down the enemy in a series of battles. Winter would force Haig to abort any further advance. During the summer of 1916 as the Somme campaign was raging, Ludendorff was concerned that if Haig was to adopt the same strategy in 1917, then Germany would not have the military resources to hold the allies back. He knew the allies had 75 Divisions on the Western Front against Germany's 40 divisions. Ludendorff realised that they would be unable to launch a German offensive. He convinced German High Command that a defensive strategy was the best strategy and conceived a plan for the withdrawal of German forces 25 miles across the Somme to newly established defensive positions. He named the defensive system the Siegfried *Stellung* after the third of the four operas in Wagner's Ring cycle. This line of fortified trenches, deeply excavated concrete dug-outs, gun emplacements protected by acres of high density barbed wire entanglements, would be known to the British as the 'Hindenburg Line'. Stretching 85 miles it was built east of Arras and went through Bullecourt to positions in the Champagne region near Soisson. By initiating a withdrawal, Ludendorff would shorten the front by 27 miles and free 10 infantry divisions to be deployed in reserve to bolster sectors where the enemy was making breakthroughs. Work commenced on building the new defensive line during September 1916, unbeknownst to the Allies. In breach of the Geneva Convention 50,000 Russian prisoners of war were forced to work on constructing the fortifications. Hague Rule No. 6 reads: 'The State may employ the labour of prisoners of war ... the work shall not be excessive, and shall have no connection with the operations of war.'

Workers were also drafted from Germany and Belgium to assist in this massive undertaking. Ludendorff ordered that work should be completed by the end of 1916 but because of the enormity of the task, this deadline was unachievable. The severe winter frosts of January 1917 forced the suspension of the construction of concrete fortifications. This certainly hindered the building of defences around Bullecourt. When British troops entered German trenches at Bullecourt, they found large holes in the ground that were incorrectly identified as tank traps. In fact these holes were dug for the foundations of concrete dug-outs and gun emplacements not completed by April 1917 because of the severe winter.

When General von Moser commanding XIV Reserve Corps arrived on the Bullecourt front on 18th March he found that work to construct defences along this sector of the Hindenburg Line had not begun and he was left to organise the construction of temporary defences. It was to von Moser's advantage that Bullecourt was positioned on a ridge, which would allow his machine gunners to look down upon the enemy once they reached these lines. Dense fields of barbed wire were positioned in v-shaped formation, which would break up waves of advancing enemy infantry and force them into carefully positioned traps where machine guns would fire upon them. General von Moser was concerned that if he placed all his troops in the trenches at Bullecourt, they would be wiped out by preparatory artillery barrages. He therefore placed only a small number of his men in the front-line trenches, holding back the majority of his force in reserve. These reserves would be held in strength in the nearby fortified villages of Hendecourt and Riencourt. If the enemy secured a foothold in the trenches then his reserve troops would be deployed. A series of underground tunnels were dug underneath Bullecourt to ensure that reinforcements could be quickly deployed to repel enemy attacks anywhere in the village.

Although construction of the Hindenburg Line was not complete, Kaiser Wilhelm signed the order to initiate the withdrawal of personnel, arms, artillery and material on 4th February 1917. Five days later the Germans began the withdrawal. The operation, code-named 'Alberich', was co-ordinated by Crown Prince Rupprecht of Bavaria, Commander of the Northern

Group of Armies. Thirty five days were scheduled to allow for the withdrawal of infantry, artillery and heavy materiel to positions to the rear of the Hindenburg Line. They kept a small force in place to slowly follow as the main contingent withdrew, to ensure that the enemy would be deceived into thinking that the lines were being held. Each village before the Hindenburg Line would be defended by trenches and wire defences to establish a temporary rear guard action as the heavy guns and equipment were being withdrawn.

Pilots from the Royal Flying Corps who were patrolling the Arras sector first saw evidence that major construction work was underway at Quéant towards the end of October 1916 when they identified fresh earth turned up. After further reconnaissance sorties a report was produced on 9th November 1916, which concluded that the enemy was constructing a trench from Quéant to Bullecourt extending to the German third defensive line at Neuville Vitasse. British intelligence were not aware at this time that the Germans were actually constructing a new major defensive line that would stretch from Arras to the Champagne sector. They failed to piece together the reconnaissance flight evidence with further intelligence received on 8th November from a Russian prisoner of war who had escaped to French lines near St Quentin. He confirmed that 2,000 of his fellow prisoners were constructing concrete dug-outs, protected by thick belts of barbed wire, near to the French town. The work on the Hindenburg Line was not fully monitored by the Royal Flying Corps because of German air superiority and poor weather conditions, which prevented them from observing the line being constructed south of Quéant. *Rittmeister* Freiherr von Richthofen, the celebrated German air ace known as

the Red Baron, was based at Douai aerodrome and posed a great threat to all aircraft from the Royal Flying Corps which flew in the skies above that region. The sorties that did manage to fly over the region might not see anything because of the many gaps in construction during the early stages of building the line. It was not until 15th February 1917 that pilots from the Royal Flying Corps confirmed that a defensive line had been built from Quéant to Bellicourt, north of St Quentin.

On 22nd February 1917, Fifth Army Headquarters had received information about a wireless transmission which was sent on 20th and 21st February to three German Divisions ordering them to prepare to move with all materials and not to leave anything behind. Staff officers from the Fifth Army thought it inconceivable that the German Army would relinquish positions which they had so resolutely defended throughout 1916. It was considered so implausible that when the information was cascaded down to I ANZAC Corps intelligence staff, they did not pass it on to its divisional commanders in the field.

The 2nd Honourable Artillery Company had been holding the line at Beaumont Hamel during the winter of 1916–17. On 23rd February 1917 intelligence reports indicated that German forces were in the process of evacuating the village of Serre. When the 1st Royal Welch Fusiliers sent patrols into the destroyed village at Serre supported by the 2nd Honourable Artillery Company and entered the German trenches, they encountered a small German presence. Private William Parry-Morris recalled:

> We suddenly discovered one night that the Germans had retreated, the German Army retreated all the

Left: **Map of German retreat to the Hindenburg Line. ('Military Operations, France & Belgium 1917' by Captain Cyril Falls: Published Macmillan 1940, map Crown Copyright)**

Above: **Hindenburg Line – Spring 1917** *(The Great War: I Was There)*

way from the Somme, right back to the Hindenburg Line. We followed the Germans up and although they were retreating, they fought what we call rear guard actions in all the villages that they retreated to, they would stop at a village and try to hold us back for as long as they could ... The village of Serre, Gommecourt, Bucquoy ... about eight or nine villages and each time we lost a lot of men in these attacks.[1]

Serre was unrecognizable and had been pulverised by British artillery. The soldiers from the 2nd HAC saw decomposed skeletal remains caught in barbed wire six months previously during the catastrophic first day of the Somme:

> Around the village of Serre were rows and rows of barbed wire, German barbed wire, which had been put up there in 1915 and 1916 and was where one of the places which the British Army attacked on July 1st 1916 and they never even got to the wire. There was so many men killed trying to get to the wire and when we went through the village of Serre in March 1917, their bodies were still hanging on the barbed wire, 30 or 40 of them.[2]

The men were disturbed to see their dead comrades left hanging there; and worse, that they had to leave them without burying them.

After leaving Puisieux, German forces withdrew to the village of Bucquoy. An aerial reconnaissance sortie confirmed that the village was lightly defended and there was evidence to suggest that the enemy were withdrawing. At 1 pm on 13th March, Lieutenant General Fanshawe, commanding 5th Corps, ordered that this village was to be captured during that night if the enemy had not withdrawn. The 2nd Queen's (Royal West Surrey) Regiment and the 22nd Manchester Regiment were ordered to capture Bucquoy. They were given short notice of nine hours, insufficient time for artillery to lay down a preparatory barrage to destroy the German wire. Patrols had been sent close to the village and four reports indicated that contrary to aerial reconnaissance reports provided earlier that day, Bucquoy was strongly held by machine gun positions behind thick barbed wire defences. The 2nd Queen's and 22nd Manchesters had just arrived on the front line and were not familiar with the ground. Major General G. de S. Barrow, commanding 7th Division, urged Fanshawe to delay the attack until dawn, but he was overruled by Fanshawe. The attack was initially scheduled to take place at 11.45 pm on 13th March, but after Fanshawe received a protest from Brigadier General Hanway Cumming, commanding the 91st Brigade, Fanshawe relented and Zero Hour was postponed to 1 am on the morning of 14th March. Brigadier General Cumming requested that the artillery

barrage be postponed until prior to the re-scheduled attack, but his demands were ignored. The British artillery did fire its pre-arranged barrage from 10 until 10.30 pm on 13th March, but it had no effect upon the German defences, and only served to alert the German defenders to the attack. In complete darkness soldiers from the 2nd Queen's and 22nd Manchesters launched their assault. Torrential rain transformed the ground into a morass. Dense barbed wire thwarted their advance and mud clogged their rifles. Machine gun fire from carefully positioned gun emplacements opened fire upon them as soon as the battle began. Small parties from the 2nd Queen's managed to find a way through the wire, as Lieutenant Colonel Longbourne, commanding the 2nd Queen's reported:

> At zero the companies were formed up on the tape previously put out by Second Lieutenant Bingham in advance of the valley tramway line; they then advanced and succeeded in reaching the enemy's front wire, the enemy's artillery fire being intense while his machine guns were active the whole time. It was very dark and raining hard, the ground was very sticky and near the enemy wire it was full of shell-holes, into which many of the men fell and so became unarmed owing to the mud on their rifles preventing the bolts from working. Eventually small groups of men from 'B', 'C', and 'D' Companies, with Captain Driver, Second Lieutenants Furze, Burdon, Smith and Limbrick, succeeded in getting through two lines of barbed wire, only to find on arrival here that their rifles were useless; it was impossible to penetrate the third line immediately in front of Bucquoy Trench.[3]

The wire was impenetrable along the front of the 22nd Manchesters but one company who were advancing on the right flank managed to find a gap in the wire and capture a sector of Arnim Trench. The fragile foothold was secured but this company could not consolidate their position because they had exhausted their supplies of bombs and the remnants found themselves surrounded and captured.

The 2nd Queen's and the 22nd Manchesters had 48 killed, 92 missing and 122 wounded. The survivors were forced to withdraw by 6.00 am. The 22nd Manchester Regiment had lost 150 men during this poorly prepared attack. As the German forces held onto Bucquoy in this rear guard action, they were ensuring enough time for the main withdrawing force to reach the Hindenburg Line.

The 2nd HAC relieved the 2nd Queen's and 22nd Manchester Regiment on 14th March 1916. Lieutenant Colonel Lambert-Ward commanding the 2nd HAC later recalled:

On the evening of March 16th we were ordered to attack the German advanced trenches. I detailed Lieutenant Abbott with his platoon to take them, which he did, meeting with slight opposition, and we handed over the line to the Royal Welch Fusiliers that same evening. The following morning the enemy retired from Bucquoy, and the Royal Welch occupied the village.[4]

Private Parry-Morris from the 2nd HAC:

First we lost some men at Gommecourt, then we had quite a pitch battle in the village of Bucquoy. The Germans tried to hold the village. We made a bayonet attack up the village street and one of my particular pals was killed there.[5]

As British patrols were sent into German trenches they found them deserted. They assumed of course that the German units were retreating, and asked the question, could the war be coming to an end? Lambert-Ward:

On the 18th it was obvious that the Germans had retired, and we moved forward in support of the Royal Welch Fusiliers and the Border Regiment, who followed closely on the heels of the retreating enemy through Puisieux and Ervillers as far as Ecoust, which was still held in strength.[6]

General Gough was keen to push forward, for he had to get his Fifth Army to the Hindenburg Line south east of Arras so that he could be in a position to assist the First and Third Armies offensive in the region, scheduled for early April.

The Australian Imperial Force was experiencing similar problems as it pursued the German withdrawal to the Hindenburg Line. On 18th March 1917 the 21st Battalion AIF had reached Vaux Vraucourt. Private Ivor Williams, a signaller from the 21st Battalion:

Moved to Le Barque, where we stayed till 11 am then moved up to the main Albert–Bapaume Road, via Bapaume to Favreuil and on until we were stopped, or at least, came in contact with Fritz about Beugnatre. We finally got a check near Vaulx-Vrancourt. It is just terrible. ... to complete the destruction, a charge of explosives was put in the cellars of each house. It is a very pretty sight as every village for miles around is in flames.

Bapaume was totally destroyed and left in flames. In fact it is still burning furiously. We are now over three miles past Bapaume. All the main roads here have big craters in them so as to block traffic, his favourite ruse is to blow up the intersecting crossroads and thus destroy four directions at a time.

All the trees lining the roads have been wilfully cut down about a foot from the ground and allowed to fall across the roads and buildings. All the fruit trees have been ringed, thus destroying them forever. Everywhere is wanton destruction and ruin.[7]

On 19th March patrols from the Lucknow Cavalry Brigade confirmed that the villages of Croisilles, Ecoust-St-Mein, Noreuil and Lagnicourt were held in strength by German forces.

During the night of 20th March Gough convened a conference with Lieutenant Generals Fanshawe and Birdwood to discuss the problem of supplying the advancing Fifth Army. The distance between the rail heads and the outposts they had captured was great. Munitions and equipment had to be brought to the advance positions by roads obstructed by trees and shell craters. Gough thought that it was a priority to restore the Ancre Valley railway to Achiet-le-Grand and for the Candas-Acheux Line to extend through Serre and Puisieux to meet at Achiet-le-Grand. In addition to re-establishing railway lines, repairs had to be carried out on the three main roads, Albert-Bapaume, the Hamel-Achiet le Petit-Achiet le Grand Road, and the Serre-Puisieux-Bucquoy-Ablainzevelle Road. This required labour, which was provided by the same troops who had been pursuing the German Army and fighting the rear guard actions. These soldiers would have spent time at the front and when they were meant to be resting in reserve they were expected to work on the communication lines. Lieutenant Colonel Lambert-Ward recalled: 'Instead of resting when we are out of the line, work had to be done on repairing the roads and filling in the gigantic craters with which the Germans sought to hinder the advance of our troops.'[8]

Initially, the German withdrawal gave rise to optimism for some. Private W.T. King who was advancing with the 2nd/2nd Battalion London Regiment wrote in a letter home on 5th April 1917 apologising for not being in contact for a few weeks: 'We must blame Fritzy for that thro' running away. We went out on the 16th to go over the top, and it was a cakewalk.'[9] Private Leslie Pezet was following the German withdrawal with the 15th Battalion AIF. He also recalled the situation when they arrived at Bapaume on 5th April 1917:

Advance of 12 hundred yards only a few casualties and dig in strong posts ... Do not see any Germans, they are on the run, but their guns find many of our lads. Here on the 5th April the Germans shell one section out of their position and at night the section loses the toss and we have to return to take it back. At dusk the fritz shells heavily and we have to go my word ... And do it. After being a bit windy we get on our way and we all get restless and hurry over the ridge, 20 of us all told, and then for two hundred yards we crawl on hands and knees through mud and slush wishing the Germans to hell with the war.[10]

The war was not coming to an end. The Hindenburg Line would be constructed by the Germans on ground of their choosing. They built the line in a way that utilized the natural terrain and would take fewer men to defend. The deep trenches would be built on ridges so that they could command the high ground.

Lieutenant Colonel Howard Denham, commanding the 46th Battalion AIF described these trenches in the post operation report after the first Bullecourt battle. 'These were of the usual type, about 7 feet deep, 2 feet wide at the bottom – duck-boarded and drained – and five to six feet at the top. There are numerous Machine Gun Emplacements – no sign of concrete whatsoever.'[11] He also described the dug-outs: 'Of the usual deep type, about 30 feet underground – boarded but not concrete.[12]

As British forces followed the German withdrawal, intelligence was being gathered from escaped allied prisoners, captured German prisoners and French refugees about the building of the strong defensive line.

As the German Army withdrew to the Hindenburg Line, German engineers embarked on a scorched earth policy. Villages were destroyed as the German Army moved east. The measures included the destruction of all houses within these villages to deny the enemy places to billet. Farmhouses were torched, wells were destroyed, the water contaminated and fruit trees were chopped down. The German Army tore up railway lines, felled trees across roads and mined crossroads, to buy time. Churches were destroyed to ensure that their towers could not be used as observation positions.

Private W.G. Bishop who was advancing with the 2nd /1st Battalion London Regiment described the scene: 'The Germans had returned to the Hindenburg Line, having first devastated the whole area, every crossroad was cratered; every rail or other carriage was destroyed. ... Houses had no doors or windows, roofs damaged, many trees felled, nothing of value left for us.'[13]

The feelings of the residents of these villages can be guessed at. Lieutenant Ernst Junger serving with the German 73rd Hanoverian Fusiliers wrote a detailed account of the bedlam that ensued as he passed through villages on the Somme as they were destroyed around the 13th March:

The villages we passed through as we marched to the front line had the appearance of lunatic asylums let loose. Whole companies were pushing walls down or sitting on roofs of the houses throwing down the slates. Trees were felled, window-frames broken, and smoke and clouds of dust

Bapaume in Ruins – 1917 *(The Great War: I Was There)*

Ruins of Bapaume Church 17th March 1917 *(The Great War: I Was There)*

rose from heap after heap of rubbish. In short, an orgy of destruction was going on. The men were chasing round with incredible zeal, arrayed in the abandoned wardrobes of the population in women's dresses and with top hats on their heads. With positive genius they singled out the main beams of the houses and, tying ropes round them, tugged with all their might, shouting out in time with their pulls, till the whole house collapsed. Others swung hammers and smashed whatever came in their way, from flower pots on the window ledges to the glass work of conservatories. Every village up to the Siegfried line was a rubbish-heap. Every tree felled, every road mined, every water-course dammed, every cellar blown up or made into a death-trap with concealed bombs, all supplies or metal sent back, all rails ripped up, all telephone wire rolled up, everything burnable burned. In short, the country over which the enemy were to advance had been turned into utter desolation.[14]

Lieutenant Colonel Lambert-Ward wrote of the scenes of devastation that the 2nd Honourable Artillery Company observed as they penetrated further into the territory deserted by their German enemy:

> The Germans had devastated the country on their retirement with characteristic thoroughness. Over all that area, which must have extended seventy miles from south to north and ten to fifty miles east to west, there was not a living thing to be seen. Every house, every church, every barn had been either blown up or pulled down. Wells had been destroyed by blowing in the sides or poisoned by dead horses. Enormous craters had been blown at all the important crossroads and in every village street. In all that area there was not a house of any kind left standing, nor was there any shelter to be had except in a few dug-outs which the Germans had failed to destroy.[15]

As British and Australian troops followed the German withdrawal, they were lulled into a false sense of security. Firstly they had no idea that this was a contrived and well planned withdrawal to a strongly fortified position. Premature thoughts of victory made Allied troops complacent as they advanced eastwards. This was very dangerous because the German troops had left trenches, villages and roads booby trapped. Private Parry-Morris who advanced with the 2nd Honourable Artillery Company recalled: 'Wherever you went you had to be careful, because if you tried to pick up something, it was booby trapped ... We lost quite a lot of men.'[16]

Partially concealed boards would be placed across the entrances of dug-outs. The top half would be sticking out so once a Tommy moved the board back into place as a natural instinct in order gain access to the dug-out, a nail behind the door would detonate a charge, killing or disabling the soldier and any comrades nearby. Sought-after souvenirs such as helmets, bayonets and regimental badges were connected to detonators. Chimneys and stoves were booby trapped so whenever a fire was lit, they would explode. An anonymous Rifleman from the Post Office Rifles wrote an interesting account of his experiences:

> In casting one's eye memory back to the German withdrawal on the Western Front in the early part of 1917, a host of place names came to mind, Miraumont, Mory, Achiet-le-Grand, Achiet-le-Petit, Gommecourt, Behagnies, Loupar Wood, to mention but a few, but with the passage of time the association of places with particular incidents has, in my case, faded. But I recall vividly the extreme caution which had to be exercised in the course of our follow-up, which was an uncanny operation in the complete absence of any activity on the part of the enemy, owing to the large number of 'booby traps' which had been set to which in the earlier days some of our chaps fell victim, in some

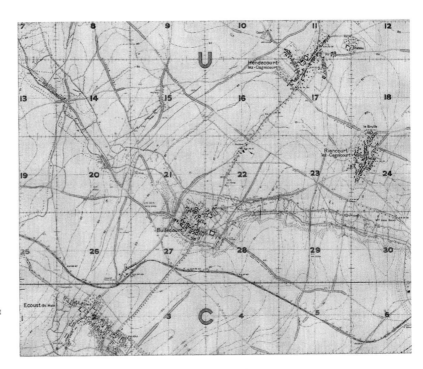

The Hindenburg line at Bullecourt. (National Archives: WO 95/3343:28th Battalion War Diary)

instances due to an over eagerness to acquire souvenirs! I remember a German helmet, left hanging temptingly on the wall of an abandoned trench, which on being lifted triggered off several explosions. Then there were the detonated duck-boards which wreaked havoc when trodden upon. This type of trap was responsible for quite a number of casualties. And there was a brazier standing outside a dug-out, neatly filled with coke and shavings and just waiting to be ignited to afford heat to a Tommy's cooker. We did not fall for this one fortunately and it was carefully dismantled, revealing a neat wad of high explosives. The entering of dug-outs was a highly dangerous undertaking because in most instances they contained traps of varying nature. We usually threw Mills bombs down the entrances of these and passed on.

Delayed action mines were another feature of this period and I remember one of these which went off at a busy crossroads probably a week or more after the German evacuation, causing destruction of divisional transport and very heavy casualties among the troops gathered there. The resulting cavity was large enough to accommodate a church! Throughout their withdrawal, the enemy practised what in later years would be described as a 'scorched earth' policy. Trees were felled across all roads, water supplies contaminated and all villages in the vacated area razed to the ground. This latter destruction was so complete that the villages were no longer recognizable as such, and in consequence it became commonplace for the British troops to erect a signboard at the entrance to each with its name, e.g. 'This is Mory'.

The optimism of many of us was sadly removed when, upon reaching the limit of the German withdrawal, we were confronted with the new strongly fortified line, which for us was to result in the grim battle of Bullecourt, in the course of which many P.O.R.s laid down their lives.[17]

Although many booby traps were left, the German attempt to slow down the pursuing enemy and cause maximum casualties failed, because British and Australian forces became aware of the problem early on. Their suspicions became aroused when they found that

Above left: **Railway Embankment from Riencourt; two trees mark position of Central Road. (Author)**

Above right: **German Trenches at Bullecourt. (AWM H12360)**

Left: **Aerial photo of Bullecourt taken on 5th April 1917. (AWM A01100)**

dug-outs had not been destroyed, so they sent in units of Royal Engineers to make such areas safe. The one distinctive German success using booby traps occurred during the night of 25th March when a mine activated by a delayed action fuse destroyed Bapaume Town Hall. When Australian units entered Bapaume, the Town Hall was considered safe to occupy after one mine had been found and removed from the cellars underground. A second mine which was not located, exploded and killed several Australians and two French officials who were sleeping in the building. The Town Hall at Bapaume was considered as a potential Fifth Army headquarters for General Gough prior to the explosion. It was just as well that this option was not chosen.

The winter frost had thawed during March and rain turned the terrain into a quagmire which would hinder the logistical operation for the British.

On 28th March the 22nd Manchesters together with the 1st South Staffordshire Regiment were ordered to capture the village of Croisilles. At 5.45 am they advanced behind a creeping barrage directed towards the village. The 22nd Manchesters' experience at Bucquoy was repeated at Croisilles. As soon as they got near to the village, German machine gunners opened fire. Only a small party led by Captain Charles Duguid got through the wire and entered the village. Duguid held onto his position for 36 hours until relieved. The South

Staffordshire's lost 10 officers and 228 men during this operation. Croisilles was taken on 2nd April by the 2nd Queen's. Casualties were incurred by the 22nd Battalion Manchester Regiment as they endeavoured to mop up small pockets of resistance within the village; they lost five officers and 39 men. These losses were mainly due to booby traps and snipers.

The Australians would encounter strong German rearguard actions at Lagnicourt, Noreuil and Hermies. German machine gunners were placed along the railway embankment south of Bullecourt. The 49th Battalion had captured the railway embankment at Bullecourt on 5th April after a heavy engagement. The Australian 14th, 16th and 46th Battalions reached the railway embankment at Bullecourt by 9.00 pm on 8th April 1917. Patrols were sent from this position to ascertain if German forces were present. The German units holding the Hindenburg Line at Bullecourt were very keen to keep a low profile until the expected allied attack took place.

The lines for the battle of Bullecourt were being drawn up as infantry from the Australian 4th Division and the British 7th and 62nd Divisions were assembling. The 27th Division from Württemberg was defending Bullecourt. They had fought well during the Somme campaign and now they were ready to repel British and Australian attacks upon their position.

NOTES

1. Imperial War Museum: Department of Sound: IWM Ref: IWM 9488: Private William Parry-Morris, 2nd Battalion Honourable Artillery Company.
2. Ibid.
3. *The History of The Queen's Royal Regiment* compiled by Colonel H.C. Wylly, Gale and Polden Ltd.
4. *The Honourable Artillery Company Journal*, Volume 1, 1923.
5. Imperial War Museum: Department of Sound: IWM Ref: IWM 9488: Private William Parry-Morris, 2nd Battalion Honourable Artillery Company.
6. *The Honourable Artillery Company Journal*, Volume 1, 1923.
7. Corporal Ivor William's (21st Battalion AIF) Diary: Courtesy of Courtesy Hugh Williams.
8. *The Honourable Artillery Company Journal*, Volume 1, 1923.
9. Imperial War Museum: Department of Documents: IWM Reference 89/7/1: Private W.T.

King 8519, 13th Platoon, 19th Company 2nd / 2nd London Regiment.
10. Private Leslie Pezet (15th Battalion AIF) Diary: Courtesy Ken Pezet.
11. National Archives: WO 95/3510: 46th Battalion War Diary.
12. Ibid.
13. Imperial War Museum: Department of Documents: IWM Ref: 79/25/1: Private W.G. Bishop 2nd / 1st London Regiment.
14. *Storm of Steel*, Ernst Junger, Zimmerman and Zimmerman, New York, 1985: p125.
15. *The Honourable Artillery Company Journal*, Volume 1, 1923.
16. Imperial War Museum: Department of Sound: IWM Ref: IWM 9488: Private William Parry-Morris, 2nd Battalion Honourable Artillery Company.
17. Imperial War Museum: Department of Documents: IWM Ref: Misc 2165: Anonymous Rifleman from the Post Office Rifles.

CHAPTER 5

THE COMMANDERS

GENERAL HUBERT GOUGH

General Douglas Haig, the Commander-in-Chief of the British Army regarded General Hubert Gough as one of his best officers. However, Gough was regarded by some then and now as an impetuous leader, who ignored the advice of the generals under his command, who highlighted their concerns for his desperate plans for frontal offensives.

Hubert de la Poer Gough was born in London on 12th August 1870. He was of Irish descent and came from a family with a distinguished military past, four of his ancestors being recipients of the Victoria Cross. He spent his childhood in Ireland. Gough was educated at Eton, and during January 1888 he began officer training at Sandhurst. After completing officer training at Sandhurst he joined the 16th Lancers in 1889. Gough took part in the Tirah Expedition and fought in South Africa 1897–98. Without official orders he led the first cavalry unit into Ladysmith during the relief of the besieged town during February 1900. In the following year he was defeated at Blood River Poort on 17th September. The failure of the action was attributed to Gough ignoring intelligence reports. He was captured after this battle, but escaped from his Boer captors on the same day.

After the Boer War Gough was appointed as a lecturer at the Staff College at Sandhurst from 1904 to 1906. He commanded the 16th Lancers from 1907 to 1911. His rapid rise through the ranks of the British Army made him at 36 the youngest Lieutenant Colonel in the British Army. In 1910 he was appointed commander of the 3rd Cavalry Brigade which was based at Curragh near Dublin.

When war broke out in 1914 Gough and his 3rd Cavalry Brigade were sent to France as part of Allenby's 1st Cavalry Division. Gough was at Mons as the Germans drove through Belgium into France pushing the British Army to Le Cateau in August 1914. As the British Army withdrew south towards the River Marne, Gough's 3rd Cavalry Brigade came under the command of Haig's I Corps and their orders were to cover the rearguard of I Corps. Gough's brigade was intact, but he was not told how to execute his orders to cover the I Corps retreat. Gough asked for orders

General Sir Hubert Gough. (*The Great War* Volume 9, 1917)

from Sir John French's General Headquarter on where he was to deploy his brigade. Sir Henry Wilson advised him to use his own discretion. 'Oh, you are on the spot, do what you like, old boy.'[1] This vague response left Gough incandescent. He wrote: 'Such orders left me to do what I liked, certainly, but did not tell me how to do it or indeed what was wanted! – and I may add, positively infuriated me'.[2]

The 3rd Calvary Brigade pursued the German Army northwards towards the River Aisne and took part in the race to the sea. Gough and his Brigade engaged in battle with Bavarian units at Messines in early October 1914. Gough performed well as a brigade commander and during the first battle of Ypres he was promoted to Major General and given command of the 2nd Cavalry Division.

During April 1915 Gough was appointed commander of the 7th Division as a temporary replacement for Major General Thompson Capper who was wounded. The 7th Division belonged to IV Corps commanded by Rawlinson. Within a month Rawlinson ordered Gough's 7th Division to attack Aubers Ridge on 9th May. When his division entered the trenches, they found that their line had been destroyed by persistent German artillery barrages. They were filled with the dead and wounded of the 8th Division. The dire state of the trenches was no platform for the 7th Division to launch an attack at dawn. Gough consulted with his brigadiers and on realising that it would be folly to launch an attack under such circumstances he took matters into his own hands, he cancelled the attack contrary to Rawlinson's order. Gough later recalled 'I had received orders to renew the attack but I recognized that the attack had not the remotest chance of success so I did not comply and reported the fact to Rawlinson'.[3] It was extraordinary that Rawlinson took no action against Gough for contravening his orders. It is ironic to note that Gough would discipline and dismiss those who disobeyed or countered his command.

Gough oversaw the 7th Division's attack on Festubert. The preliminary bombardment had not destroyed the German defences and trenches and the 7th Division sustained heavy casualties. When Major General Thompson Capper had recovered from his wounds, he returned to the Western Front to command the 7th Division during the summer of 1915. In July 1915, Gough, now 45, was promoted to Lieutenant General and given command of I Corps. Gough saw his Corps fail to make a breakthrough at the Battle of Loos partly owing to the British gas attack blowing back to his own troops, although they did succeed in capturing the Hohenzollern Redoubt.

Gough was appointed commander of the Reserve Army during May 1916. This army would become the Fifth Army. As General Rawlinson's Fourth Army began the Somme offensive on 1st July 1916, Gough was standing by for a breach in the German line to be made for the Fifth Army to advance upon Bapaume then proceed towards Arras with two infantry and three cavalry divisions.

Within two weeks of the beginning of the Somme campaign, the Fifth Army was involved in a series of attritional attacks. Gough pushed British, Australian and Canadian forces under his command into the battle to capture Pozières Ridge during July and August 1916. Gough was task-focussed and was not afraid to lose heavy casualties in order to achieve the objective. Although Gough succeeded in securing Pozières and the ridge, the Australians would suffer 23,000 casualties. Gough would drive his Fifth Army in assisting Rawlinson's Fourth Army in capturing the village of Courcelette, which would put them in a position to swing northwards and capture the village of Thiepval on 28th September 1916. During November 1916, Gough led the final offensive of the Somme campaign, known as the Battle of Ancre, when the Fifth Army captured Beaumont Hamel and secured the Ancre valley, at a cost of 125,531 casualties.

The Fifth Army pursued Ludendorff's infantry as they withdrew to the Hindenburg Line from February to April 1917. Bullecourt would become a bloody battle of attrition driven by General Gough. The attack was poorly planned and thousands of British and Australian soldiers would perish upon the bloody fields and amongst the rubble of the village of Bullecourt. About a battle fought over a period of six weeks with great loss of life amounting to tens of thousand of men, Gough would only write one sentence describing his involvement in his memoirs: 'Eventually the Fifth Army became involved in some bitter fighting round Bullecourt, in an endeavour to assist Allenby's right, but there was insufficient co-operation between the two armies'.[4]

After the Bullecourt fiasco Gough commanded the early phases of the third Ypres campaign later in 1917. His strategy to overwhelm the German forces in one fell swoop failed dismally. He pushed his men beyond their capabilities in an effort to achieve unrealistic objectives of little tactical or strategic value. Subsequently, command of the offensive was passed from Gough to General Plumer.

During March 1918 Gough was commanding the Fifth Army holding the line on the Somme Sector. When General Ludendorff unleashed the Kaiser's offensive on 21st March, the Fifth Army was overwhelmed by the might of German forces that advanced west. The Fifth Army could not withstand the hurricane bombardments or resist the German storm troops and were in disarray, being forced to retreat. Gough was considered responsible for the collapse of the Fifth Army as the German Army pushed through allied lines. Gough was subsequently relieved of his command on 28th March 1918. Haig would later admit that Gough was used as a scapegoat at the time. During 1919 Gough was appointed commander of British forces in the Baltic sent to Russia to overthrow the Bolshevik government.

Gough retired from the British Army in 1922 and would play a role in the creation of the Australian War Memorial in Canberra. He received a knighthood in 1937. When the Second World War broke out in 1939, Gough, aged 70, established the Chelsea contingent of the Local Defence Volunteers, which would later become the Home Guard. Gough retired for a second time in 1942. Gough died in 1963.

GENERAL ERICH LUDENDORFF

Erich Friedrich Wilhelm Ludendorff was born on 9th April 1865 at Kruszewnia near Posen, now Poznan in Poland. As a child he excelled in Mathematics, which would stand him in good stead when studying as a cadet at a military school in Plön. In 1885 Ludendorff was commissioned as a Lieutenant in the 57th Infantry Regiment. By 1911 he had reached the rank of Colonel and was working on the General Staff in Berlin. He was involved in assessing the Belgian fortifications of

Liège years before the war. His assessment would have a bearing on the preparation of the Schlieffen Plan. Ludendorff was the deputy chief of staff of the German Second Army when the First World War began. He was appointed to the position because of his knowledge of the Belgian defences. On 5th August 1914 the German Second Army sustained heavy casualties during a frontal assault on Liège. Belgian artillery and machine gun fire cut them down as they advanced towards the Belgian town. The commander of the 14th Brigade was killed on 5th August and Ludendorff was appointed as his successor. This moment allowed Ludendorff to demonstrate his command ability. He called for siege guns on 8th August and by the 16th all the Belgian forts surrounding Liège had fallen. Ludendorff was hailed as the hero of Liège in Germany and he was awarded Germany's highest military decoration for gallantry, the Pour le Mérite, which was presented to him by Kaiser Wilhelm on 22nd August.

The German Second Army captured the Belgian garrison at Liège and advanced towards the River Sambre. As Ludendorff was preparing to lead an assault upon the Belgian fortified town at Namur, the Russian Army was advancing from the east. Ludendorff was transferred to the Eastern Front where he served for two years. During that time he became, instrumental together with Paul von Hindenburg, in defeating the Russians at the Battle of Tannenberg in August and the Battle of Masurian Lakes in September. After his victory at the Battle of Lodz he was promoted to Lieutenant General. Ludendorff was appointed first quartermaster general of the German forces on 29th August 1916. This role in effect made him commander-in-chief of the German Army. Ludendorff would endorse unrestricted submarine warfare in order to starve Britain into submission. Realising that the German Army could not withstand the continuous British and Commonwealth offensives which were wearing down his forces during the summer of 1916, Ludendorff devised the strategic withdrawal to the Siegfried Line, the Hindenburg Line to the British.

Later during 1917, Ludendorff orchestrated the strategy to launch an offensive against Italy and in October the Germans won a crushing victory over the Italians at the Battle of Caporetto. The Italians sustained 600,000 casualties. When Russia withdrew from the war in 1917, the Eastern Front collapsed. Ludendorff participated in peace talks with the Bolshevik regime which resulted in the signing of the Brest-Litovsk Treaty in March 1918. With Russia out of the war Ludendorff could

General Ludendorff

transfer troops to the Western Front. With additional resources he could plan new offensive strategies for 1918. Ludendorff planned the Michael, Mars, St George I and St George II operations, unleashed from March to May 1918. By May, German forces were close to Paris. Their drive upon the French capital was thwarted when American forces obstructed their path and stopped them at Belleau Wood and Château Thierry. With fresh American troops brought to the front to support the worn out British, French and Commonwealth troops, Germany had lost the advantage. The tide of war changed on 8th August 1918 when 30,000 German troops were lost at the Battle of Amiens. Ludendorff recognised the 8th of August as 'a black day' for Germany and realised that the war was lost. It was the beginning of the end of the war. The allies were able to exploit the use of tanks in conjunction with infantry following creeping barrages and air support in a series of battles that brought them to the Hindenburg Line in September 1918. Ludendorff lost confidence in a German victory and encouraged peace initiatives. In an effort to obtain favourable peace terms he established a civilian government on 3rd October who would negotiate an honourable peace agreement. When the terms they negotiated were brought to Ludendorff he found them to be unacceptable and he changed his mind and decided that Germany should continue the war and concentrate on a defensive strategy. Although the war was lost, it was his view that if his forces could hold the Hindenburg Line and a small part of occupied France, they could negotiate better peace terms. Prince Max von Baden saw Ludendorff's radical change in strategy as erratic and forced his resignation on 26th October 1918. Feeling dejection at the loss of the war and nursing the belief that the defeat of Germany was caused by Jews, Freemasons and Jesuits, Ludendorff escaped across the Swedish border in disguise, where he lived in exile for a short period.

Returning to Germany in 1920 Ludendorff became involved in politics and German Nationalism. He supported Adolf Hitler's Beer Hall Putsch in Munich on 9th November 1923 and after its failure he was acquitted of any involvement. He was elected to the Reichstag in 1924 to represent the NSFB (a coalition of the German Völkisch Freedom Party and members of the Nazi Party). Ludendorff decided to run for the presidential election against Paul von Hindenburg in 1925, but lost due to poor campaigning and his association with the Beer Hall Putsch two years earlier. As Hitler gained popularity, Ludendorff considered him a danger to Germany and withdrew his support for the Nazi party. Ludendorff retired from politics in 1928. Hitler was anxious to gain public approval from Ludendorff and in 1935 the Fuhrer paid him a visit and offered to elevate Ludendorff to the rank of Field Marshal, which he declined with the comment 'a

Field Marshal is born, not made.' Ludendorff died on 20th December 1937 in Tutzing. Against his wishes, Ludendorff was given a state funeral, attended by Hitler.

GENERAL WILLIAM BIRDWOOD

William Riddell Birdwood was born in Kirkee, Maharashtra, India, on 13th September 1865. Educated at Clifton College, England, he joined the British Army and trained to become an officer at the Royal Military College, Sandhurst. After graduating from Sandhurst he was commissioned in 1883 to serve with the 4th Battalion Royal Fusiliers. In 1885 he was promoted to lieutenant and transferred to the 12th (Prince of Wales Royal) Lancers who were serving in India. He was transferred to the 11th Bengal Lancers in 1886. Birdwood participated in the Terah expedition during 1887 and was present at the Battle of Dargai. From 1891 Birdwood was serving on the Indian north-west frontier. Birdwood climbed the ranks, being promoted to Captain in 1896 and Major in 1900.

When the Boer War broke out Birdwood requested a transfer to the British Army and was given an appointment on the staff of a mounted brigade in Natal on 8th November 1899. He fought in several battles and was wounded at Machadodorp on 28th August 1900. Birdwood joined Lord Kitchener's personal staff in Pretoria in October 1900, He returned to India after the Boer War and by 1911 he had reached the rank of Major General. In 1913 Birdwood became Secretary to the Government of India, Military Department. When World War One erupted Lord Kitchener appointed Birdwood as commander of the Australian and New Zealand Army Corps, known as ANZACs and he was dispatched to Egypt to meet them and organise their training. Birdwood landed at Anzac Cove, Gallipoli on 25th April 1915. Affectionately known as 'Birdy' he earned the respect of the men that he commanded by visiting them regularly within range of the Turkish guns. To promote hygiene and cleanliness amongst the men Birdwood would frequently swim in the sea at Anzac Cove despite the Turkish shells and shrapnel. Birdwood resisted calls to evacuate from the Gallipoli peninsula but he was overruled by the overwhelming consensus amongst politicians and generals that the campaign was a failure and that there was no other option but to withdraw and utilize the ANZAC forces on the Western Front. Birdwood's coordinated plan to evacuate the peninsula was a success. When the ANZAC Corps was split into two Corps, Birdwood was appointed commander of I ANZAC Corps. On the Western Front he directed operations at Bullecourt in 1917. On 17th October 1917 he was awarded the KCB and knighted

Royal Flying Corps aerial reconnaissance photograph of Ludendorff's Hindenburg Line taken on 8th April 1917. The long lines of thick barbed wire are visible, cutting across the French countryside. (Author)

Sir William Birdwood. During the following month, when all five Australian Divisions joined together within the same Australian Corps, Birdwood became their overall commander until May 1918, when Lieutenant General John Monash took over. Birdwood became commander of the British Fifth Army for the rest of the war. Despite being involved with disastrous operations such as Bullecourt, Birdwood was one officer that was regarded highly by the Australian soldiers, for he would always argue their corner and support the men that he commanded. After the war he toured Australia and received a good reception. In 1925 he was promoted to Field Marshal and appointed Commander of the Indian Army. Birdwood died at Hampton Court Palace in England on 17th May 1951.

NOTES ··

1. *Soldiering On*, by General Sir Hubert Gough, p117.
2. Ibid.
3. Ibid, p122.
4. Ibid, p138.

PART TWO

THE FIRST BATTLE OF BULLECOURT
11TH APRIL 1917

CHAPTER 6

PRELUDE TO BATTLE

Days before the offensive had begun; Anzac commanders were expressing concerns about Gough's plan. On 31st March, Major General Cyril Brudenell White, Chief General Staff Officer of I Anzac Corp wrote, 'Between Quéant and Bullecourt the enemy's line forms a re-entrant some 1,500 yards deep. An attack there would be unwise unless Quéant were also attacked.'[1] If the Germans maintained their positions at Quéant, then the Australian advance would be horribly exposed. Birdwood thought the plan was too risky, but the Anzac concerns were overruled and it was decided that the German guns at Bullecourt could be subdued by concentrated artillery fire, while smoke would obstruct the vision of machine gunners in Quéant. Together with tank support, Gough thought the plan was viable and emphasised that Field Marshal Haig, the Commander-in-Chief, insisted that the attack took place.

Haig planned to launch an offensive along the Arras–Vimy front on 9th April 1917. General Horne's First Army was ordered to capture Vimy Ridge, which would protect General Allenby's flank as his Third Army was ordered to drive east of Arras towards Cambrai, while the Fifth Army, commanded by General Gough, would assault the Hindenburg line at Bullecourt.

On 2nd April the Fifth Army had captured the villages from Doignes to Croisilles and General Gough ordered preparations for further attacks. By the 5th the 49th Battalion had captured the railway embankment. Haig requested Gough to create a breach in the Hindenburg Line so that the 4th Cavalry Division could sweep through at Bullecourt and join the main cavalry thrust that would have broken through German lines at Arras on Allenby's Third Army front line. Gough was convinced that the German forces were in retreat and was prepared to commit his Fifth Army into a larger offensive at Bullecourt. On 5th April General Gough issued precise orders for I Anzac and V Corps to launch an attack on a 3,500-yard front, with the village of Bullecourt as the primary objective. Riencourt and Hendecourt would be the respective second and third objectives. The 4th Australian Division (I Anzac) commanded by General William Birdwood and the 62nd Division (V Corps) commanded by General Walter Braithwaite would participate in the attack supported by a company of tanks, which were assigned to the Fifth Army, with five tanks assigned to each of the Corps and two retained in reserve. General Gough considered the attack on Bullecourt to be viable provided it was launched simultaneously with Third Army's attack on the Wancourt–Fenchy Line. Once the Hindenburg Line at Bullecourt had been broken, the 4th Cavalry Division would swarm through this breach northwards capturing German artillery and trapping infantry units. If successful, they could advance onto Cambrai, then onto Belgium and win the war. This offensive on Bullecourt was scheduled to take place on 10th April. Every available gun was ordered to be brought to the Fifth Army front to support the offensive.

The Germans had not completed the fortification of the Bullecourt sector of the Hindenburg Line and during the beginning of 1917 Fifth Army Intelligence received numerous reports from German prisoners of war of the accelerated construction of concrete dug-outs, blockhouses and machine-gun emplacements. Two strongholds were established at Bullecourt and Riencourt, exploiting the advantage of a semi circular

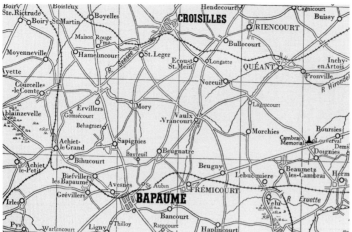

The approach to Bullecourt.
(Twenty Years After Vol.2)

British and Australian forces found it difficult to transport men, supplies, artillery and ammunition to the front line. As described earlier, German forces withdrawing to the Hindenburg Line had sabotaged the roads with mines and laid trees across them. Railway lines were miles short of the front. As a consequence there were not

ridge, which enabled them to dominate No Man's Land. In front of the trenches thick belts of barbed wire were positioned in v shaped formation, so that any attacking infantry would be channelled into a focal point in No Man's Land, where a machine gunner could concentrate his fire. A Maxim machine gun, which fired 600 rounds per minute, was capable of cutting a man in half.

Riencourt was strongly fortified with machine gun emplacements and underground cellars that sheltered troops. A small detachment would be deployed in the front-line trenches with a greater ratio of machine guns to infantry. The 27th Württemberg Division defended the Hindenburg Line between Bullecourt and Quéant, comprising the 120th Infantry Regiment in Bullecourt, the 123rd Grenadier Regiment in Quéant, and the 124th Infantry Regiment holding the line between the two villages. They had spent four weeks in training camps far from the front line at Valenciennes and their morale was high. However they became disenchanted in finding that the construction of the Hindenburg Line in the Bullecourt sector was not complete.

The Germans had nevertheless established a redoubtable defensive position at Bullecourt. Here the Hindenburg Line formed a salient and the villages of Hendecourt, Riencourt and Quéant were turned into fortresses, which could provide covering fire for each other.

sufficient heavy guns in place to cut the high density barbed wire fields. Patrols were sent into No Man's Land and reports were received by Major General White that the wire was not cut. White and Birdwood were both concerned by these reports.

Bombardment began on April 3rd, with 26 batteries of medium and heavy howitzers attached to I Anzac and V Corps operational. Delays occurred in deploying artillery to the front, so serious bombardment did not commence until 5th April when an average of 4,000 rounds per day were fired by I Anzac's artillery alone.

An air reconnaissance flight over the Hindenburg Line during the afternoon of 8th April assessed the impact of the allied barrage upon the German wire. They reported that the wire was only partially cut. At a conference held at Bihucourt Château on 8th April, Gough was advised by White that his men could not attack if the wire was intact and that eight days would be required in order to cut the barbed wire defences. Australian commanders were concerned that there was not adequate time to

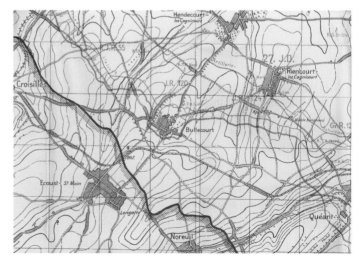

German positions at Bullecourt on 8th and 9th April 1917. (Die Osterschlacht bei Arras II. Teil Zwisch)

effectively prepare for the assault. White emphasised that Australian troops were expected to advance between two salients. They would come under heavy machine gun fire from the right and left flanks and from in front of them from Hendecourt and Riencourt as they crossed 1,500 yards before they reached the enemy trenches. German observers positioned at Hendecourt could see from this ridge the entire region, including Bullecourt, Riencourt, the railway embankment and the Noreuil valley. They could direct artillery fire anywhere within this area.

If there was sufficient time to pulverise the German wire and trenches with artillery then maybe there was a chance that the plan would succeed. Gough sanctioned the postponement of the attack scheduled for the 8th, but he forewarned them that they may be ordered to attack on the 12th.

On 9th April 6,025 rounds were fired by allied artillery. Australian patrols and air reconnaissance discovered that no gaps had been breached in the wire and that to the east of Bullecourt it averaged 30 yards in depth. The wire was reported to be 'cut about in places by our artillery fire, but no gaps yet'.[2]

The 62nd Battalion also sent patrols to ascertain the effect of allied barrages upon the German wire. During the night of 8th/9th April patrols from the 2nd/5th West Yorkshire Regiment were sent out. The 185th Brigade Report recorded that the patrols found that 'the wire was still very little damaged, and judging from the churned up state of the ground in front, the shells had been falling short'.[3] Lieutenant Arthur Wilfred Lucius Smith from the 2nd/5th West Yorkshire Regiment led another patrol at 2.15 am on 9th April. He confirmed that 'the wire was damaged but no gaps were seen'.[4] A patrol led by Lieutenant Geoffrey Skirrow was spotted by a German patrol by the wire. The Germans threw bombs and a fierce rifle duel ensued.

Lieutenant C.B. Stead and Sergeant Eagers led a reconnaissance patrol that found the wire undamaged by shell fire in some areas but in other areas they identified breaches. The 185th Brigade War Diary records:

> The information gained by this patrol states that the wire is about 15 to 18 feet thick. At 20.a.6.7. it is not very thick and is untouched by shell fire. At U.20.a.7.5 there is a gap, there are knife rests at the outer end and, ready to be placed in the gap. At U.20.a.9.4 the wire is damaged by shell fire and is lying on the ground but still forms an obstacle. The wire in the corner at U.20b.1 ½.⁴. is very strong but wire at U.20.b.15.25. is damaged by shell fire and lies in the ground. Wire is about 3ft high where untouched by shell fire. Wire is on screw pickets, no enemy movement was observed.[5]

2nd Lieutenant C.L.S. Musgrave led a patrol from the 2nd/7th West Yorkshire Regiment:

> The enemy's wire was examined from U.21.c.9.0. to U.27.a.9.5 The Outer band running between these two points is very thick, but has been very little damaged, the inner band about 75 yards inside appeared thick, and quite intact.[6]

The First Army commanded by General Horne had begun their offensive during the morning on 9th April with great success, the Canadian Corps capturing Vimy Ridge. Allenby had succeeded in capturing objectives within the Black and Blue Lines, but could not reach the third objective, the Brown Line. However, the Third Army had captured 5,600 prisoners and 36 guns.[7] Gough was receiving reports of Allenby's success and he was furious and frustrated that he could not launch an attack on Bullecourt because the wire had not been cut. Allenby's success at Vimy enforced Gough's view that Bullecourt might be less strongly defended than reports indicated. His belief was enforced by the statements he read from three prisoners of war from the 5th Dorset Regiment, who had been forced to work close to the front line and had escaped to the Australian lines near Bullecourt.

During that afternoon, Lieutenant Colonel J. Hardress-Lloyd, commanding D Company Tank Battalion, brought Gough a proposal to his headquarters at Albert, which would revise his planned attack on Bullecourt. The original plan involved pairs of tanks attacking Bullecourt along a two-mile front. This plan was not favoured by tank officers, because isolated tanks dispersed along an attacking front were considered a vulnerable and easy target. There was also a lack of confidence in a single tank's ability to make significant breaches in the wire for the infantry to break through. The proposal that Gough received from Hardress-Lloyd had originated from Major W.H.L. Watson commanding 11 Company, D Tank Battalion, who also visited Gough at his headquarters at Albert. He suggested that the twelve tanks under his command should launch a surprise attack on a 1,000-yard front, with the artillery withholding fire until they had passed the wire, so as to preserve the element of surprise. The tanks would therefore replace the artillery barrage. A concentrated attack, it was thought, would make significant gaps in the wire, as opposed to a series of smaller narrow breaches. Once the wire had been breached, infantry would charge through. The defenders of Bullecourt would then be aware that an attack was taking place, but too late. Major Watson later wrote:

> It had been arranged at the last army conference that the Fifth Army would move when the offensive of the Third Army was well launched. My tanks were to be distributed in pairs along the whole front of

the army, and to each pair a definite objective was allocated. I had always been averse to this scattering of my command. The Hindenburg Line, which faced us, was notoriously strong. Bullecourt, the key to the whole position, looked on the map almost impregnable. The artillery of the Fifth Army was far from overwhelming, and gunners had told me that good forward positions for the guns were difficult to find. I realised, of course, that an officer in my subordinate position knew little, but I was convinced that a surprise concentration might prove a success where a formal attack, lightly supported by a few tanks, scattered over a wide front, might reasonably fail. I planned for my own content an attack in which my tanks, concentrated on a narrow front of a thousand yards and supported as strongly as possible by all the infantry and guns available, should steal up to the Hindenburg Line without a barrage. As they entered the German trenches down would come the barrage, and under cover of the barrage and the tanks the infantry would sweep through, while every gun not used in making the barrage should pound away at the German batteries.[8]

Gough was now in a jubilant mood because of the Canadian victory at Vimy Ridge during that morning and Allenby's advances east of Arras. He was receiving reports confirming the achievement of the First and Third Armies when Hardress-Lloyd and Watson presented themselves at his headquarters with their proposal to launch an attack upon Bullecourt which depended entirely upon tanks. Thus gave Gough the impetus to attack. Gough was convinced that the proposal was viable and immediately approved it for the following day, 10th April. Watson recalled the conversation: '"We want to break the Hindenburg Line with tanks, General" said the Colonel and briefly explained the scheme. General Gough received it with favour, and decided to attack at dawn the following morning.'[9]

When Gough gave the go ahead, he was not taking into account the possibility that Bullecourt may be defended in depth, as suggested by the fact that the Fifth Army were encountering stronger resistance the closer they got to the Hindenburg Line. Nor did he consider the fact that although Canadian infantry were consolidating the ground they captured at Vimy and that Allenby was advancing east of Arras, the extent of their success on that day had been grossly overestimated. Gough was falsely given the impression that the German Army was disintegrating. During the past six months he had seen the tank's performance on the battlefield. The tank had enjoyed minor successes, but this was a new weapon of war, prone to malfunction. On 15th September 1916, most of the tanks broke down, and in other attacks during the later stages of the Somme campaign, their successes were very limited.

The plan proposed by Hardress-Lloyd and Watson was a new tank strategy that had not been tested and there was no time for pre-training of infantry and tanks. During this stage of the war the allies were refining and developing the strategy of infantry advancing closely behind a creeping barrage. Gough was taking a major gamble in placing complete reliance upon the tanks supporting the infantry. Although sceptical, White and Birdwood were swayed by the tank commander's plan and Gough's enthusiasm. Gough had seen the potential of tank warfare, but chose to ignore the failures. Birdwood and White had no experience of working with tanks and had to go along with Gough's plan irrespective of their reservations. Bean comments in the official history that White was impressed by the confident presentation given by Hardress-Lloyd and Watson, but these were not the men who would be driving tanks, without armoured protection, into battle.

The tanks assigned to Gough's Fifth Army came from No. 11 Company 'D' Tank Battalion and were Mark II tanks. These tanks were not intended for warfare and were originally intended for training purposes. So the external structures of these tanks were not fitted with armour plating. The tanks were positioned four miles from the front line at Mory Copse and could not be moved until dark, because of the risk of being discovered by enemy aircraft. They had arrived at Mory Copse at dawn on 6th April and were camouflaged and positioned in an old quarry nearby. However, they were not totally concealed from the enemy. Major Watson wrote:

> The quarry was not an ideal hiding-place, as it lay open to direct though distant observation from the German lines: but the tanks were skilfully concealed by the adroit use of trees, undergrowth, and nets, the hill surmounted by the copse provided an excellent background and we were compelled to make a virtue of necessity as the open downs in the neighbourhood of Mory gave not the slightest cover. The village itself was out of the question: the enemy was shelling it with hearty goodwill.[10]

The plan for the tanks to advance towards the German wire and crush the wire was supposed to persuade Birdwood and White that there was no reason to wait for more artillery to arrive at the front to blast gaps through the wire.

Watson's orders for the ill-fated Bullecourt initiative reached Lieutenant Hugh Swears at Mory Copse at 6.30 pm during the evening on 9th April 1917. Swears was left in charge of the Company while Watson visited Gough during that afternoon. They had less than twelve hours to prepare for the attack. By 8.00 pm the tanks had left the quarry. As they were heading towards Noreuil, Watson went to the Australian Divisional Headquarters at Bapaume where he presented the plan to Osborne, the G.S.O.II of the Corps.

4th Australian Division Headquarters consisted of canvas huts and it was a cold night with snow and sleet falling heavily. Watson managed to find time for a brief sleep before midnight. His testimony reveals that although he was confident of his plan, he had inner misgivings about the impending attack. He was awoken by a nightmare and the thought of failure must have prompted it: 'We turned in for a snatch of sleep, and I woke with a start – dreaming that my tanks had fallen over a cliff into the sea'.[11]

A gale was blowing, and sleet was mixed with snow. After midnight I waited anxiously for news of my tanks. It was a long trek for one night, and, as we had drawn them so recently, I could not guarantee, from experience, their mechanical condition. There was no margin of time for any except for running repairs.[12]

As the tanks were heading towards Noreuil, British and Australian patrols were sent into No Man's Land at Bullecourt in order to appraise the state of the German wire. At 8.15 pm during the night of 9th April, three West Yorkshire Battalions from the 185th Brigade sent patrols to find breaches in the wire and to seize the German front and support line trenches if they were found to be unoccupied. These patrols found the enemy wire to be strong and undamaged and they encountered heavy German machine gun fire from entrenched positions at Bullecourt. These patrols returned to their positions by 9.30 pm. The German units holding Bullecourt had been alerted to the fact that a British and Australian assault upon the Hindenburg Line was imminent. Surprise was lost. The soldiers from Australia and Yorkshire would be attacking a heavily fortified position with no artillery support and the Germans defending that position knew they were coming.

At 9.50 pm east of Bullecourt, Captain Albert Jacka VC, an intelligence officer from the 14th Battalion, led a reconnaissance patrol of two officers from the 16th Battalion, Lieutenant Frank Wadge and Lieutenant Henry Bradley plus a small detachment of six men into No Man's Land 'to reconnoitre the state of the enemy's wire and if possible ascertain the enemy's strength'.[13]

The patrol carefully ventured towards a sunken road located 300 metres from the Australian lines. Jacka had discovered this road on the night of 8th April on a previous reconnaissance. It was decided that since the enemy did not occupy the sunken road, it would provide an ideal starting point for the first wave of the attack and that the 14th, 16th and 46th AIF Battalions could be positioned their unopposed and undetected. The weather conditions that night was extremely harsh, very cold with snow blizzards. White and orange flares were constantly

illuminating the sky and No Man's Land was being strafed by sporadic machine gun fire. Jacka and his patrol proceeded farther into No Man's Land to inspect the condition of the German defences. Jacka and his patrol went far enough to hear German soldiers repairing the wire. At this point Captain Jacka proceeded alone to get a closer look. He would later report to Brigadier General Brand, 4th Brigade Commander and Lieutenant Colonel Peck at 14th Battalion Headquarters, that most of the wire was intact. Though Peck reported according to the battalion war diary that the wire was 'very badly broken and cut to pieces by bombardment'.[14] The official historian Bean records that Jacka insisted that 'other parts of the wire were intact'.[15] According to the 14th Battalion AIF war diary, Jacka's patrol found the German barbed wire in some places 'to be very badly broken and cut to pieces'.[16] Captain Longmore in his unit history entitled *The Old Sixteenth* mentions that the wire was 'smashed by shell fire in places, but it was generally unbroken'.[17] So, obviously, there was, and is, some confusion.

Jacka's search was interrupted when a German patrol appeared, forcing him to hide in the wire. The patrol passed within inches of Jacka's position, but he remained undetected. At this point Jacka stopped the reconnaissance. The men in his patrol were waiting for him in No Man's Land and Jacka led them back. Lieutenant Edgar Rule witnessed Jacka reporting to 4th Division Headquarters. He 'had told all the heads it was pure murder to attempt the operation'.[18] Jacka emphasised to his superiors that the Hindenburg Line was held in strength and the chance of a successful operation was remote. Jacka's forthright opinion greatly undermined Brand's position, and the two men clashed. Brand overruled Jacka's view. 4th Divisional Intelligence was unconvinced by Jacka's comments about the wire and ignored his comment about heavy artillery shelling from Quéant.

During the evening of 9th April reports were reaching General Birdwood that the expected Third Army breakout at Arras had not materialised. Strong German resistance at Monchy le Preux was holding up Allenby's advance. Poor weather conditions were also hindering the exhausted soldiers. With the wire question still burdening Birdwood's conscience, at 11.00 pm he asked White whether they were to proceed with the impending attack on Bullecourt knowing that the wire was undamaged and that the breakthrough on their left flank had not occurred. White conferred with Gough, who confirmed that the attack would take place.

Major General William Holmes commanding the 4th Australian Division would attack with the 4th and 12th Brigades. The 12th would attack on the left flank and follow tanks into Bullecourt with the 46th and 48th Battalions. The 4th Brigade was assigned the task of capturing Riencourt with four battalions. The 14th and

16th Battalions would form the initial waves, closely supported by the 15th and 13th Battalions respectively. They were currently resting seven miles away at Favreuil and had to march through the freezing night to reach the starting point, which was 600 yards from the German front-line trenches and 500 yards from the nearest point of the barbed wire zig zag formation. The attack was scheduled to take place one hour and 48 minutes before sunrise at 4.30 am. Artillery continued to fire the normal rate of shells until Zero Hour, and then they laid down a barrage on each flank.

The 15th Battalion began the trek to the assembly position from Favreuil at 9.30 pm on 9th April. They had to walk the seven miles across the snow carrying their packs, weapons and equipment. On arriving at 4th Brigade Headquarters at Noreuil, Captain David Dunworth accompanied Lieutenant Colonel Terrence McSharry, 15th Battalion Commanding officer, for a briefing with Brigadier General Charles Brand at midnight. It was at this meeting that McSharry and Dunworth were told that the plan for the attack had been changed, four and half hours before the operation was about to begin. Dunworth:

> We found Brig-Gen Brand apparently despondent. Then and only then we learned that the orders had been altered. The barrage had been dispensed with and a tank attack substituted. This news came as a thunderclap. Every officer and man knew his job by heart. Now we were to forego all these instructions and act on fresh ones. There was no chance to get the men together – the best we could hope for would be to get the officer's and N.C.O.s to know the new plan as well as we could.[19]

Infantry from the 4th Brigade had practised following an artillery barrage, but they had no experience of following tanks. They were initially told that their infantry would closely follow the artillery barrage and when reaching the enemy line, would fall into their trenches. The Australian commanders were unnerved by this sudden change in plan. Lieutenant Colonel McSharry requested artillery to support his infantry but was told that 'the tanks could not co-operate with artillery.'[20]

McSharry and Dunworth returned to the 15th Battalion and organised their assembly at the railway embankment opposite Bullecourt. This railway embankment would become an important feature on the battlefield because this earth wall provided a natural protection for battalion headquarters, shelter for regimental dressing stations and the starting point for attacks. McSharry and Dunworth had to brief their officers and N.C.O.s on the new plan while in the assembly position. They had to use groundsheets to cover torchlight as they studied maps and explained the new orders. The men were tired, cold and had to focus their minds on the new plan as the blizzard descended upon them.

As British and Australian battalions were heading towards the assembly positions at Bullecourt, the tanks were also trying to get to the starting points, but they were lost in the snowstorm. Major Watson had ordered Lieutenant Swears to contact him once the tanks had reached Noreuil. By 1.00 am Watson had heard no news. He was concerned because he knew that from Noreuil another ninety minutes were required for his tanks to reach their starting points along the railway embankment. An hour later, Watson was still in the same position, ignorant of the whereabouts of his tanks. Watson knew of the serious consequences if his tanks did not reach their starting positions in time for Zero Hour. Watson recalled:

> By two o'clock everybody was asking me for information. Brigade Headquarters at Noreuil had neither seen tanks, or heard them, but sent out orderlies to look for them in case they had lost their way. At Noreuil it was snowing hard and blowing a full gale. My position was not pleasant. The attack was set for dawn. The infantry had already gone forward to the railway embankment, from which they would 'jump off'. In daylight they could neither remain at the embankment nor retire over exposed ground without heavy shelling. It was half past two. I was penned in a hut with a couple of staff officers, who naturally enough, were irritated and gloomy. I could do nothing.[21]

At 3.15 am, one hour and fifteen minutes before Zero Hour, Watson received a call from Captain Wyatt who confirmed: 'We are two miles short of Noreuil in the valley. We have been wandering on the downs in a heavy snowstorm. We never quite lost our way, but it was almost impossible to keep the tanks together ... the men are dead tired.'[22] They were nowhere near to their allocated starting position near the embankment. With Australian troops descending upon their assembly areas and with no tank support, a disaster was about to happen at Bullecourt and there was no turning back.

Since 1.00 am during the morning of 10th April Livens Projectors fired shells containing phosgene gas onto the soldiers of the 120th Württemberg Regiment. They suffered 200 casualties as a result of this attack. Once the Germans had recovered they responded with a barrage of retaliatory machine-gun fire. Unperturbed, Jacka would later venture out into No Man's Land to reconnoitre east of Bullecourt with a party of scouts. At 2.15 am he positioned 'jumping off' tapes to guide the advancing infantry later that morning. He began this process from the enemy lines, then gradually worked backwards to the safety of his own trenches. He had nearly completed this task when he saw Lieutenant Reich and his orderly from the 124th Württemberg Infantry Regiment walking towards the other end of the tape. Jacka was afraid that if the tape were discovered, then the entire operation would be compromised, so he and a Lewis gunner promptly captured them. The officer resisted capture and was subdued after being pistol-whipped by Jacka. Lieutenant Reich would later complain about Jacka's treatment to Lieutenant Colonel Peck, Jacka's CO, who told him to think himself lucky to be alive, if he had been in the hands of Jacka. For his actions at Bullecourt, Jacka would be awarded a bar to his MC. His peers thought that it should have been a bar to the Victoria Cross that he had won at Gallipoli, but Jacka was a man who spoke his mind and it was because of his outspoken nature that he was denied further promotion.

The 6th Machine Gun Company bivouacking at Beugnatre were ordered to stand to at short notice. Lieutenant William Carne commanded No.2 Section, later recalled:

> At 1.30 am on the morning after arrival, the Company, without warning, was aroused and ordered to move forward for action. In the darkness, with a strong wind blowing and driving the falling sleet, it was a most disagreeable task to resume the habiliments of war: harness horses, issue rations, and march off in formation for action. Some very strong language reflecting on the peculiar ways of the staff, helped to restore a semblance of good humour.[23]

By 3.30 am the 14th and 16th Australian Brigades assembled in the unoccupied sunken road. Here the Diggers lay upon the snow-covered ground undetected. They were denied greatcoats, because they were considered too heavy and with the mills bombs and ammunition they carried, such clothing would restrict their movement during the attack. Here they patiently awaited the tanks that were to lead them through the barbed wire. At 4.15 am it was reported that the tanks were delayed by the snowstorm and that they had only reached Noreuil, which meant they required a further hour and a half to reach the start point of the attack. This delay had serious implications, because dawn was approaching, which would make the tanks and infantry clearly visible to the enemy. The element of surprise would be lost and the attacking force annihilated. Major General William Holmes, commanding the 4th Division AIF, realised that it was necessary to withdraw the Australian infantry who were already assembled in No Man's Land without alerting the enemy. He gave the order to abort the operation. The Australians were fortunate, because the snow blizzard concealed their withdrawal. However, the withdrawal was planned in haste, which resulted in a breakdown in communication. The 4th Australian Division Staff had failed to inform the neighbouring 62nd Division that the attack was aborted. Unaware of the Australian withdrawal, the West Yorkshires carried out the attack as planned. British Tanks had let down the Australian Infantry; but the Australian commanders' failure to communicate the withdrawal to their counterparts in the 62nd Division would result in tragedy for the British, who were about to advance upon the village of Bullecourt without support on their right flank.

The officer commanding the 2nd/7th Battalion West Yorkshire Regiment had received a copy of the orders relating to the attack in the early hours of 10th April. In the battalion war diary, he states that prior to receiving these orders 'a rough idea of the operation had been given to the O.C. Coys concerned.'[24]

At 4.35 am the 2/5th, 2/7th and 2/8th West Yorkshire Battalions left their trenches. As they approached the enemy wire at Bullecourt, they realised that the tanks and the Australian infantry to their right were absent. They succeeded in cutting through the first wire, but once enemy flares illuminated No Man's Land, German machine gunners in Bullecourt concentrated their fire upon the West Yorkshires. The officer commanding the

The sunken road in front of the 12th Brigade AIF frontline. (Author)

2nd/7th West Yorkshires wrote that at 4.50 am 'patrols came under heavy machine gun fire .... it [is] obvious that Bullecourt is still strongly held.[25]

Many men were entangled and trapped in the barbed wire, where they fell. Those who survived sought sanctuary in the sunken road, but even here they were not safe, for some were blown to pieces by an intense barrage from their own artillery. Braithwaite, commanding the 62nd Division, was informed of the operation's postponement at 4.55 am, which was too late. By 5.00 am the shelling had stopped. The West Yorkshires had lost 162 men. If Holme's staff had communicated to Braithwaite that the 4th Division had aborted the operation, then these men might not have died. At 5.10 am the 2/7th West Yorkshires were ordered to withdraw.

Seven wounded soldiers from the West Yorkshires caught in the wire were captured. The German commander of the 120th Regiment, *Oberst* von Gleich was concerned that the events of that morning was the beginning of a major offensive and promptly ordered an artillery barrage to target British positions along the railway embankment. A hail of shells poured down upon the 48th Battalion HQ, killing 21 men, including Major Ben Leane, 2nd in command of the battalion. Lieutenant Colonel Raymond Leane, his brother and commander of the 48th Battalion, found his body and carried it away for burial.

There were many acts of bravery that day. Riflemen Walter Gough and Benjamin Draycott were two stretcher bearers from the 2nd/8th Battalion West Yorkshire Regiment who ventured into No Man's Land to rescue a wounded artillery officer. The position was being heavily shelled. As they were carrying the officer to the safety of their own lines Rifleman Draycott was killed. Despite the loss of his mate Gough carried the wounded officer another 100 yards. If it was not for the efforts of Gough and Draycott this officer would have certainly been killed. (Note that the date given for this action is 10th April 1917 in WO 95/3075 185 Brigade War Diary. The Commonwealth War Grave Commission records the date of Draycott's death as 7th April 1917). Gough was awarded the Military Medal for his bravery.

Sergeant Thomas Henry Gower who belonged to 2nd/8th Battalion West Yorkshire Regiment was in Company reserve near the railway embankment on 10th April. On hearing Rifleman Pickard lying in an exposed position crying out for help, Gower went to his aid despite the shells that were falling on the position and brought him to safety. Gower was also awarded the Military Medal. Gower was later promoted to Company Sergeant Major and killed on 23rd November 1917. He was buried at Rocquigny-Equancourt Road British Cemetery, Manancourt.

Some retiring Australians also became casualties. It was miraculous that there were so few. Sergeant Douglas Blackburn later recounted the desperate dash as they withdrew and of their one stroke of good fortune:

> No one who took part in that 'retreat' will ever forget the ensuing scramble. Someone surely had a lucky halfpenny or a hare's foot with him that morning; for a heavy snowstorm providentially blowing up, we were able to get back across the plain in daylight with hardly any casualties.[26]

German observers on high ground at Hendecourt might not have seen the Australian troops withdrawing en masse because of the falling snow. Lieutenant Colonel Howard Denham, commanding the 46th Battalion, was convinced that the Germans could indeed see the withdrawal:

> The attacking troops were therefore ordered back, and, to the enemy's amazement, what had appeared to him a perfectly normal No Man's Land suddenly assumed the appearance of a crowd returning from a football match. So astounded were the Germans that for some considerable time not a shot was fired; however, they made up for it later, but by then most of our men had regained our front line.[27]

Private Leslie Pezet from the 15th Battalion AIF wrote of his experience of the aborted attack:

> On the evening of the 9th April we are ordered a good issue of rum, and a big dinner – all to be ready at nine o'clock in full marching order to march to the line, carrying full packs, blankets, pick and shovel, 200 rounds ammunition, and a sand bag of canteen stuff for ourselves. We get to sunken road and dump packs and rations. When attack is finished carriers will bring them along to us the fighters. We are formed in line, bayonets fixed waiting for order to come from right to charge over a distance of 1,200 yards, daybreak upon us, the order came to retire at the double, everyone is sick at heart, making up our mind to got into it and get it over. The German guns were quiet and no machine gun fire, we were mad, we start to retire, the Hun see us and now for it, machine and artillery fire etc. Terrible snow storm comes and the Hun scatter their fire and they cannot see us and we dodge it with very few men not to answer roll call on our return.[28]

Relations between the British and Australians were severely strained as a result of this catastrophe. The commanders and men of the AIF felt that they were let down by the non appearance of British tanks. The whole operation was dependent upon the advance of the tanks and their failure to appear at the scheduled time caused a great loss of confidence in the tank as a weapon of war and loss of respect for the crews that manned them. The senior commanders, Haig and Gough, who sanctioned the attack, were bitterly condemned. The Australians' confidence in Gough and Haig was seriously undermined. Those men who lay in the snow waiting for their arrival also criticized high command for their belief in the tank. The 48th Battalion history:

> Those men got up stiff and cold and cramped, damning the tanks, and the stupidity of the higher command that backed the tanks. They returned to their own trenches just as does a crowd disperse after a football match, no pretence at taking cover, no care for an enemy.[29]

The botched attempt had undermined confidence in any further attacks on this sector of the Hindenburg Line. It alerted German forces that another attack was possible and they strengthened the line at Bullecourt with reinforcements. Most importantly, the mess had a negative impact on the morale of the men who took part.

Hours after the initial attack had failed; General Gough chaired a meeting at his HQ in Albert with Corps Commanders, artillery, tank commanders and representatives from the Royal Flying Corps, at midday on 10th April. Gough announced that another attack upon Bullecourt would take place the next day. Lieutenant General Birdwood, commander of I Anzac Corps raised his concerns about further attacks – no surprise – especially when the tanks, the main element in the plan had proved unreliable. He was acutely conscious that there was not adequate time to prepare his troops; not to mention the possibility that the enemy had been alerted by the patrols during that morning and would be prepared for another attempted offensive at Bullecourt. General Gough overruled him with the argument that the tanks failed owing to particular circumstances and stated he was confident that 75% of the tanks would enter the Hindenburg Line. The plan was amended. He did not consider that the Germans would be waiting for an attack, with no explanation for such an assertion. To maintain the element of surprise for the tanks, there was to be no creeping barrage to support the infantry. There was to be no bombardment of Bullecourt, instead, the village would be shelled with poison gas prior to the assault. A normal bombardment would be carried out throughout the night, but would be suspended at 5.00

am at Bullecourt and 5.15 am at Riencourt to allow the advancing allies sufficient time to enter the villages and ensure that they did not become victims of their own artillery. Tanks would leave their starting lines at 4.30 am, followed 15 minutes later by the infantry. Once Bullecourt had been captured, six tanks would move into Bullecourt on Major General Walter Braithwaite's 62nd Division front and would assist in the advance on Hendecourt. The infantry would advance after the tanks without waiting for a signal from them indicating that they had breached the wire.

This attempt to breach the Hindenburg Line within 24 hours of the botched initial foray was a grave decision: the Germans were now alerted to the fact that their enemy had ideas of making a breakthrough in this sector of the front and they had had a day to strengthen and fortify Bullecourt. Sergeant W.D. Blackburn withdrew with the 14th Battalion under the cover of the snowstorm on 10th April, but was only too aware that the German forces defending this stretch of the Hindenburg Line were expecting another attempt to breach the line: 'Though the snowstorm saved our lives that morning, it certainly put Fritz wise to our little game, as well we knew when we returned for the second spasm 24 hours later.'[30]

The 124th Infantry Regiment holding OG 1 and OG 2 east of Bullecourt and the 123rd Infantry Regiment occupying Quéant were not aware of the two Australian Brigades' presence on the railway embankment, or of the aborted attack. The 120th Infantry Regiment in Bullecourt could see the withdrawal, although many of the soldiers in the village were suffering from the effects of gas propelled into their lines earlier that morning. They had also been attacked by men from the 62nd Division and that was evidence enough to suspect that something was imminent on this sector of the front.

During the afternoon of 10th April, German observers in the air and on the ground could see masses of troops south of Bullecourt. Considering that Bullecourt had been attacked by gas and the villages of Hendecourt, Riencourt and Cagnicourt were subjected to heavy shelling the previous night, German commanders could hardly fail to be alerted. The II Battalion of the 124th Infantry Regiment was brought forward to a position south of Riencourt. German artillery was placed on alert to counter any artillery barrages upon the villages in the vicinity. German artillery action further intensified at dusk on 10th April as their guns targeted the railway embankment on the 62nd Division's front line and continued sporadically throughout that night in anticipation that the British would assemble for another attack. After he was captured on 11th April, Captain Dunworth was told by a German Intelligence Officer.

... that had we attacked the first night with an efficient barrage we had an excellent chance of success, enabling our turning of the flank of the German forces; and that as they knew we would return to the attack they had rushed up strong reinforcements of storm troops.[31]

The 2nd /6th West Yorkshire Regiment had not taken part in the initial assault on 10th April. They were resting at St Leger on the 10th April, when they received orders that they would proceed to Ecoust-St-Mein later that night, in order to take part in an operation to capture Bullecourt and Hendecourt during the early hours of the following morning. Orders were issued at 11 pm on 10th April, but were not received by the battalion commander until 12.25 am on the 11th. The hour of attack was scheduled for 4.30 am. The plan of attack was as follows. If the Hindenburg Line was found to be evacuated by the enemy, the battalions of the 4th Australian Division would send strong forward parties on the right flank under the cover of an artillery barrage. They would be supported by tanks and their objective was to advance on Riencourt and clear the enemy from Bullecourt. As soon as the 4th Australian Division had accomplished these objectives, the British 185th Brigade would send one battalion into Bullecourt from the south west, supported by another battalion. Heavy reliance upon the Australians and the tanks entering Bullecourt and the Hindenburg Line is clear in the orders, before the 185th Brigade battalion could be sent into Bullecourt. If Bullecourt was captured, then the British would drive an advance towards Hendecourt and the Australians would head for Cagnicourt.

The operation depended upon the 4th Australian Division, supported by 12 tanks from D Battalion, Tank Corps, east of the village. Once they had entered Bullecourt from the north east, only then would the 185th Brigade send in 2nd/6th and 2nd/8th West Yorkshire Regiments. The 185th Battalion orders for the 11th April 1917 assault stated:

> Unless it is discovered during the night that the enemy have evacuated the Hindenburg Line on our front, the 4th Australian Division will push forward strong patrols under a barrage, on the morning of 11th April.

Royal Flying Corps aerial photo showing OG 1 and OG 2 Trenches at Reincourt taken on 24th April 1917. (Author)

Zero Hour will be 4.30 am.

The 4th Australian Division attack will be supported by Tanks. The objective of the 4th Australian Division will be Riencourt and the clearing of Bullecourt.

The 185th Infantry Brigade will push one Battalion into Bullecourt from the south west, with 1 Battalion in support, as soon as the operations by the 4th Australian Division make this possible, and, supported by Tanks will clear and occupy the Hindenburg Line westwards as far as U.20.b.

If we succeed in occupying the Hindenburg Line an advanced guard strength as par margin, will capture Hendecourt and move forward in the general direction of Villers-Lez-Cagnicourt, gaining touch northwards with the cavalry corps and covering the left of the ANZAC Corps, who will be advancing towards Cagnicourt.[32]

The Australians were apprehensive about the prospect of breaking into the Hindenburg Line, but they were comforted by the thought that for the first time during the war the Australian battalions would enter the battle together. Captain David Dunworth from the 15th Battalion AIF:

> When the 4th Bde learned that it was to be employed in an effort to break the much vaunted Hindenburg line it was recognized that the task set was very severe, but general pleasure was felt by the men that for the first time in France all of the battalions would be joined together in the stunt – not piece-meal, and that each battalion would give support to and receive support from one another.[33]

NOTES

1. *Official History of Australia in the War of 1914–1918* Volume 4, Charles Bean, Angus and Robertson Limited 1938: p264.
2. National Archives: WO 95/3443 4th Australian Division Intelligence Summary No123 (Appendix 35).
3. National Archives: WO 95 /3079: 185th Brigade War Diary.
4. Ibid.
5. Ibid.
6. Ibid.
7. *Military Operations France and Belgium 1917* Volume 1, Captain Cyril Falls p236.
8. *A Company of Tanks*, Major W.H.L. Watson, William Blackwood and Sons, Edinburgh and London, p21.
9. Ibid, p22.
10. Ibid, p21.
11. Ibid, p22.
12. Ibid, p22.
13. National Archives: WO 95/3494: 14th AIF Battalion War Diary.
14. Ibid.
15. *Official History of Australia in the War of 1914–1918* Volume 4, Charles Bean, Angus and Robertson Limited 1938: p276.
16. National Archives: WO095/3494: 14th AIF Battalion War Diary.
17. *The Old Sixteenth*, Captain C. Longmore, the History Committee of the 16th Battalion Association: 1929: p133.
18. E.J. Rule Diary quoted from Jacka VC, Australia's Finest Soldier by Ian Grant, Sun Books 1990: P102.
19. *Reveille*: 1st April 1933: Captain David Dunworth MC (15th Battalion AIF) Testimony.
20. Ibid.
21. *A Company of Tanks*, p22.
22. Ibid.
23. *In Good Company, An Account of the 6th Machine Gun Company AIF 1915–19*, Lieutenant William Carne: Published Melbourne 1937.
24. National Archives: WO 95/3082: 2nd/7th Battalion West Yorkshire Regiment War Diary.
25. Ibid.
26. *Reveille*: 1st April 1933: Sgt. Douglas Blackburn's (14th Battalion AIF) Testimony.
27. *Reveille*: 1st April 1933: Lieutenant Colonel Howard Denham's (46th Battalion AIF) Testimony.
28. Private Leslie Pezet Diary (15th Battalion AIF): Courtesy Ken Pezet.
29. Taken from We Were The 46th p39, extracted from the 48th Battalion History entitled *The Story of A Battalion*.
30. *Reveille*: 1st April 1933: Sergeant. W.D. Blackburn's (14th Battalion AIF) Testimony.
31. *Reveille*: 1st April 1933: Captain David Dunworth MC (15th Battalion AIF) Testimony.
32. National Archives: WO 95/3082: 185th Infantry Brigade Operational Order No.19.
33. *Reveille*: 1st April 1933: Captain David Dunworth MC (15th Battalion AIF) Testimony.

CHAPTER 7

THE 4TH AUSTRALIAN BRIGADE'S ASSAULT UPON BULLECOURT

At 10.30 pm on the night of 10th April, the 15th Battalion once again left Favreuil and marched the seven miles through the snow to the railway embankment. For Lieutenant William Boland it was a welcome relief to get moving. He was an officer with the 14th Battalion who had spent the day in a wet trench awaiting orders to repeat the operation. He recalled that 'the night was extremely cold, and we were glad to leave the wet, uncomfortable trench in which we had spent the day.'[1] Lance Corporal Bert Knowles from the 13th Battalion remembered being 'warned to leave all diaries and papers behind; and also to conserve our rations and water.'[2]

As the infantry lumbered through the snow, since 1 am Bullecourt was being attacked for the second consecutive night with gas, but according to Captain Dunworth the gas had no effect upon the Wüttembergers from the 124th Regiment who were holding the line at Bullecourt. Throughout the early hours of the morning the village was bombarded by artillery until Zero Hour. The German guns responded with their own barrage. Lieutenant Edgar Rule later recalled. 'As soon as they started, the Hun lit up the sky with Very lights, and we could plainly see our gas-bombs bursting and giving off dense clouds of gas which were slowly drifting over the village, and it was so thick that it must have caught a few Huns.'[3] During the early hours on the 11th, the exhausted Australian Infantry returned to their starting positions. Private Gallwey remembered his thoughts as he proceeded through Noreuil Valley with the 47th AIF Battalion:

> I carried my rifle in my left hand, just holding it by the sling and trailing the butt through the mud. It was too much energy to carry it any other way. Knees were giving way, and I was plodding on like in a dream ... Of what use would I be to fight tonight? My body was in a wretched state of weakness.[4]

The snow on the ground was much deeper than the previous day and they had to spend another cold, sleepless night getting to their assembly positions and waiting in No Man's Land for the tanks to arrive. They could hear the tanks approaching at 3 am. There were fears that the Germans might have heard them. After the war Lieutenant Edgar Rule confirmed that the Germans did in fact hear the approaching tanks. Lieutenant William Boland with the 14th Battalion also realised that as he heard the tanks approaching, 'the enemy doubtless heard them also.'[5]

German sentry posts on the 124th Infantry Regiment line opposite the Australian lines could hear the sound of petrol engines approaching in the distance as early as 2.00 am. The sound became audible amidst the exploding shells to the 123rd Infantry Regiment in Quéant at 3.00 am. They could see that Bullecourt was being shelled.

Captain Jacka, who had gone out onto No Man's Land on the second consecutive night to lay down jumping off tapes, had performed beyond his duties as 14th Battalion Intelligence Officer in guiding three tanks into their correct positions in front of the 14th and 16th Battalions. The first tank arrived at the rendezvous point at the railway crossing at 3.00 am. Captain Jacka guided this tank into its starting position twenty minutes later. This tank was part of the right flank advance. Jacka asked the crew if they could reach the Hindenburg Line in 15 minutes and the tank commander replied that it was impossible. Jacka realised that the Australian infantry would reach the wire before the tanks and that a disaster was about to occur. He brought the tank commander to confer with the 14th and 16th Battalion commanders, Lieutenant Colonels Peck and Drake-Brockman, whose headquarters were at the railway embankment. Drake-Brockman, horrified by the implications of the tanks being unable to support the infantry advance, immediately telephoned Major General Holmes and requested a 15-minute delay of the infantry advance to ensure that the tanks got to the objective before the infantry. Brockman's request was denied. It was too late to make any changes to the plan and Holmes ordered him 'to stick to the programme'. Drake-Brockman had to send his infantry towards the German machine guns knowing full well that the men would be leading the tanks instead of the tanks leading the men. Only four of the twelve tanks designated for the attack had reached their starting points at the scheduled time of 4.30 am. One tank was out of action and seven tanks were delayed by the severe blizzard.

As the attack commenced at 4.30 am, the three tanks assigned to advance ahead of the Australian Infantry battalions from the 4th Brigade could be heard by the enemy approaching their wire and the noise of the engines was not drowned by the sound of machine gun fire, as originally hoped. A German sentry must have seen the tanks because at 4.35 am a green signal flare was fired from Bullecourt village and a second was fired a minute later. Green and golden flares were fired from the same position at 4.40 am and German machine guns opened fire. Australian infantry were lying still in the snow in nervous anticipation of the signal to advance as these flares illuminated No Man's Land. The 124th Infantry Regiment could hear the tanks approaching and could see dense black figures in the white snow.

Despite the failure of half of the tanks assigned to the Australian front to arrive, at 4.45 am the 16th, 15th, 14th and 13th Battalions of the 4th Australian Brigade commanded by Brigadier-General Charles Henry Brand advanced in four waves at distances of 200 yards.

Men from the 16th Battalion were advancing closest to the three tanks. Half way across No Man's Land two of these tanks stopped to begin firing upon enemy positions. The enemy returned fire. Commanders in the 16th Battalion decided to press on with the advance without the tanks. As they approached the German lines hundreds of flares were launched into the sky, illuminating the snow-covered ground, making the approaching Diggers horribly visible. Jacka's report was proven correct: the wire had only been cut in some places and most of it was still intact. As they searched for gaps in the wire, many Australians fell dead and wounded. Private Edward Bentley was in the first wave as the 16th advanced towards the barbed wire. Bentley was a machine gunner. Private Thomas Sloss:

Loftus Bentley was killed instantaneously by M.G. fire on 11.4.17. He was a Machine Gunner and went over with the first wave. I was in the fourth wave and came about his body in the trench about 11 am he had three bullets through his neck close together, and from the position in which I found him, I felt sure that death was instantaneous.[6]

Sergeant George Mace from the 16th Battalion was an Englishman from Derbyshire who had settled as a farmer in Australia and had been in the patrols led by Jacka on the two previous nights and had guided his men to their jumping off positions. Mace played a prominent role in braving enemy fire to attend to the wounded and bring them to the safety of the railway embankment. His recommendation for the Military Medal recorded that 'he went out to 'No Man's Land' from our Outpost position under a veritable hail of Machine Gun bullets and attended to and assisted to bring in wounded men.'[7]

The tanks which were intended to support the 14th Battalion were slow in reaching their assembly positions and proved more of a hazard to the Australians than the enemy. Sergeant Douglas Blackburn was in charge of the Lewis gun section in the 14th Battalion:

We passed the tanks on our way to the assembly position. It is a pity they ever caught up to us again. While we were waiting in the sunken road for 'Zero' one of the tanks straddled our trench and suddenly opened up on us. One poor chap in our Lewis Gun section got such a fright that he jumped backwards and was impaled on his own bayonet. He had had it fixed and his rifle was leaning alongside him.[8]

The men from the 14th Battalion could not wait for the tanks and once it was Zero Hour the first infantry waves overtook the floundering machines. Lieutenant William Boland recalled the moments of anxiety as they waited to attack:

Battle of Bullecourt, 11th April 1917 ('Military Operations, France & Belgium 1917' by Captain Cyril Falls, map Crown Copyright).

The minutes were now dragging along to zero hour. Every man felt that it was the eve of the greatest battle in the history of the 4th Brigade, and all seemed anxious to get it over. At last the words 'one minute to go' were passed along, then simply 'Advance'. The battalion immediately moved forward in four waves, some sixty yards from the other, with each man about six feet distant from his neighbour. The ground was white with snow, which was still falling, though slightly. This advance, over 800 yards of open country as level as a table, was the most wonderful sight I have ever seen.[9]

Major Percy Black who was standing at the rear of the 16th Battalion charged to the front and with great bravado shouted 'Come on boys, bugger the tanks!'[10] This act inspired the battalion to charge across No Man's Land and cut through the wire.

As the 14th Battalion advanced, to their horror they discovered that the artillery had caused minor damage and had not formed breaches in the barbed wire. The wire defences were 25 metres deep and over a metre high, so thick that a soldier could not see through it. 'The wire was found badly damaged but no lanes had been cut right through and our troops suffered heavy casualties getting through it.'[11] Lieutenant Edgar Rule witnessed the carnage:

> As soon as it came in sight of the Huns the massacre commenced, the enemy lining his parapet and shooting down our boys like rabbits. Lots of them reached the wire, but ... had to bunch together; and they fell in heaps on the wire and in front of it. The wonder is that any of them reached the trench. But reach it they did, and took the enemy's front line.[12]

Lieutenant William Boland:

> It seemed as if every artillery piece, machine-gun and trench mortar in the entire German Army were opening on us. As for the barbed-wire, there was not a single gap in it, so it was a case of getting through as best one could. It was so thick that some chaps even tried to walk on top of it.[13]

Sergeant William Charles Groves advanced with the 14th Battalion:

> With startling suddenness, the silence ceases. With a fury of hell, the enemy machine guns spit out incessant fire. The chaps try frantically to find a way through the frightful network of barbed wire. The enemy had left zig zag passages here and there into which the men pour in dense columns to be mown down so that their shattered bodies pile up at the entrances.[14]

The 13th Battalion followed the 16th and could see the chaotic struggle of the leading wave. Lieutenant Colonel James Durrant, Commanding Officer of 13th Battalion saw how early the machine guns opened up: 'As soon as they left the shelter of the cutting losses from shell fire commenced. When about 600 yards from the 1st objective the battalion came under heavy machine gun fire, which became more intense at the first wire and officers and men fell fast.'[15]

Lieutenant Colonel Terrence McSharry commanding the 15th Battalion reported the wire in front of the first objective to be 'almost intact'[16] and that the battalion had suffered 100 casualties trying to cut through it.

Lance Corporal Bert Knowles led a party of six men and a Lewis gun section from the 13th Battalion across No Man's Land. He was following behind the legendary Captain Harry Murray, who was the AIF's most highly decorated soldier. Knowles later recounted that the fearless Murray 'was strolling along as if death was something which came with old age'.[17] Most of Bert Knowles' party was wiped out before they reached the German wire:

> A few yards further on we walked into a barrage of machine-gun fire from the village of Quéant. Glancing in that direction, I saw rows of men in the semi-darkness crumpled up. My own section now comprised two men and myself.[18]

As this murderous machine-gun fire cut down the advancing 13th Battalion, Captain Murray gave the order 'Get down, 13th, until it passes.'[19]

> We lay close to the ground in the snow for a while, and listened to a noise like thousands of bees passing overhead. I saw a tank smothered with little sparks where the bullets were striking. Various coloured star shells flashed in the rear, and overhead, where their shells were bursting, lighted up the snow covered ground, which was dotted with dead and wounded.[20]

With half their strength gone, Knowles and all those who ran, walked and crawled through this slaughter began to lose hope. They were pinned down in No Man's Land. They had to get through two belts of German wire, enter OG 1 and OG 2, link up with the British 62nd Division in Bullecourt, and hold the village for two days. There were no supporting troops behind the 13th Battalion. Achieving the objectives looked absurd and personal survival became the main priority. Captain Murray was aware of the carnage in the ranks of the 13th Battalion, but he could also see that his friend, Major Percy Black and the 16th Battalion, whom they were meant to be supporting, were still struggling to get through the wire. Knowles remembered when Murray rallied his men: 'I

Diorama depicting the Battle of Bullecourt on 11th April 1917. (Australian War Memorial: AWM ART 41022)

was brought back to realities by the same wonderful voice in front, "Come on 13th! The 16th are getting hell." And we did the next 200 yards or so at a jog trot.[21]

Murray and the 13th Battalion reached the wire alongside. Major Black and the 16th. If a gap was found in the wire then it would be swarmed by desperate Australians from both these battalions trying to get through. They were easy pickings for German machine-gunners. Lance Corporal Bert Knowles:

> It was now almost daylight, and although there was still a mist, the drizzle of snow had ceased; also our artillery fire and the enemy machine guns were having it all their own way. Anywhere, where men were grouped together trying to penetrate the barbed wire, the machine-guns simply wiped out 50 per cent, with a swish; but men lay on their sides and hacked at the wire with their bayonets. Some few had cutters: others tried to cross the top, leaping from one strand to another. Many slipped and became hopelessly entangled in the loosely bunched wire. Many were shot down half way through, and hung up on the wire in various attitudes.[22]

Knowles was fortunate to find access through the wire which was used by German patrols at the right moment:

> I managed to scramble through a gap which had been left by Fritz for his patrol to use. The machine gun which usually covered these gaps was evidently put out of action by the 16th, who had, by this time, taken their objective.[23]

The 16th Battalion had succeeded in fighting their way into OG 1 Trench, but it was achieved at a high cost. A bitter battle was fought as they entered the trench:

> I then arrived at what looked like an unfinished portion of trench, about 18 inches deep and 8 or 9 feet wide, in which many dead and wounded were lying – mostly 16th men. Others were lying along the far side, using their rifles over the top.[24]

Major Black had sent a runner back to Battalion Head-quarters: 'First objective gained, pushing on to second

objective.'[25] It was at OG 1 that vicious hand-to-hand fighting took place. OG 1 was a very wide and deep trench with earthen walls and deep dug-outs. About 60 German prisoners were captured in this trench and sent back to the Australian lines; 42 survived crossing No Man's Land, the remainder falling victim to their own machine gun fire.

Once OG 1 Trench had been captured Major Black pressed onto the second objective, OG 2, which was held by the enemy in great strength. As they advanced towards OG 2 the 16th Battalion found that the barbed wire entanglements between OG 1 and OG 2 trenches were uncut and it was here that many of Black's men became casualties or were forced to take refuge in the nearest shell hole.

The enemy offered stubborn resistance at the second objective. Major Black led attempts to find gaps in the wire under a torrent of heavy German machine gun fire. The 13th Battalion war diary recorded:

> The 16th Battalion had taken the first objective, but were seen to be in very great difficulties with the 2nd objective, the wire in front of which was uncut, and it was only too evident that the 16th Battalion had suffered enormous losses from machine gun fire in taking the first objective.[26]

Major Black suffered a fatal shot to the head as he was trying to break through the second wire. He was one of many men who were left hanging on the wire as they died. Captain Harry Murray, his comrade from the 16th Machine Gun Section, passed the body of Percy Black as he led his men from A Company, 13th Battalion through a gap in the wire into OG 2.

The 13th Battalion proceeded with remnants of the 16th Battalion towards OG 2 Trench, where they too found the second line of wire to be intact. A tank had been trapped in the wire defences before OG 1 trench and within 10 yards a German machine gun crew was firing upon Australian soldiers as they passed it. Men from Captain Murray's A Company attacked and silenced this machine gun. Survivors entered the second trench through communication trenches. Using Mills bombs they evicted the enemy from some sectors of the second trench.

Private Leonard Rzeszkowski had struggled to cut through the barbed wire, but returned to help his mates belonging to the 16th Battalion who were caught in the wire by cutting them free. Exposed to almost certain death, he defied the odds to save his comrades under horrendous enemy fire. Sergeant Leslie Boully was another man who helped comrades entangled within the high density barbed wire defences. When all the officers around him had become casualties, Sergeant Boully took control of the situation and organised two fragmented platoons as the machine guns fired upon them. He then ventured into the exposed area between OG 1 and OG 2 to rescue two wounded men.

Remnants of the battered 16th Battalion eventually broke through into OG 2 Trench by 6.30 am that morning. Among those that advanced through the wire under heavy fire was Private Thomas Caldwell. His recommendation for the Military Medal stated that 'he displayed absolute fearlessness in advancing to the objective through uncut wire in this way'.[27] German sniper and machine gun fire poured upon them from all directions, preventing any movement above the ground. The 16th Battalion war diary records that 'The fighting was most severe, continuous bombing parties having to be beaten off, while all the time Machine Guns from all directions kept up a continual fire on parapet'.[28]

Captain Murray's men were bombing westwards along OG 2 Trench and had established contact with men from the 14th Battalion on their left flank. They had achieved the impossible; they had charged from the railway embankment up a slope, under a surge of enemy machine gun and artillery fire without support from tanks or artillery, across the snow. They had fought their way through the wire and entered both OG 1 and OG 2 trenches. It was an amazing feat without tank and artillery support.

Once they had secured sectors of OG 2 Trench, the second objective, the Australians could see the enemy withdrawing to Riencourt and Bullecourt. Here they sniped and fired Lewis machine guns as the enemy retreated. It was not long before German units launched a counter attack to win back lost ground. At 7.30 am German reinforcement soldiers were heading from Riencourt armed with many bombs.

As the German bombing parties mounted continuous attacks in waves, Sergeant Leslie Boully erected a barricade within his sector of OG 2 Trench occupied by the 16th Battalion.

Private Maurice Bercovitch, 16th Battalion was in the thick of the action for most of the morning. His recommendation for the Military Medal reported:

> One Lewis Gun team was entirely annihilated. He filled some empty magazines from the pouches of

the dead and went from end to end of the section of enemy trenches held by us looking for and finding targets. This he did for four hours and did great execution amongst the enemy.[29]

Private James Walsh, also from the 16th Battalion, positioned his Lewis gun on the parapet of the OG 2 Trench despite the dangers from sniper and machine gun fire and dispersed a batch of fifty German reinforcements, suppressing their counter attack before it had gained momentum.

As the morning progressed, ammunition supplies depleted, casualties mounted and German counter attacks grew stronger as the Australian parties holding on became exhausted. A desperate close quarter battle was fought for several hours in the Hindenburg Line trenches. Bombs and bayonets were used to stem the determined German attacks. The situation was so desperate that the Australians resorted to frantically searching for any ammunition from dead and wounded comrades. Lance Corporal Bert Knowles provided a graphic account of the frenzied battle to hold onto the foothold they had gained 14 years later in *Reveille*:

> For the next four or five hours things seemed to be a sort of nightmare, consisting of throwing Mills bombs over a traverse of the trench or sap, waiting for them to explode, and then rushing into the next portion of trench with a bayonet, and shoot or chase any Hun out who was not wounded. This was repeated into the next section; or, before we were really in, we could see a shower of enemy bombs coming over, and we would get back round the corner until they had exploded, and then rush forward again before Fritz had time to occupy the disputed section. Captain Murray instructed us where to build a block in the trench. Then the enemy, with lighter bombs, would make us give way a little, but before he could cross the barrier we would be back again to meet him, and blow him out of the next section again. Meanwhile, we would help Lewis gunners over the top into shell holes on either side of us, so they could stop Fritz's carrying parties farther back along the trench. This gave us a breather occasionally, in which to drag our wounded back out of range of bombs, empty our dead pals' cartridge pouches and load panniers for the Lewis guns. Others would run back and try and collect a few more Mills bombs from dead and wounded in the rear, and find out, if possible, how the fight was going in other parts of the trench, and see if there was any chance of getting a little more help. In this way we learned that we had blocks at each end of the first and second trenches, and one sap, and were holding our own while ammunition lasted.[30]

The 14th and 15th Battalions had a similar experience as they advanced to the left of the 16th and 13th Battalions and the Central Road. The wire before OG 1 was intact and undamaged, but once this was breached many Australians became casualties as they crossed the fifty yards between the first wire and OG 1 Trench. OG 1 was promptly captured by the 14th Battalion. Lieutenant William Boland advanced with B Company, 14th Battalion:

> The Germans, shoulder to shoulder, could be seen lining their trench, and shooting as fast as they could pull their triggers. Suddenly a yell went up from some of my company ('B') as they forced an entry. Soon on either side of us men from various battalions poured into the trench, and brisk hand-to-hand fighting ensued. This was a proper test for our Mills bombs without which I am doubtful if one man could have got into the Hindenburg Line.[31]

Before the supporting 15th Battalion had reached OG 1, the 16th were already advancing towards OG 2. Many men could not penetrate the wire and would become casualties. Other men sheltered in shell holes. It was Lieutenant Thompson and a party from the 14th Battalion who led a small party through a communication trench into OG 2 and captured it. The 15th Battalion was supporting the 14th Battalion's advance and it is reported in their War Diary, 'the wire in front of first objective was almost intact on our front and it is estimated we had nearly 100 casualties on this wire from enemy enfilade M.G. fire'.[32]

Captain David Dunworth from the 15th Battalion recalled the grim sight: 'The wire looked awful with dead men strung on them like clothes pegs. Those who were kept in the dug-outs till later told me that they felt sick when they saw the blood pools in the snow.'[33] Dunworth advanced with the 15th Battalion and commented on the destructiveness of the German shells upon their advancing line:

> The German heavies were enfilading us from Quéant. I saw one section of the 15th wiped out by a heavy shell. I ordered the troops into lines of skirmishers. Without a single protective shell, we advanced. A hail of machine gun bullets met us. Fortunately, Fritz was firing a bit high. We arrived to find the 14th finishing up the first line. We pushed through and stormed the second.[34]

Dunworth organised men from both the 14th and 15th Battalions who were in OG 1 Trench and assaulted OG 2. Although wounded as he led his men over ground exposed to enemy machine gun and rifle fire he carried on. 'The 14th and 15th were thoroughly mixed owing to the heavy fighting. I collected a small body of men of both units in the first line, and made for the second line overland. I was wounded, but recovering, pushed on with the men to the front line'.[35]

The 15th Battalion fought their way into OG 2 Trench after suffering further casualties which were inflicted upon them as they tried to get through the barbed wire entanglements before the second objective, swept by incessant German machine gun fire. The 15th Battalion War Diary reported that 200 German soldiers were killed and 38 taken prisoner.[36] Twenty of these prisoners were killed by their own artillery fire.

Despite the carnage inflicted, Captain David Dunworth, 15th Battalion never forgot his orders and with great determination and tenacity he continued the advance upon Riencourt once he had reached OG 2 Trench. It was thought that Dunworth was probably the officer in the Australian 4th Brigade who advanced farthest into the German-occupied positions. Captain Dunworth, on reaching OG 2, led an attack down a communication trench called *Cannstatter Graben*, known to the Australian's as 'Ostrich Alley', which led to Riencourt. Three tanks were meant to have broken through, but Captain Dunworth proceeded in their absence. In charging across exposed ground most of Dunworth's party was killed by machine gun fire. The Germans occupying 'Ostrich Trench' soon retreated, but by that time Dunworth was wounded and was forced to crawl along this communication trench back to OG 2. He wrote:

> I gathered 14 or 15, and ordered them to follow me. My objective was Riencourt, and my idea was to push on while some N.C.O.s, to whom I had given hurried orders, collected the rest of my company and any other 15th Battalion men and brought them on. We pushed on towards the six roads. I was about 30 yards ahead of my men, who were all far out, when I was shot in the left shoulder and fell on my face. At the same moment an enemy M.G. post opened on the small party behind me. It kept a continuous fire on the party and when, later, I looked round, every man had been killed.[37]

Captain Somerville led a party from the 16th Battalion along another communication trench called *Calwer Graben*, later known to the British as 'Emu Alley' and made an attempt to reach Riencourt, but this was stopped by a thick belt of barbed wire 250 yards from the village. They too were forced to withdraw to OG 2. Any further advance towards Riencourt was deemed not to be viable, owing to heavy casualties sustained and depleted stocks of bombs and ammunition, and therefore it was decided to consolidate OG 1 and OG 2. Sandbags blocked the sections of the trenches held by the Australians.

With all his men killed, and after being hit by a bullet in his shoulder, Captain Dunworth would not concede that he was out of the fight. He got back to other Australian units:

I stayed still for some time, then crawled on my stomach to the right, reached a communication trench and worked my way back to our own line. The enemy was on our flanks and in front. His M.Gs swept the ground at the rear. A carrying party of the 15th was not able to pass through the hail of bullets ... So long as the munitions lasted so long did we drive back the enemy. Fritz bombarded us from Quéant with great accuracy, shell after shell falling into the trench. Our 'blocks' were destroyed by his trench mortars. When our munitions failed we tried to get at him with the bayonet, over the top, only to be knocked out by shell fire.[38]

By 8.30 am Lieutenant Colonel Terrence McSharry, the commanding officer of the 15th Battalion, had not received any reports from his units who were occupying the German trenches. He was unaware that Captain David Dunworth was wounded, fighting a battle to the last round as the enemy were encircling their positions. Runners were unable to cross the ground between OG 1 Trench and the Australian-held railway embankment because German machine gun fire was sweeping the area. Lieutenant Rae was ordered to establish communications with those who were occupying OG 1 and OG 2 but was wounded and could not get across No Man's Land. An officer from the 17th Lancers asked McSharry whether the wire was sufficiently breached to enable his cavalry to pass through. McSharry reported that the wire was not cut and horses would be unable to proceed. The officer from the 17th Lancers went into No Man's Land to assess the situation, but was wounded. McSharry then sent his intelligence officer, 2nd Lieutenant Frank Eugene Barnes, to try and establish some contact. He was wounded but managed to enter OG 1 Trench. Barnes was recommended for the Military Cross in 1916 for his work as a Sergeant during the Pozières battle. When a German officer and soldier were seen in No Man's Land, Barnes seized a rifle and shot the officer in the leg. He then went into No Man's Land, within 60 yards of the German trenches, to bring them into the Australian lines. When the Germans counter attacked at Bullecourt and surrounded the Australians holding onto their positions in OG 1 and OG 2 trenches, it is thought that Barnes refused to surrender and although wounded, tried to get back to Australian lines, but failed. Captain Percy Toft later wrote of Barnes during the Bullecourt battle:

Mr. Barnes was sent over into the captured trenches a few hours after they were taken. Unfortunately very few came back who had seen him, but I have had a letter from Lieutenant J Ingram, a Prisoner of War in Germany, who said he was with him until about half an hour before the Germans who counter attacked and practically surrounded the trenches, took most of them prisoners. A few men succeeded running the gauntlet and getting back to our own lines. Knowing Mr. Barnes well and often being with him in action I believe if he were not taken prisoner, and he often told me he'd never be taken, he was killed getting back to our own lines. Mr. Ingram stated he was not with the officers he saw taken ... I cannot speak too highly of Mr. Barnes, he was a model officer in every way.[39]

McSharry then sent runners and men with supplies of bombs and ammunition to the men holding on, but they did not return. Three attempts were made by McSharry to send supplies to his beleaguered men still holding out against German counter attacks. By 7.00 am Captain Dunworth and his party comprising the 14th and 15th Battalions were still holding on to their positions, but with their supplies of ammunition depleted they were pinned down by German snipers and machine gunners. Dunworth wrote: 'The enemy snipers were safely laying out in the open picking off our men, and it was heartbreaking to see man shot after man and no hope of retaliation.'[40]

Captain Dunworth sent a message by carrier pigeon, requesting more small arms ammunition and rifle grenades and a supportive artillery barrage. McSharry received this message from Dunworth at 7.10 am, but he realised the futility of sending men with supplies across the impassable No Man's Land in broad daylight and set about organising carrying parties to make the crossing under cover of darkness – if those holding onto OG 1 and OG 2 trenches could hold out. Dunworth was in OG 2 with no ammunition and no supporting artillery barrage until he was captured and the barrage fell 15 minutes too late, killing several of his men.

The 4th Brigade managed to overcome the strong German defence at great cost and secured their objectives. The 14th Battalion then endeavoured to meet up with the 12th Australian Brigade to their left. Although the Australians had penetrated and secured enemy front-line trenches, it was difficult to hold the positions. As daylight approached it became increasingly difficult to reinforce and replenish the first waves with supporting troops and supplies, although one company from the 47th Battalion did manage to reinforce the 12th Brigade. They were also denied artillery support, on the grounds that if the tanks had pushed ahead they would be hit. Orders were not changed to accommodate the changing circumstances and failure of the tanks; with artillery support, they could have held the newly-gained positions.

Communication between those holding part of the Hindenburg Line and supporting waves proved impossible, because 'machine gun fire rendered visual signalling impossible and the open ground swept by machine gun fire was almost certain death by runners, so that no messages were coming in to Battalion Headquarters'.[41] As early as 5.15 am 2nd Lieutenant John MacIntyre Rae from the 15th Battalion was wounded as he tried to reach the captured positions. He crawled back to the Australian lines and reported that 'enemy Machine Guns dominated the ground and he thought it was impossible to get back from captured position'.[42] At 8.00 am S.O.S. signals were fired by troops holding onto the captured enemy trench, requesting support, with no response. As the morning progressed the Australians were running short of bombs and ammunition. Unless they received further supplies, the attack could not progress and their gains could not be consolidated. The Germans could easily replenish their troops with bombs and ammunition.

German prisoners who had been captured were sent back to allied lines across No Man's Land only to be ruthlessly cut down by their own machine guns, including a party of 32 who were heading back towards the 16th Battalion headquarters.[43] Officers from the 14th Battalion headquarters did not realise that these men were prisoners surrendering and thought that they were a German counter attack. The 14th Battalion War Diary records 'the enemy were seen massing in the sunken road at U.22.c. and were dispersed by artillery'.[44]

Around 8.00 am Private Edmond Ashdown from the 13th Battalion was observing from the sunken road when he was mortally wounded by shrapnel from an artillery blast. This shell killed seven men from the 13th Battalion in total, including Captain Shierlaw and Lieutenant Cuyler.

Private Thomas Ensor had fought his way into the second German trench and observed German machine gun teams deliberately targeting the wounded:

> From 6.30 am to 8.30 am, of 11th April, before my capture, while in the captured German 2nd trench of the Hindenburg Line I watched German machine gunners in the village of Riencourt, steadily firing on British wounded lying in No Man's Land. The firing was regular and continuous. I watched the bullets striking the ground round the wounded as they lay or crawled from one shell-hole to another. The firing was at short range and the machine-gunners could not have failed to see that their targets were wounded men, because the latter had no rifles or equipment, and some had limbs in slings.[45]

At 8.10 am, Brigadier General Brand ordered a barrage 200 yards beyond the second Hindenburg trench and some distance beyond the right flank. This order was questioned and Lieutenant General Birdwood refused to sanction the barrage on the basis of false reports that tanks supported by infantry had entered Bullecourt and were advancing towards Riencourt. Men from the 16th Battalion sent several S.O.S. flares requesting artillery barrage support, which were ignored owing to Birdwood's decision.

At this stage the view from the starting point by the railway embankment was confusing as observers looked upon the snow covered battlefield littered with the dead, the dying and burnt-out tanks. It was not until 9 am that 13th Battalion Headquarters received a message from Captain Harry Murray written approximately two hours earlier at 7.15 am which reported that 4th Brigade had captured and was holding 900 yards of the Hindenburg Line. He confirmed it was impossible to attack Bullecourt and that they had captured 30 prisoners from the German 124th Regiment. He requested further ammunition and was confident of holding the line if British artillery supported their defence of the captured ground. Murray ended the message as follows: 'With artillery support we can keep the position till the cows come home'.[46] Bombs, small ammunition and a supporting artillery barrage were not forthcoming. Murray, who had seen German infantry reinforcements assembling at Riencourt, had ordered the firing of the flare to request an artillery barrage seventeen times without any response. Birdwood's failure to order artillery support upon the German positions during that morning would have catastrophic ramifications for his men.

General Gough was under the false impression that the operation was succeeding. At 5.35 am he had received a report from a forward observation officer that Bullecourt and Riencourt had been captured by the tanks. He had also received a report from an air reconnaissance plane which had observed several British troops on the western perimeter of Bullecourt. At 9.35 am, misguided by these reports, Gough ordered the 4th Cavalry Division to advance to Fontaine, Croisilles and Chérisy. The Sialkot Brigade assembled in a valley west of Ecoust-St-Mein. At 8.45 am they had been incorrectly informed by Divisional HQ that Bullecourt and Riencourt had been captured and that they were to follow the initial wave.

A squadron from the 17th Lancers made an attempt to break through the wire ¾ mile east of Bullecourt on the 12th Australian Brigade's front, but was prevented by heavy enemy machine gun fire, which caused 20 casualties. A dismounted unit at the railway embankment with wire cutters could not make any progress as machine gunners fired upon them killing one man and wounding 15 others before they reached the wire. The cavalry were seen by German artillery observers galloping along the Noreuil-Longatte Road, which subsequently prompted a German barrage to fall upon them killing several horses and dispersing them before reaching the battlefield. The cavalry was withdrawn in disarray at 10.30 am.

At 10.00 am the Australians were still holding onto the first and second trenches of the Hindenburg Line, without artillery support. At this time the Germans began to initiate a series of counter attacks from all sides using hand grenades. The 4th Brigade held on until their supply of bombs and ammunition was depleted. The German machine gunners aimed their sights upon the parapets, which prevented the Australians from running along the parapet and attacking the German bombers from above. The valiant Australians were caught in a trap. Runners were sent to establish communication with those holding the captured position, but the majority of them never returned. Private Percy Larratt from the 16th was one of a few runners that succeeded in delivering their messages to battalion headquarters. Larratt's recommendation for the Military Medal states:

> He knew that he volunteered for this service with very little chance of getting through the heavy barrage of Artillery and Machine Gun fire which then swept 'No Man's Land'. Nearly all the previous runners who attempted this had been shot down and he knew it. By proceeding from shell hole to shell hole he succeeded in crossing the danger zone and delivered his dispatch to battalion headquarters.[47]

Carrying parties with ammunition and bomb supplies made efforts to replenish their comrades holding the Hindenburg Line but were stopped by the German machine guns. It was decided that it was too dangerous to try any more.

With supplies of small arms ammunition and bombs exhausted and numbers reduced by enemy fire, the 16th Battalion were barely holding onto their position. The enemy sent in successive counter attacks and were surrounding these gallant and determined Australians. When Private William Richard Rogers ran out of ammunition, he went into No Man's Land and began to search through the pockets of the dead, dying and wounded who were lying amongst the wire in between OG 1 and OG 2 Trenches. So desperate was he to continue the fight and ensure that his comrades had ammunition he exposed himself to danger on several occasion in order to replenish supplies.

Lance Corporal George Ball from the 16th Battalion used his initiative to gather enemy munitions to defend his ground in OG 2 Trench. His recommendation for the Military Medal records his extraordinary resolve in the face of an overwhelming enemy:

> When the objectives had been obtained he led a bombing party along an exposed flank of the second objective and drove the enemy back fully a hundred yards. He held on until no further bombs were available. He then attempted to deal with the enemy by charging over the top but most of his comrades were immediately shot down by Machine Gun fire. He still held on however, gathered up enemy bombs lying about the trenches and returned to the attack. When the end came and all supplies of ammunition were exhausted he made a dash for freedom across bullet swept 'No Man's Land' and called on the men with him to do likewise.[48]

Ball survived the ordeal of Bullecourt, but was killed the following year at Le Hamel on 4th July 1918.

As the battle progressed the German soldiers were outflanking the determined Australians and were able to surround them. The Germans were using underground tunnels between OG 1 and OG 2 trenches. Lieutenant Colonel McSharry reported in the 15th Battalion War Diary that 'the enemy had tunnel communications about 10 feet underground between first and second lines'.[49]

By 10.45 am Captain Murray and the 13th Battalion were pinned down. German bombers were throwing their bombs into their trench and machine gunners were sweeping the parapets ensuring that the Australians did not retaliate with a bayonet charge. Lieutenant Colonel James Durrant wrote:

> At 10.45 am heavy bomb attacks by the Germans were started from the right and left of both objectives, also down the communication trench from Riencourt and a communication trench running north and south on the west of Riencourt, six attacks in all. These attacks were very severe and our bombs were quickly exhausted and our men pressed back to the centre of our position from all sides. The Germans had machine guns trained on the parapet which frustrated every endeavour on the part of our men to go along the top and attack the bombers with the bayonet.[50]

The Australians were using the High Explosive No.36 grenade. This grenade resembled a small ball with a jagged surface. The bomb thrower would pull out the safety pin while keeping the striker lever held down. The striker lever would be released once the bomb was thrown and activate the bomb which had a seven second delay before exploding. When it exploded, it broke up into small segments, which proved to be a devastating weapon in an enemy trench. The Württembergs were using the standard *Steilhandgranate*, also known as the stick bomb or potato masher. This standard German grenade consisted of a steel canister containing explosives attached to a wooden handle measuring 14 inches. The soldier would activate this grenade by unscrewing the bottom of the handle and tugging the cord inside the handle, which activated the detonator before it was thrown.

The Australians resorted to searching for hand grenades amongst the German dead. When they started to lob these into German positions, German commanders became aware that the Australians had run out of munitions. Sending further reinforcements from Riencourt, German COs knew that it was only a matter of time before the Australian defence would collapse and they would regain the Hindenburg Line trenches. Lance Corporal Bert Knowles recalled 'We were now using a few of Fritzy's bombs which we had found, and that exposed the fact that we were running short, and the enemy redoubled his efforts.'[51]

Despite having no ammunition these intrepid Australian soldiers fought off German counter attacks with the bayonet. They had gone through so much in order to get into the trenches that they were determined to hold on for as long as possible. Bert Knowles was one of those men who carried on fighting. 'Still, I never heard anyone talk of surrender, and we drove him back with the bayonet on several occasions, even clearing two or three sections of trench, only to be sent back under a shower of bombs.'[52]

S.O.S. flares were fired into the sky requesting artillery support. Captain Murray had sent runners with messages requesting urgent help back across No Man's Land to battalion headquarters by the railway embankment. Many were cut down by machine-gun fire, but some delivered their messages and returned back to Murray. Despite these messages getting through, no assistance came.

The options were either to surrender to the enemy or to make a desperate dash across No Man's Land to the railway embankment. After marching from Favreuil, which was several miles away, twice on the two previous nights, advancing across No Man's Land without artillery support, or tank support, fighting through wire under murderous enemy machine gun fire, breaking into the first trench then proceeding into OG 2 Trench where they held on to the position for several hours, many of these men were not prepared to surrender even though they were surrounded. Such was the determination of these brave souls who had travelled thousands of miles from the other side of the world to fight for the freedom and liberty of others. They fought their way out and dashed across No Man's Land. Private Maurice Bercovitch was one of those men and his Military Medal recommendation states that 'when called on to surrender, he made a dash for freedom and took his Lewis Gun with him.'[53] Other machine gunners decided to sabotage their Lewis guns rendering them inoperable. Lance Corporal Bert Knowles: 'The beginning of the end came when the Lewis guns ran out of ammunition. Gunners took the pin out of a Mills bomb, laid it on the

gun and left before the bomb exploded and destroyed the gun; other men pulled their gun to pieces and threw the parts in different directions.'[54]

Private James Walsh, also from the 16th Battalion, continued to defend his position in OG 2 Trench until all has ammunition was expended. He was completely surrounded by the enemy. Instead of surrendering, he decided to fight his way out using abandoned German bombs. He used one of these bombs to destroy his Lewis Gun and with another German bomb he courageously fought his way out of the desperate trap that he was in and made his way back to the railway embankment.

Sergeant Leslie Boully was another from the 16th who refused to surrender. His citation for the Distinguished Conduct Medal stated:

> Throughout the whole of the fighting he showed an utter disregard for his own safety and when the situation became hopeless on account of the exhaustion of the ammunition supplies he refused to surrender and led the balance of his men out of the trenches and back to our lines.[55]

By 11.20 am some of the remnants from the 16th Battalion had managed to get back and provide first-hand accounts of the situation in the German lines. The 16th Battalion had expended all supplies of small arms ammunition and bombs and had suffered 75% casualties. They had no choice but to withdraw.

A white flag was seen in OG 1 Trench and Captain Harry Murray ordered the flag to be shot down. He was not prepared to surrender; instead he decided to risk his life to reach Australian lines. Sergeant Douglas Blackburn, who had organised the Lewis gunners from 14th Battalion in OG 1 Trench, was with Murray and his party:

> As carrying parties could not get through to us from our own lines, things were looking pretty bad. About this time Major H. W. Murray, V.C., of the 13th, came along the trench. Hopping on to the parados, he addressed us something like this:-
> 'Well, men, we are just about out of ammunition, and it doesn't look as if anything more can be done. We either stay here and get skittled or be taken prisoners, or we can get out while our luck is in. What do you say?'
> Long Joe Bamford sings out: 'We're with you Harry, whatever you do.' 'Well, boys' says Murray, 'out we go. Hand over all your ammunition, except ten rounds, to the Lewis gunners; but listen you chaps' (turning to us), 'don't be too long after we go.'[56]

Lance Corporal Bert Knowles was also with Murray when he laid out the option to surrender or withdraw across No Man's Land.

Captain Murray said, 'Well, men it's either capture or go into that. Each man for himself.' We had not a bullet or a bomb among the lot of us; and only 30 of A Company got into the trench in the first attack; though it started with 166; the remainder were lying on the plain, which we now had the option of crossing a second time, this time in broad daylight, with the enemy standing above ground ready to shoot down anyone showing his head.[57]

Murray was heard to have shouted, 'Everyone for himself' as he ordered the men to withdraw. The unit history of the 13th Battalion entitled 'The Fighting Thirteenth' recorded the withdrawal:

After crossing the wire, those left rested in shell holes a while before continuing. Murray jumped into one of these holes. The remnant of the glorious 4th Bde was still being cut down. It was too much for Murray. 'This is not war; it is murder,' he exclaimed. 'Some of those men helped me to get my VC, and must help them now.' With these words he ran out into the hail to advise in order to try to save his men. And our artillery was still silent, allowing the enemy to pour his lead into us at his sweet will. Thus it was that, after fighting heroically for seven hours, dozens of splendid men were killed returning.[58]

It was miraculous that any man who decided to run the gauntlet of German machine-gun and shell fire across No Man's Land made it to the railway embankment alive. Murray was part of a 10-man party which made the dash for freedom:

Amid all the tragedy and loss there that morning, one episode gave us complete satisfaction at the time. Most of the unwounded having made a dash for the Australian lines, ten of us decided (as Germans were in the next bay of the trench) that it was time for us to go, too. So, with seventy to a hundred of the enemy chasing us, we jumped into a shell-hole on his side of the wire to finish the argument – we would have been sitting shots for them if we had tried to cross the entanglement.

There was some dust and smoke at the time, and the German machine gunners, unable to distinguish their own men from us, almost completely wiped out our would-be-captors. It has always been rather a mystery to me how we managed to cross that wire, it being too high to straddle and too thick to get one's leg through often. I ruined a perfectly good pair of breeches that morning!

I still do not let my mind dwell on the tragedy which cost the lives of so many wonderful comrades that day. Of the ten that left the German trench

together, only four got back, and one of those [Lieut. Tom Morgan] was killed by a shell as soon as he reached our front line. He was one of the best.[59]

Private Gladstone Bannatyne who belonged to Captain Murray's Company was hit as he tried to run through the hail of the bullets to escape. Private Alfred Neate who was taken prisoner in OG 2 Trench witnessed the moment when Bannatyne was mortally wounded:

He had got up on the parados to get back when he was hit by machine gun bullets in the arm – which was almost severed. He jumped back into trench. I don't know what became of him when we were taken Prisoners. I think he must have bled to death, as there was no one to attend to him.[60]

Bannatyne's remains were recovered and later buried in Quéant Road Cemetery.

Sergeant Douglas Blackburn and his party of Lewis gunners covered Murray and those men who chose to risk their lives in the dash to freedom:

Subjected to artillery and other fire, the crew was practically exhausted when the order was given to retire ... Everyone was a hero a dozen times over and when I came out I recommended the whole lot to my C.O. Of the 30 men I took in to the fight, only four besides myself came out with whole skins. Another four, wounded, managed to get to our lines.[61]

For those isolated in the Hindenburg Line and in No Man's Land what little ammunition they had possessed was rationed. Sergeant Hugh Orr was fighting with the 16th Battalion:

We were the first into the Hindenburg Line ... we got in there and fought in there until 12 o'clock. We got orders there about 11 o'clock to hand in any ammunition that we had and just keep five rounds. All the ammunition had to go back to the machine guns. We had no bombs, no artillery, just the rifle and the machine guns ran out of ammunition. So we handed in our bullets and kept five rounds. Not long after we had to hand in the rest of the ammunition and keep one round. So we did that. After about 12 o'clock we had nothing at all. We hadn't a bullet to fire or anything and the order came along that it was every man for himself to get back and we started to scramble back then.[62]

The 16th Battalion began the withdrawal before midday. Lieutenant Edgar Rule observed the enormous loss during the withdrawal.

Those who tried to break away were killed like flies, and it was only the foxy ones, who used their heads, that succeeded. Numbers leapt out and lay in shell-holes until darkness set in, but those who lay 'doggo' too close to the German lines were collected by Hun patrols and sent back to Germany.[63]

Lance Corporal Bert Knowles was not prepared to surrender:

> Many of us preferred risking 'that' to being captured. Some climbed the parapet, only to be shot down like rabbits; others like myself found gaps in the parapet made by shells, and crawled through. I lay under the shelter for a few minutes to take my bearings, made a mental note of position of shell holes between myself and the barbed wire, then dived into the nearest one, out of that and into the next. I fell over getting through the wire, and lay perfectly still among the dead around me. I lay there for a long time, almost clear of the wire; the bombing had ceased, and I knew the fight was over. Thinking it a good opportunity whilst Fritz was souveniring and putting his 'house' in order, I started my short dashes into shell holes again, getting further out of range all the time. Many bullets droned past me or dug into the earth around me.[64]

Knowles hoped that he could seek shelter in a shell hole until night and crawl back to Australian lines under the cover of darkness, but was captured later that day.

Lieutenant Colonel McSharry observed the remnants of his men retiring from OG 1 across No Man's Land around 11.15 am but many were cut down by machine gun fire before his eyes and never reached the railway embankment.

There were many Australians still occupying sectors of the Hindenburg Line after Murray had withdrawn. Some men could not hear Captain Murray's voice in the noise of the battle and continued the fight. Other units still holding on had doubted the order to retreat and continued to fight. Corporal James Corrie Wheeler, 15th Battalion, encouraged his men to 'Fight it out like Australians!' Wheeler had been wounded at Gallipoli and at Pozières. He would continue to fight until he was surrounded and captured.

Private Leslie Pezet and remnants from the 15th Battalion who had decided to remain in the Hindenburg Line trenches described their ordeal as they bitterly held on for a few more hours until forced to surrender:

> Our men are all now, getting killed and wounded, losing and regaining Sap and bay every hour, our bombs run out, no ammunition whatever, machine guns fail and we find a few hundred German bombs in a very deep dug out. When using his, he found our position critical and came down on us, our left retiring and being absolutely mowed down on our right, we see them running with their hands up. We have no alternative, we have to let him come and take us, he puts a barrage with his guns and machine guns behind us and we have to remain where we are. Several men tried but fell in their attempt.[65]

Lieutenant William Boland refused to be taken and succeeded in making the dash across No Man's Land. He later recalled the grim scenes he witnessed in No Man's Land:

> As we returned, the sight of that snow-covered No Man's Land was appalling. Dead bodies were strewn all over the place, many hanging in the German wire; and everywhere wounded men were calling for help. So ended the worst organised battle in our experience, if not the history of the war. It did more to shake the Australian soldiers' faith in the Higher Command than any other incident during those fateful years.[66]

NOTES

1. *Reveille*: 1st April 1933: Lieutenant William Boland MC (and Bar) (14th Battalion AIF) Testimony.
2. *Reveille*: 30th April 1931: Lance Corporal Bert Knowles (13th Battalion AIF) Testimony.
3. *Jacka's Mob*, Edgar Rule: Angus and Robertson Limited 1933: p171.
4. *Official History of Australia in the War of 1914–1918* Volume 4, Charles Bean, Angus and Robertson 1938: p289.
5. *Reveille*: 1st April 1933: Lieutenant William Boland MC (and Bar), (14th Battalion AIF) Testimony.
6. Australian War Memorial: Australian Red Cross Missing Files: AWM 1DRL428/0004: Private Edward Bentley.
7. Australian War Memorial AWM 28/1/198/0087: Military Medal Recommendation: Sergeant George Mace.
8. *Reveille*: 1st April 1933: Sgt. Douglas Blackburn's (14th Battalion AIF) Testimony.
9. *Reveille*: 1st April 1933: Lieutenant William Boland MC (and Bar) (14th Battalion AIF) Testimony.
10. *Official History of Australia in the War of 1914–1918* Volume 4, Charles Bean, Angus and Robertson 1938: p295.

11. National Archives: WO 95/3494: 14th Battalion AIF War Diary.
12. *Jacka's Mob*, Edgar Rule, Angus and Robertson 1933: p171.
13. *Reveille*: 1st April 1933: Lieutenant William Boland MC (and Bar), (14th Battalion AIF) Testimony.
14. Australian War Memorial: AWM 2DRL/0268: Sergeant William Charles Groves Papers.
15. National Archives: WO 95/3491 – 13th Battalion AIF War Diary.
16. National Archives: WO 95/3498 – 15th Battalion AIF War Diary.
17. *Reveille*: 30th April 1931: Lance Corporal Bert Knowles (13th Battalion AIF) Testimony.
18. Ibid.
19. Ibid.
20. Ibid.
21. Ibid.
22. Ibid.
23. Ibid.
24. Ibid.
25. National Archives: WO095/3499 16th Battalion AIF War Diary.
26. National Archives: W 95/3491: 13th Battalion AIF War Diary.
27. Australian War Memorial: AWM 28/1/198/0095: Military Medal recommendation: Private Thomas Caldwell.
28. National Archives: WO 95/3499: 16th Battalion AIF War Diary.
29. Australian War Memorial: AWM 28/1/128/0092: Military Medal Recommendation: Private Maurice Bercovitch.
30. *Reveille*: 30th April 1931: Lance Corporal Bert Knowles (13th Battalion AIF) Testimony.
31. *Reveille*: 1st April 1933: Lieutenant William. Boland MC (and Bar) (14th Battalion AIF) Testimony.
32. National Archives: WO095/3498: 15th Battalion AIF War Diary.
33. *Reveille*: 1st April 1933: Captain David Dunworth MC (15th Battalion AIF) Testimony.
34. Ibid.
35. Ibid.36. National Archives: WO 95/3498: 15th Battalion War Diary.
37. *Reveille*: 1st April 1933: Captain David Dunworth MC (15th Battalion AIF) Testimony.
38. Ibid.
39. Australian Red Cross Missing File AWM 1DRL/0428: 2nd Lieutenant Frank Barnes.
40. *Reveille*: 1st April 1933: Captain David Dunworth MC (15th Battalion AIF) Testimony.
41. National Archives: WO 95/3498: 13th Battalion AIF War Diary.
42. National Archives: WO 95/3498: 15th Battalion AIF War Diary.
43. National Archives: WO095/3499: 16th Battalion AIF War Diary.
44. National Archives: WO 95/3494: 14th AIF Battalion War Diary.
45. National Archives: WO 161/100/93: Private Thomas Ensor, 16th Battalion AIF: POW Report.
46. Official History of Australia in the War of 1914–1918, Charles Bean, Angus and Robertson 1938: p317.
47. Australian War Memorial: AWM 28/1/198/0082: Military Medal Recommendation: Private Percy Larratt, 16th Battalion.
48. Australian War Memorial: AWM 28/198/1/0085: Recommendation Lance Corporal George Ball.
49. National Archives: WO095/3498: 15th Battalion AIF War Diary.
50. National Archives: WO095/3491: 13th Battalion AIF War Diary.
51. *Reveille*: 30th April 1931: Lance Corporal Bert Knowles (13th Battalion AIF) Testimony.
52. Ibid.
53. Australian War Memorial: AWM 28/1/128/0092: Private Maurice Bercovitch: Military Medal Recommendation.
54. *Reveille*: 30th April 1931: Lance Corporal Bert Knowles (13th Battalion AIF) Testimony.
55. *London Gazette* 18th June 1917.
56. *Reveille*: 1st April 1933: Sergeant Douglas Blackburn's (14th Battalion AIF) Testimony.
57. *Reveille*: 30th April 1931: Lance Corporal Bert Knowles (13th Battalion AIF) Testimony.
58. *'The Fighting Thirteenth' The History of the Thirteenth Battalion* by T.A. White, Tyrells Limited Sydney 1924: p96.
59. *Reveille*: 1st April 1933: Captain Harry Murray's (13th Battalion AIF) Testimony.
60. Australian War Memorial: Australian Red Cross Missing File: AWM 1DRL/428/00002: Private Gladstone Bannatyne.
61. *Reveille*: 1st April 1933: Sergeant Douglas Blackburn's (14th Battalion AIF) Testimony.
62. Liddle Collection: Lance Corporal Hugh Orr interview: Reference Tape 239.
63. *Jacka's Mob*, Edgar Rule, Angus and Robertson 1933: p179.
64. *Reveille*: 30th April 1931: Lance Corporal Bert Knowles (13th Battalion AIF) Testimony.
65. Private Leslie Pezet Diary: 15th Battalion: Courtesy Ken Pezet.
66. *Reveille*: 1st April 1933: Lieutenant W.P. Boland MC (and Bar) (14th Battalion AIF) Testimony.

CHAPTER 8

THE 12TH AUSTRALIAN BRIGADE'S ASSAULT UPON BULLECOURT

While the 4th Australian Brigade attacked at 4.45 am, the 46th and 48th Battalions from the 12th Brigade remained in their positions in the snow waiting for the tanks to arrive at their starting off positions. The 46th Battalion commanded by Lieutenant Colonel Howard Denham was ordered to lead the brigade's first wave and capture the first German trench OG 1. The 48th Battalion commanded by Lieutenant Colonel Raymond Leane was ordered to follow the 46th Battalion to OG 1 then advance to capture OG 2.

Four tanks were meant to be advancing ahead of the 46th Battalion who would follow 15 minutes later. Two of these tanks were ordered to advance along the eastern perimeter of the village of Bullecourt. The 46th were expected to support these tanks, but the tanks never appeared at Zero Hour, 4.30 am. The officers of the 46th Battalion obeyed orders and kept their men in the jumping off position waiting for their arrival. The 46th Battalion had been assembled in the jump off position since 3.30 am that morning. They maintained this position during a German barrage and were ordered not to advance until 15 minutes after the tanks had passed them. However, Lieutenant Colonel Denham had not passed on the complete Brigade Orders, which were that the 46th Battalion should advance at 4.45 am irrespective of the presence of the tanks. Gough had changed the plan and during the haste of issuing new orders he caused chaos. This lack of detail caused confusion amongst his company commanders, who had thought of the doomsday scenario and asked what they should do if the tanks did not arrive. Denham verbally confirmed that they should advance with the tanks, but did not give them a time. So as the 4th Brigade advanced upon the Hindenburg Line at 4.45 am, the 12th Brigade was still waiting for the tanks and company commanders from Denham's 46th Battalion were left unsure as to when they should attack. Denham was a respected soldier with long military service in the militia; but he lacked the necessary man management and leadership skills and

his lack of attention to detail seriously jeopardized the operation and exposed the 4th Brigade's left flank. The 4th Brigade advanced thinking that the 12th Brigade would be attacking the Hindenburg line at the same time, but this was not the case.

Forty minutes after the 12th Brigade were to advance a British tank arrived at the jumping off position at 5.10 am. Captain Davies, who commanded the 46th Battalion's central section, telephoned Howard Denham to confirm: 'Only one tank has passed our jumping off trench, we can't see any of the others – are we to advance?'[1] Denham ordered Davies to advance immediately.

The men from the 48th Battalion commanded by Lieutenant Colonel Raymond Leane started to assemble in their allotted jump off positions from 3.00 am. Lieutenant Leslie Challen, commander of C Company, led his men 200 yards in front of the railway line and they were ready for the assault by 4.00 am. Each of these men carried 200 rounds of ammunition, two Mills hand grenades, two sandbags. Other items were carried amongst the company for the purpose of consolidating captured ground including 14 shovels and six picks. Two mats were also taken to lie on the wire to enable the Company to get across, but they would not be of much use. The Company was positioned in two waves as they waited in the snow for Zero Hour. The first wave comprised bombers and men ready to charge with fixed bayonets. The second wave was armed with Lewis guns and rifle grenades.

Challen reported that the barrage opened at 4.30 am and the first tank did not arrive at their position until 5.00 am, where he observed it fire upon OG 1 trench for 15 minutes. The men of the 48th Battalion were still in their positions at 5.00 am and Leane had to telephone his commanding officer to see if they were to await a signal from the tanks. He received the following response. 'You do not wait for signal from Tanks. When the first objective is taken, you go on and take the second.'[2]

Lieutenant Challen did not receive the order to advance until 5.30 am. By that time the British artillery barrage had subsided as planned, the dawn light was beginning to break through the night sky and the advancing men from C Company, 48th Battalion were exposed to enemy high explosive shells, shrapnel and machine guns. Challen:

> About 5.30 am the word to advance was given and the lads got up quickly and advanced at a quick pace, almost at a run. The enemy barrage was thick both with H.E. and shrapnel and was supported by M.G. fire, which caused heavy casualties.[3]

The 46th Battalion was sheltered in a position near to the sunken road, but the 48th Battalion lay exposed and was vulnerable to German shelling. One tank appeared and passed the 48th Battalion start line, but after going forward a little farther it opened fire upon the men of the 46th Battalion who were waiting in their jump off position. The tank stopped and the officer appeared and asked the identity of the troops. Once he established that they were Australians he got out of the tank and apologised. He asked in which direction the enemy was located, then drove off towards OG 1 Trench. Within minutes one of the crew returned to report that an enemy shell had hit this tank and that he believed that he was the only survivor.

At 5.00 am British artillery fire upon Bullecourt had stopped in order to allow the entry of tanks and infantry into the village. Dawn was breaking and with no tank support the soldiers from the 46th Battalion pressed ahead with their advance upon the German positions

The 46th and 48th Battalions from the 12th Australian Infantry Brigade advanced from the railway embankment, where the trees are lined to the left of this photo. This photo was taken from the Central Road. The sunken road can be seen running parallel to the line of trees towards Bullecourt. The Australian infantry would have received heavy machine gun fire from Bullecourt (where the church steeple is situated) and OG 1 Trench. (Author)

at 5.15 am. The Württembergs in the Hindenburg Line could observe the Australian advance up the slope and could fire at will.

As the 46th Battalion advanced supported by the 48th Battalion they suffered heavy casualties from enemy fire from machine guns in the trenches skirting the eastern perimeter of the village of Bullecourt on their left flank and directly ahead of them from OG 1 and OG 2 Trenches. Soldiers from one company of the 124th Infantry Regiment defending the German OG 1 Trench east of Bullecourt had fired 70 cartridges of ammunition each before they were forced to withdraw from the position by the advancing Australians.

The 46th Battalion veered to their right flank towards the Central Road. Heavy machine gun fire from Bullecourt on the left flank may have forced them in that direction and into the dense fields of barbed wire. To the west of the Central Road they met up with one tank heading for the Hindenburg Line. This tank may have been the one commanded by Lieutenant Eric Money. Men from the 46th Battalion followed the single tank very closely and breached the wire, where they were brutally cut down by concentrated machine gun fire from Bullecourt 300 yards distant on their left flank. The tank was caught in the wire and received four hits from trench mortars and a machine gun was able to fire into its cabin. Lieutenant William Pentland managed to struggle through a breach in the wire on the battalion's right flank and gave the order for all unwounded men to follow him towards the German trench; only two men answered. One of those men was Lance Corporal Francis Tobin and he was dying of his wounds. Tobin had received a gunshot wound near to the German wire. According to Sergeant John Paxton, Tobin had been shot in the left breast and was unable to walk or move and he had become entangled in the wire. Paxton could not reach him and Tobin had to be left there exposed to German machine gun bullets and the cold weather. Private Thomas Tyler later witnessed Tobin lying wounded in a shell hole with Sergeant Norman Pontin. Tobin either died from his wounds or exposure that day. Pontin also died of his wounds. Their bodies were never recovered.

Many soldiers from the 12th Brigade became entangled in the German wire. Among them was Private James Berry who was close to Money's tank, which got caught in the wire. Trapped in the wire Berry received a bullet wound in the groin. He was later shot in the stomach by machine gun fire. His comrades could not extricate him from the wire. Berry bled to death as the snow fell upon him.

Lieutenant William Pentland, who could not proceed with the attack with one man alone returned to Lieutenant Colonel Denham at 5.45 am. Pentland reported that 30 of his men were killed on the German wire; that the enemy was defending their position in OG 1 Trench with great strength and that he was unaware of the locations of the remainder of the attacking formations. Pentland volunteered to lead a reinforcement company and advanced once again towards the German wire. Before 6 am Denham received a further report from Major Victor Waine, commanding the right flank, confirming that his men had taken a section of OG 1 and that the men from the 48th Battalion were heading for OG 2 Trench. It is hard to comprehend how anyone could have got through the dense barbed wire fields at Bullecourt that day. Denham immediately sent a carrying party of 30 men to take supplies of rifles and grenades to the occupied positions.

Meanwhile, elements of the 46th Battalion left and central flanks managed to break through the wire. 2nd Lieutenant Clarence Wraight rallied his men despite the heavy German machine gun fire and succeeded in entering OG 1 Trench. Captain Frederick Boddington and the remnants of B Company entered OG 1 Trench and launched a ferocious attack along this trench towards Bullecourt. Armed with bombs they got to a position north east of the village. Boddington, despite being wounded, had got himself through the enemy fire. He was now fighting a desperate battle to consolidate the position he and his men from B Company had captured in OG 1 against repeated German counter attacks. Boddington was well respected by his men. Private Scott wrote that 'he was a good sort, one of the best.'[4] Scott reportedly witnessed him being killed as he fought off a German attack. Other eye witnesses report that Boddington was killed while leading a bayonet charge towards German positions. With no more bombs and ammunition left and the enemy on either side of their position, Boddington chose to launch a desperate bayonet charge. Boddington asked for volunteers to join him in this attack. Private Charles Taylor stated that 'Capt. Boddington wanted to organise a bayonet charge, and he just got up on the parapet to look and see how many men he had got when he was shot through the head and killed instantly.'[5] Other reports indicate that he was killed by sniper fire, or shell fire. In the heat of battle conflicting reports of a man's fate are in many cases difficult to resolve. Private Walter Surridge:

> We got into the front trench at Bullecourt; the German's were in part of the trench. We had no more bombs and we went for them with the bayonet. Captain Boddington just got up and fell back dead, but I cannot say what hit him. We lost that trench after holding it an hour or two longer. He was the finest officer out there, a soldier both in the trenches and out of them.[6]

Private Roger Donahue was one of the volunteers who took part in the bayonet charge witnessed Boddington's

German Maxim Machine Gun exhibited at the Jean & Denise Letaille Bullecourt Museum. This machine gun would have been fired upon Australian soldiers as they left the railway embankment on 11th April. Its 600 rounds per minute was devastating and decimated the advancing waves of Australian infantry as they headed for OG 1 Trench. (Author)

desperate and final act of courage. His testimony gives some indication of how far the party charged before Boddington received his fatal wound:

> He was hit in the head by a M.G. bullet in the forehead when taking his men out in a body to make a charge. Three or four men of my Coy were hit and killed at the same time. We had got about 50 yards from the enemy line and quite 800 yards from our own line ... The Capt was wounded about mid-day, it was a fatal hit.[7]

Boddington's body was not recovered and his name is therefore on the memorial at Villers-Bretonneux.

Major Victor Waine was also desperately clinging on to his position, fighting off German counter attacks on OG 2 Trench. All their bombs and ammunition were becoming expended fast. Without further supplies they would not be able to sustain a defence of the captured position. According to Lieutenant Colonel Denham's report 'Each man in the attack carried 220 rounds of SAA, two bombs per man, each Company Bomber carried six Mills No.5 Hand Grenades and each company had 72 No.23 Rifle Bombs.'[8]

Waine sent a runner to Lieutenant Colonel Denham at 6.25 am with the following message. 'Running out of Bombs and Rifle grenades – 48th holding part of 2nd line – we are being bombed on both flanks – our casualties very heavy.'[9] The runner got back to battalion headquarters fifteen minutes later.

On receiving this request, Denham immediately summoned all available men and sent them to Waine's position with more bombs. Denham also requested from Brigade Headquarters more units to replenish Waine's units in OG 2. Brigade headquarters dispatched a company of one officer and 50 men from the 47th Battalion with supplies of Mills bombs. As they passed the battalion ammunition dump they took 600 Mills bombs with them for their comrades. Lance Corporal Fred Beitzel belonged to the carrying party. His father was of German descent. He was mortally wounded in the first trench.

As the 48th secured the first trench, the 48th proceeded to take the second. They had to advance 1,000 yards from the start-off point to the line, which was covered by German machine gunners east of Bullecourt. Many casualties were inflicted upon the 48th, although for a period during the early stage of the advance an allied artillery barrage subdued the German positions. Leane reported:

> While the barrage remained on enemy trenches East of Bullecourt the fire was kept down, but this was lifted at 5 am to allow the tanks to operate on the flanks, consequently the enemy had every opportunity to snipe my men from 5 am to 6.19 am, which he did, inflicting great casualties.[10]

2nd Lieutenant William Blaskett was amongst the men from the 48th Battalion killed while trying to fight their way into the second German Trench. Blaskett was born in Folkestone in England and immigrated to Australia before the war. At Bullecourt, Blaskett was reported well ahead of his men after OG 1 Trench was taken and was shot in the forehead by machine gun fire.

Leane could see that his men were attempting to take their allotted objectives without tank and artillery support and were being cut down by German machine gun and sniper fire. Leane did request that the artillery continue to shell the German-held trenches on the eastern perimeter of Bullecourt, but he was told that nothing could be done, because of the prior arrangement to withhold artillery support to enable the tanks to advance. This was of no help to his men who were already committed to taking the objectives and suffering owing to the lack of support. They found the wire to be uncut, but persevered in trying to take the second objective. Private Rose, a Lewis machine gunner from the 48th recalled, 'We were being raked by machine-gun fire and shelled with shrapnel. Wounded and dead men were hanging in the wires all around me, and I noticed that the shell holes were full of wounded.'[11] Leane reported that 'No artillery barrage was on the trenches yet the men advanced despite all obstacles and made their way through the wire. This was necessarily slow work and many fell getting through it.'[12]

The 48th Battalion lost half its strength in reaching OG 2. Captain John Mott was one of the officers who bore witness to the decimation of the battalion. At one stage he was in command of the remnants as they fought and held onto OG 2 Trench. Mott received a wound to his neck and become partially paralysed. He later described how he was wounded and his unit destroyed as they fought their way into OG 2 Trench:

> I was in charge of the battalion and we managed to get through the first line of German trenches, but as we were crossing No Man's Land – about 150 yards – between the first and second lines, the Germans turned their machine guns on us, and the greater number of the battalion were wiped out. I went back to the first lines to try and get reinforcements, but whilst I was standing on the parapet, talking to the men in the first line, I was hit by a bullet in the neck, which laid me out for the time being. Previous to this I had been wounded in several places by bullets.[13]

Lieutenant Colonel Leane reported that his men from the 48th Battalion reached OG 2 Trench by 6.18 am. His nephew Captain Allan Leane, a company commander from the 48th Battalion, was amongst them. They bombed as far as the Central Road, where they established a position. Lewis guns fired effectively upon German reinforcements heading from Riencourt and several counter attacks were resisted during that morning.

One tank commanded by Lieutenant Birkett did report to Lieutenant Colonel Leane's Headquarters for orders and Leane directed the crew to assist on the 48th Battalion's left flank and drive towards the north east sector of Bullecourt. The tank did not get far and was hit by German shell fire 20 yards from Leane's headquarters. The crew quickly abandoned the tank and dashed back to Leane's position. German observers were able to direct their artillery to fire upon this tank and the surrounding area, including Leane's Headquarters. Leane recorded in a report after the operation:

> At about 6.30 am I saw a tank near my Headquarters on Railway Track, and told the officer in charge of it to go to the North East corner of Bullecourt and assist my battalion to clear up their left. We were being strongly counter attacked at this time. It was a male tank and went forward firing its six pounders as it moved. I watched this tank and after going about 300 yards it turned and returned. When about 20 yards from my Headquarters the crew left it and rushed to the Embankment. I enquired from the NCO why he had left it, and he said they had a direct hit, and I believe one man was slightly wounded by the door blowing in. He said it was going all right and could be driven away but declined to try and the crew left for the rear. The enemy put a heavy fire onto the Tank and about 7.30 am it caught on fire. I believe the Tank

could have been saved had the crew possessed the necessary pluck. They were absolutely panic stricken when they reached my Headquarters.[14]

Leane did not record in his report that Captain Thomas Fairley, who was 48th Battalion signal officer, made an attempt to move the tank from 48th Battalion Headquarters, because the position was receiving heavy German artillery fire as a result. Fairley was badly wounded by a German sniper positioned in Bullecourt.

By 7.00 am the 48th Battalion occupied 500 yards of OG 2 Trench and the 46th Battalion was in control of 300 yards of OG 1 on their left flank. Major Waine reported that 65 officers and men were holding onto OG 1, plus 12 wounded men. Signallers from the 48th Battalion had established a telephone line from Lieutenant Colonel Leane's Brigade Headquarters at the railway embankment and Captain Leane's position OG 2 Trench. Shell fire severed the line, but this was restored by Lance Corporal Dowd who was wounded in repairing the line fully exposed to the enemy.

After sustaining many casualties, Lieutenant Leslie Challen led C Company into OG 2 Trench and contrary to reports of determined German resistance in other sections of the trench, he reported little opposition. Although the Germans who had retreated from this part of OG 2 had left steel traps to inflict injury upon the men of this Company. Within half an hour of capturing this section of the trench they had successfully consolidated the position. 2nd Lieutenant Sheldon who commanded No.9 Platoon from C Company reported that Lewis guns had been positioned to cover the flanks and the riflemen had dug a fire step in the rear side of the trench. By 9.30 am Sheldon reported that there were nine officers and 218 men defending their positions in OG 2 Trench.

By 10 am as the Germans counter attacked Major Waine's and his men were in dire need for water and ammunition for the Vickers gun. He sent another message to Lieutenant Colonel Denham which read 'Must have more ammunition, Bombs and Rifle grenades. Vickers requires 4 gallons of water and at least 6,000 rounds S.A.A. Enemy massing in Riencourt – Rifle Grenades most important.'[15] Denham could only send four petrol tins containing water to Major Waine. There were no more men to send carrying small arms ammunition, Mills bombs or rifle grenades. Major Waine held on for another hour and then at 11.15 am men from the 46th Battalion were seen to be withdrawing.

By 6.50 am the 4th and 12th Australian Brigades had succeeded in achieving their objectives and had penetrated and secured a section of the Hindenburg Line, with the exception of the 48th Battalion in the support trench, who could not extend their left flank beyond the Riencourt–Bullecourt Road; and the 46th Battalion who failed to secure the right flank. One party did manage to

fight along a communications trench and get within 150 yards of Riencourt. At 7.30 am the Germans launched a counter attack, charging down the communication trench from Riencourt. The 13th and 14th Battalions stoutly resisted this onslaught and beat the enemy back to positions with 100 yards of Riencourt east of 12th Brigade's positions.

The 46th Battalion was holding positions in the first trench with small numbers and was forced to retreat without warning, which meant that the 48th Battalion, holding the second trench, was left stranded and surrounded by the enemy as they retook OG 1 Trench. Major Victor Waine was captured as the 46th Battalion line had collapsed. Captain Allan Leane did not realise that the 46th Battalion had evacuated OG 1 until 12.25 pm, when a runner from the 47th Battalion reported that this was the case. Private Herbert Dunnett acted on his own initiative when he brought this important, but disheartening message to Captain Leane. This news must have been a tremendous disappointment to Leane, after he and his men had successfully held onto their position for an hour and ten minutes. Realising it was impossible to hold onto OG 2, Captain Leane organised an attack upon OG 1 Trench to clear the German troops who had just recaptured it. Instead of surrendering, Leane hoped to clear a path for the few men who held on, to withdraw back to Australian lines. Before launching this attack upon OG 1, Leane ordered the destruction of all military papers. Allied artillery was then permitted to fire a barrage upon the enemy positions, which was so effective that it rendered the trenches untenable. This barrage came too late to be of help to those men who held onto the Hindenburg Line that morning.

Captain John Mott was still holding onto his sector of OG 2 Trench with the 48th Battalion despite being wounded. Private William Chester recalled:

I saw Captain Mott about 6 in the morning. We were then in the second line. He was limping as he was wounded in the leg. He said to me 'You stop here.' He shouted to the others to 'Stick to it,' and went forward along the trench, which ran to the left. Jack Rudd and Bill Spearwood were with him. The machine gun fire did not seem so heavy the way they went, but another Battn. retired without letting us know they were doing it and Capt. Mott and the men who had gone with him were cut off.[16]

Captain Mott received a wound to his stomach and was surrounded by the enemy.

Leane got his men to fall back, fight their way back into OG 1 Trench and clear the enemy from the first trench. They held onto this section of OG 1 until 12.25 pm when Leane realised that they could hold on to their position no longer. Supplies of bombs and ammunition had run out. Artillery from their own guns was falling around their position and German soldiers were approaching from the communication trench from OG 2 and on both right and left flanks in OG 1. Leane had one option and that was to order a withdrawal. 2nd Lieutenant Leslie Sheldon who was holding on to OG 2 Trench felt let down by the 46th Battalion. He later wrote:

> ... the trench evacuated by the 46th Battalion was cleared of the enemy. At 12.25 am, finding that the position was untenable, we retired leaving our wounded in the trench owing to the inability to remove them. Bombs were found in the line which had been occupied by the 46th, and I am of the firm opinion that they were not justified in leaving the line, and that they could have held on.[17]

Captain Allan Leane remained in the trench and covered the withdrawal of his men as they evacuated OG 1. Once they were clear of the trench Leane began his own dash to the railway embankment. German troops began to overwhelm the position. A German bomb exploded, wounding Leane as he reached OG 1 Trench. He was last observed hopping towards the wire behind stragglers, but the enemy captured him. It was later reported that he died in a German hospital on 2nd May.

Lieutenant Edwin Dennis was one of two senior officers left alive from the 48th Battalion. When his supply of Mills Bombs was exhausted he found amongst the dead German soldiers egg bombs, which he used upon the enemy to great effect. On realising that it was futile for them to hold onto OG 1 Trench, he decided that the best course of action would be to withdraw to the railway embankment. He addressed his men: 'The only thing left for us to do is to withdraw, as much as I hate to, but we can't hold out longer'[18]

Dennis initially planned for the remnants of the 48th Battalion to make the dash back across No Man's Land when the allied barrage had stopped, however Sergeant Max McDowall, who had been lying along the parapet sniping at the German bombers, suggested to Dennis that the barrage was keeping the Germans in their trenches and they would be able to use the shell fire as cover for their withdrawal:

> He agreed and told me to go back and tell the men to lighten themselves as much as possible and get ready to leave. We had well over a thousand yards to go in full view of the Boche and lives would depend on speed. I did and reported to Dennis that the men were ready.
>
> By threes or fours, at short intervals, they disappeared over the top. We listened in silence to the rifle fire that greeted them. Finally only Dennis,

Watson and myself remained. 'You had better go Watson' said Dennis, 'All right, good luck.' 'Good luck old chap' and he was gone. He was not seen alive again.[19]

Lieutenant Dennis and Sergeant McDowall were the only two men remaining in OG 1. Dennis had assumed command and refused to leave until everyone had retired to Australian lines. With the little ammunition that they had, they covered the withdrawal of their comrades. McDowall later recalled:

> Purely out of politeness I said I would follow Denny. I will always remember how he drew himself erect and said: 'Sergeant, I am in command here, and I am the last to leave; you go now.' 'Good luck, sir.' 'Good luck McDowall', and I was away.
>
> I ran at top speed and as soon as my speed slackened dived into a shell hole. After a short rest I started off again. Top speed was not possible for long and I slowed to a walk. Shortly after that I saw two figures on my right, one supporting the other. I went over and found a Corporal helping Dennis, who was badly wounded. I caught hold of Dennis's left arm to put it over my shoulder, but the movement made him gasp with pain. He urged us repeatedly to leave him, stating we would surely be shot. But Fritz was a good sport and let us go![20]

McDowall helped Dennis reach 48th Battalion's headquarters at the railway embankment. The wounded Dennis was concerned about Lieutenant Colonel Leane's reaction to their withdrawal. On arriving at Leane's battalion headquarters Dennis said 'I'm sorry we had to retire sir.' Leane shook his hand and said with a smile 'My boy, I am proud of you all, the 48th stayed in the line an hour after everyone else had left'[21] Leane demonstrated his appreciation by recommending Dennis for a Military Cross.

Lieutenant William Watson was Lieutenant Colonel Leane's Intelligence Officer and he was amongst those wounded as the remnants of the 48th Battalion made a dash back to Australian lines. Leane had sent him forward to assess the progress of the 48th Battalion fighting in the Hindenburg Line trenches. The first thing he saw was his dead brother, Lieutenant Herbert Watson, impaled on a German bayonet in OG 2 Trench. Herbert had advanced with the first wave of the 48th Battalion. Lieutenant Imlay had seen William play a prominent role in the battle but witnessed him being shot in the spine as he tried to make a dash across No Man's Land to Australian lines. Despite his wounds, he managed to crawl across the battlefield. He was later found by stretcher bearers and evacuated from Bullecourt and taken to Rouen where he died from his wounds on 28th April 1917.

NOTES

1. National Archives: WO 95/3510: 46th Battalion AIF War Diary.
2. National Archives: WO 95/3514: 48th Battalion War Diary.
3. Ibid.
4. AWM 1DRL428/00004: Australian Red Cross Missing File: Captain Frank Boddington.
5. Ibid.
6. Ibid.
7. Ibid.
8. National Archives: WO 95/3510: 46th Battalion AIF War Diary.
9. Ibid.
10. National Archives: WO 95/3514: 48th Battalion AIF War Diary.
11. *Official History of Australia in the War of 1914–1918* Volume 4, Charles Bean, Angus and Robertson 1938: p308.
12. National Archives: WO 95/3514: 48th Battalion AIF War Diary.
13. National Archives: WO 161/96/28: Captain John Mott, 48th Battalion AIF: Prisoner of War Report.
14. National Archives: 12th Brigade War Diary: WO 95/3506: Lieutenant Colonel Raymond Leane Post Operation Report.
15. National Archives: WO 95/3510: 46th Battalion AIF War Diary.
16. National Archives: WO 161/96/28: Captain John Mott, 48th Battalion AIF: Prisoner of War Report.
17. National Archives: WO 95/3510: 2nd Lieutenant Leslie Sheldon Report, 46th Battalion AIF War Diary.
18. *Reveille*: 1st May 1935: Sergeant Max McDowall's (48th Battalion AIF) Testimony.
19. Ibid.
20. Ibid.
21. Ibid.

CHAPTER 9

RECOVERING THE AUSTRALIAN WOUNDED

Colonel Barber, Assistant Director of Medical Services 4th Australian Division, was informed on 7th April that an attack upon the Hindenburg Line at Bullecourt would take place. An advanced station was set up at Vaulx. It was expected to transform the advance station at Vaulx into a Casualty Clearing Station in the event that the Fifth Army made a breakthrough at Bullecourt.

The wounded at Bullecourt would have first been taken to one of the Regimental Aid Posts by regimental bearers where the RMO (Regimental Medial Officer) and his orderlies applied dressings or gave injections to ease pain. Regimental Aid Posts were usually established close to the battlefield. The 4th Brigade established Regimental Aid posts in dug-outs within the railway embankment, while the 12th Brigade positioned their Regimental Aid Posts on the Noreuil-Longatte Road. Colonel Barber ordered: 'Regimental bearers will not be allowed in the rear of the RAPs. Ambulance bearers will not be allowed in front.'[1]

The 12th and 13th Field Ambulances were allocated to evacuate the wounded from the 4th and 12th Brigades. Ambulance bearers would then transport the wounded on stretchers from the Regimental Aid Posts farther behind the front line to Advanced Dressing Stations. The Advanced Dressing Station was positioned north of Vaulx-Vraucourt and it was a perilous journey from the RAPs to the ADS across the

Aid Post, Bullecourt. (The Great War Volume 9)

Noreuil Valley. Stretcher bearers could be seen from the German lines at Hendecourt and were exposed to enemy shelling. Doctors would assess the wound at the ADS and might decide to amputate or treat the wound otherwise depending on the nature of the injury. The ADS were located in positions where it was easy for motorized ambulances to transport patients either to a Main Dressing Station or a Casualty Clearing Station. The Main Dressing Station was established at Beugnatre and it was here that the walking wounded had their wounds dressed. Seriously wounded casualties were taken to the 3rd and 12th Casualty Clearing Stations at Grévillers. Operations were carried out at the Casualty Clearing Station and nurses were available to provide professional care until the patient was strong enough to be evacuated to hospitals in Rouen, Wimereux, or in severe cases, sent to hospitals in Britain.

As the battle of Bullecourt raged on 11th April, stretcher bearers made efforts to go out into No Man's Land to rescue the wounded entangled in the wire, while under enemy fire. Before 6.00 am medics and stretcher bearers could go out onto the battlefield under the cover of darkness to reach the wounded. At dawn, the battlefield was completely visible and anyone who ventured into No Man's Land would do so at great personal risk. After sunrise, German machine gunners and snipers showed no mercy towards Australian stretcher bearers who ventured out to attend to and recover their wounded countrymen who were lying in agony in the snow. Private George Gilson, a veteran from Pozières was one of the stretcher bearers from the 15th Battalion who risked his own life to save others. His citation for the Military Medal states that 'he brought in wounded over ground swept by enemy machine guns and controlled by enemy snipers who showed no respect to Stretcher Bearers and it was entirely due to the noble efforts of the Stretcher Bearers that over fifty of our wounded were brought back to our lines a distance of over half a mile.'[2]

Private Ernest England, a railway worker from Boulder, Western Australia, was a Regimental Stretcher Bearer with the 16th Battalion. He had won the Military Medal during 1916 and at Bullecourt he would win a bar.

Left: **Mobile stretcher used by medical teams on display at the Jean & Denise Letaille Bullecourt Museum. (Author)**

Right: **An advanced dressing station built in the bank of the main Vaulx-Bullecourt road, near Vaulx. The 7th Field Ambulance treated the wounded here, sending the serious cases by motor ambulance to the casualty clearing stations further to the rear. (AWM E00591)**

Throughout the Bullecourt battle he braved machine gun fire and shell fire to recover wounded cobbers lying in the snow in No Man's Land. This time he worked closely with three other bearers, Private Elliott Buswell, Private Rowland Taylor and Private Patrick Fox. Their courage at Bullecourt was recognised when they were all given Military Medals. Their joint recommendation:

> ... these men are Regimental Stretcher Bearers and are brought under notice for conspicuous bravery and determination displayed by them in bringing in wounded in the face of heavy shell, rifle and machine gun fire during the attack on the Hindenburg Line in front of Riencourt on 11th April 1917 and on the following day. They showed great eagerness to go out for more wounded as soon as those brought in by them were dressed and stretchers were available for use again. They succeeded in bringing in a number of wounded even during the period when all stretcher bearers who ventured into 'No Man's Land' were deliberately fired upon by the enemy's machine guns. These four men are grouped together because they work in one party. They are all recommended for distinction.[3]

Private William Affleck was another soldier from the 16th Battalion who made numerous attempts to rescue wounded comrades lying exposed to deadly German sniper and machine gun fire in No Man's Land. His recommendation for the Military Medal:

He volunteered to go out into 'No Man's Land' to attend to and bring in wounded men lying there. He continued his mission of mercy throughout the day and was instrumental in bringing in many wounded. At times he was subjected to heavy machine gun fire, but this did not deter him.[4]

At 2.00 pm during the afternoon of 11th April German medics were seen to be tending to wounded Australian soldiers entangled in the wire or lying in the shell holes in No Man's Land despite machine guns firing and British shells falling in their direction. These brave men disregarded nationality and the British artillery to reach out and tend to enemy soldiers, trapped in the German wire, or lying helpless in shell holes. Australian commanders observed the decent actions of their German enemy and ordered the artillery to cease fire. A white flag was flown and a temporary truce was negotiated for the purpose of recovering and exchanging the wounded.

At 4 pm under the cover of Red Cross flags Lieutenant James Julin and 50 stretcher-bearers from the 52nd Battalion were allowed to recover the Australian wounded without any interference from enemy snipers. The Germans displayed acts of human kindness as they assisted in this operation, covering the wounded with waterproofs to shield them from the atrocious weather. They evacuated many wounded who were caught in their wire and escorted them to their own trenches where they received attention. Many of these wounded would have been taken to

Riencourt, where there was an underground hospital. In cases where a soldier was severely wounded they were placed outside of their own wire so that the Australian stretcher bearers could reach them. Some German medics shot those wounded men who were close to death. Charles Bean records that 'they were put to death by a merciful enemy'.[5]

At 6 pm snow started to fall and the Germans, who were fearful of another attack, shouted from their trenches 'finish hospital' to indicate that the truce was over. The stretcher bearers continued their work throughout the night without being fired upon by the enemy, but this goodwill was withdrawn the following morning. Some wounded survivors crawled across the battlefield to the railway embankment in the nights that followed.

On reaching the railway embankment the wounded had to be taken to the casualty clearing stations in the Noreuil valley. German artillery shelled the valley and during the period 11th April to 17th May 1917, 224 men from the Australian Army Medical Corps were killed. Contrary to Colonel Barber's orders, Ambulance bearers, who were forbidden to go forward of a Regimental Aid Post; went to assist the Regimental bearers who were overwhelmed by the numbers of wounded. Infantry from the 47th and the 51st Battalions were ordered to act as ambulance bearers. A total of 1,090 wounded had reached advanced dressing stations at Vaulx during the first Bullecourt battle. The wounded were then taken to the Main Dressing Station at Beugnatre where the 4th and 13th Field Ambulances worked incessantly throughout that day, the exhausted men continued without taking a break or eating. Within 24 hours after the first Bullecourt battle 446 stretcher cases and 671 walking wounded were attended to at this Main Dressing Station. An unpublished history of the 4th Field Ambulance:

> All departments were kept busy. [At the M.D.S.], almost a record number of patients were put through, and the doctors with their assistants never stopped. The stretcher-bearers had one continuous stream of wounded and barely had time to eat. Every possible man helped to carry the wounded in. For the first time the method of carrying on the shoulders was adopted by all, and from that date it was never dropped. The weather kept fine till the afternoon and then the snow came and it was frightfully difficult for the bearers to pick their tracks. The men were drenched and cold, but as nothing compared to the wounded who lay out in the snow. It was a sight to see the smaller men stick to their job, backwards and forwards. Finally, with strength almost gone, a party of infantry relieved them in what was the most solid day's carrying in France.[6]

Wounded were processed at the Main Dressing Station into two categories, stretcher cases and sitters. Stretcher cases were sent to Grévillers while sitters were sent to Pozières.

NOTES

1. *Official History of the Australian Army Medical Services, 1914–1918*: The Western Front: 1940: Colonel Barber's orders: 7th April 1917.
2. Australian War Memorial: AWM 28/1/198/0057: Military Medal Recommendation: Private George Gilson.
3. Australian War Memorial: AWM 28/1/198/0094: Military Medal Recommendation Privates Elliott Buswell, Rowland Taylor and Patrick Fox.
4. Australian War Memorial: AWM 28/1/198/0090: Military Medal Recommendation Private William Affleck.
5. *Official History of Australia in the War of 1914–1918* Volume 4, Charles Bean, Angus and Robertson 1938: p340.
6. *Official History of the Australian Army Medical Services, 1914–1918*: The Western Front: 1940: p136.

Australian wounded being transported from the Bullecourt battlefield to dressing stations in the Noreuil Valley. This photo was taken on 3rd May during the second battle. The road was used by stretcher bearers during the first battle on 11th April. German observers could see the road from Hendecourt and were able to direct artillery fire upon it. Many stretcher bearers became casualties as a result of this shelling. In this photo a shell is seen exploding in the background over a stretcher party. The man in the foreground is looking back to see where the shell burst. (Australian War Memorial: AWM E00443)

CHAPTER 10

THE TANKS' DAY OF DISASTER

When Major Watson gave the officers under his command the revised orders an hour and half before the tanks from D Battalion were scheduled to set off, the change in plan at such short notice was not warmly received by some of the officers. Watson later recalled:

> All my officers were assembled in the darkness. I could not see their faces. They might have been ghosts: I heard only rustles and murmurs. I explained briefly what had happened. One or two of them naturally complained of changes made at such a late hour. They did not see how they could study their orders, their maps, and their photographs in the hour and a half that remained before it was time for the tanks to start.[1]

Watson had to brief his officers about the changes a second time. Gough's revised plan was now to attack on a 1,500 yards front, between the villages of Bullecourt and Quéant. As previously described, the 4th Australian Division would attack alone, without direct artillery support and would be led by tanks that would break through the thick wire ahead of them, then capture the first and second line of the Hindenburg Line trench system named OG 1 and OG 2. Once the Hindenburg Line had been breached four tanks would turn left and advance west towards Bullecourt and four tanks would turn east towards Quéant, each supported by Australian infantry. It was hoped that by not directly attacking Bullecourt, the enemy could be squeezed out of their strongly defended garrison by the tanks. The 62nd Division would assault Bullecourt and advance towards Hendecourt.

The Australian artillery was regarded as weak because there had not been enough time to bring sufficient artillery pieces and ammunition up to the front in time; therefore it was considered that they could not be effective in supporting the attack. Gough compensated for this problem with the provision of twelve tanks to lead the infantry. These tanks would spearhead the attack.

Major Watson, the commander of D Battalion wanted the tanks under his command to play an effective role in the battle of Bullecourt and to give the Australian infantry the support that would enable them to reach, capture and consolidate the Hindenburg line trenches east of the village of Bullecourt. Watson felt confidence in the capabilities of his tanks, but was also apprehensive and fearful of the repercussions for the Australian infantry if the 12 tanks under his command were to fail:

> I was desperately anxious that the tanks should prove an overwhelming success. It was impossible not to imagine what might happen to the infantry if the tanks were knocked out early in the battle. Yet I could not help feeling that this day we should make our name.[2]

The role of the tank was to advance ahead of the infantry and flatten sections of the German wire. When an entrance through the wire had been established the tank was ordered to display a green disc.

Studying the tank action on 11th April 1917 is extremely difficult because of the confusion that reigned during the battle, the sometimes vague account given by Major Watson and the inaccurate official account in the Tank unit's war diaries. Charles Bean probably gave a more accurate account of the tank's role during that day because when he was writing the Australian Official History two decades later, he had access to German reports. He had numbered each of the tanks and if we analyse Bean's account and consider the locations of where pieces of tanks have been found by Jean Letaille at Bullecourt, historians can now get closer to the truth. Adopting Charles Bean's numbering of the tanks, the following list can be derived:

A disabled tank at Bullecourt. (Author)

Tank No. According to Bean	Tank Number	Tank Commander	Section Commander
1	Unknown	2nd Lieutenant Puttock	Captain Wyatt
2	Unknown	2nd Lieutenant David Morris	Captain Wyatt
3	799	2nd Lieutenant Harold Davies	Captain Wyatt
4	586	2nd Lieutenant Harold Clarkson	Captain Wyatt
5	Unknown	Lieutenant MacIlwaine	Captain Field
6	Unknown	Lieutenant Eric Money	Captain Field
7	Unknown	Lieutenant Arthur Beirnstein	Captain Field
8	Unknown	2nd Lieutenant Richards or Sherwood	Lieutenant Hugh Swears
9	Unknown	2nd Lieutenant Richards or Sherwood	Lieutenant Hugh Swears
10	Unknown	2nd Lieutenant Cuthbert Birkett	Lieutenant Hugh Swears
11	800	2nd Lieutenant Hugh Skinner	Lieutenant Hugh Swears

The right flank commanded by Captain Wyatt comprised four tanks commanded by Puttock, Morris, Davies and Clarkson. They were ordered to approach the German wire and in the words of Major Watson, to 'parade up and down the German wire immediately to the right of the front attack'.[3] They had to remain by the Hindenburg Line trenches until the trenches had been captured and consolidated. With the likelihood of German reinforcements coming east from Quéant, Puttock and Morris were ordered to drive in the direction of the junction of the Hindenburg Line and Balcony Trench to head off any counter attacks. Davies and Clarkson would head northwards accompanying advancing Australian infantry in their assault upon Riencourt and Hendecourt.

Captain Field commanded the central section of three tanks commanded by Lieutenants Money, MacIlwaine and Beirnstein. They would attack along the Central Road towards the German trenches, advancing up a slight depression and exposed to enemy fire that swept the line of approach. The capture of these trenches depended solely upon these tanks, because the infantry would have been certainly cut down by machine gun fire across this depression.

The four tanks commanded by Lieutenant Hugh Swears were designated to carry the left flank of the assault. These tanks were commanded by Skinner, Birkett, Richards and Sherwood. The plan was for these four tanks to lead the attack on the Hindenburg Line defences east of the village of Bullecourt at 4.30 am. Once they had reached the first objective, they would leave men from the 46th and 48th Battalions to consolidate the captured OG 1 Trench while they proceeded onto OG 2, flattening barbed wire defences as they went along. Two tanks would then skirt the perimeter of the eastern Bullecourt sector defences with the 46th Battalion mopping up the trenches behind them. According to the 46th Battalion war diary, these tanks never reached OG 1.

The tanks crawled into No Man's Land towards the Hindenburg Line at 2 mph, closely followed by two waves of infantry. The tank crews endured terrible conditions within their tanks and because it did not have any suspension, the eight man crew inside would be tossed around the compartment, sometimes burning themselves as they fell onto the hot engine and exhaust manifolds as they drove over shell holes and rugged ground. A combination of the deafening noise, the intoxicating carbon monoxide and cordite fumes, the intense 125-degree heat generated from the uncased engine, made the cab unbearable. Some men vomited as a result of these conditions. Like their Digger comrades waiting in the snow, the tank crews were denied sleep, which would further slow their reactions. Major Watson:

By this time the shelling had become severe. The crews waited inside their tanks, wondering duly if they would be hit before they started. Already they were dead-tired for they had had little sleep since their long, painful trek of the night before.[4]

The 16th Battalion war diary confirms that the first tank arrived at the rendezvous point at the railway crossing at 3.00 am This tank was part of the right flank advance. When Captain Jacka liaised with the tank crew, concerns were raised that the tanks would not be able to reach the first objective in 15 minutes. Lieutenant Colonel Drake-Brockman requested a 15 minute delay of the infantry advance to ensure that the tanks got to the objective before the infantry. Drake-Brockman's request was denied and he had to send his infantry within range of German machine guns knowing full well that these men would be leading the tanks instead of the tanks leading the infantry.

Two of the tanks commanded by Captain Wyatt, which advanced ahead of the 4th Australian Brigade on the right flank, proved ineffective. Tanks commanded by Lieutenant Morris and Puttock were ordered to drive their attack towards the intersection of the Hindenburg Line and Balcony Trench. Their role would be to block German reinforcements from Quéant launching counter attacks from the east. Watson reported that tanks commanded by Lieutenant Morris and Puttock reached the wire, swung westwards along the wire towards Bullecourt and swept the OG 1 Trench with machine gun fire. Both tanks were the focus of German machine gunners. The right-hand tank commanded by Lieutenant Puttock experienced clutch problems, forcing it to return to the railway line. According to Bean, the tanks commanded by Morris and Puttock never reached the German wire.

Puttock struggled to get his tank back towards Noreuil amidst the storm of shells. The clutch kept slipping to the point when the tank could not move any farther. It was very dangerous for him and his crew to stay in the stranded tank as German shells landed close by. They had a choice; either to remain in the lightly armoured tank or take a risk and leave their tank for the shelter of a trench. With the intensity of shell fire increasing, Puttock chose the latter option and ordered his crew to evacuate the tank and seek shelter. At that point a German shell struck the tank again.

The tank commanded by Morris was hit by German fire and abandoned in front of the railway embankment west of the Central Road. Morris was awarded the Croix de Guerre for his role at Bullecourt. His citation records:

> For gallantry and skill in the handling of his tank at Bullecourt on April 11. This officer, under an extremely heavy and accurate fire, entered the German trenches and worked down them for over a thousand yards, destroying the machine gun emplacements at least. He then reported for further orders. He took his tank into action a second time, carried out his instructions, and finally, with considerable skill, brought his tank out of battle.[5]

A British tank abandoned at Bullecourt. The dense barbed wire defences of the Hindenburg line can be seen in the background. (Author)

Puttock managed to overcome problems with the clutch and brought his tank south of the railway embankment where it was obliterated by German artillery as it was proceeding towards Noreuil. Wreckage from Puttock's tank was found in a farmer's field close to where Bean thought it was hit, south of the railway embankment.

Lieutenant Davies' and Clarkson's tanks were ordered to break through OG 1 and OG 2 Trenches and attack Riencourt and Hendecourt. They were thought to have broken through the German lines and were advancing towards Hendecourt. According to Major Watson, allied aeroplanes observed two tanks heading towards Riencourt supported by four hundred to five hundred Australian soldiers. This fact was completely inaccurate for Davies and Clarkson never reached the German-occupied villages. However, Davies and Clarkson did succeed in reaching the German trenches. Both these officers were experienced infantrymen. Davies had served with the 14th Battalion Welch Regiment at Mametz Wood during July 1916. Clarkson served as a medic with the Royal Army Medical Corps before transferring to the Northumberland Fusiliers. He had taken part in the attack upon La Boiselle on the first day of the Somme campaign. Davies and Clarkson would have been conscious of the implications for the Australian infantry if the tanks did not play their intended role at Bullecourt that day. They did their best to help their Australian comrades despite overwhelming odds.

Clarkson in Tank 586 and in accordance with his orders had reached OG 1 Trench in front of the 16th Battalion's front. Captain Harry Murray squeezed past this tank in order to get through the German wire. Clarkson fired upon the defenders of OG 1 and was held up until 5.30 am Lance Corporal Bert Knowles was close to Clarkson's tank and later recalled the efforts of one of the tank crew in trying get this tank back in action, exposed to enemy machine-gun fire:

> A tank (the only one which got so far) penetrated the front line of wire, which, by the way, was about four or five yards across and became a hopeless wreck. In passing fairly close to it, I remember a chap standing near the front of it, with a short plank, trying to lever a piece of iron from amongst the big cogs beneath the wheels, and cursing like a bullock whilst the bullets were rattling like hail on the tank itself.[6]

Once Clarkson got his tank moving again he crossed OG 1 and headed for OG 2 Trench. It was here that he encountered direct field artillery fire from Riencourt and was forced to turn around and drive towards OG 1. It was at OG 1 that this tank was put out of action. Survivors of the crew sought refuge as German artillery continued to pour incessant shell fire onto the position. Harold Clarkson was killed and has no known grave.

British Tank 586 which was commanded by 2nd Lieutenant Harold Clarkson on 11th April 1917. (Author)

Right: Tank 586 lies abandoned near German trenches at Bullecourt. (Yves Fohlen)

Below: Tank track from 2nd Lieutenant Harold Clarkson's tank adjacent to Bullecourt Church. (Author)

Above: Tank 586 seen from German trench. These German soldiers are standing close to left side of the tank, because they could be seen from the Australian lines by the railway embankment. (Author)

Another German soldier poses by Clarkson's tank. Note the German stick grenades lying in the trench. (Author)

German soldiers inspect Tank 586 from the German-held trenches in the Hindenburg Line. (Author)

Unidentified German soldier stands by 2nd Lieutenant Clarkson's Tank 586. The same soldier is in both photographs. (Author)

Davies in Tank 799 might have been aware of the problems suffered by Puttock and Morris in their tank and may have taken it upon himself to carry out their orders, to head for the intersection of the Hindenburg Line and Balcony Trench and stop German infantry counter attacking from Quéant. Bean had accessed the German reports in the Reicharchiv in Berlin and confirmed in his Official History:

> On the Quéant flank, the advanced posts described a single tank 500 yards from the centre of their front. At a speed of about 4 miles an hour it approached the entanglements firing. After a short halt it moved along, crossed it easily ... and then enfiladed with its fire our front line. Here for the first time our grenadiers encountered one of these famous monsters ... It would be untrue to attempt to deny that the slowly advancing tank which there was apparently no means of stopping, had a strong moral effect and succeeded in crippling the resistance. But the first fright soon passed.[7]

Tank 799 crossed Balcony Trench at a position half a mile west of Quéant and then headed for a second trench where it became a target for concentrated artillery and trench mortar fire. *Leutnant* Schabel was sent from battalion headquarters with a machine gun to the line to confront the tank commanded by Lieutenant Harold Davies. *Leutnant* Schabel was credited in '*Die Württemberger im weltkrieg*' as the individual who destroyed the first tank with his machine gun. Schabel was in command of 3rd Machine Gun Company, 123rd Grenadier Regiment and positioned yards ahead of his command post manning a machine gun. He had fired 1,200 rounds of armoured piercing bullets towards the tank at a distance of 150 yards. As it turned around three bullets penetrated the petrol tank, igniting the fuselage. After the battle, this tank was carefully examined; 77 rounds were found to have penetrated the structure. The Württemberg unit history:

> The tank knocked out by *Leutnant* Schabel was the first tank to be destroyed within the German lines. For days it was the objective of officers of all ranks, some of whom had travelled long distances, to be able to cast eyes on this amazing creature. Its possession made it possible for the German commanders to obtain exact information concerning its construction, equipment and armament, as well as ways to attack it.[8]

The Württemberg unit history affirms that the tank burst into flames and that the crew who were burnt and suffering bullet wounds were captured as they tried to escape. Davies was killed and has no known grave. Years later the remains of Lieutenant Davies' Tank 799 were found in a field south east of Riencourt and west of Quéant. The turret from Tank 799 is exhibited in Jean Letaille's Jean and Denise Letaille Bullecourt Museum. The fate of Clarkson and Davies and their tank crews remains uncertain. Both these officers are commemorated on the Arras Memorial to the Missing.

The three tanks in the centre section commanded by Captain Field were designated to capture OG 1 and OG 2. Much reliance was placed upon these tanks to achieve their objective because this was the most vulnerable section of the battlefield, as they were advancing up a slope exposed to enemy fire from the front and from left and right flanks.

Money's tank was the only tank within this section that reached its designated starting point at Zero Hour. All three tanks were disabled by shells. They were silhouetted against the snow-covered depressions of the landscape, which made them easy targets. The German gunners directed their shells accurately upon these slow mechanical monsters as they crawled towards the Hindenburg Line.

MacIlwaine's tank reached the junction of the Central Road and the sunken road when a shell hit one of its tracks, immediately knocking it out of action. The crew evacuated the tank, however as daylight dawned, it was struck again by shell fire before the track could be repaired.

Lieutenant Money's tank drove through to the depression west of the Central Road, but became enmeshed in the German wire close to OG 1 trench. Once this tank was static it attracted heavy fire from German bombers in OG 1 and from German artillery. Money desperately tried to extricate himself by moving backwards and forwards, but they could not get out of the wire. At 6.00 am a shell hit the petrol tanks and exploded. These petrol tanks were positioned forward either side of the officer's and driver's seats in the Mark

Melted bullets retrieved from the inside of a British tank at Bullecourt. (Author)

II tanks. A sergeant and two of the crew escaped from the burning tank according to Major Watson. Bean recorded that 'a number of the crew tumbled out of its door, only to lie there still, evidently killed either by enemy bullets or by burning'.[9] Private Ben Bown was one of those who escaped from the burning tank, but he was soon killed by machine gun fire near to the tank. Lieutenant Money was killed by the shell and was incinerated inside the tank – one of the first of many tanks to be 'brewed up' in warfare – a terrible death for this brave man whom Major Watson called 'best of good fellows'.[10]

A shell hit the third tank commanded by Lieutenant Beirnstein as it followed Money's path and approached the German wire. The shell decapitated the driver and wounded the corporal in the arm. The inside of the cab was filled with smoke. Beirnstein was concussed and temporarily blinded. On evacuating the tank, he was disorientated. As the rest of his crew escaped a second shell struck its roof. Somehow Beirnstein got back to the Australian line where he was sent to a dressing station. A runner was sent back where he found the remainder of his crew trying salvage ammunition and equipment from the disabled tank while under heavy enemy fire.

All four tanks in the left sector commanded by Skinner, Richards, Sherwood and Birkett, tasked to capture Bullecourt, were late at Zero Hour. Two of these tanks managed to proceed beyond the railway embankment, commanded by Richards and Sherwood, but were hit before reaching the German trenches. One of these tanks was struck by a shell, blowing a large hole on its roof. The engine stopped and its commanding officer (either Lieutenant Richards or Sherwood); evacuated his crew and retired to the embankment. Apparently this officer left his crew and looked for Watson to ask for orders. As the crew was heading for Noreuil on foot, Corporal Ernie Hayward remembered that he had left his primus stove in the cabin of the abandoned tank. According to Major Watson, he valued this primus stove so highly he headed back to the battlefield with two comrades to recover it. The German guns were still targeting the abandoned tank. The three men got inside the tank and decided to make another effort to drive it to the railway embankment. To their great surprise the engine started and they drove it to Noreuil. Hayward was awarded the Distinguished Conduct Medal for recovering the tank. His citation reads: 'For conspicuous gallantry and devotion to duty. He collected his crew and brought in his Tank under heavy fire after it had been abandoned'.[11]

The tank commanded by 2nd Lieutenant Cuthbert Birkett entered the German trenches. This tank's guns provided effective support for the Australian infantry that were following. Birkett worked his tank along the German trenches towards Bullecourt and inflicted casualties. The tank was hit by German shells on two occasions with everyone inside receiving wounds.

Birkett was losing direction and was being observed by Lieutenant Swears, his section commander who was at the railway embankment. Swears ran into No Man's Land towards Birkett's tank avoiding enemy fire by jumping from shell hole to shell hole to order Birkett to alter his course towards Bullecourt. He made it; but some time soon after on that day, he was killed.[12]

Birkett continued the fight and took out a German trench mortar. With Swears, his section commander dead, Birkett returned to the railway embankment to seek further orders. Birkett's tank arrived at Lieutenant Colonel Leane's 48th Battalion HQ at 6.30 am Leane wanted him to move on the left flank and clear German infantry occupying the sunken road, as well as take out a specific German machine gun position in Bullecourt. Birkett replied 'Easily done.' The tank headed for the German machine gun position and succeeded in suppressing its fire. Birkett continued until all his ammunition was expended and he received a wound to his leg. As he withdrew the tank back towards the embankment he was hotly pursued by German soldiers. He lost his bearings as he brought the tank near to the embankment and climbed out to assess his position. Another German shell hit the side of the tank, shattering his leg. The wounded crew of this tank evacuated the burning hulk, salvaged the equipment they could carry and helped each other back to the railway embankment. The tank was struck many times by German fire and became a burnt-out wreck. Stretcher bearers went to Birkett's aid. He was evacuated and as he lay on the sunken road outside a dressing station another shell exploded nearby, wounding him for a third time. Birkett's tank was attracting heavy German fire and making Leane's HQ an accidental target. Captain Fairley, Leane's nephew tried to restart the tank to drive it away from 48th Battalion HQ, but he was wounded by a sniper.

2nd Lieutenant Hugh Skinner's tank had malfunctioned and could not get to the railway embankment for Zero Hour, but arrived at 9.00 am, four hours after the battle had begun. Skinner managed to get his tank onto the battlefield with the assistance of Lieutenant Morris, who towed his tank across the railway embankment and headed towards the German lines at Bullecourt. Skinner was the only officer who entered the village. He had assumed that the Australian infantry had captured OG 1 and OG 2 Trenches and had entered Bullecourt. Once his tank entered the village he and his crew were subjected to heavy German machine gun fire. Little flakes of metal were flying around inside the cabin as the bullets pelted the tank and slightly wounded some of the crew inside. The Tank Corps War Diary reported that 'this tank went into Bullecourt and cruised about the village, shooting any Germans visible. The enemy fled in disorder. The infantry apparently were unable to keep close to this tank'.[13]

As he brought his tank to the edge of a crater he stopped, made an attempt to reverse, but could not change gear. Skinner realised that he and his crew were isolated. The Australian and British infantry had not succeeded in entering Bullecourt. His tank was unable to move and they waited helpless behind enemy lines. German units hastily placed a trench mortar in one of the derelict houses within the ruins of the village to target Skinner's tank. Skinner ordered that the crew evacuate the tank and they made their way back to the railway embankment. 2nd Lieutenant Hugh Skinner received the Military Cross for his actions. His citation in the *London Gazette* reads:

> For conspicuous gallantry and devotion to duty, when in command of a tank. He penetrated entirely without support into a strong fortified village of Bullecourt, inflicted heavy casualties upon the enemy, and, when his tank was disabled, brought back all his crew and valuable parts of his guns and tank under heavy machine-gun and shell fire.[14]

Lieutenant Swears was reported by Watson and Bean to have gone into Bullecourt to search for Skinner and his tank. Birkett, in a letter to Swears' family, confirmed that he last saw Swears on the battlefield at Bullecourt when he relayed the order to keep going towards the village. Swears was killed at some point during the first Bullecourt battle and was never seen again.[15]

Only two tanks survived. By 7.00 am according to Bean, as for the others, 'their carcasses could be seen motionless and in most cases burning, all over the battlefield'.[16]

News of the progress of the tanks was not reaching Major Watson's headquarters.

There is little news of the tanks. One report states that no tanks have been seen, another that a tank helped to clear up a machine-gun post, a third that a tank is burning. At last R. one of my tank commanders, burst in. he is grimy, red-eyed, and shaken. 'Practically all the tanks have been knocked out, sir!' he replied in a hard excited voice. Before answering I glanced around the cellar. The Australians had been told to rely on tanks. Without tanks many casualties were certain and victory improbable. Their hopes were shattered as well as mine, if this report were true.[17]

Watson was most likely referring to 2nd Lieutenant Richards. He clearly names some officers, but in this case he refers to the officer by the first letter of his surname. Perhaps Watson was protecting his subordinate's reputation. Richards might have been suffering from shell shock.

At 7.21 am Captain Jacka informed Brigadier General Charles Brand at 4th Brigade HQ of the failure of the tanks. The Machine Gun Corps Heavy Section had sustained 52 casualties from the 103 officers and men who had entered the battle. The Germans had managed to capture Tank 799, the first intact tank they had captured, an apparent coup for German intelligence. The Germans had discovered that armour-piercing bullets could penetrate the steel exterior of the tank and as a result; all infantrymen were issued with them. However, the Germans were unaware that 799 was a training tank and did not have armour plating.

Captain Jacka compiled a comprehensive report detailing the failure of the use of tanks at Bullecourt: 'The tank co-operation in the attack made on the Hindenburg Line on the night of the 10th/11th April

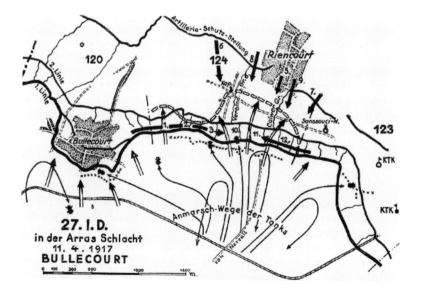

German Map showing British tank movements on 11th April 1917. (German 27th Infantry Division Unit History)

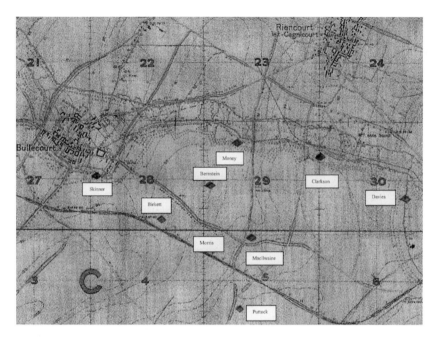

Tank positions
11th April
1917 (National
Archives: WO
95/3343: 28th
Battalion AIF
War Diary)

was useless, or worse than useless.'[18] Lieutenant Colonel Drake-Brockman commanding the 14th Battalion authorised the report. Jacka's report highlights the failure of tank commanders to bring their tanks to designated starting positions on time: 'Tanks were late in arriving at rendezvous, which meant that they were late in getting to the jumping off place.'[19] Jacka criticises the poor communication between tank crews and infantry. Jacka points out an incident where a tank was attempting to cross a deep sunken road and the tank officer ignored the advice of an Australian Intelligence Officer, which resulted in the tank being stuck and unable to move. Jacka was understandably bitter owing to the severe losses that his countryman had suffered at the hands of British commanders:

> The tank crews seemed to know little or nothing of an attack by infantry and nothing whatsoever about the particular operation they were about to participate in. For instance in the case of No.2 Tank, the Tank Commander had not even synchronised his watch; his time being five minutes behind true time as given to infantry. Further, Tank crews did not even know direction of enemy. This is verified by the fact that they opened fire on our troops, thereby causing us many casualties. One Tank in particular opened fire on our men at jumping off place, killing four men and wounding others. The organisation seemed to be bad, and no one appeared to be in direct command of the show. This was shown by the fact that Tanks wondered aimlessly about in every

direction, thereby drawing enemy fire upon us, and on all our trenches.[20]

Jacka does praise the efforts of one tank crew, probably referring to Clarkson's Tank 586 which did reach the objective and proved effective attacking the German trenches; but he criticises the lack of motivation and initiative of the other tank crews:

> One Tank only reached the objective, and did good work, but was almost immediately put out of action by direct hits from a gun in Riencourt. Commanders and crews of other tanks seemed to make no effort whatever to reach their objectives, and although their tanks were in no way damaged, even after the attack was well under way and Tanks could have given the greatest assistance in helping to connect up between us and the Brigade on our left, they made no effort to go forward, but wandered back moving along the front of our jumping off place and finally pulling up alongside one of our Dressing Stations. Other Tanks which apparently had made no effort to get up to their objectives were found in various places; on fire, although they had not been hit by shells. One crew in particular when asked why they had vacated their tank stated that, 'it had caught fire', but gave no reason for same. This same crew returned carrying two sandbags, one containing enamel ware and the other food. Personal safety and comfort seemed their sole ambition. Another crew was asked why they did not go forward to help clear

a communication trench. They replied that, 'they had no officer, so could not do so'. This showed a great lack of initiative in that the whole affair as far as the Tank was concerned seemed to be the responsibility of one man, and that man gone, the Tank could do no more, – though undamaged. One Tank returning almost to the reserve Battalion H.Q. pulled up right on the sky line in full view of Bullecourt, therefore making a splendid aiming mark, and drawing severe enemy gunfire, which made the route very dangerous for troops. The whole outfit showed rank inefficiency and in some cases, Tank crews seemed to lack 'British tenacity and pluck, and that determination to go forward at all costs' which is naturally looked for in Britishers.[21]

Although the tank assault upon the Hindenburg Line on the 11th was perceived by the Australians as an abysmal failure, intelligence gathered from reports on captured German prisoners indicated that the tank did cause German infantry a degree of 'shock and awe'. Some of the tanks did actually breach the Hindenburg Line, undermining the German confidence in the apparently impregnable defences and naturally having a negative affect upon the morale of the German infantry holding the line. One entry in a captured German officer's war diary states: 'The English have broken through ... He attacked with his tanks and had considerable success'.[22] Another captured German report reads, 'The capture by the British of the Cojeul Switch is attributed to the use of tanks and the poor fight put up by IX Res Corps'.[23]

A report entitled 'Experiences gained during English tank attack on April 11 1917 (Bullecourt Sector)' was expediently prepared and issued by V. Maur on 14th April and distributed to personnel of the 27th German Division. The report was found on captured German prisoners days after its release. It begins as follows:

The machine-guns at the fore end of the tanks open fire when within 500–100 yards of our lines. The guns of the male tanks can only fire to the front and to the side. Their arc of fire is considerable. On reaching or passing our trenches the majority of the tanks turn to the right or left, to assist the infantry in the mopping up of the trenches. Odd tanks go ahead to enable the infantry to breach our lines. Ordinary wire entanglements were easily overcome by the tanks. Where there are high, dense and broad entanglements, such as those in front of the Hindenburg Line, the wire is apt to get entangled in the tracks of the tanks. On 11.4.17 one tank was hopelessly stuck in our wire entanglement. Deep trenches, even eight feet wide ... seem to be a serious obstacle to tanks.[24]

The report may have been referring to Money's tank, confirming that wire got entangled in the tracks.

The report also confirmed the effectiveness of German batteries against the tanks. 'At long ranges by day, tanks will be engaged by all batteries that can deliver fire with observation and that are not occupied with other more important tasks. All kinds of batteries put tanks out of action on 11.4.17'.[25] The report indicates the concern of German command about this new weapon, but at the same time tries to convey a positive message:

The moral effect of tanks on the infantry is very great, it is somewhat minimised in this division by the successful repulse of the tank attack on 11/4/17. The actual effect of the tank guns and machine guns must not be underestimated, 124th Inf. Regt. suffered considerable losses from them on 11/4/17. The issue to the Infantry of plenty of armour piercing ammunition and of trench guns would put into their hands weapons which would bring to an end all tank attacks.[26]

This report demonstrates that the tanks commanded by Lieutenant Money and Clarkson did have a significant effect upon the 124th German Infantry Regiment defending OG 1 and OG 2 and confirms that these tanks inflicted severe casualties. It was circulated to other German units on the Western Front in an effort to raise awareness of the tank threat. The report was altered by German commanders of the 207th Division in an effort to reassure their infantry that the tanks did not poise such a significant danger, provided that they were armed with the necessary weapons. The revised report reads:

The moral effect of the tanks on the infantry was great when they were first used, but disappeared when the Infantry realised the value of deliberate, well directed fire. To furnish the infantry with a plentiful supply of 'K' (armour piercing) ammunition and trench guns is to give them weapons that, literally, mean the end of tank attacks. 11th April has abolished the feeling of helplessness against these fire-spitting monsters. We have recognised their weak points and know where they are vulnerable. Whenever we succeed in incapacitating a tank, the initial paralysing effect of the hitherto unknown weapon is succeeded by a feeling of exultation.[27]

Even Bean concedes in his official history that

... the tanks did help the infantry in two ways. The panic which sent part of the German garrison fleeing across the countryside as the 4th Brigade entered OG 1 was caused by their presence; and there is no question that the tanks attracted much of the attention which would otherwise have been concentrated on the infantry.[28]

Despite the detrimental affect upon morale of the German infantry, the soldiers of the Württemberg Regiments had fought with great determination. Throughout the morning of 11th April they worked their way into the trenches held by the Australians from the 12th Brigade. They outflanked and isolated them, preventing many of them withdrawing to the Australian lines. To regain these trenches was a courageous achievement; but their greatest accomplishment that day was probably the capture of two Mark II tanks.

In fairness to the tank crews, they too were let down by their commanders. Most who were ordered to attack Bullecourt were inexperienced in driving tanks and for some it was their first time in battle. The noxious interior would have made them feel extremely nauseous and would have further impeded their ability to fight a battle. They were given training tanks without armour protection, never intended to go into battle; 103 men from D Company entered the battle and 52 of those men were killed. The Company was awarded two Military Crosses, one Distinguished Service Medal and three Military Medals. 2nd Lieutenants Hugh Skinner and Cuthbert Birkett received the Military Cross. Corporal Ernest Hayward was awarded the Distinguished Conduct Medal. Sergeant C Harvey was awarded the Military Medal for 'gallantly seconding his officers in fighting his tank when all the crew were wounded and the tank had been hit twice'.[29] Private A Savage was awarded the Croix de Guerre. His citation states:

> Carrying an important message, he went from his tank in search of his section commander under heavy shell and machine-gun fire. Failing to find his section commander, who had moved, he took the message to another tank commander. This second journey was made under very heavy machine gun fire, as the tank was in the German wire and a target for all the machine guns in the neighbourhood. He displayed both gallantry and initiative. The entire crew volunteered for the message and Savage was chosen for the task.[30]

2ND LIEUTENANT HAROLD DAVIES,
COMMANDING OFFICER TANK 799 D BATTALION MACHINE GUN CORPS HEAVY BRANCH

Harold Percival Davies was born in 1893. He was the son of David and Sarah Davies who lived at 100 College Street, Ammanford, Carmarthenshire where his father was a schoolmaster. His mother Sarah was

born in the US. Harold wanted to follow his father and become a school teacher, but he answered Kitchener's call for volunteers and enlisted during 1914. He was commissioned into the 14th Battalion, The Welch Regiment. 2nd Lieutenant Harold Davies arrived in Havre, France during December 1915. He was a Company Machine Gun Officer during the Battle for Mametz Wood on 10th July 1916. Twelve officers and 350 men were lost during this battle. In December 1916 Davies was transferred to the Machine Gun Corps Heavy Branch and would train to become a tank commander. He arrived at his new billet on 31st December 1916 at Blangy. The war would end for him at Bullecourt on 11th April 1917 when he was in command of Tank 799. Davies drove his tank across the snow-covered No Man's Land. His tank succeeded in reaching the trenches of the Hindenburg Line. His tank was ordered

2nd Lt Harold Davies, D Battalion Machine Gun Corps Heavy Branch. (Courtesy Bryan Davies)

German soldiers pose in front of 2nd Lieutenant Davies' Tank 799 which was knocked out of action on 11th April. (Author).

The turret from Tank 799 was recovered by Jean Letaille close to the position at Balcony Trench west of Quéant, and south east from Riencourt. It is exhibited at the Jean & Denise Letaille Bullecourt Museum. (Author)

Tank 799 on the Bullecourt battlefield. (Author)

CORPORAL ERNEST WILLIAM HAYWARD DCM, MM 553,
D BATTALION MACHINE GUN CORPS HEAVY BRANCH

Ernest William Hayward was born in Ruyton Eleven Towns, Shropshire on 4th May 1893. Known as Ernie, he was born into a large family. The son of Francis and Susanna Hayward, Ernest was one of 13 children. In 1901 Francis was working as a gardener and the family was living in Wrottesley, Staffordshire.

Warrant Officer Ernest Hayward DCM MM D Battalion Machine Gun Corps Heavy Branch. (Courtesy Grahame & Lyn Pigney)

Ernie Hayward (left) on motorcycle. This photo was taken prior to his transfer to the Tank Branch of the Machine Gun Corps. (Courtesy Lyn & Grahame Pigney)

to crush through the dense wire and breach the two main German trenches, OG 1 and OG 2 and advance towards the villages of Riencourt and Hendecourt. Davies reached OG 1 Trench but must have headed east towards Quéant, for the remains of Tank 799 were found near to the site of the German-held Balcony Trench south of Riencourt, by local farmer Jean Letaille. The turret from Davies' Tank 799 is exhibited at the Jean and Denise Letaille Bullecourt Museum. Davies was killed during the battle. A sergeant who had escaped from the burning tank confirmed that Davies was mortally wounded and died on the roadside. Harold Davies has no known grave and his name is commemorated on the Arras Memorial.

Harold's brother, who fought at Mons, Gallipoli, the Somme, Ypres and Passchendaele, spent two years searching for information about the whereabouts of Harold's body. Jennie Harding-Roberts, his fiancée, received his diary and sword after the war. Bryan Davies, his nephew, described Harold as 'a kind and studious type, clever and sensitive. He apparently was a lover of nature like his Dad'.

Ernie worked as a chauffeur before the First World War. He enlisted to join the Royal Field Artillery in 1914 as a private. Due to his mechanical aptitude and knowledge of motor cars he was assigned to No.5 Battery, 6th Battalion Motor Machine Gun Corps. Ernie Hayward described life in the trenches as

> ... very nerve wracking, because the German's used to lob trench mortars at us ... the mud was terrific, particularly at Neuve Chapelle ... the trenches were a swamp. If you got your gumboots stuck in the duckboard which was about a foot and half down and you pulled your foot out you would finish without your gum boot.[31]

He did not have to go over the top, as a machine gunner, he provided supporting fire to advancing infantry. Ernie saw service in the line at Neuve Chapelle in March 1915 and during the second battle of Ypres in April his unit was in reserve and did not go into action. 'We thought a lot about the waste of life and static warfare and being slaughtered, it seemed all so stupid, because we did not get anywhere.'[32]

Hayward was awarded the Military Medal on 11th October 1916. He was transferred to serve in D Battalion Machine Gun Corps Heavy Branch as tank crew when his unit was disbanded. Ernie Hayward got his first introduction to tanks while in the line at Vimy Ridge when he saw a Bruce Bairnsfather cartoon:

> Bruce Bairnsfather gave a description of these tanks ... they were little forts running along on their bellies from the British lines to the German lines and as they went they picked up all the metal they could find, barbed wire and stakes holding it down, when they got to the German lines they just pitch it over and kill the lot.[33]

Hayward was a port gunner when he went into action at Bullecourt. His Mark II tank was armed with a 6-pounder naval gun. The early gunners of the Tank Corps were trained at the Royal Naval Gunnery School at Whale Island, Portsmouth and so naval terminology was used by the tank crews.

During the initial days training tanks were not available. Ernie Hayward remembered the primitive methods of training tank crews using mock up tanks made of wooden frames and canvas. 'We could not get tanks so we had mock up tanks, a wooden frame, with a canvas screen around it and go lumbering about over trenches and ditches and all sorts of things and imagine that we were in some sort of tank. It was not on wheels, but carried by the crews being trained.'[34] Hayward regarded these eccentric methods with amusement and recalled that the crews deferred to these mock up tanks

Ernie Hayward interviewed at the Tank Museum, Bovington. (Courtesy Lyn & Grahame Pigney)

as 'latrines'. He remembered that a crew of seven would be involved and 'sometimes the right gunner would fall in a hole and he would have to be dug out'.[35] The purpose of this training 'was to enable the tank commander to get familiar with his crew and give tank movement orders.'[36] Hayward was also picked to be a physical training instructor for his unit during this period.

Hayward was awarded the Distinguished Conduct Medal for his role in the first Battle of Bullecourt. He had been promoted to Corporal and Ernie formed part of the tank crew in the fourth tank in Lieutenant Swear's section. 'When we went in at Bullecourt, they did not give us enough time to get up there and the Australians were in position to make this attack, we did not get there, so they had to retire.'[37]

At Bullecourt there was no communication between the tanks, they were on their own. As they drove towards the German lines Corporal Hayward saw out of the tank through little slits in the side of the tank. His tank commander used a periscope to see where the tank was going and gave directions to the driver accordingly. Hayward recalled how noisy and uncomfortable it was to be inside:

> The noise from the outside was the worst, because inside you had your visual hand signals about selecting gears, but the noise outside was terrific, depending on how much of the battle you were in. At Bullecourt we were rattled with these Minenwerfers and a terrific noise went on, especially with machine gun fire. It was a terrific strain being inside the tank because you did not know what the Hell was going on outside, only by the amount of stuff that was hitting you.[38]

Inside the tank there was the risk of falling onto hot components of the engine, splinters were flying around inside and if bullets came through the tank, they would ricochet within. Tank crews wore a little protection. 'We did have some chain gear across the front of the helmet that stopped splinters from inside the tank from damaging your eyes.'[39]

Hayward's tank was not armour protected. 'Our tank suffered a direct hit on the top with a Minenwerfer and the bolts that were sheared went flying around, as bad as machine gun bullets, but luckily nobody got hit.'[40] The tank was struck by a shell that tore a large hole in its roof. The engine stopped and the crew all retired to the embankment. According to Major Watson in his book A Company of Tanks, as the crew was heading for Noreuil on foot, Corporal Ernie Hayward remembered that he had left his primus stove in the cabin of the abandoned tank. He headed back to the battlefield with three comrades to recover it. The German guns were still targeting the abandoned tank. The three men got inside and decided to make another effort to drive it to the railway embankment. To their astonishment the engine started and they drove it to Noreuil. 'I had a very smart gearsman when I drove this tank out of action, after it had been abandoned and they were really lively chaps. We ran the gauntlet of a six-gun German battery, straight up a hill some of the tanks were below us, and I fooled the Germans.'[41]

Hayward got the tank back to the railway embankment. It is difficult to imagine that Hayward and two other men would risk their lives to enter the battlefield, exposed to German machine-gun and shell fire, in order to retrieve a primus stove. Hayward never mentions the primus stove in his testimony. It is my opinion that Hayward showed more initiative and daring than his commanding officer, and that his real purpose for returning to the tank was to try to see if it was operational; get the tank off the battlefield and back to the railway embankment. Watson was possibly sparing the commanding officer's embarrassment by stating that Hayward had returned to the tank for the stove. Where was the commanding officer when Hayward rescued the tank? Watson suggests that the CO had left them in the Noreuil Valley to search for Watson for further orders. Watson never reveals the identity of this officer.

Hayward was awarded the Distinguished Conduct Medal for recovering the tank. His citation reads: 'For conspicuous gallantry and devotion to duty. He collected his crew and brought in his Tank under heavy fire after it had been abandoned.'[42] He received a Card of Honour signed by General H.J. Elles, together with the right to wear the distinctive red, brown and green whistle cord of the Tank Corps.

Ernie married Emily Corps on 15th November 1917 in Woking, Surrey. Ernie continued to serve with the Tank Corps and took part in the Second World War. He served as Regimental Technical Adjutant at the Lulworth Gunnery School. He retired with the rank of Captain. Ernest Hayward passed away in 1982 aged 89.

GUNNER ANGUS DRUMMOND 75921,
D BATTALION MACHINE GUN CORPS HEAVY BRANCH

Angus Mackay Drummond was born in January 1896 and raised in Tighagaraidh, Glencruitten, Oban, in Scotland. He enlisted in November 1914 and served with the Argyll and Sutherland Highlanders. After completing his basic training he was sent to France. He saw active service on the Western Front serving with A Company, 8th Battalion. He was temporarily attached to the 10th Entrenching Battalion from 20th March 1916 and then was transferred to B Company 6th Battalion Argyll and Sutherland Highlanders from 14th April 1916. He served with the 19th Entrenching Battalion until 13th May 1916 then he was returned to the 6th Battalion. He was finally transferred to this unit on 9th September 1916 and was given a new service number, 7989. Here he served as a machine gunner with B Company. The skills that he had attained as a machine gunner was recognised by officers assembling the newly formed Machine Gun Corps Heavy Branch, Tank Corps and he was transferred to this unit in December 1916. He was aged 21 when he was killed on 11th April 1917. Having no known grave, his name is commemorated on the Arras Memorial. The circumstances of his death were reported in the Oban Times on 16th March 1918:

> On the morning of the 11th April 1917, his company advanced at Bullecourt (Somme). The tank crew, of which Gunner Drummond was a member, was  seen by an airman to have been captured, and accordingly his parents had hopes that he might have been a prisoner. Unfortunately, the sad news has been received through the Geneva Red Cross that two of the tank crew who are interned in Germany saw the soldier taken out of the tank among the wounded, but a large piece of shell struck him on the head killing him instantaneously.[43]

Gunner Angus Drummond, D Battalion Machine Gun Corps Heavy Branch. (Oban Times 16th March 1918)

PRIVATE FREDERICK HARNESS 76278
D BATTALION MACHINE GUN CORPS HEAVY BRANCH

Frederick William Harness was born in Wainfleet, Lincolnshire, in 1892. He worked as a gardener before volunteering in September 1914 in Dolgelley in Wales. According to his medal index card he served with the 25th Cycle Corps Division, Cyclist Company before being transferred to the Tank Corps. However his granddaughter has a photo of him wearing the uniform of the Royal Welch Fusiliers. Frederick Harness, who was aged 24, was killed in one of the tanks on 11th April 1917. He has no known grave and his name is commemorated on the Arras Memorial.

Private Frederick Harness, D Battalion Machine Gun Corps Heavy Branch. (Courtesy Margaret Harness)

His parents Frederick and Elizabeth had to deal with a further bereavement the following year when Frederick's younger brother, John Thomas Harness, died of wounds sustained while serving with the 2nd Battalion, Lincolnshire Regiment on 25th October 1918, three weeks before the war ended. The parents went to France and visited John's grave at Awoingt Cemetery; but Frederick was missing and they had no grave at which to mourn.

The bereaved parents of Fred Harness at grave of John Harness, his brother, at Awoight Cemetery. (Courtesy Margaret Harness)

NOTES

1. *A Company of Tanks*, Major W.H.L. Watson, William Blackwood and Sons, Edinburgh and London, p33.
2. Ibid.
3. Ibid. p25.
4. Ibid. p35.
5. *The Tank Corps Honours and Awards: 1916–1919*, Midland Medals: Birmingham 1982.
6. *Reveille*: 30th April 1931: Lance Corporal Bert Knowles (13th Battalion AIF) Testimony.
7. *Official History of Australia in the War of 1914–1918* Volume 4, Charles Bean, Angus and Robertson 1938: p347.
8. Die Württemberger im weltkrieg by Otto von Moser: Published 1927.
9. *Official History of Australia in the War of 1914–1918* Volume 4, Charles Bean, Angus and Robertson 1938: p315.
10. *A Company of Tanks*, p29.
11. *London Gazette* 5188: 26 May 1917.
12. *The Blood Tub: General Gough and The Battle of Bullecourt 1917*, Jonathan Walker, Spellmount 1998: p99.
13. National Archives: WO 95/97: 1st Brigade Tank Corps Headquarters War Diary.
14. The *London Gazette* 30095: 25th May 1917 p8.
15. *The Blood Tub*, p99.
16. Official History of Australia in the War of 1914–1918, p316.
17. *A Company of Tanks*, p34.
18. National Archives: WO 95/3494: 14th Battalion AIF War Diary.
19. Ibid.
20. Ibid.
21. Ibid.
22. National Archives: WO 95/97: 1st Brigade Tank Corps Headquarters War Diary.
23. Ibid.
24. *Reveille*: 1st September 1933: p31.
25. Ibid.
26. National Archives: WO 95/97: 1st Brigade Tank Corps Headquarters War Diary.
27. Ibid.
28. Official History of Australia in the War of 1914–1918, p353.
29. *The Tank Corps Honours and Awards: 1916–1919*, Midland Medals: Birmingham 1982.
30. Ibid.
31. IWM Department of Sound: IWM Ref: 7029: Corporal Ernie Hayward DCM, MM, D Battalion Machine Gun Corps Heavy Branch.
32. Ibid.
33. Ibid.
34. Ibid.
35. Ibid.
36. Ibid.
37. Ibid.
38. Ibid.
39. Ibid.
40. Ibid.
41. Ibid.
42. *London Gazette* 5188 26 May 1917.
43. *Oban Times*: 16th March 1918.

CHAPTER 11

THE WEST YORKSHIRES GO IN

The 2/8th West Yorkshires commanded by Lieutenant Colonel A.H. James were positioned by the railway line opposite the village of Bullecourt. The 2/7th West Yorkshires were positioned on their right and the 2/5th Battalion was positioned on their left. The 2/6th West Yorkshires commanded by Lieutenant Colonel J. Hastings had marched from St Leger to join the line and were in jumping off positions by 4.30 am. This battalion was to go first, supported by the 2/8th Battalion. The assault was to take place once the tanks and Australians had entered Bullecourt. Hastings had deployed A and D Companies along the railway embankment, B Company positioned in support in houses and cellars located near the crossroads and C Company was kept in reserve on the south-east edge of Ecoust-St-Mein.

Most of the tanks had failed during that morning, but the Australian troops had nevertheless broken through the wire and entered the German trenches. They were holding their positions; however, they did not enter Bullecourt itself. Lieutenant Colonel Hastings could not see any tanks or Australian infantryman in the village. He could not order his men to proceed until the tanks had entered Bullecourt. Hastings sent reports to the 185th Brigade Headquarters at 5.15 am, 6.00 am and 7.10 am confirming 'no tanks have arrived.'[1] He added to the last message 'there [was] no word of the Australians having entered, much less cleared Bullecourt.'[2]

Hastings was left in limbo. Anxious to find out what was going on Hastings visited his companies, the Headquarters of the 2nd/7th Battalion West Yorkshire Regiment, officers at Australian Division and officers of the Indian Cavalry. He reported to 186th Brigade

> ... that the situation was obscure; that Australians had not entered Bullecourt, and were indeed said to have orders not to do so, but to work to the right of it; that one tank had approached the E. of the village and retired; and that the Indian Cavalry patrol found several machine guns posted on the S.E. fringe of the village.[3]

Hastings received a report from 185th Brigade via Lieutenant Colonel J.A. James from the 2nd/8th Battalion that conflicted with his own: 'Australians were reported to have posts in Riencourt, that tanks were at factory between Bullecourt and Hendecourt and ordering immediate action, (without waiting for tanks to arrive), to clear up the situation in Bullecourt and seize Hindenburg to the W. of the village.'[4] This same message, timed at 8.20 am was again received by Hastings from the 186th Brigade at 9.43 am. In the meantime, Hastings responded to James's report at 9.00 am stating

> ... that Australians did not seem even to have entered Bullecourt; and that awaiting reports from patrols, the C.O. was not pushing the Bn. into the village, as the instructions sent from the Brigadier appeared to be based on faulty and erroneous information and adding that he was informed that the Australians had orders to work to the right of Bullecourt and not through it.[5]

By 9.35 am, General Gough had also been misinformed about the progress of the battle. Convinced that the operation was a success he ordered the 4th Cavalry Division to advance upon the villages of Fontaine and Chérisy. The Sialkot Brigade was in position near to Ecoust-St-Mein and Brigadier General L.L Maxwell, their commander, had received messages from the 62nd Division HQ that Bullecourt and Riencourt had been captured and that they were to deploy the cavalry. Parties from the Lucknow Brigade had dismounted and went into No Man's Land three miles east of Bullecourt in an effort to make breaches in the German wire for their horses to charge through. They came under heavy German machine gun fire and were dispersed. A squadron of mounted cavalrymen from the 17th Lancers came under shell fire and could go no further than the railway embankment. They lost eight men and withdrew under enemy fire losing some horses. The cavalry failed to make any significant impact in the battle, an outcome that looks so obvious with hindsight.

The Brigadier commanding the 185th Brigade visited Hastings at Battalion Headquarters and was dissatisfied that no progress had been made. He agreed that Hastings was complying with orders, that they were to wait until the Australians and tanks had entered Bullecourt, however he ordered that the 2nd/6th Battalion send out patrols to investigate the situation.

Hastings complied with the Brigadier's orders and sent out patrols to reconnoitre the area in front of Bullecourt. They were reporting that the wire was uncut and insisting upon the dangers of launching an assault. Hastings visited one of the outposts in between the British line and Bullecourt. 2nd Lieutenant E.W. Pearson was returning from a patrol and briefed Hastings on the enemy position and the strength of the wire. On the basis of Pearson's briefing, Hastings wrote the following report to 185th Brigade Headquarters, timed at 11.00 am:

> I have just visited my most advanced company. 2nd Lieut. Pearson had at the moment returned from patrolling the S.W corner of Bullecourt and reports wire uncut except one small gap near Crucifix, active sniping from probably machine guns, smoke issuing from many chimneys and men moving about among houses. Considers attempt to capture village in daylight bound to fail and be very costly, even at night without wire cut very dangerous. I have therefore instructed O.C. the Coy. Patrol S.E. edge of village. I am informed that the wire there is very strong and quite uncut. I am of opinion that the village cannot be captured in daylight except by very great sacrifices.[6]

Hastings mentions a position called the Crucifix. This position would be obstinately held by German forces throughout early May and prevented the complete capture of the village during those weeks. Built close to the site of the village crucifix west of the village, German forces had fortified this position. Lieutenant Humphries from the 2nd/7th West Yorkshire Regiment described the site of the Crucifix 'as a mound with two entrances'.[7] Further reports were received from 2nd Lieutenant R. Frost and 2nd Lieutenant G. Charlesworth at 1.00 pm.

Charlesworth was ordered to send a patrol to position U.28.d.1.9, however heavy sniper fire prevented him from reaching it. With very little cover, it was impossible to proceed. Frost made no contact with the enemy as he led a patrol along the sunken road to a position 200 yards from the wire. Frost reported that he 'met with no resistance'. Frost also gave details of the state of the wire reporting that 'along the Eastern side of the village, the wire is low, about 2 ft. out in

places and appears to have been trampled on. Along the southern side the wire is higher, about 3 feet and is in better condition'.[8]

Frost encountered no opposition during his patrol and was not fired upon, which, according to his report 'suggested that the enemy might have evacuated the village'.[9] At 1.50 pm Hastings was ordered to withdraw his patrols, but maintain posts for observation purposes.

Further reports were received at 3.00 pm that indicated the enemy may have withdrawn from the front of the left battalion of the 185th Brigade. At 3.07 pm Hastings ordered A and C Companies to send patrols into Bullecourt to ascertain the situation and to confirm whether the enemy were actually retiring. 2nd Lieutenant V Wilson led a patrol and at point U.27.d.2.5 they made contact with German snipers who fired 12 shots at them. Wilson considered that the village of Bullecourt was lightly held. 2nd Lieutenant H. Rhodes commanding A Company's patrol also came into contact with the enemy. He reported to Hastings 'Bullecourt still held by the enemy: snipers active — shots coming from U.21.6.7.1, U.27.b.7.3 and U.28.a.2.4'.[10]

185th Brigade Headquarters ordered further patrols to take place at dusk later that evening on 11th April. These patrols discovered that the wire was only passable at one position and that it was 'a serious obstacle'.[11]

Hastings and the 2nd/6th Battalion were withdrawn from the line after dark during the evening when they were relieved by the 2nd/7th Duke of Wellington (West Riding Regiment). There was a delay in the relief because Corporal Gill and five men holding a T-shaped shell hole on A company's front were missing. This hole was considered lost because new shell holes surrounded it. Corporal Gill and his party were given up for lost; however they had been nearly buried by shell fire on two occasions and were unable to withdraw because they were pinned down by German sniper fire. They were found safe and well on the following day.

Although the battalion did not launch a full-scale attack upon Bullecourt they did suffer some casualties, with two officers killed and one wounded; 31 other ranks killed and 29 wounded.

Private Robert Haigh, 241142, 2nd/6th Battalion West Yorkshire regiment. As a member of B Company, Private Haigh was killed on 11th April during the advance. (Bradford Weekly Telegraph)

The battalion suffered these casualties throughout the day. Two men were killed and seven men wounded from D Company when a shell exploded near to their position at the railway embankment during that morning. Captain Richard Burnie Armistead was wounded with two other men while leading a patrol into No Man's Land. The majority of casualties suffered by the battalion came from B Company where a platoon in support was holding a position in the cellar of a ruined house. A German shell hit one of the gables of the house, which resulted in the house collapsing upon the platoon in the cellar. Lieutenant Charles Francis Robert Pells, together with 2nd Lieutenant Alfred George Harris and 25 men were killed and a further six wounded.

NOTES

1. National Archives: WO 95/3082: 2nd/6th Battalion West Yorkshire Regiment War Diary.
2. Ibid.
3. Ibid.
4. Ibid.
5. Ibid.
6. Ibid.
7. National Archives: WO 95/3079: 185 Brigade War Diary.
8. National Archives: WO 95/3082: 2nd/6th Battalion West Yorkshire Regiment War Diary.
9. Ibid.
10. Ibid.
11. Ibid.

CHAPTER 12

PRISONERS OF WAR CAPTURED 11TH APRIL 1917

Feelings of dejection and frustration were felt by the Australians who had advanced across the snowy terrain east of Bullecourt under heavy shell fire, fought their way through the wire into the German trenches and held on to their captured positions for several hours, only to run out of ammunition, resulting in their being surrounded and captured. They had survived the ordeal of the battle of first Bullecourt, but once captured they faced an unknown period of incarceration – in fact it would be 19 months captivity.

Some of the men who were taken were killed by Australian barrages as they were being escorted by their German captors through Riencourt to prisoner-of-war camps. Private William Belcher from the 15th Battalion made it into the German trenches where he was surrounded and captured. As he was being marched half a mile towards Riencourt an Australian shell fell nearby killing him instantly.

Sergeant Frederick Peachey, an original from the 15th Battalion, was forced to bury dead comrades in a shell hole with their identity discs by his German captors soon after being taken. 'The Germans made us bury about 200 of our own dead in the afternoon without removing discs.'[1]

Some of the wounded were killed by German personnel when they regained possession of the Hindenburg Line trenches on 11th April. Private John Lee from the 14th Battalion was captured with a hundred men who had bitterly defended the trench that they had taken for more than six hours. During his first moments of captivity he saw German medics shooting wounded prisoners. After he escaped on 5th November, Lee recalled the treatment meted out by German personnel wearing the Red Cross on their arm to Australian wounded who lay in German OG 1 and OG 2 Trenches:

There were about 100 of us taken at the same time. At the time of my capture I noticed several of our wounded lying in the trenches. Some of these men had been wounded in the stomach and some in the leg and were unable to walk, and I noticed some of

the German Army Medical Corps men deliberately go up to three of them and shoot them. As far as I noticed, all the German ambulance men, who go about with large red crosses on their arms, carry revolvers.[2]

Although this testimony gives the impression that these German medics were murderously brutal, they were arguably acting in the best interests of the wounded soldiers who were in considerable pain and who were beyond medical attention, in the opinion of the medics they were clearly not going to survive their wounds. Bean in his official history does refer to those Australian soldiers who were 'put to death by a merciful enemy'.[3] After all, the German's initiated a truce later on 11th April to ensure that the wounded were recovered from the wire. Some of them were brought to a position so that Australian medics could retrieve them. There is evidence that suggests that the Germans treated the wounded with care, attention and respect.

Captain John Mott who had been wounded in the stomach in OG 1 trench was treated with kindness by his captors from the Württemberg Regiment. However, he had to wait three days before he could be removed from OG 2 Trench:

There were a great many wounded in the trenches, which the Germans eventually retook, and it was three days before I was taken to a dressing station. During this time, however, I was given food and water. On the third day, the 14th April, I was carried away to a dressing station. Previous to this I had not noticed any infraction of the laws and usages of war. The regiment – the Württembergers – who took me prisoner behaved very well and treated us quite fairly. They could not take me away for three days owing to the large number of casualties to which they had to attend and the number of seriously wounded who had to be taken away before myself. I was taken to a dressing station where my wounds were bandaged, and from there I was shifted to another dressing station.[4]

German Aid Station at Hendecourt. Wounded Australian prisoners of war would have received medical treatment here after the first Bullecourt battle on 11th April. (Yves Fohlen)

As soon as they were captured some of the men were stripped of valuables and personal belongings. Anything of no intelligence value or material value they were allowed to keep. Private John Lee recalled: 'The men who took us prisoners searched us, and one of them took away the gold wrist watch I was wearing, together with my letters and papers, but left me my money. I also managed to retain my pay-book, as I had it tucked under my puttees.'[5]

Lance Corporal C.W. Stewart was Captain Harry Murray's runner. He was wounded in the leg during the battle and unable to withdraw to Australian lines. He was wearing his Military Medal ribbon on his tunic. A German soldier who was souvenir hunting tried to take it from him. Stewart resisted and there was a commotion. A German officer rebuked the German soldier and Stewart was allowed to keep his decoration.[6]

Sergeant Hugh Orr from the 16th Battalion AIF, who was captured on 11th April having held the Hindenburg Line for several hours, was taken to Marquion where he was robbed of valued personal possessions by German officers:

They took us to Marquion and the day after we were captured we went out into a paddock and there was a big long row of tables with about 20 German Officers there and we had to hand out everything that we had in our pockets on to these tables and what they wanted to they kept and what they didn't want they gave you back.[7]

Private Leslie Pezet recalled that the first line soldiers who captured him treated him well, probably out of respect for the determined defence of the trenches which they had captured, but as they were passed to reserve troops the treatment from their captors changed:

The first line soldiers treating us very well, but being handed over to his reserve men, they being very rough, knocked and kicked us. Whatever they wanted doing, no one understanding German we suffered severely and innocently were being punished. Taken from here [Riencourt] we were marched 12 kilometres to HQ. Here a German officer insults our officers, almost refusing my officer Lt. Binnington a drink of water and after calling us swine etc. he searches us, tearing up all letters and photos with absolute murder in his face.[8]

On 12th April many of the Australian prisoners of war captured at Bullecourt were taken to the notorious Fort Macdonald in Lille, which was used by the Germans as a prison. Known as 'the Black Hole of Lille', those Australian POWs who were incarcerated in the fort for several days received harsh treatment at the hands of their captors. On arrival they were threatened by the commandant in charge of the prison, to instil fear into the new inmates and prevent escape attempts. Sergeant Percy Fleming from the 15th Battalion recalled: 'I do not know the name of the officer in command. He was a very short man on a black horse. He greeted us with the observation "the guns are loaded: he who attempts to escape will be shot".'[9]

They were held in large numbers in small cells with poor sanitary conditions, starved and given no opportunity to exercise. Private John Lee gave a graphic account of the overcrowding and unhealthy living conditions at Fort Macdonald:

There were about 95 of us altogether. We were very overcrowded and were made to sleep on the bare floor and were not given any blankets. The sanitary arrangements consisted of tubs in the room. There were no washing facilities, and I never got a wash the whole six days I was here. The food was very poor and consisted of a slice of bread and a drink of water for breakfast, hot greasy water – without any nourishment whatever – for dinner, and a slice of bread again in the evening.[10]

Private Claude Benson from the 16th Battalion was wounded in the left leg and taken to Fort Macdonald:

> The treatment was very bad there; we were put 100 into a room meant for 20. We had to eat out of our tin helmets. The food was very poor, we were not allowed out into the yard and the sanitary arrangements were anything but good.[11]

Sergeant Hugh Orr would spend three weeks imprisoned in Fort Macdonald, where within a short space of time he quickly suffered from the effects of malnutrition and living in such abominable conditions:

> It was an unpleasant place I can assure you of that. We had a loaf of bread to eight men and they gave you no dishes to eat out of. If you had a tin hat with you, you were luckier. You could get a bit of soup in the tin hat and that was all you had. Just black bread and soup for about three weeks. I think that we lost a stone to two stone up there in weight.[12]

Many of the prisoners were sent to camps near to the front line where they were put to work. They were deliberately sent to work within range of British guns in reprisal for alleged mistreatment of German prisoners working near to the British trenches. Private Leslie Pezet remembered what a German officer told them:

> You men are here for punishment, no beds to sleep on, and cask for latrine, no water to wash, and very little food to eat. You are punished because England refuses to listen to our appeal, to stop working our German prisoners in her firing line, we are going to punish you further by sending you to our firing line where you will get killed and wounded by your own English shells. We are going to make you work very hard and all hours. You will get very little food, no beds, no soap, no clothes nor boots ... If you refuse to do anything, no matter how small, we will shoot you.[13]

Private John Lee was sent to work near Brebières which was 8 kilometres behind the German front line at Arras for three months. 'Our work consisted of making roads, dug-outs and burying German dead. There were always a heap of German dead in the cemetery waiting to be buried. The hours of work were 7.00 am to 6 pm.'[14]

Private Claude Benson was sent to a civilian prison at Douai where he was imprisoned from 18th April to July 1917. Here he was sharing a cell built to accommodate one prisoner with 13 other soldiers. During the three months that he was imprisoned he was forced to work:

> I was about three months here and we had to work on the roads or at ammunition dumps, the work was very hard, the hours very long and we were being knocked about by the guards the whole time and were under our own shell fire the whole time. No one in my particular party died but I heard that eight or nine in other parties did.[15]

After spending three weeks in Fort Macdonald Prison in Lille, Sergeant Hugh Orr joined some of the British POWs captured on 3rd May at Marquion north west of Cambrai, where he was put to work. Opportunities existed to acquire food while joined to work parties. French civilians would assist and provide food when the Germans were not looking. Orr later remembered, 'Well, we had bad treatment in Lille. It wasn't too bad in Marquion because we could get quite a lot of stuff. Men went out working there on working parties and they could bring back some food that they managed to scrounge off the French.'[16]

Australian and British POWs captured soon after the Battle of Bullecourt on 11th April were sent to the civilian prison at Fort MacDonald in Lille. They remained here for several days where they received harsh treatment. (Yves Fohlen)

Although extra food could be obtained from French civilians by some prisoners, it was difficult for many others. The regime at Marquion was harsh, the accommodation crude, the hygiene abysmal. Being overworked and underfed made the prisoners weak and undermined their immune systems making them vulnerable to disease. Sergeant Percy Fleming from the 15th Battalion wrote of the appalling conditions endured by prisoners at Marquion on his arrival on 23rd April:

> We were then sent to Marquion and put in a camp which had just been vacated by Russian prisoners and was half occupied by French prisoners. The conditions of it were most frightful. The latrine was an old moat which had been used by the prisoners for two years. Anywhere in the lines you could see vermin crawling. No arrangements were made whatever for feeding. We went all day without anything to eat. The men were glad to pull nettles and boil them up. Next day rations were issued, and the men were put out to work on various jobs such as railway dumps, loading munitions, railway work etc.[17]

It was difficult for them to carry out the physically demanding work. Sergeant Fleming: 'The men were very weak, and it was almost impossible for them to do the heavy work. The Germans would use the butt of a rifle on them on the least provocation.'[18]

Working close to the German lines meant that many of the Australian soldiers captured at Bullecourt were exposed to British shell fire. Private John Lee: 'We were under British fire the whole time and one day seven of our fellows got killed, amongst them Fraser, of the 48th Battalion, and Hutchins of the 15th Battalion.'[19]

Private George Fraser from the 48th Battalion was killed by British shells while working for the Germans on 1st May. Private Matthew Holder, also from the 48th Battalion and captured at Bullecourt belonged to the same work detail and witnessed Fraser's death:

> He was one of eight being practically blown to pieces by one of our own shells when in a working party (of which I was one) some five kilometres behind the line between Brebières and Douai. I was about 20 yards from them and saw the bodies about half an hour after, but they had been burnt by the subsequent explosion of a dump and were then unrecognisable.[20]

With their nerves strained from shell fire and exhausted from overwork the Australian POWs quickly grew weaker and the treatment meted out by the German guards made it worse. Private John Lee: 'Some of the guards in charge of us treated us all right, but some

thought nothing of hitting us with the butt of a rifle if we left off working for a minute.'[21]

Some guards went further and committed murderous atrocities. Private Joe Miller from the 16th Battalion was murdered by a German soldier. Miller, known as Paddy, an Irishman from Wexford, was desperate for food. Details of this incident were provided by Private Thomas Ensor in his testimony: 'Joe Miller, of the 16th Battalion AIF, was shot and killed by a German sentry while pulling potatoes out of the ground for food for himself.'[22] Miller had climbed over the wall of the camp to dig for potatoes then return. Private Harry Kyle, who was captured with Miller at Bullecourt, witnessed the execution of his mate. 'At Valenciennes, Pte Miller 16th Battalion who was in a starving condition, attempted to take some potatoes growing in a field, close by and was shot dead by one of the sentries.'[23] Private Thomas Leiper confirmed:

> At St Saulves Camp about July 1917, he got out of the camp to dig up some potatoes or anything he could get to eat. He was on his way back, when shot by sentry at wall of camp. Hit in heart. They took four of our men out of camp to carry his body in. he was then taken to hospital for burial.[24]

A document in his Red Cross Missing file tells a different story. The report of the Commandant 158 Field Post read:

> The English Prisoner of War Joseph Miller, 6897, escaped on the night of the 6/7 July 1917 from the prisoner camp St Saulve, and was shot by the sentry whilst escaping because he failed to halt when given the order. Death followed the shot injuries on 7th July between 12.15 and 12.30 am.[25]

If he had been starving, Miller would not have had the will or the energy to commit to an escape attempt. Miller was buried at Valenciennes (St Roch) Communal Cemetery.

As mentioned earlier, the Germans did explain why they were being forced to work near to the German front lines. Private John Lee:

> We were told by the Germans that the reason we were put under such conditions was because the British government were working the German prisoners right up in the firing line and though they had been asked to do so, had refused to move them, and in consequence we should be kept there until they consented to shift the German prisoners.[26]

During the middle of July the British Government agreed to concede to the requests and confirmed

British and Australian Prisoners at Douai Prison. Private Claude Benson was among the Australian prisoners who were taken to this civilian prison soon after capture at Bullecourt. (Die Osterchlacht bei Arras II. Teil Zwisch)

that they would move all German prisoners of war 25 kilometres from the British front line. The German authorities then moved all British and Australian prisoners of war away from the German front line to Belgium and Germany.

When they arrived in camps in Germany, life for the soldiers captured at Bullecourt improved. They were better fed, received Red Cross parcels, they were housed in wooden barracks and got better treatment from their guards. Morale improved. Sergeant Percy Fleming arrived at Fredericksveldt camp in Germany on 1st October 1917:

> We went in a truck to Fredericksveldt. On arrival there we were searched and our boots were taken and wooden clogs were served out to us. We were put in barracks which were quite all right – long wooden huts. We were put into the barrack with the other British. They looked after us and gave us underclothes and boots or slippers.[27]

Escape attempts were made by the soldiers who were captured at Bullecourt. Private Claude Benson from the 16th Battalion escaped from Aachen, Germany, on 1st October 1918. Captain John Mott recovered from his wounds and successfully escaped from Germany to Holland. He was the first Australian officer to escape from a German POW camp and returned to the 48th Battalion to become its Commanding Officer. Sergeant Percy Fleming also escaped from Fredericksveldt Camp on 1st October 1918. Private John Lee escaped from

Quartes in Belgium on 5th November 1917 and after three weeks on the run he crossed the Dutch border on 25th November 1917.

Sergeant Frederick Peachey was wounded in the head and left lying in No Man's Land at Bullecourt for two days before he was found by a German patrol on 13th April. Peachey recovered from his wounds and later escaped from the POW camp at Limburg, Germany during November 1917. He reached Holland that same month.

Captain George Gardiner was not so fortunate. He had succeeded in escaping from his POW camp, but was caught before crossing the German border and remained a captive until the Armistice.

One of the most intriguing stories concerns Private Thomas Taylor from the 14th Battalion who was captured in the Hindenburg Line trenches on 11th April and escaped from a German prisoner of war camp – all the way to Russia.

Corporal Percival Job, Privates John Parsons, G Stewart and Edward Smith from the 16th Battalion escaped from Parchin POW Camp on 19th May 1917. They reached the German border on 22nd May, where they decided to separate. Job and Smith were captured and sent back to their prisoner of war camp. Parsons and Stewart managed to evade their captors and reach the Australian front line near Riencourt, held by the 32nd Battalion. The sentries on duty shot at them. Stewart received a wound in the shoulder but they managed to identify themselves.

Many of the prisoners contracted pulmonary tuberculosis. Private Amos Dyer from the 13th Battalion was afflicted by this illness and would die in 1924 in Randwick, New South Wales, at the age of 42, as a consequence.

SERGEANT JACK PAXTON 430,
13TH BATTALION AIF

Jack Johnson Paxton was born in Dumbarton, Glasgow, Scotland during 1885. Paxton was aged 29 and working as an engineer Based in Sydney prior to the war. He enlisted at St Kilda, Victoria to join the AIF on 25th September 1914. His service record stated that his wife Dorothy lived in Falkirk, Scotland. He embarked aboard the troopship HMAT *Ulysses* at Melbourne on

Sergeant Jack Paxton, 16th Battalion AIF. (Courtesy Ross Moon)

22nd December 1914. Paxton landed on Gallipoli with D Company, 13th Battalion on 25th April 1915. Three days later he sustained gunshot wounds to his left wrist and hand, which resulted in him being evacuated to England to recover. He returned to the 13th Battalion when he had recovered from his wounds. Paxton fought his way into the German trenches at Bullecourt on 11th April. During the battle he sustained a gunshot wound to his nose and eye. After his capture he was imprisoned at Saltau POW Camp in Germany. He returned from Germany to England on 19th January 1919. Paxton was discharged from the AIF on 28th March 1919 while in London.

PRIVATE THOMAS TAYLOR 5782,
14TH BATTALION AIF

Thomas Edward Taylor was born in Neerim, North Gippsland, Victoria, in 1896. He was known as Tommy and prior to the war, he worked as a farmer at Neerim. He was aged 20 when he enlisted to join the AIF on 16th March 1916. Private Tommy Taylor began his long journey which would take him to Russia on 4th May 1916 when he embarked aboard HMAT *Port Lincoln* from Melbourne. He arrived in England in 10th June 1916.

Taylor left England for France on 22nd September. He arrived at Etaples in France on 4th October and was assigned to the 14th Battalion AIF. The following day he was attached to the 1st Canadian Tunneling Company. Ten days later he fell ill with mumps and was sent to hospital. He returned to the 14th Battalion on 11th November.

Taylor would experience action for the first time at Bullecourt on 11th April. He charged across the snow with the 14th Battalion towards the German lines under heavy machine gun fire. Taylor was among those soldiers who fought their way into the Hindenburg Line trenches and with dogged determination held their ground for six hours before being surrounded and forced to surrender. Taylor had been wounded in the hand during this fierce battle. His wound was so severe that the German surgeon who attended Taylor contemplated amputating the hand. Taylor persuaded him not to amputate. Instead the surgeon operated on

his hand without anaesthetic. Tommy was bound to a table as the surgeon carried out the operation. After a period of recuperation in a German hospital he was transferred to a hospital for POWs:

> I was transferred to a hospital for prisoners of war, and there the effects of the bad food and black bread were very evident. Dysentery was carrying off the invalids in scores, especially the Russians who seemed to be accorded worse treatment than other Allied prisoners. I counted as many as 15 deaths in the Russian quarter in one week. The way in which their remains were treated showed us that they were evidently treated contemptuously as a people by the Hun. Their ward was in an upper floor of the building and each unfortunate, as he died, was taken by the legs or an arm and dragged down the stairs and thrown into one huge common grave. Even now I can hear the dull thuds and humps of those lifeless bodies. Several English Tommies died at the same hospital while I was there, but they were treated with more respect and were carried out decently and buried in separate graves.[28]

Tommy Taylor's time in captivity meant poor rations, which mainly constituted a daily portion of black bread. During the summer of 1917 Taylor was listed as missing and his family in Neerim did not know his fate. The anxiety of not knowing was alleviated when on 4th August 1917 a message was received in London confirming that Taylor had been captured at Riencourt and was being held at Limburg Prisoner of War Camp in Germany. At least his family knew he was alive.

On 9th October 1917 he was transferred to Heilsberg Lager POW camp in Germany. He was given the prisoner number 255369. He sent a message to his relatives, which was dated 28th April 1918 but received in London on 2nd July 1918: 'I am quite well; I have been a prisoner for 12 months and have not received any parcels yet.'[29]

While at Heilsberg Tommy Taylor was sent out to work on a German farm. He worked with two Russian POWs. The woman who owned the farm was left alone to tend the farm because her husband and two sons were fighting the war. While Tommy and his fellow prisoners worked here they received better food from this lady. Influenza was spreading throughout Germany during the autumn of 1917:

> The flu was raging throughout Germany at that time. There was not much that I missed, and, of course I didn't miss getting the flu. For two weeks I lay very near to the 'borderland' I think, with no medical attention whatever. No one came near to help me, save my companions, and they were only

Private Thomas Edward Taylor, 14th Battalion AIF. *(Peregrinations of an Australian Prisoner of War, the Experiences of an Australian Soldier in Germany and Bolshevik Russia by Private T.E. Taylor, published 1932)*

there after working hours. One of them in particular (a Russian) did more to help me than all the others, and to him, in a great measure, I owed my recovery.[30]

By the summer of 1918 Tommy had been a prisoner of war for a year. He had received a letter from home which confirmed that his mate from the 17th Battalion, Private Joseph Newman who had been captured at Lagnicourt on 15th April 1917, had escaped from a POW Camp and reached Petrograd on 13th June. The news of a successful escape motivated Tommy Taylor. He was being held eight miles from the Polish border. If he escaped he would have to travel across Germany into France. He considered it impossible to cross the trenches to reach allied lines. So he and the Russian prisoners decided to head east across Poland towards the Russian border:

For some considerable time some of us had been thinking seriously of making a bid for freedom. One Russian prisoner had secured a compass, whilst another had a map, and together we studied and discussed that map. From information we got from time to time from Russian prisoners who had escaped and had been recaptured, we decided that our best course was to make for Minsk, which was situated on the border of Poland and Russia. Once over the border we thought we would be safe. Of course we knew nothing whatever at that time the state of affairs in Russia. Our German guards had at times told us contradictory tales of affairs in the outer world, and had even told us that the Russians had deserted their Allies, and that the country was in a state of chaos, but we did not believe anything.[31]

Unaware that the war would be over within two weeks and with no knowledge of the revolution in Russia, Taylor and three Russian prisoners made a dash for freedom as they escaped from Heilsburg Lager on 3rd November 1918. It was tough going as they headed in the darkness towards the Polish border. Once the camp guards were aware of their escape they knew that they would be vigorously pursued and hunted down. It was important for them to get as far away from the camp as possible during the first night of their escape:

At about 7 o'clock in the evening, I and three Russians started off to the Polish border, which was about eight miles east of us. When we reached the vicinity of Sawalki we had no cover whatever, and travelled for a considerable distance over ploughed fields. We wanted to go well beyond that district before dawn, and as it was heavy going, we decided to make for a nearby metalled road, thinking it easy enough to make off the road for safety if we heard anything approaching. That went on very well for a

good few miles, but the heavy going and continuous plodding had made us all very tired, and we rested for a while on the roadside. Of course, we all meant to keep very much awake and have our wits about us, but we had scarcely sat down, it seemed, then we had all fallen asleep. How long we slept I don't know, but we were rudely awakened by the sound of approaching horses, which were so near that we had no time to make ourselves scarce. We did not know what to do, so did the most natural thing under the circumstances – nothing. And it was well we did (or didn't for the slightest movement would have been our undoing). They were a party of Uhlans patrolling the road, we could just distinguish their peaked caps in the dawning light. One of them remarked as they were opposite to where we were lying that 'those black objects look like men', and we strained our ears for the reply. As we were lying amongst some very large stones, the other mistook us for stones, and, to our unbounded relief, they took that for granted and passed on. We managed to reach a small wood beyond a village shortly after daybreak, quite exhausted, and there we slept well into the evening.[32]

On crossing the Russian border two of the Russians in their party went in another direction. Taylor was left with a Russian prisoner who had been his workmate on the farm. It was he who had helped Taylor when he was ill with the flu in the prison camp. Taylor shared his food with the Russian. When Taylor found himself in Russia, he of course had difficulty speaking the language and when bartering for food he was being charged extortionate prices. Taylor felt that he could trust his Russian friend with what little money that he had and depended upon him to buy food. The Russian soldier left him and stole the money. After suffering the ordeal of Bullecourt and 18 months of captivity as a prisoner of war, Taylor found himself alone in a country in the throes of a civil war.

Suffering from hunger and exhaustion Private Tommy Taylor reported to the British Consul in Moscow on 9th December 1918. A cable was sent to Melbourne that Taylor had escaped from a camp in Germany and that he had reached Moscow, but Mr Selby at the FO Russia department in London was unable to confirm his exact whereabouts in Moscow and there would be an investigation that was to last for several months.

News that Taylor had escaped arrived in London in the New Year. Private H Harrison 4th Machine Gun Company also escaped that night and communicated on 16th January 1919 the following information about Taylor to the Red Cross:

This man was with me in East Prussia, Heilsberg Lager, working on a farm. We both tried to escape, left the same night, 3rd November 1918. I went with an Englishman through Russia to Finland, and he went with three Russians. I think making for Petrograd. They were to cross the border east of where we did. He started half an hour before us, and I have no idea how they got on ... He was in good health and they took all the food that they could carry.[33]

Earl Curzon of Kedleston tried to get further information about Taylor's whereabouts soon after this report was received. Gerald Spicer from the Foreign Office in London wrote on 3rd March: 'Lord Curzon desires me to add that he is also causing such enquiries as are possible to be made in regard to the present position of Private Taylor and that it is understood that this soldier is still in Moscow.'[34] On 4th March 1919 the following communication was released by the Foreign Office in London:

Lord Curzon is not in possession of definite information as to whether Private Taylor is at present in prison there [Moscow], or whether he is allowed to move freely in that city, but from the latest reports received he is inclined to believe that he is at present employed as a messenger by Mr. Mucukaln, who is in charge of His Majesty's Consulate-General at Moscow.[35]

Definite confirmation was received in London on 11th April 1919, exactly two years to the day he was captured at Bullecourt. The Foreign Office received the following letter written by Taylor:

No doubt you will be surprised to get a letter from me here. You remember sending them a letter to Germany telling me of my mate Joe Newman getting away. Well, when I received it I decided to try my luck and here I am. I left Moscow on the 7th March and am now held up here in quarantine. We think we will go on next Tuesday so we ought not to be long before we reach England. Would you be so kind as to let my people know that I am coming home as they don't know what has become of me and by doing same you will greatly oblige.[36]

Taylor left Moscow by train for Helsingfors in Finland on 7th March 1919. He reported to the Red Cross in London on 12th April. A cable was sent to Melbourne on that day confirming to his family, 'Arrived London, well'. On arriving in London Tommy Taylor was subjected to three weeks interrogation about his experiences in Bolshevik Russia. He left England on 7th July aboard Chemnits, and arrived in Melbourne on 5th September 1919. Tommy was discharged in Melbourne from the AIF on 26th October 1919.

PRIVATE HUBERT DEMASSON 6501,
16TH BATTALION AIF

Hubert Peter Demasson was born in Guildford, Western Australia in 1881. He worked as a railway guard in Guildford and married Lillian Minchin in 1909. They had five children. Demasson enlisted to join the AIF on 23rd June 1916. On completing his basic training he embarked aboard HMAT *Suffolk* on 13th October 1916 from Fremantle for the war in Europe. He arrived in England during December 1916. Assigned to the 16th Battalion he embarked for France from Folkestone aboard SS *Princess Victoria* on 8th February 1917.

Demasson advanced across No Man's Land at Bullecourt, got through the wire and fought his way into the German trenches. At midday when all their ammunition had been expended his unit was given the choice to withdraw which meant risking life, running the gauntlet across No Man's Land or they could wait in the trenches and surrender to the enemy. Eye witness Private Thomas Sloss 6582 from the 16th Battalion later reported:

All I know of Demasson is that when we left the trenches about 12 noon 11.04.17 after receiving the order to take our choice of surrendering or retiring, Demasson decided to stay behind and he was then unwounded.[37]

Demasson was captured and imprisoned at Limburg in Germany. While in captivity he was taken ill and sent to a hospital in Langensalza on 19th September 1917 where he died. Cause of death was attributed to inflammation of the kidneys and chronic inflammation of the intestines, while his Australian Red Cross Missing file indicates that he died of dysentery. His inability to fight off illness and disease was brought on by malnutrition. Private Campbell Stewart, 14th Battalion recalled: 'I saw Pte Demasson H. 16th Battalion die at Langensalza from starvation.'[38]

He was buried initially at Langensalza Cemetery; however his remains were exhumed and buried at Niederzwehren Cemetery, Cassel. The record of where Demasson was buried within Niederzwehren Cemetery was lost as well as those of six other soldiers interred there. A special memorial commemorating Demasson was created in the cemetery. The inscription reads:

Private Hubert Demasson, 16th Battalion AIF. (Australia's Fighting Sons of the Empire)

TO THE MEMORY OF THE SEVEN SOLDIERS
OF THE BRITISH EMPIRE,
WHO DIED AS PRISONERS OF WAR
IN 1917 AND WERE BURIED AT THE TIME IN
LANGENSALZA P.O.W. CEMETERY NO.2
BUT WHOSE GRAVES ARE NOW LOST.
THEIR GLORY SHALL NOT BE BLOTTED OUT[39]

SERGEANT ALEXANDER GLOSTER 6458,
16TH BATTALION AIF

Alexander Burns Gloster was born in Seymour, Victoria in June 1885. He was educated in Seymour and later Brighton. Prior to the war he was a publican/hotel keeper in Osborne, Western Australia. Gloster was aged 40 when he enlisted on 1st March 1916 at Busselton, Western Australia. He trained at Blackboy, Bunbury and Belmont Camps. By September 1916 he had quickly climbed the ranks to Sergeant. He embarked aboard HMAT *Port MacGuarie* at Fremantle on 13th October 1916 and sailed for England. He arrived at Plymouth, England on 12th December 1916. He was sent to France during January 1917 and joined the 16th Battalion. He saw action in Flers during February 1917. Gloster was captured at Bullecourt on 11th April. He remained a POW in Germany until the end of the war. After spending two months in captivity he was anxious to get a message to his wife Grace in Australia to let her know that he was a POW in Germany. He had sent letters but was not receiving any replies. In a letter dated 21st June 1917 Gloster wrote to his cousin Mrs. A Westlake, who was living in Orpington in Kent, England:

Dear Cousin, I wrote to you by letter on 22/4/17 and again on 25/5/17 by postcard stating that I was a P. of W. and in both letters I asked you to cable to

my wife Claremont W.A. informing her of the fact and that I was well and at the same time I wished you to forward me a parcel of food weekly, so far I have had no reply to my letters and no parcel so presume that my letters have never reached you, as I feel sure you would have written and done what you could for me. I will now ask you again in the hope of a reply some day, because if more food is not obtained and we have to work, some of us will never survive the coming winter – we are merely existing.[40]

Sergeant Alexander Gloster, 16th Battalion AIF. (Australia's Fighting Sons of the Empire)

When he was transferred to Friedrichsfeld Camp life became more bearable for he wrote on 21st October 1917: 'Parcels now arriving more regularly and prisoners consequently in better heart, they feel quite satisfied that they will see the war through. I am well with the exception of bad hands.'[41] He was repatriated back to England via Denmark during December 1918. He arrived in Australia on 17th March 1919.

PRIVATE HARRY KYLE 2012,
16TH BATTALION AIF

Harry Bruce Kyle was born in Beechworth, Victoria. He was educated at Scotch College. When he was aged 18 and still a student he enlisted to join the Army at Kalgoorlie on 18th February 1915. After completing his basic training he boarded HMAT *Hororata* at Fremantle and sailed for Egypt on 26th April 1915. He took part in the Gallipoli campaign with the 16th Battalion during 1915 and saw action on the Somme during the summer of 1916. Kyle was captured at Bullecourt on 11th April 1917. He was interned at Schneidemuhl Camp where he was subjected to harsh treatment and starvation as a prisoner of war. Malnutrition was a problem for many men in captivity and Kyle complained of his diet as soup which was made of grass instead of vegetables. He returned to Australia during June 1919 and became a dentist in Perth after the war.

Private Harry Kyle, 16th Battalion AIF. (Australia's Fighting Sons of the Empire)

PRIVATE ERNEST RAWLINGS 5173
16TH BATTALION AIF

Ernest James Rawlings was born at Toodyay, Western Australia. Prior to the war Rawlings worked as a labourer. He enlisted in Perth on 7th January 1916. On 31st March 1916 Rawlings boarded HMAT *Shropshire* at Fremantle and sailed for England. On 19th August 1916 he joined the

Private Ernest Rawlings 16th Battalion. (Australia's Fighting Sons of the Empire)

16th Battalion in France. Rawlings was captured at Bullecourt on 11th April 1917. He was initially interned at Limburg Camp and by October 1917 he had been transferred to Friedrichsfeld Camp in Germany. He was repatriated back to England on 31st December 1918. Rawlings returned home to his wife Florence in Australia in 1919. He passed away on 29th August 1955.

PRIVATE EDWARD MCKERNAN 6059,
16TH BATTALION AIF

Edward Walter McKernan was born on 3rd October 1892 in Bunbury, Western Australia. He worked as a boatman before the war. McKernan enlisted on 21st March 1916 at Blackboy Hill. After completing his training, McKernan sailed from Fremantle aboard HMAT *Miltiades* for England on 7th August 1916. He arrived in Plymouth on 25th September 1916. After completing his training at Codford Camp he was sent to France on 21st December 1916. His right hip was shattered and he suffered a compound fracture to the thigh in the trenches of the Hindenburg Line at Bullecourt on 11th April 1917, where he was captured. His German captors evacuated him to hospital. McKernan succumbed to his

wounds and died from blood poisoning at the Valenciennes Military Hospital at 1.15 pm on 13th June 1917. McKernan, who was aged 25, was buried in Valenciennes St Roch Communal Cemetery.

Private Edward McKernan 16th Battalion. (Australia's Fighting Sons of the Empire)

PRIVATE EGBERT REEVES 6084,
16TH BATTALION AIF

Egbert Robert Reeves was born in Geelong, Victoria. He was educated at Jarrahdale and on leaving school he became a fitter. Prior to the war, he had belonged

to a rifle club and was able to develop his ability to shoot. Reeves enlisted on 8th March 1916. On completing basic training he embarked aboard HMAT *Miltiades* at Fremantle and sailed for England on

Private Egbert Reeves 16th Battalion. (Australia's Fighting Sons of the Empire)

7th August 1916. After arriving in Plymouth on 30th September, Reeves spent three months training at Codford. During December 1916 Reeves was sent to France and joined the 16th Battalion on 2nd January 1917. Reeve's was captured at Bullecourt on 11th April. By May, Reeves was interned at Dulmen Camp and by August 1917 he had been transferred to a camp at Gustrow. He spent 20 months as a prisoner of war in Germany. After repatriation to England he had to wait seven months before he could begin the journey home to Australia. He arrived in his homeland on 16th September 1919.

CORPORAL JOHN (JOCK) WILLIAMSON MM 2053,
16TH BATTALION AIF

John Williamson was born at Springhill, Lanarkshire in Scotland on 23rd March 1893. Known as 'Jock' to his family he was one of five brothers and five sisters. He was raised at Carfin Byers, a dairy farm near Motherwell. Although his family was not affluent Jock received an adequate education, which would stand him in good stead for when he emigrated to Australia. Jock's parents died when he was aged fifteen and for a short period he lived with his eldest sister Margaret McInnes and her husband at Banks Farm, Inverkip near Greenock. His brothers William and James emigrated to Alberta in Canada during 1909. During that same year, Jock decided to emigrate to Australia. His sister Jenny recalled that Jock drank beef tea in order to build himself up before leaving Scotland for Australia. Margaret was distraught, when he left – she cried for weeks. The next time she would see her brother was when he returned to Scotland dressed in an Australian army uniform.

Jock arrived at Fremantle, Australia during January 1910. He found work as a timber cutter where he demonstrated that he was a hard working, industrious individual. Such was his dedication to his job, that his workmates would frequently urge him to take a break. When the First World War broke out Jock was working on the construction of the Trans-Australia Railway Line east of Kalgoorlie. He enlisted to join the AIF on 18th February 1915. After completing basic training at Blackboy Hill he boarded the troopship HMAT *Hororato* on 26th April 1915. On arrival in Egypt he joined Australian units guarding the Suez Canal against the threat of

Corporal Jock Williamson 16th Battalion AIF after enlistment during 1915. (Courtesy John Williamson)

Corporal Jock Williamson 16th Battalion AIF after receiving MM, 1916. (Courtesy John Williamson)

Corporal Jock Williamson's Escape Map. (Courtesy John Williamson)

attack from Turkish forces. It was during this period that Jock learnt to swim in the Canal. On 28th July 1915 Jock arrived on the Gallipoli Peninsula where he joined the 16th Battalion AIF. On 6th August 1915 Jock took part in the failed operation to capture Hill 971. On 27th August he was wounded when he was part of the assault force from the 16th Battalion attacking Hill 60. Jock was evacuated to St Andrew's Hospital, Malta. He was transferred to Cardiff Military Hospital in Wales when the wound turned septic. Jock recovered from his wound and was discharged from hospital on 26th October 1915. He was given leave for one week and it is probable that this was the time when he visited his family at Carfin Farm. His sister Jenny later recalled that Jock came home on leave twice during the war. On the first occasion he attended his sister Christina's wedding and acted as best man. The other occasion was one of great sadness for Christina died while giving birth to her first child and Jock attended her funeral. Jock returned to the 16th Battalion at Tel-el-Kebir in Egypt on 9th March 1916. The battalion was sent to France during June. On 9th August Jock took part in the battle for Pozières when the 16th Battalion succeeded in capturing trenches north of the village. They held onto the trenches despite heavy German bombardment on 10th August and repelled a German counter attack on the 11th. Jock was promoted to Lance Corporal on 24th August. From the night of the 28th/29th August until the morning of the

31st August Jock and another man resisted a German assault from the 5th Prussian Foot Guard upon Point 77 near to Mouquet Farm. Jack regarded the Prussians as good soldiers who respected the rules of war. It was during this engagement that Jock earned the Military Medal. His recommendation stated:

Corporal Jock Williamson stands amongst seven POWs from the 16th Battalion at Friedrichsfeld Camp in Germany in September 1918. From left to right: Corporal Jock Williamson, Sergeant Charles Turner MM, Private Joseph Wallbank and Corporal Walter Sanders. Sitting from left to right: Private George Isbister, Sergeant Hugh Orr and Private Aubrey Whittington MM. Williamson, Wallbank, Sanders, Isbister, Orr and Whittington were all captured at Bullecourt on 11th April. Sergeant Hugh Orr made a successful escape attempt to Holland. (Courtesy John Williamson)

Lance Corporal John Williamson of the Lewis Machine Gun Section ... had his gun at the advanced point of 77. His gun team consisted of himself and one other man. He remained in this position, which is within the German lines, from the night 28/29th August until the morning 31st August. During the period this portion was constantly under fire from aerial torpedoes and rifles at close range. He directed and himself took part in digging operations during this period. He is recommended for his devotion to duty in remaining in his post for the period indicated.[42]

Jock was promoted to Corporal on 8th September. The 16th Battalion was transferred to the Ypres front after Pozières but returned to France in late October. The 16th Battalion supported the 13th Battalion's attack upon Stormy Trench on 2nd February 1917.

On 11th April Jock advanced across No Man's Land. When all their ammunition was expended he was one of those Australian soldiers who made a brave attempt to return to Australian lines. When he dived into a shell hole for cover he found a hand sticking out of the ground. He frantically dug the man from the earth and found that he had sustained a severe head wound. In a valiant effort to rescue this injured soldier he carried him on his back and headed for the Australian lines by the railway embankment. Jock received a bullet wound to the thigh and both the men were captured. Jock carried the man to a German casualty station before getting his own wound dressed. He assumed he had died from his wounds, however, years later after attending an Anzac Day Ceremony in Perth the wounded soldier recognised Jock and shook his hand with vigour. Jock mislaid the

POWs at Friedrichsfeld; Corporal Jock Williamson standing 5th from left, 2nd row from top, 3rd March 1918. (Courtesy John Williamson)

contact details of this man, but the soldier never forgot Jock who saved his life at Bullecourt.

Jock's wound to the thigh was tended by a German doctor who spoke fluent English. After experiencing harsh treatment during the initial period of his capture Jock was transferred to Friedrichsfeld POW Camp close to Essen in Germany. During his captivity Jock made two escape attempts. He had acquired a map from a French POW cook in the camp. The first time he escaped at dusk and waded through creeks in order to throw the prison dogs off the scent. He returned of his own accord with a camp work party. His second escape attempt took place during the winter. He managed to get close to the Dutch border but he was apprehended while he was asleep in a haystack by a pitchfork-wielding German farmer who had followed Jock's footsteps in the snow. Jock was fatigued and weakened by starvation having been living on raw swedes and turnips while on the run. When German prison guards came from Friedrichsfeld he was handcuffed and taken on a train. He was refused food, until some sympathetic German women passengers berated his guards persuading them to give him food. On his arrival at Friedrichsfeld Camp he was told that he would be shot if he made any further escape attempts. Jock was repatriated to England on 22nd November 1918. He then returned to Scotland where he attended the funeral of his sister Christina, who died in childbirth. He left the UK on 18th January 1919, arriving in Fremantle in February.

Being an ex-serviceman Jock was eligible to be allocated one of the dairy farms at Harvey, south of Perth. When Edward, Prince of Wales (future King of England) toured Australia, he visited Jock's farm at Udoc Road. Andy Ochiltree, another Bullecourt veteran from the 16th battalion also ran a farm nearby and a close friendship developed between Jock and Andy. During the late 1920s both men would move to Wiluna where they worked underground in the gold mines. In 1934 Jock was introduced to Andy's sister Isabella and they married two years later. During the Second world War Jock served with the Australian Reserve Signals Corps. In 1944 Jock took over a milk round in Northam. Jock and his wife Belle opened a delicatessen in West Leederville in 1945, but with a growing family of three children he decided to return to work in the gold fields and moved the family to Big Bell. Jock was suffering from heart problems in 1954 and gave up work in the minefields finding employment in the PMG Midland Junction. On 11th September 1965 Jock Williamson passed away at the Hollywood Repatriation Hospital at Nedlands, Western Australia. His son, John Lachlan Williamson, never knew that his father had won the Military Medal until after his father had died.

PRIVATE ARTHUR ZOWE 5471,
16TH BATTALION AIF

Arthur Percy Zowe was born in Kapunda, South Australia on 3rd August 1892. Arthur worked as a butcher before enlisting to join the AIF at Blackboy Hill, Western Australia, on 4th December 1915. Zowe left Australia aboard HMAT *Aeneas* on 17th April 1916 from Fremantle. He arrived in Egypt on 10th May. Private Arthur Zowe was assigned to the 16th Battalion. After spending two months in Egypt, he was sent to France on 10th June to the Somme and while taking part in the battle

Private Arthur Zowe, 16th Battalion AIF.
(*Australia's Fighting Sons of the Empire*)

Kriegsgefangenenlager Limburg.

POW Camp at Limburg, Germany. Many prisoners captured at Bullecourt were held there. (Author)

for Pozières Zowe received a gunshot wound to his left thigh on 11th August. He was transferred to a Military Hospital in Rouen before being sent to 3rd London General Hospital, in Wandsworth, England, to recover. By November he had recovered from his wounds and returned to his battalion.

Zowe entered the German trenches at Bullecourt on 11th April 1917 where he was wounded and captured. He was interned at a camp at Verden near Hannover. Arthur Zowe sent a postcard from the camp on 25th April 1917 which got through to London on 8th June. He wrote:

> I was shot through the cheek by machine gun and bullet came out back of neck, fracturing jaw bone. I was picked up by German stretcher bearers and taken prisoner. I would be glad if you could send my people in Australia a cable and let them know what has happened to me and charge to my account.[43]

By 5th June 1917 he had been transferred to Soltau. As a result of his wounds he was repatriated to Switzerland on 27th December. A few months later he wrote a message confirming 'My wound has healed up at last and I am beginning to feel my old self again.' He remained in Switzerland until the Armistice was signed. Zowe returned to England on 9th December 1918 and went home the following year. He was discharged from the AIF on 9th June 1919.

NOTES

1. Australian War Memorial: AWM 1DRL428/009: 2nd Lieutenant James Proctor, 15th Battalion AIF, Australian Red Cross Missing File.
2. National Archives: WO/161/99/194: Private John Lee, 14th Battalion AIF: Prisoner of War Report.
3. *Official History of Australia in the War of 1914–1918* Volume 4, Charles Bean, Angus and Robertson 1938: p340.
4. National Archives: WO 161/96/28: Captain John Mott, 48th Battalion AIF: Prisoner of War Report.
5. National Archives: WO/161/99/194: Private John Lee, 14th Battalion AIF: POW Report.
6. *Reveille*: 1st April 1933: Captain Harry Murray.
7. Liddle Collection: Sergeant Hugh Orr interview: Reference Tape 239.
8. Private Leslie Pezet Diary: Courtesy Ken Pezet.
9. National Archives: WO/161/100/494: Sergeant Percy Fleming, 15th Battalion AIF: POW Report.
10. National Archives: WO/161/99/194: Private John Lee, 14th Battalion AIF: POW Report.
11. National Archives: WO/161/100/479: Private Claude Benson, 16th Battalion AIF: POW Report.
12. Liddle Collection: Sergeant Hugh Orr interview: Reference Tape 239.
13. Private Leslie Pezet Diary: Courtesy Ken Pezet.
14. National Archives: WO/161/99/194: Private John Lee, 14th Battalion AIF: POW Report.
15. National Archives: WO/161/100/479: Private Claude Benson, 16th Battalion AIF: POW Report.
16. Liddle Collection: Sergeant Hugh Orr interview: Reference Tape 239.
17. National Archives: WO/161/100/494: Sergeant Percy Fleming, 15th Battalion AIF: POW Report.
18. Ibid.
19. National Archives: WO/161/99/194: Private John Lee, 14th Battalion AIF: POW Report.
20. Australian War Memorial: AWM 1DRL428/00013: Australian Red Cross Missing File: Private George Fraser, 48th Battalion AIF.
21. National Archives: WO/161/99/194: Private John Lee, 14th Battalion AIF: POW Report.
22. National Archives: WO 161/100/93: Private Thomas Ensor, 16th Battalion AIF: POW Records.
23. National Archives of Australia: Private Joseph Miller Service Record.
24. Australian War Memorial: AWM 1DRL428/000023: Australian Red Cross Missing File: Private Joseph Miller.
25. Ibid.
26. National Archives: WO/161/99/194: Private John Lee, 14th Battalion AIF: POW Report.
27. National Archives: WO/161/100/494: Sergeant Percy Fleming, 15th Battalion AIF: POW Report.
28. *Pereginations of an Australian Prisoner of War, the Experiences of an Australian Soldier in Germany and Bolshevik Russia*, Private T.E. Taylor, Published 1932.
29. National Archives of Australia: Private Thomas Taylor, 14th Battalion AIF, Service Record.
30. *Pereginations of an Australian Prisoner of War, the Experiences of an Australian Soldier in Germany and Bolshevik Russia*. Private T.E. Taylor, Published 1932.
31. Ibid.
32. Ibid.
33. Australian War Memorial: AWM 1DRL428/00035: Australian Red Cross Missing File: Private Thomas Taylor.
34. Ibid.
35. National Archives of Australia: Private Thomas Taylor, 14th Battalion AIF, Service Record.
36. Australian War Memorial: AWM 1DRL428/00035: Australian Red Cross Missing File: Private Thomas Taylor.
37. Australian War Memorial: AWM 1DRL/428/00009: Australian Red Cross Missing File: Private Hubert Demasson.
38. National Archives of Australia: Private Hubert Demasson Service Record.
39. Ibid.
40. Ibid.
41. Australian War Memorial: AWM 1DRL428/00014: Australian Red Cross Missing Files: Private Alexander Gloster.
42. Australian War Memorial: AWM 28/1/183P/0085: Military Medal Recommendation: Lance Corporal John Williamson.
43. Australian War Memorial: AWM 1DRL428/00039: Australian Red Cross Missing File: Private Arthur Zowe.

CHAPTER 13

ASSESSMENT

The first Battle of Bullecourt was a disaster for all the allied units involved. A large proportion of the blame was placed with the tanks The overall failure of the tank at the First Bullecourt resulted in committing the Australian infantry into attacking the formidable Hindenburg Line without adequate artillery support, advancing up a slope, with the wire defences in front of them only partially cut.

The tanks' capabilities had been greatly exaggerated by their commanders and no allowance for their mechanical failure had been made. Only a small number of the tank crew had any battle experience in a tank, the remainder of the tank force had little experience of driving one. Nor were they able to deal with malfunctions.

The tanks, however, were only part of the reason for the tragic failure. Gough's decision to drive an attack through a narrow front, exposed to enemy fire on both flanks, was a strategic blunder. Rushing through with the attack, denying his men the chance to become familiarised with the plan, as well as not waiting for artillery units to get to the front line, were also reasons for failure. Gough could argue that he wanted to expedite the attack in order to assist Allenby's Third Army drive east of Arras. He could also put forward the argument that had he waited for more artillery to get to Bullecourt, Ludendorff would be allowed more time to strengthen the defences along this section of the front. However, Gough did not make provisions for the tanks failing to arrive on the battlefield. Infantry commanders were not given orders to refer to if the tanks did not show. Gough did not consider the scenario if the tanks malfunctioned.

General Birdwood, commanding the I Anzac Corps, cannot escape censure. Although he did challenge Gough prior to the operation about the feasibility, as the first assault on Bullecourt was being fought he chose to ignore the SOS flares requesting artillery support that were sent by Australian units trying to hold on to their positions in the Hindenburg Line which they had fought so hard to capture. If he had ordered artillery support then maybe they could have held on. Edgar Rule, an officer from the 14th Battalion later wrote:

As a rule, nearly all schemes of military operations look nice on paper, no matter how rotten they are,

but this one was an exception; at any rate, all our Australian chiefs were opposed to it. Maybe it looked all right to General Gough, whose army we formed part of, but he took no notice of General Birdwood and the rest of the Aussie Generals when they implored him to change the scheme and give the men a chance. Later, at our Mametz camp, I heard both General Birdwood and General Brand apologise to the men who were left, and with tears in their eyes tell them how they had done everything in their power to have the plan altered, but without success.[1]

Birdwood was devastated by the failure of the Bullecourt operation. He recognised that the men had been asked to achieve the impossible and on 18th April he wrote the following letter of consolation to Major-General William Holmes at 4th Australian Division headquarters:

You know well what my feelings are as regards the magnificent work done by your Division in the attack on the Hindenburg Line on the 11th, and I have already endeavoured to express these in the messages which you sent for me to the Brigades. Having heard, however, so many more details on the subject since then, I feel I must send you a line to again let you know my feelings of intense admiration for, and pride in, the officers and men in their really magnificent and gallant work that morning. No words can, I think, describe the reckless bravery with which they tackled the wire before them and went through everything in going in – in the desperate fighting they had while in the enemy's trenches, and again in the necessary retirement, which in the hands of inferior and less determined troops might well have led to panic and disaster.

We can none of us ever sufficiently regret the losses which we sustained, but we of course, every one of us, recognise that such are essential, when we are playing a part in the huge battlefield from Arras to Champagne.

I have been particularly struck with the way in which all company and platoon commanders conducted the most difficult retirement, seeing their men quietly through the wire as they did, and then following after they had seen all safely through. It is through doing their duty nobly like this that I am afraid that we have lost so many valuable officers. That officers should have thus willingly sacrificed themselves for their men speaks for itself, and no episode in the annals of the AIF will ever stand higher than the behaviour of the officers and all others on this occasion.[2]

As the First World War fades into distant history the men who were sacrificed in this, on the face of it, futile act must never be forgotten. The 4th Australian Division was decimated, losing 3,500 men, including 28 officers and 1,142 men captured. Bullecourt saw the largest number of Australians captured in one engagement during World War I.[3] The large number captured is significant because those who were wounded beyond the first wire failed to escape.

The 4th Australian Brigade was almost annihilated, sustaining 2,339 casualties out of 3,000 who participated. The 12th Australian Brigade suffered 950 casualties. Many of the battalions suffered heavy casualties. The 16th Battalion began the battle with a fighting strength of 20 officers and 797 men and left the battlefield with three officers and 97 men. The 13th Battalion lost 510 men from 750. Approximately 750 men from each battalion had taken part in the attack on 11th April. A proportion of officers, NCOs and men were held back who could form a new battalion in the event that the attacking forces were mauled.

Major-General William Holmes (HQ 4th Australian Division) wrote a letter to General Robertson on 12th April:

The fact that we could not 'stick it' in the line, was due to bad luck, and cannot be regarded in any way as a reflection on your Brigade, which fought magnificently, and in my opinion performed, under all circumstances, a herculean task in getting there at all and staying as long as they did.[4]

The men who had fought at Bullecourt and who got back to the railway embankment would march back the long distance to Favreuil cold, dejected and grieving for many comrades. Captain C Longmore described the first battle of Bullecourt as 'one of the most gallant and hopeless efforts in the history of warfare'.[5]

Major-General William Holmes, commanding 4th Australian Division wrote the following report summarizing the Bullecourt disaster:

1) Owing to the tanks giving no assistance whatever to the Infantry, the latter had to advance under heavy machine gun fire across open ground and clamber over wire which was in many places quite undamaged. This caused heavy casualties and the troops, when they reached their objectives, were in considerable confusion and very reduced in numbers.

2) Owing to the tanks failing to do their work, a large gap was left between the two Brigades, which could never be closed and whence the enemy delivered repeated counter attacks.

3) Owing to Bullecourt not being attacked, and the idea of 'squeezing it out' with the help of tanks being an impractical one, it commanded the open ground and made it quite impossible for carrying parties to get forward with bombs etc., although large forward dumps had been formed North of the railway line.

4) If Bullecourt had been attacked, as originally intended, and if our attack had been carried out under an Artillery barrage – even with the wire only partially out as it was – I am confident that the ground gained could have been held.[6]

Lieutenant Colonel Denham commanding the 46th Battalion listed the reasons for the failure at Bullecourt in the battalion war diary: shortage of bombs and small arms ammunition to consolidate captured positions and the inability to send carrying parties across machine-gun-swept open ground to ensure that men in these positions had enough to enable them to continue the fight and hold on. Denham produced an inventory of all ammunition held at the forward battalion store dump, which listed:

4,000 No.5 Mills Hand Grenades
800 Mills No.23 Rifle Grenades
50,000 rounds S A.A.

Only 720 Mills Hand Grenades, 350 Mills Rifle Grenades and approximately 5,000 rounds of small arms ammunition reached the men holding onto OG 1 and OG 2 Trenches.

German losses were estimated to have amounted to 750 men. They had captured Tank 799 and Tank 586, the first British tanks to be captured by the Germans, within their lines. They claimed to have captured 1,137 men and 27 officers. Bullecourt was regarded as a German victory. The 27th Württemberg Division casualties were six officers and 132 men killed with a further 11 officers and 520 men wounded. The 124th Regiment lost 434 men. General Otto von Moser commanding Group Quéant was awarded the Pour le Mérite for leading the defence of Bullecourt.

Captain Louch, intelligence officer for the 51st Battalion, wrote of the attitude of his men towards the tanks. 'The verdict of our troops was that the crews were as game as Ned Kelly; but the tanks were no good. And it was a long time before they changed their opinion.'[7]

Lieutenant-Raymond Leane thought that the tanks made no contribution in support of his 48th Battalion:

> What was achieved by this battalion was in no way due to the assistance given by the Tanks. In fact they were a hindrance not a help. The men would have gone forward at once under cover of darkness, instead of having to wait in the open from 4 am until 5.16 am by which time it was daylight, for Tanks that never advanced. Had we been able to get forward half the casualties would have been saved.
>
> ... I am of the opinion that the Tanks absolutely failed to carry out their part in the attack. I consider had they shown more dash and initiative things would have been better and perhaps we might have been still holding the line captured today.[8]

The tanks were a new weapon of warfare and it was hard for senior officers in the British Army who were trained during the Victorian era to fight wars with cavalry to understand how to use these new weapons. They did not understand their capabilities or their vulnerabilities. Corporal Ernie Hayward Knew this: 'The Generals did not understand about tanks, they were not convinced, any more than they were convinced about cavalry going in on horses.[9] Corporal Hayward identified the other command shortcomings: 'When we went in at Bullecourt, they did not give us enough time to get up there and the Australians were in position to make this attack, we did not get there, so they had to retire.[10]

It would take a year before the Australians would have the confidence to use tanks in an offensive again. Jacka concluded his report on the disastrous performance of the tank by making suggestions on how they might be effectively used:

> In our opinion Tanks armed by the bravest of crews, if placed directly under Infantry Officers concerned in operations would be of great help, but they should never be relied upon as the sole arm of support in an attack by Infantry. Further, when Tanks are got into position we think it absolutely necessary that a heavy barrage be put up by our guns to deaden the sound of Tanks. In our case not a shot was fired when Tanks were taking up their positions, and so the whole show was given away to the enemy.[11]

Major General Monash who was appointed Corps Commander of the Australian Forces in France in 1918 would refer to Captain Jacka's report on the use of tanks and acted upon his recommendation that tank crews be commanded by the commanding officer of the infantry battalion they were attacking with. Monash and his staff studied Jacka's report before the attack at Le Hamel on 4th July 1918 when he used tanks in conjunction with infantry, artillery and aerial support to capture the German position known as the Wolfsberg within an hour and a half. The tactics used by Monash at Le Hamel would be used again during the final four and half months of the war. Until then, the tanks would not be highly regarded or trusted by the Australian troops.

The fact that Australian infantry got through the wire and managed to get into OG 1 and OG 2 trenches and hold their ground until all ammunition had been expended was a remarkable feat. The final word must go to the Australian commanders. Lieutenant Colonel Raymond Leane wrote the following message to the remnants of his battalion and highlighted their accomplishment:

> It was an achievement of the very highest order and is well worthy of the Battalion. Our casualties are heavy, both in Officers and O/Ranks, but we proved again that we are more than a match for the Hun. To have successfully broken into and held the great Hindenburg Line is something indeed to be proud of. We have all of us have lost Comrades and Brothers yet we must not think the sacrifice in vain, but rather let it make us firmer in our resolve to use every effort to beat him to his knees.[12]

Major General William Holmes commanding the 4th Australian Division also recognised the bravery of the men under his command. Holmes wrote the following communication to Brigadier General James Robertson commanding 12th Infantry Brigade:

> Will you please accept yourself and convey to the Officers and other Ranks of the units under your command who took part in yesterday's operations, my sincere thanks for their gallant services, and my congratulations on the success achieved in breaking the formidable Hindenburg Line, notwithstanding the failure of the Tanks from which so much was expected in the direction of preparing the way.[13]

General Birdwood commanding 1st ANZAC Corps wrote the following message to his men on 11th April:

> The Army Commander fully appreciates the splendid effort made this morning by the 4th Australian Division, which so nearly achieved a great and very important success. Even though we have not gained any ground locally, the Army Commander is satisfied that the effect upon the whole situation by the ANZAC attack has been of great assistance. I am sure you all know how fully I appreciate the really good work done by every man who took part

in this morning's operation. We have no cause to be disheartened at having failed to retain our footing in the face of overwhelming odds. Rather can we feel proud of the magnificent bravery displayed.[14]

Fifteen years later Lieutenant Colonel Raymond Leane remembered the Bullecourt battle in *Reveille*. His later assessment is personal and not muted by military considerations:

> Such was the first battle of Bullecourt – a glorious failure; glorious because the Australians were asked to do the apparently impossible and they did it. They penetrated the great Hindenburg line, and held it for hours. It was an ill conceived venture, and the lives of good Australians were sacrificed.[15]

Lieutenant Colonel Howard Denham paid this tribute to the Australian soldiers who took part in the assault on Bullecourt, also in *Reveille*:

> Personally, I cannot speak too highly of the bravery and loyalty shown by all ranks. The casualty lists of 12th and 4th Bdes. were exceedingly heavy, many of my own personal friends being included therein. I always feel that the best commentary on Bullecourt of April 11, 1917, is contained in those well-remembered lines:

> Theirs not to reason why
> Theirs but to do or die.[16]

The significant losses sustained by 4th Australian Division amounting to two thirds of its strength resulted in the division being withdrawn from the front line for four months while it recovered, and assimilated and trained reinforcements. It is not surprising that Australian commanders and their men became embittered by the failure of the British tank and disillusioned about British commanders such as General Gough. Although first Bullecourt, together with Gallipoli and Pozières would seriously undermine Australian confidence in their British commanders, they continued to fight loyally for King and Empire.

NOTES

1. *Jacka's Mob*, Edgar Rule, Angus and Robertson 1933: p164.
2. National Archives; WO 95/ 3494: 14th Battalion War Diary.
3. *Official History of Australia in the War of 1914–1918* Volume 4, Charles Bean, Angus and Robertson 1938: p342.
4. National Archives: WO 95/3510: 46th AIF Battalion War Diary.
5. *The Old Sixteenth*, Captain C. Longmore, the History Committee of the 16th Battalion Association: 1929: p136.
6. National Archives: WO95/3443 HQ: Branches and Services General Staff, 4th Australian Division Nov 1916–June 1917 Appendix 39 written by Major General Holmes.
7. Brigadier T.S. Louch 51st Battalion, IWM Ref: 12281 p271.
8. National Archives: WO 95/3506:12th Brigade War Diary: Lieutenant Colonel Raymond Leane's Post Operation Report.
9. IWM Department of Sound: IWM Ref: 7029: Corporal Ernie Hayward DCM, MM, D Battalion Machine Gun Corps Heavy Branch.
10. Ibid.
11. National Archives: WO 95/3494:14th Battalion AIF War Diary.
12. National Archives: Lieutenant Colonel Raymond Leane: WO 95/3514: 48th Battalion AIF War Diary.
13. National Archives: WO 95/3514: 48th Battalion AIF War Diary.
14. National Archives: WO 95/3506: 12th Brigade War Diary: General Birdwood's message 11th April 1917.
15. *Reveille*: 1st April 1933: Lieutenant Colonel Raymond Leane, 48th Battalion AIF.
16. *Reveille*: 1st April 1933: Lieutenant Colonel Howard Denham's account, 46th Battalion AIF.

CHAPTER 14

THEY FOUGHT AT THE FIRST BULLECOURT: THE AUSTRALIANS

PRIVATE WILLIAM ARTERY 2121,
13TH BATTALION AIF

William Albert Artery was born on June 1872 at Chain of Ponds, Oberon, New South Wales. He was the fifth child born to William and Ann Artery. William Artery was unmarried and worked as a labourer before the war. He was aged 44 when he enlisted to join the AIF in Essington, New South Wales on 26th February 1916. Private William Artery was assigned to the 45th Battalion. He embarked aboard the HMAT *Wiltshire* on 22nd August from Sydney. He arrived in Plymouth on 13th October and was sent for further training via Wool in Dorset to Codford. On 15th February 1917 Private Artery left Folkestone for Boulogne aboard SS *Victoria*. Arriving at the camp at Etaples the following

day, he would spend two weeks preparing him for life in the trenches. On 2nd March 1917 he was allotted to the 13th Battalion. Artery was killed at Bullecourt on 11th April 1917. He has no known grave and his name is commemorated on the Australian National Memorial at Villers-Bretonneux.

PRIVATE DOUGLAS GRANT 6020,
13TH BATTALION AIF

Douglas Grant was an aborigine born on the Bellenden Ker Ranges, Queensland. His POW record records that he was born on 7th January 1889 in Atherton, Queensland. According to his service record he was aged 30 when he enlisted in 1916. His aborigine name was Peppin Jerri. His parents were killed during a tribal fight

Private William Artery pictured with his comrades from the 13th Battalion. He is the soldier standing back row second from right. (Courtesy Wilma Artery)

Private Douglas Grant (left), Private Harry Avery and another in captivity. (Australian War Memorial: AWM P01692.001)

when he was a child. A native soldier was about to kill Peppin who was 12 months old, but he was rescued by Robert Grant who was in Queensland on a collecting expedition for the Australian Museum in Cairns. Grant brought the infant home to his parents in Lithgow, New South Wales, where Peppin was adopted and named Douglas Grant. He received a good education, acquiring an appreciation for the works of William Shakespeare, learned to play the Scottish bagpipes and developed his talent as an artist. In 1897 he won first prize for his drawing of a bust of Queen Victoria. On leaving school Douglas trained as a mechanical draughtsman and worked for Mort's Dock and Engineering Company in Sydney. He left the company in 1913 and worked as a wool classer at Belltrees station, Scone.

Grant enlisted on 13th January 1916 in Scone, New South Wales. After completing basic training Grant boarded HMAT *Wiltshire* on 22nd August at Sydney. He arrived in Plymouth, England on 13th October. During the next four months he was based at Wool, Dorset and on 8th February 1917 he sailed from Folkestone to Boulogne, France. On passing through Etaples he was allocated to the 13th Battalion.

Grant was wounded in the German trenches at Bullecourt on 11th April, where he was captured. He was first sent to Lille then he was interned at a camp in Dulmen, Germany. He remained there for the duration of the war. Grant attracted the attention of German scientists because of his aboriginal race. As a POW, Grant was placed in charge of relief parcels by his fellow prisoners because he was respected by his peers for his honesty and integrity. After the Armistice he went back to England on 30th December 1918. Grant visited the family of his foster parents in Scotland before embarking on a ship that would take him home to Australia. He arrived on 1st June 1919 and was discharged from the Army on 9th July 1919. Grant returned to his job at Mort's Dock as a draughtsman and years later he relocated to Lithgow where he found employment in a small arms factory. His foster parents passed away during the early 1930s and he returned to Sydney where he worked as a clerk at the Callan Park Mental Asylum. As he grew older he became the victim of racial prejudice, which caused him great frustration. With no wife and no family, he would drown his sorrows with alcohol. Douglas Grant died in the Prince Henry Hospital, Little Bay of subarachnoid haemorrhage on 4th December 1951. He was buried in Botany Cemetery.

PRIVATE OSWALD MCCLELLAND 6777,
13TH BATTALION AIF

Oswald Oscar McClelland was born in Nowra, New South Wales, in 1895. He worked as a farm labourer before the war at Beaumont, Nowra, New South Wales.

On 8th June 1916, aged 21, Oswald enlisted to join the AIF. On completing his basic training he boarded the troopship SS *Port Nicholson* at Sydney on 11th November 1916 and set sail for Europe. He arrived at Devonport, England on 10th January 1917. After spending a month in England, McClelland was sent to France where he was assigned to the 13th Battalion AIF. McClelland was captured at Bullecourt and interned at Limburg. After the war ended he went back

Private Oswald McClelland. (Courtesy Aaron Pergram & Mary Newin)

to England arriving in Ripon on 18th December 1918. McClelland arrived in Sydney on 14th May 1919.

PRIVATE GEORGE MOPPETT 6835,
13TH BATTALION AIF

George Sydney Moppett was born in Kemp Town, Brighton, England in 1880, his family migrating to Australia at the end of the century. In 1914 George Moppett was a headmaster of a school in Copmanhurst, New South Wales.

Moppett had been captain of a rifle club and knew how to handle a rifle well. He was keen to play his part in the war and several times he tried to enlist, but was turned away by recruiting officers because he was in his mid-thirties, older than the average soldiers being recruited. Recruiters also took into consideration the fact that he was a widower with three children dependent upon him. As the war progressed the pressure upon the Army to recruit men to replace those lost at Gallipoli was immense and he was permitted to enlist on 10th June 1916 at Lismore, New South Wales. Moppett, aged 36, was given the rank of private. After completing basic training he embarked aboard SS *Port Nicholson* in Sydney on 8th November 1916 and sailed for England. Arriving at Devonport in England on 10th January 1917, Private Moppett spent four weeks at a training camp in Codford. He sailed from Folkestone to France on 15th February and spent a month training at Etaples. Moppett joined the 13th Battalion in the field on 15th March 1917.

On 11th April, Private George Moppett was killed at a dressing station in the sunken road while waiting for medical

Private George Moppett. (Courtesy Alan Beattie)

attention. According to Private Mitchell he was waiting to advance upon the Hindenburg Line at Bullecourt when a shell killed him. His remains were not found and he was therefore listed as missing in action. Private Mitchell testified that he saw Moppett being taken by stretcher to a dressing station, but he was clearly dead.

Another version of events was given by his mate Lance Corporal Clempson, who was adamant that Moppett was wounded during the battle of Bullecourt on 11th April and that he reached the Dressing Station in the sunken road, where he and the doctor were killed by shell fire. Clempson saw the remains of Moppett at about midday.

CAPTAIN HARRY MURRAY, VC, CMG, DSO and BAR, DCM, CROIX DE GUERRE,
13TH BATTALION AIF

Henry William Murray was born in Evandale in northern Tasmania on 1st December 1880. He was the most decorated soldier in the Australian Army. He was a strong, disciplined warrior who was highly respected by the men that he commanded. Known as Harry, he was the eighth of nine children born to Edward and Clarissa. His great grandfather, Kennedy Murray, was of Scottish descent and was transported to Australia as a convict after being convicted in Glasgow in 1786 for burglary. He was sentenced to 14 years in a penal colony and served his sentence on Norfolk Island, New South Wales. The colony provided food for the garrison at Sydney Cove.

Harry Murray was educated at Evandale State School until he was aged 14. His father Edward removed him from school in order to help on the struggling family farm. Clarissa continued his education; however, Harry bore great resentment throughout his life towards his father for interrupting his education.

During his early years living in Tasmania, Murray developed soldiering skills well before the First World War. He was competent in the use of firearms from the age of 10, shooting possums on the farm and from 1902 until 1908, he served in the Launceston Volunteer Artillery Corps. With the family farm still in decline, in 1908 Harry followed his two brothers and migrated to Western Australia where there were better employment prospects for a young man.

Captain Henry Murray VC DSO DCM. *(Australia in the Great War)*

He worked on a wheat farm owned by his brother Charles in return for food and lodging until he found work as a courier for a mining company at Kookynie, near Kalgoorlie. He later relocated to Manjimup where he established a timber cutting business. Using axes to chop wood helped to develop his physique, but it was a dangerous occupation and the life was tough. This experience would strengthen his character, resilience and his resolve. When war erupted on 4th August 1914 Harry Murray wanted to enlist immediately, but he had to conclude his business commitments before he could proceed. He was in a position to enlist on 30th September 1914. He gave his occupation as a bushman, however he lied about his age. He was aged 33 years old and 10 months, and told the enlisting officer he was 30. Maybe he was afraid that he would be deemed too old to serve. He was assigned to the 16th Battalion. Murray had demonstrated his ability to manage men in his business, so the army, recognizing his leadership potential, offered him a commission, but he refused. He was given the service number 315 and began basic training at Blackboy Hill Camp. He was accepted by the battalion's machine gun section where he met Percy Black, who would become a close friend.

Murray experienced war for the first time at Ari Burnu, Anzac Beach, Gallipoli, on 25th April 1915. As they approached the landing beach in a whaleboat amidst Turkish machine gun fire, 10 men were hit amongst Murray's party. The boat grounded on a rock and was unable to move. They were sitting targets and vulnerable to being completely wiped out. Not waiting for the order to disembark, Murray jumped out of the whaleboat and was completely submerged under the blood red waters of Anzac Cove. He struggled to the beach where he found Percy Black had set up a machine-gun position. Murray later recalled:

Up to now, our experience of war had been limited to the naval bombardment. Now we were to witness actual consequences in the shape of men wounded, dying, and dead; and other feelings took possession of us. War meant the wounding, mutilation and killing of men – and they were our own men who lay there before us.[1]

The trauma of being confronted with the horrific sights and ear splitting sounds of battle changed Harry and the men around him instantly:

Life was being blotted out every minute, hot blood spilt and still none of us could even guess how the fight was faring. Glancing at the faces of my comrades, their change of expression made me think. The brief experience had transformed them into killers. Lips were tightly compressed, jaws set, eyes alight with blood lust – these were not the boys with whom I had been playing 'banker' a few short hours ago.[2]

Murray would spend the first week of the Gallipoli campaign defending Pope's Hill against Turkish counter attacks. He manned a machine gun with his cobber, Percy Black. Black was No.1 machine gunner in the crew, firing the weapon, and Murray was his No.2 who passed ammunition boxes.

On the night of 2nd May Murray took part in the attempt to capture a ridge known as 'the Bloody Angle' when the 16th Battalion was severely mauled, reduced to the size of a company. He would later draw comparisons between this action and the calamitous Bullecourt:

> And so the game went on, up to the fateful night of May 2nd, when we were scheduled to take the Bloody Angle and other spots ahead of the eastern fork of Monash Valley. Sheer military impossibilities with such troops and munitions as were at our disposal, but one must learn by bitter experience, not that we need telling, even then. It was a blunder, and, excepting Bullecourt in April 1917, the worst stunt I was ever in. Because of a slight wound, my sergeant would not let me do much. It was a sad and terrible business, and I feel like hurrying over it. The machine gunners advanced with the infantry, and as we topped the ridge, our men fell like grass before the sweep of an expert mower; but most tragic of all, one of our own machine-guns was firing too low, and added to the massacre until we got the message back and stopped it. Disaster on disaster, following fast and following faster. Our leaders still had something to learn about the Turk and the strength of his defence; particularly in country such as this.[3]

Murray was engaged in further action from 9th to 31st May in the Gaba Tepe region. Resisting Turkish attacks he inflicted many casualties upon the enemy despite being wounded. He was awarded the Distinguished Conduct Medal for his bravery during this period. His military career nearly came to an end when he received a gunshot wound to his right knee on 30th May. Evacuated from Gallipoli to Abassia Hospital in Alexandria, Egypt, his wound healed, but his knee stiffened making him unable to bend his leg. He was deemed by doctors medically unfit for military service and was sent to a hospital ship which was to return him home to Australia. On 3rd July 1915, while being driven to the ship that was to take him home, he persuaded the ambulance driver to drive him to a ship which would take him to Gallipoli instead. Despite his stiff knee, Lieutenant Colonel Harold Pope commanding the 16th Battalion accepted him. Although his knee gained some flexibility he would suffer from this wound throughout his life.

Murray was back in action again on the Gallipoli peninsula. During 8th August the 16th Battalion was heavily engaged in close quarter bayonet fighting. Corporal Murray led a charge against a Turkish trench with the bayonet. Murray could not extract his bayonet from a Turkish soldier's body. As Murray struggled to retrieve it, another Turkish soldier charged towards him. At that point he thought that he was about to die until a Gurkha swung his Kukri and decapitated the Turk.

Five days later, on 13th August, Murray was transferred to the 13th Battalion as a replacement Machine Gun officer. He received two promotions on that same day, being promoted to Sergeant and then to Temporary Lieutenant. On 21st August Murray took part in the attack on Hill 60 and inflicted heavy casualties upon the Turkish enemy with his machine gun. Although he was fighting on the front line, Murray was drained and suffering from dysentery. Sickness would overwhelm him and Murray was evacuated to hospital in Egypt to recover. After regaining his strength, Murray returned to Gallipoli on 7th December 1915. After spending two weeks on the peninsula he was one of the last of the Anzacs to withdraw on 20th December 1915.

The 13th Battalion returned to the Egyptian desert where they began training for their eventual deployment to the trenches in France. Murray received confirmation of his permanent promotion to Lieutenant on 20th January 1916. A shortage of officers in the 13th Battalion due to their assignment to create the new 45th Battalion provided Murray an opportunity for further promotion within the 13th Battalion and he was made a Captain on 1st March 1916.

Murray and the 13th Battalion embarked aboard HMAT *Transylvania* at Alexandria on 1st June 1916. They arrived in Marseille several days later. On arriving, Murray had to quell an act of disobedience when a group of soldiers from the 4th Brigade made an attempt to leave the docks and enter Marseille for some unofficial leave. Drawing his pistol, he persuaded them to return to quayside and wait as ordered.

Later that month, when the 13th Battalion entered the line in a quiet sector of the Western Front at Bois Grenier, near Armentières, Captain Murray often ventured into No Man's Land reconnoitring. He captured his first German prisoner while in this sector.

Murray took part in an assault on Mouquet Farm on 29th August 1916. He led his company on the left flank as the 13th Battalion assaulted German positions. German artillery fired upon the lines held by the 13th Battalion from morning until night. It was recorded that 'by his personal example, [Murray] inspired confidence and resolution into his men throughout the day'. Despite sustaining heavy casualties they captured their objective and although severely weakened by the assault, they held onto their positions against determined German counter attacks. The Somme mud played havoc with their rifles and clogged up the mechanisms rendering them useless. Murray organised a defence using the supply of bombs they had with them. This resistance would hold out for an hour.

Murray and his men would resist three further German counter attacks. Murray engaged in a close-quarter battle with two German soldiers in the trenches, shooting them both dead. Unable to hold onto the trenches, Murray, who had sustained two wounds during the savage fight, assessed the situation and on realising the futility of holding on to the position he decided to evacuate the remnants of his party. Murray remained on duty when he returned to Australian lines until the following morning when he fainted from loss of blood. The exhausted Murray was forced to hand over command to another officer. Murray's Distinguished Service Order citation records:

> For conspicuous gallantry in action. Although twice wounded, he commanded his company with the greatest courage and initiative, beating off four enemy counter-attacks. Later, when an enemy bullet started a man's equipment exploding, he tore the man's equipment off at great personal risk. He set a splendid example throughout.[4]

Murray recovered from his wounds and returned to the 13th Battalion. During the night of 4th/5th February 1917 Murray was ordered to lead an assault upon Stormy Trench, which was north east of the village of Geudecourt, on the Somme. It was regarded as one of the bitterest engagements fought by the 13th Battalion. Murray had led patrols to assess the German wire days prior to the attack and was well prepared to take this important position, which provided its German occupiers with good observation of the Somme. The day before the attack on Stormy Trench, Murray had been suffering from influenza with a temperature of 103 degrees, but refused to come off the line when Major R.C. Winn, the regimental medical officer, made arrangements to evacuate him to a hospital. 'You can cut that out. I'm not going away.' Winn was fearful that his influenza may develop into pneumonia and responded, 'Not going. You'll get pneumonia if you don't. In fact I'm not too certain you haven't got it already.' Murray defied this sound medical advice and defiantly declared: 'Pneumonia or not, I'm not going to hospital. I'm going to take Stormy Trench tomorrow ... and what's more let me tell you. I'm going to keep it.'[5]

After a preparatory barrage which softened the German positions Murray and four companies attacked Stormy Trench at 10 pm. They got into the German trenches. German infantry ascended from their deep

dug-outs to resist the 13th Battalion's onslaught with egg grenades. Murray held off the German counter attacks until they gave up further attempts to regain Stormy Trench. For his courage at Stormy Trench, Murray was awarded the Victoria Cross:

> For most conspicuous bravery when in command of the right flank company in attack. He led his company to the assault with great skill and courage, and the position was quickly captured. Fighting of a very severe nature followed, and three heavy counter-attacks were beaten back, these successes being due to Capt. Murray's wonderful work. Throughout the night his company suffered heavy casualties through concentrated enemy shell fire, and on one occasion gave ground for a short way. This gallant officer rallied his command and saved the situation by sheer valour. He made his presence felt throughout the line, encouraging his men, heading bombing parties, leading bayonet charges and carrying wounded to places of safety. His magnificent example inspired his men throughout.[6]

Within weeks of earning the Victoria Cross, Murray, who was also a recipient of the DSO and DCM would continue to display great courage and leadership at Bullecourt on 11th April. He was a motivational force who played a pivotal role in getting his men into the Hindenburg Line trenches and defending them during that morning. He led the remnants of the 13th Battalion to break out from their predicament. His conduct at Bullecourt would earn him a bar to his DSO. His recommendation stated:

> He led his company with great courage and skill through 1200 yards of shell and machine gun fire and he and his company still kept on although they lost 75% of their strength before reaching the second objective. Captain Murray being the senior officer of the 4th Brigade in the 1st and 2nd objectives, went along the whole frontage, 900 yards, organising and directing the defence, always encouraging the men of all units by his cheerfulness and bravery, and always moving to the points of danger. When the bomb supply was running out and the men gave ground, he rallied them time after time and fought back the Germans over and over again. When there was no alternative but to surrender or withdraw through the heavy machine gun fire, Captain Murray was the last to leave the position. He is not only brave and daring, but a skilful soldier possessing tactical instinct of the highest order.[7]

Murray was promoted to Major on 11th April and was now in command of 13th Battalion. On 2nd June 1917 he received his Victoria Cross and a Distinguished Service

Order with bar from King George V in a ceremony held in Hyde Park in London.

Murray was appointed commander of 4th Machine Gun Battalion during March 1918 and led them for the duration of the war. Murray returned to his native Tasmania during March 1920. During World War Two Murray served as commander of the 26th Battalion (the Logan and Albert Regiment) based in north Queensland. During the early phase of the war, the threat of a Japanese invasion of Australia was real and this battalion would play a defensive role and patrol the outback until the threat receded in 1942. During that year he was appointed commander of the local Volunteer Defence Corps with the rank of Lieutenant Colonel until he retired in February 1944. Murray was involved in a car accident on 6th January 1966 and he died of heart failure the following day at Miles District Hospital in Brisbane.

LANCE CORPORAL ERNEST CHRISTIAN TRY 6364,
13TH BATTALION AIF

Ernest Christian Try was born in Adaminaby, New South Wales in 1887. He was the son of Mary and John Try. Ernest worked as a baker in Campsie and married Annie Falconer before the war. He was father to Adrian, Isla and Madge. Ernest enlisted to join the AIF in Campsie on 29th April 1916. After completing basic training Private Ernest Try embarked on HMAT *Euripides* from Port Sydney on 9th September 1916.

Try arrived in Plymouth, England on 26th October. He was assigned to the 4th Training Battalion, was sent to Codham then from 17th November was based at a training camp in Wool, Dorset. Within six weeks he was heading for the Western Front. He left England aboard the *Princess Clementine* from Folkestone, bound for Boulogne. He was then marched to the camp at Etaples for further training, arriving there on 22nd December 1916. On 2nd January 1917 Try joined the 13th Battalion. He was promoted to Lance Corporal on 19th February 1917. Try was killed at Bullecourt on 11th April. He has no known grave and his name is commemorated on the Villers-Bretonneux Memorial. His wife Annie was left to raise their three children. His son Adrian would be killed on 8th May 1943 while serving as a Signalman in the Australian Corps of Signals during World War Two.

Lance Corporal Ernest Try.
(Courtesy Max Try)

DRIVER JAMES SWASBRICK 135,
13TH BATTALION AIF

James Drummond Swasbrick was born in Albury, New South Wales in 1890. Known as Jim to his family, he was the son of William and Jean Swasbrick, pioneer settlers from Broad Ribb. They raised a family of fifteen children and worked a farm. Jim left the family farm at Broad Ribb and drifted within the area finding employment as a labourer and worked on other farms as a horse breaker. He then ventured to Queensland where he became a dam building contractor. According to his service record, before the war Jim Swasbrick worked as a bush contractor, living in Proston, near Wondai in Queensland. Swasbrick enlisted on 24th August 1914 and joined the 1 Light Horse Brigade Train (5 Company ASC [Army Service Corps]).

He left Brisbane aboard HMAT *Omrah* on 24th September 1914 bound for Egypt. On 15th April 1916 he was transferred to the Anzac Patrol Corps. Within six weeks he was bound for England departing Alexandria on 22nd May aboard the HMAT *Corscian*. He arrived in England on 8th October and was assigned to the 1st Training Battalion. On the following day he was sent to France and began preparations for life on the Western Front at Etaples. After 10 days training at Etaples, Swasbrick was assigned to the 13th Battalion.

During the first Bullecourt battle James Swasbrick and his brother Private David Swasbrick belonged to No.5 Platoon, B Company, 13th Battalion. He advanced with his brother towards the Hindenburg Line on 11th April. Driver James Swasbrick was killed at the German wire while his brother was alongside him. Private Horace Stevenson observed the moment when he was hit by German machine-gun fire:

> He was just behind me when I saw him fall, hit by a machine gun bullet in head. I turned round and asked if he was hit, but got no answer. I am morally certain he was killed outright.[8]

Left to right, **James, David and Peter Swasbrick.**
(Courtesy Pat Swasbrick)

His remains were not recovered and his name is commemorated on the Australian Memorial at Villers-Bretonneux. Private James Williams remembered that 'Swasbrick was very popular amongst his mates.'[9]

PRIVATE DAVID SWASBRICK 2216,
13TH BATTALION AIF

David Henry Swasbrick was the brother of Driver James Swasbrick. David was born in 1884 in Bogong, Victoria. Before the war he worked as a farmer at Eskdale, Victoria. David enlisted to join the AIF on 14th September 1915 and belonged to the 4th Light Horse Regiment. After basic training he embarked aboard HMAT *Katuna* from Melbourne on 9th March 1916. He was assigned to the 13th Battalion in January 1917 and would join his younger brother Jim who had also been transferred to the same battalion. Known as Dave to his mates in the battalion he advanced across No Man's Land during the Battle of Bullecourt on 11th April. He was near to his brother Jim when he was killed by German fire by the wire. Dave received a gun shot wound to his right arm. He left his dead brother on the battlefield and was evacuated to England to convalesce. He returned to his battalion in June 1917. After the war he married Florence Porter, an English girl, in St Andrew's Church, Lambeth, London on 6th September 1919. He brought his English wife home to Australia to settle in 1920. He established a dairy farm on land adjacent to his father's property at Broad Ribb. David and Florence would raise two sons and five daughters. David Swasbrick passed away aged 70 in 1955 and was buried at Mitta Mitta.

PRIVATE WILLIAM BIRTHISEL 6472,
14TH BATTALION AIF

William John Birthisel was born at Burkes Flat, Victoria, in 1888. His parents were Matthew and Emily. William, known as 'Bill', was the eldest of ten children, five boys and five girls. His embarkation record states that he was a farmer from Gre Gre village, Victoria, before he enlisted to join the Australian Infantry Force on 16th May 1916.

He arrived in France in January 1917 and after completing further training at Etaples, he joined the

Private William 'Bill' Birthisel. (Courtesy Shane Birthisel)

14th Battalion AIF. Birthisel was to die at the Battle of Bullecourt on 11th April. He got through the first belts of German wire and entered the first line of trenches. Private Walter Ware was advancing with Birthisel and later wrote:

> Casualty was in the advance at Bullecourt. He got into the first German line and was advancing to the 2nd. He was caught through the barbed wire and was hit by a machine gun bullet and he dropped back onto the wire leaving himself in a very exposed location. I am not certain if casualty is dead, but if the first bullet never killed him – which I am nearly certain did – he would have sure to have been riddled with bullets afterwards.[10]

Private William Birthesel has no known grave and his name is commemorated on the Australian Memorial at Villers-Bretonneux.

SERGEANT DOUGLAS BLACKBURN 416,
14TH BATTALION AIF

Douglas Wilkie Blackburn was born in Nhill, Victoria, in 1895. Douglas was a 19-year-old electrician from Camperdown, Victoria, when he enlisted to join the AIF on 14th September 1914. After completing his basic training he boarded the troopship HMAT *Ulysses* at Melbourne on 22nd December 1914 and began the long passage to Egypt. Private Douglas Blackburn was assigned to the 14th Battalion. Being one of the originals who joined the AIF in September 1914, Blackburn landed at Gallipoli and fought on the peninsula during 1915. By April 1916 Blackburn had reached the rank of Sergeant. When the 14th Battalion was sent to the Western Front in France he was wounded at Pozières on 9th August 1916.

Sergeant W.D. Blackburn. (Reveille, 1st April 1933)

He was in charge of the Lewis Gun section in the 14th Battalion at Bullecourt on 11th April. He recounted his experience at Bullecourt for *Reveille* 15 years after the battle:

> We hopped off at 4.45 all the Lewis guns were going in the second wave ... My section was a bit scattered, but we managed to keep some sort of line until we ran into the German wire. We had a few casualties up to the time we got to within striking distance – 80 yards from the German front line. Then we advanced

under heavy machine-gun and rifle fire. Just in front of the German front line the enemy had constructed tank-pits – big holes dug in the ground – about 9 ft deep and measuring 10 yards by 6 yards across. We were lucky enough to miss them.[11]

Within half an hour of the beginning of the assault and by the time that Sergeant Blackburn reached the first German trenches he had lost half of his Lewis Gun section including all his NCOs. Lance Corporal Norman Buckman was killed on arriving at the first objective. Corporal Ken Miller received wounds to his neck, chest and leg. Bill Nicholls was incapacitated when he was wounded in the thigh and later captured. Pressure mounted upon Blackburn to control the remnants of the battalion's Lewis gun section:

> I took one of my teams round to the left. Going along a sap which led in the direction of Riencourt, we turned into a trench held, on the right, by 'D' Coy. To the left was a dug-out, which, we discovered, had an exit on the other side of the chamber, leading to a second trench. I showed this to Capt. Wadsworth and Coy.-Sgt.-Major Lou Garcia, and, supported by my gun-crew, we went along this trench until we ran into a mob of Germans. We retired a few yards and sent back for bombs. After bombing for about 15 minutes and gaining about 20 yards, we decided to barricade the trench and hold the position with the Lewis Gun.[12]

Captain Wadsworth was mortally wounded and Charlie Parker, one of Blackburn's Lewis gunners, was also killed. Blackburn left Private Branigan Mitchell in charge of a Lewis gun while he took Private George Brooks to another Lewis gun in order to cover their right flank. Here they found that ammunition was in short supply. Company Sergeant Major Lou Garcia was asking those who were holding on to their fragile position 'How much ammunition have you got?'[13]

Blackburn used his initiative to find ammunition in the trenches and get it to the machine gunners. He also helped Lance Corporal Bamford in repositioning his Lewis gun where he could keep the enemy's head down:

> The trenches on the right were being shelled, and one Lewis Gun under L/Cpl. Bamford, was in a bad way. He and another man, firing for their lives, were just about out of ammunition. I managed to get some more for them, and then, after three attempts, we set the gun in a fresh position, close in front of the trench, whence we were able to force the enemy opposing 'A' Coy. to keep his head down while our chaps repaired the trench and had a blow.[14]

Within a short time, Blackburn and Bamford ran out of ammunition and their Lewis gun position became untenable. They were both compelled to withdraw to the section of OG 1 that the remnants of the Australian battalions were holding. 'Before long we again ran out of ammunition, and therefore, being unable to rake up more than would fill a single magazine – 45 rounds – withdrew to the trench.'[15]

It was Blackburn and his small party of Lewis gunners who held onto their positions in OG 1 who provided covering fire for Captain Harry Murray and those men who elected to risk life to withdraw to the Australian lines. Blackburn took 30 Lewis gunners into the Bullecourt fight. Blackburn and four other men came out of the battle unscathed and four were wounded. He lost 22 men:

> It is remarkable what peculiar things men will do in tight corners. Merl Cattledge got his waterproof cape caught in the barbed wire coming out, and he stayed there fully two minutes under heavy fire to disengage it, instead of slipping his arms out of it and going on. I, too, couldn't have been in my right senses. In the hurry to get clear, I shook my tin hat off. Ten or 15 yards further on, I suddenly thought to myself that I might want it, so I went back for it.[16]

Blackburn continued to serve with the 14th Battalion after surviving Bullecourt. When the battalion was holding the line on the Warneton sector he was gassed on 31st January 1918 and was sent to the Eastbourne Military Hospital in England to recover. Blackburn distinguished himself in the 14th Battalion's last engagement of the war when he was awarded the Military Medal for his bravery in the assault on the Hindenburg Line at Ascension Wood on 18th September 1918. His recommendation signed by Major General E.G. Sinclair Maclagan (Commanding 4th Australian Division) states:

> For conspicuous gallantry and devotion to duty near Ascension Wood on 18th September 1918. Shortly after crossing the Red Line, owing to heavy enemy machine gun fire, the advance was delayed. By immediately taking forward a Lewis gun and engaging the enemy guns he enabled his Company to work forward with minimum loss. On two other occasions he afforded covering fire to the Coy which materially assisted them in their advance. By his initiative, skilful handling of his gun and cool daring he not only set a fine example to his section, but was responsible to a large extent for the success of his Coy.[17]

LANCE SERGEANT HARRY CATTERSON 3294,
14TH BATTALION AIF

Robert Henry Catterson was born at Sailors Hill, Daylesford, Victoria, on 26th January 1878. Known as Harry to his family, he was the eleventh child of Cuthbert and Mary Jane Catterson. Harry lists on his Army Service Record under previous military service that he belonged to the school cadets. On leaving school Harry trained as a barber and in 1895 he moved to Maffra where he opened a hairdressing and tobacconist saloon. Sixteen years later, he moved to Hamilton where he opened another saloon. Harry gained experience with firing rifles when he became a member of the Maffra Rifle Club for 14 years and continued by joining the Hamilton Rifle Club. Harry was such a proficient rifleman he was selected to tour the Western district with the club, displaying his marksmanship.

The Gallipoli campaign had been in progress for three months when Harry responded to a national call for more volunteers to enlist in the Australian Army. He enlisted on 6th July 1915. His service record stated that Harry was 27 years and 5 months, in fact he was 37. Within two weeks of enlisting, Harry married Mary Gibbons on 21st July 1915 at St Joseph's Church, West Brunswick. His shooting skills gained with the rifle clubs at home in Hamilton were obvious when he arrived at the training camp in Australia; he gained the distinction of best shot in the Company and was chosen as a sniper. When he later arrived in France he trained men as an instructor at sniper's school. On completing basic training, Private Harry Catterson embarked from Melbourne on the HMAT *Nestor* on 11th October 1915 bound for Egypt. He was part of the 11th Reinforcements of the 14th Australian Infantry Battalion. Harry wrote to his mother in early 1916 from the Australian Army Training Camp in Egypt of his ambitions for promotion:

> We are in the Battalion now, the 11th, have been in a little over a week but I have been in about 6 weeks, I came down before the others; we are ready to go to the front any time now but I don't suppose we will for another month or so. One has to wait for promotion, 'tis very hard to get promotion over here unless one has extra special ability or very lucky. I know I am not lucky and I suppose the Heads do not

Lance Sergeant Harry Catterson. (Courtesy Noeleen Ridgeway)

think I have the extra special ability, but it will come in time ... 'Tis no use talking War as we get very little news, you get much more than we do.[18]

He left Alexandria in Egypt on 1st June 1916 bound for France and the Western Front aboard RMS *Transylvania*. During this passage he wrote a postcard to his mother dated 4th June:

> We are on another sea voyage but only a short one as we expect to land in a few days but we cannot say where our destination is but it is where I thought in my last, where all the fighting is. This is a grand boat we are travelling by, not a movement in here. I am keeping very well and am in good condition so I should not notice the cold where we reach the firing line. Hope you are keeping well.[19]

He arrived in Marseille on 8th June 1916. Within a month of arriving in France he was promoted to Corporal. While fighting in the battle for Pozières on 14th August 1916, Harry received a gun shot wound to his right leg and was evacuated to a military hospital in Rouen to recover. He soon recovered from his wound and returned to serve with the 14th Battalion on 17th September 1916. Harry received a further promotion to Lance Sergeant during November 1916. He wrote a letter home to his mother on 10th February:

> Just received a couple of letters from you dated the 10th Dec. also the 22nd Dec. very pleased to receive them, I also got a parcel sent on the 11th of Nov. with a tin of Biscuits, pair of socks, mittens, 3 Handkerchiefs and a tube of vaseline, many thanks for the things they came in very handy. I have not received any of the other parcels which you mention having sent. I got two just before Xmas with a Knife in each, but there must be a couple on the road yet.
>
> We have been in the trenches for the last eighteen days but are back a little (still within the firing line though) doing fatigues just now, that will give us a chance of a little spell and a clean up.
>
> It was very cold in the trenches this last time, we have had snow for the last fortnight or more with a heavy frost every morning, I saw ice this morning over two feet thick, not bad eh. I saw dust on the roads this morning and all over the country was snow, not often one sees that but the frost had dried up the roads well and made them as hard as glass and just as slippery.
>
> I am going to a school in a day or two (an instruction one) it will last for a month and should be a very fair change. I will be away from the noise of the guns for a month and that is something.[20]

Catterson would fight his last battle at Bullecourt on 11th April. Private James Wilfred Lucas, 14th Battalion, witnessed Catterson being wounded in the German front-line trench. Private Albert Cecil Squires saw Catterson returning to the dressing Station on the 11th. 'While advancing at Bullecourt, I met him returning to our line with two fingers off. He had been in the wave before us. He was very cheerful when I saw him. He had to cross a zone swept by heavy M.G. fire to reach the Dressing station.'[21]

At some point, Harry Catterson was killed at Bullecourt. He has no known grave and his name is commemorated on the Villers-Bretonneux Memorial. His name was also commemorated on the war memorial in the place of his birth in Daylesford, in Burke Square. It reads:

> For King and Country – A grateful tribute to the men of the Daylesford district who gave their lives in the Great War 1914–1919: Remembrance is little to offer for sacrifice but is all we have to give.

Harry's name is also commemorated on the memorials of Maffra and Hamilton. The following obituary appeared in the *Hamilton Spectator* during late 1917:

> He was loved and respected by a large circle of friends both in Maffra and Hamilton, where his true worth was best known, and sincere and widespread sympathy will be felt for his relatives. The late Sergeant Catterson made the supreme sacrifice in noble fashion. Though badly wounded, he rushed to the assistance of his comrades when he saw them being surrounded by Germans, and this high impulse cost him his life. But he died as no doubt he would have wished best, helping his pals in a tight corner and in upholding the honour of his native land.[22]

COMPANY QUARTERMASTER SERGEANT ALFRED LESLIE GUPPY MM 201,
14TH BATTALION AIF

Alfred Leslie Guppy was born in Benalla, Victoria in 1888. Known by his family as Les, he worked as a farmer at Moor Park, Benalla before enlisting to join the AIF on 16th September 1914. After basic training he departed from Melbourne aboard HMAT *Ulysses* on 22nd December 1914 bound for Egypt. He was assigned to the 14th Battalion AIF and during February 1915 Guppy was promoted to Lance Corporal.

On 25th April 1915 Guppy landed with the 14th Battalion AIF at Gallipoli. Guppy would take part in the attacks on the Turkish lines on 2nd and 19th May. On 27th May 1915 he was promoted to Corporal. He would

continue to play a role during the campaign, taking part in assaults on Turkish lines on 6th, 8th, 21st and 27th August 1915. During the month of August Guppy received another promotion to the rank of Sergeant. While serving in Gallipoli, Guppy was seconded to the British 163rd Brigade, 54th Division on special sniping and scouting duties. Guppy remained in Gallipoli until the 14th Battalion was evacuated from the peninsula on 18th/19th December 1915. As he waited to embark on evacuation boats from Gallipoli, his thoughts for his friends that had died there overwhelmed him, more than the failure of the campaign:

> Sleep sound, old friends – the keenest part
> Which, more than failure, wounds the heart,
> Is thus to leave you – thus to part.[23]

After spending six months in Egypt preparing for the Western front, Guppy departed Alexandria, Egypt on 1st June arriving in Marseille on 8th June 1916. In August Guppy took part in his first actions on the Western Front when the 14th Battalion engaged in the Battles of Pozières and Mouquet Farm. It was for his role in ensuring that rations and munitions were brought to the front-line units of the 14th Battalion that he was awarded the Military Medal. Lieutenant Colonel John Peck wrote the following recommendation:

> During the whole of Q.M.S. Guppy's service, all his actions have shown an unflinching and gallant devotion to duty. At Pozières whilst acting Q.M.S. he was instrumental in bringing rations to the front line, which at that time, owing to heavy enemy artillery fire, was a most difficult and dangerous duty. He is a man upon whom I would place the greatest reliance. Whilst under my direct personal command, his conduct and influence, particularly in action, has been a splendid example of keen, courageous and intelligent devotion to duty on all occasions.[24]

Quartermaster Alfred Guppy MM. (Courtesy Russell Williams)

On 18th September 1916 he was promoted to Company Quartermaster Sergeant. He received the Medaille Militaire for his role during the campaign in France on 13th February 1917. Guppy spent three weeks in hospital from 1st to 19th March 1917. During that period he received the Military Medal.

Quartermaster Sergeant Alfred Guppy would fight his last battle of the war during the assault on Bullecourt on 11th April. He succeeded in entering the German trenches, but was surrounded and was captured later that day. Private Francis Dolan, a comrade from the 14th Battalion confirmed that Guppy had entered the first trench and that he may have been captured:

> He was last seen in the German line. He was all right then but the lads who were nearest to him that returned reported that he had got taken prisoner, but in his case it is difficult to say so positively, as there was a general mix up, but all the lads agree that he was left there, and as we had to retire, they all think he must be a prisoner.[25]

After his capture at Bullecourt, Guppy was interned at the POW Camp at Gefangenenlager in Dulmen, near Essen in Germany. He wrote the following message on a postcard to Miss M Barnett, who was living in Horseferry Road, Westminster, London on 20th May 1917:

> Perhaps you will have heard before this of my captivity, perhaps not. I think that they should know at our Headquarters, whom I have advised, as through them is the only way we can receive parcels of money. I of course lost everything I possessed. It is hard luck to be taken prisoner after such a long run and when my prospects were good, but must make the best of it and hope for the end of the war. Not badly off, but miss many things.[26]

Guppy was then transferred to camps in Minden, Westphali and to Soltau Z3036 near Hannover. Guppy managed to send a message from Soltau dated 15th October 1917, which was received in London on 24th November in which he wrote: 'I am keeping in excellent health now as all our boys here are – am receiving my food parcels regularly and in good order.'[27]

Quartermaster Alfred Guppy MM photographed with fellow prisoners of war. Guppy is standing back row, third from right. (Courtesy Russell Williams)

He returned to England on 26th December 1918. In January 1919 he was admitted to the 3rd Auxiliary Hospital suffering from gastritis and bronchitis. After suffering the horrors of Gallipoli, Pozières, Bullecourt and enduring 18 months as a POW Les Guppy left England on 31st March 1919 to return home to Australia. He arrived in Melbourne on 12th May 1919. He returned to farming at Moor Park and in 1920 married Helen Cumming, who was a teacher at Benella High School. They raised three daughters, Leticia, Isabel and Lesley. His wife Helen passed away in 1942. He did not remarry, but ensured that his daughters were all educated to tertiary standard. While working as a farmer he suffered from the effects of mustard gas and the malnutrition he endured while a prisoner. Despite his own health problems he was very generous and publicly spirited and was always ready to help those in need. His daughter Isabel paid this tribute to her father:

> He was an excellent farmer, concentrating on wool and cereal crops. However the after-effects of war and imprisonment began to take their toll. Mustard gas ruined his lungs and ulcers made him very ill at times. He involved himself in the community and council affairs and was known for his ready smile, helping other returned soldiers when needed.

Les Guppy passed away in 1968 aged 78.

Alfred Guppy photographed in later life. (Courtesy Russell Williams)

CAPTAIN ALBERT JACKA VC, MC and BAR
14TH BATTALION AIF

Albert Jacka was born on 10th January 1893 at Layland, Victoria. After leaving school he worked as a labourer for the Victorian States Forestry Department. Jacka enlisted soon after the war began on 18th September 1914. Jacka was given the service number 465 and assigned to the 14th Battalion. After completing basic training, Jacka embarked aboard HMAT *Ulysses* at Melbourne on 22nd December 1914 and sailed for Egypt.

Captain Albert Jacka VC. (*The War Illustrated, Volume 6*)

He landed at Anzac Beach during the afternoon on 25th April 1915. Jacka had attained the rank of Acting Lance Corporal and it was while serving on the Gallipoli peninsula that Jacka established a reputation as an effective soldier. It was at Courtney's Post during the night of 19th/20th May 1915 that the Jacka legend was born, in the action that would earn him the Victoria Cross. Jacka, aged 22, was the first Australian recipient. Seven Turkish soldiers had launched a counter attack against trenches held by the Australians. They had made a breakthrough into the trenches and several counter attacks launched by the Australians failed to dislodge

them. After a diversion was made at one end of the trench held by the Turks, when bombs were thrown into their sector, Jacka leapt into the other end and launched a counter attack all on his own. He killed all the occupants and recaptured the position. His Victoria Cross citation:

> Lance Corporal Jacka, while holding a portion of our trench with four other men, was heavily attacked. When all except himself were killed or wounded, the trench was rushed and occupied by seven Turks. Lance Corporal Jacka at once gallantly attacked them single-handed and killed the whole party, five by rifle fire and two with the bayonet.[28]

Jacka would climb the ranks as he demonstrated his ability to lead men. On 28th August 1915 he was promoted to Corporal and during November 1915 to Sergeant Major. He remained on the Gallipoli Peninsula until the 14th Battalion was evacuated on 18th December. While in Egypt during the early months of 1916, Jacka attended officer training school, where he excelled passing examinations with high marks. Subsequently he broke through the ranks to be promoted to 2nd Lieutenant.

Jacka, a man of great dash and courage established a reputation for bravery and was widely respected by the men of the 14th Battalion. He was also very outspoken and was a man of conviction, who would say what he felt. He was never reckless and his moves were calculated. It was such a premeditated move during August 1916 at Pozières that turned defeat into victory for the Australians. Jacka had led his platoon into OG 1 Trench at dawn on 6th August while German guns were pounding Pozières Ridge. They settled in a dug-out in OG 1 close to where the Windmill Memorial now stands today. Some men were sleeping when a loud explosion

Jacka's Victoria Cross Exploit at Courtney's Post 19th/20th May 1915. (*Deeds that Thrill the Empire*)

Captain Albert Jacka and fellow Victoria Cross recipient Private Martin O' Meara from the 16th Battalion. This photo was taken while they recovered from wounds received at Pozières in August 1916. (*The Great War, I Was There*)

inside the dug-out awakened them the next day. German infantry swarming over the ridge had thrown a bomb into the dug-out. Two men were killed while the others were concussed or badly maimed. Jacka suffered concussion but soon regained consciousness, firing two shots with his revolver up the stairway to the dug-out entrance. Without hesitation Jacka rushed up the stairway followed by eight men. They had to pass over two badly wounded colleagues as they entered OG 1 Trench from the dug-out. Jacka also had to shoot dead the German sentry that was posted outside the dug-out. They found the trench to be deserted, the Germans having rushed over the trench and advanced towards Australian lines to the rear. Jacka and his party were behind the German lines. Soon after entering OG 1, Private Billy Williams, who followed Jacka, observed a group of Australian prisoners from the 48th Battalion being escorted by German soldiers – approximately 60 men – approaching their position. Jacka prudently decided not to attack immediately; but it was not Jacka's nature to surrender or do nothing, so he waited until the party of prisoners got to within 30 yards of OG 1 then charged at the German escorts from the rear. Startled, some of the German guards threw down their arms and surrendered immediately. They were unaware that such a small force was attacking them. Many German guards decided to fire back and each man in Jacka's party including Jacka received bullet wounds. Privates Finlay and Williams were shot as soon as they left their trench, which left Jacka with five men. The remaining five were all hit, but continued the fight with vehemence. Sergeant Edgar Rule recorded Jacka's own account of the action in his memoirs. Rule obtained the account from a friend of Jacka given in confidence:

> There were four Huns in a shell-hole. All I could see were their heads, shoulders, and rifles. As I went towards them, they began firing point-blank at me. They hit me three times and each time the terrific impact of bullets fired at such close range swung me off my feet. But each time I sprang up like a prize fighter, and kept getting closer. When I got up to them, they flung down their rifles and put up their hands. I shot three through the head and put a bayonet through the fourth. I had to do it – they would have killed me the moment I turned my back.[29]

Jacka's audacious counter-attack against a vastly superior force inspired others to join him and forced the Germans to retreat. Lance Sergeant Cyril Beck from the 48th Battalion witnessed Jacka's attack and led a small party from his position into the battle to support Jacka. The prisoners under escort from the 48th broke from their guards, took their weapons and fought

alongside Jacka. Other Australian units joined the fight. Men from the 15th in the north and the 14th in the west converged upon the German positions. They became intermingled and the fight became a mass skirmish where Germans and Australians fought each other face-to-face with the bayonet. The use of rifles and machine guns ran the risk of hitting colleagues. The fight was dispersed along the ridge. Sergeant Edgar Rule from the 14th Battalion:

> Through my glasses I could see some of our boys standing up and firing point-blank at other men. Some figures I could see on their knees in front of others praying for their lives, and several were bayoneting Huns. It was one of the queerest sights I've ever seen – Huns and Aussies were scattered in ones and twos all along the side of the ridge. It was such a mix up that it was hard to tell who were Huns and who were Aussies. Each Aussie seemed to be having a war all on his own.[30]

Private Leslie Pezet from the 15th Battalion also witnessed the German counter attack and Jacka's bravery:

> After midnight, seventh of August, the Germans send over a terrible barrage and curtain fire, another attack on our right 48 Battalion. We all stand to rush into front line. The Germans run in a charge at the lads on our right ... to our horror we see our lads captured. Jacka and his bombers rush out wild and call us for help. Here is a mix up, bombs, bullets, bayonets and shrapnel all mixed Germans frightened to death, killed coldly in fair fight. Jacka wounded, McGee our officer gets off free, ours recaptured by us, and 100 Germans, many on both sides killed, our wounded stream in, it is getting too hot, The Germans want the windmill back.[31]

The tide had turned and the Germans were surrendering to the Australians. At the end of this savage fight Jacka's platoon had just four unwounded men. There were three survivors from the party of seven who fought with Jacka during his spectacular charge, Privates Miller, Williams and Fitzpatrick.

At one point Sergeant Rule had received an incorrect report of Jacka's death. Jacka was a casualty, sustaining several bullet wounds. One bullet went beneath his right shoulder and a shell fragment wounded his head. Jacka lay out on Pozières Ridge for some time before being found by a stretcher bearer, who did not have a stretcher. Jacka had no choice but to crawl to company headquarters.

Bean wrote: 'Jacka's counter attack, which led directly to this result, stands as the most dramatic and effective act of individual audacity in the history of the AIF.[32] It was the opinion of Rule and other men from the 14th Battalion that Jacka should have received a bar to his Victoria Cross for his leadership and courage at Pozières, but a Military Cross was the recognition given to him. It is interesting to note that the 14th Battalion War Diary does not mention Jacka in the report of the action. It maybe because of his abrasive manner and his uneasy relationship with his superiors, Major Fuhrmann and the CO Lieutenant Colonel Dare, that his name was omitted. Lieutenant Colonel Leane recorded in the 48th Battalion war diary that 'a party of the 14th who were on my left under Lt. Jacka attacked on the right. Between them Jacka and Sgt. Beck (of the 48th) the Germans were captured and the prisoners to the number of 54 including two officers passed through my HQs for despatch to the rear.'[33] Although officially Jacka did not receive the accolade of another VC, his peers knew the significance of Jacka's work and its impact upon the outcome of the battle that day.

Jacka's citation stated for the Military Cross stated: 'He led his platoon against a large number of the enemy, who had counter attacked the battalion on his right. The enemy were driven back, some prisoners they had taken were recovered and 50 of the enemy captured. He was himself wounded in the attack.'[34]

After Pozières, Jacka was evacuated to England where he recovered from his wounds for several months at the 3rd London General Hospital at Wandsworth, London. Due to the heavy officer casualties within the 14th Battalion, Jacka was promoted to Lieutenant while he was recuperating. During December 1916 Jacka was deemed fit for active duty and returned to his battalion in France. Soon after his return, a new commanding officer was appointed to command the 14th Battalion. Major John Peck was the new man and Jacka was pleased with this decision. Peck recognised Jacka's qualities as a soldier and a leader and within weeks he promoted Jacka to Captain and appointed him battalion intelligence officer.

At Bullecourt, Jacka would distinguish himself again. Three days prior to the first Bullecourt battle he led reconnaissance patrols beyond the railway embankment into No Man's Land. As intelligence officer it was his role to assess the German defences of the Hindenburg Line and during his patrols he discovered the sunken road at Bullecourt, which he identified as a suitable jumping off position for the 14th, 16th and 46th Battalions. Jacka got very close to the German wire on 9th April, so close that he could hear German fatigue parties mending sections of the wire destroyed by British artillery. Jacka returned to report to Brigadier-General Brand that most of the wire was intact and that it would be 'pure murder to attempt the operation'. Brand was not accustomed to being talked to by a subordinate officer so directly and ignored Jacka's counsel. Jacka returned to No Man's Land hours later during the morning of 10th April to lay jumping off tapes. During this process he came into contact with a German officer named Lieutenant Reich and his orderly, engaged with them and captured them. Jacka pistol-whipped the German officer who complained to Peck. Peck replied to the German officer that he was lucky to be alive, if captured by Jacka.

Jacka had questioned one of the tank commanders in the early hours of the 11th April and learned that the tanks could not reach the scheduled start time. Realising that Australian infantry would be attacking a formidable German defensive system without tanks and artillery support, Jacka informed Peck at 3.05 am urging him to warn Major General Holmes at 4th Division Headquarters. Holmes replied that it was too late to change the plan and the attack must take place with or without the tanks. Despite his reservations about the operation, Jacka got the men from the 14th Battalion to their starting positions and reported to Peck as the disaster ensued before his eyes. Jacka would receive a bar to the Military Cross which he had earned at Pozières. His citation recorded that 'he carried out a daring reconnaissance of the enemy's position and obtained most valuable information. Later, he rendered invaluable assistance in guiding troops to their assembly positions.'[35]

After the Bullecourt fiasco, Jacka wrote a report, condemning the role of the tanks. If it were not for Jacka's abrasive personality and his uncontrollable ability to aggressively challenge the leadership of his superiors in a manner which undermined their authority, he may have been awarded two bars to his Victoria Cross for his actions at Pozières and Bullecourt. His peers and those who served under him on the battlefield were of the opinion that he should have been awarded three Victoria Crosses.

When Peck was transferred to 3rd Division as a Staff Officer, Major Fuhrmann was reappointed as commander of the 14th Battalion. Jacka had clashed with Furhmann earlier during the war, so when the new CO reorganised the structure within the battalion, he passed over Jacka for promotion. Jacka was very disappointed, for he was transferred from Intelligence Officer to commander of D Company. Jacka was ambitious and realised his own worth, and expected promotion to Major, but Peck had to contain this outspoken warrior and moved him sideways. Within weeks Furmann was replaced by Margolin.

Jacka was also denied further awards. Prior to the Battle of Messines Jacka and Captain Reg Jones from B Company went on a reconnaissance mission. Jones was awarded the Military Cross, but despite being recommended for the same award by Margolin, Jacka was not given any recognition. Margolin's recommendation for Jacka to receive the MC details the significant role that Jacka played at Messines:

> During the recent operations beyond Messines on 11th-13th June 1917 Capt. Jacka VC MC was in charge of D Coy 14th Battalion which occupied a section of the Green Line. According to his usual practice he personally led a patrol out into the hostile area, successfully drove back several snipers who were harassing our lines, seized a Machine Gun and occupied Deconinck Farm. He sent back the most lurid and comprehensive information and throughout displayed his usual coolness and judgment.[36]

Margolin's recommendation failed to mention that Jacka had captured a field gun during the battle. D Company, under Jacka's command had captured 600 yards of German occupied territory.

On 8th July 1917 Jacka was wounded when a German sniper fired a bullet into his leg at Ploegsteert Wood and he was taken out of the line to recover. Jacka returned to his battalion and took part in the third Ypres campaign. He was recommended for an award for his actions at Polygon Wood on 26th September 1917, but the recommendation was turned down and he received no honour. The recommendation written by Lieutenant Colonel Smith stated:

> For conspicuous gallantry and untiring energy during the operations at Zonnebeke on 26th September 1917. After the capture of the Second (Objective) he became the 'soul' of the defence, personally coordinating the work of the Stokes Guns, Vickers and Lewis Guns in such a way that heavy losses were inflicted on the enemy in three counter-attacks. When the position was ceaselessly bombarded he maintained, by his example, a fine spirit amongst all ranks.[37]

Brand, who was one of Jacka's adversaries, bore witness to Jacka's contribution to the success of the operation. Despite his feelings towards him, he did say to Jacka that he had recommended him for a Distinguished Service Order for the role that he played at Polygon Wood, but no recognition was forthcoming. Jacka continued to serve with professionalism despite being passed over for promotion and awards. Jacka was wounded during a German gas bombardment at Villers-Bretonneux during May 1918.

Jacka returned home to Australia during September 1919 and was demobilised from the AIF in January 1920. He returned to St. Kilda where he set up business with two former comrades from the 14th Battalion exporting and importing electrical products. The business operated successfully for a decade until it went into voluntary liquidation in 1930. Jacka was elected to St. Kilda Council in 1929 and in 1930 he was elected Mayor. He was commended for his work in assisting the unemployed to find work.

After suffering from kidney disease Jacka passed away on 17th January 1932 at Caulfield Military Hospital. He was aged 39. His coffin was passed by 6,000 as it lay in state, and it was carried by eight VC recipients at his funeral. He was proclaimed as 'Australia's greatest front-line soldier' at his funeral service. Jacka was laid to rest at St Kilda's Military Cemetery; his legend still resonates through Australian military history.

PRIVATE JACK STEWART 384,
14TH BATTALION AIF

Jack Stewart was born David William Stewart in 1893 in Myamyn, Victoria. He was known to his family as Jack and served in the AIF under the name Jack Stewart. He was the son of Andrew and Elizabeth Stewart, living in Wallacedale, Condah, Victoria. After attending the State School, Jack worked as a labourer in Condah. When war broke out, he was one of the first to enlist. He joined the AIF on 10th September 1914. After completing his basic training he left Melbourne aboard HMAT *Ulysses* on 22nd December 1914.

Private Jack Stewart was wounded at Anzac, Gallipoli on 3rd May 1915 while serving with the 14th Battalion which was holding Courtney's Post, when he received multiple gun shot wounds and shrapnel wounds from a shell explosion. He was evacuated from Gallipoli and on the 7th May 1915 he was admitted to No.17 General Hospital in Alexandria in Egypt. His service record reports that: 'He was struck on the right thigh by fragments of an exploding bomb. There was no fracture of any bones. The abdominal (post operative) wound discharged for about 12 weeks. There is a fragment of metal on inner border of patella. He was in hospital 10 weeks'[38]

Another report stated that he had sustained:

Private Jack Stewart, seated right, Private Tom Newton, seated left. (Courtesy Lesley Desborough)

Shrapnel wound right knee. Bullet entered inner aspect of leg, just above right knee and has not been removed. Now complaining that he cannot walk any distance without pain in knee joint.

Bomb wound abdomen. Two pieces of bomb entered abdomen and were removed by median incision. Was 12 weeks in bed and wound required draining.[39]

On 7th June 1915 he was sent to England and on 19th January 1916 he was sent back to Australia. While Jack Stewart was recovering from his wounds, his family was mourning the loss of his brother, Trooper James Stewart, who was killed at Gallipoli on 7th August 1915 while serving with the 8th Light Horse Regiment. He has no known grave and is name is commemorated on the Lone Pine Memorial.

As Jack Stewart tried to gain some mobility after his wound, he found that with the bullet still lodged above the right knee, could not walk far. Doctors declared him not fit for active service, but fit for Home service in England or Australia.

Stewart returned to duty on 6th June 1916. Contrary to the doctors' recommendations he would return to active service on the front line with his old unit, the 14th Battalion. He left Melbourne for the last time on 1st August 1916 aboard HMAT *Miltiades*. During this passage to England he was promoted to Corporal and he was appointed Military Police Corporal while aboard the troopship. He arrived at Plymouth, England, on 25th September 1916.

After training in England he left Folkestone for Boulogne on 4th December aboard the *Princess Victoria*. The following day he was marched for further training to Etaples. Stewart was pleased to be back with his mates when he rejoined the 14th Battalion on Christmas Eve, 24th December 1916.

During the Battle of Bullecourt, Private Jack Stewart saved the lives of his commanding officer and comrades when he assaulted and knocked out a German machine gun position which was holding up their advance. Stewart fell dying at the moment he destroyed the enemy position. He has no known grave and his name is commemorated on the Australian National Memorial at Villers-Bretonneux.

Private Bertram Harry Perry 487 was Jack Stewart's mate. He too was wounded in 1916, returned home to Australia, then rejoined the 14th Battalion. He wrote the following letter of condolence to Jack's mother Elizabeth:

Dear Mrs Stewart,
I expect that by now you are acquainted with the sad news of Jack's death in action. I know I shall be opening an old wound but felt that I could not let

it pass without letting you know of the appreciation of his comrades. I was his intimate pal, invalided home to Australia and came out again with Jack August 1 1916. He had the respect of both officers and all the boys in our Coy. We went out together in the fight on April 11th and Jack won everyone's praise in jumping at a machine gun that was troubling us. He probably saved our lives and an officer's, who was himself killed afterwards and would have recommended him for bravery. Jack got the machine gun but unfortunately fell. He suffered no pain but his thoughts were of home.

I will not say any more but all that gets out of the fight in our company will remember him as a man who died as good as he lived helping his pals. I am sorry it was impossible to get his belongings owing to a counter attack by the Germans.

May God comfort you in your troubles and if in his mercy God sees fit for me to return I will visit you as I would like to see the people of a dear pal.[40]

Elizabeth Stewart had lost two sons during the First World War. She had one remaining son, Charles, serving on the Western Front with 57th Battalion. After Jack was killed, she wrote to the Australian Army requesting Charles be removed from the front line. Charles was transferred to serve at the 1st Australian General Hospital.

CAPTAIN HAROLD WANLISS DSO,
14TH BATTALION AIF

Harold Boyd Wanliss was born in Ballarat, Victoria on 11th December 1891, son of Newton and Margaret. Wanliss was studious, non-smoking and teetotal. After completing his education at Ballarat College, Harold travelled to Europe with his father. When he returned to Australia in 1912 he attended the Hawkesbury Agricultural College, New South Wales for one year. In 1913 he bought a farm near Lorne, Victoria. His career as a farmer ended when World War One began. Breaking his leg after

Captain Harold Wanliss DSO. (The Distinguished Service Order 1916–1923)

falling from his horse he was unable to enlist in 1914. He was determined to join up. While he was convalescing he studied the theory of war in preparation for service.

Wanliss was 23 years and living in St Kilda, Victoria, when he enlisted on 28th April 1915. He was selected for officer training and sent to Broadmeadows. Promoted to 2nd Lieutenant on 16th July 1915, Wanliss was assigned to the 29th Battalion. On completing his basic training he embarked aboard the troopship HMAT *Demosthenes* from Melbourne on 29th October 1915 and sailed for Europe.

During March 1916, Wanliss was transferred to the 14th Battalion and he was promoted to Lieutenant during the following month. Wanliss received his baptism of fire when he led a raid to capture German prisoners on the Bois Grenier sector during the night of 2nd/3rd July 1916. There was tremendous complaint from 2nd Lieutenant Albert Jacka VC who knew that Wanliss had no combat experience and was perturbed that he was passed over to lead this raid. Jacka's protestations were ignored and Wanliss led the raid. Despite a preliminary mortar barrage, they were unable to penetrate through the German wire, which was uncut and German machine gunners and artillery shells poured upon them. Battalion scouts and some of the wounded men were reported to have thrown their bodies upon the wire to create a bridge for their comrades to cross the wire. They only had ten minutes to get into the German trench, capture any prisoners and get out before British artillery bombarded the German lines to cover their withdrawal. Despite being wounded in the face and neck, Wanliss managed to find a way through the German wire and get into a German trench, which he cleared. He remained in the trench to cover the withdrawal of his men. They failed to secure any German prisoners. Wanliss received gunshot wounds to the face, neck and chest and had to be carried off the battlefield. Despite the failure of the operation to capture prisoners, according to Edgar Rule, Wanliss and his raiding party had killed approximately 50 soldiers from the 50th Reserve Division. Wanliss received the Distinguished Service Order for his leadership and courage. If it was not for his determined spirit and his command abilities the withdrawal could have resulted in severe casualties. Wanliss was the first officer from the AIF holding the rank of Lieutenant to receive this award. The recommendation for the Distinguished Service Order signed by Lieutenant-General Birdwood states:

> This officer displayed most conspicuous bravery and resolution during a raiding attack carried out against hostile trenches in the Bois Grenier district on the night 2-3/7/16. The attack was unexpectedly held up by the fact that our Mortars had failed to cut or damage the two belts of wire entanglements protecting the enemy trenches and the enemy brought a heavy enfilade machine gun fire, also a barrage of shell fire, to bear upon these entanglements in the direct path of these assaults. This officer who was in immediate command of 60 Officers and men instantly resolved to push on with the enterprise and ordered an immediate assault through the barbed wire. While himself struggling

through the wire he was wounded in the face but pushed on encouraging his men to follow and took up his prearranged position on the enemy parapet at the point of entry while his party leapt into and raided the trenches inflicting many casualties on the enemy. While directing operations from this point he was again wounded by a bullet in the neck. But he carried on coolly until the conclusion of the prearranged time when he gave the 'Out' signal and supervised the withdrawal of the raiding party. He then himself withdrew and while struggling through the enemy wire he was hit a third time in the side and had to be carried in. Had this Officer given up before the task was finished there is every probability that the withdrawal would have ended in confusion with heavy loss.[41]

His citation states:

> For conspicuous gallantry and determination when leading an attacking party during a raid. He forced the wire which was uncut, entered the trench, inflicted heavy loss on the enemy and supervised the withdrawal. While forcing the wire he was wounded in the face, later he was wounded by a bullet in the neck, and finally when withdrawing he was again wounded and had to be carried in. He set a fine example to all with him.[42]

Wanliss was transferred to England and admitted to the 3rd London General Hospital in Wandsworth. The medical report from the hospital stated that he received 'GSW to right side of face. The bullet entered left side of neck and came out through the right cheek.'[43] Most of the upper right set of his teeth were knocked out.

After recovering from his wounds Wanliss joined the 14th Battalion on 27th September 1916. Wanliss was mentioned in Sir Douglas Haig's dispatch issued on 13th November 1916 for 'Distinguished and gallant services and devotion to duty in the field.'

He became the Battalion Adjutant in February 1917 and Captain on 6th March 1917. At Bullecourt, as adjutant he was expected to remain with his CO, Lieutenant Colonel Peck in the battalion HQ; however, when news of the 14th Battalion's assault upon the Hindenburg Line came through, Wanliss became anxious to get to the front line to help his comrades. On numerous occasions during that morning he pleaded with Peck to allow him to go to the front line. His final request:

> I'm going to ask you once again, Colonel, to let me go. We've a good idea now of what's happened, and I can't be any use here. I feel I ought to be up there doing what I can to help the fellows. God knows what has happened to Jacka and the rest of them, and I can't stand the suspense.[44]

Peck refused Wanliss's request. Knowing that the men were already committed to the desperate struggle to retain the trenches, he was anxious to keep back one of his best officers, not only to ensure that the battalion had experienced officers – he was aware of Wanliss's potential to become a national leader after the war ended.

Wanliss took part in the Battles of Messines during June 1917. On 26th September 1917 Wanliss was killed by machine gun fire from a machine gun emplacement he was trying to locate and destroy during the Battle for Polygon Wood. He was aged 25. He has no known grave and his name is commemorated on the Menin Gate. Wanliss was highly respected by the men that he commanded for Edgar Rule testified that he was 'a gentleman in the best sense of the word, whom everybody liked and admired'.[45]

It was thought that had he survived the First World War he would have played a prominent role in the future of post-war Australia. When on leave Wanliss would spend his time studying industry. When the 14th Battalion was off the front line he organised lectures and debates on Australia after the war. His former commanding officer Lieutenant Colonel Peck proclaimed: 'Many brave men, many good men I have met ... but he was the king of them all.'[46] Chaplain Rolland wrote: 'He would have been Australia's leader in days when she will surely need one.'[47]

PRIVATE FREDERICK MORLEY 1531,
15TH BATTALION AIF

Frederick John Morley was born in St Pancras, London, on 19th February 1893. Morley emigrated to Australia and worked as a farm labourer. He enlisted at Lismore, New South Wales on 29th December 1914. He embarked aboard HMAT *Seang Choon* on 13th February 1915. He joined the Mediterranean Expeditionary Force on 12th April 1915 in Egypt and took part in the Gallipoli campaign. He served on the peninsula with the 15th

Private Frederick Morley. (Courtesy Kevin Morley)

Battalion until the evacuation in December 1915. Morley arrived in France on 8th June 1916 and was sent to the Western Front on the Somme. He was wounded on 8th August 1916 when the 15th Battalion captured a communication trench which ran in front of Mouquet Farm. Morley was evacuated from the battlefield. He was first taken to the 44th Casualty Clearing Station with a gunshot wound to the knee. On 10th August he was admitted to the No.3 Canadian General Hospital in Boulogne. He recovered from his wounds and returned to the 15th Battalion on 23rd September 1916.

Morley would fight his last battle on 11th April at Bullecourt. Morley advanced towards the German positions during that morning with C Company. He crossed the machine gun swept No Man's Land but fell when he reached the first German line. Private Charlie Evans from the 15th Battalion was C Company runner declared:

> I saw him fall, pitched forward on his face. He was next to me at the time. This was about 300 yards from enemy's 1st line of wire in No Man's Land. Was shot by machine gun fire. I could not swear it was Morley, but I always took it to be him. He was always next to me and he was never seen again.[48]

Corporal M.L. Goodyer was more certain about Morley's fate:

> I was with Morley all away across in the attack till reaching the German first line of wire. I saw him fall as if killed instantly. I did not stop but went on, he would be about three yards in front of me when I saw him fall, I did not see anything of him again.[49]

Morley was initially listed as missing. There was no trace of his remains. During October 1917 he was still considered as missing. After a court of inquiry convened in November 1917 Morley was listed killed in action. His remains were not recovered until 1920. Some investigation had to take place before Morley's remains were positively identified, because on his person was found a watch and identity disc bearing the name of Lieutenant Edward Wareham. During the Gallipoli campaign Morley was batman to Wareham until his death on 10th May 1915. It was Morley's intention to return this disc to Wareham's family when he returned home from the war. Wareham's father wrote:

> The disc undoubtedly belonged to my late son, and the newspaper cutting referring to him which accompanied the disc was a cutting from the *Brisbane Courier*. The F.J. Morley mentioned is the Private No.1531 as surmised by you; he was my late son's Batman when he went to Gallipoli,

and wrote giving me the full account of my son's death. The watch did not belong to my son, therefore presumably was Morley's own property. I am therefore returning the watch to you. Morley undoubtedly intended to bring my son's disc back to us had he lived, because in a letter we received from him after my son's death, he mentions he would bring back his field glasses and anything else belonging to him that he could.[50]

Subsequently the remains of Private Frederick Morley were identified and he was buried in a grave bearing his name at Quéant Road Cemetery.

PRIVATE LESLIE PEZET 3416,
15TH BATTALION AIF

Leslie Robert Pezet was born in Milton New South Wales in February 1893. He was a 22-year-old carpenter from Mullumbimby, New South Wales, when he enlisted in Brisbane, Queensland, on 17th August 1915. Private Pezet was allocated to the 15th Battalion. After completing his basic training he embarked from Brisbane aboard HMAT *Seang Bee* on 21st October 1915. Although they received a jubilant send off, Pezet was aware that he was going to war and that there existed the real prospect that he may never see his family or friends again, for he recorded in his diary that day:

> The Queensland people gave us a splendid send off, about 3,000 all told, streamers being in abundance and a beautiful afternoon, and two bands keeping us alive and in good spirits, whilst waiting for our final and last goodbye to our many friends whom we may never see again.[51]

It was a six-week passage across the Indian Ocean to Egypt. Pezet arrived on 29th November. His deployment

Private Leslie Pezet. (Courtesy Ken Pezet)

to Gallipoli was cancelled when the evacuation of the peninsula began in December and so he remained in the desert for five months. In June Pezet was sent to France. Arriving in Marseille he embarked on a 65-hour train journey to Bailleul in northern France. He experienced life in the trenches on the Western Front for the first time at Bois Grenier near Armentières. The 15th Battalion was sent to Warloy for a week towards the end of July 1916 where they trained hard prior to be sent into the Battle of the Somme. Whilst there Pezet recorded that 'hearing the roaring and thundering of the guns day in and day out makes one want to get along and get finished with it without so much talking about it.'[52]

On 1st August 1916 the 15th Battalion received orders to march to Pozières. Pezet mentions in his diary that the men lost their appetites as apprehension overwhelmed their senses:

> We march off feeling brave, but at this time one gives more thought to those he loves best … Here we see what the Germans are doing in hunger and hatred. The shells fall among us, but here we remain for the night in this bivouac, [at] daybreak we put our packs on and march in artillery formation through Sausage Gully, helping the wounded, covering the killed as we go. Now we are among all our guns tied wheel to wheel and the noise is terrific and the sound of determination from both sides, hastens one to be away either for the best or worst.[53]

Pezet entered the reserve line at Pozières while German artillery was pounding the remnants of the village on 4th August. The sound of the shells exploding made it impossible for Pezet to hear his comrades:

> One becomes sick from the odour and the sight of the ground. One feels as if all the world is being churned up this last two hours, the roar from the guns deafens us all. We do not speak, only making signs and shouting to one another, our officers and comrades leave one by one, will we ever see them again, one never knows.[54]

Pezet described the horrendous barrage as a 'curtain of fire' as they headed for the front line near to the Windmill at Pozières. He continued to write of his ordeal when they arrived in the front line:

> The officers orders every man to find his own way into the line as the Germans are preparing to attack us, the fire is bearing down on us and shortly men are taken one after the other in rapid succession and the officers lead us through the barrage now that it is following the curtain, we rush headlong into it. Through it and now we are running towards the line

in order, but from all directions. Here we stay with bayonets fixed, rifles in good working order, we find we are in front and on the right of the Wind Mill, who will forget that, and what of thirst, all cry for water. A few men left out of a ration party bring us water in petrol cans, we drink heartily and when finishing, ask if it is petrol. The officer said it was the best to be got, and we made the best of it, as thirst made us glad of anything that looked watery. We passed a terrible night, men never loved one another's company as much as at this time, nothing was too much to do for one another, here we talked to keep our mind from what laid [sic] in front of us.[55]

Pezet and the soldiers from the 15th Battalion remained on the line for another three days. His diary is a tremendous historical record of his experience in the trenches. The Germans were desperate to capture the strategically important Windmill at Pozières and continued to shell the Australian lines for three days prior to a major counter attack:

Heavy shells are falling all round us wounding many and sleep no not until after midnight so we shut our eyes after many a little word of prayer, all men say prayers now. Three more days find us in the same position, we now begin for our big attack, dirty shaky beards, aching dirty feet, water not enough for one's insides.[56]

Pezet describes how men who had no faith before the war were trying to find comfort through religion and prayer.

On 7th August Pezet was in the line with the 15th Company as German infantry swarmed through lines being held by the 48th and 14th Battalion AIF. He saw Jacka's courageous counter attack from behind German lines to release comrades from the 48th Battalion. Pezet and the 15th Battalion were called to assist Jacka in this effort.

On the following day, during the evening of 8th August, Pezet and the 15th Battalion launched an attack on a communication trench known as Park Lane, west of Mouquet Farm Track. They succeeded in driving out the Germans holding this position and successfully entered the OG Trench system but the failure of the 7th Suffolk's to attack along Western Trench to enter Ration Trench had left them exposed on their left flank. There was no choice but to withdraw from Park Lane. Pezet was among the first wave to attack Park Lane Trench. He gave a very graphic account of this attack:

Now four o'clock, trench mortars open, artillery opens, machine guns open, rifles open, all from both sides, plans come up to officers and final orders.

Oh is it cancelled, to God they would, now 9.20 pm the barrage lifts and charge in waves and masses, our wave the first. The guns boom, we stand too anxious, not afraid, not discouraged, but oh what one would give to have it over, three minutes to go lads, the barrage lifts and we charge helter skelter through bombs, bullets, shrapnel, and on all run, making for the German trench, the light is as if the sun was shining, the frightened Germans, the screech from shells overhead was weird, our men fall in hundreds. We reach the trench, Germans squeal and cry and beg mercy, say they have wives and children, others say they sick. Not too sick to shoot our lads and we charge them. Some we take prisoners but nothing done in cold blood. Those that did not have their hands [sic] suffered death, they are dirty these men, shot down our wounded and stretcher bearers. We swore to kill and murder every German before us, but to do the deed we couldn't. We kicked them instead and sent them back, 150 of the swine.[57]

Pezet's party was reduced to eleven men and as they advanced forward through German shell fire they become disorientated and lost. Pezet was wounded when he received a gunshot wound in the right arm. The bullet entered his wrist and exited at his elbow:

I get wounded and drop. I laid down to get away from the shrapnel not losing my senses and crawled with one hand to a shell hole where there was a man crying for water, as I enter two others enter. I supply him with a little water having a drink myself. Oh but my poor arm broken, bleeding and bursting over everything and everyone around me. Here were five of us, bombs, bullets, shells, shrapnel flying all round us; we do not know what to do, lost. Hell is hard, my arm is paining terrible now being a little numbed after I was hit. I get afraid of the amount of blood coming from it. The other lads tie their wounds helping one another and they attend to mine now, I can't stand to wait any longer. They were sorry as my arm is badly broken, they did not know they had bad flesh wounds, so I let them finish, theirs was on the leg, mine an arm. I could keep it free from dirt; they tie ligatures and bind tightly with one of my puttees, and make a sling out of two white handkerchiefs.[58]

Pezet and his wounded comrades sheltering in the shell hole were unaware of their position, not knowing whether they were behind German lines. For several hours they remained in the shell hole pondering how they were going to get out. Pezet wrote of his fears and how they extricated themselves:

Now we get worried we want to find out where we are, we all suffer too much pain to stay here, we look over the shell hole, we see flares all round us, we think we are behind the Germans, we crawl out and hear someone else. We don't know what to do, we lay still, on he comes, and one of our wounded mates shouts 'who goes there' and two more wounded lads come crawling with a leg broke and crying with agony asks where our lines are. Here we are, seven wounded and thirsty, lost and almost done. All of us losing much blood our clothes now saturated and stiff. We decide to lay in a hole till day light in one large enough for all. Here we settle down, there two hours and three of them get wounded again. One is wounded for the fourth time and then gets killed, another killed. Day break comes and we are afraid to move, if we are in front of our own lads and they see us stir they will shoot. Another man wounded for the second time, and we have to risk if we are to be killed, we will be done going home in the attempt. One lad and I crawl first to find our way. We get out thirty yards from the hole with the other lads and we shout to them our lads in behind you, they crawl towards us, and we run as hard as we can, our lads fire on the Germans to keep them down, but they sniped us luckily missing, but putting the fear of God into us, as the bullets just whizzing by our ears and ploughing the dirt up at our feet, my foot is very painful when I get in.[59]

After his death-defying dash towards Australian lines he was taken to a field dressing station where his wounds were tended before heading for the Red Cross wagon in Sausage Valley, which transported him to a Casualty Clearing Station at Puchevillers. He had a gunshot wound in his right forearm and a pellet in his back. After a train journey to Boulogne he was sent to England where on the 24th August 1916 Pezet was admitted to Norfolk War Hospital.

After recovering from his wounds he returned to the 15th Battalion in France in December 1916. He would see action at Guedecourt during early 1917. Pezet was with the 15th Battalion when they pursued the German retreat to the Hindenburg Line from February to April. Pezet took part in the aborted attempt to attack Bullecourt on 10th April 1917:

We are formed in line, bayonets fixed waiting for order to come from right to charge over a distance of 12 hundred yards, daybreak upon us, the order came to retire at the double, everyone is sick at heart, making up our mind to got into it and get it over. The German guns were quiet and no machine gun fire, we were mad, we start to retire, the Hun see us and now for it, machine and artillery fire etc.

Terrible snow storm comes and the Hun scatter their fire and they cannot see us and we dodge it with very few men not to answer Roll Call on our return.[60]

Pezet was not pleased to hear that he and his comrades would have to repeat the same exercise the following night. Feeling exhausted and dejected owing to the failure of the first attempt, Pezet had mentally and physically to prepare himself to go through the ordeal once again. Arriving at the railway embankment during early morning on the 11th, Pezet was detailed as runner to 15th Battalion Adjutant, Captain Francis Leslie. His battalion had to wait on hands and knees on the cold snow for the tanks to arrive. The moment to advance arrived:

Wave after wave, the Germans make it as if the sun is shining with their red flares, men are falling in terrible masses, the artillery and machine gun fire from the Germans is terrible, but we push on, our lads are fighting and falling in great numbers. The tanks are put out of action one after the other, the only artillery from our men is the heavies to cut the wire and they cease and they leave us to the mercy of the Germans who have an open go at us.[61]

Despite Captain Leslie being killed in the advance towards the German first line trench, Pezet and the remnants of the 15th Battalion continue to attack:

Attacking now in disorder and mad stretcher bearers are rushing to help doing noble work, many never reach their lads who they seek, we reach his front line and find only one tank to be there and put out of action, here a fight goes on, we bayonet what Huns don't surrender in a twinkle of an eye. Two hundred we get and we have to go on to his second line. Here we reach with only a quarter of our division left to put up a fight, here we fight him with bombs and rifle and bayonet, no prisoners here, and here we have to stay, no officers.[62]

Officers from the left flank made contact with Pezet's party in the German lines. Lieutenant Watkinson ordered Pezet to dig a funk hole into the side of the sector of German trench they occupied. Pezet was too fatigued to carry out this order. 2nd Lieutenant Edward Binnington ordered Pezet to gather as many men as possible to resist further German counter-attacks. Pezet returned with few men and was met by Captain Harry Murray who was organising the defence of the captured German lines. Murray rallied these men ordering them to stand to and to resist any counter-attack 'saying that we can beat him easy'.[63]

Pezet continues to defend the trench until the point where the ammunition supplies have run out and there is no hope of escaping back to Australian lines:

> Bombing starts, we throw till not a bomb remains ... We find the Hun in great force and holding his third line very strongly and fighting very hard, our bombers are put to a very severe test, every bomb has to be effective, our men are all now, getting killed and wounded, losing and regaining sap and bay every hour, our bombs run out, no ammunition whatever, machine guns fail and we find a few hundred German bombs in a very deep dug out. When using his, he found our position critical and [they] came down on us, our left retiring and being absolutely mowed down on our right, we see them running with their hands up. We have no alternative, we have to let him come and take us, he puts a barrage with his guns and machine guns behind us and we have to remain where we are. Several men tried but fell in their attempt.[64]

Trapped between determined Württembergs and German artillery, Pezet and the remnants of the Australian units holding OG 1 and OG 2 Trenches were forced to surrender. He and his fellow captives were treated well by the Württembergers who captured him in the Hindenburg Line trenches. They most likely respected them for their strong defensive fight. However they were ill treated by Württembergers in the reserve lines. They were held in a church behind the lines during the first night of captivity. Their captives were the Prussians, their opponents during the battle for Pozières in 1916. Exhausted and hungry, they were fed meagre rations:

> ... at 8 pm a big gray clothed hog brings to us, bread five men to one loaf, black in colour and sour in taste, we only have very little of it, and two tubs of black coffee, we drink this out of our steel helmets, and terrible stuff it was.[65]

He was taken to the notorious prison at Fort MacDonald in Lille:

> Here we suffer only what one other place could make for mankind and that is hell, of fire of hunger, here we are almost thrown in one by one, a dirty dusky dungeon, tiled walls, tiled floors, no beds, boards about nine inches wide and ten feet long are brought into us for beds, but we have to lay them out, spacing about twelve inches and cross way and we sleep or try to on this bed, for first two nights and days we sit down and then walk to get warm, drenched to the skin, we complain, only, for something to eat, bread comes in a piece about

three or four ounces in weight and coffee, the guards tramp loudly, whistling and singing over the prey they have in their merciless power.[66]

The conditions within which Pezet and his fellow captors were incarcerated were unsanitary: 'In a corner a large barrel is placed for our latrine, for two hundred men, and most of the men being ill, this is flowing on the floor by the morning and the smell is terrible, all ventilation being blocked off'.[67]

Within weeks Pezet was sent to the front line to carry out manual work for the German army, deliberately positioned near to where British artillery shells were falling. As mentioned earlier, the German authorities were using prisoners captured at Bullecourt in this way until the British government gave assurances that German prisoners of war were not treated in a similar way behind the British line. Pezet unloaded shell cases at Corbehem, worked on roads at Vitry and unloaded ammunition from trains at Douai.

Pezet was registered as a POW on 11th June 1917 and was taken to the camp at Fredfrickfeld where he received better treatment, although hunger still remained a problem. Food packets from England were being received but they were not enough. Pezet put his thoughts into the following verse:

> I fought at Bois Grenier, Pozières that is a tale to tell,
> Returned and fought at Guedecourt and Lagnicourt as well,
> But that attack at Riencourt nipped my fighting in the bud,
> And never in those fields of blood, did I such hunger ken
> As I have, since Freedom changed for Kreigagefangenan.
>
> Yet still I have a lesson learned and hard tho it maybe,
> I've learned to humble crusts of bread to bow the lowly knee.
> And if inclined to grouse at times, I always think of when,
> For scraps of bread my Soul I'd sell, when Kriegagefangenan.
>
> I've told you how as captives we hungered oft and sore,
> And after meals, we always looked eagerly for more,
> In passing now I tell you how we hailed with loud acclaim,
> The day of Glory, the day der Grosser Packets came.
>
> Bully, biscuits, butter, jam, the humble pork and beans
> And vacant coffins everywhere that once had held sardines,
> For tins of honey tins of Milk and tins without a name,
> Were in profusion on the day,
> Der Grosser Packets came.

For brows were wet, with honest sweat as over fires we
    toiled,
And strove to fry the bacon crisps and cans of rice we
    boiled,
Oh hearts were light and eyes were bright as rose the
    ruddy flame,
That cooked that dear Australian food, the day,
Der Grosser Packets came.[68]

During December 1917 Pezet was transferred to Gustrow
Lager in Mackemberg where he was sent to work at the
Howaldt Works shipyards on the Kiel Canal. He remained
there until the Armistice. Pezet arrived in England on
30th December 1918. He returned to Australia on 2nd
March 1919. He married Lottie Louisa Rae on 2nd August
1919 and they would raise six children. Leslie moved his
family to Newmarket in Brisbane, where he established a
construction business. His grandson Ken recalled: 'Leslie
never really recovered from either his experience or his
injuries. My father told me that Leslie never spoke about
the war, but during thunderstorms, he would disappear
and they would find him curled up in the foetal position
behind the earth closet down the back yard.'

  For the remainder of his life Leslie would suffer
periodic spasms when his right arm would freeze
with his palm open. He would regularly need his arm
to be opened, cleaned up and resewn. This ongoing
problem would eventually lead to him succumbing to
tuberculosis and premature death on 11th March 1940,
aged 47. He was buried in the Toowong Cemetery in
Brisbane, Queensland.

2ND LIEUTENANT PERCY TOFT MC & BAR, MM,
15TH BATTALION AIF

Percy John Gilbert Toft was born in Bundaberg,
Queensland in 1894. Prior to the war he worked as a
civil servant in Bundaberg and was married to Grace.
He had previous military service serving for five years
as a cadet and two years in the 4th Infantry Battalion
C.M.F. He enlisted to join the AIF on 22nd October 1914
as a private. He left Melbourne on 22nd December 1914
aboard HMAT *Ceramic* for Egypt. On arriving in Egypt he
was assigned to the 15th Battalion.

Private Percy Toft first saw action
when he landed at Anzac Cove,
Gallipoli with the 15th Battalion
during the late afternoon on 25th
April 1915. Toft was involved
in consolidating and defending

**Captain Percy Toft MC and Bar
MM. (Courtesy Lloyd Toft)**

the Anzac beachhead. Within two days of landing at
Gallipoli he saw a friend killed by a sniper while in a
trench close to Russell's Top:

> I sat down and decided to have a snack before I tried
> to sleep. I had just finished opening a tin of bully
> beef with my bayonet when I heard a plop. Looking
> up I saw my mate crumpling and sliding to the
> bottom of the trench. One look and I saw that his
> head had been cut off in a straight line above the
> ears, from his eyebrows. A sniper's bullet must have
> hit a pebble on the parapet of the trench and the
> bullet ricocheting made the ghastly severance.[69]

Toft received a gun shot wound to his arm on 21st
May. He was admitted to a hospital in Alexandria to
recover. He returned on 2nd August and soon received
promotion to Corporal. Toft took part in an attack upon
a Turkish-held strongpoint, Hill 971. They had captured
this position at great cost to the battalion, but were
forced to withdraw when overwhelmed. On 7th October
1915 Toft was promoted to Sergeant. Toft served on the
Gallipoli peninsula until the battalion was withdrawn in
December 1915.

  The 15th Battalion spent five months in Egypt before
embarking aboard the troopship Transylvania for France
on 1st June 1916. They arrived in Marseille on 8th June
and boarded trains which would take them to the
Western Front.

  During August 1916 Toft was in the Somme and took
part in the Battle of Pozières. He was recommended for
the Military Medal for his actions there:

> This N.C.O. performed excellent work on nights
> 8/9th and 9/10th August during operations N.W. of
> Pozières. He was always cool and courageous, and
> showed a fine example to his men. He consistently
> displayed splendid qualities throughout and
> handled his men with much ability, and was of great
> assistance to his Coy. Commander.[70]

Toft was promoted to 2nd Lieutenant on 19th August
1916. On 11th April 1917 he took part in the attack on
German OG 1 and OG 2 trenches. Toft was the Brigade
Intelligence officer during this period. Before the
attack it was discovered that 38,000 bombs designated
for the Bullecourt battle were brought to the front
without any detonators. It was Toft who supervised the
15th Battalion placing the detonators. Soon after the
Bullecourt battle Toft was promoted to Lieutenant.

  Lieutenant Toft and the 15th Battalion played a role
in the Battle of Messines from 7th to 14th June 1917.
Toft distinguished himself once again and was awarded
the Military Cross. His citation in the *London Gazette*
reported that 'He displayed great dash and enterprise in

capturing and consolidating an enemy advanced post which was causing casualties to our front-line troops. He had no opportunity of previously reconnoitring the ground and success was entirely due to his coolness and determination.[71]

On 15th October 1917 Toft was promoted to Captain. He would continue to serve with the 15th Battalion throughout 1918 and took part in the battles for Le Hamel, Amiens and the Hindenburg Line. In September 1918 he was awarded a bar to his Military Cross:

> For conspicuous gallantry and devotion to duty when in command of a company. By his skilful arrangements an enemy raid in considerable strength and under cover of intense bombardment was beaten off with heavy casualties. During the night he drove the enemy from the front where they were established. Later, he fought the enemy throughout the greater part of the day with bombs and rifle grenades, and prevented them from establishing machine guns. Throughout he showed untiring energy, and by his courage and cool behaviour set a splendid example to his men.[72]

MAJOR PERCY BLACK DSO, DCM, CROIX DE GUERRE, 16TH BATTALION AIF

Percy Charles Herbert Black was born in Beremboke, Victoria, on 12th December 1877. Percy was one of 11 children born to William and Ann Black. William, a farmer, was of Irish descent and emigrated from Antrim. Percy was educated at Beremboke State School and after completing his education he became a carpenter. During the years 1901 to 1913 Percy worked as a prospector and miner in the goldmines of Western Australia.

When war broke out Percy Black enlisted to join the AIF as a Private at Blackboy Hill in Western Australia on 8th September 1914. He had poor teeth and was accepted on the provision that his stumps were extracted. Black was sent to the 16th Battalion. Within weeks of enlisting he was promoted to Lance Corporal. Black and his friend Harry Murray were attached to the machine gunner section and underwent six weeks of training. Black was reported to have been able to set up

Major Percy Black DSO DCM. (*The Old Sixteenth* by Captain C. Longmore)

a machine gun ready for action in 13.4 seconds, which according to Charles Bean was 'the fastest time known for this operation.'[73]

He left Melbourne aboard HMAT *Ceramic* on 22nd December 1914 for Egypt. After spending several months there he joined the Mediterranean Expeditionary Force heading for the Gallipoli Peninsula on 12th April 1915.

Black landed at Anzac Cove at 5.30 pm on 25th April 1915. As soon as he landed on the beach he dug a trench and set up his machine-gun. After climbing Monash Valley to Pope's Hill, Black set up his machine-gun on the side of the hill and fought off numerous Turkish counter-attacks during the following days. Harry Murray wrote:

> Many of our boys were shot, often by invisible marksmen, which is enough to try the stamina of any troops, but the survivors still held their ground. Black never missed a chance with his machine-gun and he was a deadly shot. If any man could claim to have done more than another in stopping the Turkish counter attacks on April 26th and 27th, it was Percy Black. Only for his deadly gunning and determination I am convinced that the Turks would have succeeded in turning our flank and so forced us off Gallipoli.[74]

Holding onto his position with stubborn determination Black withstood a torrent of Turkish shell fire and despite being wounded he carried on. He became a legend during the Gallipoli campaign and his reputation would be enhanced by his actions at Pozières on the Somme and cemented by his sacrifice at Bullecourt. Harry Murray:

> As the day wore on, the Turks tried to cross some open country and Black caught them in enfilade lines. They simply sank and died. In one case, when overtaken by the death rain, they hunched together in protection and very few escaped. This drew on Black a concentrated 'hate' from the Turks. A mountain gun shelled him. He got a shrapnel wound through the ear, and another through his hand, both painful wounds which bled profusely, but still managed to deliver his lethal spray whenever opportunity offered. His gun casing was now holed with rifle bullets. Suddenly a party of 70 Turks jumped out of a small depression some 80 yards in front. 'Here they come,' roared Percy, and a steady stream of fire roared from his gun. The nearest of them got to within forty yards of us before collapsing. All were exceptionally brave men who pushed home the attack in the name of Allah, but none was able to get back.[75]

Black's machine-gun was damaged so severely by rifle fire that it was rendered inoperable. He had to go back to Anzac Beach to get it repaired:

> There was a heavy demand on the machine-guns, and Black's weapon was so often hit that it became unworkable. He just put it on his shoulder and walked back to the beach to see if it could be repaired by a ship's armourer, but had the good luck to exchange it for another one instead. The new gun was all brass, and shiny – and what a picture of a returning warrior Percy made as he came up the hill! He might have been Diomede striding back over the plains after interviewing Paris, a splendid physical specimen, afraid of nothing on earth and glorifying in his strength and power. Although his arm was in a sling and his head swathed in bandages, his eyes were beaming with joy at the success of his quest; now he could carry on with the good work and we needed him badly.[76]

Lance Corporal Percy Black would distinguish himself during the disastrous attempt to capture the Bloody Angle ridge, near Kaba Tepe during the night of the 2nd/3rd May. He advanced with the machine gun section and held onto his machine gun position despite all his comrades being killed. He was surrounded by the enemy, but continued to fire his machine gun until all ammunition was expended. He brought back his gun to safety. He was believed to have killed 500 Turkish soldiers during that night and was awarded the Distinguished Conduct Medal for his actions. He received a battlefield commission when he was promoted from Lance Corporal to 2nd Lieutenant on 2nd May 1915.

Black was Mentioned in Dispatches on 5th August 1915 and appointed temporary Captain on 9th August. On 26th August he was attached to the 25th Battalion until 8th October when he returned to the 16th Battalion at Mudros.

On 4th December he was attached to the 14th Brigade Machine Gun Section. He was with the last units to leave the trenches during the evacuation of Gallipoli on 18th/19th December 1918. He was mentioned in dispatches: 'For services in connection with the preparations for, and the execution of, the operation of re-embarkation. Was a member of the 'C' [final] party to leave the trenches.' Black and the 16th Battalion arrived in Alexandria on 30th December.

In the early months of 1916 Percy Black would climb the ranks at a rapid rate. Promoted to Lieutenant on 1st January 1916, on 20th January he was elevated to Captain. While at Serapeum on 27th April he had reached the rank of Major.

On 1st June 1916 Major Black and the 16th Battalion left Alexandria aboard HMT *Canada* and arrived in Marseille on 9th June. Black played a prominent role in the fight for Pozières and Mouquet Farm during August 1916. He took part in an attack on German positions during the night of 9th/10th August. Black's actions during that night are explained in detail in his recommendation for the Distinguished Service Order:

> For very gallant leadership on the night of 9/10th August 1916, when he led his Company over 'No Man's Land' in a charge against a German strongpoint; this charge was in addition to being a very gallant action a very difficult feat, as it necessitated a change of direction after passing one German strongpoint under very heavy Artillery and Machine Gun fire; and subsequently supervising the work of consolidation not merely on the frontage of his own Company, but the consolidation of the frontage of two other Companies, and subsequently on the night of 10/11th August for seizing under a very heavy barrage of Artillery fire, with the assistance of the Battalion Bombing Platoon, a further strong point some 200 yards in advance of the firing line. This officer displayed great gallantry and marked powers of leadership during the operations 9/12th August 1916 and I strongly recommend high distinction.[77]

Black received gun shot wounds to the head and forearm at Mouquet Farm on 30th August 1916. He was evacuated and arrived at Boulogne the following day. On 1st September he was shipped to England and was sent to the 4th London General Hospital in Denmark Hill, south London.

On 14th November 1916 he received notification of his award of the DSO which was listed in the *London Gazette*. 'He led his Company over 'No Man's Land' against an enemy's strongpoint which he captured and consolidated under very difficult circumstances and under heavy artillery and machine gun fire.'[78]

On that same day he was sent back to France and arrived at Etaples. Black rejoined his battalion on 16th November. On 16th December Major Black received the Croix de Guerre from the French President.

Black would fight his last battle at Bullecourt on 11th April. On the night before the battle, Black told his friend Captain Harry Murray from the 16th Battalion he had a premonition that Bullecourt would be his last battle.[79] Black who was standing at the rear of the 16th Battalion charged to the front and with great bravado shouted 'Come on boys, bugger the tanks!' This act inspired the battalion to charge across No Man's Land towards the German wire. Black managed to find a way through the first German wire defences and fight his way into the first German trench OG 1. As he proceeded

Death of Major Black by Charles Wheeler.
(Australian War Memorial: ART03558)

to lead his men towards OG 2 Trench, he became entangled in the wire and received a fatal machine gun bullet to the head. Captain Harry Murray, his cobber from the 13th Battalion, passed him as he advanced towards OG 2 Trench. Murray later paid this tribute to him: 'He was the bravest man I ever knew, and I knew hundreds of them.'[80] Major Percy Black was 38 when he died at Bullecourt. His remains were not recovered and has no known grave. His name is commemorated on the Australian National Memorial at Villers-Bretonneux.

PRIVATE WILLIAM CAMPBELL 6492
16TH BATTALION AIF

**Private William
Campbell. (Courtesy
Jean & Denise
Letaille Bullecourt
Museum)**

William Flemming Campbell was born at Pitkevie Farm, Leslie, Fife in Scotland on 5th June 1889. He was the youngest of four children and his mother Amelia tragically died a few days after he was born. His father Ewen was left to raise him, his brother David and sisters Annie and Margaret. William and David emigrated to Australia. Prior to the war William worked as a teamster. William enlisted on 14th April 1916 and joined the 16th Battalion as a private. He arrived in France on 8th February. William fought his way into OG 1, where he was wounded on 11th April. He continued to fight and hold his position against German counter attacks. Private Horatio Ganson testified:

He was a mate of mine. On 11th April 1917 at Bullecourt in the enemy's 1st line he was hit by a piece of bomb close to the heart. He and I continued fighting for over an hour after. Campbell was then told to go and get bandaged up, he left to go to the Dressing Station in trench. I never saw him again. He seemed to have a nasty wound, but from the way he carried on, I thought he would get better. I heard afterwards from some of our men that Campbell had been left at a German Dressing Station in the first village we went through behind the line [to the right of Riencourt].[81]

Campbell was captured and died of his wounds during the following day. He has no known grave and his name is commemorated on the Villers-Bretonneux Memorial.

SERGEANT HENRY CHOULES MM 1794,
16TH BATTALION AIF

Henry Leslie Choules was born in Oldham, Hampshire, England in 1896. He was educated at Pershore. On completing his education he emigrated to Australia. He enlisted at Black Boy Hill on 29th January 1915, aged 19 and gave his occupation as a contractor. After completing basic training he was sent to Egypt. On 19th April 1915 he left Fremantle aboard HMAT *Argyllshire*. Choules would see action when he was sent to Gallipoli with the 16th Battalion. While on the peninsula he caught a fever and was sent to No.3 General Hospital in Wandsworth, London, England to recover. He was sent back to his battalion in Egypt in 1916 and went to France in June. By March 1917 he had attained the rank of Sergeant.

At Bullecourt he fought his way into the trenches, held his ground for several hours then retired to the railway embankment uninjured. His courage was recognised when he was awarded the Military Medal. His recommendation states:

He showed great coolness and excellent leadership in steadying his men and keeping them well in hand during the advance. In the enemy trenches his organisation of the counter bomb work went far towards enabling us to hold on as long as we did. Throughout the whole operation he displayed a magnificent courage and devotion to duty.[82]

Choules received gunshot wounds to his right arm on 26th September 1917 during the Ypres campaign. He was sent to No.2 Military Hospital, Canterbury, England. On 16th February 1918 Choules returned to the 16th Battalion in France. He returned to Australia on 7th April 1919.

Sergeant Henry Choules.
(*Australia's Fighting Sons of the Empire*)

PRIVATE CECIL HIDE 3476,
16TH BATTALION AIF

Cecil Hide was born in Eastbourne, England in 1888, the son of Samuel and Sarah Hide. Cecil was educated at the Higher Grade School in Eastbourne. He emigrated to Australia and his service record states that he was a 27-year-old shop manager from Kalgoorlie, Western Australia, where he sold boots. Cecil enlisted to join the Australian Infantry Force on 9th August 1915. After completing basic training he left Fremantle aboard HMAT *Benalla* on 1st November bound for Egypt. During early March 1916 he joined the 16th Battalion. After training in Egypt he left Alexandria on the HMT *Canada* bound for Marseille on 1st June. After the week-long passage across the Mediterranean, he arrived at Marseille on the 9th.

Private Cecil Hide would see active service at Pozières and Mouquet Farm during August 1916. On 11th April 1917 Hide was killed during the first battle of Bullecourt. He was with a Lewis Machine Gun section when he was killed by a sniper as he was advancing towards the Hindenburg Line. Witnesses confirmed seeing his body lying near to the German front-line trenches. His remains were not recovered and he was listed as missing. Private Hide has no known grave and his name is commemorated on the Australian National Memorial at Villers-Bretonneux.

Private Cecil Hide. (Australia's Fighting Sons of the Empire)

PRIVATE ARTHUR MORRIS 5751,
16TH BATTALION AIF

Arthur Stanley Morris was born in Sydney in 1889. Arthur worked as a bricklayer in Fremantle. He enlisted to join the AIF on 18th February 1916. After completing his basic training he embarked from Fremantle aboard HMAT *Seang Bee* on 18th July 1916. Private Morris joined the 16th Battalion on 30th October. He was captured during the Battle of Bullecourt on 11th April. A message was sent to London on 26th July 1917 confirming that he was interned at a POW Camp in Limburg, Germany. His wife Maggie was unaware of her

Private Arthur Morris. (Australia's Fighting Sons of the Empire)

husband's fate. Her anxiety was eased when she received official notification on 24th September 1917 that her husband Arthur was being held as a prisoner of war.

He was later transferred to Schneidemuhl Camp. Morris sent the following message dated 25th February 1918, received in London on 22nd March 1918. He wrote: 'I and the rest of the Australian boys with me are well. I have not been very fortunate with my parcels; I have had none for a month now'.[83]

He was repatriated to England on the 18th December 1918 and arrived in Australia on 10th April 1919.

PRIVATE ANDREW OCHILTREE 6131,
16TH BATTALION AIF

Andrew Ochiltree was born in Edinburgh, Scotland, in 1898. When he enlisted to join the AIF on 3rd March 1916 Ochiltree was 18 and working as a horse driver in Perth, Western Australia. He embarked aboard the troopship HMAT *Miltiades* at Fremantle on 7th August 1916. After spending several months in England he was sent to the Western Front on 21st December. Ochiltree joined the 16th Battalion on 2nd January 1917. Prior to going over the top at Bullecourt he met his future brother-in-law, Corporal John (Jock) Williamson, another Scotsman serving with the 16th Battalion. Ochiltree said something that gave offence to Williamson and there was a heated exchange that nearly turned into a brawl, until their comrades persuaded them that it was better to use their energies for fighting the Germans instead of fighting each other. Jock would marry Ochiltree's sister Isabella after the war. Ochiltree would distinguish himself at the Battle of the Menin Road on 26th September 1917 when the 16th Battalion attacked German positions near Zonnebeke. Ochiltree was awarded the Military Medal for his role during this battle. After the war he returned to Australia in 1919. He worked as a dairy farmer, and then later worked in the goldmines.

Private Andrew Orchiltree. (Courtesy John Williamson)

PRIVATE CHRIS PARTLON 3542,
16TH BATTALION AIF

Christopher Joseph Partlon was born in Fremantle on 4th September 1898. He was known as Chris to his family and was brought up in Fremantle. He was educated at the Christian Brothers School. The regime at the school was governed by harsh discipline which did

Private Chris Partlon. (Courtesy Lesley Reid)

not suit Chris's strong personality. He therefore left the school aged fifteen and became a labourer. Tragedy struck the family when his father died on 7th July 1914.

When World War One broke out a few months later, Chris was keen to play a role. According to his granddaughter Lesley Reid her grandfather was 'an adventurous, spirited young man' who found the idea of enlisting and fighting for his country very appealing. Chris was aged 16 and too young to enlist. Undeterred, he lied about his age and enlisted to join the Australian Imperial Force on 26th July 1915 in Perth. His embarkation record states he was aged 18.

He left Australia 1st November 1915 from Fremantle aboard HMAT A24 *Benalla*. He formed part of the 11th Reinforcements for the 16th Battalion. Private Partlon was with the battalion when they took part in the battle of Pozières in August 1916. He again saw action during the first battle of Bullecourt on the 11th April. He belonged to A Company and was one of the few men who overcome the barbed wire defences and attacked the German trenches during that day and managed to withdraw back to Australian lines.

Chris witnessed terrible sights and saw the loss of many friends at Bullecourt. However, Chris recounted to his wife Alice one moment of levity amidst the horror. His granddaughter Lesley heard how 'the mud caked 16th soldiers stumbled into a lingerie factory and found bottles of wine after trudging miles from the trenches. My grandfather had joyfully related the fun and skylarking the boys got up to, getting out of their army gear and putting on the women's apparel.'

While in England, he visited his relations in Ireland on leave. The conflict between the Irish nationalists and the British left Chris in a very uncomfortable situation, mistaken for a British soldier and suspected of being a spy working for the British authorities. Anne Partlon his niece remembered that her Uncle Chris did not speak much about the war; but he did mention the tension in Ireland:

He had some fast talking to do to convince his relatives that he had joined up purely for the adventure. After that 'Kit', as he came to be known in Ireland, was warmly welcomed. He was even urged to stay on and not return to France but felt honour-bound to go back and fight for his country.

When he gained the confidence of his Irish relations, one of them whispered to him that 'there were enough guns and munitions hidden in the hills to blow up all

Ireland.' His Irish hosts referred to him as the 'mad Australian' and the entire village watched him swim across a lough fabled to have been the home of a fearsome monster.

Chris Partlon continued to serve with the AIF until the end of the war. After the Armistice, while still in France, he suffered from the pneumonic plague and was confined to a stretcher. During December 1918, while he was lying on a stretcher awaiting to be transferred onto a train which would transport him to the embarkation port, he overheard an announcement over a loud-hailer that only the walking wounded were allowed on the train and would be evacuated back to England. Chris was convinced that he would not survive another day if he remained in France, so he summoned up the strength to get on his feet and struggle on the train. He would later tell his family that this inner strength that enabled him to board the train saved his life. He arrived in England on 17th December 1918.

Chris Partlon arrived back in Australia on 3rd March 1919 and was discharged from the Australian Army on 26th April. He returned to Fremantle where he worked as a labourer and in August 1920 married Alice Mary Carter. Later that year, their only child, Alice, was born. Chris eventually worked for Massey Fergusson. While working for this company he trained as a tractor mechanic. During the Depression Chris was out of work. In order to make ends meet during those difficult Depression years he set up a business with his brother Bernie delivering fruit and vegetables from a horse drawn cart around the streets of Fremantle. His wife Alice would bake pies and pasties and Chris would sell these door-to-door. Once the Depression came to an end he found work in numerous assembly line jobs, including working for Ford Motor Company, before returning to his job as a tractor mechanic.

Chris was a man of many talents. He taught himself Esperanto, French and some Latin. He was also a practical man and was a keen carpenter and built small boats, caravans and caravanettes, which he sold. His granddaughter Lesley recalled, 'it's my enduring memory as a child of my grandfather with a hammer in his hand and in shorts and a singlet.' Chris was not a religious man, but he was very spiritual and a deep thinker. He was a passionate supporter of the Labour party and would attend political rallies.

Chris Partlon was always a publicly spirited man and was a Red Cross blood donor for most of his life. In 1946 he received a letter of acknowledgement from the Red Cross congratulating him on his many years of donations. Chris was able to buy a small cottage with the help of a War Service Loan and lived there for all his life. He died of leukaemia on 8th June 1969 in the Repatriation Hospital for Returned Servicemen with his family around him.

PRIVATE FRANK RUNNALLS 5783,
16TH BATTALION AIF

Francis Robert Runnalls was born in St Peter's Port, Guernsey. The family emigrated to Australia. Prior to the war Runnalls was a grocer. Runnalls enlisted on 20th

March 1916. After completing basic training he sailed for England on 18th July 1916 aboard HMAT *Seang Bee*. He was wounded at Bullecourt on 11th April and was taken to the Norfolk War Hospital in England to recover from gun shot wounds. He rejoined the 16th Battalion in France during December 1917. On 12th June 1918 Runnalls was wounded at Le Hamel. He regarded Australia as home and returned on 8th July 1919.

Frank Runnalls.
(Australia's
Fighting Sons of
the Empire)

PRIVATE LEONARD RZESZKOWSKI 3037 MM,
16TH BATTALION AIF

Private Leonard Ignatious Rzeszkowski was born in Jamestown, South Australia in 1896. Leonard's father, Ignatious Arthur Rzeszkowski, was Polish and emigrated to Australia from Poznan. Ignatious arrived in Australia with his parents Casimir and Julia in January 1854 and by 1872 Casimir and Ignatious owned many acres of farmland around Belalie near Jamestown. Ignatious and his wife Susan had 10 children of whom Leonard was the youngest. Unfortunately by the time Leonard was seven both his parents had died leaving him an orphan to be raised by his sisters.

Rzeszkowski worked as a hairdresser in Balaklava, South Australia before he enlisted to join the AIF on 10th June 1915. He embarked from Adelaide on 14th September 1915 aboard HMAT *Ballarat* bound for Alexandria in Egypt. He was then transported from Alexandria to Gallipoli on 4th November 1915 where he was assigned to the 16th Battalion. Rzeszkowski served in Gallipoli during the last two months of the campaign, while the battalion was engaged in patrols in No

Man's Land. The 16th Battalion was withdrawn in phases over three days from 18th to 20th December. He left Gallipoli on the second day of the phased withdrawal and would spend

Private Leonard
Rzeszkowski. (Courtesy
Judi Eggers & Norma
Rzeszkowski)

several months in Egypt before being sent with the 16th Battalion to serve on the Western Front arriving in Marseille on 9th June 1916.

Rzeszkowski was with the 16th Battalion when they were deployed to the Somme and played an active role in the fight for Pozières and Mouquet Farm. At midnight on 9th August they attacked and captured Circular Trench situated north of Pozières. They overwhelmed the determined German defenders capturing 70 German prisoners and three Maxim machine guns. Many casualties were inflicted upon the battalion as German artillery responded with a heavy barrage. On 11th August the 16th Battalion repelled a concerted effort by the Germans to recover the ground that they had lost. Later that day, Rzeszkowski and the remnants of the battalion were relieved. The battalion returned to the front line on 29th August and was involved in a failed attempt to capture Mouquet Farm.

Private Rzeszkowski would distinguish himself during the Battle of Bullecourt. By then Rzeszkowski had become a battle-hardened solder through his experiences during the Gallipoli evacuation and the battles on the Somme. He set an example to the less experienced soldiers. Seeing men get caught in the wire he braved enemy fire to return and free many of them. Rzeszkowski was awarded the Military Medal for his selfless actions. His recommendation stated:

> This man was conspicuous amongst many brave men for his coolness and courage during the assault on the HINDENBURG Line on the morning of the 11th April 1917. After getting through the enemy's barbed wire entanglements, he helped other men also to get through at the risk of almost certain death from enemy Machine gun fire which was pouring in from all directions. His fine bravery and example and devotion to duty under most trying circumstances is worthy of the highest commendation and went far towards keeping up the courage of many younger soldiers, for whom this was their first fight.[84]

Rzeszkowski received his Military Medal from General Birdwood on 15th May 1917. On 29th September 1917 he was promoted to Corporal. Several months later Rzeszkowski made Sergeant.

During February 1918, Rzeszkowski attended the 2nd Army Musketry Course. On 4th July 1918 he would take part in his last action of the war, the successful attack upon Le Hamel. At Bullecourt he had witnessed how the tank had let down the Australian Infantry. At Hamel, as part of the Australian Corps commanded by Monash, Rzeszkowski saw how the tank could be successfully used in modern warfare when in conjunction with artillery, air support and infantry. Rzeszkowski received a severe gun shot wound to his left wrist and had to be evacuated to a hospital in Rouen. Two days later he was transported to Southwark Military Hospital in London, England. He convalesced there until 24th August when he was transferred to Harefield Hospital. Although he was a patient he was still under military jurisdiction and liable for punishment if he violated any rules. On 29th September 1918 he went absent without leave from the hospital from 20.00 hours until 18.00 hours the following day. Lieutenant Colonel C Yeatman, who presided over his court martial, realised that this man had earned some time to himself, after going through the trauma of Gallipoli, Pozières and Bullecourt, and decided a reprimand was sufficient together with a fine of one day's pay.

After serving three years and 94 days overseas, he left England on 16th December 1918 for home. He was discharged from the Australian Army in February 1919. After the war and despite the wound to his wrist he resumed his career as a barber running a business in Balaklava and later in Adelaide.

In 1924 Rzeszkowski married Doreen Howard and they settled in Balaklava and bore two sons, Howard and John and two daughters, Marie and Pauline. During the Second World War he re-enlisted in the Australian Army and holding the rank of Sergeant Major he trained soldiers in Queensland. Leonard Ignatious Rzeszowski passed away in 1968 aged 72. He was buried in Centennial Park Cemetery, Adelaide.

LANCE CORPORAL SAMUEL WADESON 2714,
16TH BATTALION AIF

Samuel Jackson Wadeson was born in Diamond Creek, Victoria, in 1887. He was a 27-year-old miner from Meekatharra, Western Australia when he enlisted on 24th June 1915. He was sent to Blackboy Hill for basic training. Four days after he enlisted he wrote the following letter to his mother, Harriet:

Lance Corporal Sam Wadeson.
(Courtesy John Wadeson)

Pt S.J. Wadeson
8th Reinf. 16th Batt.
28/6/15

Dear Mother
No doubt you will be surprised when you hear that I am down here at Blackboy Hill, the training camp for the Expeditionary forces of W.A. I have been out here at the camp for five days now. I left Meekatharra a week ago today. Would have wired to you when leaving there but was not too sure how I would get on with the doctor out here. If I had not passed I intended to go straight back as my job was right up there. But it's far better Mum to go to the war and take a chance than to meet a certain death at the hands of the fat dividend grabbers. And it's up to me to go. I have health and strength. And a lot of the finest men I have met have gone from Meeka.

I was in Perth for a day before coming out here. And had five teeth out. They stung a bit for a while. But are alright now ...

Now dear Mum must tell you that they lined a few hundred of us up today on the parade ground and [they] called for volunteers for the 8th reinforcements for the 16th Battalion. I was one they accepted which will tell you I am looking pretty fit when they only wanted a dozen. We are supposed to leave here in about two or three weeks so are not going to be here very long which is a good job as it is awfully cold and wet here. It has rained off and on ever since I came here. Dear Mother you will want to write right away as soon as you get this as we might have to go at any time. I will find some way to let you know when we sail by wire. I have not been able to get any leave since being here. Now Mum I must tell you and Dad not to fret or worry about me. Remember that there is thousands doing the same and I reckon to do my best when I get to the front. Give my love to all at home and Ede and Ive. Remember me to Don and Andy.[85]

After basic training he embarked on HMAT *Anchises* at Fremantle on 2nd September 1915 for Egypt. Wadeson left Alexandria for Mudros on the 18th October 1915. He joined the 16th Battalion on 24th October. On 2nd November the 16th Battalion returned to Gallipoli and Wadeson would experience life in the trenches for the first time. Wadeson in B Company and the rest of the battalion were sent to garrison 2 sector of the line at Aghyl Dere, which was sub-divided into four sectors known as Franklin's Post, Warwick Castle, Beck's Bluff and Newbury's Post. While posted in this sector Wadeson would have been involved in strengthening the line, securing existing trenches and digging underground dug-outs for accommodation during the cold winter months. Turkish forces dominated No Man's Land and patrols were sent out and in some instances there were skirmishes. During the latter part of November, the evacuation of Gallipoli was in the process of being planned. The 16th Battalion received orders not to fire upon the enemy for a given period of 48 hours and then this period was extended for a further 48 hours. With no Australian shots being fired at

Turkish lines, Turkish soldiers became complacent, their heads and shoulders being visible above their trenches and they were observed walking freely in No Man's Land. The men from the 16th Battalion were eager to shoot but showed great restraint and obeyed orders. At the end of the second 48-hour period they were permitted to fire. A further period of non activity was ordered a few days later which lasted for 96 hours. The purpose of withholding fire was to deceive the Turks into believing quiet periods along this front were part of normal practice, so that when the evacuation did take place, the enemy would not be suspicious and attack the Australians withdrawing. (For the full story of the only success at Gallipoli for the invading forces – the deception before the evacuation – see *Conceal, Create, Confuse* by Martin Davies.) On 14th December Wadeson and his comrades first heard rumours of an evacuation. During the latter part of the month the 16th Battalion withdrew. Captain C Longmore recorded in the 16th Battalion unit history *The Old Sixteenth* how the Turkish units were deceived into thinking that the Australians were still occupying their trenches:

> Automatic rifles were arranged in the trenches so that a desultory fire could be continued for some 20 minutes or so after the last troops had departed. The 16th arranged some by leaving tins of water each with a small hole in the bottom, standing over the tops of empty tins, each of the latter being attached to the trigger of a loaded rifle. The bottom tin, when it filled with sufficient weight of water, would automatically release the trigger and fire the rifle.[86]

Wadeson belonged to the first party from the battalion to leave Gallipoli. He was evacuated at 10.40 pm on 18th December. Arriving in Alexandria he remained in Egypt for several months. He arrived in Marseille on 9th June 1916.

Wadeson took part in the battle for Pozières, when on the 9th August 1916, the 16th Battalion overwhelmed Circular Trench and captured 70 prisoners and three machine guns. The following day, the battalion came under heavy German artillery fire, but this did not prevent them from further advances. The 16th Battalion consolidated their gains and established a communication trench from the captured positions back to Australian lines.

The 16th Battalion was placed in reserve for the next two weeks, but returned to the region to attempt to capture Mouquet Farm during the night of 29th August. Wadeson belonged to B Company commanded by Major Percy Black. After the preparatory bombardment, the 16th Battalion stormed the objective. Although Mouquet Farm was captured, the soldiers from the 16th battalion found themselves isolated from their own lines when German infantrymen appeared behind them from the labyrinth of underground tunnels and passageways which had not been cleared. Wadeson and the 16th Battalion were in no position to hold onto Mouquet Farm and were compelled to fight their way back into their starting trenches.

Sam Wadeson was promoted to Lance Corporal on 3rd March 1917. At Bullecourt he was carrying a Lewis Gun across No Man's Land when he was hit, either by machine gun fire or shrapnel 50 yards before the wire. Several comrades recorded Wadeson's last moments. Sergeant James McMahan:

> I was to the right of him when we went over at Bullecourt on April 11th. Corporal Pratter of B Co. told me he got knocked a few yards after we went over, in the arm. Pratter went and spoke to him. He said 'Go on, I'm all right'. He was in a shell hole. Pratter took his Lewis Gun from him. He thought that he would get back to the Dressing Station all right. I always thought that he had gone through a Dressing Station. He was only slightly wounded.[87]

Company Quartermaster Robert Battison reported that 'I saw him fall seriously wounded right in the German barbed wire. He was in my section and I passed right over him.' He was hit in the legs and shoulder – badly hit.'[88] Lance Corporal Samuel Jackson Wadeson was buried at Quéant Road Cemetery.

PRIVATE HERBERT CLARK 462,
46TH BATTALION AIF

Herbert Clark was born on 21st December 1885 at Seasowes Farm, Stretton in Staffordshire, England. In 1888, his family emigrated to Australia and settled in Carlton, a suburb of Melbourne. Prior to the war he moved to Colac, a town situated west of Melbourne. Here he worked as a coach painter and served for five years with the Colac Garrison Artillery, a part-time territorial force. Herbert Clark enlisted on 19th August 1914 aged 31. After completing his basic training he left Australia for Egypt on 19th October.

He was attached to the 8th Battalion initially and joined the Mediterranean Expeditionary Force on 5th April 1915. Clark and the 8th Battalion landed at Anzac during the morning of the 25th April as part of the second wave assault force. He braved Turkish artillery fire and sniper and machine gun fire from Turkish troops entrenched on the cliff tops. On 5th May the 8th Battalion was redeployed to Cape Helles to assist the British with their attack on Krithia. Herbert Clark would take part in another landing at Gallipoli disembarking from landing barges near to the River Clyde at V Beach.

Soldiers recuperating in either France or England, with Private Herbert Clarke in the wheelchair second from left holding up the mug. Clarke was wounded at Bullecourt on 11th April 1917. (Courtesy Helen Turnball)

The 8th Battalion landed at Cape Helles with minimal casualties and promptly headed inland. The battalion suffered 38 casualties for small gains during this offensive. The 8th Battalion was later sent back to Anzac Beach to secure the beachhead.

Private Clark was admitted to hospital on various occasions while at Gallipoli. Diarrhoea was suffered by many soldiers who fought in the trenches at Gallipoli. Clark succumbed on 30th August and was admitted to the 1st Advanced Casualty Clearing Station at Mudros. His illness soon developed into gastro-enteritis and he was transferred to the 25th Casualty Clearing station at Imbros. He was transferred by hospital ship to Malta and admitted to St Patrick's Hospital with debility and varicocele. He was then sent to England arriving on 20th October when he was sent to the 1st Southern General Hospital in Plymouth. After he was fully recovered Clark returned to the 8th Battalion. The battalion had been evacuated from Gallipoli and was now in Egypt. Clark left Plymouth aboard a troopship on 22nd February 1916 and arrived in Alexandria on 5th March. He was hospitalised once again on arrival in Egypt and rejoined the 8th Battalion on 11th March. He only spent days with his old battalion and because of his experience he was transferred to the newly formed 46th Battalion.

The 46th Battalion departed from Alexandria on 2nd June 1916 bound for France. They arrived in Marseille on 8th June. On 20th July Private Clark was charged with being unshaven while on parade. He was docked one day's pay.

During early August, the 46th Battalion were deployed to positions near to Pozières on the Somme and worked in carrying and fatigue parties. On 12th August the 46th Battalion launched an attack upon the German Switch Line at Pozières. On 13th August

he was admitted to the 7th Field Ambulance with shell shock.

After more periods in hospital, the war ended on 11th April 1917 for Private Herbert Clark when he suffered a gun shot wound to the right leg. Evacuated from the battlefield, he was admitted to a military hospital in Rouen on 13th April. His wounds were so bad that he was transferred to England and sent to the 1st Birmingham War Hospital. Clark was sent back to Australia from Weymouth on 28th August 1917. He arrived back in Melbourne, Australia on 22nd October. Clark was discharged from the AIF as medically unfit for service due to disability caused by military service on 25th February 1918.

PRIVATE ALBERT DAVIES 4480A,
46TH BATTALION AIF

Private Albert Henry Davies was born in Balnarring, Victoria on 8th February 1894. Known as 'Harry', he was the eldest of four children born to Albert and Maud Davies. A year after Harry's birth, the family moved to Mornington. Harry was educated at Mornington State School. After leaving school Harry worked around the Mornington area until. During August 1911, aged 17 he moved to Richmond where he began an apprenticeship as a bootmaker for H. Perry and Co. When World War One broke out Harry joined the City Military forces 56th Infantry, based at Richmond. Harry served on a part time basis and would attend weekend training camps and evening drills.

Harry enlisted on 29th July 1915. After completing four months of basic training he was assigned to the 15th Battalion, 14th Reinforcements, at Williamstown. By the end of 1915 he was heading for the war in Europe. Harry left Melbourne on 28th December 1915 aboard HMAT *Themistocles* bound for Egypt. He arrived in Alexandria on 22nd February. While in Egypt he joined a training battalion for two months. On 21st March Davies was assigned to the newly created 46th Battalion based at Serape, near Alexandria. On 2nd June the 46th Battalion sailed for Marseille. They arrived in France on 8th June.

Harry experienced war for the first time when the 46th Battalion took part in the battle for Pozières during early August. Harry formed part of the carrying parties that brought supplies and ammunition

Private Albert Davies. (Courtesy Kevin Davies)

to front-line battalions. He also experienced two periods holding the front-line trenches at Pozières. After surviving on the Somme and the harsh cold winter on 1916–17, Harry Davies would take part in his final battle when the 46th Battalion attacked Bullecourt. He was aged 23 when he was killed on 11th April. He has no known grave and his name is commemorated on the Australian National Memorial at Villers-Bretonneux.

PRIVATE CLAUDE JONES 1938A,
46TH BATTALION AIF

Claude Powell Jones was born in Newport, Victoria in August 1889. He was a carpenter from Newport, Victoria when he joined up on 1st April 1916. After completing his basic training he embarked aboard HMAT *Medic* at Melbourne on 20th May. He arrived in England in July. He was based in Rollerstone while in England until the end of September when he was shipped to France. He joined the 46th Battalion on 19th October.

Private Hall reported seeing Jones on 11th April:

> I saw him in the German 1st line trench at Bullecourt on April 11th 1917, daylight. He had been hit in the stomach. I spoke to him but he was just about done. He had been bandaged and asked to be allowed to remain where he was, as he felt that he was done. We lost the ground the same day. Jones was left behind.[89]

Private R. Pilkington, another mate who referred to Jones by his nickname 'Clarry' confirmed 'he had been shot through the abdomen by a bullet. I don't think he could live many minutes as he looked very low and was in great pain.'[90]

Private Claude Jones' remains were not recovered. His name is commemorated on the National Australian Memorial at Villers-Bretonneux.

PRIVATE JOHN ORD LAING 2284,
46TH BATTALION AIF

John Ord Laing was born in St. Kilda, Victoria, in June 1894. He worked as a grocer before the war. Laing enlisted in Coburg on 23rd March 1916. He had completed his basic training during the summer and on 16th August embarked aboard RMS *Orontes* at Port Melbourne bound for England. He arrived in Plymouth,

England, on 2nd October 1916. After spending two months in England training, Laing was sent to France. He embarked aboard *Princess Clementine* on 4th December and sailed for Boulogne. He was sent to Etaples for further training from 5th to 29th December. Laing joined the 46th Battalion AIF on 29th December.

Laing was last seen in the German trenches at Bullecourt on 11th April, limping with a wound to his foot. Private Albert Smith from the 46th Battalion later reported: 'On the 11th April 1917 I saw No. 2284 Pte Laing lying wounded in the trench at Bullecourt. The trench was taken by the Germans and in my opinion Pte Laing would be made a prisoner as he only appeared to have a foot wound.'[91] Private H.R. Dellar from the 46th Battalion reported:

> The last I saw of No. 2284 Pte. Laing J.O. 46th Battalion was about 11.20 am on April 11th 1917, in the Hindenburg Line in the vicinity of Bullecourt, just previous to the evacuation. He was wounded in the foot and limping badly and was proceeding in the direction of a German dug-out in which were other wounded men. Whether he left the trench or not I cannot say.'[92]

Laing was killed during that day and his remains were not recovered. Laing was aged 23 and his name is commemorated on the Australian National Memorial at Villers-Bretonneux.

PRIVATE FRANCIS WILLIAMS 2005,
46TH BATTALION AIF

According to his service record Francis was born in Melbourne. He had served in the town cadets for four years and had previously tried to enlist, but was refused because his chest measurement did not meet the required criteria. The fact of the matter was that Francis Williams was a boy and too young to serve in the AIF. Nonetheless he persevered and enlisted on 27th March 1916. He gave his age as 18 but he was he was 15. He gave his occupation as a grocer working at Moonie Ponds, Victoria. On completing his basic training he was sent to England for further training. He arrived in France on 13th March 1917 and joined the 46th Battalion. Private Francis Williams was aged 16 when he

was killed on 11th April. He has no known grave and his name is commemorated on the Villers-Bretonneux Memorial.

Private Francis Williams. (Courtesy Jean & Denise Letaille Bullecourt Museum)

PRIVATE ARTHUR TOFT 2726,
47TH BATTALION AIF

Private Arthur Toft MM. (Courtesy Lloyd Toft)

Arthur Stanley Toft was born in Bundaberg, Queensland, in May 1896. He worked as a clerk and served with the Territorial Army in Bundaberg before the war. He enlisted on 22nd June 1916.

Toft embarked aboard HMAT *Marathon* on 27th October 1916 from Brisbane bound for England where he carried out further training. On 28th March 1917 he sailed to France from Folkestone and was assigned to the 47th Battalion on 7th April. Within four days he would experience active service for the first time when the 47th Battalion took part in the attack on Bullecourt.

Toft received a severe gun shot wound to his left leg on 12th October 1917 during the Battle of Passchendaele. He was admitted to Horton County of London War Hospital in Epsom on 18th October. On 25th May 1918 Toft was transferred to 45th Battalion. He would play a role in the final months of the war. On 8th August 1918 he distinguished himself at the Battle of Amiens. Toft was awarded the Military Medal on 12th August 1918. His recommendation stated:

> During the operations East of Hamel on 8th August 1918, this soldier was a member of a mopping up party in Caroline Wood, whilst clearing several dug-outs he was fired on from one of them. At great risk he rushed this dug-out, killed two of the occupants, and took the remaining six prisoners. This soldier has always done good work and his courage and coolness are remarkable.[93]

Toft and the 45th Battalion would fight their last battle of the war on 18th September 1918 at Le Verguier where they assaulted and captured the German line that guarded the approach to the main defences on the Hindenburg Line. Toft was wounded a second time during this battle. He was evacuated to England on 21st September 1918 and was admitted to Reading War Hospital. Toft was discharged from the Army on 19th March 1919.

LANCE CORPORAL HAROLD BEECHEY 200,
48TH BATTALION AIF

Harold Reeve Beechey was born in 1891 at Friesthorpe Rectory, at Friesthorpe, Lincolnshire, England. He was the son of the Reverend Prince William Thomas and

Lance Corporal Harold Beechey. (Courtesy De Aston School)

Amy Beechey from Lincoln. Harold was educated at De Aston School. After completing his education he worked in agriculture. In 1912 his father died and during the following year, when Harold was aged 22, following his brother Christopher, he emigrated to Australia where he became a farmer.

Beechey enlisted to join the AIF on 9th September 1914 at Helena Vale, Western Australia and was attached to the 16th Battalion. After completing his training Beechey embarked with the 16th Battalion aboard HMAT *Ceramic* at Melbourne on 22nd December and set sail for Egypt.

He joined the Mediterranean Expeditionary Force that took part in the landing at Anzac Cove, Gallipoli on 25th April 1915. Within a month he was struck down by influenza and dysentery. He was suffering from dysentery so badly that he was sent back to Egypt where he recovered in hospital. He returned to the 16th Battalion on 22nd July and was sick in August once again and hospitalised between 22nd and 29th August. He was sent back to Egypt on 9th September and admitted to a hospital in Cairo with diarrhoea, then to a hospital in Cardiff, Wales.

During this period, Harold was grieving for his brother Sergeant Bernard Reeve Beechey who was killed on 25th September 1915 while serving with the 2nd Battalion Lincolnshire Regiment. Bernard has no known grave and his name is commemorated on the Ploegsteert Memorial in Belgium.

After regaining his health Harold was sent back to Egypt where he was assigned to the newly formed 48th Battalion on 26th April 1916. He arrived in Marseille in June 1916. Within weeks the 48th Battalion received their baptism of fire on the Somme. During the attack on Pozières on 6th August while carrying messages Beechey suffered gun shot wounds to his chest, face and left arm as well as suffering from a fractured jaw. He was evacuated from the battlefield to Boulogne the following day and was admitted to the 5th Southern General Hospital in Portsmouth on 12th August. Beechey wrote in a letter home: 'Very lucky, nice round shrapnel through arm and chest, but did not penetrate ribs. Feel I could take it out myself with a knife.'[94]

While recovering from his wounds, Harold learned that another brother, 2nd Lieutenant Frank Collett Reeve Beechey, was killed on 14th November 1916 while serving with the 13th Battalion East Yorkshire Regiment. He was buried at Warlincourt Halte British Cemetery, Saulty.

On 25th November 1916 Beechey returned to the 48th Battalion in France. He was denied the opportunity to go on leave prior to returning to his battalion on the Western Front. He complained to his mother, Amy: 'To deny a fellow the right of a final leave seems to me to be a miserable spitefulness on their part.'[95]

Beechey was promoted to Lance Corporal on 5th January 1917. Harold Beechey was killed on 10th April. He was digging a dug-out close to the Railway Embankment when he was killed by the same shell that killed Major Ben Leane. Corporal Stanley Smith reported:

> ... the Germans sent a couple of shells over and he was severely wounded about the body and legs. He died two hours afterwards and was unconscious most of the time. He was a L/Cpl at the time and very popular amongst the men. I knew him well. I did not see the grave but was told he was buried about 50 yards away from place where he was killed. I saw him before he died and also after his death. Pte. Martin 48th Battn. A Coy. who was a Runner told me he saw him buried near Major Leane's grave, same shell killed both men.[96]

Beechey was 26. His remains were not recovered, which meant that he has no known grave. His name is commemorated on the Memorial at Villers-Bretonneux. His mother Amy wrote to Harold's friends:

> Thank you very much for your kindness in sending me details of the death of my son L/Cpl HR Beechey 48 Battalion. I am thankful that he did not suffer long. Poor boy, he had been invalided twice and wounded once and we hoped he would come through.[97]

Cruelly, unbearably, Amy would suffer further bereavement when a fourth son, Private Charles Reeve Beechey, served with the 25th Battalion, Royal Fusiliers was killed on 10th October 1917 and was buried Dar Es Salaam War Cemetery, Tanzania.

2ND LIEUTENANT WILLIAM BLASKETT
48th BATTALION AIF

William George Blaskett was born in Folkestone, England on 18th April 1895. Blaskett attended the Simon Langton School in Canterbury. In 1913 aged 17 he sailed to Australia aboard the *Omrah* to seek a new life. He settled in South Australia and prior to the war he worked as a clerk in Bowden. Blaskett enlisted

2nd Lt William Blaskett photographed when he held the rank of Sergeant.
(Courtesy Malcolm Blaskett)

on 2nd August 1915. Although he was 20 years old his mother Elenor wrote a letter confirming her consent to her son joining the AIF. Blaskett was accepted as a private, given the service number 3232 and assigned to the 16th Battalion. After completing basic training he embarked aboard HMAT *Benalla* at Adelaide on 27th October 1915 and six weeks later he arrived in Egypt. On 9th March he was transferred to the newly formed 48th Battalion. Blaskett climbed quickly through the ranks and during April 1916 he was promoted to the rank of Sergeant. On 11th May he received a gun shot wound to his left hand. The wound may have occurred during a training exercise in the Egyptian desert. Blaskett was sent to France with the 48th Battalion in June 1916. On 8th August Blaskett received a gun shot wound to his back while in action at Pozières. Once he had recovered from his wounds he returned to the 48th Battalion on 20th November. On 23rd February 1917 Blaskett was commissioned as 2nd Lieutenant. On 11th April Blaskett led No.5 Platoon, B Company at Bullecourt. He was killed by machine gun fire as he fought his way into the German trenches. He sustained a bullet wound to the head which killed him instantly. Blaskett has no known grave and his name is commemorated on the Australian National Memorial at Villers-Bretonneux. His bereaved parents William and Elenor Blaskett named their home at Ninth Street in Bowden, South Australia 'Bullecourt'.

PRIVATE WILLIAM DOYLE 2649,
48TH BATTALION AIF

William Doyle was born in Geraldton, Western Australia, in 1898. Doyle worked as a labourer before enlisting on 19th May 1916. On completing his basic training he left Australia on 30th October for England aboard HMAT *Melbourne*. He arrived at Devonport on 28th December. Arriving in France in January, Doyle joined the 48th Battalion on 10th February 1917. He was aged 19 when he was killed at Bullecourt. Private D. Hanley later recalled:

Private William Doyle.
(*Australia's Fighting Sons of the Empire*)

We were in front of the enemy's wire before the 2nd line trench, he was hit by Machine Gun bullet in the shoulder, bullet penetrated down into his body. I bandaged him up, later he was killed outright by a minnie shell, was not knocked about. I saw him after this happened, he was dead. We were taken prisoner of war later in the day. His body would be left in the field.[98]

He has no known grave and his name is commemorated on the Memorial at Villers-Bretonneux.

LIEUTENANT COLONEL RAYMOND LEANE, COMMANDING OFFICER
48TH BATTALION AIF

Raymond Lionel Leane was born on 12th July 1878 at Prospect, Southern Australia. He was educated at the North Adelaide Public School. He became a commercial traveller. In 1905 his work brought him to Albany where he joined the 11th (Perth Rifles) Infantry Regiment commissioned with the rank of 2nd Lieutenant. Three years later he bought a retail business at Kalgoorlie, where he joined the local Goldfields Infantry Regiment, reaching the rank of Captain in 1910.

He joined the 11th Battalion AIF as a Company Commander with the rank of Captain on 25th August 1914. Affectionately known as 'Bull' by the men he commanded Raymond Leane was in command of A Company, 11th Battalion during the landing on Anzac Cove on 25th April 1915.

On 4th May Leane led a dangerous beach assault upon the Turkish Fortress at Gaba Tepe. The Turkish forces defended the trenches with great determination thwarting any opportunity of establishing a beachhead. Leane and his party of 110 men were pinned down by heavy machine gun fire and were unable to get off the beach. Leane sustained a bullet wound to his hand, withdrew his men and rescued the wounded under heavy Turkish fire. Although the operation failed, Leane was awarded the Military Cross for his role at Gaba Tepe.

Leane was wounded during an attack upon Bolton Ridge during 28th June 1915. Within a month Leane was back in action again. On 31st July Leane led a successful attack upon a Turkish trench. It became known as Leane's Trench. Leane received wounds to his head from a shell. During August he was promoted to Temporary Major and in September 1915 he was appointed temporary commander of the 11th Battalion. Leane was promoted to Major in October and the following month he was promoted to the rank of Lieutenant Colonel. During March 1916 he was appointed commanding officer of the 48th Battalion. Several of his relatives also served in this battalion, including his brother Ben and nephew Allan. It was therefore known as the 'Joan of Arc Battalion' because it was made of 'All-Leanes'.

The five Leane brothers. Edwin, seated left, served in the ordnance service. Allan Leane, seated right, commanded the 28th Battalion and was killed on 4th January 1917 at Delville Wood. Major Ben Leane standing left, was the youngest brother and was second in command of the 48th Battalion when he was killed by shell fire near the railway embankment at Bullecourt on 10th April. Earlier during the war while serving with the 10th Battalion on Gallipoli he had been wounded in the right arm and was unable to effectively fire his rifle. Determined to help his comrades in arms he endeavoured to carry boxes of ammunition while under fire. Lieutenant Colonel Ray Leane (standing centre) found his brother Ben's remains and buried them. Ernest Leane standing right served with the 27th Battalion. One of his sons, Allan, was wounded in OG 1 where he was last seen. He was captured but it was later reported that he died in a German hospital on 2nd May 1917. (AWM – P02136.001)

During 1916, Leane led the 48th Battalion at Pozières, Mouquet Farm and Geudecourt. At Bullecourt during the following year, he established his headquarters near to the railway embankment. Bullecourt was a national tragedy for Australia, but it was a personal tragedy for Lieutenant Colonel Leane: he lost his brother Ben and his nephew Allan. 'His loss cast a heavy gloom over the whole battalion.'[99]

Leane personally searched among the dead bodies for his brother Ben. Ben's head and leg was all that he found. Ben's head and face appeared to have been uninjured despite the rest of his body being pulverised by the shell. Lieutenant Colonel Leane carried his brother's remains in his arms back to Australian lines where he dug his grave and buried him. Captain N.G. Imlay, the 48th Battalion's Lewis gun officer wrote:

> Major Ben Leane was missing, and despite the widest searches for him, he could not be found. It was not until the following morning when the battalion was again in position for the jump-off, that Col. Leane discovered Ben's body. Ben had evidently collected a shell all to himself the previous day.

After the temporary interment, and standing bareheaded for a few minutes, the Colonel said, 'I'll attend to you again, later, Ben, old man'. He then resumed command of the situation.[100]

Major Alban Moyes, 48th Battalion, paid this tribute to Leane:

> There are men who grip you by their very personality. They radiate strength, put fresh courage into the weary, and give renewed spirit to the hopeless. Such a man was Raymond Lionel Leane, CB, CMG, DSO, MC, the commanding officer of the 48th Battalion at Bullecourt ... Stern and unrelenting in his sense of duty, a man who if he knew the meaning of fear, kept his knowledge well hidden under an iron will, his very demeanour an inspiration to those who had the honour of serving with him.[101]

Captain Norman Imlay wrote that Leane 'was made of case-hardened steel; he was a marvel both physically and mental, but did not know it. He never went sick, and nothing could turn him from his set purpose, provided he was convinced of the rightness of such purpose.'[102]

Leane continued to lead his battalion through the battle of Messines during June 1917 and in the autumn in Flanders. On 12th October 1917 Leane was severely wounded at Passchendaele and spent three months recovering from his wounds. On 1st June 1918, Leane was promoted to Brigadier-General and appointed commander of 12th Brigade until the end of the war. He was awarded the Military Cross, the Distinguished Service Order and bar, as well as a Croix de Guerre. On returning to Australia after the war, Leane was appointed South Australia's Police Commissioner in March 1920. Leane served during the Second World War as senior officer of the Volunteer Defence Corps. He retired from the police during 1944 and was knighted in 1945. Raymond Leane lived in retirement in Adelaide until his death on 25th June 1962.

CORPORAL TOM LOXTON MM 4164,
48TH BATTALION AIF

Thomas Samuel Loxton was born in 1894 at Leigh's Creek, South Australia. Tom worked as a labourer in Mannum, South Australia. Tom enlisted to join the AIF on 1st September 1915 as a Private in an Adelaide recruiting office. After completing his basic training he embarked aboard the troopship HMAT *Borda* at Adelaide on 11th January 1916 and sailed for Egypt. He was initially assigned to the 16th Battalion but after he had arrived in Egypt he was transferred to the 48th Battalion. During early June he was sent to France aboard the troopship HMAT *Caledonia*. Arriving in Marseille on 9th June he continued his journey to the Western Front.

Loxton saw action for the first time at Pozières on the Somme during August 1916. During the 5th August the 48th Battalion was ordered to recover wounded men from other battalions from OG 2 Trench under heavy German artillery fire. The battalion had suffered 598 casualties as a result of this torrent of German shells. In the days that followed Loxton would have endured further German shelling on Pozières Ridge. On 7th August German infantry overran positions held by the 48th Battalion. Many were captured, but at a pivotal point in the battle Lieutenant Albert Jacka and a small party of men from the 14th Battalion led a counter attack against the advancing Germans and altered the course of the battle in favour of the Australians. No doubt Loxton was there and would have played some role in this action. Towards the end of August 1916, the remnants of the 48th Battalion defended ground captured at Mouquet Farm.

He was promoted to Corporal on 13th October in the field. On 26th November Loxton was one of six men from the 48th Battalion who were wounded during a patrol near Flers. Loxton was admitted to a military hospital in Rouen with gun shot wounds to his hand and fingers. After recovering from his wounds he returned to his battalion on 19th January 1917.

On 11th April Corporal Loxton advanced with the 48th Battalion. Loxton was one of the first men from the

Battalion to reach OG 1 Trench. He fought bravely and was responsible for inflicting many casualties with his Lewis gun. He retired from the German lines but was later wounded that day. Lieutenant Colonel Raymond Leane recognised

Private Tom Loxton. (David Bomford)

Loxton's role at Bullecourt by recommending him for the Military Medal. His recommendation states:

> At Bullecourt for gallantry and devotion to duty during the attack on the Hindenburg Line on 11th April 1917. Cpl. Loxton went forward carrying two panniers and a Lewis Gun and was one of the first to reach the objective. He immediately got his guns into action and inflicted casualties on the enemy. Retiring he showed great coolness and presence of mind and set a fine example of soldierly bearing and devotion to duty. He was eventually wounded.[103]

He was transferred to Colchester Military Hospital in Essex on 18th April with gun shot wounds to the neck. After recovering he returned to the 48th Battalion on 25th August. He received promotion to Sergeant on 9th October.

Sergeant Loxton's war would come to an end when he was wounded in early March 1918. He was admitted to the 2nd Casualty Clearing Station on 5th March suffering from a gun shot wound to the right thigh and pneumonia. He was transferred to England and was sent to a military hospital in Bury St Edmunds. Loxton's wounds necessitated the amputation of his right leg from the knee. He returned aboard the hospital ship *Kanowna* to Australia on 30th June and was discharged from the army later that year. Tom Loxton resumed life as a civilian at Moorook on the River Murray, where he established an orange orchard. He still kept in contact with the men from the 48th Battalion after the war. He became great mates with Brigadier-General Raymond Leane and named one of his own sons Ray. After Tom Loxton died, his widow was denied a service pension by the authorities. Brigadier-General Leane intervened in the matter and helped Tom's widow get the pension.

When he passed away, Tom Loxton was buried in the West Terrace Cemetery, Adelaide, South Australia, in the Soldiers Memorial section. His headstone bears the insignia of the 48th Battalion.

PRIVATE ALFRED OXMAN 4684,
48TH BATTALION AIF

Alfred William Oxman was born in Perth during 1892. He went to school in Narrogin. Oxman and joined the AIF in Perth on 20th November 1915. Prior to enlistment he was a labourer living in Narrogin,

Private Alfred Oxman.
(Australia's Fighting Sons of the Empire)

Western Australia. He was 24 at the time of enlistment. Oxman left Fremantle on HMAT *Miltiades* on 12th February 1916, arriving at Port Suez on 11th March. He was assigned to the 48th Battalion at Serapeum and in June he embarked on the HMT *Caledonia* from Alexandria, bound for Marseille.

Private Oxman was carrying bombs and ammunition with Private Eric Kelly across No Man's Land to their comrades of the 48th Battalion holding onto their positions in the Hindenburg Line when he was shot and killed by machine gun fire. Kelly recalled the moment when his pal Alfred Oxman was killed:

> We were in a carrying party taking ammunition to a trench that we had recently occupied. The machine guns were firing at us all the way across when I was hit on the arm and looking round to tell Oxman I saw him lying on the ground. He took two deep breaths and then never moved again. The Germans were all around us by this time, so I took cover in a shell hole and had to remain there from 7.00 am until it was dark when I crawled out and Oxman was still there as he had been in the morning.[104]

Oxman was listed as missing and his name is commemorated on the Australian National Memorial at Villers-Bretonneux.

PRIVATE JAMES MCCABE 2706,
48TH BATTALION AIF

James McCabe was born in Glasgow, Scotland in 1888. He emigrated to Western Australia where he worked as a coal miner at Collie. McCabe joined the AIF on 23rd May 1916. He left Melbourne on 30th October arriving at Devonport, England on 28th December. He joined the 48th Battalion in France on 6th April 1917. McCabe was killed in his action at Bullecourt on 11th

April, aged 28. His body was seen in the trenches of the Hindenburg Line, but was never recovered. He has no known grave and his name is commemorated on the Memorial at Villers-Bretonneux.

Private James McCabe.
(Australia's Fighting Sons of the Empire)

PRIVATE WILLIAM PARSONS 5849,
48TH BATTALION AIF

William Gordon Parsons was born in Orroroo, South Australia in December 1894. He was the son of Thomas Herbert and Annie Maria Parsons. Known as Gordon

to his family, he worked as a labourer before the war. He enlisted in Morchard on 18th April 1916. He served 2½ years in the 24th Light Horse.

He embarked from Melbourne aboard the HMAT *Barambah* on 27th June 1916. He arrived in Plymouth on 25th August. He spent several weeks with the 3rd Training Battalion and then was sent to France on 14th October. After two weeks further training at Etaples he joined the 48th Battalion.

William Parsons was aged 23 when he was killed at Bullecourt. His remains were not recovered and his name is commemorated on the Memorial at Villers-Bretonneux.

PRIVATE GEORGE PURDIE 1973,
48TH BATTALION AIF

George Gardner Purdie was born in Bute, South Australia in 1896. He worked as a farm labourer. Purdie enlisted on 6th March 1916. He embarked from Adelaide aboard HMAT *Seang Bee* on 13th July for France. On 4th December he was assigned to the 48th Battalion.

During the night before the first battle of Bullecourt Private George Purdie belonged to a party of men digging hop-over trenches near to the railway embankment. (A hop-over trench was a small trench where assaulting infantry could take shelter from enemy shelling before an attack.) As they were digging these trenches in the snow, the enemy would have known what they were doing as they could see the freshly dug earth above the snow, even under the cover of darkness.

Purdie was the second man in a Lewis gun team and he carried panniers of ammunition and a rifle. As Purdie advanced across No Man's Land a shell burst behind his comrade Private Wilfred Nankivell. As mud oozed down his leg it was assumed that Nankivell had been wounded, so he was carried away on a stretcher. Purdie received a gun shot wound to his right knee. Purdie's knee was shattered. As Nankivell was evacuated it was realised that he was not wounded and he was therefore reassigned as a stretcher bearer. Nankivell came to Purdie's assistance.

Private George Purdie.
(Courtesy Judi Eggers & Norma Rzeskowski)

Purdie was sent to the base hospital in Havre by train. His right leg was amputated from the middle of the thigh. Discharged from the Australian Army as medically unfit for service on 13th July 1917, he returned to Australia. George Purdie recalled his experience of being transported to hospital to his son Colin Purdie:

> He always joked that the train had square wheels because by the time he reached the base hospital his knee was by now not only mutilated but bent at a 90 degree angle. The doctor took a smell of his knee and sent him straight to the operating theatre to have it amputated. It was already becoming gangrenous and the death rate for wounds with gangrene was very high. Scars around George's stump were from the cutting of the surgeons who were taking away the gangrene or allowing the poison to escape.[105]

When he returned home he met and married Coral Berriman who was a nurse working at the Bute hospital. Coral's family had some hesitancy about her marrying him because they did not think he would be able to support her or raise a family following the amputation. George would prove that he was able to work and provide for his wife. He first worked as a Post Master at Port McDonnell, and then he moved to Truro and worked in another post office. As the years passed he still suffered from his wounds. He left his position with the Post Office and bought a delicatessen in Laura which he managed with Coral. George would take deliveries of fruit and vegetables around to different homesteads in the district. George also worked as an agent for Radiola to earn more income and sold and repaired radios and electrical goods. Coral was a very supportive and understanding wife for she cared for George and the kept the business going at the same time. George and Coral had three daughters and a son, Joan, Norma, Valda and Colin.

George's daughter Norma Rzeskowski recalled that her father seldom spoke of his experiences with her or her sisters. George suffered leg tremors and his stump would sometimes shake and jump. At other times he could feel his full 'phantom' limb. He would use a wooden leg. The leather straps that were attached would occasionally break and he would fall down. George had numerous operations on his leg in order to help with the scarring and ease the discomfort. His daughter Valda recalled:

> I heard him mention how the nurses frequently pinned his bandages to the stump of his leg by mistake as it was difficult to keep the bandages on. I'm not sure if his stump was numb or so painful he didn't register the pin pricks.

George Purdie would reflect upon his war experiences and recall to his children the times in the trenches when they starved. His daughter Valda remembered:

> Dad didn't speak much about the war except when we children wouldn't eat our meals or wasted our food. He would tell us how the soldiers would lay in trenches of muddy water and if they were lucky enough to have a loaf of bread they would have to squeeze the muddy water out of it before being able to eat it.

George Purdie died aged 77 on 13th February 1974.

SERGEANT ROBERT RAFFERTY MM 2694,
48TH BATTALION AIF

Robert Scott Rafferty was born in Paisley, Scotland in 1893. He was a carter from Victoria Park, Western Australia. He enlisted to join the Australian Army on 21st June 1915 as a private of the 16th Battalion. On completing his basic training he left Fremantle on the HMAT *Anchises* on 2nd September 1915 bound for Egypt.

He was transferred to the newly formed 48th Battalion on 3rd March 1916. Rafferty was promoted to Corporal during June. Arriving in Marseille on 9th June Rafferty and the 48th battalion were sent to the Somme region. He was wounded during the Battle of Pozières on 14th August 1916. Weeks later he was promoted to temporary Sergeant and by early December he became a full Sergeant.

During the Battle of Bullecourt, Rafferty was heavily involved with the fighting to retain the sections captured in OG 1 and OG 2 trenches. When he was ordered to withdraw he saw a wounded officer sheltering in a shell hole. Instead of saving himself and heading for the Railway Embankment he went to the aid of this officer, stayed with him until it was dark and brought him to the safety of Australian lines later that evening. Lieutenant Colonel Raymond Leane recommended Rafferty to receive the Military Medal:

> At Bullecourt on 11th April 1917 for gallant conduct and devotion to duty during the attack and occupation of the HINDENBURG LINE. When the order to retire was given he fell back in good order with his men, but seeing a wounded officer in a shell hole near enemy wire he remained until dark and carried him into safety.[106]

Rafferty received a commission and was promoted to 2nd Lieutenant on 4th May 1917.

Sergeant Robert Rafferty MM.
(Courtesy Noeleen Ridgeway)

PRIVATE HORACE SHEPHERD 2243,
48TH BATTALION AIF

Horace Reginald Shepherd was born in Hindmarsh a suburb of Adelaide on 23rd August 1889. Known as Reg to his family, he was the son of Charles Robert and Ida Elizabeth Shepherd. Before the war he worked as a joiner in Mount Gambier. Shepherd enlisted to join the AIF aged 28 on 28th April 1916. After completing his basic training he embarked on the troopship HMAT *Ballarat* on 12th August 1916 from Adelaide. Private Reg Shepherd arrived in Plymouth, England on 30th September to undergo further training. He left Folkestone on the SS *Victoria* en-route to Boulogne in France on 20th November 1916. After spending two weeks training at the notorious Etaples camp Shepherd was assigned to the 48th Battalion and joined them on the front line on 4th December.

Shepherd had dark straight hair and was known as 'Darky' to his mates. The assault on Bullecourt on 11th April would be his first and last action. He was acting as a stretcher bearer during the battle when he was killed. He served in the army for less than a year. Reg Shepherd has no known grave and his name is commemorated on the Memorial at Villers-Bretonneux.

Private Horace Reginald
Shepherd photographed in
1916. (Courtesy Jillian Thomas)

PRIVATE ALBERT SHILLABEER 1731,
48TH BATTALION AIF

Albert Arthur Shillabeer was born in One Tree Hill, South Australia in May 1894. He was the son of Andrew and Elizabeth Shillabeer. Prior to the war he worked as an engine driver. He was aged 21 when he enlisted to join the AIF in Adelaide on 6th March 1916

He left Adelaide aboard the HMT *Aenaes* on 11th April bound for Egypt. After training in Egypt he embarked from Alexandria on the HMT *Franconia* on 6th June 1916 and arrived in Plymouth England, on 16th June. He spent the following months in England then was sent to France aboard the SS *Victoria* from Folkestone. After arriving in Boulogne he was sent for further training at Etaples. He was assigned to the 48th Battalion on 10th February.

On the 11th April, Shillabeer was a signaller and his comrades from the 48th Battalion confirmed that

Private Albert Shillabeer.
(Courtesy Rose Shillabeer)

he successfully crossed No Man's Land and reached the first line of German trenches. Private C.H. Wisse saw him die on reaching the second trench. 'In enemy's 2nd trench, he was shot by sniper, hit in the forehead and killed outright. I saw it happen. His body was left there. We were taken prisoner about two hours later.'[107]

Albert Shillabeer's remains were not recovered and he was listed as missing. He has no known grave and his name is commemorated on the Australian National Memorial at Villers-Bretonneux.

PRIVATE NORMAN SIVIOUR 1989,
48TH BATTALION AIF

Norman Rollond Siviour was born in Redhill, South Australia on 25th August 1897. He was the twelfth child and youngest son of Richard and Clementine Siviour and was one of the first students enrolled at the Stokes School, situated on the Eyre Peninsula, East of Cummins in South Australia. He was a keen football player during his youth. On completing his education he worked on 'Hillside', a property east of Cummins. From his embarkation record it states that he was a farmer from Cummins, before he enlisted to join the AIF on 22nd February 1916. He embarked on 13th July from Adelaide on the troopship *Seang Bee* bound for England. After training he was sent to France on 28th December 1916. He embarked aboard the troopship named *Princess Clementine* from Folkestone, Clementine was his mother's name. On arriving in France he marched to Etaples where he received further training in preparation for joining the 48th Battalion on the front line. On 11th April, Private Norman Siviour

was killed at Bullecourt. His remains were not recovered and his name is commemorated on the Memorial at Villers-Bretonneux.

Private Norman Siviour.
(Courtesy Maurice Siviour)

PRIVATE HENRY WOOD 712,
6TH MACHINE GUN COMPANY

Henry Wood was born in Dorking, Surrey, England, on 19th October 1895. He was known by his family and his

comrades as Harry. When World War One broke out Harry was living in Melbourne, Australia and he was one of the many British men who enlisted to join the AIF. He enlisted on 15th February 1915 as a private. He stated

Private Henry Wood. (Courtesy
Dave Cooper & Eileen Ring)

that his trade was a tea blender. During the period while he was training, he married his fiancée Mabel Brett on 24th April 1915. Harry embarked aboard the troopship HMAT *Ulysses* on 10th May 1915, sailing for Egypt. He was not to see his wife again. Arriving in Egypt during June 1915 he was assigned to the 22nd Battalion. He joined the Australian Depot stores at Ghezireh from 30th August 1915. A year later he was sent to England, where he was transferred to the 6th Training Battalion at Parkhouse. Wood was sent to France via Folkestone aboard the troopship SS *Victoria* on 11th November. The brutal regime at Etaples, where all soldiers were sent to prepare them for life in the trenches on the Western Front, must have made an impact on Harry. He felt compelled to write to his family a final letter, which would be sent if he was killed. It was written in November 1916:

Dearest Mother and Dad, Daisy, Charles and Marjorie, – You are reading this because I have gone under. I know you will one and all feel terribly cut up and you will feel this new sorrow for some considerable time to come. But I don't wish you to be sorry for me, dear ones, and you must very soon try and shake this off.

Remember I have answered duty's call and God saw fit for me to pay the greatest price by giving my all for this righteous cause in which the whole manhood of our Empire are involved. Do not lose heart because of me, but like the painting of Lord Kitchener's death, with his arm extending from a wave holding a sword on which are the words 'Carry on'. Therefore dear ones, I pass these words on to you. Carry on with this glorious work and fellows who are leaving for the Front cheer them and let them realise theirs is a glorious work. You must console yourself – each one of you. I am happy and at rest, whereas, who can tell what my future might have been had I lived.

Although I have not lived to see victory I am confident in Him that it will come to our arms and our results will live in future generations, and they will realise we have not laid down our lives in vain.

My life was not a long one, but it is not the span of life so much that counts but what have you done in your space of living. Have you done your best and so made the most of life in the correct sense of the word?

Some persons may say 'Poor fellow with no chance in life'. Not so; we have had a great chance in the building and remoulding of our great Empire. What better or more noble cause could a man die for than for his country and loved ones? I wish no better death: much better than dying in bed.

Now I must thank each one of you for your kindness and love to me in past years, in my early youth, when I could not help myself. My childhood days were happy, and I am happy still – the day I gave my all, because I have tried to pay back a very little of what I owe you all by helping to give liberty and safety in your future years.

Now, I have said a lot, and it will pain you to read all this. I wanted to comfort and help you, but remember, God knows best. Look to Him for comfort and strength.

To me, it's the easiest thing to give my life: to you all the most difficult because you remain in sorrow. Yet be of good courage. Life was dear to me with prospects in front, but all these I lay on the altar of self-sacrifice willingly for each of you ... May His Blessing rest on you all and in that great beyond, where I am now with the silent hosts of my comrades I await you all. Therefore adieu.[108]

Harry would serve approximately four months before he paid the ultimate sacrifice at Bullecourt and he carried this letter with him in the hope that it would be found upon his body and forwarded to his family if he was killed.

Private Harry Wood was transferred to the 6th Machine Gun Company on 8th December 1916. On 11th April 1917, the day before he died, Harry wrote home. He was only hours away from entering his first and last battle. He wrote 'You wonder how I am getting on. "Good", best of health, spirits and muscle and ready for any Hun. eh!'[109]

Although he had been in the front line for a short while, he was in close contact with the horrors of war, and it appears that he was adapting to life on the front and was, like many soldiers, becoming desensitised by witnessing such terrible sights. He wrote:

I've often wondered what people really meant by 'nerves of steel', I can realise now. Some of the sights one sees the meaning in full. Although its terribly strange how that saying 'a 9 days wonder' is correct. I remember the first time I saw a dead soldier on the field, not as you would look on a dead person, but mangled as we know, only I felt anything but brave but time and sights harden one to such an extent that you take no notice of them in time and you might say 'poor beggar' as you pass to your chum with you.[110]

In this final letter Harry indicates how he felt to be woken up to take part in the botched attempt to attack Bullecourt during the night of the 9th/10th April 1917:

Well to use a true soldier's term on tonight's climatic conditions 'its a devilish night'. We are 'bivouacking' out in Farmer Jones' paddock and it's been raining, hailing, snowing and at times a bitter north wind blowing – all in 4 days so you can guess we've had a stomach full of weather for a time. Fancy this experience happening to you, second night here it was cold and we turned in about 8pm. 20 minutes to 1 o'clock I awoke with 'turn out No. 2 Battery, pack up in fighting order and be ready to process up the line in ½ hour'. You can guess one's feelings waking up in the dark and receiving such an order and the line was 6 miles from this camp. Anyway with a good heart we turned out in record time. Everything was bustle. The moon was shining and it was snowing at intervals, the whole camp was busy harnessing horse limbers and transports, rattling orders being given. Guns etc. etc. were soon on the road and off we started. I might say I did not have to stay up with the guns and only help them to carry ammunition etc. Passed several villages (ruins of course. German Culture) and when we got near the line things began to warm up. Well we dump our stuff and come back to camp. You can guess by the time we left here, and it was 7am when we got back, how far it was and we were going all the time. Good Friday we had ½ days holiday and Easter Sunday we marched roughly about 15 miles so you can guess we were tired when we got here that night. Monday (Easter Monday) night was the night we were called out so you can guess we spent a good Easter Holidays. Generally speaking I am in good health – our tent tonight is covered in snow and outside its snowing hard and there's about three inches thick on the ground so its fairly cold.[111]

Harry and the 6th Machine Gun Company would repeat the same journey the following night and under the same terrible weather conditions to attack on the 11th. Sixteen guns from the 6th Machine Gun Company provided covering fire for the 4th Australian Division, protecting their right flank and firing upon enemy targets in OG 1 and OG 2 Trenches during the first two hours of the battle. Private Harry Wood was part of machine gun crew from No.2 Section positioned along the railway embankment. Each gun crew comprised a sergeant and four other ranks and was firing 1,500 rounds per hour towards Riencourt.

During the evening of 10th April No.2 section were ordered to relocate their machine guns farther east along the embankment in order to protect the Australian right flank from possible counter attacks. German artillery observers may have spotted their movement. A German artillery barrage fell upon their position before midnight. Sergeant Albert Payton and Corporal Sid Deakin formed part of the machine gun crew Harry Wood belonged to. Unperturbed by the heavy shelling they endeavoured to mount their machine in the new position towards the end of the railway cutting. So severe was the shelling that they were forced to seek shelter. As Payton and Deakin sheltered behind the embankment the nose of a shell cap struck Payton across the face wounding him. Private Harry Wood was killed when a German 4.2 inch shell exploded as he left the shelter of the embankment to retrieve a spade. Lieutenant Pallin, Harry's commanding officer, wrote a letter of condolence to his parents:

> Since Harry joined our company, I can assure you that I was proud to have him on the same gun as myself. He was always ready for anything: a finer soldier an officer could not have had. I write to lighten, if possible, your grief at the death of your son. Words are very helpless things, and quite fail to express all that I feel, but I trust it will be some comfort to you, to have through me, the sympathy of the 6th Machine Gun Corps. Your son always did his duty faithfully and well, and was well liked by his fellow gunners. It was in the execution of his duty in the front line that he met his death. As your son's officer I have nothing but praise for your boy, and as a man my heart goes out to you in deep and sincere sympathy. Please try hard not to give way to grief – it is very hard not to do so, but I would be happier if I thought you found comfort in the brave and honourable memory of your son. Please accept every comforting good wish.[112]

Private Henry Wood has no known grave and his name is commemorated on the Memorial at Villers-Bretonneux. He is also commemorated in the United Reform Church in his home town of Dorking and on the war memorial in that town, where each year his family lay a cross in remembrance of him.

LANCE CORPORAL RAYMOND RICHARDS 2368,
48TH BATTALION AIF

Lance Corporal Raymond Richards. (Courtesy Christine Parker)

Raymond Martin Thomas Richards was born on 8th July 1887 at Balaklava, South Australia. He was the eldest of five sons born to Albert and Annie Richards. He attended Roseworthy Agricultural College, but worked for his father's business in Owen as a draper. Raymond married Mary McLachlan on 1st September 1909 and they raised three daughters, Annie, Jessie and Gladys. When war broke out in 1914 his youngest brother Vyvyan enlisted on 25th August. Raymond was reluctant to enlist immediately and declared to his family that he would only enlist if the war continued.

Raymond enlisted on 28th March 1916 aged 28. He boarded HMAT *Anchises* at port Adelaide on 28th August 1916. As he sailed for the war in the Europe Raymond's younger brother Vyvyan, who was a Sergeant serving with the 10th Battalion was killed in action on 26th September 1916. Raymond arrived at Plymouth, England on 11th October. He spent time at a training camp at Codford before he was sent to France on 28th December. He joined the 48th Battalion and would reach the rank of Lance Corporal. Raymond Richards was killed in action at Bullecourt. He has no known grave and his name is commemorated on the Australian National Memorial at Villers-Bretonneux.

CORPORAL ALBERT RICHARDS 2016,
48TH BATTALION AIF

Albert Stanley Richards was born on 30th March 1895 at Balaklava, South Australia. He was the third of five sons born to Albert and Annie Richards. Known as Stan to his family he worked as a draper in his father's drapery business in Owen. He enlisted on 2nd March 1916. He embarked aboard HMAT *Seang Bee* at Adelaide on 13th July. On arriving in France he joined the 48th Battalion. His brother Raymond also served in the same battalion. Stan was promoted to Lance Corporal on 13th February 1917 and two days later received a further promotion to Corporal.

Stan and his brother Raymond advanced upon the German trenches on 11th April. Raymond was killed on that day. Stan received a gunshot wound to his abdomen and was evacuated to England. He died at the 1st Australian Auxiliary Hospital at Harefield, Middlesex from primary tuberculosis on 1st December 1917. Corporal Stan Richards, aged 22 was buried at Harefield (St. Mary) Churchyard. The burial report recorded that:

> The deceased soldier was accorded a Military Funeral and firing party by the Guard Administrative Headquarters, Australian Imperial Force, London and Bearers by the staff of Harefield Hospital.
>
> A service was conducted in the church by Rev. Terry attached to Harefield Hospital.
>
> The 'Last Post' was sounded by 2 buglers of A.I.F. Captain Renwick and 50 patients followed the procession from the Hospital to the graveside.
>
> A representative of Administrative Headquarters, London attended the funeral.[113]

Lance Corporal Raymond Richards and Corporal Stan Richards. (Courtesy Christine Parker)

NOTES

1. 'Three Weeks on Gallipoli' by Harry Murray, *Reveille*, 1st April 1939.
2. Ibid.
3. Ibid.
4. *London Gazette* 14th November 1916.
5. *Reveille*, February 1938: R.C. Winn.
6. *London Gazette*: 10th March 1917.
7. Australian War Memorial: AWM 28/1/198/0004: Captain Harry Murray Bar to DSO Recommendation.
8. Australian War Memorial: AWM 1DRL/428/000034: Australian Red Cross Missing File: Private James Swasbrick.
9. Ibid.
10. Australian War Memorial: AWM 1DRL/428/00004: Australian Red Cross Missing File Private William Birthisel.
11. *Reveille*: 1st April 1933: Sgt. Douglas Blackburn's (14th Battalion AIF) Testimony.
12. Ibid.
13. Ibid.
14. Ibid.
15. Ibid.
16. Ibid.
17. Australian War Memorial: AWM 28/1/246/0070: Sgt. Douglas Blackburn's Military Medal Recommendation.
18. Letter from Private Harry Catterson to his mother Mary Jane Catterson: Courtesy Noeleen Ridgway.
19. Ibid.
20. Ibid.
21. Australian War Memorial: AWM 1DRL428/00006: Australian Red Cross Missing File: Lance Sergeant Harry Catterson.
22. *Hamilton Spectator* 1917.
23. Company Quartermaster Alfred Guppy papers, courtesy Russell Williams.
24. Australian War Memorial: AWM 28/1/198/0018: Sergeant Alfred Guppy Military Medal Recommendation.
25. Australian War Memorial: AWM 1DRL428/00015: Australian Red Cross Missing File: Sergeant Alfred Guppy.
26. National Archives of Australia: Letter to Miss M Barnett, Horseferry Road, Westminster, London: dated 20th May 1917: Sergeant Alfred Guppy Service Record.
27. Australian War Memorial: AWM 1DRL428/00015: Australian Red Cross Missing File: Sergeant Alfred Guppy.
28. *London Gazette*: Issue 29240: 23rd July 1915.
29. 'Sergeant Rule', quoted from *Jacka's Mob*, Sergeant Edgar Rule, Angus and Robertson Limited, 1933: p72.
30. Ibid.
31. Private Leslie Pezet diary, courtesy Ken Pezet.
32. Official History of Australia in the War of 1914–1918, Volume 4:by Charles Bean, Angus and Robertson Ltd 1938: p720.
33. National Archives: WO95/3514: 48th Battalion War Diary.
34. *London Gazette*: Issue 29824: 14th November 1916.
35. *London Gazette*: Issue 30135: 15th June 1917.
36. Australian War Memorial: AWM 28/2/308/0040:MC recommendation: Captain Albert Jacka.
37. Ibid.
38. National Archives of Australia: Private Jack Stewart 384, 14th Battalion AIF Service Record.
39. Ibid.
40. Letter from Private Bertram Harry Perry to Mrs Elizabeth Stewart, courtesy of Lesley Desborough.
41. Australian War Memorial: AWM 28/2/78/0004: Distinguished Service Order Recommendation: Lieutenant Harold Wanliss.
42. *London Gazette*: Issue 29684: 25th July 1916.
43. National Archives of Australia: Wanliss Service Record.
44. *Jacka's Mob* by Edgar Rule: p177: Published 1933 by Angus and Robertson.
45. Ibid, p51.
46. Official History of Australia in the War of 1914–1918, Volume 4: p828, Charles Bean, Angus and Robertson Ltd 1938.
47. Ibid.
48. Australian War Memorial: AWM 1DRL428/00024: Australian Red Cross File: Private Frederick Morley.
49. Ibid.
50. National Archives of Australia: Service Record of Private Frederick Morley.
51. Private Leslie Pezet diary, courtesy Ken Pezet.
52–68. Ibid.
69. 'Playing a Man's Game': Article in the Queensland Digger by Captain Percy Toft MC: 2nd December 1935: Courtesy Lloyd Toft.
70. National Archives of Australia: Captain Percy Toft's Service Record.
71. *London Gazette*: Issue Number 30251 25th August 1917.
72. *London Gazette*: Issue Number 30901: 13th September 1918.
73. Official History of Australia in the War of 1914–1918, Volume 1, Charles Bean, Angus and Robertson Ltd 1922: p499.
74. 'Three Weeks on Gallipoli' by Harry Murray, *Reveille*, 1st April 1939.

75.   Ibid.

76.   Ibid.

77.   Australian War Memorial: AWM 28: Distinguished Service Order Recommendation. Major Percy Black.

78.   *London Gazette*: 29824: 14th November 1916 DSO Citation Major Percy Black.

79.   *Reveille*: 1st April 1933.

80.   *Reveille*: 1st April 1933: Captain Harry Murray.

81.   National Archives of Australia: Service Record of Private William Campbell.

82.   Australian War Memorial: AWM 28/1/198/0085: Recommendation: Sergeant Henry Choules.

83.   Australian War Memorial: AWM 1DRL428/00024: Australian Red Cross Missing File: Private Arthur Morris.

84.   Australian War Memorial: AWM 28/1/198/0086: Recommendation MM: Private Leonard Rzeszkowski.

85.   Letter from Sam Wadeson to his mother Harriet, dated 28th June 1915. Courtesy John Wadeson.

86.   *The Old Sixteenth*, Captain C. Longmore: Published 1929.

87.   Australian War Memorial: AWM 1DRL428/00036: Australian Red Cross Missing File: Lance Corporal Samuel Wadeson.

88.   Ibid.

89.   Australian War Memorial: AWM 1DRL428/00018: Australian Red Cross File: Private Claude Jones.

90.   Ibid.

91.   Australian War Memorial: AWM 1DRL428/00020: Australian Red Cross File: Private John Laing.

92.   National Archives of Australia: Private John Laing's Service Record.

93.   Australian War Memorial: AWM 28: Military Medal Recommendation: Private Arthur Toft.

94.   Courtesy of De Aston School, Lincolnshire.

95.   Ibid.

96.   Australian War Memorial: AWM 1DRL428/00002:

97.   Ibid.

98.   Australian War Memorial: AWM 1DRL428/00010: Australian Red Cross Missing File: Private William Doyle.

99.   *Reveille*: 1st June 1935 Captain N.G. Inlay MC (48th Battalion AIF) Testimony.

100. Ibid.

101. *Reveille*: 1st April 1933: Major Alban George Moyes MC (48th Battalion AIF) Testimony.

102. *Reveille*: 1st June 1935 Captain Norman Imlay MC (48th Battalion AIF) Testimony.

103. Australian War Memorial: AWM28/1/198/0133: Recommendation MM: Corporal Tom Loxton.

104. Australian War Memorial: AWM 1DRL428/00027: Australian Red Cross Missing Files: Private Alfred Oxman.

105. Courtesy Judi Eggers (nee Judith Britten Rzeszkowski), granddaughter of George Purdie and daughter of Norma Rzeszkowski (nee Purdie).

106. Australian War Memorial: AWM 28/1/198/0132: Recommendation MM: Sergeant Robert Rafferty.

107. Australian War Memorial: AWM 1DRL428/00032: Australian Red Cross Missing File: Private Albert Shillabeer.

108. Private Henry Wood papers: Letter to family, dated November 1916: Courtesy Dave Cooper and Eileen Ring.

109. Private Henry Wood papers: Letter to family, dated 11th April 1917: Courtesy Dave Cooper and Eileen Ring.

110. Ibid.

111. Ibid.

112. Private Henry Wood papers: Letter of condolence from Lieutenant Pallin: Courtesy Dave Cooper and Eileen Ring.

113. National Archives of Australia: Corporal Stan Richards Service Record.

       Australian Red Cross Missing File: Lance Corporal Harold Beechey.

Captain Albert Jacka wins the Victoria Cross at Gallipoli, 19th/20th May 1915. (*Deeds that Thrill the Empire*)

PART THREE

THE SECOND BATTLE OF BULLECOURT
3RD MAY TO 17TH MAY 1917

CHAPTER 15

PREPARATION

Although Haig had launched a British offensive in the Arras sector, Nivelle was unable to begin his offensive on the Chemin des Dames owing to adverse weather conditions. Haig learnt from Nivelle on 12th April that the French Northern Army Group had postponed their offensive for 24 hours.

On that day Haig wrote a supportive letter to Nivelle appraising the situation on the Arras front and expressing his commitment to push forward in the Arras sector to aid the impending French offensive:

> I understand that these postponements have been forced on you by the very unfavourable weather, which we also are experiencing. My intention, which has not been modified in any way, is to push forward in the direction of Cambrai as rapidly and energetically as possible. I regret that owing to the bad weather and the consequent state of the ground my troops have not been able to follow up the successes already gained as rapidly as would have been possible under better conditions. The enemy has therefore had time to bring up reinforcements and is offering strenuous opposition, to overcome which, without great sacrifice of life, it is necessary to bring forward artillery, a slow and difficult task. Every endeavour is being made to overcome these difficulties but it is still doubtful within what time I shall be able to organise an attack in force, adequately supported by guns against the Quéant-Droucourt line, on the defences of which the enemy is working with great energy. It will be attacked as soon as possible and I will inform you as soon as I can form a reasonable estimate as to when the attack can be launched.[1]

As Haig wrote this letter to Nivelle, Gough was making preparations for another assault on the Hindenburg Line at Bullecourt. Allenby had made a breakthrough at Monchy on that same day and Gough was confident that his Fifth Army could initiate a breakthrough this time. During the evening of 11th April, preparations were being made by the Fifth Army for a further attack on this sector. The next operation was scheduled for 15th April, but the German breakthrough at Lagnicourt prevented these plans from being implemented.

While Gough was preparing for another initiative to capture Bullecourt, General von Moser launched a retaliatory counter attack upon a 13,000-yard front with the objective of knocking out Australian artillery batteries positioned between Noreuil and Lagnicourt. General von Moser was aware that the Australian position along this sector was weak and with the 3rd Division being sent to reinforce his own line, he was confident that he could deliver a significant breakthrough.

This attack upon Lagnicourt began at 3.30 am on 15th April with an artillery barrage. At 4.30 am 23 battalions from the 2nd Guard, 38th Ersatz Division and 3rd Guard 4th Ersatz Division advanced through lines held by Australian 1st Division; 16,000 German infantry broke through the lines, which were defended by approximately 4,000 men. Among the weapons used by these Ersatz Divisions was the formidable flammenwerfer.

Despite being attacked by overwhelming numbers, the 1st Division AIF repelled the German attack. The 3rd Battalion AIF held onto their positions with courageous determination, dispersing the advancing German infantry and forcing them to withdraw in chaos. The 4th Battalion also held their resolve until they were overwhelmed by the flammenwerfer. The weakest point in the Australian line was the sector held by the 12th and 17th Battalions. It was here that the 2nd Guard Reserve Division drove their advance through the 17th Battalion's line and captured Lagnicourt and continued south into the valley, where the guns of the 1st and 2nd Australian Field Artillery Brigade were positioned. Their comrades from the 12th and 17th Battalions being pursued by German infantry, they were reluctant to fire for fear of shelling their own troops. The gunners had no choice but to withdraw, removing the sights and breech blocks from their guns.

The Australians launched an attack in response later that morning when the 9th and 20th Battalions were brought forward to help the 17th Battalion restore the line. Lagnicourt was recaptured and the Australian guns recovered. All the 1st Australian Field Artillery Brigade's guns were taken without damage. Only five out of twenty one guns from the 2nd Australian Field Artillery Brigade were damaged.

A rifle grenade section distinguished themselves on 15th April by inflicting substantial casualties upon the enemy and capturing 52. The section comprised Private Albert John McMahon, Private Ernest Elliott, Private Thomas Bourke and Private Sydney Bond of the 20th Battalion were recommended to receive the Distinguished Conduct Medal, but they were each awarded the Military Medal. Their recommendation stated:

> Those men are members of a rifle grenade section which did excellent work during the operations of 15th April at Lagnicourt. The section was advancing through the village when a strongpoint was discovered in the right of the village – a trench about 20 yards long. They attacked the strongpoint vigorously and caused the garrison of 25 to surrender. Continuing the advance along a sunken road on the right of the village they came upon a number of the enemy strongly entrenched on a ridge. They immediately attacked the position with rifle grenades inflicting severe casualties on the enemy and caused the remaining 27 to surrender.[2]

Private Ernest Elliott was born in London, England and was killed two weeks later on 3rd May 1917. The Australian 1st Division lost 1,010 casualties including 300 prisoners during the battle for Lagnicourt. The German casualties amounted to 2,313. Four Australian battalions had resisted 23 German battalions.

Once the German attempt to capture Lagnicourt had been thwarted, Gough resumed his preparations for another initiative to capture Bullecourt. After several postponements the next major offensive was scheduled for 3rd May. It would be part of a further British offensive in the Arras region that would involve 14 Divisions from the First, Third and Fifth Armies attacking on a 16-mile front from Vimy to Quéant, with the aim of pushing the

Aerial photo of Bullecourt taken on a reconnaissance sortie made by the Royal Flying Corps on 22nd April 1917 at 1,000 feet. (Author)

Members of the 22nd Machine Gun Company near Bullecourt. Lieutenant (Lt) W.A. Shelley (right), is looking for movement in the gaps made by Australian artillery in the German wire. Left to right: 371 Private J Findlay (foreground), the next two men unidentified, Pte J MacDonald (sitting, centre foreground), 296 Corporal P.N. Kidgell, Lt Shelley. (Australian War Memorial: AWM E00604)

German line to the Drocourt–Quéant Switch. Gough's Fifth Army would attack simultaneously with Allenbys' Third Army carrying the right flank.

The Royal Flying Corps sent pilots on reconnaissance sorties to photograph the Hindenburg line after 11th April. Baron Manfred von Richtofen with six fellow pilots from the 11th *Jagdstaffel* Squadron shot down six Royal Flying Corps pilots who were trying to photograph the Drocourt–Quéant Switch and two escort planes which were meant to be protecting them in a single day, 15th April. Richtofen operated in the Arras–Bullecourt sector throughout April and shot down many RFC aircraft. New British aeroplanes were brought to the sector on 23rd April to counter the threat from Richtofen and his squadron.

On the ground, patrols were sent into No Man's Land to reconnoitre the area. On the night of the 14th/15th April, Lieutenant Leon David Goldseller, the signal officer from the 2nd/5th West Yorkshire Regiment, led a patrol south west of Bullecourt. This patrol got through the German wire, however their presence was discovered by the enemy and they were fired upon. One of the parties was wounded by a gunshot to the hand. Lieutenant Goldseller received a mortal wound to his stomach. Goldseller was accompanied by Private Edward Rust and Privates Carter, Chapman and Crabtree. Rust and the other men managed to carry the dying Goldseller into a nearby unoccupied German trench for cover. Private Carter was sent to British lines to bring a stretcher bearing party to help them evacuate Goldseller. As Privates Rust, Chapman and Crabtree waited patiently with Goldseller in this trench, German Very lights were illuminating the sky and ground for an hour. Under sporadic bursts of machine gun and sniper fire Private Rust and his comrades got Goldseller through the wire. Carter guided a stretcher bearing party to meet them 200 yards from the German line. Goldseller was brought back to Ecoust-St-Mein but died shortly after arriving at a dressing station. Lieutenant Goldseller was buried the following day by a Jewish Chaplain at Mory Abbey Military Cemetery on 15th April 1917. Private Edward Rust was awarded the Military Medal for his actions during the patrol.

As Gough's Fifth Army was preparing to launch another assault upon Bullecourt General Nivelle launched his offensive on 16th April at 6 am under atrociously wet weather conditions. Nivelle's strike at the German lines on the Chemin des Dames was intended to inflict a decisive defeat upon the enemy and bring the war to a speedy conclusion. Nivelle's offensive had taken more ground than any previous French offensive, resulting in the capture of 28,500 prisoners and 187 artillery guns; but losing 122,000 French casualties within the first days of the campaign, Nivelle realised that his initiative had failed. Low morale was prevalent throughout the French Army, which threatened the Allies' very ability to continue the war. Haig's Arras offensive had been orchestrated for the purpose of assisting Nivelle's campaign on the Chemin des Dames. Haig was therefore anxious to close down operations in Arras and launch an offensive in Flanders. Realising that a significant breakthrough was unrealistic and sympathetic to General Nivelle's predicament, Haig agreed at a meeting with Nivelle at Amiens on 24th April that an attritional offensive was the way forward. The French Army would continue to push forward attacks in the Chemin des Dames on the Aisne Front while the British would attack German lines on the Arras front. This strategy would initiate the Third Battle of the Scarpe and Second Bullecourt with Haig ordering Allenby and the Third Army to drive an advance to the Drocourt–Quéant Line and Gough's Fifth Army to capture Bullecourt.

The failure of the first battle at Bullecourt had taught Allied Command lessons. In contrast to the initial attack, which was ordered at short notice with very little preparation, the second attack was carefully planned. Concise, detailed orders were issued and contingency plans were prepared to adapt to any eventuality. Infantry units practised tactics in advance near to the village of Favreuil where the enemy defences of Bullecourt were recreated. Each man would know positions of trenches, wire and machine gun emplacements. The 2nd/6th and 2/5th West Yorkshire Regiments carried out intensive training from 13th April until 2nd May, rehearsing attacks on Behagnies and Gomiecourt, villages similar to Bullecourt behind Allied lines. Although it was good to prepare, there was one disadvantage in that there was time, almost too much time, to make many changes to the plan of attack. Lieutenant Colonel Hastings wrote 'The length of time from the 14th of April to the 3rd May and the large number of alterations to the Order had a tendency to make the attack appear more complicated than it had done at first sight'.[3]

The numerous changes to the plan and the confusion it caused Battalion commanders was addressed by daily conferences where the changes were discussed and explained. Aerial photographs of Bullecourt were circulated to ensure that Battalion commanders were familiar with the sector they were assigned to assault.

It was apparent from the daily intelligence that Bullecourt was strongly defended. Concerns were raised by Lieutenant Colonel Hastings, who considered his battalion to be under strength. He wrote in the battalion war diary:

> Intelligence received, however, brought forward almost daily, the fact that the village was much more strongly defended than such intelligence had at first discovered. This consideration and the strength of the Battalion, at which time was only about 400 trench strength, resulted in an appreciation of the situation being forwarded to Brigade Headquarters.[4]

One can sense his apprehension and anxiety. Many of the men who served in the 2nd/6th Battalion had actually worked for Hastings' business pre-war. Hastings was very familiar with these men and their families and could foresee the awful risks. In a detailed memorandum for the benefit of staff officers at Brigade Headquarters entitled 'Appreciation regarding points in connection with projected operations against Bullecourt', he listed the following ten concerns:

1. The strength of the 2/6th Bn West Yorkshire Regiment is probably too small for the task set it, if the village should be strongly held.
2. The fighting strength of the Coys. is
   'A' Coy.   85   'B' Coy. 60.
   'C' Coy.   105.   'D' Coy. 90.
3. 'B' and 'C' Coys. are detailed to capture the earliest objective, and should probably be able to do so, but may suffer casualties in the 2 mins. before Zero.

4. Advancing with these Coys, one platoon of 'A' Coy. on the right is to clear the trench on the East of the village, (with a strong point at the S. end). This trench is 500m long, has at least a dozen dug-outs, and three machine Gun Emplacements – a severe task for 25 or at most 30 men.

5. The remaining two platoons of 'A' Coy. (each 25 to 30 men) move through the village to the E. of the château. They have to clear and mop the trench, U.28.a.3.6. to U.28.a.6.7., for which they can spare 1 section (say 10 men at most) if they are to leave any force to deal with the final objective. Ten men for mopping this trench (200x are not enough).

6. Of 'A' Coy. there remain at most fifty men (even allowing for no casualties. These 40 or 50 men have to clear and mop the network of trenches U.22.c.7.4 to U.22.c.95.35, to construct blocks, three on the east of the final objective, and to put out at least one battle outpost. They may also have to provide escorts for prisoners and to send back for bombs etc. The strength is insufficient.

7. 'D' Coy. have to reduce the château with it four dug-out entrances in front and one in rear, and its great, well built cellars.

8. 'D' Coy. has only three bombing sections, yet in addition to mopping the château, it has to clear up the trenches from X.U.27.b.8.2. to U.27.b.95.55, and U.27.b.8.6 to U.28.a.x.6., together about 500 yards.

9. This Coy. has then with what is left of it to press through the village under and up to the barrage, and to capture and consolidate the final objective and to put out battle outposts.

10. It is clear that it has no bombers left for the work and inadequate force of other men.

11. The following alternative courses suggest themselves:-
   (a.) that a special party from the supporting Bn. Should take the mopping of the trench on the E. side of the village leaving 'A' Coy. all its strength for the village and final objective.
   (b.) That at the earliest moment, the supporting Bn. should relieve 'B' and 'C' Coys. In the trench captured on S. side of village, thus freeing B and C Coys. to go forward in support of A and D to the final objective.
   (c.) That the objectives of the 2/6th Bn should be S. edge of village, the trench behind the château. And that the supporting Bn should provide the waves to go, by leap frog and capture and consolidate the N. edge of the village.

12. Unless the village is lightly held, the alternative 11 (c.) is the only safe one.[5]

Hastings received a response the following day to his concerns. Brigade Major R.N. O'Connor wrote the following response on behalf of the Brigadier commanding the 185th Battalion, dated 18th April:

> The Brigadier recognises that your battalion is much below establishment, but he also considers it to be strong enough to carry out the task allotted to it.
>
> In the event of your 'A' and 'B' Coys. being unable to get through, reinforcements from the support Battalion will of course be put in, the whole idea of a support being to give fresh impetus to the attacking troops if required.
>
> Two tanks are to assist in the attack, and details of their action will be issued as soon as received.
>
> Your 'B' and 'C' Coys. should of course be re-organised as quickly as possible and if necessary be sent forward in whole or in part to assist 'A' and 'D' Coys in their advances.
>
> Your Battalion is also supported by machine Guns and two Trench Mortars (Stokes are held in readiness to assist in reducing enemy strong point which may hold out.
>
> The Brigadier does not propose to adopt either of the alternatives suggested by you.[6]

The Staff officers of the 2nd Australian Division studied the experiences of the 4th Australian Division at Bullecourt on 11th April and they recognised the importance of ammunition supplies. If the men who had fought so valiantly to get into the Hindenburg Line trenches on 11th April had had continuous ammunition supplies they may have held out longer and secured the captured ground. Therefore, each soldier would carry six grenades in their tunic pockets and once that had reached their objective would place two of these grenades in a designated ammunition dump. They would also carry six sandbags for the consolidation stage of the operation.

Bombers and rifle grenadiers would take ten grenades and designated bomb carriers would bring 24 grenades with them. The German stick grenade was capable of being thrown at a greater range than the Mills Bomb; therefore rifle grenades would be taken. Any captured German stick grenades would be used in conjunction with the Mills Bombs. At first Bullecourt, when the Australians had run out of Mills Bombs and used stick grenades, the Württembergers were alerted to the fact that they were short of ammunition.

The 2nd Australian Division rehearsed the attack on 27th April at Favreuil where problems of assembling and keeping direction were highlighted. Therefore a further practice took place on 30th April in the presence of Gough, Gellibrand and Birdwood. Performance during this rehearsal had greatly improved.

This time the Australians would not be attacking alone. They were tasked to capture OG 1 and OG 2 trenches while the British 62nd Division was designated the task of capturing Bullecourt on their left flank. OG 1 and OG 2 trenches were assigned to 2nd Australian Division commanded by Major-General N. Smyth. The 62nd Division was designated to capture Bullecourt and the line to the Fontaine–Moulin Sans Souci–Quéant Road. The third objectives were to capture Hendecourt (62nd Division) and Riencourt (2nd Australian Division). Ten tanks would support the 62nd Division. Tanks were offered to the Australians, but after the debacle of the first Bullecourt, they were reluctant to trust them.

They would be supported by a considerable artillery bombardment. Artillery would be reinforced with 28 batteries supporting I ANZAC Corps and 20 siege and heavy batteries covering the V Corps assault. A creeping barrage, a tactic that proved very successful in the capture of Vimy Ridge on 9th April 1917, would shield the infantry at a rate of 100 yards in three minutes, then as the infantry progressed this would be reduced to 100 yards in five minutes. In addition to increased artillery support, an unprecedented 96 machine guns would support the infantry advance providing overhead and flanking barrage fire. Once OG 1 and OG 2 trenches had been captured bombing parties would advance along the trenches and link with British units in Bullecourt.

The logistical problem of bringing equipment and ammunition to the front had eased, roads were strengthened with metal supports and a rail line had been built as far as Vaulx by 30th April. In the weeks preceding the second battle, Allied artillery increased its bombardment of the wire, enemy batteries, and roads that carried supplies and reinforcements to the front. Bullecourt, Riencourt and Hendecourt were reduced to rubble. The church and houses in Bullecourt were totally destroyed. All that remained in the village were the low remains of walls and underground cellars that provided shelter for the battered German troops. The ruins of Bullecourt would provide ideal places for the enemy to conceal themselves. The labyrinth of linked cellars and dug-outs underneath the village would be the scene of violent and incessant fighting in the weeks to come. The Germans were desperate to retain control of the village and even utilised the cemetery, removing the dead from graves and using the graves as sniper nests and machine gun emplacements.

With more guns, the artillery was able to cut breaches in the German wire. From 14th April, parties from the 62nd Division and the 2nd Australian Division had gone into No Man's Land and had exploded several Bangalore torpedoes under some sectors of the wire. These were long tubes containing ammonal that were pushed into the barbed wire and exploded creating lanes for infantry to pass.

This new onslaught was subjected to numerous postponements. Initially, there existed great resentment and distrust of the use of tanks by the Australian Infantry and they preferred to work without them. The Australian decision therefore required a very intensive and systematic artillery bombardment, which delayed the attack. General Gough was also reluctant to launch this second offensive upon Bullecourt until Allenby's Third Army reached the River Sensee.

The incentive behind the first Bullecourt was to exploit the success of the Third Army's advance during the Arras offensive; the motivation for their second attack was to assist the Third Army as part of its right wing. The order for the attack was issued on 12th April, scheduled to take place on 15th April. As a result of the delays, the attack did not start until 3rd May, at a time at when Field Marshal Haig had made the decision to bring the Arras Offensive to a conclusion and transfer his resources to the Flanders campaign. The attack at

German soldiers stand outside Bullecourt Church during 1917. (Author)

Bullecourt Church 2009. When the war ended the church was rebuilt. (Author)

German soldiers standing amongst the ruins of Bullecourt Church. This photo was taken during 1917, probably between the first and second battles. (Author)

Bullecourt was part of a British offensive carried out in the Arras region on a 25-mile front. The purpose of the attack at Bullecourt, together with the other operations carried out on the 3rd May, was to force the enemy to concentrate a sufficient force in the Arras region, holding them to this ground, while the French Army continued their attacks in the south. This action would also encourage the French to maintain the momentum of their attacks.

A special company of Royal Engineers took advantage of favourable wind direction to unleash gas into Bullecourt and Quéant for three days from 27th to 29th April. During the night of 1st May the Royal Engineers exploded 144 drums of ammonal in the wire west of the Central Road.

Haig had held a meeting on 2nd May at Bavincourt with Gough and Allenby in attendance. It was at this meeting that Zero Hour was agreed for the combined attacks, 3.45 am during the following day.

While Haig was in conference with his commanders, a German reconnaissance plane flew over the 21st Battalion AIF assembled in the sunken road behind the railway embankment. The plane was shot down by ground fire. Australian soldiers crowded round the fuselage to find both the pilot and the observer still alive. One of them asked 'When was Zero Hour?' Captain McDonald from 20th Battalion replied that 'There's no Zero!' Private Ivor Willams recalled in his diary: 'About sunset we brought down a Hun plane. When the occupants were passing us, one who could speak English, called out to us that they would be waiting for us in the morning. How they get to know these things I do not know.'[7]

General von Moser was aware that Gough was going to make another strike at Bullecourt. The masses of men and munitions crossing the Noreuil valley and assembling close to the railway embankment were clearly visible to German observers at Hendecourt. The intensive artillery barrages were indications that an offensive was imminent. General von Moser deployed the 27th Württembergers in OG 1 and OG 2 trenches east of Bullecourt; and the 2nd Guard Reserve Division were ordered to hold the Quéant Spur and Balcony Trench. The Cockchafers Division of the Kaiser's personal bodyguard was deployed from the Eastern Front to bolster the defences. The Kaiser sent them the following message. 'I call upon you now, my Cockchafers, to meet an enemy more brave, more resolute, more hardy than any you have yet seen. I call upon you to defeat them.'[8]

The arrangements for evacuating the expected high casualties were reviewed. The casualty clearing station at Grévillers remained in its original location. A second casualty clearing station was created at Achiet-le-Grand. The Main Dressing Station at Beugnatres was moved to Vaulx, where the 5th Field Ambulance were detailed to attend to the walking wounded, while the 6th Field Ambulance concentrated their efforts on stretcher cases. The railway line to Vaulx would help in transporting the wounded to Bapaume where they could either be sent to the casualty clearing station at Grévillers or to the rest station at Pozières. An advanced dressing station was positioned south of the village of Noreuil. Regimental Aid Posts were retained in dug-outs in the railway embankment.

The weather had changed significantly since the first battle. Winter was giving way to spring. First Bullecourt was fought in the snow, but it was now melting away.

German troops at Bullecourt 1917 (Author)

NOTES ···

1. National Archives: WO 158/137: Haig to Nivelle 12th April 1917.
2. Australian War Memorial: AWM 28/1/86/0032. Private Albert John McMahon, Private Ernest Elliott, Private Thomas Bourke and Private Sydney Bond DCM recommendation.
3. National Archives: WO 95/3082: 2nd/6th Battalion West Yorkshire Regiment War Diary.
4. Ibid.
5. Ibid.
6. National Archives: WO 95/3082: Major R.N. O'Connor's response to Lieutenant Colonel Hastings: 2nd/6th Battalion West Yorkshire Regiment.
7. Corporal Ivor William's diary: Courtesy of Courtesy of Hugh Williams.
8. *To the Last Ridge*, W.H. Downing, H.H. Champion Australasian Author's Agency 1920, p67.

CHAPTER 16

THE AUSTRALIANS HOLD THE HINDENBURG LINE: 3RD MAY 1917

During the night of 2nd May engineers laboured in No Man's Land laying down jumping off tapes to mark the line of advance. Captain Steele from the 5th Field Company inspected these tapes and confirmed that everything was in place at 1.45 am Captain Walter Gilchrist inspected the 5th Brigade's tapes at 2.00 am. Brigadier General John Gellibrand commanding 6th Brigade had set up his headquarters in a dug-out in the railway embankment and would remain there throughout the heavy shell fire for the next two days.

During the early hours of 3rd May the Australian 5th and 6th Brigades prepared for their assault upon the trenches east of Bullecourt. By 2.45 am leading waves had ventured into No Man's Land and were getting into position at their starting points. The 5th Brigade was on the right flank and the 6th Brigade the left. Absolute silence was maintained except for when it was necessary for officers to issue verbal instructions after passing the starting point. As they assembled they were played upon by a searchlight from Hendecourt sweeping its beam of light along the entire front. German artillery bombarded the Australian starting points with lachrymatory shells from 2.25 am until 3.00 am. Among those that were suffocated by this gas was Private Joe Heady, born in London, serving with the Australian 22nd Battalion. His friend Private Stephen Hayhurst recalled:

I knew Joe Heady. We joined up together. My No. was 6091 and his 6092. He was a barber from Sydney. He belonged to my Coy and Pltn. We were together at Bullecourt where he was gassed on 3rd May 1917. The day we took Bullecourt he was in the wind side in No Man's Land, I was on the left or clear side. It was about three o'clock in the morning, daybreak. I did not actually see him drop, suffocated, but men of my company who were with him told me that Heady (and several other men from my Coy.) got the full force of the gas wave and were done for.[1]

Within half an hour the Australians were in position. German artillery carried out their usual bombardment of the line at 3.32 am, a daily occurrence around this time as a precautionary measure in case of any offensives. The Australians had anticipated this barrage and positioned the 2nd Division ahead of it. The German bombardment lasted for ten minutes. During this time the 21st Battalion of the 6th Brigade in the rear lines suffered casualties. During the early hours, the Germans did not discover the assembled Australian troops in No Man's Land.

At 3.45 am the Australian guns opened fire, which was a signal for the 5th and 6th Brigades to begin the attack. Private Oswald Blows, 28th Battalion AIF recalled: 'At about day-break our bombardment started. It was very heavy and continued for some time – about the heaviest bombardment I have been in.'[2]

They advanced from the positions by the railway embankment in four waves, two lines in each. Opposing them were the Cockchafers and Prussian Guardsmen. Within a minute German red flares were being shot into the sky calling upon German artillery to respond to the Allied barrage.

The 6th Brigade advanced on the left flank west of the Central Road. The 22nd and 24th Battalions led the advance, followed by the 21st and 23rd Battalions. The 25th and 26th Battalions were held in reserve by the railway embankment.

German artillery responded at 3.49 am with concentrated fire upon the 6th Brigade's advance with a barrage of shrapnel and high explosive shells directed at rear waves. The 28th Battalion which was held in reserve at Noreuil felt the full force of this barrage with shrapnel falling upon them. By 4.00 am the 28th Battalion war diary recorded 'enemy retaliation now very heavy on roads and in valley.'[3] This caused severe problems for the 21st and 22nd Battalions advancing on the extreme left flank of the assault. Their advance was split in half by effective German shelling.

Captain Joseph Slater from the 22nd Battalion was killed by shell fire as he led D Company. Slater was a footballer from Geelong. He was last seen by Private Alexander Bruce: 'I saw him blown to pieces about 10 yards in front of me in the attack ... One of the most popular officers in the battalion.'[4]

Private Oscar Hart from B Company gave further details of Slater's last moments. 'A shell burst overhead on 3rd May 1917 and I saw the shrapnel hit him and think a machine gun played on him. I saw him wounded in the barb wire and he could not get out of it.'[5]

Private Henry Harrington also advanced with D Company and received three bullet wounds to his body and one in his thigh. Such was the ferocity of the German machine gun fire that it was impossible to evacuate him from the battlefield. His mate Private Edward Carroll last saw him in a shell hole where he bled to death.

C Company, commanded by Captain Eric Gordon Hogarth, suffered 90% casualties that morning. Hogarth and Private William Griffin were hit by the same shell. Griffin recalled: 'I was wounded close to the German wire. Capt. Hogarth was lying next to me. He was lying on his side with no helmet on, and the right side of his head was blown away. He was of course quite dead.'[6]

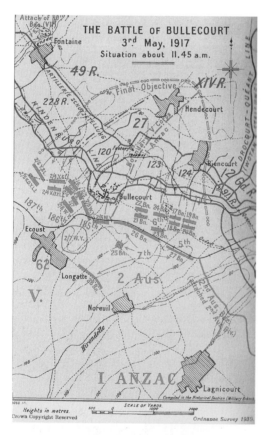

Position of British and Australian Infantry Battalions at Bullecourt on 3rd May 1917. ('Military Operations, France & Belgium 1917' by Captain Cyril Falls, map Crown Copyright)

Such was the severity of the machine gun fire that Private Griffin had to wait in a shell hole until dark, when he could crawl back to Australian lines. 'I crawled away into a shell hole where I had to stay for 16 hours after which I crawled away and escaped.'[7]

Lieutenant Sydney Scammell from Bradford-on-Avon, England, of D Company, was another officer casualty. He was wounded by a bullet in the stomach, within 10 yards of OG 1 Trench. Despite his wounds he carried on and sheltered in a nearby shell-hole. Determined to carry on with the fight he raised his head from the shell-hole to fire at a German soldier when he was shot in the head by a German sniper and killed. Heavy machine gun fire fired from Tower Trench, which skirted the eastern perimeter of Bullecourt, prevented the left flank of the 22nd Battalion from reaching OG 1 Trench, its first objective. They were experiencing the same problem encountered by the 48th Battalion on 11th April.

Captain Alderson's company from the 22nd Battalion and Captain Russell's men failed to keep up with the barrage, so that when they reached OG 1 Trench they had no option but to engage in a fierce rifle battle with the German defenders holding the trench. They took with them three trench mortars; the Germans saw these mortars and made attempts to capture them. Alderson had to order the destruction of one mortar in order to avoid it falling in German hands.

The 22nd Battalion was being mauled as they advanced. Chaplain Francis Durnford was actively tending to the wounded, carrying out ministrations under heavy fire for the following 24 hours. He was to earn a Military Cross for his actions. By his 'fearless conduct and his cheerful bearing he helped to maintain the spirit of the troops in a most valuable manner.'[8]

Australian line at the railway embankment south east of Bullecourt, 8th May 1917. This was the position of Lieutenant Colonel Leane's headquarters on 11th April. A tank abandoned during the first battle can be seen in the rear. On 3rd May, Brigadier General Gellibrand set up 6th Infantry Brigade Headquarters here. (Australian War Memorial: AWM EO1408)

German POWs and Australian wounded in the Noreuil valley close to Vaulx, photographed on 3rd May 1917 as the second battle of Bullecourt was raging. Close to this point was a dressing station. A motor ambulance is passing. (Australian War Memorial: AWM E00491)

The 22nd Battalion's right flank entered OG 1 Trench at 4.01 am. By 4.18 am they had fought their way into OG 2 Trench where they captured 18 German prisoners. Private Frank Joseph reached the objective but was wounded while he retreated. He lay in a shell hole for two days before he was found and evacuated to a dressing station.

Lieutenant Hubert Percy Fraser was leading his platoon from A Company from OG 1 into OG 2 Trench when he and two other soldiers, Privates William Barker and William Morrison, received fatal machine gun bullet wounds at 5.30 am. A bullet passed through Fraser's mouth via both his cheeks. He was conscious for a while but he had to be left in a shell hole where he died from his wounds.

Private Oswald Blows was waiting with the 28th Battalion in reserve and observed the wounded coming from the Bullecourt battlefield towards the Noreuil for medical attention:

Walking wounded of the 5th and 6th Bde's began to come through – on and on they came, scores of them in a steady stream, some with bandaged arms, some hands, some heads, some hobbling along helped by other wounded – those men hit in the legs, and shortly after stretcher cases. It is a hard sight to see this and an awful sight, but one must harden his heart.[9]

Within thirty minutes half of the objectives in the Hindenburg Line were secured on the 6th Brigade's front. Captain Bland from the 22nd Battalion and Captain Kennedy from the 21st Battalion led their men close to the barrage, through the enemy wire without any problems. Together these units entered OG 1 at 4.00 am after encountering little German resistance because

the German soldiers who were sheltering in dug-outs had no time to reach the parapet and fire upon the advancing Australian infantry. They were soon followed by the 23rd Battalion.

The 24th Battalion advanced on the right flank of the 6th Brigade. At 3.45 am they followed close to the Australian barrage towards OG 1 Trench west of the Central Road, supported by the 23rd Battalion following behind. The 24th Battalion went through the German wire with ease. Australian artillery had cut breaches.

The 24th Battalion with the right half of 22nd Battalion proceeded to OG 1 capturing sections of this enemy front-line trench and fired success flares at 4.10 am from the positions they had captured. At the same time the Germans fired SOS signals. The remnants of the German units near to OG 1 Trench sent up an SOS flare, which signalled to German artillery and machine gunners to concentrate minenwerfer and machine gun fire from the eastern side of Bullecourt. The left flank of the 22nd Battalion suffered from the German response to breaking into OG 1 Trench. They lost direction as a result of the German fire and deviated towards the left. They managed to capture a small section of OG 1 Trench, but they would be engaged in a bomb fight throughout the day.

Once the first objective had been captured two trench mortars brought up with the right flank were put to work immediately from OG 1. One mortar was

Central Road looking north towards the German lines. The Australian Memorial Cross is on the left in between the two tall trees. This track would become the artery for bringing supplies of ammunition and reinforcements to Australian units holding the Hindenburg line on 3rd May. Note that the Australians were afforded some protection from machine gun fire from Quéant by the high bank. They were still exposed to enemy fire from Bullecourt in the west and to German forces holding onto their positions in OG 1 and OG 2 Trenches. (Author)

put out of action after firing only one round. The other fired rounds onto German positions which were causing havoc amongst the advancing units of the 5th Brigade on their right.

Once the four Australian Battalions from the 6th Australian Brigade had reached OG 1, they reorganised and then followed a barrage towards the second objective, OG 2 Trench. More resistance was encountered in the second trench system, but the Germans were overwhelmed when the Australian waves descended upon them from the parapets. Signal flares indicating that OG 2 Trench had been entered and captured were fired at 4.26 am. However, some sections of the 22nd Battalion were stopped by enemy machine gun fire from a position just south of OG 2 Trench and had to retire at 4.30 am.

2nd Lieutenant Walter Filmer led a carrying party of 30 men from 22nd Battalion across No Man's Land bringing ammunition and supplies. By the time they had reached the German trenches the party had been annihilated. Four men were left, then three when Filmer himself was killed.

At 4.26 am soldiers from the 24th Battalion and some elements of the 22nd Battalion fought their way into OG 2. Their success was overshadowed by the fact that they could see that battalions from the 5th Brigade on their right flank were withdrawing. This was a strong indication that the attack had failed, verified by a telephone communication received from 5th Brigade Headquarters at 4.40 am. The situation on the left flank did not look too good either. Signal flares being fired from Bullecourt at 4.50 am indicated that the 62nd Division had not succeeded in capturing the village.

As the 24th Battalion consolidated their position, the 23rd Battalion passed through them and secured positions in shell holes located between OG 1 and the German-occupied OG 2. A report was received at 5.30 am confirming that parties from the 21st Battalion had entered OG 2 Trench and that many officers were casualties.

By 5.30 am Captain Gordon Maxfield leading D Company, 24th Battalion comprising of two officers and 30 men, was advancing beyond OG 2 Trench towards the tramlines, running from the six crossroads towards Hendecourt. Maxfield sent up flares to signal that this objective had been captured. Maxfield was covered by two Lewis machine guns led by Lieutenant Robert Desmond from the 3rd Machine Gun Corps. Captain Pascoe from 23rd Battalion was holding positions at the six crossroads and had secured Maxfield's right flank. Maxfield did not have enough men to launch an attack upon Riencourt and had set up a defensive position along a line 200 yards from the six crossroads. Here they fought numerous enemy counter attacks killing 40 German soldiers until both the guns were knocked out. Lieutenant Desmond; and all his crew were killed with the exception of Private

McDonald, who walked backed to the Australian lines at 11.30 am carrying his damaged gun.

Maxfield's left flank became exposed. Maxfield received a bullet wound in the face. He was able to get into a shell hole to take cover from the machine gun fire. Attempting to retire to the second line he was struck by a piece of shrapnel and killed. When the remnants of D Company withdrew, it was thought too dangerous to return to search for him because of enemy snipers. It was decided to look for Maxfield under the cover of darkness. Lance Corporal George Higham from D Company: 'He was so well liked that the boys went out and made a special search for him and succeeded in finding a piece of his tunic with the three stars and the MC ribbon, this was on the right of Bullecourt.'[10]

The 6th Brigade continued its advance and by 5.45 am they had reached the second objective at the junction of Fontaine-Moulin Sans Souci Road and the Central Road at six crossroads, which was 400 yards to the west of Riencourt. The intensity of the barrage and the smoke made visibility poor. Captain Percy Parkes: 'The inferno then started two or three minutes after we started to advance. The noise of our artillery, rifle and MG fire was frightful – one could not see six feet ahead on account of smoke.'[11] It was here that Captain Francis Henry Dunn MC was killed while advancing with the 23rd AIF Battalion. Dunn's body was never recovered after the battle, but his identity disc was found 72 years later near to the six crossroads by a local farmer in June 1989.

Since no advance was possible beyond the Blue Line objective, a barrage was requested at 5.47 am. The 24th Battalion had penetrated the farthest. Captain John Lloyd had hastily established 24th Battalion headquarters in OG 2 Trench at 5.10 am. Reports were received that soldiers from the 21st Battalion were retreating; the 22nd Battalion's advance was checked by a strongly-held machine gun position and could proceed no farther. The 24th Battalion had expended most of its supplies of ammunition. Divisional Headquarters was advised that it was not prudent for 24th Battalion to continue the advance until the left flank had been reinforced and Bullecourt taken. A report was sent recommending this course of action at 6.20 am. The message got through very quickly and at 6.28 am the 25th Battalion was ordered to advance on the left flank and drive the German defenders from Eastern sector of Bullecourt to support the British 62nd Division.

Since 4.45 am walking wounded were heading towards rear lines near Noreuil. The 28th Battalion war diary reported: 'Numbers of wounded came through, but none were able to give any definite definition as to the success or failure of the attack.'[12]

Brigadier-General Gellibrand commanding the 6th Brigade received the following information about the progress of the attack at 6.00 am:

About 400 men and 2 M.G. holding the general line
   of the tramline and Sunk road to OG 2.
About 700 men, 4 M.G. and 2 T.M. holding OG 2 and
   OG 1.
About 250 men, 2 M.G. and 2 T.M. facing W from
   OG 2 to about the wire angle in 29b.[13]

Gellibrand had received reports that the British had made a breakthrough in Bullecourt and that the German defenders had been routed. These reports conflicted with what he could actually see from the 6th Brigade Headquarters at the railway embankment. Gellibrand had gained a negative impression of the Major-General Braithewaite, 62nd Division's Commander, from his days at Staff College and therefore did not rely upon his reports.

At 8.00 am 25th Battalion was ordered to attack Bullecourt from the south east. This would support the 5th and 6th Brigades trying to break out from OG 2. By 8.30 am the 25th Battalion was scythed down in its frontal assault on the south east trenches by heavy German machine gun fire. It was apparent that any further attempt to dislodge the enemy from this position was futile.

Major William Trew had established headquarters for the 23rd Battalion in OG 1 Trench along the road and through the Tramway line westwards by 8.30 am. At that same time Captain Lloyd had established 24th Battalion Headquarters in OG 2 Trench and his troops were in control of the Tramway line alongside soldiers from the 23rd Battalion.

At 8.30 am a report was received at 6th Brigade Headquarters from the 23rd Battalion reporting that German units were advancing between the 5th and 6th Brigades at OG 1. A report was also received from the 21st Battalion confirming that they had consolidated their position in OG 1, but they had sustained heavy casualties.

By 9.15 am the 24th Battalion was in a very precarious situation because the 5th Brigade on the right had lost control of OG 2 Trench, leaving their right flank exposed. At 9.55 am Lieutenant Colonel Herbert Collett, commanding the 28th Battalion, confirmed that his men would try to recapture OG 2 Trench by sending bombing parties eastwards along OG 1 and OG 2 Trenches in an attempt to help the 5th Brigade. The 24th Battalion launched their initiative to recapture OG 2 Trench on their front at 11.07 am. German artillery concentrated their firepower upon soldiers from the 23rd and 24th Battalions who were already consolidated in OG 1 and OG 2 west of the Central Road. The German shelling was so intensive that it forced parties from the 23rd and 24th Battalions to withdraw from the Tram Line. Soldiers from these battalions held on to their position in OG 1 and OG 2 despite the ferocity of the

barrage. An Australian barrage was ordered to counter the German barrage while the 24th Battalion fought off two companies of German infantrymen advancing north from Riencourt.

Captain Ewan Bland had captured a section of OG 1 Trench close to the eastern perimeter of Bullecourt with a small party of men from the 21st Battalion. By midday, they were unable to hold their position and were compelled to withdraw eastwards towards the 24th Battalion-held positions in OG 2. They had lost seven officers and 200 men. Out of 14 runners, only two managed to get messages through.

As the 21st Battalion was withdrawing stretcher bearers from the 7th Australian Field Ambulance made brave efforts to recover the wounded from the battlefield. Three of the men from this unit received the Military Medal for their endeavours. Lance Corporal George Coutts continued to carry the wounded despite being wounded himself for several hours before being evacuated to a Casualty Clearing Station. Private Robert Rowley was another stretcher bearer wounded. Private Allan Maguire carried men through the barrage to the 21st Battalion Regimental Aid Post repeatedly throughout the day.

At 12.45 pm the 24th Battalion fought off another German counter attack from the direction of Quéant.

Communications during that afternoon were very poor. A message timed at noon, reporting that a small party of men from the 22nd Battalion led by Captain Victor Alderson was still holding onto a small section of trench east of Bullecourt was received nearly four hours later at 3.50 pm. Those men eventually withdrew to the railway embankment at 8.15 pm that evening. By 2.00 pm not a man could be spared by the 6th Brigade, which meant that the wounded lying in No Man's Land could not be recovered.

Seventeen replacement officers were brought forward at 5.00 pm. German units launched a major counter attack on the right flank and succeeded in forcing the 28th Battalion back to the sunken road by 5.40 pm. An hour later German forces launched an attack from Riencourt upon the right flank held by the 23rd and 24th Battalions. The Australians succeeded in repulsing this attack at the cost of heavy losses. Lieutenant Robertson cannibalised two damaged Minenwerfers and made them into one working weapon which he got into action. German artillery maintained the pressure by bombarding the railway embankment in an effort to prevent Australian reinforcements from getting to the front line.

Another counter attack was initiated at 6.30 pm when German shells pounded OG 1 and OG 2, followed by an advance by German infantry from the direction of Riencourt. Men from the 24th Battalion held off the German advance, which was repulsed with severe losses. The remnants of this German attack were observed retreating back to Riencourt in disarray.

By 7.00 pm ammunition and bomb supplies were depleting rapidly amongst the Australians holding positions in OG 1 and OG 2. At 8.15 pm the 1st, 2nd, 3rd and 4th Battalion commanders were given orders to relieve the 6th Brigade battalions. The 3rd Battalion was given the unenviable task of taking over at OG 1 and OG 2.

At 8.32 pm the 28th Battalion was withdrawn and beat a hasty retreat to the railway embankment. This left the soldiers from the 21st, 22nd, 23rd and 24th Battalions who were still holding onto their captured sectors in OG 1 and OG 2 exposed.

A further German counter attack was expected from the north west. From 9.00 pm until 11.00 pm German artillery bombarded Australian positions. There was concern for the defence of the railway embankment. During the early hours of 4th May the 6th Brigade Battalions were relieved by the 1st and 3rd Battalions from the 1st Australian Brigade. This relief was successfully carried out by 4.00 am. The 5th Brigade advanced east of the Central Road. The 17th and 19th Battalions led the advance upon OG 1 and OG 2 trenches supported by the 18th and 20th Battalions.

The 6th Brigade was more successful than the 5th Brigade because the ground was lower than that crossed by the 5th Brigade. The Central Road was sunken and enabled men on its eastern bank to stand without exposure to enemy gunfire. Lieutenant Edward Smythe leading a Company of the 24th Battalion towards OG 1 Trench saw that the 5th Brigade had failed and led his men to 5th Brigade objectives along this trench without enemy opposition for 200 yards, when they were confronted by German machine gun emplacements. With insufficient numbers they exchanged fire. He deployed his men to block the trench preventing any enemy counter attacks on 6th Brigade's right flank.

The 5th Brigade attacking on the Australian right flank suffered from German artillery bombarding their advance so that they had shells falling in front of them from their own creeping barrage and enemy shells falling upon them at the same time. Private George King advanced with the 19th Battalion in the first wave and became a casualty. Blinded by smoke, confusion ensued as it became impossible for advancing infantry to keep direction. King advanced 30 yards then fell into a shell hole wounding his face, right arm and chest. Stunned by the fall he remained in the shell hole until his comrades withdrew back to the railway embankment. [14]

Those that survived the barrage hesitated at the wire and their advance failed. Once the barrage subsided the Germans could sweep No Man's Land with heavy machine gun fire from the right flank and inflicted many casualties amongst soldiers who were bunched in large numbers at the wire. Many enemy guns were positioned on Quéant Ridge. Men were forced to seek refuge in shell holes and the pace of the attack was lost. Officers tried to regain momentum but were cut down by machine gun fire. German soldiers, lined along the parapet of OG 1 Trench targeted officers and NCOs. This fire caused chaos amongst the advancing Australian ranks and the battalions were being dispersed and becoming mixed. Apparently, one unidentified officer had lost his nerve and ordered the men to 'Pull out – retire – get back for your lives.' One soldier questioned the authority of this individual, but he replied 'Never mind, but get back. I'm an officer of the __th Battalion'.[15] This order to pull out reverberated along the line. At 4.20 am one officer and a party of men returned to the railway embankment and reported the order to retire and that men were streaming back. The reporting officer was sent back into the battle, but this did not stop further units from retreating. By 5.00 am, 400 dejected and disorganised stragglers without officers had withdrawn to the sunken road (the Bullecourt–Quéant Road). The situation was chaotic.

Despite this major setback small elements from the 5th Brigade managed to break through the wire and reach OG 1 and OG 2. A party from the 19th Battalion including Captain Taylor, Lieutenants Hinds and Cant had managed to break through the wire and reach a German sap that was within bombing range of OG 1. Captain Goff with a party and four Stokes mortars infiltrated German lines on the right flank. This party was pinned down from enemy fire directed from an observation post within the structure of a disabled tank from the first battle at Bullecourt. On the left flank a party led by Sergeant Temple succeeded in entering OG 1 from the Central Road and bombed their way along a short stretch of the trench, but a German counter attack pushed them back. This was the only success of the 5th Brigade. An hour after the attack began the majority of 5th Brigade was back at the starting line.

General Gellibrand commanding the 6th Brigade could see that the failure of the 5th Brigade could jeopardise the position of his own Brigade, who had made some advances into the German line. Anxious to ensure that the 6th Brigade's advances were consolidated, he sent Captain Walter Gilchrist, an intelligence officer from 6th Field Company, to reorganise the remnants of the 5th Brigade. They were duly reorganised and further attacks were made. Out of the 400 men who returned to the sunken road, Gilchrist organised a unit which amounted to 200 men, including a company from the 26th Battalion from 7th Brigade which was being held in reserve by the railway embankment. The remainder of the returned men must have been wounded and would have headed to Regimental Aid Posts. At 5.45 am Gilchrist sent his unit to support the faltering left flank of the 5th Brigade on the east side of the Central Road.

This advance was checked just before OG 1 Trench with the exception of a small party led by Captain Gilchrist who on the left flank entered the first German line. Here they succeeded in linking up with a party from the 24th Battalion (6th Brigade) where Gilchrist (wearing no coat or protective helmet) took overall charge of the situation. OG 1 was discovered to be empty and Gilchrist led his men eastwards from the Central Road along the trench. At the same time Gilchrist tried to organise disjointed units sheltering in shell holes in No Man's Land, tying in vain to coax fellow diggers to rejoin the attack. Machine gun fire from Quéant was too severe and they could not be encouraged to leave their refuges. At 5.47 am Brigadier-General Gellibrand ordered 'Blue Barrage' to commence. This was a protective bombardment to be implemented if 5th Brigade failed to capture its first objective. This barrage did not actually begin until 7.00 am.

Only the 6th Brigade in OG 1 and OG 2 had secured a small foothold, 400 yards west of the Central Road. The Central Road was a vital artery for the Australians to send supplies and reinforcements to secure captured ground. Once beyond the sunken road the Central Road was protected by an embankment 7 foot high. This would provide adequate protection from machine gun fire from Quéant; however they were exposed from enemy fire in Bullecourt and in OG 1 and OG 2.

The Germans still possessed 500 yards of trench running from Bullecourt. By 6.28 am Major General Smyth ordered the 25th Battalion from 7th Brigade to attack the south east corner of Bullecourt. Instead of sending an entire battalion, two platoons were sent to test if a breakthrough could be achieved. These platoons suffered heavily with survivors trapped in No Man's Land. This disaster prompted Smyth to abort the attack upon Bullecourt.

On the right flank Captain Gilchrist and the remnants of 5th Brigade were engaged in ferocious hand-to-hand combat in OG 1 until the attack lost momentum and they were forced to retreat to the Central Road. Captain Gilchrist was killed in this action. A barricade was established in a support trench 150 yards east from the Central Road. Efforts were made to bomb west along OG 1 towards Bullecourt, but their courageous attempts were thwarted by the enemy at the Riencourt–Bullecourt Road. The enemy attempted a counter attack here but they were strongly resisted.

Major Trew established 23rd Battalion headquarters in OG 1 at 8.30 am and Captain Lloyd formed 24th Battalion headquarters in OG 2. Reports were being received by the 2nd Australian Division that the British had failed to break into Bullecourt and advising that any further attacks upon the village should be made from the south west of the village instead of attacking the strongly fortified south-east corner.

At 8.50 am The German 124th Infantry Regiment launched the first of numerous counter attacks upon the Australian 6th Brigade that involved the use of flame-throwers. The rapid implementation of a counter attack proved that the Germans had expected this offensive. As the morning progressed, the 6th Brigade was left more and more vulnerable with the 62nd Division having failed to capture Bullecourt on their left and the 5th Brigade failing in their objectives on their right. The situation was not helped by British artillery accidentally shelling the 6th Brigade's positions. The remnants of this party were called back and a barrage was raised to protect the Australians defending their positions in OG 1 and OG 2.

At 9.55 am the 28th Battalion began to make preparations for an attempt to bomb eastwards along these trenches to try to achieve the 5th Brigade's first objective and the effort was made at 11.07 am.

During that morning, the 28th Battalion from the 7th Brigade was placed under the command of Brigadier General Robert Smith and was tasked to capture and secure 5th Brigade's original objectives, OG 1 and OG 2. Major Arnold Brown was given command of a detachment from 28th Battalion and at 7.00 am they were ordered to move to the railway embankment. As they assembled close to the railway embankment the battalion came under high explosives. At 10.45 am Smith spoke to Major Brown on the telephone and ordered him to take his entire 28th Battalion to OG 1 and OG 2 trenches to support the remnants of the 5th Brigade. At 12.15 pm 28th Battalion ventured along the Central Road and assembled in captured sectors of OG 1 and OG 2. When the 28th Battalion arrived, the remnants of the 5th Brigade was under the misapprehension that they were there to relieve them. Brown reported in the battalion war diary:

> The men of the 5th Brigade were under the impression that we had come to relieve them. I could not find any officer of the brigade in the trenches of along the Road U29 Central. The consequence was that before I could stop it, all the 5th Brigade men had left ... in the direction of the railway. I do not know whether any liquor had been issued to these men of the 5th but numbers of them appeared to be under the influence of the same.[16]

At 2 pm the 28th Battalion advanced along the Central Road to trenches OG 1 and OG 2, where they launched a bombing operation along the trenches eastwards Private Oswald Blows of the 28th Battalion:

> Our men went on the bombing stunt and they practically cleared the trench, and twice they were repulsed. Again they partly cleared it, and again

pushed back. The Germans fought throughout as a man with his back to the wall – their reinforcements were men who volunteered for the job of stopping the Aussies.[17]

Brown made several requests from the 5th Brigade Headquarters for more ammunition. It was not until late afternoon that carrying parties brought boxes of bombs to their position. To Major Brown's dismay, most of the bombs contained no detonators:

> I first saw three 5th Brigade officers whom I at once asked to detail me some men for examining bombs, also for carriers for when we started to bomb OG 1 to the 2nd line. They replied that their men were laid out and that they would not ask them to work. I at once detailed a 5th Brigade Sergeant and 15 or 20 men who started work. Shortly after, the party had dwindled until there were none left.[18]

Stretcher bearers from the 28th Battalion made intrepid efforts to recover the wounded. Private Oswald Blows recalled: 'The Germans were sniping stretcher bearers – of one section of 80, 35 were casualties by 4 o'clock, and one stretcher bearer of my (C) Coy, was deliberately sniped.'[19]

Despite the poor support from the 5th Brigade, Brown continued the fight. By 6 pm they had succeeded in capturing the length of trenches to the Noreuil–Riencourt Road. All ground captured by the Australians that day was sustained by the single link of the Central Road. 2nd Lieutenant William Conroy was among the party from the 28th Battalion holding on to the ground taken. He held on for four hours despite being wounded. He was awarded the Military Cross and his citation records:

> He displayed great courage and determination in leading bombing attacks. On two occasions he repulsed enemy counter attacks. He was wounded on three occasions, but stuck to his post till ordered to go to the dressing station. His disregard of personal safety was marked.[20]

At 6.10 pm General Smyth commanding Australian 2nd Division ordered that they hold on through the night. The 28th Battalion and the 5th Brigade were to hold the trenches to the right of the Central Road while the 6th Brigade held those on the left.

On three occasions they managed to reach the Noreuil–Riencourt Road located 500 yards east from the Central Road and three times they were driven back by the tenacious German defence. As evening approached a barrage fell upon the region south of OG 1 and remnants of 5th Brigade lying in shell holes retired with haste. The remnants of Major Brown's party misread the situation and thought that the Germans were launching a counter attack. They thought that the 6th Brigade were retreating and were vulnerable to being surrounded. The 124th Regiment was advancing from the west while their comrades in the 123rd Regiment approached from the east.

General Otto von Moser had deployed stormtroopers and during that evening they were sent to Ostrich Avenue, a trench that lead from Riencourt to OG 2. At 9.00 pm the 28th Battalion withdrew, with the exception of Captain Jack Roydhouse. He continued the fight and headed for Captain John Lloyd's position in OG 2.

During two assaults 18th Battalion lost 12 out of 22 officers and 61 out of 84 NCOs.

Within 24 hours the four battalions of the 6th Brigade had been reduced to the strength of a single battalion losing 68 officers and 1,524 men. Charles Bean described the 6th Brigade's determination to hold as having 'few parallels in the history of the AIF.'[21]

At 4 pm on 4th May Lance Corporal Walter Hopwood from the 3rd Field Ambulance crawled across No Man's Land while an enemy bombardment was taking place to reach and rescue two wounded men. Private Samuel Rixon from the same unit made numerous trips across the shell-shattered landscape. After 24 hours, and with his exhausted unit given leave to rest, he single-handedly continued to bring casualties back to safety.

The Main Dressing Station near to Vaulx-Vraucourt was overwhelmed by the number of casualties pouring from the Bullecourt battlefield. Within nine hours they had tended to 1,700 wounded soldiers.

The 2nd Division fought off 18 German counter attacks in 24 hours. Australian dead and wounded was sprawled across the battlefield. Private Walter Downing from the 57th Battalion recalled that 'the ground was hideous with its dead. There were many times more Germans than Australians rattling in the shell holes and the trenches; nevertheless the latter lay in thousands.'[22]

NOTES

1. Australian War Memorial: AWM 1DRL428/00016: Australian Red Cross Missing File: Private Joe Heady.
2. IWM 10798 81/91/1: Private Oswald Blows, 28th Battalion AIF.
3. National Archives: WO 95/3343:28th Battalion War Diary.
4. Australian War Memorial: AWM 1DRL428/00032: Australian Red Cross Missing File Captain Joseph Slater.

5. Ibid.
6. Australian War Memorial: AWM 1DRL428/00017: Australian Red Cross Missing File: Captain Eric Hogarth.
7. Ibid.
8. Australian War Memorial: AWM 28/1/1/87/0267: Recommendation Military Cross: Chaplain Francis Durnford.
9. Imperial War Museum Department of Documents: IWM 10798 81/91/1: Private Oswald Blows, 28th Battalion.
10. Australian War Memorial: Australian Red Cross Missing File: Captain Gordon Maxfield.
11. Forward Undeterred, History of 23rd Battalion, Ron Austin, p117.
12. National Archives: WO 95/3343:28th Battalion War Diary.
13. National Archives: WO 95/3322: 6th Brigade War Diary.
14. Australian War Memorial: AWM PR83/018 Private George Edward King.
15. Official History of Australia in the War of 1914–1918, Volume 4, Charles Bean, Angus and Robertson Ltd 1938: p435.
16. National Archives: WO 95/3343: 28th AIF Battalion War Diary.
17. Imperial War Museum Department of Documents: IWM 10798 81/91/1: Private Oswald Blows, 28th Battalion.
18. National Archives: WO 95 / 3343: 28th Battalion War Diary.
19. Imperial War Museum Department of Documents: IWM 10798 81/91/1: Private Oswald Blows, 28th Battalion.
20. London Gazette: Issue 30188: 17th July 1917.
21. Official History of Australia in the War of 1914–1918, p488.
22. To the Last Ridge, W.H. Downing, H.H. Champion, Australasian Author's Agency, Melbourne, 1920, p63.

CHAPTER 17

THEY FOUGHT AT THE SECOND BULLECOURT

BRIGADIER GENERAL JOHN GELLIBRAND

John Gellibrand was born in Lleintwardeinse, Ouse, Tasmania on 5th December 1872. He graduated from the Royal Military College, Sandhurst in 1893. Gellibrand could speak German and French fluently and qualified as an interpreter during the same year. On 21st October 1893 he was commissioned as a 2nd Lieutenant and posted to the 1st South Lancashire Regiment. Gellibrand was promoted to Lieutenant two years later. In 1900 he was transferred to the 3rd Battalion Manchester Regiment. Gellibrand served in the Boer War in 1900 and took part in the relief of Ladysmith. After the Boer War he returned to Sandhurst where he attended Staff College. He graduated from Staff College in 1907. He was posted to Ceylon, but resigned his commission. He returned to Tasmania where he became an orchardist. When the First World War broke out in 1914 Gellibrand was appointed to the Administrative Staff of the 1st Australian Division with the rank of Major. He landed at Gallipoli in April 1915 and was wounded twice. He was evacuated to Egypt to recover and returned to serve on the peninsula in May 1915. In December 1915 Gellibrand was transferred to the staff of the 2nd Australian Division. During that month he was promoted to Lieutenant Colonel and appointed commander of 12th Battalion AIF. In 1916 Gellibrand was awarded the Distinguished Service Order for his work on Gallipoli. While in Egypt he was promoted to Colonel then Brigadier General in March 1916. He was appointed commander of the 6th Infantry Brigade. During May 1916 Gellibrand was wounded in France. He continued to lead the 6th Infantry Brigade during the battles for Pozières and Mouquet Farm during the summer of 1916. Gellibrand was awarded a bar to his Distinguished Service Order for his role at Bullecourt on 3rd May 1917. He returned to England and during 1917 he played a role in reorganising the AIF. Gellibrand returned to France in November 1917 where he assumed command of the 12th Infantry Brigade. He left the AIF during May 1918 with the rank of Major General and returned to his farm in Risden, Tasmania. Gellibrand would hold various government and military posts throughout his life after the war. Gellibrand died on 3rd June 1945 at Balaclava, Victoria.

LIEUTENANT BENNO CARL LEHMANN MC,
3RD MACHINE GUN COMPANY

Benno Carl Lehmann was born in Maitland, South Australia during 1880. His parents Emil Hindrick and Augusta Henreitta Lehmann were of German descent. Prior to the war he worked as a marine engineer and lived with his wife Eliza Jane in Palmyra, East Fremantle, Western Australia. When the First World War began and because he was of German descent, Benno's loyalties would be tested. His parents were Germans living in Australia and he had a sister living in Germany. However despite his German ancestry Benno Lehmann enlisted to join the AIF on 16th September 1915. After completing basic training Lieutenant Lehmann embarked aboard HMAT *Miltiades* on 12th February 1916 from Fremantle bound for Europe.

Lehmann was assigned to the 11th Battalion but on arrival in England he was transferred to the 3rd Machine Corps Company. Lehmann would tell Private C Last, his batman, that he would remove the second 'n' from his name if he shot one of his compatriots from Germany. Lehmann shot

Brigadier General Sir John Gellibrand. (Australian War Memorial: AWM P01489.001)

Lieutenant Benno Lehmann MC. (*Australia's Fighting Sons of the Empire*)

his first German soldier during the Second Battle of Bullecourt on 6th May 1917. During that day he fought his way into OG 2 Trench. He was wounded twice. Despite his wounds he continued to fight and hold his position. His MC recommendation states:

> For conspicuous bravery and devotion to duty at O.G.2 (Hindenburg Line) Riencourt and Lagnicourt front on the morning of the 6th May, during the enemy counter attack Lieutenant Lehmann first moved his gun to a new position, under heavy shell fire and at great personal risk and brought accurate fire to bear on the enemy by so doing dispersing them in the trench. He then, seeing his gun in danger of being captured organised and led a _____ attack until the enemy were repelled. After being wounded a second time he remained with his gun in the front line for 24 hours after, by which time the enemy had been finally driven off.[1]

His Military Cross citation cited in the *London Gazette* on 16th August 1917 states that:

> During an enemy attack he brought his gun into action at great personal risk. On seeing his gun in danger of being captured he led a bombing attack, and though twice wounded, remained until the enemy was repulsed.[2]

Lehmann was evacuated with a gun shot wound in his right buttock and another wound to his thigh. He arrived at a hospital at Le Treport on 8th May. He remained here until 17th June, when he was transferred to another hospital in Dieppe to convalesce. On 2nd July 1917 he was discharged from hospital. On that same day, he was informed that he had been awarded the Military Cross. He spent a week in a camp at Havre and then he rejoined the 3rd Machine Gun Company on 17th July.

Lieutenant Lehmann took part in the Battle of the Menin Road on 20th September 1917. This action was one of many during the Third Ypres campaign, General Haig's plan to break through the German line at Passchendaele and capture the Belgian ports of Bruges and Zeebrugge, which were the bases for submarines from the Flanders Flotilla wreaking havoc amongst allied merchant shipping. During the battle he was slightly wounded in the arm by shrapnel in Glencorse Wood. He received attention and doctors wanted to evacuate him from the front line. Lehmann refused further medical attention and insisted on returning to the front line and rejoining his men. On the following day, 21st September 1917, while on his way back to his unit in Glencorse Wood, Lehmann received shrapnel wounds to his face, body and legs which killed him instantly. The testimonies of the men that served with

him demonstrate how much Lehmann was respected. Private James Augustine Madden:

> It was the morning on the 20th, not 21st, for the attack began on the evening of the 19th with us – quite early, that I saw him wounded in the arm, but he carried on. Later in the morning he went with his batman to a D/S [Dressing Station] in a pillbox which he had captured. I was told later by Sergeant Tendley DCM, that as he and his man were coming out after his arm had been dressed a whizzbang caught him full in the chest and killed him. The batman was severely wounded and has been invalided home. He was buried in Glencorse Wood. I have seen his grave. He was very much liked and admired in the company, although he was German by birth and has a sister in Germany. He shot his first compatriot in Bullecourt and he turned to us and said: 'I've wiped out one 'n' off my name with that'. He was my section officer and a good one.[3]

Lehmann was aged 37 when he died. He was buried by three officers from the 1st Australian Machine Gun Battalion near to Clapham Junction. The grave was marked with a wooden cross; but the third campaign was fought for a further three months and the grave was lost. Lehmann's name is therefore listed on the Menin Gate Memorial at Ypres.

SERGEANT GORDON CHICK MM 1901,
17TH BATTALION AIF

Gordon John Chick was born in Tenterfield, New South Wales in 1892, the son of John and Theodosia. He belonged to the local rifle club for three years and was served in the Light Horse for 2½ years. Prior to the war he worked as a cheese factory manager. Chick enlisted as a private on 15th June 1915. On completing basic training he boarded HMAT *Runic* at Sydney on 9th August 1915 and departed for Egypt. He spent several months training in the Egyptian desert until he was sent to France in June 1916. Chick had the necessary leadership skills developed before the war and consequently he climbed the ranks very quickly. In October 1916 he was promoted to Lance Corporal, two months later he was elevated to Corporal and on 4th April 1917 he was given a third stripe and promoted to Sergeant.

During the pursuit of the German Army to the Hindenburg Line on 13th March 1917, Sergeant Chick

Sergeant Gordon Chick MM.
(Courtesy Jean & Denise
Letaille Bullecourt Museum)

distinguished himself when he reconnoitred the village of Grévillers, under heavy enemy shell fire to search for dug-outs and accommodation for wounded troops of the 17th Battalion. The information that he had obtained during this mission saved many of the casualties. He was awarded the Military Medal for this deed. He received notification of his award on 5th April 1917

Chick advanced on the German trenches at Bullecourt on 3rd May 1917. According to eye witness Sergeant Hugh Hanna, 17th Battalion Chick was seen to have been killed instantly by an exploding shell at 4.00 am that morning:

> On 3rd May 1917 I was in charge of a Platoon in B Coy. 17 Btn and in company with Sgt Chick. He was killed by a splinter of shell when about 50 yards from OG 1. His body rolled into a shell hole. On passing the point an hour later I saw his body was partly covered with earth. I do not know what become of his body afterwards.[4]

Another informant, Private John Kearney, saw him bomb his way along an enemy-held sap, Chick was standing by an Australian bombing dump when two German shells exploded nearby blowing him to pieces. Private Arthur Sullivan saw Chick wounded while trying to get through the wire.

He was meant to have been decorated with the Military Medal in the afternoon of the 3rd May, but he never lived to receive it. Lieutenant Charles Hannaford wrote that 'he ranked very high in the estimation of the men as well as myself.'[5] He has no known grave and his name is commemorated on the Villers-Bretonneux Memorial.

PRIVATE FRANCIS ELLISON DARE 1897,
18TH BATTALION AIF

Francis Ellison Dare was born in Granville, Sydney in 1892, the son of Francis Henry and Ella Eugene. Known to his family as Ellison he was educated at Kings School, Parramatta. He then worked for the Commercial Bank as a bank clerk. Ellison enlisted on 5th August 1915 aged 23. He arrived at Goulburn Training Camp on 7th March 1916.

Ellison embarked on the journey to Europe aboard HMAT *Barambah* from Sydney on 23rd June 1916. He arrived in Plymouth on 25th August 1916. While he was sailing

Private Francis Ellison Dare.
(Courtesy Scott Wilson)

towards England, his brother Herbert Scot Dare was fighting at the Battle of Pozières on the Somme with the 3rd Battalion AIF. Herbert was wounded in the arm during the engagement.

Based at Hurdcott in England he was assigned to the 14th Training Battalion where he was trained as a signaller. He enjoyed being in 'the mother country' so much he went absent without leave from 3rd February until 12th February 1917. He was confined to barracks for 10 days as a punishment. Weeks later Ellison was bound for France. Leaving Folkestone on 28th February aboard the troopship SS *Golden Eagle*, he arrived in Boulogne. In a letter to his mother written on 1st March 1917 Ellison wrote of the crossing of the English Channel:

> We had an awfully good trip over from Folkestone. It was as smooth as going out to Manly. We passed Dover and were over in Boulogne in about ½ hour. We marched up through the town to a rest camp for the night.
> Of course we were out at night down the town. We had some food at a French restaurant. The fellows I was with so funny, they are frightened to eat and think the people are always swearing at them. It is just like any English sea port. I can always understand them even if I don't venture to speak to them. They have good YMCAs and canteens in the camp here and very good concert parties perform. We marched down to the train this morning and we are now in horse trucks, about 40 each, on the way to the base.[6]

Ellison wrote this letter on the train journey to the notorious training camp at Etaples, known as the Bull Ring. All soldiers were put through a rigorous course of physical training, drill and basic field skills. The training camp at Etaples gained its bad reputation because the drill sergeants bullied and intimidated the men Ellison did not seem to mind. Two days after his arrival at the camp he wrote to his mother, 'We were out in the Bull Ring yesterday; I spent the day in the signallers' dug-out sending messages. We have good concerts in the YMCA and there is a large Picture Show here.'[7]

He spirits remain high in a letter he wrote two weeks later to his mother on 17th March 1917:

> We are still having a good time down here near the sea. The weather is fine and I have not been having much in the way of work. There has been some splendid concerts during the week. We expect to be sent up the line at any time now.
> I discovered a good library in one of the YMCAs here and got some French books out. I have been speaking to some of the sellers of chocolates etc in the Market Square here.[8]

Ellison left Etaples for the Somme in March 1917 and was transported to a camp near Albert. He wrote to his mother on 24th March:

> On Tuesday we left our base by the sea, for the front. We were up about 4am, had breakfast and marched to train. ... We embarked in cattle trucks about 10am and travelled till 4.30pm. I had a good seat on top of the car although it was bitterly cold we passed thru some large towns with splendid cathedrals, and later arrived at the base. A large town much shelled by Fritz, the same name as one of our allies Kings, you may have often seen pictures of the church with the Madonna hanging from the top towards the ground.[9]

The church with the Madonna 'hanging from the top' was in fact the famous statue of the Golden Virgin that once stood above the steeple of the Basilica of Notre Dame de Brebieres in the town of Albert. German guns had dislodged the statue in January 1915; and the Golden Virgin was left hanging from the steeple. The statue was secured at right angles to the steeple by French engineers and the myth was that the war would end when the statue fell. It was a common sight for all British and Australian soldiers marching to the trenches on the Somme, as they passed through Albert. The Golden Virgin bolted uncomfortably at 90 degrees to the steeple has become an iconic image of the Great War. The statue did fall, in April 1918, due to British shell fire, eight months before the Armistice. His unit spent one night in Albert: 'We stayed the night there in tents, walked round the town in the thick mud and managed to get a bottle of vin rouge which was not at all bad. It snowed hard during the night and we covered the guns at the front.'[10]

The following day Ellison marched north along the Albert–Bapaume Road. He was crossing the battlefields of Pozières:

> In the morning we set off across the battle fields of last July and had lunch in the first of trenches where Bert [his brother] was wounded ... Nothing appears for miles but burnt stumps of trees and old trenches and shell holes filled with water, old shells, ammunition, wrecks of aeroplanes and motor lorries etc.[11]

In another letter to his mother written on 24th March he provides a more detailed description of the Somme battlefield:

> We march about over old battlefields where Bert was last year. Everything is just as in the drawings of London papers; huge shell holes, wire entanglements, shell cases, dead Fritzes, broken rifles, ammunition,

blown up dug-outs, some very elaborate furnished flats in fact.[12]

Ellison thought that the enemy was in retreat and was unaware that the Germans were withdrawing for strategic purposes in order to shorten their front and to occupy the newly constructed Hindenburg Line:

> We stayed the night in wooden huts where Fritz was four weeks ago and where there was some elaborate wicked dug-outs. We spent a perishing night and next day set off across duck boards thru many villages of which nothing remains to a large town which fell a while ago. The Battalion I am in now being the first to enter. Fritz is still fleeing and has not been seen yet.[13]

Ellison was referring to Bapaume and it was here that he was assigned to another battalion in a reorganisation to bolster weaker units, the 18th Battalion:

> When we arrived at the town our 300 men from our Brigade were split up and 50 went to each Battalion of another Division. I am now in the Battalion Addison was in I think at Gallipoli, it is the best Battalion in the best Brigade in the best Division so they tell us. The colours are purple and green in a diamond shape.[14]

Ellison had to endure the harsh winter weather. 'We also get sheepskin gloves which you need in this freezing place, not at all la belle France at this time of the year.'[15] He spent a miserable 25th birthday sheltering in a former German position. 'I spent my birthday in one of Fritz's muddy dug-outs, in mud and rain.'[16]

On 10th April, he was hospitalised in a Division Rest Station with a skin illness known as the 'chats' and was sick for two weeks. This was a most uncomfortable and unpleasant illness: 'I have been scratching myself to pieces.'[17] Ellison rejoined the 18th Battalion on 28th April.

Ellison was about to take part in his first and only battle at Bullecourt on 3rd May 1917, as a signaller with No.12 Platoon, C Company as the 18th Battalion advanced from the railway embankment just east of the Central Road, towards OG 1 Trench. The battalion was following the 17th Battalion. Ellison was in the thick of the Second Battle of Bullecourt. German guns of the 124th Infantry Regiment were firing and they were receiving enemy gunfire from the right flank, the same unit holding Balcony Trench. Private Charles Adams recalled the events relating to Ellison's death in a report to the Australian Red Cross:

> On 3/5/1917 the Battalion was in action at Bullecourt. They hopped over at 4 am. About half an hour later

Dare was alongside of [Adams]. Heavy firing was going on and [Adams] said to Dare, 'Things are pretty hot'. He also asked Dare where the other members of the Platoon were and Dare replied that he did not know. Dare then got ahead of [Adams] and almost immediately a shell burst in front of [Adams] and killed some boys. It is [Adams'] opinion that Dare was one of those killed, but he could not say for certain, as it was still dark. He never heard of anybody who again saw Dare, who was posted 'Missing'.[18]

Ellison's death was not officially announced until February 1918. Herbert and his two sisters would never speak of Ellison after his tragic death. Ellison's name is commemorated on the Villers-Bretonneux Memorial.

PRIVATE CHARLES ROSENWAX 2236,
19TH BATTALION AIF

Charles Henry Rosenwax was born in Carlton, Victoria in 1888. Before the war he worked as a labourer in Dubbo, New South Wales. He enlisted in Orange, New South Wales on 7th January 1916. After training he left Sydney on 11th July 1916 aboard HMAT *Vestalia* bound for England. He arrived at Plymouth on 9th September 1916. After spending some months in England he was sent to France on 20th November leaving Folkestone aboard SS *Victoria*. After arriving in Boulogne he was sent to Etaples for further training prior to going to the front line. He was assigned to the 19th Battalion on 3rd December 1916.

Private Rosenwax took part in the Battle of Bullecourt on 3rd May 1917. He somehow got back to Australian lines and was last seen by Private Alban Carter from the 19th Battalion:

> He was in the advance on Bullecourt on 3.5.17 and was not seen again until the following morning when he was found again in a dug out near the village of Noreuil. He was killed on 3rd May 1917 at Bullecourt. He remarked that he was unwounded, but completely knocked up and wanted to rest there for a few minutes. He was never seen after that.[19]

Private Edgar Davies from the 19th Battalion gave a testimony to the Australian Red Cross which indicates that he was killed by shell fire behind the

Private Charles Rosenwax. (Courtesy Judy Rosenwax)

Australian lines: 'I saw the body of Private Rosenwax after he had been killed by a shell near Lagnicourt, behind the line. I do not know where he is buried'.[20]

Private Charles Rosenwax has no known grave and his name is commemorated on the Australian National Memorial at Villers-Bretonneux.

LANCE CORPORAL ARCHIBALD CURVEY 4675
20TH BATTALION AIF

Archibald John Curvey was born in Tenterfield, New South Wales in 1886. Curvey served as a police constable at Hughendon, Queensland, prior to the war. He enlisted on 26th October 1915. Once he had completed basic training he embarked aboard HMAT *Ceramic* at Sydney on 13th April 1916 and sailed for Europe. On 15th December 1916 Curvey was promoted to Lance Corporal. Curvy was killed by a shell as he reached the first German wire defences at Bullecourt on 3rd May 1917. He has no known grave and his name is commemorated on the Villers-Bretonneux Memorial. Private Harold Cowling, 20th Battalion wrote that he was 'one of the finest chaps I ever had anything to do with, a real straight goer'.[21]

Lance Corporal Archibald Curvey. (Courtesy Jean & Denise Letaille Bullecourt Museum)

CORPORAL IVOR WILLIAMS 538,
21ST BATTALION AIF

Ivor Alexander Williams was born in Ballarat, Victoria during 1897. Williams worked as a clerk prior to enlisting in the AIF on 18th January 1915. After completing his basic training Private Ivor Williams left Melbourne on 8th May 1915, and boarded the troopship HMAT *Ulysses*. Arriving in Alexandria on 9th June 1915, Williams recounted that the ranks were so incensed that only officers and sergeants were granted to permission to go ashore, they swarmed down the ropes and gangways to the shore and spent the early evening exploring Alexandria. On 14th June 1915 he was promoted to Lance Sergeant.

Williams was attached to the 21st Battalion and during September he was sent to Gallipoli. He was aboard the

Corporal Ivor Williams. (Courtesy Hugh Williams)

troopship *Southland* en-route to Gallipoli when she was torpedoed by a submarine on 2nd September 1915. Williams recalled in his diary:

> It was 9.50 am. Just as I was fastening up my watch the boat gave a lurch, a wiggle, shook violently and then gave a sound of a terrible explosion. On the top of this came a deluge of water and spray. About a minute after this happened the 'ABANDON SHIP' Signal was given. This meant every man for himself as we were torpedoed and it looked as if the ship would go under any minute. The boys took it quite calmly as they stopped and lowered all the boats. Everyone went down below, got their lifebelt and stood at their boat stations as if it was a drill move instead of being in earnest.[22]

Williams was recovered and within a week he and the 21st Battalion landed at Gallipoli at 11.30 pm on 7th September. They were taken to a place to rest: 'We woke at 3.30 to find we were in a very dangerous position. All were liable to be sniped by the enemy as we were in full view of his front line.'[23]

After spending several months in the Gallipoli trenches exposed to Turkish snipers, machine gunners and artillery the 21st Battalion began preparations to withdraw from the peninsula. Williams recalled on 15th December 1915: 'The destruction of war materials and ammunition is enormous. Thousands of pounds of material is being destroyed by tearing up the clothing and blankets and smashing all other material.'[24] Four days later, on the 19th December 1915 the 21st Battalion withdrew:

> We rose at 2am and at 2.45 started for the pier. After passing through the deep saps which were carpeted with torn strips of blankets to deaden the sound arrived at the pier.(likewise covered) at 3.45am. At 4.45am we boarded a lighter which took us to the HMS 'HEROIC' A bonza and very fast boat.[25]

In March 1916, the 21st Battalion arrived in Marseille and on 8th April they entered the front-line trenches for the very first time on the Bois Grener sector:

> I went through the front line today. Owing to the great amount of water in the ground, the trenches are about three feet deep and then built up with breastworks. What little is dug is full of water. Duckboards are placed all along the trenches. In places there are about six inches of water.[26]

In July 1916 Williams was in the line at Pozières. On the 31st he was knocked to the ground by a six-inch shell which burst ten yards from him. During the following days he would endure further German bombardments and as a signaller, Williams was busy repairing telephone lines severed by German shelling. On 1st July he wrote:

> Our headquarters and trenches were bombarded without ceasing today. It was terrible. The number of shells in the air at one time is simply outstanding. We are out all day mending the telephone wires which are broken as fast as we lay or mend them.[27]

On 25th August the 21st Battalion was preparing to move to trenches near to Mouquet Farm. The shelling continued and at one point Williams found himself buried by earth from a shell explosion:

> The floor ... is as soft as butter with the dead that have been buried. The whole surrounding country is littered with corpses that have been thrown out of the trench when it was the front line. The amount of abandoned material here is terrible. Just as we turned round to go back, a piece of shell hit me on the helmet and made a dint in it 3 in long and about half wide. It stunned me for the time being. Eventually, we arrived at our destination. At 4 am tomorrow morning our Battalion is to go over in this position. The shelling here is cruel.[28]

As British and German artillery pounded the battlefield at Mouquet Farm on 26th August, Williams, accompanied by his mate Reg, tried to get a message across open ground to the new front line being held by the 21st Battalion. During this attempt, he was wounded:

> During this trip I was sniped in the arm with a machine gun bullet. Owing to loss of blood I could not go any further, so had to get into a shell hole while Reg went on, on his own. Just as he left me a shell burst in the hole in which I was sheltering and I got a piece of this in the back. At the same time as this another shell landed into the hole in which Reg was. I thought he was gone. To my surprise when I was coming in with the stretcher bearers who should pop out of a shell hole but Reg. I was pleased to see him too. Whilst I was in this shell hole I was buried for about 15 minutes by a shell which burst on the side and blew it in. Anyhow I soon managed to get out again and returned to the old place. Here we sat along with about 200 or 300 wounded in the quarry just waiting to be wounded again and again as many were and to watch our mates getting blown to bits. The shells are just pouring into this place. We have hardly any Officers left and precious few men. The stream of wounded is constant. 9 am, the shelling has eased

off slightly. There are very few of our Battalion left now. They have been caught in some sort of trap. This is something awful. Taking advantage of this lull in the shelling all those who could walk or even crawl made for the dressing station about half to ¾ of a mile away. All the way back along the Kay Sap are the fresh dead. These are those who tried to get back during the heavy shelling but were killed. Just before we left, we could see the Hun massing for a big counter attack so we turned the Stokes mortars on him and inflicted terrible severe casualties. One could see the Hun sailing through the air every time a mortar exploded. When about half way down the Sap on our way to the dressing station a shell burst in front of us. It blew the head of the man in front of me right over my shoulder, but the two leading ones were never seen again. Of this lot I received a piece in the left shin. So now I am lame and cannot walk.[29]

Williams was evacuated from the battlefield and within two days he was sent to No.1 Australian General Hospital at Rouen. The doctor classified him as a 'cot case' bound for Britain. On 31st August 1916 Williams arrived at No.3, Western General Hospital, Cardiff. A doctor confirmed that the wound had damaged his lung and that a piece of shrapnel was still lodged in his chest. On 12th September he was transferred to Harefield Hospital. On 1st October Williams witnessed a Zeppelin fall to the earth in flames after being shot down. Williams was sent back to France in January 1917. On 3rd May Williams, who was now a corporal, would see action once again when the 21st Battalion took part at Bullecourt:

At last a day of adventures. 1 am. We moved forward to the front line, where we extended at 3 am and proceeded to move off across 'No Man's Land'. Previous to this we had to hand in all our overcoats, spare gear etc, and go over with two water bottles and bare fighting equipment with extra ammunition and bombs.

We had not gone across 'No Man's Land' more than 50 yards when Fritz spotted us, our attack was no longer a secret, so he shelled us terribly, causing terrible casualties.

3.45 am, our bombardment opened accompanied by Fritz as well. All the furies of hell could not be worse. 4 am. Somehow or other something has gone wrong. Instead of being 5th wave we are all mixed up with the 1st wave and are now in our own as well as Fritz's barrage. Men are literally being wiped out as they advance. Some blown clean off the earth.

As the lines advance, they are just dissolving like ice in front of a fire. We have now reached his wire

entanglements which our artillery has completely destroyed. Casualties are heavy. A few minutes past four. We have no Officers left. Casualties are increasing and we are now just pouring into the famous Hindenburg Line. 4.15 am. Getting rather strong resistance. The trench is full of dead Fritz's.

The English on our left and the Australians on our right have failed, so our position is precarious, but we are holding on and fighting on all four sides. 7 am. After two hours bombing, we have succeeded in getting him out of a couple of posts.

There are 26 of us opposing heaven knows how many. 7.15 am. Fritz is causing us to retire. Our supply of bombs has given out but more are on the way.

An Officer from one of the other Battalions and I crawled out over the top and took all the bombs and ammunition from the dead and wounded lying around. We also got a Lewis gun which we are now using against him. As fast as our men get up to snipe they are killed.

The Officer has just been killed leaving me in charge of about five men. All the others are killed. Ours is a very important post now as we are not only protecting the flanks but the whole Battalion from being cut off, also saving the only means of communication. We are up level with Reincourt (at our 2nd-last objective) but do not think it advisable to go any further. 7.30 am. We have a new supply of bombs and about 15 more men and are pounding him with mortars. 7.35 am. He is retiring. 9.30 am. Fritz is launching an enormous counter attack on us (about the sixth since we got into the trench). We are sniping and bombing for our lives. The attack seems to be coming on three sides.

The Australians on our right are recovering and are now advancing while the Tommies on our left are retiring even from their old front line, a fine lot these?

Noon. The right has failed again but with persistent and hard fighting are now gaining ground inch by inch. 3.pm. Gas shells are now being fired at us. Have been rushing round bandaging wounded and putting on their gas helmets.

Fritz is attacking again. We are now practically wiped out. 4.30 pm. We have now held this position for 12 hours and have consolidated. We have succeeded in clearing the old Hun from behind us, so breaking the square and giving us a path back to Headquarters.

I have to go back at the orders of an Officer who has just turned up, to Headquarters with a dispatch and to explain things to the C.O. We had to go back over the newly captured ground [over 2,300 yards] where dead and wounded lying around is something awful.

Fritz is sniping the wounded and stretcher bearers as they go out. On arrival at Headquarters, I was kept there for a rest. 9 pm. Fritz is shelling us awfully and the English are retiring on our left. We had to help them back into their line. Midnight? The terrific bombardment still continues. How I am living at the present moment is nothing short of a miracle. All our own guns have opened on us in response to the S.O.S. signal on our left. The casualties are terrific. We are now under our own fire and our men are getting our shells from the rear and Fritz's from the front. We have now about 70 left out of about 1090 men. Our fate now seems inevitable, just to wait here till we are all finally killed or wounded.[30]

4th May:

On an average of about every ½ hour our phone wire is being broken and we have to go out to mend it. All the Headquarters section are gone. We have 'Stood To' all night. The men in the front line were relieved at 4 pm. Out of our 1090 men there are now a full muster of 53 Officers, N.C.Os and men. Reinforcements are arriving this afternoon.[31]

Williams next saw action during August 1918 when he entered the line at Cappy. On 26th August 1918 he recorded that 'The shelling was just hell.'[32] During the following day Williams went on a patrol. Most of the patrol members were killed and Williams and the Sergeant were the only survivors. Later that day he was part of an attack on German positions and after hard fighting between 2,000 and 3,000 yards had been captured. Williams would make four further patrols during that day.

Williams would engage the enemy during the following day on 28th August 1918 and his diary gives details of enduring bombardments, gas attacks, walking into a German position and being targeted by snipers:

Rained nearly all the morning. 4 am. We advanced after some very heavy fighting, a further 1000 yards. No prisoners. 9.30 am. Fritz gave us a very heavy bombardment with gas to which we replied with one twice as heavy.

10 am. We had rather a hard fight but gained a further couple of woods and a few more hundred yards. My mate and I had rather a narrow escape. We walked right into a Fritz post. Lines were terribly troublesome; also a few snipers who had been missed in the advance. About 3 pm. a sniper put a bullet clean through my tin hat.

4 pm. we went over with a party of 50 and after some heavy fighting again and heavy machine gun fire, captured the village of Frise with 70 prisoners,

14 machine guns and three Minenwerfers and a 77mm gun. 9 pm. we were relieved and went back to Cappy. During the day I got a fair dose of mustard gas so tonight have lost my voice and am nearly blind.[33]

On the 1st September Williams would fight his last day near to Ommiecourt-les-Clery:

We have been surrounded 100 yards behind enemy front line. Have had a solid hour's fighting. Everyone is wounded, self included, only a little one through the arm. 2.15 am. still fighting hard. I am afraid we shall never get out of this lot. Out of our party of 20, 14 are now dead. Just got our Lewis gun working so have a good chance of getting out now and cutting our way through to our own lines. 4.30 am. Arrived back at our lines in time to hear we were going over the top at 6 am. 6 am. under way. The enemy is resisting terribly. They are the best fighters we have struck. 7 am. Casualties are fearful.

The Division on our right is suffering heavily. As they are getting wounded, they are falling into the swamps and drowning. 8 am. Held up by machine gun fire and bombs. 8.55 am. Just finished an hour's bombing. Casualties are increasing every minute. We are now up against it and right in front of a big brick wall which is infested with machine guns.

At last it has happened. My mate and I were sitting in a shallow trench and a 5.9 shell fell in beside us and wounded us both. I was carried out to the dressing station and from there to a field ambulance (5 km) by four Fritz prisoners.[34]

His service record stated that he had sustained gunshot wounds to his left arm and both his legs. He was taken to Daours, where his wounds were dressed, and from there to Rouen by hospital train. While at No.10 General Hospital at Rouen, Williams was classified as a 'Blighty cot case' and he was sent to England to recover. The war had ended when Williams had recovered. He was sent home aboard HMAT *Aeneas* and left England on 18th December 1918. Ivor Williams arrived at Port Melbourne on 5th February 1919.

After the war he continued to suffer from his wounds. He worked for Melbourne City Council for most of his life and retired in January 1962.

PRIVATE ROBERT JOHNSTON 3854,
22nd BATTALION AIF

Robert Johnston was born in December 1892 in Beaufort, Victoria. He worked as a blacksmith in Raglan before the war. Robert enlisted to join the AIF on 12th July 1915. After completing his basic training he left

Melbourne aboard the HMAT *Warilda* on 8th February 1916 and sailed to Egypt. On 21st March Private Johnston embarked for France. He arrived in Marseille on 27th March. On 7th July he joined the 22nd Battalion. Within the month he saw his first action at Pozières where he

received a gunshot wound to the right arm, shoulder and buttock on 5th August. He was sent to Britain via Boulogne to hospital, being admitted to the Welch Metropolitan War Hospital, Whitechurch, Cardiff. Johnston returned to the 22nd Battalion on the Western Front on 7th April 1917. He was killed at Bullecourt on 3rd May. He has no known grave and his name is commemorated on the Australian National Memorial at Villers-Bretonneux.

Private Robert Johnston. (Courtesy Christine Baker)

LANCE CORPORAL WILLIAM LAYBURN 5117 MM, *22ND BATTALION AIF*

William John Alfred Layburn was born in Sawyers Bay, near Dunedin, New Zealand 1890. He was the son of John and Jane. His father ran a small tannery business and William joined him in partnership in 1908.

William relocated temporarily to Australia during 1913 to learn the wool trade by working at several large sheep stations in Queensland and Victoria. When the First World War began, William was anxious to play a role and made two attempts to join the AIF, but was rejected for medical reasons. Despite being rejected twice, he was determined to enlist. In a letter to his sister May 15th 1915 from Mt. Marlow Station, Queensland, William wrote that he

> ... was seriously thinking of enlisting again as soon as I got back to Melbourne. I did twice at the beginning of the war but was rejected on account of chest measurement; but they won't reject me now as I am 34-in normal at present. The Victorians have gone under in their first engagement according to the wires we have received here, it is a wonder a lot of

these shearers don't go, they are big fine strong young fellows, if I was in the same condition in Melbourne as I am at present, no doubt I would have been well amongst it by now.[35]

William Layburn in 1918. (Courtesy Wilf Layburn)

He was aged 25 when he enlisted on 1st December 1915. He said later he never expected the war to last as long as it did. After completing his basic training Private William Layburn, known as 'Bill' to his mates, boarded the HMAT *Ayrshire* at Melbourne on 3rd July 1916 – 13th Reinforcements 22nd Battalion – and began his journey to the war. He arrived in Plymouth on 2nd September 1916. William was sent to Rollerstone Camp for training. On 19th September 1916 he wrote home of the tough training and of a visit to London:

> On the 5th Sept I was sent up to London to A.I.F. Headquarters with the pay books, papers etc. One of the Staff accompanied me as escort, and we were there for two days. Gee London is a great place and I liked it immensely, especially the underground electric railways. At night it was very dismal as nearly all lights are out, so as not to attract Zeppelins.
>
> The training here is very hard and I am now doing outside work. This week I am Coy Orderly Cpl.
>
> Last Friday every one of us Sgts were reduced to L/Cpls and the Cpls to Privates, on account of joining up with our original Battalion; but the first opportunity we get them all back again. The Battn. Adjutant told me that I was pretty certain of getting them back before very long. I think we'd shall be going to France about the end of November, gee it will be cold then.

No 5 Platoon, 22nd Battalion AIF photographed on 8th September 1917. William Layburn wrote on the back of this postcard: 'This is our fighting strength when we go into the line this week. I am signaller to the Officer Lt. G.O. Grieg so will have a decent time. 16 of these boys were through Bullecourt & 4 that were wounded are back again. As I told you before, 13 of us were left. I hope we have better luck this time.' Layburn is pictured third row from bottom on the extreme left, folding his arms. (Courtesy Wilf Layburn)

This is an enormous Camp and there are thousands of Australians here. The Camp must be about fifteen miles long and about one and a half in breadth.[36]

Within months of arriving in England he was writing of his hopes that the war would end soon. When he learnt that he was to be transferred to Battalion Headquarters during October 1916 he wrote home:

Sometime this week I am going to be transferred to Battalion Headquarters here; so I won't be seeing the firing line now, at least not for six months or more and I hope the war is well over by then.[37]

Weeks later, while he was still at Rollestone he wrote:

Yesterday I was taken out of the Draft that is under orders for France and am now awaiting my transfer to 6th Training Battn. Headquarters. This means I have got a decent inside job for the winter and won't be going to France before March or April 1917, sincerely hope the war will be over by then.[38]

While serving with the 6th Training Battalion at No 25 Camp, Larkhill, William wrote of his ambitions to getting his Sergeant's stripes and gaining a commission:

Am still a Corporal, but don't get extra pay for it, but there is a chance of me being a Sgt. again before long. I am also studying hard and it is my greatest wish to get a Commission, but I think they are much easier got in the firing line than in this Camp.[39]

Layburn was dispatched to France via Folkestone during March 1917. On 14th March he arrived at the training camp at Etaples. In a letter home to his mother written on 16th March 1917, Bill wrote:

At present I am at a Base Depot, but am going up the line in the morning to join the Battalion, so shall soon be with my old mates again.

We are living in tents here and the nights are very chilly, so I miss my little room in 'Blighty' very much but I'll soon get used to that. Our 2nd in Command that I came over from 'Aussy' with is here, and he was pleased to see me.

The days are getting very much better now and it won't be long before we have the summer weather ... As all letters are strictly censored I can't say very much ...

The 'natives' here are very amusing, wish I could speak and understand their 'lingo' like [his brother] Tommy.[40]

After a brief time at Etaples he was assigned to the 22nd Battalion AIF on 17th March. Layburn and the 22nd Battalion were deployed to the Bullecourt front line shortly after the first battle had taken place on 11th April. On 12th April, Layburn wrote to his mother of his feelings as he entered the front line for the first time. He may have been freezing cold on the front and was anxious and fearful of war, but tried to be optimistic for the benefit of his mother:

Have been with the Battn for some weeks now and in the morning we are going up to the firing line to relieve the Division that went in last week. They got knocked about a bit so I hope the good God will bring me safely through, anyhow I am not afraid of the future ... We have had a great deal of snow lately and tonight it is snowing like fury; but strange to say I don't feel the cold very much, in fact it is quite mild.[41]

On 3rd May 1917 Private Bill Layburn experienced war for the first time when his platoon was part of a fatigue party carrying ammunition across No Man's Land towards the captured trenches held by the 22nd Battalion. On 24th May 1917 he wrote to his mother detailing his Bullecourt experience:

Our Battn went over the top in a big charge [this] month and done great work, but the losses were pretty heavy (mostly wounded). I did not take part in the charge being in Reserves, but we used to go up to the new front lines with ammunition etc. Fritz used to shell us with his big guns something fearfully; thank God I came out without a scratch, although I had a close call the last day we were up; but you always get them so I don't take any notice. Something seems to tell me I shall come through safely so I'm not afraid when I'm in the line under fire or doing fatigue work out in the open under fire. Death has no terror for me Mother; perhaps my Religion accounts for that, in fact I am sure it is for I seem to be praying all the time and quickly reconciled to the inevitable. (Enough of war.)[42]

He also wrote of his thoughts regarding the second Bullecourt to his brother Tom on 25th August. 'I had plenty of experiences on the Somme but thank God I came through safely. I was at Bullecourt and I can tell you it was a hot place. I don't think we shall ever see another 'stunt' like it.'[43]

Bill Layburn wanted to progress his career within the Army. In a letter to his mother dated 24th May 1917, he wrote: 'I am attending an NCO's class and a Signalling Class (Morse Telegraph) so I have things cut out a bit for me.'[44]

By 25th August 1917 Bill had passed the signallers course. He had impressed the officers he served. They gave him plenty of encouragement to develop within the Army. He wrote on 25th August to his brother Tom:

> I am signaller to our 2nd in Command and attached to Coy Hdqts. It is a good job, also the Sig. Officer has taken a great liking to me and there is every chance of me getting a comm. if I keep going and study hard. As a matter of fact it was promised me if I make good, and as I have heard things from other quarters it looks like as if it is to be so.[45]

Attending the signaller's course had delayed his chance of promotion to Sergeant for on 9th September 1917 he wrote to his mother telling her that he would leave the signallers to return to his old platoon in order to get it. 'I am going to leave the Signallers and go back to the Platoon for I will get on much quicker. If I hadn't been in the Sigs I could have held my three stripes again by now and been confirmed at that.'[46]

During early September the 22nd Battalion was billeted in St Omer and preparing to play its role in the third Ypres campaign. Although they were miles away from the front Layburn and the battalion were exposed to German planes that bombed their positions. On 8th September, while billeted in St Omer, Bill reported the bombing raids in a letter to his brother Tom:

> We are still here Tommy but it is only a matter of a few days before we are moving and are going straight into the line. From what our O.C. tells me we are in for a pretty warm time as things are just 'hell let loose' up the line now.
>
> Fritz has been coming over almost every night this week and bombing us. One landed within 200 yds of our billet and about a dozen others landed all around within the radius of a mile. St Omer generally catches it and he has dropped papers to say that he will level it to the ground. It is a pretty sight watching an aerial barrage but unfortunately none of the blighters get knocked down before they drop their bombs.
>
> The ones he dropped to get us around here were the very latest. The 5th Div. Dug down 24 feet for a dud and it was a 13.5 armour piercing shell. I picked up pieces near the crater he made out here and it caused no end of arguments, however experts have cleared the matter up and that is big shells converted to bombs.
>
> We done a big gas 'stunt' this morning and I was glad to get my helmet off at the finish. Gas is going to be our chief obstacle up here.[47]

Bill was prepared for the oncoming Ypres offensive but hoped that he would survive the ordeal. He wrote on 9th September to his brother Tom:

> We are moving from here on Tuesday and going straight up to the line, a few days there then we partake in the biggest 'stunt' that will ever be held here. All afternoon Artillery has been passing here going up and from what the O.C. told me it is going to be hell with a vengeance so I only hope I am spared to see it right through for it means a three months spell again.[48]

He wrote again to Tom on 16th September of his hope to get through the next battle alive:

> The troops are all merry this afternoon we move up closer to the line and tonight we go in, on Monday morning I think it is 'over the top' with the best of luck. It is going to be the biggest battle of the war Tom and I hope the Good and Merciful God will spare me to come through safely. All the 'Aussys' will be in the 'stunt' and will all come out together in 5 days time.[49]

On 16th September, as the 22nd Battalion was moving to the front line along the Menin Road, Layburn lost his mate Corporal Hector Morrison:

> On Sunday night we moved up to the trenches (supports) and got a warm time going in. Poor old Morrie that was C.S.M. with me when I left 'aussy' got killed and several were wounded. When we were in the trench we had to do a bit of consolidating and five of us were working in a sap when a 'whiz-bang' came over and knocked us flat, luckily only one of us got slightly wounded.
>
> Early on Sunday morning when he was shelling us heavily, a 4.5 hit the side of the trench and wounded our platoon Com. 2 Sgts and a L/Cpl. Unfortunately our Officer died very shortly after reaching the dressing station. I was in a funk hole about 10 yards away.
>
> Altogether he got four hits on our little bit of a trench and knocked out some M.G. from another Btn. Post gun and all.
>
> On Tuesday night we were relieved and I wasn't a bit sorry for we had a very rotten time and I thank God that I have come through safely so far.
>
> Early on Wed. morning we got back to some huts for a rest and left again that same evening and bivouacked behind the lines for the night. The 'hop over' this morning was a great success so we shall be moving up shortly to relieve the chaps who took the final objective.

The artillery fire is terrific and Fritz is putting over a lot of heavy stuff. Our barrages are very deadly and must shake the hun up to some order. I had some close calls on Sunday night going in and considering everything our Ptn. were lucky to come out as they did, and I can only thank the good God for sparing me.[50]

Private Layburn would be involved in two actions, the first being the Battle of the Menin Road on 20th September, and the second engagement, the Battle of Polygon Wood, on 26th September 1917. He wrote to his mother:

I think your prayers must have saved me this time from being killed by the beastly Huns and I also thank God and the Blessed Virgin Mary with all my heart that I am safe and well.

We have been twice in the thick of it within a fortnight and it was terrible. No sleep, no rest, only the roar of guns and bursting shells. Thank goodness the weather has been fine otherwise the conditions would have been awful.

I kept splendid through it all and was as cool as possible, although most of our chaps were badly scared; indeed I prayed hard at times for all of us. The first time in we lost our Officer and five wounded out of our own platoon, the second time we only had three casualties (one death).

My chum Morrie who went up to Yorkshire with me got killed going up to the line. His brother came here to see me the day before yesterday. Poor chap he got an awful shock. I know where he is buried so the two of us are going up on Sunday if we can get permission ... At present we are a few miles behind Ypres having a rest; but next week we shall be at it again ... Must say I am keeping splendid and eat like a horse. Fritz's bombardments did not stop me from having my regular meals in the line. I guess our guns put the 'wind up' him properly this time. They surrendered in hundreds.

The 'Heads' are awfully proud of us. I wish they had to face it like we do, guess the war would be finished long ago, but somehow I don't think it will last much longer as the Hun is getting a very hot time indeed and I hope they make it as hot as old Nick for him ...

Saw dead Huns lying about everywhere especially around the 'pill boxes' (strong posts), poor beggars they must have got an awful time from our guns.'[51]

On 4th October 1917, Private Layburn was again in action at the Battle of Broodseinde when he acted as a runner and earned the Military Medal. His recommendation states:

For conspicuous courage and devotion to duty on 4/10/17 at Broodseinde and during subsequent operations. This man acted as a runner and made many trips with dispatches under very heavy shell fire. Although twice buried and physically exhausted with exposure and fatigue he remained on duty in spite of the fact that he had been given permission to report to the nearest dressing station for medical attention.[52]

On 7th November Layburn suffered a shrapnel injury to his knee after slipping off a duckboard, which necessitated his evacuation to a hospital in England. While he was recovering from his wounds notice of his award of the Military Medal awarded to him was published in the London Gazette on 14th January 1918 and on 3rd March Layburn was promoted to Corporal. Layburn returned to France on 31st July 1918 and rejoined the 22nd Battalion on 5th August. Layburn survived the action at Herleville on 18th August that decimated his Company:

There were nine in our little party and we fought our way past a wood that was a nest of M-guns. I accounted for four Huns myself and as we were getting surrounded we were forced to retire hurriedly and fight our way back. I was the only one of our Platoon to come out alive and only four of our party got back.[53]

Ten days later, Layburn was killed on 28th August 1918 in the Battle for Mont St Quentin during the capture of the village of Herbecourt. was shot through the head by a German Captain, death being instant. His friend Private Edward Percy Hayes was by his side when he fell:

I was right alongside him when he was killed at Herbecourt by a shot from a German Officer, who came running out of a house, dressed in shirt and trousers. We were attacking the place with bombs. At the time he was buried where he fell, but later his body was moved to a grave in the cemetery at Cappy and a cross erected over the grave.[54]

Another comrade Private E.C. Cooke wrote:

I saw Cpl. Layburn shot through the head and killed instantly by revolver by Hun S/M within few yards of me about midday in a sap leading to the village of Herbecourt. We were bombing at the time, trying to clear the Huns and we landed suddenly on six or seven of them.[55]

The German officer was killed soon after he fired the fatal shot at Bill Layburn, who was aged 28. Layburn had survived several battles, only to be killed within two months of the Armistice. He has no known grave and his name is commemorated on the Australian National Memorial at Villers-Bretonneux.

PRIVATE HENRY OLSEN 5651
22ND BATTALION AIF

Henry Victor Olsen was born in Burwood, New South Wales, Australia in 1896. Prior to the war he worked as a labourer. He enlisted on 17th April 1916. After completing basic training he embarked aboard HMAT *Shropshire* at Melbourne on 25th September 1916. Arriving in France during December 1916 he joined the 22nd Battalion. He managed to get into the German trenches at Bullecourt on 3rd May 1917, but was very badly mutilated by shell fire. One witness testified that he last saw him wounded in a German trench. Another informant saw him being carried by two German soldiers to their own lines. It was likely that Olsen died as he was being taken to a German casualty station for Private Thomas Widger positively identified his body when he found it while in No Man's Land. Widger recalled:

> On the morning of the 3.5.17 I was working near Bullecourt with a party of the 6th Field Company Engineers (Australian), I saw the body of an Australian soldier lying on its face in a shell hole. I went close to the body and found it was Private Olsen, whom I knew personally in the 22nd Battalion and in Australia. He appeared to have been struck in the back by a piece of shell, his tunic was torn, there was a deal of blood on his clothing. He was apparently dead. I did not report the matter to any person at the time, neither did I remove his identity disc, we were under heavy shell fire at the time. I do not know what became of the body afterwards as I went forward with the remainder of the working party. I could identify him quite easily as it was fairly light at the time.[56]

Private Henry Olsen's body was never recovered and therefore has no known grave. His name is commemorated on the Villers-Bretonneux Memorial.

Private Henry Olsen. (Courtesy Jean & Denise Letaille Bullecourt Museum)

SERGEANT JOHN WHITE 4802,
22ND BATTALION AIF

John James White was born in Maldon, Victoria in 1887. Known as Jack to his family he worked as a

Sergeant John White. (Courtesy Jean & Denise Letaille Bullecourt Museum)

blacksmith. Jack married Lillian and they raised a son named Colin and a daughter, Myrle. He was aged 29 when he enlisted on 20th January 1916. After leaving his family in Australia he arrived in France via England on 6th September 1916 and three days later he joined the 22nd Battalion. Sergeant John White was killed at Bullecourt on 3rd May 1917. His remains were found by a local farmer ploughing his fields during December 1994. Amongst the personal possessions found with him were his identity disc, a lock of his wife's hair and a wallet containing a letter to his wife that was still legible. Sergeant Jack White was buried with full military honours at Quéant Road Cemetery on 11th October 1995, 78 years after he died at Bullecourt, in the presence of his daughter Myrle, residents from the local villages and representatives from the Australian Embassy. Myrle was ten months old when her father Jack left Australia to fight in Europe. The eminent historian, the late John Laffin, helped Myrle who had travelled from Tasmania for the ceremony, to write his epitaph:

> DEEP PEACE
> OF THE QUIET EARTH
> SO FAR FROM THE LAND
> THAT GAVE YOU BIRTH

CAPTAIN FRANK DUNN MC ADJUTANT
23RD BATTALION AIF

Francis Henry Dunn was born in 1893 in Cheltenham, Victoria. Known as Frank to his family, he was the son of Francis and Eleanor Dunn. He worked as a commercial traveller prior to the war, living in Parkville, Victoria. He enlisted to join the AIF on 20th February 1915 as a private and was given the service number 117.

During basic training he was promoted to Corporal on 30th April 1915. He embarked aboard HMAT *Euripides* at Melbourne on 10th May 1915 and began the long journey to Egypt. He

Captain Frank Dunn. (Courtesy Janet Hawkins)

Captain Frank Dunn's ID Disk found by a farmer in 1978 near to the intersection of the six crossroads. (Courtesy Janet Hawkins)

Junction of the six crossroads, the site where Captain Frank Dunn's identity disc was found. The tree line was the location of the Australian positions during both battles on 11th April and 3rd May. The track on the left leads to the central road which went across No Man's Land. (Author)

For distinguished work as Adjutant of the Battalion during the operations of the Brigade since the 26th March 1916, when he proved himself an energetic and capable Officer with an excellent influence on his comrades. He distinguished himself during the Pozières operation by the cool conduct under heavy fire, especially in organising a bomb counter attack on an enemy party attacking our lines, and later in controlling movements throughout the enemy barrage on the 4th August.[57]

On 12th August 1916 he was promoted to Captain. On 10th January 1917 he was appointed Battalion Adjutant. During February 1917 Captain Dunn was granted leave to attend an investiture ceremony at Buckingham Palace where he was to receive the MC from King George V personally. The ceremony was postponed and he did not receive the award from the King.

On 3rd May 1917, Captain Frank Dunn, commanding C Company, led the seventh wave over the top in the assault upon the German trenches east of Bullecourt. Dunn was killed on that day approximately 8.15 am when he was close to reaching the second objective. Dunn sustained a mortal wound to the abdomen caused by a shell explosion. There were many eye witnesses who saw Dunn being killed that day. Sergeant Harry Pettit recalled:

> Capt. Dunn was leading his men in an attack on the right of Bullecourt on May 3rd 1917 about 7 am. It was quite light. A piece of shell smashed the lower part of his body. He fell in a shell hole and it was impossible to attend to him. He was so shockingly injured and I am of the opinion that he lived a few minutes. We retired and the body was not buried by us.[58]

Private Frederick Frost saw Dunn receive his mortal wound: 'I saw him hit up at Bullecourt, he was badly wounded in the stomach and a couple of chaps pulled him down into the shell hole. He was unconscious and practically dead.'[59]

As he was being evacuated from the shell hole on a stretcher and taken back to Australian lines he was shot in the head by a wounded German sniper who was lying in a shell hole. He was indiscriminate when identifying targets, whether they were wounded or stretcher bearers. Sergeant David Kaye reported:

> At Bullecourt, Captain Dunn was being taken out on a stretcher wounded, when he was killed outright by a sniper. I saw him being carried out, but it was generally known how he was killed, the sniper was getting the stretcher bearers as well. Six of us went out and got the sniper killing him with our bayonets. I was up there but did not see him killed.[60]

was assigned to the 23rd Battalion. Frank would see action when the 23rd Battalion fought at the battle of Lone Pine where he was wounded. On 29th August 1915 he was promoted to Sergeant and transferred to Regimental Headquarters.

On 8th December 1915 he was commissioned with the rank of 2nd Lieutenant. He was also wounded on that day in Gallipoli. His service record mentions 'Anzac' as the place where he was wounded, so he may have been wounded at Anzac Cove when the 23rd Battalion was in the process of preparing for the evacuation from the peninsula. After recovering from his wounds in Egypt, he arrived in Marseille on 26th March 1916.

On 1st May 1916 he was promoted to Lieutenant. During the summer of 1916 the 23rd Battalion was sent to the Somme front where they took part in the battle for Pozières. It was here on 4th August that Frank Dunn would distinguish himself and earn the Military Cross. His recommendation states:

Private Frank Brown provided further details:

> Capt. Dunn O.C. C Coy., was in the attack on May
> 3rd, near Bullecourt and near the second objective
> he was sniped by a wounded German who had been
> left in a shell hole and who also shot and wounded
> Capt. Dawson and killed three others.[61]

Frank Dunn was 24 when he was killed and as he has
no known grave his name is commemorated on the
Australian National Memorial at Villers-Bretonneux. His
family had no grave to visit and the ship transporting
his personal effects was torpedoed and sunk so they
never reached his family. The Dunn family had to
endure one tragic event after another.

Captain Dunn's story however, does not end there.
After Frank Dunn was killed at Bullecourt, his mother
Eleanor commissioned an artist to make a small
oil painting from a photograph of her beloved son
and this was passed down to his great niece, Janet
Hawkins As the owner of this, and also a miniature of
his Military Cross, Janet always felt a responsibility for
the preservation of his memory. She photographed
the painting and added it to the information she had
collected about Frank but not having children to pass
it on to, wondered where it would end up. In 1988 she
decided to travel overseas to visit the area where Frank
had fought and died in France. With her she took the
portrait in the hope that it might be of interest to Jean
Letaille who had established a museum at Bullecourt.
Unbeknown to Janet, ten years before her visit, a local
farmer named Jean Francois Mercier had discovered
Captain Dunn's identity disk in a field near to the
intersection of the six crossroads where Frank had been
killed. Janet recalls arriving at the museum and her first
meeting with Jean Letaille:

> When I arrived I began in much rehearsed French
> to tell him that I had something he may like to
> consider for his collection. Luckily, I needed to
> say only a few words for as soon as I mentioned
> the name 'Dunn', M. Letaille became very excited.
> 'Dunn' he exclaimed, 'Was he Capitane?' I assured
> him that he had indeed been promoted to the
> rank of Captain in the year before he had been
> killed. I was immediately led to one of the display
> panels and there to my amazement were all Frank's
> army records, identical to the ones I had brought
> with me to accompany his picture. 'Look' exclaimed
> M. Letaille, 'we have been searching for some
> relative for many years. We wrote to Canberra
> but they could not find anyone. We have had
> an amazing find; a farmer was ploughing and he
> found this identity disk that is clearly marked
> 'Captain Frank Dunn, 23rd Aus. Inf'. And there it

was pinned in the centre of his records, a small
brown disk not much bigger than a 10c piece. It
had been found 72 years after Frank had been
killed in the exact spot where the records indicate
he had fallen. It is hard to express the emotions we
all shared. M. Letaille's attempt to locate a relative
of Frank's was an example of the commitment he
has to his museum and the care he gives to all it
stands for.

The photo of Captain Dunn is now displayed in the Jean
and Denise Letaille Bullecourt Museum and in October
2007 Janet paid a return visit to present M. Letaille with
the miniature of Frank Dunn's Military Cross.

LANCE CORPORAL JOSEPH KENNEDY 1175
23RD BATTALION AIF

**Lance Corporal
Joseph Kennedy.
(Courtesy Ron
Wilson)**

Joseph Kennedy was born in
Balranald, New South Wales
in 1893. Joseph worked as a
chemist's assistant at Warragal,
Victoria. He enlisted to join
the AIF on 15th March 1915.
After completing basic training
Private Joseph Kennedy boarded
the HMAT *Euripides* together
with 2,250 other soldiers at
Melbourne on 10th May 1915
and sailed for Egypt. On 9th
June 1915 while at Port Said,
Kennedy was confronted with
the awfulness of war for the first
time. He recorded in his diary 'Saw a wounded Australian,
one eye out.'[62] During the following day HMAT *Euripides*
left Port Said and sailed for Alexandria where they
arrived at 9.00 pm that evening. They disembarked from
the troopship on 12th June and headed for a camp at
Heliopolis. A week later, Kennedy visited Cairo while on
leave. He visited the Pyramids where the temperature
was 120 degrees in the shade. The intense heat would
hinder training. Being so hot, Kennedy and his comrades
would march for seven miles during the night, when the
temperature was a lot cooler in the desert. Kennedy was
assigned to the 23rd Battalion AIF and they embarked
aboard the troopship *Southland* from Alexandria bound
for Gallipoli during the evening on 30th August 1915.
For the first 24 hours of the passage, the *Southland* was
detailed for submarine guard. During early morning
on 2nd September a torpedo fired from a German
submarine struck the port side of the *Southland* as it
was sailing across the Mediterranean towards Gallipoli.
This was an unexpected drama, before Kennedy reached
the trenches of Gallipoli which he recorded in his diary
in great detail.

About 9-50 am a great crash was heard. I looked up and saw steam and smoke coming from the funnels. It shook like a terrier after coming out of the water. It was a torpedo that hit right under the bridge on the port side. Everyone was perfectly cool; most of us were singing songs. S.O.S. signals were sent out and answered by 7 vessels. When we were hit a boat was in sight but it soon disappeared. The small boats were lowered very quickly. In 1 hour a ship was seen coming up at full speed, it was the hospital ship Neuralia. As it got near in amongst some others were put into a collapsible boat. We had a machine gun and ammunition. We got clear of the *Southland*, but had not gone very far before our boat capsized. I was on the side that went under first; consequently I had a good few on top of me under the water. I could see all about me, so I dived down again. I got a few kicks and I thought that I was never coming to the surface. After what seemed like an hour to me, I saw the upturned boat a few yards from me. So I set out for it. And we were on that for over 2 hours. Waves were fairly high at times and we had to dig our fingernails in to hold on. It was not warm sitting there, and I for one don't want to go through that same experience again. A small boat came along side and picked us up. The hospital ship was the one we got on, and it was just on 3 pm I have no boots, socks, trousers, shirt, tunic or hat. I have only a singlet and a pair of shorts to my name. I came into this world with nothing on and am not far short of same now. A few men were drowned but the number is not yet known. [30 lost.] The *Southland* is not yet sunk, but it is gradually going down. They will have time to get nearly everything off. Six other boats came up and picked up a good few. I am walking about like Jonah; I have blankets slung around me for clothes. After we got on board they had a feed for us, and as I was very hungry I enjoyed it very much. A few of my mates are here, but I think the others are all safe. The Neuralia brought us into Mudros just at sunset. Everywhere there are battleships, cruisers and gunboats.[63]

Kennedy was taken to Lemnos where five days later he boarded the troopship *Prince Abbas* and sailed across the Aegean towards Gallipoli. He and his comrades from the 23rd Battalion were given iron rations expected to sustain them for three days. Iron rations consisted of an emergency ration of preserved meat, biscuit, cheese, tea, sugar and salt for them to eat and drink in the event that they would find themselves cut off. As they approached the Turkish coastline Kennedy heard the sounds of gunfire as searchlights beamed eerily into the dark sky. They arrived at Anzac Cove at 9.30 pm during that evening. They had to wait for smaller craft to come alongside to transfer them from the *Prince Abbas* to

Joseph Kennedy as a private. (Courtesy Ron Wilson)

Anzac Cove. The battalion began to land at Watson's Pier at 11.00 pm. Kennedy at midnight on 7th September. As they disembarked from the *Prince Abbas*, they marched passed the graves of their fallen countrymen who had fallen at Gallipoli during the early part of the campaign. On 7th September 1915 Kennedy wrote in his diary:

> At 4pm we left Lemnos in the *Prince Abbas*. Firing heard. Battleships shelling, searchlights flashing every few minutes. Landed at Watson's pier at 12pm. Passed a number of graves. The first division deserves every credit for the position they now hold. A few bullets whizz by and make you duck. Now we are here we can realise the hard job the first lot had.[64]

Kennedy spent his first night on Gallipoli in a dug-out in the second line trenches. Since they were new to the peninsula they were given the task of defending the second line defence. On 9th September, Kennedy wrote 'Doing fatigue, Miles of trenches. Got lost a few times'.[65]

Within days of arriving at Gallipoli Kennedy was hit by flying debris when a Turkish shell exploded nearby. 'A few shells flew over our heads, one burst about 25 yards behind me and I got hit on the back from one of the stones that flew up.'[66]

Kennedy entered the first line trenches for the first time on 16th September on the ridge known as 400 Plateau or Lone Pine, because of the sole pine that grew there. At that time the trenches being held by the 23rd Battalion came under heavy German shell fire; 16th September:

> In the first line of trenches, Lone Pine for 50 hours. Saw a dead Turk just in front of my lookout. They are good shots, five of our periscopes broken. At dinner time seventeen 75's came flying around, got covered in dust. One chap was lying down and one lobbed not 2 feet above his head, luckily it did not burst. A few bombs were thrown in our trenches. One of our trenches was infiltrated, they blew up the coverings but we fixed it up at night.[67]

For the following months Kennedy would spend two days in the front-line trenches followed by two days in reserve. While in the front-line trenches, he would spend two hours there followed by four hours rest, however during those hours of rest, there was little difference from being on the front line because of Turkish shell fire.

During November 1915 he was promoted to Corporal. The following month the Australian, British and French forces evacuated the peninsula. On 18th December Kennedy and the 23rd Battalion left Lone Pine during the afternoon:

> Leave Lone Pine at 2-30pm never to see place again. Issued with iron rations. We had tea at 4-30 pm for the last time on the peninsula. We put strips of blanket around our boots so that we will not make much noise when we are marching to the beach.[68]

On 19th December 1915 the ordeal of Gallipoli ended for Kennedy as the 23rd Battalion marched to Watson's Pier where they boarded the troopship *Reindeer* and sailed for Mudros:

> 1 am All ready to leave. We begin to march to the pier. We boarded the *Reindeer*, not sorry to drop our packs. As the ship leaves I look at the place where thousands of Australians have been killed. Beachy Bill fired a couple of shots farewell when we were leaving, but never got any of our men. He is still there though; the war ships have done their best to put him out of action. Just a few lights were burning, a few men who would be last to leave the place. No lights on our boats, smoking was not allowed on deck, as we were getting away from the place. A few nasty words were said about the place where thousands of lives were lost. We arrived at Mudros Bay at 7 am and were transferred to a larger ship. We were given hot water to make tea with, and while I was there I saw some nice things that I could have eaten. At 2 pm we landed on Lemnos Island and had to walk about 4 miles with our packs on, we were glad when we arrived at the place. We had the pleasure of sleeping in a tent, the first time in 4 months and my first bath for 10 weeks.[69]

During January 1916 Kennedy was back in Egypt where the 23rd Battalion spent two months in the desert carrying out further training in preparation for their deployment to France. Kennedy's journey to France began on 20th March 1916 when he left Alexandria aboard the troopship *Lake Michigan*. Both the 23rd and 24th Battalions were aboard this small troopship and the decks were very crowded. Kennedy mentions the presence of German submarines and the loss of one troopship during the six-day passage across the Mediterranean. His experience of sinking on the *Southland* the previous year must have borne heavily on his mind. Arriving in Marseille on 26th March the 23rd Battalion headed north to the Western Front.

On 10th April the 23rd Battalion relieved soldiers from the 16th Battalion Royal Scots in their trenches near Fleurbaix. They had left the intensely hot temperatures of the desert and they now had to acclimatise to the harsh winter of northern France. They had left the sandy desert for mud. Kennedy was not pleased with his new environment: 'A miserable day, very muddy, not enough dug-outs.'[70]

By July 1916 the 23rd Battalion was in the Somme region and supporting the Australian initiative to dislodge the German forces from the village of Pozières and Mouquet Farm. He wrote of the attack on the Ovillers–Courcelette Track. 'Lined up and numbered off, we go in the first wave (midnight). We advanced four hundred yards, and dug in. Our company lost more than 50% casualties.'[71]

Despite feeling drained from the exertions of battle Kennedy and B Company were placed in support the following day and had to dig trenches under shell fire. They were physically drained, their nerves strained. Although Kennedy was in reserve trenches he was struck by a piece of shrapnel from a shell:

> 1 am The 7th Brigade advanced on our right, but had to retire. Consequently we had to make another trench. It was a very misty morning which helped us. All of us tired, can hardly keep awake. I carried a can of water with me, it came in very useful. We were relieved by A company at 7-30 pm At 9-00 pm they began an artillery duel which lasted for 8 hours. B Company were in support lines. Around where we were fritz's shells fell pretty frequently. I had had my water bottle blown almost in half by a piece of shell, hit on my back, 2 chips broken[72]

Kennedy spent the morning in the support lines before being relieved. He recorded in his diary:

> 30th I helped to carry a mate to the dressing station. At 8-00 am we left support lines and came into Sausage Gully, all of us knocked up. We have to go in again tonight and extend our line to the right, put off. Saw 31 aeroplanes up during the evening.[73]

After spending the day resting, 23rd Battalion returned to the front line to dig trenches while German artillery was pounding their lines with shells. Kennedy was with them, but acted as a stretcher bearer during that night:

> 31st Very hot day, resting. We went up to our line and dug a trench 500 yards long to the right. It is to be used by the 7th brigade, to hop off from. Heavy bombardment all night, we finished at 3-30 next morning. I was stretcher-bearer for the night. Not many of our boys hit during the night.[74]

Kennedy was still in the front line during the first week of August. German artillery persisted in shelling the Australian lines:

> 1st A warm day. In no-man's land. On our way up we got covered in dirt several times. Shells were bursting on all sides of us; some were too close to be pleasant. About 250 more yards were dug. Fritz sent up plenty of flares. At first we had to duck down when flares were up but a little after midnight our artillery had a bit of a stunt. Fritz replied and it was not long before the smoke was thick enough to hide us from the flares without our ducking. They sent us some tear shells. We finished about 3-00 am Next morning and on our way back fritz tried to help us on our journey. I got a bit of my skin lifted, got more dirt down my neck. A few of the boys in our company wounded.
>
> '2nd A warm day. A German prisoner brought down here this morning. At night we go to Dinkum Alley as reserves, artillery drill.
>
> 3rd A warm day. Reinforcements for the 23rd Battalion arrive. Bombardment all-night and kept it up till morning. Both sides at it. The sky illuminated with flares.
>
> 4th A warm day. Our artillery active. Most likely part of the 2nd division will attack tonight. At 9-00 pm the 22nd battalion with the 24th in support attack with the 7th brigade. They gained their objective, namely two lines of trenches. Heavy artillery fire all night, a good few casualties. I am stretcher-bearer carrying men from the firing line. We had a good few shells fall close to us at times, often got covered in dust.[75]

On 21st August 1916, Kennedy was promoted to Lance Corporal. By May 1917, Kennedy was a battle hardened soldier. He had survived the debacle at Gallipoli in 1915 and endured the nerve shattering barrages at Pozières during 1916. These experiences would prepare them for the trauma of Bullecourt.

On 3rd May 1917 Kennedy was again in the thick of battle when the 23rd Battalion attacked the German trenches at Bullecourt. He advanced across the machine gun swept and fought his way into the German first and second line trenches, then repulsed 3 German counter attacks. He recorded the following entry in his diary on that day:

> At 3-30 am we were lined up in the order we were to attack. We began the advances at 4-00 am Most of Fritz's entanglements blown to pieces, we get plenty of machine gun, high explosive and shrapnel. We took the first and second line of trenches known as the Hindenburg line. We captured a few prisoners. Fritz made 3 counter attacks during the

day, but failed each time. Most of it was hand to hand fighting, throwing hand grenades at each other. We were to have gone further but those on our right and left flank were held up. We gained ground to the extent of 1 km in depth. Our brigade suffered very heavily. In the morning Fritz was sniping at our stretcher-bearers, and wounded who could walk. Just before dusk our artillery put up a barrage about the village in front of us and made things very hot for Fritz. It was a clear day and we could see everything that was happening.[76]

The 23rd Battalion held onto their captured positions in the Hindenburg line until the afternoon on 4th May 1917 when they were relieved. By that time Kennedy and his comrades were exhausted. They withdrew to the railway embankment; however, there was no respite from German artillery and gas barrages as they rested in dug-outs:

> 4th At 2-00 pm we were relieved by the 3rd battalion and then made our way back to the railway embankment, which was our original front line. All of us worn out and weary, some of the lads fell asleep, very hard to wake up, which had to be done on account of gas shells dropping behind our line. A fine day. A few more prisoners brought in. About 9-00 pm began shelling the embankment and kept at it all night, he made things very uncomfortable for us. It was almost as severe as the bombardment we got the night after we advanced at Pozières.[77]

On 5th May the battalion was withdrawn to the rear. Kennedy was very fortunate for he was granted some leave to England.

Kennedy was back in France with the 23rd Battalion during 1918. On 23rd July 1918 he was wounded by gas. After convalescing at the 49th Casualty Clearing Station he rejoined his battalion on 10th August. Kennedy would see further action during the closing months of the war as the 23rd Battalion took part in the Battle for Mont St Quentin and in their final battle of the war at Beaurevoir on 3rd and 4th October 1918. Kennedy left the front line for the last time during 5th October 1918. On 19th October 1918 Kennedy was promoted to Corporal. Within weeks the armistice would be declared and his war would be over. He left England on 29th January 1919 and began the long passage home to Australia.

Joseph Kennedy would spend the next forty years working as a signalman on the Victorian Railways. When World War two broke out in 1939 he did not sign up saying 'he had enough of it the first time round'. Joseph never married and when he retired in 1958 he lived with his widowed sister in Warragul. He died in 1980 aged 87.

PRIVATE THOMAS OLDFIELD 1245,
23RD BATTALION AIF

Private Thomas Oldfield. (Courtesy Philip Whitehead)

Thomas Henry Oldfield was born in Leeds, England, in 1892. His parents were Thomas and Mary Oldfield and they raised nine children. Thomas was educated at Knaresborough Council School and Knaresborough Grammar School. In 1910, when he was aged 18 the family emigrated to Australia where they settled in Koyuga, Victoria. Four of their sons would serve in the AIF during the war. Thomas worked as a grocer's apprentice from 1914. He enlisted on 6th March 1915. After completing basic training he embarked aboard HMAT *Euripides* from Melbourne on 10th May 1915. He was attached to the 23rd Battalion and arrived on Gallipoli on 30th August 1915. Oldfield remained on the peninsula until the evacuation during December 1915. After spending several months in the Egyptian desert Oldfield was sent to France in June 1916. He sustained gun shot wounds to both legs when the 23rd Battalion fought at Pozières on 28th July 1917. Oldfield was evacuated from the Somme and two days later he was admitted to the 14th General Hospital at Wimereux, near Boulogne. He was then sent to the Northumberland War Hospital, Gosforth, Newcastle, England, where he recovered. He returned to the 23rd Battalion in France on 6th December 1916. Private Thomas Oldfield was killed in action at Bullecourt on 3rd May 1917. He has no known grave and his name is commemorated on the Australian memorial at Villers-Bretonneux. Oldfield is also commemorated on the Tongala War Memorial, Tongala, Victoria, Australia. The memorial is on a modern red brick block outside the Returned Servicemen's League (RSL) Club, with two white marble tablets for each of WW1 and WW2.

WW1 has 33 names including OLDFIELD T. H. Thomas is seated in the photo with his brother Farrar Oldfield. Farrar was one of the originals, a true Anzac who landed at Gallipoli on 25th April 1915. He was awarded the Military Medal for his role in the battle of Dernancourt during March 1918.

PRIVATE GEORGE WILSON 5716,
23RD BATTALION AIF

George Thomas Wilson was born in Sydney, New South Wales, in 1883. Before the war he worked as an agricultural labourer at Tallangatta, Victoria. He enlisted to join the AIF on 2nd February 1916, aged 33.

After completing basic training Wilson sailed from Melbourne aboard HMAT *Shropshire* on 25th September 1916, heading for Europe. Arriving in Plymouth on 11th November 1916, Wilson only spent a month in England. On 13th December he boarded the troopship *Princess Henrietta* at Folkestone and sailed for Boulogne. After spending three days at Etaples he was assigned to the 23rd Battalion and was sent to join them on the front. On 5th April 1917 Wilson was suffering from bronchitis and spent five days in hospital before rejoining his battalion.

On 3rd May 1917, at Bullecourt he suffered a gunshot wound to the left leg and was sent to England to recover. He was admitted to VAD Hospital, Cheltenham, on 5th May 1917, where he remained until 20th July 1917, when he was sent to a camp at Perham Downs. Instead of going straight to No. 1 Command Depot at Perham Downs, Wilson went absent without leave from 8.30 pm on 20th July until 3.30pm on 23rd July. He was fined four days pay and punished with five days confined to barracks. Wilson knew he was going to be sent back to the front now that his wound had healed. He had taken the opportunity to have some time to himself because he knew he may not get the chance again once he was back in France. On 1st September 1917 he left England for Havre in France. He rejoined the 23rd Battalion in Belgium on 9th September 1917. The battalion was

Private Thomas Oldfield is seated with his brother Farrar Oldfield. Farrar was one of the originals, a true Anzac who landed at Gallipoli on 25th April 1915. He was awarded the Military Medal for his role in the battle of Dernancourt in March 1918. (Courtesy Philip Whitehead)

Private George Wilson 1916, back row far right. (Courtesy Fay Pirotta)

based near the front at Ypres and was preparing to take part in the Third Ypres campaign. Wilson saw action again when the 23rd Battalion took part in an assault on Château Wood from 21st to 23rd September 1917. Within three weeks Wilson took part in another attack when the 23rd Battalion participated in the Battle of Broodseinde Ridge on 9th October 1917. They were involved in the capture of Daisy and Busy Woods.

Private George Wilson was killed on 10th November 1917. British artillery was firing a barrage into the German lines. German artillery responded and some of their shells fell upon positions held by the 23rd Battalion killing four men, including Wilson. His remains were never recovered from the muddy quagmire of Passchendaele and therefore his name is commemorated on the Menin Gate at Ypres, Belgium.

PRIVATE ARTHUR GRAHAM 3827,
24TH BATTALION AIF

Arthur George Graham was born in Wentworth, New South Wales on 27th September 1897. Before the war, he worked on the paddle steamer *Gem*, which operated on the Murray River. He joined the AIF on 4th December 1915 aged 18. His service record confirms that he had made one attempt to enlist but was rejected on medical grounds. The service record also confirms that he was a labourer from Melbourne and married to Elizabeth. After completing basic training he embarked from Melbourne on 8th February 1916, on the troopship HMAT *Warilda*. Private Arthur Graham was assigned to the 24th Battalion AIF and he served as a Lewis gunner. He was wounded during the battles for Pozières and Mouquet Farm during August 1916. He was patched up and returned to the front line promptly. However, he was seriously wounded in the back and lost a finger on his right hand on 3rd May 1917 while advancing at Bullecourt.

Graham was initially sent to hospital in Rouen and then was returned to England on 12th May 1917 aboard the troopship Essequibo from Boulogne. Two days later he was admitted to the 1st Southern General Hospital, King's Heath, Birmingham. A frequent visitor to the hospital was the young daughter of King George V. HRH The Princess Royal and she was a great favourite of the Australian servicemen, who appreciated her visits. Arthur Graham was sent back to Australia, departing from England aboard the troopship H.T. *Paketa* via New Zealand,

Private Arthur Graham.
(Courtesy Elsie Graham)

and arrived at Melbourne on 22nd October 1917. On arrival in Australia he was taken to the Repatriation Military Hospital at Caulifield, where he was taught to use his hands again. As part of his rehabilitation therapy Arthur made many things while he was in hospital including a small wool tapestry mat and a wooden case still owned by his daughter-in-law Elsie Graham. He was discharged as medically unfit on 28th November 1917.

He would be haunted by the horrors of the war throughout his life. His daughter-in-law Elsie Graham:

> Arthur was badly gassed and suffered from war neuroses. This affected him while he was sleeping during the night, he would relive the battles, and the shouting would wake the family, and they lived through the battles too. This must have happened in more homes in Australia than not? But the Australians never spoke about it.

Arthur would not march through Melbourne on Anzac Day, but would instead assist others in attending marches and luncheons. Elsie Graham recalled:

> I know Arthur did not march on Anzac Day in Melbourne. Instead he would use his car as a taxi, and work behind the scenes collecting disabled men for the Anzac Luncheon that took place at the end of the march. These luncheons were very personal reunions and seemed almost like a pilgrimage, by men who found mutual respect and humility in the memory of their comrades. 'Lest We Forget'.

In later life he took pleasure in making fishing nets. He enjoyed fishing for trout on the Murray River, reminiscing about the days when as a lad he worked on the steamer *Gem*. He died at Coburg, Victoria on 12th October 1949, aged 52.

CAPTAIN JOHN EDWARD LLOYD MC AND BAR,
24TH BATTALION AIF

John Edward Lloyd was born in Melbourne on 13th April 1894. Known as Jack, he qualified for appointment as a 2nd Lieutenant on 1st January 1914 and was attached to the 49th Infantry Battalion.

He enlisted to join the AIF on 1st May 1915 with the rank of Lieutenant and was posted to the 23rd Battalion. He embarked from

Captain John Lloyd,
'Bullecourt Jack'. (Courtesy
Jean & Denise Letaille
Bullecourt Museum)

Melbourne on 18th May 1915 arriving in Alexandria, Egypt, on 12th June. On 30th August 1915 Lloyd was sent to Gallipoli and within a month he was promoted to Captain. Stricken by typhoid on 11th November he was evacuated from Gallipoli and transferred to hospital in Alexandria where he recovered. He spent most of the following year in Egypt. He arrived at Plymouth on 20th September 1916. After spending several weeks with a training battalion in England, Lloyd was sent to France on 15th October and was transferred to the 21st Battalion. During December 1916 Lloyd was transferred to the 24th Battalion.

In May 1917 Lloyd led his soldiers from the 24th Battalion into the Hindenburg Line trenches and held his position against persistent German counter attacks. Lloyd was recommended for the Distinguished Service Order for his role at Bullecourt, but was awarded the Military Cross. His recommendation stated:

> For conspicuous gallantry, ability and determination in command of his battalion during the attack on the Hindenburg Line on 3rd May 1917 and the subsequent consolidations of the captured position.
>
> Dealing with a difficult situation on both flanks he displayed excellent judgment, in selecting the frontage which he held against repeated counter attacks until relieved, inflicting most severe losses on the enemy.
>
> After an exhaustive fight against superior numbers when the troops on his flanks had failed to make good the ground gained he brought his men out of action with losses amounting to 60 per cent, but still ready for action.[78]

After being awarded the Military Cross he was known affectionately by his men and fellow officers as 'Bullecourt Jack'.

Five months later Lloyd saw action again during the Third Ypres campaign at the battle of Broodseinde Ridge on 4th October 1917. Lloyd was an experienced soldier and was not daunted when events did not go according to plan. He was able to adapt to changing situations. Lloyd could reorganise his men and continue the attack in the face of overwhelming odds. As they were waiting for the barrage to lift prior to the advance on Broodseinde Ridge Lloyd steadied the men, reorganised the units and successfully led them in capturing two enemy pill boxes. During the battle Lloyd received gun shot wounds to his right shoulder and thigh. This did not deter him. Lloyd was awarded a bar to the Military Cross he had won at Bullecourt:

> For conspicuous bravery in the leading of his Company in the advance on Broodseinde Ridge

on 4th October. On the right flank whilst waiting for the lift of the barrage from the Red protective line this officer saved much confusion by skilful and quick re-organisation of units. By personal direction he was able to guide his Company with success in the mopping up of two Pill Boxes. At all times this officer moved about utterly regardless of personal danger, and along with his cheerfulness, was responsible for the keen spirit of resistance shown to the enemy. He personally reconnoitred ground in front of the advanced position, and located an enemy strong post which was subsequently blown out and two prisoners captured. Though wounded twice this officer remained on duty for 48 hours and has since been evacuated.[79]

Lloyd was taken to the 3rd General Hospital in London on 11th October. Days later he learnt that he was recommended to receive a bar to his Military Cross for his role at Broodseinde Ridge. While recovering from his wounds he was promoted to Major on 22nd October. On 12th February 1918 he was given a commission in the Indian Army. As the war ended in 1918 and his fellow countrymen were preparing to return to Australia, Lloyd would become embroiled in fighting in the Afghan War in 1919.

After a distinguished war service Bullecourt Jack returned to civilian life and became an analytical chemist. During the Second World War, Lloyd served Australia again as a Brigadier-General serving in the North African desert and on Kokoda Track in New Guinea.

He enlisted on 17th June 1940 with the rank of Major. During the following month he was attached to the 2/28th Battalion and promoted to Lieutenant Colonel. For the second time in his life Bullecourt Jack left the shores of Australia to sail 12,000 miles to fight in a World War for the freedom and liberty of others.

Embarking aboard a troopship on 3rd January 1941 he arrived in the Middle East on 2nd February. He continued to serve with the 2/28th Battalion throughout 1941 until he was seconded to 24th Brigade Headquarters. Lloyd was awarded the Distinguished Service Order for the role he played in the defence of Tobruk. His recommendation stated:

> At Tobruk during the period 26 Mar to 31 Jul 1941 Lt-Col. Lloyd has been in command of 2/28 Aust. Inf. Bn. Early in April during the withdrawal to this area of our forces Lt-Col Lloyd skilfully placed and handled his Bn. enabling our forces to withdraw from the perimeter defences occupied by his Bn. and hold off enemy forces during readjustment

and organisation of the Tobruk defences. With the exception of 9 days in reserve since 1 April his Bn. Has occupied front line defences in every sector of the Tobruk area during which time the activity of his unit in defence works raids and fighting patrols has been of an outstanding nature. Throughout the period Lt-Col Lloyd has been almost continuously among his forward troops by day and by night and by his fearlessness, cheery and untiring disposition and decided ability despite the undoubted strain to which he had been subjected he had done much to build and retain the undoubted efficiency and high morale which exists in his Bn.[80]

His DSO appeared in the *London Gazette* on 30th December 1941 together with a mention in dispatches. Lloyd returned to the 2/28th Battalion in January 1942.

On 7th March 1942 Lloyd was promoted to Brigadier and appointed commander of the 16th Australian Infantry Brigade. Three days later he left the Middle East and sailed for Ceylon for deployment in the Far East, arriving there on 27th March 1942. Lloyd was sent to Port Moresby in New Guinea during September. It was here that Lloyd effectively commanded his brigade in the battle against Japanese forces. He had fought at Gallipoli, Bullecourt, Broodseinde Ridge, Tobruk and in New Guinea he inflicted a decisive defeat upon the Japanese at Tempikton's Crossing and Kora Creek during the period October to December 1942. In December 1942 Lloyd contracted malaria and was sent to Australia to recover. After recovery in early 1943 he served as Chief Instructor at LHQ Tactical School and in September 1943 he was attached to HQ New Guinea Force. During November 1943 he arrived in New Delhi, India where he was transferred to South East Asia Command HQ. On 23rd December 1943 Lloyd was made a Commander of the Order of the British Empire, CBE. He continued to serve through the war and returned to Australia on 29th March 1945. He was demobilised in December 1945, placed on the reserve list as Brigadier. Jack Lloyd died on 24th December 1965.

LIEUTENANT EDWARD PITTARD MC
24TH BATTALION AIF

Edward James Pittard was born on 3rd October 1888 in Burnley, Victoria. He worked as a civil servant in the State Treasury Department prior to enlisting on 14th May 1915. He was commissioned as a 2nd Lieutenant. Pittard completed basic training at the Officer Training School at Broadmeadows. He was commissioned as a 2nd Lieutenant during November 1915. He embarked aboard the troopship HMAT *Warilda* at Melbourne on

Lieutenant Edward Pittard MC. (Courtesy Jean & Denise Letaille Bullecourt Museum)

8th February 1916 and sailed for Europe. While in France he was promoted to Lieutenant on 20th August 1916. Pittard led his men towards the trenches at Bullecourt on 3rd May 1917. Pittard received a gun shot wound that fractured his right leg. He continued to fight until he collapsed. Pittard was awarded the Military Cross for his courage and resilience. His citation stated: 'Though severely wounded, he continued to lead his men in the assault until he collapsed on reaching his objective. His fortitude and determination had a splendid effect upon his men'.[81] He was taken to the Military Hospital at Rouen and then transferred to a 3rd General London Hospital at Wandsworth, London, England.

PRIVATE NATHAN LEGGETT 5608,
25TH BATTALION AIF

Private Nathan Leggett. (Courtesy Ian Pinder)

Nathan Thomas Leggett was born at Bacton, Suffolk, England in October 1893. He was the son of Charles and Caroline Leggett. When war broke out the family was living at Hazel End Farm, Farnham, Bishop's Stortford, Hertfordshire. Nathan had emigrated to Australia where he worked as a labourer in Lismore, New South Wales.

Nathan enlisted to join the AIF as a private on 8th April 1916. After completing his basic training he embarked aboard HMAT *Clan McGillivray* on 7th September 1916 from Brisbane. He arrived at Plymouth England on 2nd November 1916. He was sent to France on 12th December 1916 and joined the 25th Battalion during February 1917.

He was killed on 3rd May 1917. Private Nathan Leggett was buried by Chaplain F.H. Divinford (attached to 6th Battalion AIF) opposite the railway embankment, however his grave was lost. Therefore Leggett, who was aged 24, has no known grave and his name is commemorated on the Australian National Memorial at Villers-Bretonneux.

CAPTAIN JACK ROYDHOUSE
28TH BATTALION AIF

Jack Roydhouse was born in Adelaide, South Australia, in 1892. He studied science at the University of Western

Australia. Prior to the war, Jack Roydhouse was a school master. He enlisted in Perth on 11th June 1915 aged 23. He left Australia aboard HMAT *Medic* from Fremantle on 18th January 1916 and arrived in Plymouth on 12th February 1916.

Assigned to the 28th Battalion he climbed the ranks and by 11th October 1916 he had been promoted to Captain. He received a gunshot wound to his left knee on 18th February 1917 at Flers and was sent to hospital in Rouen. He returned to his battalion on 9th April 1917 as a Company Commander.

During the Second Battle of Bullecourt on 3rd May 1917 he made determined onslaughts upon the German positions. Captain Roydhouse received the Military Cross for his work at Bullecourt. His citation records 'He displayed great courage and determination in organising and carrying out bombing attacks setting a splendid example to his men. His work helped materially to hold our positions.'[82]

He was buried by a shell explosion on that same day and would suffer shell shock and trench fever. He was admitted to the London General Hospital in Wandsworth, England, on 18th May 1917.

He returned to the 28th Battalion on 16th August 1917 and would suffer from the effects of gas during September 1917. During 1918 he worked for Major General Monash. He was mentioned in dispatches three times. When the war ended he was appointed Brigade-Major. He returned home to Subiaco, Western Australia, after the war.

PRIVATE GEORGE CHITTY 4993,
28TH BATTALION AIF

George Edward Chitty was born in Toodyay, Western Australia in 1893. He enlisted in February 1916. Chitty sailed for England on 17th July arriving in England in September 1916. Chitty was sent to France in November 1916. He saw action at Armentières, Bapaume and Bullecourt, where he was wounded. After recovering from his wounds he returned to the 28th Battalion. It is tragic that Chitty had travelled so far away from home and survived Bullecourt to be killed by the accidental discharge of a live round from a Lewis machine gun.

He was mortally wounded during training on 11th June 1918. He died on 13th June 1918 and was buried at Vignacourt British Cemetery. Private Thomas Riley witnessed the fatal accident:

> At Bertancourt during the Machine Gun instruction the accident occurred in a billet as it was a wet day. I was there at the time and saw it all. One of the party was practising with blank ammunition and by a mistake a live round got into the breach. Chitty was sitting directly in front of the gun and a bullet passed through his chest and out of his back. He was moved to Vignacourt C.C.S. where he only lived about 24 hours. He was well liked by everyone.[83]

PRIVATE ALFRED LLEWELLYN GREEN 5861,
28TH BATTALION AIF

Alfred Llewellyn Green was born in Northam, Western Australia, in 1879. Before the war he was a grocer from Northam and was married to Mary when he enlisted on 25th April 1916. Green embarked aboard HMAT *Suffolk* from Fremantle on 13th October 1916. He arrived in Plymouth on 20th December. During training in England he succumbed to tuberculosis and was in hospital from 20th February until 5th April 1917. He left Folkestone for France on 5th April and spent two weeks at Etaples. He joined the 28th Battalion on 19th April 1917. Within weeks he was in battle. On 4th May 1917 he was wounded in the face and sustained a compound fracture to his thigh. He had been in action for less than 36 hours. He was taken to a casualty clearing station where died of his wounds the following day on 5th May 1917. Private Alfred Green, who was aged 28, was buried at Grévillers British Cemetery.

LIEUTENANT EDWARD SMYTHE MC & BAR,
24TH BATTALION AIF

Edward Vivian Smythe was born in 1891. He was known as Viv to his family. He enlisted along with his three brothers. Viv went to Officer Training School and spent a year in Australia. Before leaving Australia he married his long-term sweetheart Clytie. On 2nd November 1915 he left Sydney aboard the troopship HMAT *Euripides* and sailed towards the war in Europe. During August 1916 he took part in the battle of Pozières.

In our last stunt the Batt did good work and a number of distinctions are to be awarded. As the O.C. couldn't differentiate between us, myself and the other sub in A coy tossed up for who would be recommended. I lost. Gambling is not my strong point so I have to wait for it until another opportunity offers but I assure you I'm not looking for anything beyond doing my job and getting safe home again. I've too high a regard for this precious skin of mine to risk it for the purpose of hanging a metal tag on myself. The stunt we were in was described by the papers as a neat piece of work. We hopped over at dusk and occupied our objective which was two lines of trenches about 100 yds apart. Captured and sent back the occupants, about 80, with little loss but as usual we had to hang on.[84]

During February 1917 Viv would distinguish himself during the battle for Dinkum Spur, near Warlencourt, where he led a strong patrol from the 24th Battalion into Camp Trench and held the position until nightfall under heavy enemy machine gun fire. Viv was awarded the Military Cross for his bravery.

On the 3rd May 1917, Viv advanced with the 24th Battalion. He gave a detailed description of his experience at Bullecourt in a letter he wrote to his father on 8th May 1917:

The stunt has 'been and went' as we used to say and still I am whole and undamaged. It was the stiffest fight my battalion has had yet and our own losses were proportionate but the men were splendid. We went out into No-Man's Land in single file and formed up in lines 500 from the Bosche Line. Fritz expected us and showed it by the numerous flares, the intermittent chatter of his machine guns as they searched for us and by the two search-lights which played over the ground every now and again. As we were in the lead we had to be out some little time to allow the rest to form up also, but this part of the operation went on smoothly and except for a little shelling without hindrance. After seeing that the men were in position and knew their direction we lay down and waited for the moment to advance. Five minutes

The Smythe Brothers, from left to right, Vern, Bert, Percy and Viv. (Courtesy Jacqui Smythe)

before time word was passed down the line to get ready. Almost before it reached the last man the sky, low down, behind us, burst suddenly into a flickering blaze of light as the guns behind us woke suddenly to life. In a few seconds a torrent of shells screamed overhead and burst like a sparkle of jewels in front. We rose and moved slowly forward, fixing bayonets as we went. No one hurried as there was plenty of time before that deadly hail was shifted back behind the first line trench, our objective. We overtook the barrage near the wire, but within a few seconds it shifted on and was now concentrated on the famous Hindenburg line, a hundred yards ahead.

Before this the slowly advancing waves had been seen by the defenders and a continuous crackle of machine gun bullets whipped and tore the air around us. But not for that would the advance stop. Calmly and coolly the men picked their way through the blasted wire and absolutely ignored the frantic machine guns. Once through the wire we were supposed to lie down and wait until the barrage lifted, but with the enemy so close in front few thought of anything but getting at him and so they pressed on through our own barrage and were fighting in the front line three minutes before the barrage lifted. As soon as the trench was cleared up we pushed along to both flanks to connect up with or assist the people attacking on either side. We soon found that except for a certain distance to the left where part of a battalion had got in, we were the only successful part of the attack and in a few minutes bombing operations were in full swing on both sides. Meanwhile the waves had passed through and soon the success signal was seen from the second line. Following the slowly advancing barrage, the last wave of our battalion steadily advanced and at the scheduled time signalled its occupation of our furthest objective. So far we were completely successful while on our right and left partial success only had resulted.

On our right the attack was twice renewed but each time it wilted and failed at the wire. The light had increased as daybreak approached and as the barrage had gone on advancing the Boche machine guns and automatic rifles were undisturbed, except on the extreme end of their defence where our bombers were at work. However, the attack had left us numerically weak for the length of line we held and we could do little more than hold our own. As the day advanced and it was seen that there was no chance of bringing the line up level with our furthest advance, we had to withdraw and be content with holding both lines of trenches. This we did, bombing almost continuously and holding off his desperate efforts to nip us off. During the night

Bert's lot came in and relieved us. I didn't see him but my C.O. did and told him I was O.K. We moved back to support and then to reserve and are now on our way out for a spell (we hope). Bert was OK the day after we were relieved, as I heard from the Q.M.S. of his company. As soon as I get time I'll hunt him up, but that won't be until we get to a place where we can stay a day or two.[85]

Viv was unaware that his brother Bert had been killed when the 3rd Battalion was relieving his battalion on 3rd May. He was still unaware of this tragic news when he wrote home to his father. It was not until the 13th May that he was told of his brother's death.

Viv was promoted to Captain and on 9th October 1917 he took part in the attack on Daisy Wood near Broodseinde in Belgium during the third Ypres campaign. When all company commanders and platoon officers had become casualties it was Viv who organised the men and coordinated the attack upon Daisy Wood. He was awarded a bar to his Military Cross. The recommendation states:

Throughout the day, he, at great personal risk supervised the whole battalion front as all other Company Commanders and many platoon officers had become casualties. His sound judgement made communication with all Companies possible and at all times he kept in close touch with Battalion Headquarters. His personal reconnaissance materially aided the clearing of Daisy Wood. Thoroughness and clear initiative inspired all ranks to offer material resistance to the enemy and eventually permitted the formation of a defensive line.[86]

Viv had attained the rank of Major by the end of the war. He returned home to Australia and later became a farmer. When the Second World War broke out in 1939 he was recalled to serve, retaining his rank as Major.

CORPORAL HERBERT SMYTHE 1175,
3RD BATTALION AIF

Herbert Andrew Smythe was born in Toorak, Victoria in November 1888. Known as Bert to his family, he was born into a family of nine children.

Bert was an experienced horse-man and a good shot with a rifle. In 1911 he left school and started work with the Postmaster General's Office where his three other brothers

Corporal Herbert Smythe.
(Courtesy Jacqui Smythe)

worked. Here they all learnt Morse code and Bert would become a telegraphist. During September 1912, Bert joined the Australian Rifles. By the time World War One began he had served less than two years with the militia.

He enlisted at Kensington in New South Wales with his brother Vern on 21st August 1914. Bert was given 1175 as a service number. Vern was 1174. On completing his basic training he and Vern embarked aboard HMAT *Euripides* at Sydney on 20th October 1914. The Army utilised Bert's experience as a postal official, for when they arrived in Aden. Bert, together with his brother Vern, were given the task of sorting the mail amounting to 15,000 letters which was to be sent from the *Euripides* back to Australia. They arrived at the mouth of the Suez Canal by 1st December 1914. They proceeded along the canal and disembarked at Alexandria. The 3rd Battalion was then taken to Mena Camp, close to the Pyramids near Cairo, where they would train.

On 4th April the 3rd Battalion entrained for Alexandria and boarded the SS *Derflinger*, a captured German vessel which was used by the Australians as a troopship. Bert was amused by the irony that he was being transported on a German ship. 'This is a boat that's been captured from the Germans _ _ _. That's insult to injury – using a German boat to take her enemies to the front.'[87] Bert was heading for Mudros for the impending Gallipoli campaign.

During the morning of 25th April 1915 Bert, his brother Vern and the 3rd Battalion AIF formed part of the second wave which landed on the beaches at Anzac Cove. Bert gave a graphic account of his first horrific experience of war. He saw the blood of dead comrades even before he landed on the beach:

We got on a destroyer and she took us pretty close in, and then we got into rowing boats and thus got on shore. When I first got on the destroyer I was as right as rain until I saw my first sight of the harvest of war. I saw blood oozing from beneath a tarpaulin and a sailor told me there were 4 dead men under it – killed by shrapnel on the destroyer before they even landed. When the boats got into 3 ft of water, we all jumped out and waded ashore feeling mighty thankful that we'd got so far.[88]

Bert dodged the Turkish bullets and shell fire as he dashed from the sea across the beach to the bottom of the cliffs. Here they had to take cover from Turkish troops firing from the cliff tops. Heavily laden with extra rations and ammunition Bert and his comrades from 3rd Battalion had to climb steep cliffs under this enemy fire:

Hills! They're awful. We simply had to pull ourselves up hand by hand, and to improve matters we had 50 rounds of extra ammunition, three days rations, and some firewood. Presently we got to a plateau with a lovely trench in it that the Turks, with commendable foresight had provided for us.[89]

Fortunately for the 3rd Battalion, the cliffs which towered over their landing beach were lightly defended by Turkish units. Bert ascended the cliffs and took part in the consolidation of the Turkish trenches which the 3rd Battalion had captured. The next four days would be spent defending their positions. Their Turkish opponents denied them the opportunity to settle down and they were unable to rest. Bert lost most of his belongings during the first days of the campaign. In a letter to his parents he confirmed that: 'I've lost every mortal thing I own except the clothes I used to stand in and my great coat. Had four different rifles during the fighting. The beggars never gave us a moment's peace the whole time I was there.'[90]

Turkish artillery pounded the Australian positions. During his fourth day on Gallipoli a shell exploded close to an observation post Bert was occupying. A mass of earth was propelled into the sky and fell upon the observation post burying Bert and his fellow occupants up to their necks.

Bert was wounded five days after landing at Anzac. As British Tommies were relieving the 3rd Battalion on the 30th April, Bert received a gunshot wound to the right shoulder:

> A concussion shrapnel landed right in the trench fair opposite us and buried us up to our necks in dirt. I scrambled to my feet to see if I was hurt and was mighty thankful to find I wasn't ... Whilst having tea a bit after dark I had to take an officer to a trench he did not know! Only expected to be away 10 minutes so I left haversack, water bottle, rifle and all behind me. While away the enemy suddenly threatened us with a bayonet charge so we all rushed to the front line. I grabbed a rifle – a broken one too – fixed the bayonet and hopped in with them ... Later we had to cross over about a hundred yards under fire to reach safety at the rear of a hill so we rushed over. About ten yards from the safety trench I stopped to walk when I got a knock in the shoulder like the kick of a 12-inch gun. I didn't want another, and tumbled into the trench mighty quick. Got the wound dressed and was led back to the rear. I'm hanged if I know where the beggar could have been. He must have been almost under me, and the valley beneath us was full of our own boys. The bullet went in at the back of my armpit and came out near the top of my shoulder in front.[91]

When Bert arrived at the rear he was pleased to see his brother Vernie who comforted him by making him a cup of tea. Doctors considered it necessary for him to be evacuated from the Gallipoli peninsula and on 3rd May he was transferred to the hospital ship Galilon, which took him to Alexandria, Egypt. Bert was transferred to the Goorkha on that same day and sailed for Southampton, England.

As Bert was being transported back to England, his brother Vernie continued to fight against the Turks. In a letter to his mother on 9th May 1915, he tried to reassure her that Bert was alright, despite being wounded:

> Today completed our fourteenth day of battle, and up to the present I have not received a scratch. Don't worry about Bert. His wound is in the shoulder but is only a flesh wound, and was made by a clean bullet. Had it been a dum-dum it would have blown his arm off. Some of the chaps have been frightfully torn about by dum-dums.[92]

On 20th May 1915, aged only 20, Vern received a battlefield commission and was promoted to the rank of 2nd Lieutenant.

On arrival in England Bert was admitted to 1st Southern General Hospital in Birmingham on 16th May 1915. He wrote of the pleasure of travelling by train from Southampton to Birmingham and of the warm reception he received from the English people:

> We arrived at Southampton, Sunday 16th May. They put us in a lovely hospital train. You ought to see the English scenery. In Spring – well words can't describe it. Lovely green fields fringed in almost every case by either beautiful hedges or trees ... We got a great reception at Birmingham. As soon as we got off the platform there was a long line of motors waiting for us, and an enormous crowd and they cheered us all a treat. It was the same all the way to the hospital. Everybody we passed waved to us and gave us a smile of welcome. It was particularly cheerful after being outside of civilisation since we left dear old Australia.[93]

While he was recovering from his wound, Bert had time to reflect on the five days which had spent on Gallipoli. The brief experience had changed Bert as a man and his outlook on war. He wrote:

> I've seen enough to convince me that it's a horrible ghastly business and all the glamour leaves it when you look over the sights with the bullets from the enemy cracking all around and you see your dead and dying mates near and hear the wounded moaning. I've come throu the first chapter O.K. for I consider my shoulder wound nothing.[94]

It took two months for Bert to recover from his wounds. On 21st July 1915 Bert sailed aboard the troopship Grampian from Weymouth back to Egypt to rejoin the Mediterranean Expeditionary Force. Arriving in Alexandria on 2nd August he was sent to a camp at Mustapha, near to the Egyptian port. On the 10th August he boarded the troopship Cawdor Castle which would take him back to Gallipoli. By 15th August, Bert had rejoined the 3rd Battalion on Gallipoli and was back in the trenches. There was a reunion with his brothers Vernie and Percy in dug-outs at Shrapnel Valley, at Lone Pine. On the 17th August 1915, he wrote to his family from Gaba Tepe:

> Well I'm back in this unhealthy hole again but I'm glad to say it hasn't had any ill effect on me so far. Arrived here last Sunday 15th about 3am and moved into the trenches at 9am and am now enjoying 48 hrs leave with the others after 48 hrs of the other thing.[95]

Gallipoli was indeed an unhealthy place to be. While in front-line trenches Bert had to sleep in his clothes, so that if the Turks launched an attacked he would be dressed to fight. Keeping himself clean was a difficult task because Turkish snipers were close by and there was very little water to drink, let alone to wash. Flies would also cause problems for Bert and his comrades in Gallipoli:

> 'The flies here are something awful. They stop on your tucker all the way to ones mouth and then they have to be threatened with death by mastication before they'll depart to something else you are waiting to eat. Things can't be too good with them tho, cos they commit suicide in thousands wherever they can find hot tea. Poor things I suppose they have their troubles too. Perhaps they are unhappily married or something. Who can tell?[96]

It was not long before the insanitary conditions would affect his health. Together with nerves being fraught and shaken by the daily dangers of exploding shells and gunfire, being tired by daily life in the trenches Bert's resistance would diminish making him susceptible to any illnesses that were circulating through the trenches. On 15th September 1915 Bert was admitted to hospital at Mudros with bronchitis. His condition deteriorated to influenza and dysentery. As a consequence Bert was sent back to England to recover. He was admitted to the 3rd London General Hospital in Wandsworth. Although he was pleased to be away from the front, Bert was ambitious and several times he missed out on promotion due to ill health. During March 1916 Bert was sent to Egypt to rejoin the Mediterranean Expeditionary Force. He rejoined the 3rd Battalion at Tel-el-Kebir. During

April 1916 Bert had been promoted to Corporal. The following month Bert saw advertisements for qualified telegraphists for which he applied and was accepted by the Signal School at Perham Downs, in Hampshire, England. He arrived there during June 1916 and the following month he was transferred to the Signal School at Weymouth, Dorset and trained to become an instructor in telegraphy until September 1916. He was sent to a training camp based at Perham Downs. Here he trained battalion signallers, but Bert was anxious to go to France. He made efforts to get to the Western Front but his requests for active service were declined. In a letter home of 27th September 1916 he wrote:

> I felt that it was my duty to get over to France if possible and with that in view I approached the Signal Officer but he has turned me down – refuses in fact to hear of it, so for a while at least you can imagine me safe and snug in Eng whilst the others are in France doing their bit – and mine.[97]

Bert Smythe was sent to France on 13th March 1917, leaving Folkestone by troopship to Boulogne. The following day he arrived at Etaples. On 1st April 1917 he rejoined the 3rd Battalion.

Within the next few weeks, Bert Smythe would see action with the 3rd Battalion when he came under heavy German shell fire near Hermies:

> Was in a bit of a stunt the other day when another Bn and C & D coys of ours took Hermies. [Canal?] to be in it cos I had a fatigue party carrying up iron rations to feed the M. Guns. Fritz threw a lot of metal at us – it was the worst I had up till then experienced, but we came throu O.K. Gave Fritz a severe towelling and got quite a lot of prisoners. A few mornings later he put a barrage behind us and bombarded us but nothing much came of it. A great number of HEs fell very close to us, but owing to the softness of the earth, only 2 went off. One of the ones that didn't go off was so close that when it stuck it violently shook our dug-out. just before day break the same morning a party of about 40 Fritz tried to get around on to the right flank of No 1 platoon, and apparently unaware of our position, ran almost into us and although it was dark, still at 200 yds they were a pretty good target and so they came the proverbial G. Our Lewis gun chopped them up more than a little bit. I bagged one. Had pretty rotten weather nearly all the time we were in. At present we are out just behind the line having a spell with only an occasional shell from Fritz.[98]

On 3rd May 1917 the 3rd Battalion entered the front line at Bullecourt relieving the 24th Battalion in the OG

1 and OG 2 trenches. Bert's brother Viv, serving with the 24th Battalion was leaving the front as Bert and the 3rd Battalion was going in. The brothers did not come into contact with each other that day. Bert Smythe was killed on 3rd May 1917.

Lieutenant Viv Smythe was told about Bert's death. In a letter to their brother Percy, Viv wrote:

> I rode over to look Bert up the day before yesterday and was informed when I found his batt that he had been killed on 5th instant in the Hindenburg Line E

of B – where we had got in and where Bert's lot had relieved us. After several counter attacks had been beaten off, the captured position was very heavily shelled and in this shelling Bert crossed over. Death was instantaneous, so he felt no pain and knew nothing of the terror of approaching the brink.[99]

Bert was buried near to the location where he fell on the Bullecourt battlefield. The grave was lost and his name is commemorated on the Australian National Memorial at Villers-Bretonneux.

NOTES

1. Australian War Memorial: AWM 28//1/24P2/0071: Lieutenant Benno Lehmann: MC Recommendation.
2. *London Gazette*: Issue 30234: 16th August 1917.
3. Australian War Memorial: AWM 1DRL428/00021: Australian Red Cross Missing File Lieutenant Benno Lehmann.
4. National Archives of Australia: Sergeant Gordon Chick Service Record.
5. Australian War Memorial: AWM 1DRL428/00007: Australian Red Cross Missing File: Sergeant Gordon Chick.
6. Private Francis Ellison Dare papers, courtesy Scott Wilson.
7. Ibid.
8. Ibid.
9. Ibid.
10. Ibid.
11. Ibid.
12. Ibid.
13. Ibid.
14. Ibid.
15. Ibid.
16. Ibid.
17. Ibid.
18. Australian War Memorial: AWM 1DRL428/00009: Australian Red Cross File Private Ellison Dare.
19. Australian War Memorial: AWM 1DRL428/00030: Australian Red Cross Missing File: Private Charles Rosenwax.
20. Ibid.
21. Australian War Memorial: AWM 1DRL428/00009: AWM: Red Cross Missing File: Lance Corporal Archibald Curvey.
22. Corporal Ivor William's diary: Courtesy of Hugh Williams.
23. Ibid.
24. Ibid.
25. Ibid.
26. Ibid.
27. Ibid.
28. Ibid.
29. Ibid.
30. Ibid.
31. Ibid.
32. Ibid.
33. Ibid.
34. Ibid.
35. Letter from Private William Layburn: 15th May 1915: Courtesy Wilf Layburn.
36. Ibid, 19th September 1916.
37. Ibid, 17th October 1916.
38. Ibid, 3rd November 1916.
39. Ibid, 8th January 1917.
40. Letter from Private William Layburn to his mother Jane: 16th March 1917.
41. Ibid, 12th April 1917.
42. Ibid, 24th May 1917.
43. Letter from Private William Layburn to his brother Tom: 25th August 1917.
44. Letter from Private William Layburn to his mother Jane: 24th May 1917.
45. Letter from Private William Layburn to his brother Tom: 25th August 1917.
46. Letter from Private William Layburn to his mother: 9th September 1917.
47. Letter from Private William Layburn to his brother Tom: 25th August 1917.
48. Ibid, 9th September 1917.
49. Ibid, 9th September 1917.
50. Ibid, 20th September 1917.
51. Letter from Private William Layburn to his mother Jane: 27th September 1917.
52. Australian War Memorial: AWM 28/1/95P2/0018: Private William Layburn MM recommendation.
53. Lance Corporal William Layburn Papers, courtesy Wilf Layburn.
54. Australian War Memorial: AWM 1DRL428/00021: Australian Red Cross File Lance Corporal William Layburn.
55. Ibid.

56. Australian War Memorial: AWM 1DRL428-00027: Australian Red Cross Missing File: Private Henry Olsen.
57. Australian War Memorial: AWM 28/1/69/0071: Captain Frank Dunn MC recommendation.
58. Australian War Memorial: AWM 1DRL428/00010: Australian Red Cross File: Captain Frank Dunn.
59. Ibid.
60. Ibid.
61. Ibid.
62. Private Joseph Kennedy's diary. Courtesy Ron Wilson.
63–77. Ibid.
78. Australian War Memorial: AWM 28/1/87/0084: Captain Jack Lloyd MC recommendation.
79. Ibid.
80. National Archives of Australia: Brigadier John Lloyd's service record.
81. *London Gazette*: Issue 30188: 17th July 1917.
82. Ibid.
83. Australian War Memorial: AWM 1DRL428/00007: Australian Red Cross Files: Private George Chitty.

84. Letter to his wife Clytie: 11th August 1916: Lieutenant Viv Smythe Papers, Courtesy Jacqui Kennedy.
85. Letter to his father, Ted Smythe: 7 May 1917: Lieutenant Viv Smythe Papers, Courtesy Jacqui Kennedy.
86. Australian War Memorial: AWM 28/1/95P2/0041: Lieutenant Viv Smythe bar to MC recommendation.
87. Corporal Bert Smythe Papers, Courtesy Jacqui Kennedy.
88. Ibid.
89. Ibid.
90. Ibid.
91. Ibid.
92. Private Vernie Smythe Papers, Courtesy Jacqui Kennedy.
93. Corporal Bert Smythe Papers.
94. Ibid.
95. Ibid.
96. Ibid.
97. Ibid.
98. Ibid.
99. Lieutenant Viv Smythe Papers.

Bullecourt Jack attending an Anzac Day Parade during the Second World War. (Courtesy Jean & Denise Letaille Bullecourt Museum)

CHAPTER 18

THE 62ND DIVISION'S ASSAULT ON BULLECOURT: 3RD MAY 1917

The 62nd Division commanded by Major-General Walter Braithwaite comprised the 185th, 186th and 187th Brigades, which had never taken part in a major offensive. The Division was supported by 10 tanks from D Battalion Machine Gun Corps Heavy Branch and the 22nd Brigade from the 7th Division was seconded to 62nd Division as a reserve.

Preparatory British barrages were falling upon German positions along the Bullecourt front during the morning of the 2nd May. German guns retaliated with shelling upon British lines and as a consequence cut all communication lines on each brigade sector.

The 185th Infantry Brigade was ordered to capture the German trenches of the Hindenburg Line, including the village of Bullecourt. On their left the 186th Infantry Brigade would drive through the Hindenburg line and capture Hendecourt, while on the far left flank the 187th Brigade would form a defensive perimeter around Hendecourt.

On the 1st May 1917, Major-General Walter Braithwaite, conscious that this was the first battle of the 62nd Division, sent the following message to the division:

As the Division will be shortly be going into action to take part in the first great battle, the Divisional Commander desires to assure all ranks of his complete confidence in their ability to defeat the German troops opposed to them. That the 62nd (West Riding) Division will maintain its reputation for staunchness and grit – qualities for which Yorkshiremen have ever been famed – that they will gain all objectives and defend them against the most determined counter-attacks, is the firm conviction of the General Officer who is proud to be their Commander.[1]

185TH BRIGADE FRONT

The 2nd/6th Battalion left their billets at Ervillers at 7.30 pm on the evening of 2nd May 1917. They were ordered to take part in the assault on the south eastern sector

of Bullecourt. Battalion strength comprised 20 officers and 380 men. On arriving at Mory at 8.30 pm they received a hot meal before they entered the line and their jumping off positions. Lieutenant Colonel Hastings set up his battalion headquarters in a German dug-out located on the Longatte – Bullecourt Road and all his men were in place by 3.10 am on 3rd May.

The attack was scheduled to take place at 3.45 am on 3rd May. The advancing infantry battalions from the 62nd Division would be supported by a creeping barrage. Artillery would focus their guns upon the German wire defences at a rate of 100 yards in three minutes. British infantry would follow this barrage closely.

The 185th Brigade was commanded by Brigadier-General Vigant William de Falbe. The units from the 185th Brigade were in their jumping off positions by 2.10 am. By 3.30 am all units from the 62nd Division were in their assembled positions waiting for Zero Hour. The moon was shining strong that night and the German observers saw their movements and became suspicious of an imminent attack. They sent several very lights into the sky. Five minutes before Zero Hour, the Germans had pre-empted an attack and launched their own artillery barrage at 3.40 am. This barrage would be intense until 4.50 am that morning and would cause many casualties amongst the British troops waiting for Zero Hour.

The 185th Brigade had the difficult task of capturing the heavily fortified village of Bullecourt. The 2/6th West Yorkshire Regiment advanced on the right flank with the 2nd/5th West Yorkshires on the left flank. The 2nd/7th West Yorkshires was held in reserve. Four battalions from the Duke of Wellington's Regiment, supported by the 2nd/8th West Yorkshire Regiment, were designated to capture trenches south west of Bullecourt and advance towards Hendecourt. Heavy belts of wire covered this area and were within range of carefully positioned machine guns that would fire upon troops as they were filtered by V shaped wire formation into designated killing fields.

At 3.37 am the 2nd/6th West Yorkshire Regiment moved to their starting line. Many casualties had already been suffered due to the German shelling. Two minutes after the Yorkshire battalions left their jump off positions German machine guns were firing through the barrage towards the advancing British troops. They had to dash across 200 yards before they reached the German wire. They advanced behind a creeping barrage moving at a rate of 100 yards every four minutes. When they were held up at the wire, the British barrage continued to creep towards Bullecourt. With the advance thwarted by the German wire, the Yorkshire men were unable to keep up.

The 62nd Division achieved limited success in its assault upon Bullecourt; units from the 187th Brigade managed to temporarily capture parts of the Hindenburg Line trenches, but were soon repulsed by the enemy.

It was emphasised to Lieutenant Colonel Hastings commanding the 2nd/6th West Yorkshire Regiment that it was important his battalion should link up with the 22nd Battalion AIF and communication between the units was established prior to the assault.

The 185th Brigade advanced upon Bullecourt in four waves using the leapfrog system, carrying the right flank they had fought their way into Bullecourt, but their attempts to consolidate captured ground was frustrated by soldiers from the 27th Württemberg Division concealed within the rubble, dug-outs and underground cellars in the village. The men of the 27th Württemberg Division had been stationed in the village since the first battle in April and were tired, shell shattered and hungry, but determined to hold.

Smoke from shells and dust were blown into the faces of the soldiers from West Yorkshire by a north-easterly wind. They were blinded, which caused the 2/6th West Yorkshires lose their intended course, intermingling with the 2/5th West Yorkshires on their left flank. German machine gun fire from the direction of an abandoned British tank also caused the 2nd/6th Battalion to alter their intended course. The 2/6th West Yorkshires sustained heavy casualties as they advanced upon the village. Some men were killed by friendly fire from their own creeping barrage. Many others were killed by German machine gun fire. The 2/6th West Yorkshires were annihilated during their baptism of fire. According to official reports 287 out of 393 men were casualties, including every officer. Sixty four years later Private Willie Greaves wrote that his 'most vivid war memory is of the Battle of Bullecourt

Private Willie Greaves in later life. (Courtesy Judith Lydon)

(3/5/17) ... a black day for many Bradford families.'[2] Greaves, who belonged to the 2nd/6th Battalion West Yorkshire Regiment acted as a runner during that fateful day when we was wounded. In a letter to a Yorkshire newspaper editor he provided an emotive and detailed account of his ordeal. When he was aged 84 he recalled the experience which haunted him:

We had taken up our positions during darkness the previous night with no undue trouble, which ought to have made us suspicious, but we ordinary lads didn't think about it – 'Jerry' was very quiet, but when we started to move at Zero Hour, 3.45 am on the 3rd May, all hell was let loose – and shells rained on the German lines. Their shells and machine gun bullets rained on us – we had not previously experienced such density of fire. We could not see very clearly, but those of our comrades who had already gone forward, seemed to be dropping like flies and struggling in the barbed wire, which, although pretty well cleared by our barrage, was still not easy to surmount under fire! How anyone at all came through that morning was a miracle! I learned afterwards that out of 405 men who went 'over the top' scarcely 100 men came back, all our 12 officers being either killed or wounded.

I considered myself fortunate having been detailed as a 'Runner' with a chap called Tom Illingworth. Our job was to reach a pre-arranged point and then stay put, ready to rush back any messages given to us by an officer. I don't know how long the battle had been raging when an officer gave Tom and I a folded message and shouted 'HQ quick' – who he was I never knew as he was filthy and quite unrecognizable, even though I knew them all. We dashed off, excitement dominating our fear of the bursting shells and bullets which buzzed around us like thousands of angry hornets.

Soon we were out of bullet range, but not before one hit me – it felt as if somebody had laid a red-hot poker across the calf of my leg. The wound was not bad enough to hold me up, so after putting a 'Field Dressing' on it we carried on from shell-hole to shell-hole, getting what brief respite and shelter we could. Soon again, getting out of a shell-hole into which we had just jumped, I was hit once more, this time (I found out later) by a small piece of shrapnel in one of my nostrils. It felt as if an Elephant had kicked me – blood spurted profusely all over my tunic and for a while I was knocked out. How glad I was to have a 'Pal' – when I eventually came round there was Tom doing what he could for me. Somehow he had not received a scratch and although I suggested he carried on with the message he refused to leave me and insisted on half-walking me to half carrying me. In spite of the danger, he kept going until we reached Battalion HQ. I had lost so much blood that as we arrived at the 'Dug-out', I must have passed out because the next thing I remembered was waking up in the Casino Hospital in Boulogne, many miles behind the front.[3]

The loss of officers made it difficult to know what was going on. It was very dark; the dust which was caused by the British and German barrages also impeded the vision of observers at the railway embankment. Lieutenant Colonel Hastings did not receive any news until after 6.00 am. He had sent officers and runners to get news of the progress of his battalion, but none had returned.

In the post operation report, Lieutenant Colonel Hastings wrote of how his battalion was decimated during the early hours of that morning:

On the right, owing to the darkness and dust thrown up by the barrage, direction was lost. Although attempts were made to correct this in 'A' Coy, very few men succeeded in reaching the objective. Those who did were promptly counterattacked, and killed, wounded or made prisoners. B Company were also driven away from their objective and were mostly killed, wounded or prisoners. The survivors of the right of the Bn's attack were very few in number, and I may state, fighting very severely, but the odds were against them.[4]

2nd Lieutenant Robert Bickerdike and 2nd Lieutenant V. Wilson led C Company from the 2nd/6th West Yorkshire Regiment did manage to fight their way into a trench just south of the village of Bullecourt. Bickerdike and his men destroyed three German dug-outs and caused many casualties amongst the occupants. German forces made numerous counter attacks from the east of the

Barbed wire pickets still in use during 2009 in fields south of Bullecourt. Over 90 years ago this was a killing field where soldiers from Yorkshire were mown down by German machine gun fire. (Author)

village, pushing them towards the 2nd/5th Battalion. Bickerdike was wounded as he held onto his position. An article appeared in the 20th June 1917 edition of the *Harrogate Herald* which described how Bickerdike narrowly escaped death during this battle:

Lt Bickerdike had a miraculous escape. A bullet passed through the front of his helmet, and came out at the back, leaving a huge bulge. The missile just grazed the top of his head, narrowly escaping the brain.[5]

C Company was forced to retire due to lack of ammunition. Bickerdike was awarded the Military Cross for his conduct at Bullecourt. His citation states:

For conspicuous gallantry and devotion in an attack, when he destroyed three hostile dug-outs causing many casualties and finally, although wounded himself, took command of his company, holding his ground against superior numbers until his ammunition ran out.[6]

Bickerdike retired to the railway embankment. Within months of being wounded at Bullecourt he was promoted to Captain. He was killed during the Battle of Cambrai on 20th November 1917. He was aged 29 and buried at Sains-Les-Marquion British Cemetery near Cambrai. The Colonel of his regiment wrote the following condolence letter to Bickerdike's brother:

Please accept my great sympathy on your brother's death in action on the 20th. He was killed instantaneously whilst leading his company to the assault of Havrincourt. I cannot tell you how much I regret his loss. He was absolutely reliable

Bullecourt from the south. Soldiers from the 2nd/5th and 2nd/6th West Yorkshire Battalions advanced either side of this road towards the village on 3rd May 1917. (Author)

and absolutely fearless, and was invaluable to his company both as a trainer and leader of men.[7]

D Company had leap-frogged C Company and fought their way northwards through to Bullecourt. It is assumed that all the officers belonging to this company were killed or wounded. There is a report which states that men from this company reached the ruins of the church in the centre of the village where they established posts under the command of an officer from the 2nd/5th Battalion West Yorkshire Regiment. What happened to these men is uncertain. Lieutenant Colonel Hastings wrote, 'How long these posts held out, or what was their ultimate fate, no one has been procurable.'[8]

2nd Lieutenant Robert Frost led remnants from his platoon numbering six men along the south trench before Bullecourt and was engaged in a savage bayonet fight, carrying on until they were all wounded and forced to retire. For his bravery Lieutenant Frost was awarded the Military Cross. His citation states: 'For conspicuous gallantry and devotion to duty. Although wounded he gallantly led a few men forward, and himself accounted for the enemy.'[9] The recommendation for the Military Cross shows more detail about the brutal engagement which took place between Frost and the enemy. It highlights the bitter fight to the death in which Frost was engaged:

> In the attack on Bullecourt at 3.45 am on the 3rd May 1917 his platoon having been divided he went along the trench on the S. side of the village with six men meeting Germans suddenly, he bayoneted one, the bayonet breaking in him, and the man drawing his pistol, Lieut. Frost brought him down with the butt end of his rifle, then he shot two others with his revolver. Carrying on a Lewis Gun was brought into action though himself was wounded in two places, and saved from three other wounds by his equipment he stood firm against odds until all his men were casualties when he retired.[10]

2nd Lieutenant H. Rhodes went forward despite his head wound and rallied five men sheltering in shell holes exposed to enemy machine gun fire. Leading them through the wire to join elements of his company in Bullecourt he was once again wounded in the arm, but he still persisted in the attack. He was forced to withdraw once he received his final wound to his knee. For commitment to duty he was awarded the Military Cross.

Lieutenant Cecil Denbigh Hannam, West Yorkshire Regiment, was another officer recommended for the Military Cross for bravery. His recommendation for the award states that:

Before Bullecourt on the morning of 3rd May 1917 he carried out a reconnaissance of much value under heavy machine gun fire to maintain touch with troops attacking Bullecourt and was invaluable in keeping his commanding officer informed of the position at a time when communication was very difficult indeed. Later, although severely wounded in the head he set a fine example of cheerfulness to his men under very heavy shell fire and refused to relinquish command of his Company until he had been relieved.[11]

At 7.10 am a Company from the 2nd/7th Battalion was sent to reinforce the depleted ranks of the 2nd/6th Battalion, but they were held up by the same German machine gun which was positioned by the abandoned tank and swept the line of advance. This Company had sustained heavy casualties and was forced to return back to the railway embankment.

Further attempts were made to bolster the 2nd/6th Battalion's front, but they were stopped by German machine gun fire. Only a few individuals managed to make an advance by crawling from shell hole to shell hole. The 6th Australian had broken into German trenches east of Bullecourt on the right flank of the 2nd/6th Battalion but was unable to advance westwards into the village to join them.

The 2nd/5th West Yorkshire Regiment was positioned on the left flank of the Hastings 2nd/6th Battalion. They were in their jump off positions by 2.45 am on the 3rd May. An hour later, Josselyn's 2nd/5th Battalion advanced towards Bullecourt. As soldiers from A and B Companies promptly crossed No Man's Land they discovered that the wire had been successfully cut by the Allied bombardments before the attack. They fought their way into the German trench and proceeded westwards along the trench towards the Crucifix. As they continued to fight through this trench north of the Crucifix, they captured one officer and 31 German troops.

Men from C and D Companies leap-frogged A and B Companies and entered Bullecourt, where they succeeded in establishing two strong positions in the centre of the village. D Company met up with soldiers from the 2nd/6th Battalion party and established a position near to the derelict church in the north of the village. German resistance intensified as heavy machine gun fire was brought upon them. The 2/5th West Yorkshires advanced through the village and secured further posts along the northern perimeter of the village, however they could not be held as the day progressed, because units were unable to follow and support them, leaving them cut off. A message carried by pigeon was received from an officer who was holding onto a position in Bullecourt. It was timed at 5.15 am. He confirmed that he was in a German communication trench with 40 of his men from the 2nd/5th Battalion and 4 men from the 2nd/6th West Yorkshires. He reported the presence of several German machine gun positions. At 6.35 am the German defence grew more ferocious as they tried to clear the West Yorkshire battalions from Bullecourt. At this stage the majority of officers within the 2nd/5th Battalion were casualties. Captain Green took command. Supported by Company Sergeant Major William Rathke they held a line of posts established within the rubble and shell craters that pocketed Bullecourt. Rathke had been wounded in the assault, but with disregard for his wounds he organised an attack upon enemy positions. His citation for the Distinguished Conduct Medal reads:

> Although himself wounded, he collected and successfully led a small party against a strong enemy bombing attack upon our trenches. His promptitude saved the situation at a very critical time. With great determination and coolness, he remained at his post, indifferent to his wounds, until his company was relieved.[12]

By 4.00 pm the 62nd Division had been expelled from the village and was back at the starting position by the railway embankment.

THE 186TH BRIGADE FRONT

The 186th Brigade, commanded by Brigadier-General F Hill, was assigned the objectives of securing the Hindenburg Line, then the Quéant-Fontaine Road (otherwise known as the *Artillerie Schutztellung*), before taking the village of Hendecourt. Prior to Zero Hour white flares were being propelled into the dawn sky by the Germans. All troops from the 186th Brigade were in position on their jump off tapes by 3.15 am on 3rd May. Enemy shelling of the lanes had declined and the brigade formed up without sustaining any casualties. As soon as the British barrage began, dust and debris made observation difficult for the battalions to advance in the right direction. Disorientated, the battalions of the 186th Brigade suffered the same problem as other battalions advancing upon Bullecourt that morning. Brigadier General F.F. Hill, commanding the 186th Brigade reported:

> From the time our barrage opened, the maintenance of direction was found to be a matter of extreme difficulty. Clouds of dust enveloped the whole area, and troops were unable to distinguish either the exact line of the barrage in the case of leading waves, or the location of troops in their immediate front in case of the remaining waves.[13]

As the British barrage lifted, the advancing soldiers from the 186th Brigade were within the sight of the German machine gunners who poured murderous fire upon their lines. They encountered a machine gun position near to the Crucifix that caused a large number of casualties. The 2/5th Duke of Wellington's Regiment linked with elements from the 185th Brigade, but suffered heavily from machine gun fire at the wire. The right flank had no problems in crossing the wire, however, on the left flank the enemy had successfully repaired many areas of the wire and small pockets of German infantry covered places where breaches still remained. Brigadier-General Hill:

> A very heavy machine gun fire was opened along the whole Brigade front as soon as the barrage lifted off the German front line. This undoubtedly contributed largely to the heavy casualties incurred. One case is known of at about U.21.c.8.8., where an Officer led his men through a gap in the enemy's wire, and, on reaching the German support line at about U.21.b.0.3., he found himself the sole survivor, the others having been wounded by Machine Gun Fire. This Officer returned and brought up a fresh party of men from the German front line, but only four of these succeeded in reaching the support line. A portion of our troops undoubtedly reached the 1st objective from U.21.d.5.6. to U.21.b.0.3., but were driven back from this by enfilade machine gun fire from both flanks.[14]

Many of these men were caught in the cross fire from the well placed German machine gun positions. Private A. Wilson:

> The artillery started on the attack fourteen days previously and they bombarded the German lines, there was 200 yards of barbed wire at least in front of the German line, as far as the eye could see either to the left or right of us. There was apparently a gap and to look out and to see the dirt flying and the barbed wire twisted and thrown all over the place during the course of each day it looked impossible for even a blade of grass to exist, never mind a German machine gunner. But at 4 o'clock in the morning ... we all had to go over, of course, but I had my Lewis gun and that was quite a work of art to carry a Lewis gun over conditions like that ... [I] was right opposite the one hundred yards gap in the wire and I got through without much trouble until I got installed, and got my machine gun inside one of the trenches, but afterwards there was such a congestion on that gap and such a slaughter went on because the Germans sprung up all over the place with machine guns, and I believe that the

historians will know the amount of men that we lost that day, but in my battalion there was only five of us left.[15]

The 2/6th Duke of Wellington's advancing on the left flank experienced difficulty in crossing the uncut wire and like their Australian comrades east of Bullecourt, were forced to shelter in shell holes. Support waves caused further confusion as desperate attempts were made to seek refuge in these crowded shell holes. Men from A Company got into their objective and held that part of the German trench until 4.00 pm. C and D Companies were pinned down in shell holes.

Company Sergeant Major Charles Hermon Gartside had led his men into the first German trench west of Bullecourt. After consolidating this captured position, Gartside gathered another party to attack the second German trench. As they charged this hostile position many men were cut down by heavy machine guns. The attack lost momentum and Gartside was unable to reach this trench. He returned to defend the first German trench and held out despite German counter attacks. He held on until dusk when he was ordered to withdraw. Gartside was awarded the Military Cross for his courage. His citation featured in the *London Gazette* on 14th August 1917: 'For conspicuous gallantry and devotion in organising and leading attacking parties under heavy fire. His total disregard of personal safety and for soldierly spirit greatly encouraged all with him'.[16]

Sergeant J.T. McLeod was another NCO from the 2nd/6th Duke of Wellington Regiment who was recognised for his courage. His citation for the Distinguished Conduct Medal records that he

... showed conspicuous gallantry and devotion to duty during the whole of the 3rd May. This NCO in charge of a machine gun section worked through the final hostile trench W of Bullecourt but was bombed out. He reorganised another party and went forward. When they had all become casualties he returned and collected another party of all units and again attacked the trench. His party met the same fate. Sergeant McLeod remained in the enemy line using his gun till dusk when ordered to withdraw. During the whole day he showed great courage, gave valuable assistance in reforming the men returned and great qualities of leadership. His gallantry and fine spirit was an example to see.[17]

Concrete enemy machine gun posts caused further delays in the advance and Company Sergeant Major Maude from the 2/6th Duke of Wellington Regiment bravely captured two of these menaces destroying the guns and dispersing their occupants. His recommendation for the Distinguished Conduct Medal reports that 'he entered the enemy machine gun emplacements, bayoneted the occupants and destroyed the guns. After being bombed out he took up a position in shell holes in the enemy's line and held out during the day only withdrawing when ordered at night'.[18]

The 2/6th Duke of Wellington Regiment had no choice but to establish their posts in these shell holes. Men from C and D Companies who were pinned down had to wait nightfall to withdraw.

The 2nd/7th Duke of Wellington's exploited the success of the 2/5th West Yorkshire Regiment on their right flank by entering Bullecourt and headed towards the northern sector of the village. They left their trenches at 3.37 for their objective, the road from U.22.b.8.5–U.16.c.4.5 and village of Hendecourt and a line running from U.12.c.7.7–U.11.b.8.0.–U.9.d.2.4. The battalion advanced with 14 officers and 430 men in two waves with C Company leading the right flank, supported by D Company. A Company led the right flank followed by B Company. As they advanced, units from the 187th Brigade lost direction and were cossing their advance. This did not deter the 2nd/7th Duke of Wellington's and they pressed ahead. Allied shells falling short caused a many casualties. Only small sections of the wire were demolished by the Allied guns. Despite these setbacks and sustaining many casualties some did fight their way into the first German trench. As a consequence of losing so many officers, the attack became disorganised. Remnants of the 2nd/8th West Yorkshire Regiment and the 2nd/5th Duke of Wellington Regiment joined forces with the 2nd/7th Battalion

Battalions from the Duke of Wellington Regiment attacked this sector of the Hindenburg Line at Bullecourt on 3rd May. Note the dense fields of barbed wire and shell holes south west from the village. (Author)

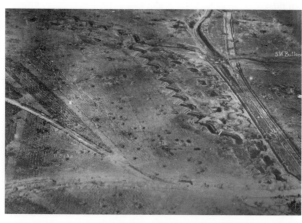

Duke of Wellington's. The German defenders offered stout resistance forcing the Yorkshire Battalions to withdraw from the fist German trench and establish positions in nearby shell holes. It was here that German artillery zeroed all calibre of shells, including fire shells, which burnt some of the wounded.

One party from the 2nd/7th Duke of Wellington Regiment did manage to drive their advance through the first and second line of trenches. The Aerial reconnaissance confirmed the presence of 2nd/7th Duke of Wellingtons in the vicinity of the factory in the north. Three missing officers were assumed to have been with this party of men. None of them returned. The 2nd/7th Duke of Wellington Regiment war diary reported that 9 out of the 14 officers who took part in the attack were casualties. Only two officers returned unhurt. They also lost two-thirds of the men. The remnants of the battalion fell back to their start off points at 9.30 pm as ordered. The 186th Brigade had captured one German officer and 31 men.

187TH BRIGADE FRONT

The 187th Brigade commanded by Brigadier General Taylor was to provide a defensive left flank not advancing beyond the Quéant–Fontaine Road. They had been shelled and some casualties were incurred as they assembled at the start off positions, including Lieutenant Colonel F Blacker who was commanding the 2nd/4th York and Lancaster Regiment. By 1.45 am the 187th Brigade was in position between the railway embankment and the outposts and ready to launch their attack north west of Bullecourt. At 3.45 am soldiers from the 2nd/5th Battalion advanced across No Man's Land as British artillery poured shells upon German trenches.

They shared the same experience as the 186th Brigade in losing direction. The sky was black and a strong wind blew dust and smoke into the faces of the advancing troops. Some officers completely lost direction and were leading their men in circles. Small parties from A and B Companies from the 2/4th York and Lancaster's on the right advanced to an enemy support trench. The 2/5th York and Lancaster's crossed the first trench but without realising and found itself at the Lagnicourt–St Martin Road. Their advance was halted as they met heavy machine gun fire trapping some men in the sunken road and forcing others to withdraw to the railway embankment. There was mayhem as masses of soldiers form the King's Own Yorkshire and Lancashire Infantry searched for gaps in the wire.

Such was the state of confusion that many of the men who had lost their officers and confidence in this botched assault decided to think of their own salvation and withdrew. Discipline was breaking down and Lieutenant Colonel William Watson who advanced with his battalion, the 2nd/5th Kings Own Yorkshire Light Infantry, was forced to stop the retreating men. Brigadier General R. Taylor, commanding officer of the 187th Brigade reported:

> In to this scene of confusion now came Lt. Col. W. Watson, who accompanied his Battn, the 2/5th K.O.Y.L.I. He found men beginning to retire, took out his revolver and attempted to get all to go forward again.[19]

The regimental history of the KOYLI recorded:

> Into the scene went Lt-Col W. Watson, already severely wounded, to rally his men and lead them through; with the help of other officers he restored order and re-organised the advance, seeking to carry the trenches by weight of numbers.[20]

The efforts of Lieutenant Colonel William Watson did little to hold back the retreating men. Taylor continued his report in the 187th Brigade War Diary: 'It was now about 4.20 am — the barrage was lifting from the support trench and Lt. Col. Watson was almost killed immediately.'[21] Lieutenant-General Sir Walter Braithwaite recounted that Watson 'went into the open in full view of the enemy under very heavy fire, and was killed while making a heroic effort to put things straight.'[22]

Watson was dead and most of his officers had become casualties. Taylor described how the attack ground to a halt:

> From that moment the attack was a failure. Sections and platoons were mixed up. Officers and men began to be hit. Platoon Commanders in the confusion were unable to get any grip of their platoons; the individual soldier was left largely to his own initiative. This seems to have induced a feeling of 'We seem to have got it all wrong somehow - what are we to do now?' The result was that though many stayed in shell holes in the wire, or in the sunken road in U.20.b. about 300 men of the Brigade came back to the Railway Cutting.[23]

His second-in-command Major Oscar Cyril Spencer Watson was sent forward to the railway cutting to take command of the 2nd/5th KOYLI. Major Watson was also accompanied by the men he had rallied in the rear who belonged to carrying parties and details from the 187th Brigade. Captain C.H. Hoare, the Brigade Major was also sent forward to appraise the situation. Taylor:

The situation was somewhat obscure – that is to say, it was not known whether our men were holding parts of the first trench or not, or whether the survivors were all in shell holes in front of it. The one thing that was clear was that the men in the Railway Cutting were not beaten men. They were cheerful – perhaps too indifferent.[24]

The fact that Lieutenant Colonel Watson forced these men at gun point to advance, then was soon killed, may suggest the possibility that he was not killed by German bullets. There were 300 men at the railway cutting and Captain Hoare thought there was a chance to re-organise them and lead them in another attack. At 8.25 am, supported by an artillery barrage, Hoare led these men forwards. They had orders to pick up soldiers from the battalion who were in shell holes and capture the German support trench. German machine gun fire stopped them and they never got beyond the sunken road. Major Watson carried on alone until he was severely wounded when he reached the enemy barbed wire. The remnants did hold a line of shell holes in No Man's Land, but no substantial gains were made on the 187th Brigade front. Without fresh troops and munitions, they were trapped, unable to advance, unable to withdraw because of the concentrated enemy machine-gun fire. The survivors of this failed attack began to trickle back to the railway cutting in twos and threes at 8.00 pm. Major Watson was left wounded in a shell hole near to the German wire and was not recovered until dusk the following day. The 187th Brigade was badly mauled, losing 55% of its officers and 48% of its men. The 2nd/5th Battalion KOYLI lost four officers killed and seven wounded. Amongst the other ranks casualties 35 were killed, 69 listed as missing and 156 wounded. The 2nd/4th Battalion KOYLI lost one officer killed and nine wounded, together with 11 killed, 15 missing and 94 wounded amongst the other ranks.

Despite the failure of the 187th Brigade to break through, honours were awarded. Major Oscar Cyril Spencer Watson received the Distinguished Service Order. His citation states that 'he reorganised men of all units, inspired the men with his own coolness and confidence, and personally led them forward for a second attack. He was severely wounded.'[25]

2nd Lieutenant Cubitt Austin Ireland from the KOYLI received the Military Cross: 'Although wounded he led his men forward with the greatest gallantry and determination. He undoubtedly saved a critical situation.'[26]

Reconnaissance sorties were flown over the ruins of Bullecourt to assess whether any units from the 2nd/5th and 2nd/6th Battalions West Yorkshire Regiment were holding on. No evidence was found and it was assumed that men who had entered Bullecourt were either killed or taken prisoner.

The reason for the failure of the assault on 3rd May 1917 was primarily the fact that German machine gun positions positioned in the gap between the Australian and British front lines were not dealt with. The fact that Zero Hour was scheduled to take place in the dark at 3.45 am made it difficult to control the operation, to observe progress and made it extremely difficult for the assaulting battalions to advance in good order in the right direction. The northerly direction of the wind made matters worse because it blew the dust raised by the barrage into the faces of the advancing British infantry. Lieutenant Colonel Hastings wrote of the failings of the 3rd May attack:

> Of attached troops, the Australian Medium Trench Mortar Battery had their ammunition dump and guns blown at 5 am on the railway embankment. Tanks, which co-operated, were able to render little assistance, many being damaged or destroyed.'[27]

However, Hastings praises the artillery saying that 'the action of the Artillery throughout the whole of the time was magnificent, and liaison was good.[28]

Hastings entered the second battle of Bullecourt with 340 men. When the 2nd/6th West Yorkshire Regiment was relieved by the 2nd H.A.C. later that day the battalion had only 100 survivors. They left the line at Bullecourt at 9.00 pm and spent the night recovering from their ordeal in the caves at Ecoust-St-Mein. When the battalion returned to Ervillers during the evening of the 4th, Lieutenant Colonel Hastings was warned that despite their losses, they could be called for duty on the front line to hold on the 62nd Division's sector. Brigadier General Taylor:

> The night was very dark, the darkness being intensified by the dust from the bursting shells, and by the smoke barrage. Thus the attack became a night attack, and not a dawn attack, and a night attack is a very difficult operation for even the most highly trained troops. The difficulties of this attack were beyond the capacity of the Platoon commanders to control, though many of them showed great individual gallantry. The individual soldier, left largely to his own initiative, apparently lost all power to exercise it. The result was a failure, and a costly failure.[29]

COMPANY SERGEANT MAJOR WILLIAM RATHKE 201195 DCM,
2ND/5TH BATTALION WEST YORKSHIRE REGIMENT

William Ernest Rathke was born in 1882 in Leeds. He was the son of Ernest, a German migrant who married Emiz Hodgkinson, a local girl, bearing four children.

William spent the early part of his life travelling. His trade was a carpenter. His name appears on a 1907 ship's manifest sailing from Vancouver to San Francisco. Eventually he returned to England and settled in Stoke-on-Trent where in 1912 he married.

When war broke out, William and his elder brother George tried to enlist. William later told his son Peter that he found it extremely difficult to enlist in the British Army because of his German surname. William succeeded in joining the Army and by May 1917 he was a Company Sergeant Major serving with the 2nd/5th Battalion West Yorkshire Regiment. During the Second Battle of Bullecourt Rathke was wounded as he entered the village on 3rd May. By 6.30 am almost all officers within the 2nd/5th Battalion had become casualties. Despite his wounds Rathke gave strong support to Captain Green, who was the only surviving officer. Establishing a line of posts amongst the rubble and shell craters that pocketed Bullecourt, they fought off numerous German counter attacks. Rathke was awarded the Distinguished Conduct Medal. His citation was published in the *London Gazette* on the 17th July 1917 and states:

Above: Company Sergeant Major William Rathke DCM. (*Harrogate Herald* 20th June 1917)

Below: Rathke in later life. (Courtesy Peter Rathke)

Although himself wounded, he collected and successfully led a small party against a strong enemy bombing attack upon our trenches. His promptitude saved the situation at a very critical time. With great determination and coolness, he remained at his post, indifferent to his wounds, until his company was relieved.[30]

Rathke was sorry to leave the Army after the war. For a period of two years his wife was the breadwinner, which made him feel very uncomfortable. Rathke eventually resumed his career as a carpenter and would become a foreman. In 1930 he was employed by Stoke-on-Trent City Corporation as a Building Inspector. William Rathke died in 1951.

COMPANY SERGEANT MAJOR JAMES HORNER 200013,
2ND/5TH BATTALION WEST YORKSHIRE REGIMENT

James Henry Howard Horner was born in 1877 in Harrogate, the youngest son of James H Horner. He was married to Annie and they raised three children. James Horner served in the Army for 25 years. When war broke out, he was attending a Territorial Army training weekend in Scarborough. In January 1917 he left for France with the 2nd/5th Battalion West Yorkshire Regiment. By that time he was a Company Sergeant Major. Horner was aged 41 when he was killed on 3rd

May. He has no known grave and is commemorated on the Arras Memorial. Captain Cross wrote the following letter of condolence to his wife Annie.

Company Sergeant Major James Horner. (*Harrogate Herald* 11th July 1917)

Dear Mrs Horner, As promised I have been making enquiries regarding your husband, and the enclosed letter (which kindly return) has just come from Capt. Heaton, who followed me as adjutant. I sadly am afraid the worst has happened; over a month has gone by and the only evidence available confirms our worst fears. I need hardly say how deeply my sympathy is for you and your children, and as you will, I hope, understand, this is much more than a mere expression of feeling. From early in 1900 to last year I had the privilege of being intimately and closely associated with your husband, and two men cannot soldier together for such a length of time without getting, as it were, an inside knowledge of each other. Your husband more than merited the regard and respect he was held in by the Commanding Officer to the last joined recruit. For the long period I was an officer in the company of which he was so great an ornament, I acknowledge with gratitude the unselfish help he gave to one and all, and especially to me as his former company commander, and other officers who followed have on every possible occasion told me what a tower of strength he was. He knew his work, he helped everyone, he was unselfish in the extreme, he was patient and painstaking, never lost his temper, never used a foul word or expression, and always did far more than mere duty imposed on him. Such is the record of my old friend and comrade, Howard Horner. He was better than most and inferior to none. Any further information I can get I will see reaches you without delay – Again with much sympathy, yours very truly, E. F Cross.[31]

COMPANY SERGEANT MAJOR ARTHUR PICKARD 241525,
2ND/5TH YORK and LANCASTER REGIMENT

Company Sergeant Major **Arthur Pickard** was killed on 3rd May. The majority of soldiers who were killed at Bullecourt have no known grave. Pickard was one of the few soldiers who fell at Bullecourt who is buried in a Commonwealth War Graves Cemetery. Pickard was buried at Ontario Cemetery, Sains-Les-Marquion.

Company Sergeant Major Arthur Pickard. (Bradford Weekly Telegraph)

CAPTAIN ERIC GREGORY
2/6TH BATTALION WEST YORKSHIRE REGIMENT

Eric Craven Gregory was born in Scotland in 1888. His parents were James and Martha. His father was a congregational minister who brought his family to live in Bradford. Captain Gregory led a party from D

Company into the rubble of Bullecourt on 3rd May. Here they established contact with the elements from the 2nd/5th West Yorkshire Regiment, but soon after Gregory was wounded by crossfire.

Captain Eric Gregory. (Bradford Weekly Telegraph)

PRIVATE FREDERICK COPLEY 202474
2ND/4TH BATTALION DUKE OF WELLINGTON REGIMENT

Frederick Copley was born in Sheffield in 1879. He was severely wounded during the battle. His face was shattered by a gunshot wound causing dreadful disfigurement. He was evacuated back to Sidcup Hospital in England where during the course of four years it would take 38 operations to reconstruct his face. Copley was discharged on 27th March 1919. Frederick Copley died in 1963, aged 84. The photos show how his face was reconstructed after being wounded. The scars borne would remind him of Bullecourt for the rest of his life.

Top left: Private Frederick Copley after Bullecourt.
Bottom left: Private Frederick Copley, 30th January 1918.
Right: Private Frederick Copley photographed in 1920, three years after Bullecourt. (Jean & Denise Letaille Bullecourt Museum)

SERGEANT MAJOR JOSEPH MAUD 265530 DCM
2ND/5TH DUKE OF WELLINGTON REGIMENT

Company Sergeant **Major Maude** from the 2/6th Duke of Wellington Regiment captured two enemy machine gun positions destroying the guns and dispersing their occupants. His recommendation for the Distinguished Conduct Medal:

Company Sergeant Major Joseph Maude DCM. (Bradford Weekly Telegraph)

He entered the enemy machine gun emplacements, bayoneted the occupants and destroyed the guns. After being bombed out he took up a position in shell holes in the enemy's line and held out during the day only withdrawing when ordered at night.[32]

His citation for the DCM was posted in the *London Gazette* on 24th July 1917 and stated: 'For conspicuous gallantry and devotion to duty. He rallied several parties of men, under heavy fire and succeeded in destroying two enemy machine gun emplacements.'[33]

LANCE CORPORAL ARTHUR FITZ-JOHN 242801,
2ND/5TH BATTALION DUKE OF WELLINGTON (WEST RIDING REGIMENT)

Arthur Thomas Fitz-John was born in Hull in 1879 to Thomas and Eliza. He married Alice in 1908 and they bore two sons, Arthur and Eric. Arthur worked as a labourer in Hull. At the start of each year Arthur would write a few lines in the family album. In his final entry on 1st January 1913 he wrote:

Above left: Lance Corporal Arthur Fitz-John

Above right: Arthur Fitz-John with wife Alice

Right: Arthur Fitz-John and family. (Courtesy Rob Fitz-John)

Time that is past thou canst never recall;
Of time to come thou knowest not all.
The present only is within thy power,
And therefore now improve the shining hour.

Arthur served with the 2nd/5th Duke of Wellington (West Riding Regiment). He was aged 37 when he was killed on 3rd May. He has no known grave and his name is commemorated on the Arras Memorial.

PRIVATE HERBERT HUGGINS 242069,
2ND/6TH BATTALION WEST YORKSHIRE REGIMENT

Private Herbert Huggins was wounded at Bullecourt and was evacuated to a hospital in Rouen for medical attention. Huggins died of his wounds on 7th May 1917 and was buried at St Sever Cemetery Extension in Rouen.

Private Herbert Huggins.
(Bradford Weekly Telegraph)

LANCE CORPORAL GEORGE TWIVY 341321,
2ND/6TH BATTALION WEST YORKSHIRE REGIMENT

George Albert Twivy was born in Bradford, Yorkshire in 1894. His father Tom was a builder. George joined the 2nd/6th Battalion West Yorkshire Regiment. At some stage during the war he was wounded and sent to hospital. The photo of him wearing hospital blues indicates this. By the time he took part in the attack on 3rd May he had attained the rank of Lance Corporal. He was aged 32 when he was killed on that day. His remains were not recovered. George Twivy has no known grave and his name is commemorated on the Arras Memorial.

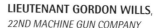

Lance Corp George Twivy.
(Courtesy Keith Twivy)

LIEUTENANT GORDON WILLS,
22ND MACHINE GUN COMPANY

Arthur Gordon Wills was born in Birmingham in 1891. Known as Gordon to his family he was the youngest of four children. His father was an affluent lawyer practising in Birmingham. They were brought up in Barnt Green. Gordon attended Lickey Hill School, and

Lieutenant Arthur Gordon Wills, standing centre. (Courtesy John Wills)

then he went to Uppingham School where he learnt to shoot. Gordon studied Greek and Latin at Cambridge and after graduating in 1913 he joined Sharp and Pritchards in Birmingham where he trained to become a solicitor. He worked for this firm for less than a year, for in June 1914 Gordon and his sister Lucy embarked on a long holiday to South Africa. They were in Durban in August 1914. Gordon was so desperate to play his part in the war that he got on a train to Johannesburg and enlisted in the South African Army. He joined the Transvaal Scottish as an unpaid corporal. He recalled to his grandson that after completing his basic training he 'was very fit and the colour of a Red Indian'.[34]

On 7th September the Transvaal Scottish were sent to Cape Town where they embarked on the cruise liner Galway Castle. Sailing for Luderitz Bay in Namibia, they landed on the beach unopposed on 19th September. German forces were fearful of Royal Navy battleships bombarding their positions along the Namibian coast, so they withdrew 130 km inland to Aus. After establishing a beachhead the Transvaal Scottish and the South African force advanced inland across the Namib Desert towards Aus across the harsh desert. They were hindered by sandstorms. Water was in short supply. By 8th November they had reached Tschaukaib, 32km inland where they quickly overwhelmed the German forces and captured the railway overhead water tank.

On 26th February 1915 the Transvaal Scottish captured the town of Garub. After serving for several months with the Transvaal Scottish, Gordon was tired of wearing the Scottish kilt. He transferred to the Machine Gun Section. In a letter to his brother Jack he confided:

I had taken up machine gunning, chiefly to get a pair of trousers. For some reason, unknown to me, kilts were considered unsuitable for machine gunners and as I detested kilts under any circumstances, I applied for the vacancy in the machine gun corps and got it.[35]

Gordon was not content serving with the South African Army. In a letter home to his mother he described its soldiers as 'an appalling armed rabble'. He wrote of his yearning to 'come home and get a Commission in a real regiment'.[36] His mother was well connected and was able to pull strings in order to get Gordon home to England where he could enlist in the British Army as an officer. Gordon left South Africa in April 1915. He had played a role in defeating German forces in South West Africa that culminated in the German surrender in July 1915.

Gordon arrived home and after ten day's rest he joined the Cambridgeshire Regiment at Rayleigh in Essex. In November 1915 Gordon was assigned to the 1st Battalion Cambridgeshire Regiment in Newmarket. On 2nd March 1916 he married Murial Evans. A few weeks after his wedding day Gordon was transferred to the Machine Gun Company based in Grantham, Lincolnshire.

Lieutenant Gordon Wills was sent to France towards the end of August 1916. He arrived in Boulogne and spent three weeks at Etaples. He joined the 22nd Machine Gun Company at Woirel on 11th September. He was a section leader and was responsible for seven machine guns. Gordon was told with horrible honesty by his superiors that this unit had been wiped out three times since the first day of the Somme on 1st July 1916 and that they were known as the 'suicide club', because a Machine Gunner only lasted seven days on the front line until he was either killed or seriously wounded. Their high casualty rate was because they were a principal target for German artillery.

Lieutenant Wills spent six weeks in the trenches at Ploegsteert Wood, Belgium, during which time he experienced a German Phosgene gas attack and was the target of German snipers – when hunting for pheasant and partridge! Towards the end of November 1916 he was transferred to trenches on the Somme. He spent Christmas day at Serre and fell off a duckboard into the mud. He found himself up to his waist and it took his men two hours to extract him.

Lieutenant Gordon Wills took part in his first major battle on the Western Front during the assault on 3rd May. After fighting for 24 hours he was wounded:

I remember the incident very plainly. I and one of my gun teams were sheltering in an old German gun emplacement, probably a foolish place to shelter as they had the range exactly and knocked hell out of us as a result. I did not know anything about the shell that knocked me out but in addition to wounding me it killed the whole of my gun crew. I had been on the go, marching and fighting for about 24 hours so I had dozed off in spite of the bombardment. In the afternoon my Orderly came and woke me up with a cup of tea and a slice of bread and jam. After the shell burst I came to and I said to no one in particular 'Some swine has spoilt my tea!' because the jam was covered with dust and earth. I went to the nearest CCS and the doctor there lifted my shirt, as, like all good soldiers, I was hit in the back and pulled a bit of shell about one and a half inches long out of the muscles of my shoulder, painted it with iodine, stuck a piece of plaster on it and sent me back to my unit. I was sent down to the nearest Field hospital and turned loose. I remember the chief effect that it had on me was that I could not stop talking until one of the doctors gave me a drink, followed by a second one, which must have had some knock out dope in it because I went to sleep and did not stir until 12 o'clock the following day.[37]

Gordon wrote home nonchalantly describing his wounds to his mother as 'a couple of scratches' from a game of football. Wills was hospitalised for a month and returned to his unit on 5th June in billets near Arras. He and 14 other men from the 22nd Machine Gun Company were gassed at Glencorse Wood on 2nd October during the Third Battle of Ypres. He was returned home to England to convalesce. In December 1917 Lieutenant Wills was awarded the Military Cross. He was not informed for what action he was awarded this decoration. After recovering from the gas attack at Ypres he spent the remainder of the war in Grantham where he became a Staff Captain Instructor.

SERGEANT OSBORNE GOUGH 241190,
2ND/5TH KINGS OWN YORKSHIRE LIGHT INFANTRY

Osborne Leonard Gough was born in 1885 at Pentre Broughton in Wales, the son of David and Anne. David was a coal miner and the family lived at Poplar Cottages, Gwersylt, Wrexham. In 1901, aged 16 he followed the family tradition and became a collier. He married Sarah Jones, known as Lizzie, in 1906. By 1911 Osborne and Lizzie were the parents of three children and during that year the family moved to Castleford, Yorkshire. Their fourth child was born that year. Osborne enlisted some time after October

Sergeant Osborne Gough. (Courtesy Phillip Rogers)

1915. He joined the 2nd/5th Kings Own Yorkshire Light Infantry and had attained the rank of Sergeant when was killed on 3rd May. He has no known grave and his name is commemorated on the Arras Memorial.

PRIVATE JAMES RILEY 242748,
2ND/5TH BATTALION KING'S OWN YORKSHIRE LIGHT INFANTRY

James William Riley was born in 1897 in Derby. He attested on 10th December 1915 under the Lord Derby Scheme prior to his 18th birthday. He was allowed to continue working for the Midland Railway Company until he was called up for service on 10th October 1916. Riley joined the 2nd/5th Battalion King's Own Yorkshire Light Infantry and they arrived in France on 14th January 1917. On 3rd May Riley sustained a bullet wound to his left arm. Riley returned to duty and would serve in the 1st/4th and 10th Battalions of the KOYLI for the remainder of the war. He was wounded a second time during the Battle of Passchendaele in October 1917. He was reported as killed, but later awoke from a coma in a Glasgow hospital. After recovering from his wounds he returned to the Western Front and was wounded a third time by a bullet to the foot. He returned to France later in 1918 and took part in the advance to victory. By war's end he had attained the rank of Acting Sergeant. He continued to serve with the Army of Occupation in Germany after the war with the 2nd KOYLI. On 17th October 1919 he was transferred to Class Z reserve. After the war he returned home to Derby and found a job with his pre-war employer, the Midland Railway Company at the Carriage and Wagon Works. He was initially a spring maker and he later transferred to the upholstery department. He married Eva Wye on Christmas Day. James Riley died on 23rd October 1973.

Above: Private James Riley

Right: Private James Riley wearing three wound stripes. (Courtesy Christopher Preston)

NOTES ⋯⋯⋯⋯⋯⋯⋯⋯⋯⋯⋯⋯⋯⋯⋯⋯⋯⋯⋯⋯⋯⋯⋯⋯⋯⋯⋯⋯⋯⋯⋯⋯⋯⋯⋯⋯

1. National Archive: WO 95/3087: 2nd/6th Battalion Duke of Wellington's Regiment.
2. IWM: Ref: MISC 95(1457) Private Willie Greaves, 2nd/ 6th Battalion West Yorkshire Regiment: Letter 25th July 1981.
3. Ibid.
4. National Archives: WO 95/3082: 2nd/6th Battalion West Yorkshire Regiment War Diary.
5. *Harrogate Herald*, 20th June 1917.
6. *London Gazette* issue 30234, published 14th August 1917.
7. *Harrogate Herald*, 12th December 1917.
8. National Archives: WO 95/3082: 2nd/6th Battalion West Yorkshire Regiment War Diary.
9. The *London Gazette* 30204 24th July 1917.
10. National Archives: WO 95/3079: 185th Brigade War Diary.
11. Ibid.
12. The *London Gazette* Issue 30188: published 17th July 1917.
13. National Archives: WO 95/3084: 186th Brigade War Diary.
14. Ibid.
15. IWM Sound Archives: IWM Reference: 4260: A. Wilson.
16. *London Gazette*: Issue 30234: 14th August 1917.
17. National Archives: WO 95/3087: 2nd/6th Duke of Wellington's Regiment War Diary.
18. Ibid.
19. National Archives: WO 95/3088: 187th Brigade War Diary.
20. *The History of the King's Own Yorkshire Light Infantry*, H.C. Wylly, 1926.
21. National Archives: WO 95/3088: 187th Brigade War Diary.
22. *The History of the King's Own Yorkshire Light Infantry*, H.C. Wylly, 1926.
23. National Archives: WO 95/3088: 187th Brigade War Diary.
24. Ibid.
25. *London Gazette*, Issue 30204 24th July 1917.
26. Ibid.
27. National Archives: WO 95/3082: 2nd/6th Battalion West Yorkshire Regiment War Diary.
28. Ibid.
29. National Archives: WO 95/3088: 187th Brigade War Diary.
30. The *London Gazette*: Issue 30188: 17th July 1917.
31. *Harrogate Herald*: 4th July 1917: Letter from Captain E.F. Cross to Annie Horner.
32. National Archives: WO 95/3087: 2nd/6th Duke of Wellington's Regiment.
33. The *London Gazette*: Issue 30204: 24th July 1917.
34. *World War 1 Experiences of my Grandfather*, Gordon Wills, 2005.
35. Ibid.
36. Ibid.
37. Ibid.

English dead in German trenches at Bullecourt, taken on a sector of the Hindenburg Line held by the 121 German Infantry Regiment. This regiment held the line during 1917 and 1918. (Author)

CHAPTER 19

THE TANKS ENTER BULLECOURT: 3RD MAY 1917

Eight tanks from Nos 9 and 10 Sections, No.12 Company from D Battalion, Machine Gun Corps Heavy Branch were assigned to assault Bullecourt on 3rd May 1917. These tank crews had taken part in the attack on Vimy Ridge in support of the Canadians, but the shell-cratered terrain prevented them from providing effective assistance. Many of them became trapped in the craters and were unable to reach the German lines. Major Watson wrote:

> The ground was impossible and the tanks 'ditched', They were dug out, hauled out, pulled out, one way or another under a cruel shelling, but they never came into the battle. It was naturally a keen disappointment to Ward, and he and his company at Behagnies were spoiling for a fight.[1]

The tanks were brought to Mory Copse during the night of the 1st/2nd May. The following night they were moved to the railway embankment at Ecoust-St.-Mein where they arrived at 1.45 am, two hours before the hour of attack. At 3.35 am six tanks advanced towards the village of Bullecourt to support infantry from the 62nd Division.

At night, it was impossible to monitor the progress of the tanks. It was not until 6.10 am that Lieutenant Colonel C.K. James commanding the 2nd/7th West Yorkshire Regiment received a report that one tank had been seen operating near to position U.27.b.38.

Lieutenant Hardress Lloyd, commander of D Battalion Heavy Branch Machine Gun Corps, made the following interesting observation: 'The conditions (except in Bullecourt, which was impassable from shelling) were perfect for tank operations. It was a great disadvantage that Zero was as early as 3.45 am; as it was impossible to see the ground until 4.30 am at the earliest.'[2] A further six tanks were reported to be seen withdrawing from positions U.27.c. and d. and were eventually confirmed to be out of action.

Men from the 2nd/7th West Yorkshire Regiment established contact with two tanks at 7.30 am. These tanks were known as Daisy and Dragon. The officer commanding Dragon was requested to move his tank along the eastern perimeter of the village in an effort to reach Australian battalions who were driving their attack in that direction. Both Daisy and Dragon were knocked out of action; however, the officer commanding Dragon returned to his lines and brought another tank into action. At 7.45 am a tank was observed entering the village of Bullecourt and Lieutenant Colonel C.K. James, commanding the 2nd/7th West Yorkshires wrote:

> It is presumed that this Tank was got into action by the Officer i/c Dragon by re-organising crews from the remnants of other Tanks and it is considered that great credit is due to him, as this re-organisation was performed under heavy M/G and shell fire. This officer (name unknown) was in the Buffs.[3]

Three tanks entered Bullecourt; one spent ninety minutes in the village but was hit as it withdrew. Second Lieutenant Charles Knight commanding another replaced his four wounded crew members with four fit men from a tank that had broken down and continued the fight. Lieutenant Colonel James may have been referring to Knight in his report. A third tank reached the southern perimeter of the village. At one point the tank commander left his tank to try to persuade supporting infantry to follow him, but was unsuccessful. On returning to the tank he discovered that most of his crew had been wounded by armour piercing bullets, which meant that the tank did not have sufficient hands to drive it. Other tanks entered the north west of the village, but were either out-run by the infantry or deserted by men retiring to allied lines. Major Watson:

> The third tank ran into the thick of the battle, escaping by a succession of miracles the accurate fire of the German gunners. It crashed into the enemy, who were picked troops, and slaughtered them. The Germans showed no fear of it. They stood up to it, threw bombs and fired long bursts at it from their machine guns. They had been issued with

armour-piercing bullets, and the crew found to their dismay that the armour was not proof against them. Both gunners in one sponson were hit. The corporal of the tank dragged them out of the way – no easy matter in a tank – and manned the gun until he in his own turn was wounded. Another gunner was wounded, and then another. With the reduced crew and the tank encumbered by the wounded, the tank was practically out of action. The tank commander broke off the fight and set out back.[4]

A 'Report on Tanks in Action 3rd May 1917' was produced for the purpose of staff officers at 1st Tank Brigade Headquarters. Accounts of each of the eight tanks are provided in this interesting document. According to this report all the tanks left their designated starting off positions at Zero Hour at 3.45 am.

This photo features three of the Tank commanders who took part in the Battle of Bullecourt on 3rd May 1917. 2nd Lieutenant Ralph Cooney (standing left), Lieutenant E.J. Smith (standing right) and 2nd Lieutenant Herbert Chick (seated right). (Tank Museum E2001.767.11)

Tank No. 791; Crew No. D/42: Commanding Officer Lieutenant William Sinclair McCoull

Tank 791 advanced along the eastern perimeter of Bullecourt and successfully entered the village. At this stage visual contact with this tank had been lost. At 5.45 am Lieutenant McCoull was seen returning with this tank to his starting off position. As they were returning to British lines German shells were targeting the tank. Several shells hit the tank and McCoull evacuated his crew. Taking their Lewis Guns with them they took refuge in a nearby shell hole. When the fire subsided, McCoull and his crew returned, but just when they were seen to be leaving the disabled tank again, it was hit by two shells and the tank was on fire. Lieutenant McCoull and his crew were never seen again and were presumed killed. Their names are commemorated on the Arras Memorial to the missing.

Tank No. 793; Crew No. D/41: Commanding Officer: 2nd Lieutenant Charles Martel Knight

Knight showed tremendous courage and determination during the attack. Leaving the starting off point at Zero Hour, Tank 793 drove along the western perimeter of the village before turning into Bullecourt. On reaching a stretch of German trench which ran from position U.27.b.4.0 to U.28.a.6.7 Knight found no German infantry beyond the front German line. At this stage, while in the centre of Bullecourt, Tank 793 was receiving heavy fire from German armour piercing bullets. Knight brought Tank 793 along the German trench defending the southern sector of the village. They drove along this trench backwards and forwards. At one point Tank 793 became lodged in a shell hole. When Knight and four of his crew were wounded Knight made the decision to withdraw. As they headed towards the rallying point, Knight met the disabled tank and as previously described he substituted his four wounded men for four men from the other tank. Knight then brought Tank 793 back into Bullecourt. Lance Corporal Wateridge, the driver of Tank 793, was not wounded and stayed with Knight as he drove back into Bullecourt. Wateridge kept his nerve in the driving seat as armour piercing bullets were being fired at the tank and he was awarded the Military Medal. His citation states:

> When this driver's tank was in a deep crater in Bullecourt, his skilful driving under heavy fire from armour-piercing bullets enabled the tank commander to extricate himself and continue in action. The tank, owing to casualties in personnel, was brought back to starting point and the wounded crew were replaced. This driver, however, continued at his post during the succeeding operations and was in action seven hours.[5]

Private J. Anderson who was wounded had refused to be evacuated and was awarded the Military Medal. His citation stated that 'although wounded and blinded in one eye he continued to work his gun with great determination and kept up a steady fire on the enemy. He asked not to be evacuated until the action was over, and made a second journey into Bullecourt'.[6]

Private A.E. Ashdown also volunteered to remain with Knight aboard Tank 793 for the second attack. He was also awarded the Military Medal for his courage. His citation records that 'he showed great devotion to duty and did excellent work, and though four of the crew were wounded he cheerfully volunteered and went into action a second time'.[7]

On his second venture into Bullecourt Knight discovered that there was no German infantrymen occupying the front trench and that the position had been evacuated. After suffering three further casualties aboard Tank 793, Knight returned to the rallying point at 7.55 am. 2nd Lieutenant Knight was awarded the Military Cross. His citation states:

This officer went into Bullecourt and came under heavy continuous fire from armour-piercing bullets. After he and four of his crew were wounded, took fresh men on board, and went back into Bullecourt, where he remained in action until so many of his crew were wounded that he could not carry on. He brought back his tank to starting point; all his crew were wounded. He was in action seven hours.[8]

Tank No. 598; Crew No. D/43: Commanding Officer 2nd Lieutenant Andrew Ralph Lawrie
Lieutenant Lawrie in Tank 598 proceeded well ahead of the infantry units. When Lawrie and five of his crew were wounded near to position U.27.b.5., Lawrie decided to return to the rallying point. Tank 598 was hit five times by shell fire and was put out of action and Lawrie and his wounded crewmen had to evacuate the tank, which was burnt out. He succeeded in leading his men back to British lines. Lawrie would be killed on 22nd August 1917 during the Third Ypres campaign. He has no known grave and his name is commemorated on the Tyne Cot Memorial at Passchendaele.

Tank No. 596; Crew No. D47: Commanding Officer Lieutenant Tom Westbrook
Tank 596 left the start off position at 3.45 am and crossed the British front line at 4.10 am. On reaching the German trenches at U.27.b.4.5 Westbrook could see soldiers from the Yorkshire Regiments fighting in the trenches. An English officer reported to Westbrook that there was a German machine gun position on their left flank. Westbrook left Tank 596 to join this officer to assess the best route to approach and

subdue the machine gun. Armour piercing bullets were being fired at Westbrook and at the tank. Three of his crewmen were wounded by these bullets. Westbrook got back into the cabin of the tank and instructed the infantry officer and his men to follow him as they advanced towards the machine gun position. The infantry did not follow, but Westbrook is thought to have attacked nevertheless. With no infantry supporting him, he brought the tank back towards the German wire and found another enemy machine gun position. Westbrook received a wound to his right hand. Sergeant Joshua Weeks took Westbrook's place and acted as brakesman. At this stage, four of the crew was wounded, five of the Lewis Machine guns had been put out of action, the radiator had been perforated and the engine had been shot through the casing and would not cool. Tank 596 was disabled and Westbrook, greatly assisted by Sergeant Weeks, evacuated his four wounded crewmen and the remaining Lewis Gun to a nearby shell hole for cover. Weeks carried on firing this Lewis Gun as they withdrew to British lines until German bullets knocked this gun out of action. Weeks would be awarded the Military Medal. His citation records:

When his officer was wounded he took his place in the brakesman's seat and was responsible for getting the car as far as it did. When he left the car he looked after the wounded by placing them in safety in shell-holes and getting them water. He also got a Lewis gun and ammunition out of the tank and helped a man to a shell-hole. All this was done under very heavy machine-gun fire.[9]

The crew of Tank 596 got back. Westbrook was awarded the Military Cross. Sergeant Joshua Weeks would be killed on the 22nd August 1917 during the Third Ypres Campaign.

Tank No. 795; Crew No. D/44: Commanding Officer 2nd Lieutenant F.J. Lambert
Tank 795 left its allocated starting point 45 minutes after Zero Hour. It entered the battle at 4.30 am, but after travelling 500 yards gas shells landed around the tank. 2nd Lieutenant F.J. Lambert and his crew were blinded. Lambert managed to get Tank 795 to the German trenches at a position U.21.d.23. He observed small parties of British soldiers withdrawing from Bullecourt. He also saw other parties were pinned down by German machine-gun fire, but was unable to help them due to loss of power caused by a punctured radiator. Lambert who was wounded with two of his crew, turned the tank around and struggled back to British lines.

Tank No. 785; Crew No. D/48: Commanding Officer 2nd Lieutenant Herbert Robert Chick

Tank 785 is on display at the Tank Museum at Bovington. It is the only surviving Mark II Tank and was first used at the Battle of Arras on 9th April 1917 and had reached the first German line where it became stuck for a short period. It continued to open fire on the enemy before returning. On 3rd May Tank 785 left its starting off position at 3.45 am and within 20 minutes of the attack commencing encountered large numbers of British infantry returning from the German lines, 600 in strength. Their commanding officer confirmed that they were unable to pass through the think belts of wire and heavy German machine-gun fire. These infantrymen were denied artillery support from Zero Hour until 6 am. Chick and Tank 785 were in a position to help them break through the German wire and knock out the machine-gun positions.

The post-operation report records that Chick 'arranged with the subaltern to attack strong point, and was given to understand that infantry would support him 200 yards in the rear. He got into the strong point and waited some time for the infantry, knocking out several machine guns and emplacements, but the infantry were unable to advance.'[10]

Chick's performance at Bullecourt proved that tanks could work effectively with infantry. With four of his crew wounded, Chick decided to return to British lines at 7.30 am. Tank 785 was later converted to a supply tank and served F Battalion. It was given the number F53 and called 'The Flying Scotsman'.

Tank No. 580; Crew No. D/49: Commanding Officer 2nd Lieutenant Ralph Cooney

2nd Lieutenant Ralph Cooney had seen action as an infantryman with the 2nd Battalion Royal Scots Fusiliers in October 1916 and as a tank officer at Vimy Ridge on 9th April 1917. On 3rd May at Bullecourt, Cooney brought Tank 580 to the German trenches and neutralised a strongly held enemy position. After spending a considerable time in this area, four of his crewmen had become casualties after the tank had been hit by a shell. Cooney later recalled:

> We were going to our objective, which was a line on a map on the other side of the Bosch lines with the idea of putting the infantry onto their successive objectives and we lost touch with our infantry and we struggled on. We eventually ran into some difficult bits of work and eventually I had to get out and try and get the machine across a very difficult trench. There were no Bosch there and there were no infantry, but we just went on until we got hit by a shell actually. I think it a chance hit. It laid me out and one or two others. I stayed outside the tank for a good hour. ... A fellow called Tom Westbrook and I got hold of the infantry. They lost themselves, they did not know where they were going or what they were doing ... we did the best we could, but again it was a very unsatisfactory operation. The infantry did not go where it was supposed to go at the time they were supposed to go and you could not see anything because there was a colossal artillery fire going on. Sand, dry sandy soil had been thrown into the air all the way everywhere you were. It was very hot.[11]

Cooney witnessed a British officer preventing infantrymen retreating by shooting two men with his revolver.

Tank 785, commanded by 2nd Lieutenant Herbert Chick. Tank 785 was later converted to a supply tank and served F Battalion. It was given the number F53 and called 'The Flying Scotsman' and is the only Mark II Tank in existence. It is displayed at the Tank Museum at Bovington, Dorset. (Author)

Driving seat of Tank 785. (Author))

It did happen, when we were out we did find them going back in large droves and this fellow Tom Westbrook and I, he was a commander and when you are in command you have got to stop them and you get your gun out and anybody who does not go forward, shoot him and he did. He shot one or two of them, he got control of them. ... It was the old story of two or three chaps do a bunk and everyone sees them and they all go and the more go the more join in. Fortunately he stopped it in time and got them back.[12]

Cooney brought the tank back to its starting position at 7.45 am.

Tank No. Unknown; Crew No. D/46: Commanding Officer Lieutenant E.J. Smith
The tank was also listed as Tank 795 in the official reports. This was another tank which was late reaching its starting position. It arrived at 4.30 am and its objective was to break through the German wire and trenches and advance towards Hendecourt. It received a direct hit, which caused a fire in the cabin. Smith was burnt and three of his crew was wounded. He ordered his crew to abandon the tank. He sent the three wounded men back to the starting off position to seek medical attention. Smith returned to his tank and successfully extinguished the fire. Sergeant James Gully and Private W. Roberts were also wounded, but they stayed with their commanding officer and helped him to extinguish the fire and get the tank moving. Gully's citation for the Military Medal reports that

When his tank was set on fire, by a direct hit and had to be abandoned, he, though wounded, returned with his officer and two of the crew (all wounded), and assisted in putting out the fire and driving the tank back to the starting-point. During the whole of the time the car was subjected to heavy shell and machine-gun fire[13]

Lieutenant E.J. Smith drove back to the starting position at 8 am.

Analysing the numerous Military Medal citations awarded the men who crewed the tanks, further stories of heroism and courage can be found. Tales of men wounded and carrying on with the task to capture Bullecourt are numerous. Corporal William Edward Harry Levy had been wounded in the head; however he kept firing his Lewis machine gun at the hoards of German infantrymen who were charging his tank with bombs.

Lance Corporal Ernest Jagger had received a wound to an eye, but despite being partially blinded he remained at his post and continued to drive the tank.

Having to evacuate the tank he continued to show great courage by bringing back Private Whitehall, who was severely wounded, under heavy enemy machine gun fire.

Sergeant A. Davidson was also blinded in one eye during the action, but when his tank had fallen into a cellar, he left the tank under heavy machine gun fire and assisted in dislodging it, enabling it to go forward.

When three of his crew was wounded during the battle, Private N. Hewlett continued all three men's work until the tank was abandoned. He brought these wounded men to safety in a shell hole under heavy fire. As they dashed towards British lines Hewlett stayed in the shell hole and provided covering fire.

Private A. Loades opened his protective shield to assess why his tank had got stuck. As he did so he was shot through the eye by German machine-gun fire. Before he lost consciousness he was able to right the tank.

D Battalion Tank Corps entered the battle on 3rd May with 64 men and sustained 33 casualties.

2ND LIEUTENANT HERBERT ROBERT CHICK MC

Herbert Robert Chick worked as a clerk for Thomas Cook and Son in London prior to the war. As soon as war broke out Chick joined the Royal Naval Division as an Ordinary Seaman on 6th August 1914. He was assigned to Hawke Battalion on 22nd August. By 15th September he had been promoted to Able Seaman. During October 1914 Chick took part in the defence of Antwerp. Chick was sent to Gallipoli and Hawke Battalion arrived at the allied bridgehead at Cape Helles during the night of 27th May 1915. During the nights of 31st May and 1st June, 400 men from Hawke Battalion were ordered to dig communication trenches near to the Achibaba nullah. Their first operation took place during the night of 19th June when the battalion attacked Turkish trenches south of Achibaba under the cover of darkness. On 29th August Hawke Battalion was holding the line between Gully ravine and the Krithia nullah when they fought off a Turkish patrol sustaining heavy casualties. During the autumn of 1915 Chick was hospitalised with rheumatism and spent some time convalescing on the

Captain Herbert Chick. (Tank Museum E2001.767.7)

island of Mudros. Chick was in hospital when Hawke Battalion was evacuated fro the Gallipoli Peninsula. Hawke Battalion was redeployed to France and Chick arrived on the Western Front in May 1916. He had been promoted to Petty Officer.

On 30th August 1916 Chick was transferred to serve with the 8th Battalion East Kent. During early 1917 Chick transferred to D Battalion Machine Gun Corps Heavy Branch and began training to command tanks. On 3rd May 1917 2nd Lieutenant Chick was in command of Tank 785 when he and his crew helped infantry from the 62nd Division to overwhelm German machine gun positions west of Bullecourt.

While serving with the 16th Battalion by October 1917 he had attained the rank of Temporary Lieutenant and was Acting Captain when he took part in the action at Vaux-Andigny. Chick was awarded the Military Cross for his courage. His citation states:

> For gallantry and devotion to duty on October 17, 1918, at Vaux-Andigny. This officer was in command of a section of tanks, and owing to the fog and other reasons which made the situation obscure, found himself in action earlier than expected. He personally led his tanks into action under heavy shell and machine-gun fire, and at great personal risk, and regardless of danger, kept them on their proper course and indicated to each one what points to attack. He at the same time took charge of the infantry in his particular area of operations, showing them where to go and generally assisted them in a marked degree. His fine conduct and example without regard to personal safety are well worth recognition.[14]

NOTES

1. *A Company of Tanks*, Major W.H.L. Watson, William Blackwood and Sons, Edinburgh and London, p36.
2. National Archives: WO 95/97: 1st Brigade Tank Corps Headquarters War Diary.
3. National Archives: WO 95/3082: 2nd/7th Battalion West Yorkshire Regiment War Diary.
4. *A Company of Tanks*, p41.
5. *The Tank Corps Honours and Awards 1916–1919*, Midland Medals, Birmingham 1982.
6. Ibid.
7. Ibid.
8. Ibid.
9. Ibid.
10. National Archives: WO 95/97: 1st Brigade Tank Corps Headquarters War Diary.
11. IWM Department of Sound: IWM Ref: 494: 2nd Lieutenant Ralph Cooney.
12. Ibid.
13. *The Tank Corps Honours and Awards 1916–1919*, Midland Medals, Birmingham 1982.
14. Ibid.

Interior of Tank 785; a hot, claustrophobic and poisonous place to be. (Author)

CHAPTER 20

BRITISH PRISONERS OF WAR CAPTURED AT THE SECOND BULLECOURT

The British soldiers captured at Bullecourt experienced similar mistreatment as their Australian allies a month earlier, after the first battle. Private Alfred Lister from the 2nd/6th West Yorkshire Regiment was captured on 3rd May. Before the war he worked as an Export House Manager in Bradford and was able to speak German. Immediately after his capture at Bullecourt he was detained for four days at Douai. On 7th May he transferred to Fort Macdonald in Lille. In an interview he gave after repatriation when the war ended he maintained that 'The conditions there were deplorable.'[1] On arrival at this notorious prison, the British were told that were not to be treated as Prisoners of War. Private Lister:

> On arrival of 200 of us, British prisoners, at Fort Macdonald, Lille, we were formed up in the courtyard and addressed by a man in the khaki uniform of a British private, who, however we all believed to be a German, as he spoke imperfect English with a foreign accent, and had the look of a German, and appeared to enjoy greater liberty of movement about the place than the British prisoners. He stated: – We were to be treated not as ordinary prisoners of war, but more as criminals, the reason being (he said) that the German Government had sent a note to the British Government protesting against the British practice of working German prisoners in the front line within range of the German gun fire and that the British Government had taken no notice of the protest. For this reason they

[would] mete out this treatment to us, viz., that we should be made to work in the German front lines under British fire, and that the conditions of the work would be made exceedingly hard for us and he intimated that we should be made to write home to our people describing in full our treatment and the conditions under which we worked.[2]

The captured prisoners from the West Yorkshire Regiment endured poor treatment in unsanitary conditions while incarcerated in Fort Macdonald. Private Lister was held there for ten days from 7th to 17th May:

> On the first night 135 men, and afterwards 101 men were confined in the underground cell ... The ventilation (from a single window) was wholly inadequate; the atmosphere was foul day and night. The sanitary provision in the fort consisted of a large tub in the cell for urine, close to the men sleeping. There was no provision for washing in the fort.[3]

The prisoners were starved, their daily diet consisted of one loaf of bread per day for six men. They would be given ersatz 'coffee' at seven in the morning made of roasted barley and acorns. At noon they were fed thin soup made from mangel wurzels and some barley. They would receive the same soup at six in the evening. When these prisoners were sent out for light work party duties on the seventh day of their captivity, Private Alfred Lister remembered that 'on the seventh day of our detention

Corporal A Hall from the West Yorkshire Regiment was a POW captured at Bullecourt. (*Harrogate Herald* 18th July 1917)

Sergeant J.W. Abbott, POW captured at Bullecourt. (*Harrogate Herald* 11th July 1917)

Lt W. D Muirhead 2nd/8th Battalion West Yorkshire Regiment Prisoner of War. He had only been on front for two weeks prior to his capture. (*Sheffield Weekly Independent* 16th June 1917)

we were taken out for a light fatigue duty outside. Our men were then weak from confinement and want of food, and staggered and reeled in their walk. I saw three Englishmen collapse who were taken away in an ambulance.'[4]

Their German captors worked them hard, fed them little food, then paraded them in front of French citizens in an effort to humiliate them and break their morale. By parading these captured British troops starved and in a state of fatigue, the German occupiers hoped that they convince the French that the British soldiers were in no fit state to liberate them. An article in the 29th January 1919 edition of the *Harrogate Herald* recorded the experience of Corporal A. Hall, who was captured at Bullecourt on 3rd May while fighting with the West Yorkshire Regiment:

> It appears that the object of the Hun was to march the prisoners backward and forward, starve and ill-use them, and then parade them before their people as samples of Englishmen, Hall being one of the 1,800 treated to this exhibition. They were kept working behind the lines from 6am to 6.15pm with only one meagre meal a day. Whilst the English in this case, however, had an eight hours day, the Russians had 6 and the French 10. After a spell of processions to and from Fort MacDonald, they were sent to Germany.[5]

Many of the British prisoners were put to work building railways or working in mines, farms and factories. Although they were not on the front line, they were exposed to harsh physical abuse and were at risk from bombing raids carried out by the Royal Flying Corps upon the factories. Private Bernard Middlewood, from the West Yorkshire Regiment was captured on 3rd May:

> He was engaged on heavy railways first, and his rations consisted of 300 grammes of bread and a small quantity of thin vegetable soup each day. They were than taken back 25 kilometres to make munition dumps and railways. Meanwhile things were made pretty lively by the Allies' airmen. After

five months they were mustered up at Marchines and taken to Friedrichfeld Camp and then by rail to Gustow. Here they were examined by a doctor, and those fit for work were sent to farms and down the mines. Those unfit were marked for hospital work. He remained here for six weeks, and was then transferred to an officers' camp at Furstenburg. Here he did well and received all his back parcels, though it was over nine months before he received any parcels or letters from home. Like other prisoners, Middlewood experienced some rough treatment behind the lines, the guards resorting to their favourite method of butting them with their rifles on the slightest pretext, whilst French people who endeavoured to give the prisoners food were similarly treated, and even fired at through their windows.[6]

Lister was taken to a work camp at Meurchin, 16 kilometres from Lille on 17th May. Here he worked constructing railway lines within range of British shells. The camp consisted of huts made from stone and timber surrounded by barbed wire. They were expected to sleep on the cold stone floors with no mattress or blankets. The daily routine started at 5 am with coffee substitute. They were given a ration of black bread meant to last them for two days. Worked from 8 am until 4pm without a break these men were starved and exhausted as they dug the railway and carried railway sleepers. 'The men were so weak they dropped from exhaustion.'[7]

After several months Corporal Hall was taken to Prisoner of War camps in Germany and life improved:

> Disinfection, inoculation and examinations were the order of the day, Hall being inoculated no fewer than five times. After five weeks he was sent to a NCO's camp – Eaton Moor, a much better camp than the average, where he remained 14 weeks. His next habitation was Bokeleh Camp, 25 kilometres from Bremerhaven. It was a bit rough here at first, but improved towards the finish. The prisoners had no scheduled work and passed the time in knitting, unravelling mufflers or any woollen things, and making socks. Washing was difficult, as no soap was to be had. Whilst here the English were fortunate, and able to get passes through the agency of the Danish Ambassador, but the French and Russians had to take 'French leave'. He had the good luck to get parcels from England within a fortnight of their being despatched, and Hall gave every credit to the postal authorities for this excellent despatch. The only things that were missing were tobacco and cigarettes. The NCO's camp was under the large Soltau Camp.

On the armistice being signed they entrained for Holland, staying at Enschede on the frontier one and a half days. They were well treated by the Dutch until they sailed on the Paissy from Rotterdam. Here a fine system of cleansing is in vogue, 300 prisoners being fed, bathed and equipped within two hours. They arrived at Hull on Sunday week, and passing through Harrogate, Hall threw out a postcard, which someone kindly took to his wife, and he reached home last Wednesday at noon little the worse for his captivity.[8]

Some troops were not sent to work, but within a month of capture they were in camps in Germany. Private Richard Lund from the West Yorkshire Regiment was reported missing on 3rd May 1917. He sent his family a postcard dated 15th May: 'I have arrived at the above address wounded, but in good spirits. There is no need to worry at all. Am being treated as well as can be expected.'[9]

Private Charles Malthouse was also captured on 3rd May and sent a message informing his wife Alice, and parents that he was a prisoner of war in Germany. 'Just a little line to let you know the wound in my arm is going on nicely, so don't worry about me. Keep smiling and look on the bright side.'[10]

Anxiety was turned into joy when Mrs J.E. Abbott living at Oatlands Mount, Harrogate, received a letter from her son Sergeant J.W. Abbott (West Yorks), who had previously been reported taken prisoner by his Sergeant Major, and then by the War Office that he was missing and wounded on 3rd May. Her son sent her a letter dated 1st June 1917 reassuring her that he was a POW, that he was not alone and with comrades. Abbott was at Gefangenenlager, Dulmen, I, Westfalen:

You will think I am a long time in writing, and wondering what has happened, but we are only allowed to write once a fortnight, and this is the first opportunity I have had of writing to you. Of course, I have sent you a postcard, which I think will have eased your mind by now ... I came across 'Pop' Jewitt the other day and he is in the next camp to me, so I am able to see him pretty often. Sergeant Wharton, from New Park is here with me, and belonged to the same company so you see I have a good chum ... remember me to all enquiring friends. I think this is a pretty decent camp by what I can see up to now.[11]

Private Walter Rowe from the 2nd/5th Battalion Duke of Wellington's was not so fortunate. He was wounded on 3rd May at Bullecourt and was captured. He died from his wounds on 23rd June 1917 and was buried at Tournai Communal Cemetery, Allied Extension in Belgium.

PRIVATE CHARLES MALTHOUSE 38066,
WEST YORKSHIRE REGIMENT

Charles Malthouse was born in 1887. He lived in Knaresborough and worked as a plumber before the war. Married to Alice they raised two children, Eileen and Walter. Walter was born in 1915 and was named after Charles's brother; who was killed on 9th May 1915 aged 20 while serving with the 1st/5th West Yorkshire Regiment at the Battle of Aubers Ridge. He enlisted to join the West Yorkshire Regiment on 29th November 1915. Two years later Charles was wounded and captured during the second battle of Bullecourt.

Whilst a prisoner of war he fell on his head and for years he would experience pains. During his captivity Charles worked on a farm in the Black Forest. He remembered kind treatment from the German family who owned the farm. Charles was discharged on 19th July 1919. When he returned home to Knaresborough, Charles established his own window cleaning business.

The horrors of war would haunt many veterans. Charles was no exception. His wife later told her son Walter: 'Charles had nightmares and if he turned on his stomach in his sleep he threw the pillows as if he was throwing grenades.'[12] During the Second World War Charles would serve his country once again as an air raid warden. Charles Malthouse passed away in 1971.

Private Charles Malthouse photographed with his family. (Courtesy Janet Coatman)

NOTES ··
1. National Archives: WO 161/100/250: Private Alfred Lister, 2nd/6th Battalion West Yorkshire Regiment POW Report.
2. Ibid.
3. Ibid.
4. Ibid.
5. *Harrogate Herald*: 29th January 1919.
6. Ibid.
7. National Archives: WO 161/100/250: Private Alfred Lister, 2nd/6th Battalion West Yorkshire Regiment POW Report.
8. *Harrogate Herald*: 29th January 1919.
9. Ibid: 20th June 1917.
10. Ibid.
11. *Harrogate Herald*: 4th July 1917: Letter dated 1st June 1917.
12. Private Charles Malthouse papers, Courtesy of Janet Coatman.

CHAPTER 21

THE 2ND HAC AND ROYAL WELCH FUSILIERS COUNTER ATTACK: 3RD MAY 1917

Efforts were made throughout the day to reach and support units that had broken through and established positions in Bullecourt. Without support these units could not consolidate captured ground and were either killed, wounded or forced to surrender. The 62nd Division had committed all its battalions and had suffered approximately 3,000 casualties. It was no longer in a position to engage in a counter attack. Without the capture of Bullecourt, the Australian 6th Brigade's hold on OG 1 and OG 2 near to the Central Road was precarious. Time was running out and something had to be done quickly to support the Australians in consolidating the gains they fought so hard for to the east of the village.

Later that morning Gough convened a meeting by the side of the Ervillers–St. Leger Road with Lieutenant-General Sir Edward Fanshawe commanding V Corps and Major-General Thomas Shoubridge commanding 7th Division. Shoubridge had been recently appointed commander after Gough dismissed the previous commander, Major-General Barrow, for not attacking the villages of Bucquoy and Croisilles.

Gough, Fanshawe and Shoubridge agreed that in order to maintain the momentum, another attack was urgently required and that the 7th Division would initiate it. At 12.45 pm the 7th Division was ordered by Fanshawe to enter the line where the 185th Brigade had fought early that morning. Shoubridge went in person to the 22nd Brigade Headquarters at Mory and ordered Brigadier-General J. McSteele to launch an attack later that day at 6.30 pm. The plan would involve advancing along the Bullecourt–Ecoust-St-Mein road and making a night assault on Tower Trench, which skirted the southern perimeter of Bullecourt.

The 2nd Honourable Artillery Company and the 1st Battalion Royal Welch Fusiliers from the 22nd Brigade were the battalions to attack the village. Lieutenant Colonel Albert Lambert-Ward commanding the 2nd HAC and Lieutenant Colonel W.H. Holmes commanding the 1st Royal Welch Fusiliers were summoned to the Headquarters of Brigadier-General Steele, commander of the 22nd Brigade and ordered to capture Bullecourt at all costs. As the 62nd Division had failed to gain a foothold in the village, it seemed a desperately hopeless task to expect these two battalions to succeed where an entire division had failed, but Gough wanted results. They were scheduled to attack at 6.30 pm, but this did not allow them sufficient time to appraise the situation and observe the extent of the wire or identify any breaches before the assault. Lambert-Ward raised his concerns about the limited time available and persuaded Brigadier-General Steele to postpone the operation to 10.30 pm.

The 2nd HAC and the 1st Royal Welch Fusiliers were in position along the railway embankment by 7.45 pm. The 2nd HAC was to attack the right flank advancing along the Longatte–Bullecourt Road, while the 1st Royal Welch Fusiliers attacked on the left flank. A and B Companies from the 2nd HAC were ordered to capture Tower Trench, which was the first German line and the trench that extended from OG 1 and formed the southern perimeter from east to west. Once this objective had been secured, C and D Companies would pass through their sister battalions and capture Bullecourt.

A Company from the 2nd/7th West Yorkshire Regiment was attached to the 22nd Infantry Brigade to reinforce the right flank of the 2nd HAC. Their orders were to capture Tower Trench and OG 1, which cut through the centre of Bullecourt. The 2nd HAC was to establish contact with the 6th Australian Infantry Brigade on their right flank, while the Welch battalion dug into their positions on the western perimeter of the village and formed a defensive flank facing north west. Assuming that this attack would prove successful a second wave involving the 20th Manchester Regiment and the 2nd Royal Warwickshire Regiment would pass through the first wave at 4.00 am and push the line northwards into Bullecourt.

Company commanders from the 1st Royal Welch Fusiliers went forward from the railway embankment to familiarise themselves with the terrain. Lieutenant Colonel Albert Lambert-Ward and Captain E.J. Amoore, Adjutant from the 2nd HAC, went into No Man's Land to reconnoitre. They could see that in particular the German artillery was targeting the railway embankment because they knew it was the assembly area. Lambert-Ward and Amoore found shelter in a ditch where they could assess the position. It was apparent to them that if they assembled their battalion by the railway embankment their men would be obliterated before the attack had begun. Lambert-Ward used his own initiative to assemble his men 300 yards behind the railway embankment, out of range of the shells, and ordered them to advance three minutes prior to Zero Hour at 10.30 pm. His common-sense approach saved the lives of many of his men.

At 10 pm reports were being received that German forces had begun a counter attack against the 6th Australian Infantry Brigade east of Bullecourt. It was considered whether to postpone the attack that night, but further reports indicated that the Australians were holding their ground and it was decided to go ahead.

Captain R. M. Stevens who was waiting with the 1st Royal Welch Fusiliers mistakenly thought that the 2nd HAC was not in position. Stevens was not aware of Lambert-Ward's decision to assemble his battalion farther back, but was soon told that the Honourable Artillery Company were not far from their position and that the 1st Royal Welch Fusiliers was to advance at a slow pace.

At 10.30 pm, the 2nd HAC and 1st Royal Welch Fusiliers led the advance 300 yards across No Man's Land towards Bullecourt, which was covered with shell holes and the bodies of the fallen comrades from West Yorkshire killed earlier that day.

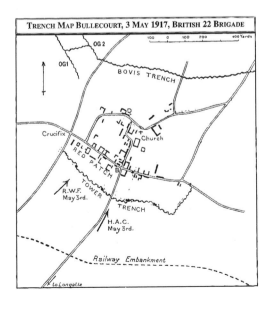

In the dark the soldiers from these two battalions, charging with fixed bayonets, were cut down by heavy German machine gun fire from Bullecourt and from strongly held machine gun positions in the German trenches. They were supported by a creeping barrage moving at 400 yards every four minutes; however, the wire became so entangled that instead of clearing a path for the advancing troops, the barrage actually impeded their attack and they were unable to pass beyond the wire. Visibility was greatly reduced due to smoke from the barrage, a problem encountered earlier that day exacerbated by the darkness. The 22nd Infantry Brigade war diary reported that 'The dust and smoke from our own barrage was so intense that men actually fell into the German trench before seeing it.'[1] Private William Parry-Morris:

> We went over at ten o'clock at night, a frontal attack, a bayonet attack. We got into the German trenches, but they were too strong for us and we were pushed out again. They saw us coming over at once. They started machine gun fire at once ... terrible machine gun fire.[2]

The 1st Royal Welch Fusiliers could only capture the first trench. They and the 2nd HAC battalions reached their first objective and entered Tower Trench where they captured 50 German prisoners. The 22nd Brigade war diary mentions the 'severe hand-to-hand fighting'.[3]

At 11.50 pm Captain Julian Soames commanding C Company, 1st Royal Welch Fusiliers reported that he had entered Tower Trench. A Company faltered on their left flank when they got entangled in the wire. Since there was no one on C Company's right flank, Soames was forced to withdraw his men from the trench.

Once A and B Companies had reached Tower Trench, C and D Companies from the 2nd HAC advanced into the village. The Australian battalions on their right flank suffered severely, exposing the advance of these companies. Eventually these men were receiving enemy fire from the flanks and from the rear as German infantry hidden in underground dug-outs appeared. Officers were identified and targeted by snipers hiding in the rubble of Bullecourt. Many of the 2nd HAC found themselves encircled.

Lambert-Ward had established battalion head-quarters in a ditch to the rear of the railway line near to Ecoust-St-Mein, accompanied by two signallers. With shells consistently falling heavily between Bullecourt and Ecoust-St-Mein it was impossible for messengers

2nd Honourable Artillery Company and 1st Royal Welch Fusiliers assault upon Bullecourt on 3rd May 1917 at 10.30 pm. (National Archives)

HAC Officers from the Reserve Battalion photographed in 1915. From left to right: standing, Lieutenant E.J. Amoore, 2nd Lieutenant F.C. Satchwell, Captain E. Boyle, 2nd Lieutenant W.G. Hoare, Lieutenant R. Corfield, 2nd Lieutenant W.A. Stone, 2nd Lieutenant G.M. Van der Byl, 2nd Lieutenant C.M. Humble-Crofts, 2nd Lieutenant B.W. Noble; 2nd Lieutenant C.J. Bolton, Lieutenant W.E. Clare, Colonel R. Farrington, Colonel L.R.C. Boyle, Surgeon-Colonel W. Culver James, Major L. Wright, Lieutenant R.P. Gosnell, 2nd Lieutenant H. Ommundsen; on the ground 2nd Lieutenant C.O. Sturgis, 2nd Lieutenant R.J. Drury, 2nd Lieutenant H.M. Worsley, 2nd Lieutenant R.C. Hawkins. Amoore, Satchwell and Drury took part in the Battle of Bullecourt. (Courtesy Sigrid Duly)

2nd Battalion Honourable Artillery Company photographed in June 1916 (Tank Museum E2001.1153)

to bring back reports from units who had entered the village. At one point a shell exploded close to Ward's position killing the two signallers and rendering him temporarily unconscious. Two Brigade signallers came to his assistance and enabled him to establish communications with Brigade Headquarters. Lambert-Ward had temporarily lost the use of his hearing and could not use the telephone. He was joined by Major Wright, Captain Amoore and Lieutenant R Heather. Here they anxiously waited for reports from their companies. The first report confirmed that A and B Company were holding Tower Trench, but C and D companies were held up in the village. At 12.30 am on the 4th Ward received reports that C Company had been driven back to Tower Trench by a strong German counter attack from the east.

More bombs and ammunition was requested by companies holding onto Tower Trench at 1 am on 4th May. The message was received by Lambert-Ward at Battalion HQ who promptly ordered a party of men to go to the Brigade bomb supply positioned 200 yards to the rear of the railway embankment. The HAC unit history recorded that 'with horror it was discovered that

all the boxes thought to contain bombs were empty, and there were none to be had anywhere.'[4] As the battle progressed, British shells were falling on the German wire where the 1st Royal Welch Fusiliers were trying to break through.[5]

By 2 am on the morning of the 4th German counter attacks using the stick bomb were driving 2nd HAC and 1st Royal Welch Fusiliers backwards. They attacked the 2nd HAC through the gap in the line between the 2nd HAC and A Company from the 2nd/7th West Yorkshires, which was brought in to support the 2nd HAC and reinforce the line; before they arrived, the 2nd HAC had been forced back. At 2.00 am Captain Theodore Clifford Bower commanding B Company sent a message to Lambert-Ward reporting that the German forces had launched a heavy attack. He had lost contact with the West Yorkshires on his left flank and with the Australians on his right.

During the attack, men from the 2nd HAC stumbled across a party of soldiers from the West Yorkshire Regiments commanded by Corporal R.F. Billington. Billington had assembled some stragglers who were withdrawing from Bullecourt during the morning on 3rd May in a shell crater. They fortified the crater and held it. When the 2nd HAC advanced towards Bullecourt he led his men in carrying bombs and munitions in support of the 2nd HAC. Billington was awarded the Distinguished Conduct Medal for 'conspicuous gallantry and devotion to duty. He rallied his men under heavy fire, and throughout the day set a magnificent example of courage and determination.'[6] Billington's recommendation for the Distinguished Conduct Medal in 185th Brigade Orders written by commanding officer V.W. de Falbe provides more detail:

> During the morning of the 3rd May 1917 when troops were returning from Bullecourt he collected stragglers into a crater where they dug themselves in and held out. In the evening when the Hon. Artillery Company attacked he led his party forward carrying bombs to the German first trench and assisted that Regiment, remaining some hours with them. His action and example were soldierly and encouraging to others.[7]

By 2.30 am both the 2nd HAC and the 1st Royal Welch Fusiliers were driven out of Tower Trench. Overwhelmed by German forces, Private William Parry-Morris from the 2nd HAC remembered: 'We had to retire because we were outnumbered. There were too many of our men killed and wounded. When the Germans came into the trench, they were double the number of us. We had to retreat.'[8]

It was difficult for men from the 2nd HAC to retreat because they were pinned down by machine gun fire.

Private Parry-Morris was forced to crawl back to the British line:

> I was pushed out of the German trench and I got about 10 yards from the German trench into a shell hole and the Germans were firing machine guns and shelling all the time. The only way I got back to our own line was by crawling on my stomach 100 yards. At the end of that battle we had 98 that was left.[9]

Captain R.J. Drury from the 2nd HAC arrived wounded at Lambert-Ward's headquarters. He reported that the battalion had been annihilated. He personally verified the written message sent by Bower to Lambert-Ward that the remnants of the battalion had been badly beaten back from positions they had briefly held in the village. Drury was left with 30 men and they were forced out of the village and were now holding positions in trenches and shell holes outside the German wire.

At 3.30 am the 2nd HAC was ordered to withdraw. The battalion lost 11 officers and 200 men in the engagement. Morale was low after the terrible losses. Parry-Morris remembered that a 'lot of wounded men were left on the open ground, until they were collected the next day.'[10]

British shells bombarding positions north of Tower Trench at 3.40 am caused further casualties amongst the small parties of 1st Royal Welch Fusiliers that were still holding on. They lost four officers – 2nd Lieutenants Arthur Starkey Lewis, David Arthur Thomas, Daniel Thomas Jones and Alfred Montague Syrett – and 20 men were killed. 2nd Lieutenant H.L.M. Ellis died from his wounds at Achiet-le-Grand. The battalion also lost 65 in the ranks wounded and 22 missing.

The attack launched by the 2nd HAC and the 1st Royal Welch Fusiliers was a failure. They had lost heavily and German forces still controlled Bullecourt.

PRIVATE MONTAGUE CALDER 9041
2ND BATTALION HONOURABLE ARTILLERY COMPANY

Montague William Calder was born in April 1888. He was the son of William and Charlotte from Streatham Hill, London. Prior to the war Calder worked as an accountant and was living in Denmark Hill, South East London. Calder joined the Honourable Artillery Company on 30th November 1915. He

Private Montague Calder. (Courtesy Jean & Denise Letaille Bullecourt Museum)

joined the 2nd Battalion on the 25th September 1916, arriving in Havre, France on Christmas Day 1916. Calder regularly kept in contact with the Anerley Bicycle Club, of which he was Captain, and in one letter to the club he described his experience as a member of a relief party going to the aid of a small British force that had captured a sector of German trench:

> I suppose it would have taken 15 minutes to walk straight over, but it took us five hours to effect that relief. The Huns had the wind up badly and kept star shells continually in the air. This meant that it was only occasionally we could move forward. Then there was the difficulty of reaching the exact place in the Hun line held by our men. Our guide got uncertain of exactly where we were so we had to be down for 1½ hours without being able to speak while he and our officer crawled up and located the spot. This was eventually successfully accomplished, but it was a very trying time, with a machine gun coughing out lead every time the Verey lights showed us up. When we got into the post our officer decided that we should try and push further down the trench, so we amused ourselves for an hour or so bombing Fritz. We had, however, to withdraw to our original position as machine gun fire prevented us from consolidating. Next night we tried again and completely succeeded in driving everyone out and capturing the whole trench, giving us access to a sunken road that led into the town that was our objective. We were relieved and the town was captured early next morning with very few casualties. Everyone was pleased with our work and we were congratulated by the General.[11]

Calder was serving with D Company when he was killed on 3rd May. He has no known grave and his name is commemorated on the Arras Memorial. The members of the Anerley Bicycle Club mourned his loss and wrote this emotive tribute to their former Captain:

> The Anerley have been happy in their Captains, but to put it temperately and simply no previous holder of the office has been more enthusiastic and efficient, more of a sportsman and a gentleman, nor more esteemed and loved by every member fortunate to meet him, than M. W. Calder, who died on May 3rd 1917, a soldier in the Honourable Artillery Company, one of the best Captains we can ever hope to have.[12]

William Calder, his father, who had also lost another son, presented the Calder Shield to Anerley Bicycle Club in honour of his son Montague. The Anerley Bicycle Club still exists today.

CAPTAIN FRANK SATCHWELL,
2ND BATTALION HONOURABLE ARTILLERY COMPANY

Frank Henry Sandom Satchwell was born in London in 1878. Educated at Christ's Hospital, Frank Satchwell joined the Honourable Artillery Company on 29th January 1900. He served in South Africa during the Boer War and was awarded the South African Medal with five bars. In 1906 he married Gertrude Russell in Brixton. He received a commission on 14th October 1914. Satchwell served with the 3rd Battalion during the early years of the war. He was sent to France on 28th April 1917 where he joined the 2nd Battalion. Satchwell was killed on 3rd May when his battalion launched the night assault on Bullecourt. He was aged 38. Satchwell has no known grave and his name is commemorated on the Arras Memorial. He left a son aged nine and two daughters aged eight and six who at that time were living in Hendon, London. Gertrude was told that he was missing and held out a forlorn hope that her husband would return. She placed appeals in newspapers containing his photo and an address to write to if anyone knew the whereabouts of her husband. She wrote the following poem in remembrance of her fallen husband:

> And still for him thy service waits,
> Tho' earth's last fight is fought.
> God did not give thy noble soul
> To end at last in naught.
> That steadfast tender heart
> Was not for this brief life alone:
> 'Tis as a soldier he will stand
> Before the Great White Throne.

Above left: **Gertrude Satchwell placed many advertisements in newspapers seeking information about her beloved husband Captain Frank Satchwell after she was notified that he was listed as missing. (Courtesy Sigrid Duly)**

Right: **Captain Frank Satchwell leads a route march with the 3rd Battalion HAC in 1915. (Courtesy Sigrid Duly)**

MISSING.

Captain F. H. S. Satch-well (H.A.C.), missing. Write 125, Sunny-gardens, Hendon, N.W.

Gertrude died of a broken heart in 1922, leaving their 15-year-old son to look after their two younger daughters.

Captain Frank Satchwell with his wife Gertrude and his family at Bisley. (Courtesy Sigrid Duly)

LANCE CORPORAL RONALD JEAFFRESON 5019,
2ND BATTALION, HONOURABLE ARTILLERY COMPANY

Ronald Percy Jeaffreson was born in Islington, London on 5th October 1897. He was the son of Henry and Edith and they would later live in Enfield. Ronald enlisted to join the Honourable Artillery Company in September 1915. He joined up weeks before his 18th birthday. Ronald chose the army because he wanted to be close to his older brother Bryan who enlisted on 15th August. Bryan was a medical student and was now training with the 1st Battalion, Honourable Artillery Company. Ronald hoped to have been sent to his brother's battalion, but was attached to the 3rd Battalion instead. Ronald began his training at a camp in Blackheath, and then another in Richmond. Since the 1st and 3rd Battalions were training together Ronald was able to share the same billet until Bryan was sent to France in January 1916.

Since Ronald was under 19 years of age, he was not eligible to be sent to the front for active duty. He had to remain in England until October 1916. Ronald was sent to France, but not to join his brother in the 1st Battalion but to the 2nd Battalion. He spent his 19th birthday in a railway cattle truck en route to the trenches. On 12th November 1916 Private Ronald Jeaffreson wrote:

> We have been on the move again, and are a considerable distance from the firing -line. I am very well, and have got used, more or less, to this life. I find a private's life is much harder than I expected, and am sorry for many reasons that I did not take a commission when I had the opportunity.[13]

Ronald was anxious to be with his brother and applied to be transferred from the 2nd Battalion to the 1st. The application was delayed, but Ronald did find an opportunity to meet Bryan when the 1st and 2nd Honourable Artillery Company Battalions were near to each other, but this was only for a few hours. This would be the only time that Ronald would spend with his brother in France and the last time that he would ever see him.

During March 1917 the 2nd Honourable Artillery Company was following the German retreat. It was a very exhausting time for Ronald as they had to dig in to positions and create billets each day as they followed the German withdrawal:

> I have never worked so hard in all my life. Being planted in the middle of a field, with no cover, we had to dig furiously to get down into the earth to protect ourselves from the shells and cold wind. I worked hard all night and had to stop at day-break. We were very thankful all the next day for the work we had done during the night, as we had fine cover.[14]

Ronald was promoted to Lance Corporal in April. He would send postcards each day to his parents in Enfield reassuring them he was well. The last postcard they received was dated 1st May 1917. On 3rd May Lance Corporal Ronald Jeaffreson advanced with the second wave of the 2nd Battalion. Ronald was seen approaching the second line of German barbed wire and not seen again. He has no known grave and his name is commemorated on the Arras Memorial.

Within a week Ronald's parents would soon learn the painful news that their beloved son was listed missing in action. Marie Therese Jeaffreson, a relative wrote:

> The whole platoon felt very deeply by his loss, as he was universally popular and loved by all. His was a very lovable character, and a charming personality from earliest childhood. Affectionate, considerate, unselfish and deeply religious, he was a favourite with all who knew him. He was very musical, and as a boy, the possessor of a beautiful voice. For several years he was a member of the choir at St Mary Magdalene, Enfield, where he generally sang the treble solos in the anthems, and sang with such feeling, that it was easy to realise that he fully meant what he sang.[15]

His bereaved parents dedicated a memorial stained-glass window in the church of Saint Mary Magdalene in Enfield inscribed, 'To the Glory of God, and in

Lance Corporal Ronald Percy Jeaffreson. (Author)

ever loving memory of our beloved son, Ronald Percy Jeaffreson, H.A.C., who was killed in action at Bullecourt, France, on the 3rd of May, 1917, aged 19 years.'

LANCE CORPORAL EDWIN BULL 6893,
2ND HONOURABLE ARTILLERY COMPANY

Edwin Hayley Bull was born in Vauxhall, London in 1893. Known as Eddy to his family, he was one of the soldiers from the 2nd Honourable Artillery Company who fought his way into Bullecourt during the night of 3rd May and was captured in enemy trenches on the 4th. He was imprisoned in Soltau Camp in Germany for the remainder of the war. On 23rd May 1917, his commanding officer Captain Theodore Clifford Bower wrote to his parents informing them that Bull was missing:

> I deeply regret to have to inform you that your son L/C E H Bull is posted as missing. I fear he was killed in an attack on May 3rd. If I hear anything further I will write to you. He had been with us since we had been sent without intervals in hospital ... Please accept my deep sympathy.
>   Yours very sincerely
>   Captain T C Bower
>   OC B Coy[16]

Lance Corporal Edwin Bull. (Courtesy Ross Moon)

Private Edwin Bull was held at Soltau Prison after his capture at Bullecourt. This photo was taken at roll call at Soltau POW Camp. (Courtesy Ross Moon)

Lance Corporal Edwin Bull (second from left) in captivity at Soltau POW Camp in August 1918. (Courtesy Ross Moon)

Many such terrible letters were written during the war. MIA creates a horribly tantalising No Man's Land all of its own. Bull had been captured and heartbreak would transform to joy when he was repatriated after the war ended. He would never talk of the war or his experiences at Bullecourt.

PRIVATE LIONEL BRADDICK 4373,
2ND HONOURABLE ARTILLERY COMPANY

Lionel Frank Braddick was born in Camberwell, London in 1897. When Braddick was a child his family lived in Wembley. He was aged 18 when he enlisted on 29th September 1915. Given the rank of private he joined the 3rd Battalion. Transferred to 2nd Battalion during September 1916, he was sent to France on 1st October 1916. Private Lionel Braddick was mortally wounded in the assault on Bullecourt during the night of 3rd May 1917. Evacuated from the battlefield he died from his wounds later that evening. He was buried at Bailleul Road East Cemetery, St. Laurent-Blangy.

Private Lionel Braddick. (Courtesy Honourable Artillery Company Archives)

SERGEANT NORWOOD BROWN 3789,
2ND HONOURABLE ARTILLERY COMPANY

Norwood Alfred Edmond was born in Edinburgh in 1889. When he was 12 years old his family relocated to Aberdeen. He joined the Honourable Artillery Company on 9th June 1915. He was assigned to the 2nd Battalion and quickly rose through the ranks. When the battalion left England for France

Sergeant Norwood Brown. (Courtesy Honourable Artillery Company Archives)

on 1st October 1916 he was a Sergeant. Brown was wounded during the night attack on Bullecourt on 3rd May 1917. He was evacuated from the battlefield and taken to a hospital at Abbeville where he succumbed to his wounds, aged 27. Sergeant Norwood Brown was buried at Abbeville Communal Cemetery Extension.

PRIVATE ERNEST BUCKERIDGE 9945,
2ND HONOURABLE ARTILLERY COMPANY

Ernest George Buckeridge was born in St Pancras, London in 1882. In 1901 At 18 he was working as a banker's clerk. When World War One was being fought Buckeridge was living in Highgate, North London and working at the National Bank in Old Broad Street, London. Buckeridge enlisted on 18th January 1917 as a private and on 3rd April he was serving in France with the 2nd Battalion Honourable Artillery Company. He was killed in the assault on Bullecourt on 3rd May. Originally listed as missing, Private Ernest Buckeridge has no known grave and his name is listed on the Arras Memorial. He left a widow and one child.

Private Ernest Buckeridge. (Courtesy Honourable Artillery Company Archives)

2ND LIEUTENANT ALFRED SYRETT,
1ST BATTALION WELCH FUSILIERS

Alfred Montague Syrett from the 1st Battalion Royal Welch Fusiliers was aged 29 when he fell at Bullecourt. Syrett was in 1888 and was educated at Dulwich College. He was destined for the legal profession, but chose music as a career. Syrett had spent time in Paris, Germany and Romania prior to the war. During the war he joined the Artist's Rifles Officer Training Corps and was commissioned as 2nd Lieutenant on 22nd November 1916. He was attached to the 1st Battalion Royal Welch Fusiliers and joined them on 16th February 1917. Within days he would see action as the battalion followed the German retreat to the Hindenburg Line. Syrett took part

2nd Lt A. M. Syrett. (By kind permission of the Governors of Dulwich College)

in the battle for Puisieux on 26th February 1917 and was wounded and suffered shell shock from his first experience of battle. Syrett was killed on 4th May 1917 while leading a platoon in an attack on Tower Trench. He has no known grave and his name is commemorated on the Arras Memorial.

PRIVATE ALBERT HANNAH 53888,
1ST BATTALION ROYAL WELCH FUSILIERS

Albert Hannah was born in West Derby, Liverpool in 1898. He was the son of Ernst and Lilley Hannah. Albert had two older brothers Fred and John and a younger sister Josephine. His father Ernest died aged 25 in 1903 when Albert was four years old. A photo exists of Albert in Army uniform which is listed as Bedford 1914. If he had enlisted in 1914, then he would have been under age to serve. The story was passed down the family that he was a dispatch rider. Albert was aged 18 when he took part in the Second Battle of Bullecourt on 3rd May 1917. He was mortally wounded on 4th May. He was taken to a casualty clearing station but died from his wounds. Private Albert Hannah was buried at Achiet-Le-Grand Communal Cemetery Extension in France. Hannah's epitaph reads: 'I KNOW THY SPIRIT / HOVERS NEAR ME / I FEEL IT / THROUGH THE DAILY STRIFE.' He is commemorated on the Hawarden War Memorial; mistakenly under the name Albert H Littler. His mother had remarried and Littler was her surname from her second marriage. Lilley made a pilgrimage to France to visit Albert's grave at Achiet-Le-Grand.

Private Albert Hannah. (Courtesy John Hannah)

Private Albert Hannah's grave at Achiet-le-Grand Communal Cemetery Extension. (Courtesy John Hannah)

Royal Flying Corps aerial photo of Bullecourt and Hendecourt taken on 24th April 1917. The mound on the left of the photo on the edge of the village is the German strongpoint known as the Crucifix. The photo was taken south of Bullecourt and shows the remnants of the village after the first battle. The 2nd Honourable Artillery Company and the 1st Royal Welch Fusiliers advanced north either side of the Bullecourt–Ecoust-St-Mein Road during the night of 3rd May 1917. (Author)

NOTES ....

1. National Archives: WO 95/1661: 22nd Infantry Brigade War Diary.
2. IWM Department of Sound: IWM 9488: Private William Parry-Morris, 2nd Battalion Honourable Artillery Company.
3. National Archives: WO 95/1661: 22nd Infantry Brigade War Diary.
4. The Honourable Artillery Company 1914–1918, Major G. Goold Walker.
5. National Archives: WO 95/1665: 1st Battalion Royal Welch Fusiliers War Diary.
6. London Gazette: Issue 30204: 24th July 1917.
7. National Archives: WO 95/3079: 185th Brigade War Diary.

8. IWM Department of Sound: IWM 9488: Private William Parry-Morris, 2nd Battalion Honourable Artillery Company.
9. Ibid.
10. Ibid.
11. Private Montague Calder Papers, Jean and Denise Letaille Bullecourt Museum.
12. Ibid.
13. Pedigree of the Jeaffreson Family with Notes and Memoirs, Marie Therese Jeaffreson 1922. Courtesy Saint Mary Magdalene Church, Enfield.
14. Ibid.
15. Ibid.
16. Lance Corporal Edwin Bull papers: Courtesy Ross Moon.

CHAPTER 22

THE 20TH MANCHESTERS AND 2ND WARWICKSHIRES ENTER THE FRAY: 4TH MAY 1917

The attacks made on 3rd May had faltered and the two battalions which were intended to pass through the 2nd Honourable Artillery Company and 1st Royal Welch Fusiliers were brought up to the front line to initiate another attack on Bullecourt. At 3.10 am on 4th May 1917 soldiers from the 20th Manchesters and the 2nd Royal Warwickshire Battalions assembled close to the railway embankment. The Warwickshire's managed to establish some pockets on the right flank of the Welch lines. Small parties of 1st Royal Welch Fusiliers held onto positions near to Tower Trench, until they were ordered to retire to allow bombardment to take place prior to the counter attack to be carried out later that morning by the 2nd Royal Warwick's and 20th Manchesters.

The Regiments were ordered to recapture Tower Trench. As the soldiers from Manchester and Warwickshire formed up in their starting positions they were heavily shelled by German artillery resulting in substantial casualties. The 20th Manchester Regiment sustained 80 casualties as a result of this barrage. Major G. Goold Walker wrote: 'A few minutes after 4 the enemy put down a barrage, completely blowing the Manchesters off the ground. It was a most appalling scene – men were falling in all directions.'[1] Lieutenant Colonel Lambert-Ward from the 2nd HAC witnessed the devastation and carnage:

At 3.30 orders came from Brigade to withdraw, as the Manchesters and Warwick's were about to attack under a barrage forming up on the same line, viz, the railway. At 3.30 during a lull in shelling, the Manchesters and Warwick's came up in rear of us and formed up ready to advance upon the railway ... The whole place was obscured in a fog of dust, and smoke, through which men could be seen staggering, falling and running in all directions. The Warwick's, who were not exposed to the full blast of the barrage, got away and reached the enemy's wire outside Bullecourt, but the Manchesters never even

started – about 75 per cent of the Battalion being knocked out on the starting line.[2]

Private Arthur Burke 20th Manchester Regiment in a letter home to his brother recalled. 'I've seen some fighting this last 18 months, but never so terrible as we went into last Friday.' He waited during the day learning of the terrible disaster that befell the 62nd Division, then the Regiment

... got orders that our brigade would attack and try and take the village which a full division and eight tanks failed to do. At 10.30 pm two battalions went over, we moved up to take our position for the stunt at 1 am timed to go over at 4.00 am news came through that so, and so and so, were fighting a terrific hand to hand battle and were slowly retiring. One battalion took their objective four times – each time being bombed out, at last they had to retire having run short of bombs. Whilst we were waiting our time to go over, the wounded were coming down in dozens, and we were under the severest bombardment I have ever known Fritz to send over. We knew it was certain death for all of us – orders are orders in the army and we had to obey them ... At 4.00 am we advanced but owing to other battalions retiring (coming towards us) we were hopeless and could not get through his barrage ... Our company went in 104 strong, came out 44.[3]

The attack began at 4.00 am and the 22nd Brigade War Diary records that 'confused fighting followed.'[4] The situation was obscure and unbeknown to the Brigade Commander, the second assault was also a failure. Some men from the 20th Manchesters fought their way into the south-eastern sector of the village but could not hold on.

The reason why the 7th and 62nd Divisions' attempts to capture Bullecourt were thwarted was that the Germans had developed new tactics. The trenches were no longer manned during the day or night; instead, sentries would be posted at entrances to dug-outs, while units would shelter in underground bunkers safe from allied shelling. As soon as allied infantry advanced towards the village they would emerge and repel the attackers. Once they had repulsed an attempt, before confronting the next onslaught, the exhausted and hungry men from the 27th Württemberg Regiment scavenged food from the dead British and Australian soldiers. Some German soldiers found themselves trapped and isolated in their dug-outs as their entrances were blocked by debris from barrages. Many men were forced to dig their way out to the surface.

The 2nd Royal Warwickshire Regiment was not affected by the German barrage and cut through the enemy wire and entered the village. German counter attacks pushed the Warwick's back. By 5.00 am no reports had been received and it was difficult to ascertain whether this initiative was a success or a failure; 50% of battalion runners were lost in the German barrage. It was decided that the 1st Royal Welch Fusiliers and 2nd Royal Warwickshire Regiments should regroup and send patrols into Bullecourt. 200 men were collected and reorganised. These patrols pushed forward towards the sunken road to the west end of Bullecourt. A message was received from a runner at 6.15 am at 20th Brigade HQ confirming that some officers and men were digging into positions in the wire in front of Bullecourt. An officer from Brigade Headquarters was sent to reconnoitre. No news came back. At 1 pm one officer from each battalion involved in the previous night's attack was ordered to go into No Man's Land and report on the positions of their units. These officers found that their units were in positions near to the Crucifix and it was decided that another push in the direction of the Crucifix could succeed. The Crucifix was a fortified mound located on the western perimeter of Bullecourt where the village of Crucifix once stood. It was a formidable position, which commanded good observation over the ruins and it would take two weeks for British forces to capture it. D Company from the 1st Royal Welch Fusiliers and the Royal Warwickshire's were ordered to launch a bombing attack from the sunken road towards the Crucifix. The attack was launched at 11 pm on 4th May. The 2nd Royal Warwickshire Regiment war diary recorded:

> The enemy held his fire until they reached the 2nd belt of wire, which was uncut, and then opened strong rifle and machine gun fire which cause heavy casualties. Communication was impossible, as the signalling lamp was broken by shell fire and both pigeons had died of shell shock. The attack was a failure.[5]

They were forced back to their starting positions. The 2nd Royal Warwickshire Regiment entered the battle

with battalion strength comprising 20 officers and 609 men. When they had left the line at Bullecourt, the battle had reduced their strength to eight officers and 362 men.[6] The reasons for the failure were set down in the 2nd Royal Warwickshire's war diary:

1. Concentration probably observed by the enemy as he put down a heavy barrage at 3.40 am which had to be passed through.
2. Sudden alteration of plans which only allowed hurried consultation with O.C. Coys on place of deployment.
3. Position held heavily by machine gun and second belt of wire uncut on front attacked by battalion.
4. It appeared that the village was honeycombed with dug-outs and underground passages which allowed the enemy to get behind our men. One sergeant described it as like being in a maze.
5. The fact that the enemy outranged us with his egg bombs.
6. The difficulty of obtaining information was very great owing to open nature of the ground and the large number of machine guns and snipers, 50% of runners becoming casualties.
7. The ... heavy enemy shelling on whole front in addition to three heavy barrages he put down along the line of track from U.27.a.8.2 to U.27.a.2.4.
8. The smoke and dust caused by shelling made it difficult to see any distance.[7]

The 8th Devonshires took control of the positions being held by the 1st Royal Welch Fusiliers. At 5 am on 4th May the 8th Devonshire's were given orders that they were to send strong patrols into Bullecourt at 2.30 pm. Reconnaissance aircraft were ordered to observe, but they were unable to fly over the first German trench due to heavy machine gun fire and could not assess progress.

The 22nd Brigade was relieved at 9 pm on 4th May. As they left the line, they were unaware that a party of ten men from the 2nd Honourable Artillery Company, led by Corporal Reginald Billingham, was holding onto a position within the ruins of Bullecourt, isolated and surrounded by the enemy.

LANCE CORPORAL WALTER DAKIN 18369,
20TH BATTALION MANCHESTER REGIMENT

Walter Dakin worked as a piecer at Mutual Mill in Heywood, prior to the war. He enlisted on 16th January 1915 and was assigned to the 20th Battalion Manchester Regiment. Dakin was sent to France on 9th

Lance Corporal Walter Dakin. (Courtesy Judith Wheatley)

November 1915. He became a signaller and later an instructor. Dakin saw action during the first day of the Somme campaign when the 20th Battalion Manchester Regiment attacked Fricourt on 1st July 1916. The attack was launched at 2.30 pm; several hours after the first waves were decimated when they went over the top early that morning. The Germans anticipated the 20th Manchesters' advance and were waiting for them with their machine guns. The battalion entered the battle with 460 men. The attack on Fricourt had reduced their numbers to 150. Dakin also took part in the battle for the village of Ginchy on 3rd September. The 20th Battalion entered Ginchy but a German counter attack forced them to withdraw to their start line at Guillemont. Walter was given compassionate leave to visit his wounded elder brother John Robert Dakin who had served with the 12th Battalion Manchester Regiment. John had been severely wounded by a shell and Walter visited him in a hospital in France before he was transferred to the 3rd Western General Hospital at Newport. Walter's granddaughter Judith Wheatley recalled: 'I remember him saying my great uncle had holes in his back "I could put my fists in".'

Walter was buried alive and posted as missing presumed killed. When he managed to get out he sent postcards home to reassure his family. He would draw an image of Charlie Chaplin which was a coded message to let his family know that he was fine.

Walter remembered some of the lighter moments and told his family: for example, the regimental mascot, an ape, jumped on his back during one dark night. On one occasion when he was out of the line, Dakin was looking forward to eating a tin of pears. Communication problems had occurred, and the locals supplied him with peas. At one point he was granted a brief leave and spoke of returning home full of lice.

As the 20th Manchesters assembled by the railway embankment prior to the assault on the village scheduled to begin at 4.00 am on the 4th, German artillery unleashed a ferocious barrage upon their lines wiping out 75% of the battalion. Dakin was fortunate to come through this terrible ordeal. Weeks later Dakin was mentioned in dispatches for conspicuous bravery during the night of 4th/5th July 1917. In the summer of 1917 Dakin attended an instructor's course and on 26th September 1917 he received a certificate confirming that he was qualified as an assistant instructor of signalling.

On 18th August 1919 he was transferred to the reserve with the rank of Corporal. On leaving the Army he returned to Heywood. He retired during the 1960s and indulged his love of gardening and sport. He supported Morecambe Football Club because he became fond of the Morecambe area when he trained with the Manchester Regiment during the war. Walter Dakin died in October 1977. His great grand-daughter is a serving Royal Naval officer who has seen active service in the Gulf and Afghanistan, 90 years after Walter Dakin served.

PRIVATE ALBERT HILL 17924,
20TH BATTALION MANCHESTER REGIMENT

Albert James Hill was born in Wolverhampton, Staffordshire in 1896. His father Isaac was a joiner and relocated the family to Salford. Albert attended St Luke's Church, Weaste, Salford and was Sergeant in the Church Lad's Brigade. Prior to the war he worked as a plumber for Schofield and Co in Manchester. He enlisted in November 1914 and joined the 20th Battalion Manchester Regiment as a private. He trained at Grantham and Salisbury during 1915. While on leave Albert married Frances Gibson on 3rd November 1915 at St Luke's Church. Six days later he entrained for Folkestone where he and the 20th Manchesters embarked on a troopship for Boulogne. The battalion arrived at the front line on 1st February at Morlancourt and on the following day was deployed in reserve trenches south of Fricourt on the Somme. It was likely that he fought with the 20th Manchesters at Fricourt on 1st July, at Mametz Wood on 4th July and at Ginchy on 3rd September. Private Albert Hill was killed at Bullecourt on 4th May 1917. He has no known grave and his name is commemorated on the Arras Memorial.

Private Albert James Hill. (Courtesy Neil Conduit)

SERGEANT ROBERT SMITH 18031 MM
20TH BATTALION MANCHESTER REGIMENT

Robert Samuel Smith was born in Manchester in 1893. Known as Sam, he worked as a builder prior to his enlistment on 16th November 1914. Smith saw action at Fricourt on 1st July and at Ginchy on 3rd September 1916 during the Somme campaign. He was wounded on

4th May 1917 at Bullecourt by German shell fire as the men assembled along the railway embankment prior to the attack on the village. The severity of Smith's wounds necessitated his return to Britain on 18th

Sergeant Robert Samuel Smith MM. (Courtesy Paul Fitzgerald)

May. Smith returned to France in April 1918 and was assigned to the 10th Battalion, Manchester Regiment. He was wounded again in the Battle of the River Selles on 20th October 1918 and returned to Britain on 28th October. The war was over within weeks and in February 1919 he received the Military Medal, presumably for his bravery during 1918. After recovering from his wounds and demobilisation he established a business as a pet store proprietor. Smith would serve his country a second time with the Home Guard during World War Two and was awarded the Defence Medal and the War Medal. Sam Smith passed away on 11th May 1955 at the age of 62.

NOTES

1.   *The Honourable Artillery Company 1914–918*, Major G. Goold Walker.

2.   *The Honourable Artillery Company Journal*, Volume 1, 1923.

3.   Imperial War Museum Department of Documents: Ref IWM 6/5/17: Private Arthur Burke, 20th Battalion Manchester Regiment.

4.   National Archives: 22nd Infantry Brigade War Diary: WO 95/1661.

5.   National Archives: WO 95/1664: 2nd Battalion Royal Warwickshire Regiment War Diary.

6.   Ibid.

7.   Ibid.

CHAPTER 23

SURROUNDED BY THE ENEMY: 3RD–7TH MAY 1917

The 2nd Honourable Artillery Company withdrew from Bullecourt during the morning of 4th May, but remarkably a party of men from this Battalion commanded by Corporal Reginald Billingham remained in the ruins of Bullecourt, surrounded by German forces for four nights and three days. During the night of Thursday 3rd May, Billingham led a bombing section from B Company of the 2nd HAC into Bullecourt. The section consisted of a corporal and five men and their orders were that once they had captured the first German line, they were to push on another 150 yards and establish an outpost position. During the attack, Billingham found himself on his own:

> Having reached our first objective I rallied my section (Now reduced to four) and went forward. Shelling was heavy and I soon found myself alone. I came across a communication trench down which the enemy were retreating. After lobbing in two Mills bombs I made off to the left in search of the L.G.s to whom I attached myself. As far as I recall we were now in a party of six, or maybe eight, occupying a fairly big crater as an outpost to comply with orders.[1]

Two other men would join Billingham and his party in the crater. They had done what was expected of them. However, they were unaware that the attack had failed and that the 2nd HAC had been ordered to withdraw. Billingham and his party of ten men fortified themselves in the ruins of a German billet, which they defended throughout the following days. Numerous German attacks were sent to clear them, but they successfully repulsed each one. Their only source of food and water was from dead comrades and dead German soldiers.

Billingham later wrote 'During the night two more stragglers joined us. The night was noisy and we realised that the Germans were counter attacking, but we had no reason to think our chaps were being driven out of the trenches they had so recently captured.'[2]

It was not until the following morning, on Friday 4th May, at dawn that they became aware they were on their own and surrounded. 'When dawn broke we were able to see something of our position and to our surprise found that the trench on our right was occupied by the enemy. During the day it became clear to us that we were cut off, as the trench in our rear was swarming with Bosche.'[3] They were unable even to address the calls of nature and were forced to keep their heads down until nightfall. 'We lay low, so as not to disclose our position. Only at night were we able to move to relieve ourselves.'[4]

> By this time we were getting terribly thirsty. Our water bottles had been full when we left Courcelles some days before, but we had no chance of replenishing them since, and the tension, fumes and dust of battle parched our throats. The question of how to break out was constantly in our minds, though no plans were discussed at this time. We were keeping a strictly defensive attitude with sentries posted throughout.[5]

It was during the second night behind enemy lines that Billingham's party came into direct contact with the enemy:

> On the second (Friday) night a party of three or four of the enemy appeared within a few yards and we challenged them. Their surprise was almost comic. They halted dead and stood motionless until, perhaps seeing the glint of steel in the moonlight, they turned and fled screaming back to their own trench. We fully expected to see the Germans send out a mopping-up party and wipe us out, but they contented themselves with the firing of rifle grenades and a few trench mortar bombs. They had not got our exact position, for luckily none of their shots dropped onto our post.[6]

German infantry did not try to remove Billingham's party from the crater at this point. During the night slight rain fell and they had to use their initiatives to capture this life saving resource:

> During the day the tension relaxed gradually when we found that no attack was forthcoming. Our water had given out and we were suffering badly

from thirst. The days were extremely hot, with no shelter from the sun. Saturday night brought a few drops of rain and we spread our ground sheets to catch some of the precious moisture.[7]

On the third day they talked of a breakout, but the Germans decided to make escape from the isolated outpost almost impossible:

> The situation was desperate and we discussed the chances of escape. We decided to wait till dark and then make a dash through the Hun lines. This was pretty hopeless but better than dying like rats in a hole. The Bosche seemed to have guessed our intentions because during dusk we could see them putting up more wire in front of their trench and mounting machine guns. This made us alter our plans and stay on for still another night.[8]

They would now be confronted by another danger, from their own artillery. During the morning of 7th May British artillery was firing upon positions in and around Bullecourt. Such was the severity of this bombardment that Billingham thought that he was going to die under friendly fire:

> Just before dawn a terrific bombardment opened from our own guns and our position between the German front and support lines got the full force. It was awful and I spent the whole time praying for deliverance. My prayers were answered because in spite of the intensity of the barrage only three of our chaps were wounded.[9]

Once the barrage lifted, it was a great relief for Billingham and his party to see men from the Devonshires and 2nd Gordon Highlanders advance into Bullecourt:

> It was, of course, the prelude to an attack and when the hurricane had passed and we could raise our heads, we saw with great joy some British soldiers on our right. We lost no time in making them understand we were not the enemy and in getting across the open to them. I managed with difficulty, because of the weakness and shrapnel in my left leg, to get over the churned up ground to the comparative safety of their trench.[10]

Billingham and his party had held onto the positions they had captured for four nights and three days. Billingham had to brief many officers and he was even brought before General Gough:

> I had to give a detailed account to umpteen staff officers and was finally brought up before the Corps

Commander, General Gough, who, after I told him the story, praised our action, and, patting me on the back, said 'I am very proud of you boys and I'm giving you all the Military Medal.'[11]

When General Gough presented the Military Medals, he said:

> It was one of the finest performances he ever remembered. These few men had held their position, although surrounded by the enemy, for three days and four nights and returned only when relieved by another regiment. They then brought back their Lewis Guns and spare parts, which was most creditable.[12]

When the Gordon Highlanders established contact with these courageous men they found a party of 10, armed only with one Lewis gun. Brigadier-General Steele commented that they 'had held on under most adverse conditions, without water, under heavy shelling and beaten off two attempts of the enemy to capture them. These men came out with their Lewis Gun and full equipment in good order.'[13] Their exploits were reported to Divisional and Corps Commanders. The Honourable Artillery Company unit history reported that 'the Corps Commander ordered that each one of them should receive the Military Medal on the spot.'[14] The men were Privates H.W.C. Bartlett, A.E. Williams, J.C. Humphrey, A. Platt, A.J.L. Ead, H.G. Payne, H.B. Trotter, Albert Victor Lindley, and A. Watson. Private Albert Lindley died of the wounds on 8th May 1917. He was buried at Achiet-le-Grand Cemetery.

CORPORAL REGINALD BILLINGHAM MM 5445,
2ND BATTALION HONOURABLE ARTILLERY COMPANY

Reginald Starmer Billingham was born in Northampton during early 1889. Known as 'Rex' to some, he joined

the 2nd Honourable Artillery Company on 22nd November 1915. He went to France with the battalion on 1st October 1916. He had attained the rank of Corporal by the time his battalion reached Bullecourt in 1917. During the evening of the 4th May he led a party in an assault. He lost

**Sergeant Reg Billingham.
(Courtesy Gill Maud)**

contact with his party during close-quarter fighting with the enemy amongst the ruins. He established contact with another party of men from the same battalion. They soon became surrounded by the enemy and cut off from their own lines and for four nights and three days Billingham with his party held onto their positions until relieved by the 2nd Gordon Highlanders. Billingham was awarded the Military Medal, presented to him by General Gough. He was promoted to Sergeant and during November 1917 he and the battalion served on the Italian Front until the end of the war. When the war ended Rex began a career in banking and was a bank manager when he retired. He died at his home in St Alban's on 26th December 1965. The photo of Billingham wearing Sergeant's stripes was taken during June 1917, a month after his ordeal at Bullecourt.

NOTES ....

1. *The Honourable Artillery Company Journal,* Volume 37, 1960.
2. Ibid.
3. Ibid.
4. Ibid.
5. Ibid.
6. Ibid.
7. Ibid.
8. Ibid.
9. Ibid.
10. Ibid.
11. Ibid.
12. Ibid.
13. National Archives: WO 95/1661: 22nd Brigade War Diary.
14. *The Honourable Artillery Company 1914–1919,* Major G. Goold Walker, Seeley, Service and Co. Ltd.

CHAPTER 24

HOLDING THE LINE: 4TH–6TH MAY 1917

While the British attempted to capture Bullecourt, the German 124th Regiment persistently tried to recapture OG 1 and OG 2 trenches from the 6th Brigade using Eierhandgranate (egg grenades) to bomb them out. The Australians responded with 'leap frog bombing'. This tactic required seven men – two bombers, two carriers, two bayonet men and an observer – fighting from trench traverse to traverse. A bomb would be thrown from one traverse into another. After the bomb exploded the bayonet men would charge around the corner to bayonet any survivors. The risk of being killed either by the explosion of the bomb or by unwounded men was enormous.

The battalions of the 2nd Australian Division had succeeded in obtaining a foothold in the Hindenburg Line trenches but they were exhausted and it was necessary to deploy battalions held in reserve from the 1st Division. General Birdwood expressed his concerns to Gough that if Bullecourt was not captured soon, the Australian 2nd Division would not be able to hold on. Major Shoubridge's 7th Division was in the process of attacking Bullecourt during the 4th and as mentioned previously parts of Bullecourt had been taken. The remnants of the 2nd Division holding OG 1 and OG 2 were exhausted and needed relief, therefore on the 4th, the 1st, 2nd and 3rd Battalions from the 1st Brigade of the 1st Australian Division relieved battalions of the 2nd Division. Brigadier-Generals Smith and Gellibrand remained in control of the Australian front although their Brigades had been relieved. The soldiers of the 1st Brigade could see the carnage caused by the previous day's battle. The narrow trenches were badly battered and were full of dead comrades. In order to get to their lines they had no option but to tread on their corpses.

Before dawn the 2nd Division's Pioneer Battalion had dug a communication trench adjacent to the Central Road towards OG 1. Many men were lost in digging this trench through enemy rifle and shell fire, but this trench played an important role, used by the 1st and 3rd Battalions of the Australian 1st Brigade to relieve the 6th Brigade; who tirelessly and with great tenacity had captured and held the position. The New South Wales 3rd Battalion AIF occupied OG 2 while the 1st Battalion AIF entered OG 1. The 3rd Battalion found OG 1 full of wounded men who could not be evacuated because men could not be spared to carry them back to the railway embankment.

The 1st Battalion comprising 19 officers and 400 men reached OG 1 by 3.30 am. The battalion war diary reported that 'the enemy were on both our flanks. The line was in very bad order being badly knocked about by shell fire.'[1] Within 30 minutes

Sentries of the 8th Battalion in the western portion of the Hindenburg Line (OG I looking east), captured in the fighting for Bullecourt. Identified is Lieutenant W.D. Joynt VC, standing right, closest to camera. (AWM EO0439)

they were resisting a German counter attack. German commanders deployed the dreaded flammenwerfer.

Just as the 6th Brigade was leaving the trenches the Germans counter attacked without a prior bombardment. The III 120th Infantry Regiment and assault troops from the 124th Infantry Regiment supported by flammenwerfer attacked on the eastern flank. At 4.00 am German flamethrowers fired jets of burning oil into OG 1. The 1st Battalion held onto its position for five minutes and the German counter attack failed.

At 4.30 am the Germans launched a counter attack on the 3rd AIF Battalion holding OG 2. A savage fire-fight took place for the following 30 minutes involving Mills bombs and stick bombs, resulting in the Germans withdrawing. An estimated 30 German soldiers were killed and one prisoner captured. Lance Corporal Alonzo Hudson fought off German assaults from two directions on the right flank. Initially his party lost ground to the enemy, but after reorganising the remnants of the unit he led a counter attack, forcing the Germans to retreat. He captured the lost ground plus 20 prisoners. His recommendation for the Distinguished Conduct Medal stated that 'it was due to the initiative and boldness of this junior leader that a very critical situation was saved'.[2] Hudson was severely wounded by a bomb shortly after this action and would subsequently lose a leg. On the left flank Sergeant Patrick Kinchington supervised the defences behind a barricade that blocked the sunken road running through OG 2. A Lewis Gun together with a captured German machine gun was in position, so when a group of 150 Germans without rifles were seen approaching Kinchington ordered his men to hold fire until the enemy got nearer. The Germans struck first, once they were 40 yards from Kinchington's position a flammenwerfer fired a jet of hot flame. Kinchington shot the carrier through his abdomen. The bullet went through his body igniting the flammenwerfer can on his back. The Australian machine gunners opened fire and a dozen Germans fell upon the carrier, catching fire. Kinchington's men found a supply of German egg bombs and used them to disperse the enemy. One German got to within five yards of Kinchington's post before withdrawing. Kinchington's party had accounted for 80 German dead.

Exhausted elements from the 123rd Infantry Regiment who had been fighting the 62nd Division in Bullecourt attacked the 1st Battalion holding the left sector of OG 1. Captain Charles Somerset was occupying Pioneer Trench. He was out of the line of the flames. It was dark, but the flames revealed the location of the advancing 123rd Infantry Regiment. Somerset threw several bombs. The Germans were unaware of Somerset's position in the dark. He had the advantage and they did not know where to throw stick bombs in response. Somerset continued to throw his bombs, destroying the flammenwerfer and killing five of the enemy.

The Germans would fiercely contest the lines captured on 3rd May and so long as Bullecourt was in German hands the Australians would not be able to hold onto trenches OG 1 and OG 2. It was still imperative that the village be captured. Battalions from the British 7th Division had tried to flush out German positions during the early hours of 4th May but had failed.

During that morning on the 4th May, east of Bullecourt, the Australian 2nd Battalion was waiting in Pioneer Trench for orders. While they were waiting they could see a wounded soldier west of the trench, close to Lieutenant Money's abandoned British tank in No Man's Land, to the west of the Central Road and in the wire south of OG 1. The wounded soldier was waving a handkerchief. Two stretcher bearers, Private Harold Ringland and Private Granville Johnson from the 2nd Battalion went to his aid. German snipers and machine gunners opened fire. Undeterred, they got the man on the stretcher, but Ringland fell dead. Johnson was left with the wounded man in No Man's Land. He called for assistance and Private Arthur Carlson leapt from Pioneer Trench in a valiant effort to assist Johnson in bringing the wounded man to safety. Carlson and Johnson got the soldier – a German – to Pioneer Trench. This rescue was seen by Australian soldiers wounded in the previous day's fighting sheltering in shell craters. They began to gesticulate for help. After resting for a few minutes Carlson went back into No Man's Land on three occasions to rescue three men. On a fourth trip, he tried to assist an elderly soldier suffering from a smashed thigh. He bandaged his leg in full view of German guns in OG 1. Private James Paul, bringing a stretcher with him, went to Carlson's aid but was shot by a German sniper in the head. Paul was from Kirktown, St Fergus, Aberdeenshire in Scotland. According to one eye witness Private William Gardiner, 1st Machine Gun Company, 2nd Battalion, Carlson and Paul were acting under a 'flag of truce'. Private Charles Wood would testify that the strapping James Paul was 'a fine fellow, always in the thick of it'.[3] Paul's remains were not recovered.

Carlson got the man on his shoulders and dashed from shell hole to shell hole in a desperate bid to get him to Pioneer Trench. A bullet hit Carlson in the thigh and he fell into a shell hole. Despite being wounded and in defiance of the enemy guns, he was able to crawl to Pioneer Trench, while dragging the wounded man. Lieutenant Colonel Nelligan, commanding 2nd Battalion, recommended Carlson for the Victoria Cross. Carlson was not awarded the VC but was given a Distinguished Conduct Medal. The reason given for not awarding the Victoria Cross was because it was understood that the Victoria Cross was not awarded for life saving. This was not true for three of the Victoria Crosses awarded on 1st July 1916 to Lieutenant G.S. Cather, Captain John Green, Private Billy McFadzean and Private Robert Quigg. In August 1916, at Guillemont, Noel Chavasse had won the first of two Victoria Crosses for saving life. So Carlson was eligible and had surely carried out a deed worthy of the most prestigious award.

At 1 pm on 4th May 2nd Lieutenant Tom Richards led a party of 16 men to bomb west along OG 1. While the 1st Battalion was bombing their way along OG 1, the 3rd Battalion was carrying out a similar assault along OG 2 westwards and they met up with Lt Richard's party. Richards was an international rugby player who played for Australia and England prior to the war. During this fight Richards and his party captured 250 yards of OG 1 and had killed 25 German soldiers and captured 12. They then fought along another sector of trench. Overall, they extended their gains by 725 yards from the Central Road. The 123rd Grenadier Regiment defending the position was paying a heavy price. The 4th Company, which entered the line with 110 men, was reduced to 12. The remaining companies of the 123rd Grenadiers had no reserves. So desperate was their situation that they had to call upon batmen, orderlies and support staff to take up arms and defend their headquarters located in a dug-out close to the junction with the diagonal road.

The battalion war diary praised Richards for the role he played in capturing sections of OG 1. 'Very good work and excellent leadership was shown by Lieutenant Richards during these operations.'[4] 2nd Lieutenant Tom Richards was awarded the Military Cross and Corporal Percy Moore received the Military Medal. Richard's citation states: 'For conspicuous gallantry and devotion to duty. He was in charge of a bombing party, and despite strenuous opposition, succeeded in extending the line 250 yards and holding a strong post. He set a splendid example throughout.'[5]

The 2nd Battalion began an assault to drive east along OG 1 at 2.00 pm and had succeeded in establishing a position 300 yards from the 1st Battalion's right flank. German forces had been pushed 80 yards north of OG 2 along Ostrich Avenue.

The 3rd Brigade took over the 2nd Battalion lines soon after this attack. At 4.30 pm artillery shelled the lines held by Australian battalions in OG 1 and OG 2 as well as the railway embankment.

During that evening German infantry units began another initiative to expel the Australians from the Hindenburg Line trenches. The counter attack began at 9.00 pm. Fresh troops from the II Battalion 98th Infantry Regiment, 207th Division, attacked the Australian-occupied sectors of the Hindenburg Line east of Pioneer Trench. The II Lehr Regiment attacked west of Pioneer Trench and the 124th Infantry Regiment, exhausted by the previous day's fighting, bombed its way northwards from Ostrich Trench. Their orders were to 'recapture under all circumstances the whole of the lost ground'.

Elements of the 3rd Battalion were driven from OG 2, which meant that the 1st Battalion's left flank was dangerously exposed. A Company had lost so many casualties that night that they had to be withdrawn during the morning of 5th May and replaced by D Company.

German shells pounded OG 1 where remaining elements from the 3rd Battalion were holding on from 9.30 pm until 11.15 pm on the night of the 5th. The shelling succeeded in severing the H.P. buzzer earth wires, which meant that the only communication with Brigade Headquarters was by runner.

A further attempt to regain the trenches was made during the following morning at 10.30 am on 6th May when 40 German soldiers tried to bomb their way along OG 1 Trench. This attack faltered in the face of stout resistance offered by the 1st Battalion using rifle grenades. These German forces were forced to retire to a sunken road behind German lines.

At 11.30 am Major Philip Woodforde commanding the 1st Battalion received a fatal wound and command was given to Captain Alexander Mackenzie.

At 1.00 pm another party of 40 German infantry attempted to force their way through OG 1 but was fought off after a 10-minute engagement. A stronger counter attack was launched three hours later at 4.00 pm and with greater determination German parties managed to get within hand-bombing distance of the 1st Battalion on three occasions during the 45-minute engagement. Stokes mortar fire assisted the Australian soldiers in defending their position.

The medics at 2nd AIF Battalion aid post at the railway embankment worked continuously from the 3rd to 5th May. Lance Corporal R. Morgan:

> The aid post was a small place built overnight [May 3rd] by the Pioneers – one sandbag overhead, not enough to stop the smallest shell made, and we had for the most part to tend wounded in the roadway, fortunately sunken, with a little shelter from the banks. At times the shelling was so fierce that we were all forced to lie alongside the bank. Casualties passed through our hands in one endless procession; mangled bodies and shattered limbs, but one cannot but be callous and indifferent as practical assistance is needed here, not sympathy. To be sympathetic one would soon become useless. Working practically for 48 hours without rest and very little food, blood to the elbows as there is not enough water to drink, much less to wash.[6]

The front line was quiet during the night of the 5th/6th May but at 5.00 am the counter attacks resumed. The 1st Battalion war diary recorded that 'the enemy used a new bomb on this occasion. It was shaped like a stick bomb but apparently was filled with flammable material. The enemy's attempt failed.[7]

Another German attack followed at 6.00 am with an artillery barrage, followed by an infantry assault at 6.30 am. This initiative was fought off in a battle which lasted for 30 minutes. Two German officers and 25 soldiers were found dead after the assault. The 1st Battalion war diary:

The fighting was at close quarters and consequently grenades played a most important part, rifle grenades proving to be an absolute necessity, undoubtedly it was greatly owing to the range of these that the enemy were prevented from approaching our flank posts in sufficiently large numbers to rush them.[8]

The 1st Battalion suffered heavily during those three days defending OG 1. The battalion entered the line with 19 officers and 400 men. At Bullecourt they lost five officers and 44 men killed, 29 men missing, eight officers and 232 men wounded:

The enemy shelling during the period was exceptionally heavy, destructive and constant and I cannot speak too highly of the spirit in which all ranks bore it, nor of the cool and able manner in which they coped with the enemy attacks using all weapons with judgment and skill.[9]

NOTES

1. National Archives: WO 95/3217: 1st AIF Battalion War Diary.
2. Australian War Memorial: AWM 28/1/24P1//0055: Lance Corporal Alonzo Hudson DCM recommendation.
3. Australian War Memorial: AWM 1DRL1:428/00027: Australian Red Cross Missing: Private James Paul.
4. National Archives: WO 95/3217: 1st AIF Battalion War Diary.
5. *London Gazette*: 14th July 1917.
6. *Official History of the Australian Army Medical Services, 1914–1918*: The Western Front: Published 1940: p148.
7. National Archives: WO 95/3217: 1st AIF Battalion War Diary.
8. Ibid.
9. Ibid.

CHAPTER 25

THE GORDON HIGHLANDERS LINK UP WITH THE AUSTRALIANS: 7TH–8TH MAY 1917

Although the British offensive at Arras had lost momentum during early May 1917, the battle for Bullecourt would continue. The 7th Division was again ordered to launch an attempt. Historians have asked why Haig allowed Gough to persist. Plans were already being made for the Flanders offensive, scheduled to take place during the summer. Gough had been appointed commander of this offensive on April 30th, in between the two battles of Bullecourt. The two major initiatives to wrestle the village from German control had failed at the cost of heavy casualties. Whether Bullecourt was in British or German hands during May 1917 would not have a direct impact on bringing the war to a conclusion. Haig nevertheless ordered Gough to continue the Bullecourt battle to act as a diversion prior to the campaign in Flanders.

The next attack upon Bullecourt was ordered on 5th May, and two days of bombardment carried out by the guns of V Corps and I Anzac Corps followed. Gough planned for the attack to start at 3.45 am on 7th May with the 20th Brigade from the 7th Division leading a direct assault upon Bullecourt from the south east and Australian 1st Brigade attacking the village along OG 1 from the north east. Limited objectives were set to capture the front-line trench and the south-east corner of the village. The purpose of this drive was to protect the isolated Australian positions being held in OG 1 and OG 2 with the hope that these trenches would be taken completely. This was a daunting task because the Australians were being attacked from the north by the Lehr Regiment.

If this operation were successful they would have a platform to launch a further attack to clear the stubborn German defenders from Bullecourt. Major-General Shoubridge commanding the 7th Division requested the support of the 2nd Australian Division to launch a simultaneous attack along OG 1 and OG 2 upon the village.

At 9.00 pm on 5th May the 20th Brigade – the 2nd Gordon Highlanders commanded by Lieutenant Colonel Percy Brown DSO and the 9th Devonshire Regiment – relieved battalions from the 20th Infantry Brigade in trenches south east of Bullecourt. The 2nd Border Regiment was held in reserve. The 8th Devonshire Regiment had been attached to the 22nd Infantry Brigade on 4th May and was already in position south of Bullecourt.

C Company from the 8th Devonshires commanded by Captain Stanley Renton was in forward positions north of the railway embankment. Another Company was positioned by the railway embankment with the two remaining companies held in reserve in the rear in a nearby quarry and in cellars in the village of Ecoust St-Mein. It was considered that after the second attempt to remove the German forces from Bullecourt, by the evening of the 4th May 1917, that the village was being held by a small contingent of German infantry during the day. The village was actually being held by fatigued units from the German 27th Division. At noon on 5th May patrols were ordered to venture into the German-occupied trenches. C Company was assigned to push patrols towards Bullecourt from their outposts to ascertain the strength of the enemy in the village because they would have less ground to cover. As they proceeded across No Man's Land, they attracted immediate German artillery fire. Captain Renton left C Company Headquarters to oversee the progress of his patrols. He had barely covered 100 yards before he was killed by German machine gun and rifle fire. Renton, who was an MC recipient, was buried at Mory Abbey Military Cemetery.

The 2nd Border Regiment was in reserve and the battalion war diary reported that 'enemy shelling was continuous and was especially vigorous from 9 pm to 10 pm.'[1] The shelling killed six men and wounded 25 from the 2nd Borders. Since German forces holding the village were seen to be on a high state of alert, further attempts to enter the village were abandoned for the day. Overall the 2nd Borders lost nine officers killed with four wounded. They also lost eight men killed and 35 wounded, of which two were suffering from shell shock.

The 3rd Battalion AIF occupying OG 2 was exhausted by the day's fighting and there were no fresh reserves that could be called upon by the 1st Brigade. It was decided that the 9th Battalion AIF, which was the last supporting battalion of the 3rd Brigade, would take part in the impending attack.

The first Bullecourt Victoria Cross was won while the 1st Battalion was about to be relieved. On 6th May, Corporal George Howell from 1st Battalion reported to HQ at 6.00 am that the battalion on his right flank was withdrawing, which would expose his battalion. All available men including batmen and signallers were called to bear arms. When a force of German soldiers and two officers entered his trench, Howell ascended the parapet, then ran along the trench dropping bombs onto the enemy causing them to retreat in panic. Howell pursued them and running out of bombs, charged at them with his bayonet. Wounded several times, he fell into OG 1. The men from 1st Battalion were inspired and followed his example by engaging in close quarter fighting to reclaim the trench. Lieutenant Tom Richards was amongst those men; armed with a Lewis machine gun he poured deadly fire into the enemy in support of Howell. Howell survived to receive the Victoria Cross.

At 4.00 pm on 6th May while in reserve at Noreuil, the 1st Australian Brigade was notified that they would be attacking that night at 9.30 pm. This was too short notice so it was decided that the attack would coincide with the British assault. During that afternoon the 1st and 3rd Battalions were relieved by the 2nd and 4th Battalions.

Once it was dark the 9th Battalion advanced to OG 2 on the left flank so that it would be in a position to assist the British assault on Bullecourt the following morning. Most of the battalion was positioned in OG 1, from where the main thrust of the Australian attack would be westwards towards the village. Major Wilder-Neligan was in command of the 9th Battalion and at 10.30 pm he had his men prepare bombs, rifles and equipment for the attack near to the barricade in OG 1. An hour later he gave his final briefing to officers. Lieutenant Sydney Shaw was in command of B Company from the 9th Battalion. He was an Englishman, born in 1880 in Sheffield and had emigrated to Australia prior to the war. He was horrified to discover that the bombs did not have any fuses in them:

The Gordon Highlanders and the Devon's were to attack the village at the same time as we bombed down the trench. The password was 'throw hard'. I made enquiries about the supply of bombs. They had been drawn from brigade for the operation and were under sheets of iron in a big shell hole. To my amazement and dismay I found that they had no fuses in them and were therefore just as useless as stones to throw. A party was immediately sent to brigade for a fresh supply, but all they returned with was fuses.[2]

Lieutenant Shaw ordered a corporal and two men to fuse the bombs then went off to ensure that the men in his company had sufficient rations for the impending attack. He was not gone for long before he heard an explosion. An enemy shell killed the men he had ordered to fuse the bombs and destroyed the supply. More bombs were brought forward before Zero Hour.

Orders were received by Lieutenant Percy Brown DSO for the 2nd Gordon Highlanders to attack Bullecourt from the south east and secure the Blue, Green and Red Lines, a triangle covering the south-eastern sector of the village. Two companies from the 9th Devonshire Regiment were placed under Brown's command to support the Gordon Highlanders. Their designated role was to follow behind and mop up pockets of enemy resistance and consolidate the initial objective once captured. The Blue line denoted Tower Trench, the sector which ran from OG 1 Trench in the east and defended the southern-east sector of the village. The Green Line denoted the section of trench that formed part of OG 1 in the east and ran westwards into Bullecourt. The Red Line denoted the Riencourt–Bullecourt Road. Before these units got into their start off positions, it was necessary for the Company from 8th Devonshires holding outpost positions in No Man's Land to be withdrawn to the railway embankment to ensure that they were not hit by the supporting artillery barrage. The 8th Devonshire Regiment war diary confirmed: 'Great difficulty was experienced in this withdrawal, owing to the number of men occupying these Posts, the brightness of the moon, and the alertness of enemy machine guns. One Platoon was unable to withdraw until the following night.'[3]

German artillery was very active that night and the 2nd Gordon Highlanders experienced heavy shelling as they assembled. Major D.W. Palithorpe MC belonged to the Royal Army Medical Corps and was attached to the battalion:

On the night of the 6th May the battalion marched in along the railway embankment – there was a considerable amount of shelling going on over all the area in front and in the rear of the embankment – we felt particularly naked behind the last company of the battalion as we waited in the open for the main body of the battalion to pass along the embankment and file up the narrow trenches leading to the outskirts of the village – we stood some 300 yards from the railway embankment for what appeared to be hours and was probably about five minutes. The sweat dropped off me and I would have given much to have doubled off with my staff to the embankment where we should be more or less under cover but this would not have helped the morale of our reserve company so we stood fast. At last we got there and the company started to digging in furiously – I watched for a few minutes and then claimed one of their holes as my Aid Post – the two Gordon diggers looked rather disconsolate so I said 'Well, what will you do if you get hit round here?' 'Come to you Sir' – I replied 'Now you've given me a spot you can come to.' They were consoled and soon got dug in nearby – actually as they saw later they were well out of this particular place. We found a company of Australians on our right whose presence was reassuring.[4]

The battalions got into their start off positions during the night of the 6th/7th May. The cloudless night was bright with a full moon. The Gordon Highlanders were in position by 3.15 am. In Bullecourt the German 3rd Guard Division had completed the relief of the German 27th Division and was fortified amongst the ruins. This unit had distinguished themselves at the battle of the Somme. The 9th Grenadier Regiment had suffered 50% casualties during the defence of Thiepval. They participated in the battle of Lagnicourt in April 1917 along with the Landwehr and Guard Fusilier.

German artillery were bombarding the British lines as the 9th Devonshires were assembling and several casualties were sustained, including Captain Symes who was wounded. The battalion successfully reached their start off positions by 3.45 am. Soldiers from the 8th Devonshires did not play a role in the attack that day but they endured a German High Explosives barrage as they were held in reserve in dug-outs by the railway embankment. The battalion sustained very heavy casualties while in reserve despite the deeply excavated dug-outs.

At 2.00 am a German counter attack succeeded in driving back an outpost held by men from the 4th Battalion AIF in OG 1. Despite the full moon illuminating the night sky, the 2nd Gordon Highlanders had crawled undetected to the jumping off tapes that were located 300 yards from the village.

At 3.45 am the 2nd Gordon Highlanders began their assault behind a rolling barrage. They fought their way onto Tower Trench, led by the Canadian Captain Maitland Lockhart Gordon. Little opposition was encountered. 2nd Lieutenant David Palithorpe from the Royal Army Medical Corps was attached to the 2nd Gordon Highlanders and had set up a Regimental Aid Post in a shell hole close to the railway embankment. Thirty bandsmen were detailed as stretcher bearers to support Palithorpe. Palithorpe described the scene at this Regimental Aid Post soon after the attack commenced:

The attack went off before 4.00 am and as usual we soon had the first stream of fairly lightly wounded men who said it was bloody murder in front. Two men stopped at our spot, slightly wounded – they both had first field dressings on but thought that they would like more attention. I advised them in the vernacular to get back as soon as possible as the embankment was no quiet resort but they waited a few minutes puffing cigarettes – then the disaster happened – there was a direct hit, a high velocity shell, right into my arena – both the wounded men were killed instantly. One had a bit of shell through his chest but I found no fresh wounds on the other so I think they were actually done in the force of the explosion. Kerr, my dresser, got a small bit in his neck, not for the first time but was quite useless to him as a wound. I was hurled on the ground unhurt – Sergeant Blacker and Foster were a few yards away untouched. Rather shaken, I gave some neat whisky from my flask to Kerr and swallowed some myself.[5]

Aerial photo of Bullecourt taken on 29th April 1917. (Courtesy Gordon Highlanders Museum)

Map of operations at
Bullecourt 7th May 1917
('Military Operations, France
& Belgium 1917' by Captain
Cyril Falls, map Crown
Copyright)

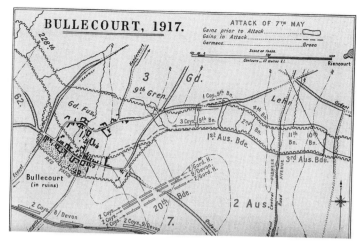

Palithorpe ventured along the embankment to seek better shelter. On reaching 80 yards to the right of his Aid Post he met an Australian Company commander. Palithorpe recalled: 'He had a dug-out of sorts heavily protected by sandbags – I asked him if I could use it – he said he would like to say yes but as his company was in reserve and had a wire to their front line it was impossible.'[6] It was perhaps fortunate for Palithorpe that he did not move his Aid Post 80 yards along the embankment because the Australian company commander was killed an hour later:

I went back and we stayed in the same spot, building up a sort of parados to stop back bursts. It was many thousands to one against our getting another direct hit. About an hour later an Australian soldier deposited some fresh bread on my 'parados', said it was from his officer and volunteered no further explanation. I went down again to the Australian company commander – the appearance of bread here seemed uncanny. Outside his dug-out was a dead officer lying with a waterproof sheet covering his face and head – the company commander told me that soon after I had left, his subaltern went outside for a minute and had been hit through the brain by a shrapnel bullet. He added 'I thought you might as well have this ration.'[7]

The Gordon Highlanders were supported by two companies from the 9th Devonshire Regiment led by Captains Raffin and Fergusson, who followed behind and mopped up pockets of resistance as they advanced. These battalions from the British 20th Brigade were covered by 24 guns of the Australian artillery that provided a barrage 100 yards ahead of them. Once a foothold had been gained in Tower Trench bombing parties from the 2nd Gordon Highlanders fought their way north eastwards along the trench in an effort to establish contact with the 2nd Australian Division. By 5 am leading waves of the Gordon Highlanders had penetrated as far as the Green Line, where a series of Lewis Gun posts was set up. German artillery responded to the success of the Gordon Highlanders by pouring

shell fire onto their positions. German machine gunners and snipers in the ruins of Bullecourt also made efforts to dislodge them from the newly gained positions along the second objective. Shell fire forced them to retire to a position close to the Ecoust-St-Mein to Hendecourt Road.

A Times correspondent wrote: 'The Devon's ... made a particularly stout attack on one of the stiffest positions we have had to tackle. They made their ground, forcing the enemy back in hard hand-to-hand fighting and held on against repeated counter attacks of a most desperate character, utterly refusing to give way.'[8]

The Australian 9th Battalion in OG 1 waited 14 minutes after Zero Hour before attacking along OG 1 so that the barrage had passed clear. They started to bomb their way along OG 1; Charles Bean describes the scene in the trench as 'an inferno of bursting grenades'[9] in his official history. They adopted the leap frog method of attack: the first wave platoon captured a section of trench and stopped to consolidate while a supporting platoon passed through and advanced onto the next section. Lieutenant Sydney Shaw led B Company into the German trench system:

Dawn was breaking on a lovely morning; and skylarks were singing as only they can, when we threw our first bombs and hopped over the bags. Before our hail of bombs the occupants of the trench had run down the steps of their dug-outs. This was a fatal mistake for them, as we followed them with bombs. The dug-outs were large, with oaken steps and beams and contained a number of men. Soon the trench was captured and we sent back a couple of dozen prisoners; all of the other occupants of the trench had been killed.[10]

The men from the 9th Battalion fought their way 70 yards along the trench. At one point they were nearly

Mills Bomb lying beside Bullecourt–Riencourt Road between the village and the Bullecourt Digger Memorial in 2006. (Author)

encircled by German snipers, machine gunners and bombers armed with egg bombs, stick bombs and pineapple mortars in shell holes outside the trench. Australian Lewis gunners countered. The Australians were also armed with Mills Bombs and rifle grenades. A fierce fight embroiled the 9th Battalion. As the Australians proceeded, they encountered parties armed with flamethrowers. One of these was destroyed by an Australian Mills Bomb. Within minutes the frequency of the German bombs diminished as they expended their supplies and were forced to withdraw back towards OG 2. The Australian attack wore down the German defence. The 9th Battalion positioned Lewis Guns in shell holes in No Man's Land. German machine gun parties were withdrawing from the Australians, but were heading in the direction of the Gordon Highlanders.

Sergeant William Porter bombed along the German sector that was still being held in OG 2 with little resistance. When they were held up by a German bombing party Porter organised and led an attack, killing and capturing many prisoners. Porter had captured 900 yards of enemy trench. He consolidated the position and held on until relieved. His courage was rewarded with the Distinguished Conduct Medal.

As the 9th Australian Battalion bombed along OG 1 and OG 2 towards the north-east sector of Bullecourt, the Gordon Highlanders were bombing from the

Group of soldiers from the 2nd Battalion Gordon Highlanders who took part in the assault on Bullecourt on 7th May. (Courtesy Donald MacCormick)

south west. Captain Maitland Lockhart Gordon was concerned that the Australians might mistake his Gordon Highlanders for the enemy, so he leapt up onto the parapet so that they were aware of their presence. At 5.15 am the Australians linked up with a party of Gordon Highlanders led by Captain Gordon. Lieutenant Sydney Shaw, an Englishman serving with the 9th Battalion AIF, reported that 'both Scotties and Aussies fraternized gladly.'[11]

German observers could easily see the glistening wet helmets of their enemy as rain was falling. German artillery then bombarded their positions and hindered the process of consolidation. Soon Captain Gordon was killed as he led a party of Highlanders and Australians to capture another enemy position. The battle continued throughout the day as German reinforcements entered the village from the north west. There was much confusion that day, but once the artillery barrage from both sides had subsided it was ascertained that the Gordon Highlanders were still holding onto the front-line trench and positions in the south-eastern sector of Bullecourt. A breakthrough into this seemingly impregnable village had been made at last. The Gordon Highlanders were amazed to discover the party from the 2nd Honourable Artillery Company led by Corporal Reginald Starmer Billingham mentioned earlier, which had been holding an isolated position amongst the ruins of the village for three days and four nights, without food or water. Despite this success the Germans still retained

Stretcher bearers of the 8th Battalion carrying wounded back along the trenches during the fighting at Bullecourt, in May. They are seen here in the trench at OG 1, looking east. (AWM EO00440)

Officers from the 2nd Battalion Gordon Highlanders, 1916/early 1917. Lt J.G. Graham (front row, first right), Lieutenant J. Riddler (rear row, third right) and French Interpreter (rear row, first right). (Courtesy Gordon Highlanders Museum)

their hold upon the south-west corner of the village. The 9th Battalion AIF had secured 650 yards of OG 1 capturing three machine guns, three trench mortars and three flamethrowers. As well as capturing 250 to 300 rifles with ammunition they had captured rations which would feed 200 men occupying the dug-out. They found between 35 and 40 dead German soldiers including two German officers laid out in the captured trench. Many of these men were killed by bombs. They had also captured one officer and ten German soldiers. Major Wilder-Neligan wrote of the conditions in the captured OG 1 in the post-operation report:

The enemy trenches were well provided with large deep dug-outs. They are very wide and have been considerably battered about by shell fire. In rear of the trenches are large deep pits about 20 feet square. These pits are probably tank traps. They have been very much battered about and most of them are no longer recognisable as pits.[12]

These were not in fact tank traps but uncompleted dug-outs. Wilder-Neligan confirmed in his report that 20 yards of OG 2 had been captured by the 9th Battalion AIF. Twenty German soldiers were found dead in this trench another 150 rifles with ammunition were captured.

The cost was high in human life. The 9th Devonshires had lost 130 men. The 9th Battalion AIF lost one officer and 159 men. The 2nd Gordon Highlanders had lost seven officers and 179 men, but they succeeded in consolidating the Australian left flank. They had captured 106 prisoners, three machine guns and had counted 50 dead German soldiers. On the following day the 2nd Gordon Highlanders received a visit from

Lieutenant J.G. Graham and a platoon of the 2nd Battalion Gordon Highlanders. Lieutenant Graham is seated second row seventh from the right. (Courtesy Gordon Highlanders Museum)

Drums and pipes of the 2nd Battalion Gordon Highlanders. These men acted as stretcher bearers at Bullecourt. Among them is Drum Major William Kenny (middle front row). He was awarded the Victoria Cross for his bravery at Ypres on 23rd October 1914 and took part in the recovery of the wounded at Bullecourt. (Courtesy Gordon Highlanders Museum)

General Gough who congratulated and thanked them for their achievement at Bullecourt. Major David Palithorpe, the regimental doctor, discovered a perfect example of esprit de corps:

> I found there were many men slightly wounded chiefly with small bits of high explosive who had said nothing about these wounds as they feared to be sent on - not to the U.K. but to the base alone and then back to some strange battalion. I managed to arrange with the nearest Field Ambulance to give them Antitetanic serum - it was deadly dangerous not to do this - and of the many who had it most came back straight away to us.[13]

LIEUTENANT COLONEL PERCY BROWN DSO,
2ND BATTALION GORDON HIGHLANDERS

Percy Wilson Brown was born on 12th October 1876. After completing his education at Uppingham, he trained at Sandhurst. On receiving his commission he was assigned to the Gordon Highlanders as a 2nd Lieutenant on 4th November 1896. Two years later he was promoted to Lieutenant and from 1899 to 1902 he served in the Boer War in South Africa. Brown had attained the rank of Major by 11th December 1914. On 12th July 1915 he was appointed commanding officer of the 1st Gordon Highlanders and given the rank of Temporary Lieutenant Colonel. Seven days later he led the battalion in the attack on Hooge on

Lieutenant Colonel P.W. Brown CMG DSO. (Courtesy Gordon Highlanders Museum)

the Ypres salient. A mine exploded under German trenches on the ridge at Hooge. When the one and a half tons of ammonal was exploded at 7.00 pm, the 4th Middlesex Regiment charged to capture the further lip of the crater, supported by the Gordon Highlanders, who bombed their way along the German trenches. From 25th to 27th September 1915, Brown saw action once again when the 1st Gordon Highlanders took part in the Battle of Loos. He was mentioned in dispatches on several occasions and on 1st January 1916 his award of the DSO was gazetted for 'Distinguished Service in the Field' while CO of 1st Gordon's. In May 1917 Brown led the 2nd Battalion Gordon Highlanders in the attack upon Bullecourt.

2ND LIEUTENANT JAMES RIDDLER,
2ND BATTALION GORDON HIGHLANDERS

James Riddler had seen action with the 2nd Gordon Highlanders since 1914 in France. He served in the ranks, but would later earn a commission. He was a 2nd Lieutenant when he took part in the assault on Bullecourt on 7th May 1917. He was wounded at that day.

Captain J Riddler. (Courtesy Gordon Highlanders Museum)

2ND LIEUTENANT LEONARD CECIL PLEWS,
2ND BATTALION GORDON HIGHLANDERS

Leonard Cecil Plews was the battalion signalling officer during the attack on Bullecourt.

2nd Lieutenant Leonard Cecil Plews. (Courtesy Gordon Highlanders Museum)

2ND LIEUTENANT J.G. GRAHAM MC,
2ND BATTALION GORDON HIGHLANDERS

Graham was a Lewis Gun officer during the Bullecourt battle on 7th May. He was awarded the Military Cross for his role in the Third Ypres campaign, several months after Bullecourt.

Lieutenant J.G. Graham (later Capt) MC. (Courtesy Gordon Highlanders Museum)

PRIVATE JAMES DUFFUS S/40109 MM,
2ND BATTALION GORDON HIGHLANDERS

James Strachan Duffus was born in Aberdeen in 1891. After leaving school he began an apprenticeship as a baker. After completing his apprenticeship he emigrated to Westerly, Rhode Island in the US. Duffus worked for a small family bakery owned by a German immigrant couple, who treated him as if he was their son. When World War One broke out in 1914, Duffus felt compelled to do his bit. The German couple tried to convince him that it was not his fight, but despite their advice he returned to Scotland and enlisted. After completing basic infantry training at Ripon he joined the 2nd Gordon Highlanders. Duffus served with this highly disciplined regular battalion throughout the war and was present at the Somme battles during 1916 at Mametz, Bazentin, High Wood, Delville Wood, Guillemont, during the Ancre operations and during the closing phase of the campaign.

At some stage, the battalion recognised Duffus's skills as a baker and he was transferred from the rifles companies to the battalion

Private James Duffus. (Courtesy Colonel [Retd] Jim Duffus)

cookhouse and became a Sergeant Cook. Feeding the battalion might have been safer than serving with rifle companies in the front line; however working in the battalion's rear had its dangers. He was exposed to German shelling as he brought food to the front line. On one occasion he and the Quartermaster remarked on the number of duds in the salvo landing close to their horse-drawn wagon; they quickly realised that the shells falling around them were not duds, but gas shells. After the battalion had been engaged in intensive fighting and lost many casualties, Duffus prepared more meals than required. As he searched for sub units he was often told that the few Jocks huddled in a field were the survivors of an entire company. Duffus was reduced to the ranks and sent back to a rifle company for his attempt to beat the mail censor with unflattering correspondence to a magazine about poor conditions.

Amongst the anecdotes he recounted was the arrival of Jocks on leave at Aberdeen Station, still wearing their muddy and lice-infested kilts. Bereaved widows and mothers would ask to scrape the mud off their kilts as mementos of their dead relations.

Duffus endured the cold harsh winter of 1916/17 at the front. He remembered the edges of the frozen kilt and kilt apron would cut into the back of his knees.

It is impossible to confirm when Duffus was transferred to catering duties, but he was serving with the battalion during the pursuit of the Germans to the Hindenburg Line in March 1917 and the battle of Bullecourt in May. He was also present when the battalion took part in the Third Battle of Ypres at Polygon Wood on 4th October. The battalion was transferred with the rest of the 7th Division to the Italian Front after the defeat at Caporetto. In 1918 Duffus was awarded the Military Medal during operations to cross the River Piave and during the final battles which defeated the Austro-Hungarian Army in northern Italy.

James Duffus intended to return to the USA after the war ended, but instead returned to Aberdeen where he married and worked as a baker until his death in 1946.

PRIVATE JOHN MACCORMICK 26097
2ND BATTALION GORDON HIGHLANDERS

John MacCormick was born on the Gaelic-speaking island of North Uist in the Outer Hebrides, Scotland, in 1887. MacCormick left North Uist in 1902 when he was 15 and lived in Glasgow. He then moved to Falkirk for several years, where he worked for Carron Iron Works. Prior to the war he worked as a salesman with Barr's Irn Bru. He enlisted in 1916 and joined the Cameron Highlanders before being transferred to the 2nd Gordon Highlanders. MacCormick took part in the Battle of Bullecourt when the battalion captured the village on

John MacCormick seated with his younger brother Angus who was aged 18. Angus was badly wounded during the war; the family received a telegram stating that he was missing presumed killed. His grieving family received a second telegram three weeks later confirming that he had survived. (Courtesy Donald MacCormick)

Private John MacCormick is seated left. Private Keyes, seated right, was reputed to be the best sniper in the battalion. (Courtesy Donald MacCormick)

Postcard sent by Private John MacCormick showing the campaigns of the 7th Division. (Courtesy Donald MacCormack)

7th May. Towards the end of 1917 MacCormick and the 2nd Gordon Highlanders were deployed to the Italian Front where they remained for the duration for the war. After the Armistice, MacCormick lived in Ireland for a short while. He returned to Falkirk and to employment at Barr's Irn Bru. In 1936 he married and had a son, Donald. MacCormick moved the family to Edinburgh in 1942 where he worked for Scottish Brewers until he retired in 1955. John MacCormick died aged 83 in 1969 in Edinburgh.

2ND LIEUTENANT MONTAGUE SANDOE,
9TH BATTALION DEVONSHIRE REGIMENT

Montague William Augustus Sandoe was born in 1895. His father Dr John Worden Sandoe was a doctor with a practice in Broadclyst, near Exeter in Devon. Montague was the eldest of three brothers. He began his education at All Hallows School, Honiton in 1908. In 1913 he studied medicine at Guy's Hospital and Durham University. He also served as a Corporal in the Officer Training Corps. When war broke out a year later he enlisted to join the Artist Rifles. He spent three months with the Artist Rifles before being transferred to the 9th Devonshire Regiment with a commission.

As the 9th Battalion was advancing towards the railway embankment Sandoe was killed by a shell. 2nd Lieutenant Charles Stewart was a friend of Montague Sandoe and he wrote of his sadness of losing him at Bullecourt:

I am very sorry poor Sandoe is dead – killed by a shell before the advance began. He was a very cheery and well liked fellow in my old D Company … The last time I saw Sandoe was at Mory. I was just setting out for that railway embankment of evil memory, to build a battalion HQ as best I could with half a dozen snipers. I went up in the afternoon – the battalion followed later and Sandoe was killed that same night. I can vividly recall how he stepped into my tent just before I left – 'What do you think of this stunt. St … St … Stewart?' he asked (he always stuttered the devil).'Not much', said I. 'From what I've seen of the arrangements, you're going over with D Coy., aren't you?'
'Yes, I think it will be something of a box-up', and he smiled in that attractive way of his. 'All these stunts seem like that at the beginning. Anyhow, I'll have to be off. – hard luck old man', he laughed. A few hours later he was dead.[14]

His commanding officer wrote in a letter of condolence to his father:

Your son was a most excellent officer in every way. His men thought a great deal of him and he is a great loss to me. He was hit by a piece of shell and though he did not die immediately, he did not suffer.[15]

2nd Lieutenant Montague Sandoe. (Courtesy Roger Sandoe)

An unnamed fellow officer who served with Sandoe paid this tribute to him. 'We miss in him a real friend and companion. He was always so cheery and happy, even after the most trying day, and helped us to laugh at billets that seemed hopeless against the weather in the villages we passed through.'[16] 2nd Lieutenant Montague Sandoe, aged 21, was buried in HAC Cemetery.

2nd Lieutenant Montague Sandoe. (Courtesy Roger Sandoe)

CORPORAL GEORGE HOWELL 2445 VC, MM,
1ST BATTALION AIF

George Julian Howell was born in 1893 at Enfield, Sydney, New South Wales. Educated at Burwood Public School, on completing his education he became an apprentice bricklayer. Howell enlisted on 9th June 1915 and was sent to Egypt on 14th July. He joined the 1st Battalion on Gallipoli on 1st November. He remained on the peninsula until the evacuation in December 1915. After spending several months in Egypt Private Howell was sent to France in March 1916. Wounded at Pozières in July 1916, Howell was evacuated to England to a hospital in Sheffield. After recovering from his wounds he returned to the 1st Battalion in France on 26th November 1916. During the following month he was promoted to Lance Corporal. Known as 'Snowy' he was promoted to Corporal in February 1917. On 9th April the 1st Battalion captured the village of Demicourt. It was here that Howell distinguished himself and won the Military Medal. His recommendation stated that he was recognised for

Lance Corporal Howell VC MM. (*The War Illustrated*)

... courage and devotion to duty displayed while leading his rifle bombing section in the operation against the German position. On several occasions when held up by machine gun fire he overcame the position by sound offensive tactics and good use of his weapons, and continued to advance. He, with his section, was in the lead throughout and was of great assistance to his company in the capture of its objectives.[17]

At Bullecourt Howell distinguished himself again when he received the Victoria Cross. At 6.00 am on the morning of the 6th May 1917 he observed German counter attacks on the battalion on the flank in the Hindenburg Line. Flammenwerfer was being used to force out Australians from their positions and they were withdrawing. Realising that the 1st Battalion's flank was seriously threatened, without hesitation Howell alerted 1st Battalion Headquarters in OG 1 and assembled all available personnel including batmen and led a counter attack. German egg and stick bombs rained down upon this headquarters' position. Howell leapt onto the parapet, ran along the trench, exposed to enemy fire and threw many Mills bombs onto the Germans occupying the trench. He fell into the trench with machine gun wounds to both legs and received 28 wounds in total. His bravery was witnessed by many soldiers from his battalion and altered the course of the engagement. His citation for the VC:

Seeing a party of the enemy were likely to outflank his Battalion, Cpl. Howell, on his own initiative, single-handed and exposed to heavy bomb and rifle fire, climbed on to the top of the parapet and proceeded to bomb the enemy, pressing them back along the trench. Having exhausted his stock of bombs, he continued to attack the enemy with his bayonet. He was then severely wounded. The prompt action and gallant conduct of this N.C.O. in the face of superior numbers was witnessed by the whole Battalion and greatly inspired them on the subsequent successful counter attack.[18]

Howell was sent to Norwich War Hospital in England. He was so badly wounded that he was deemed unfit for active service and was discharged from the AIF on 5th June 1918. While recovering he received his Victoria

Site of Howell's VC Action and where OG1 Trench crossed the Central Road. The Central Road was the principal route to Australian-occupied sectors of the Hindenburg Line. German observers were positioned at Hendecourt (where the trees are situated on the horizon) throughout the Bullecourt campaign and were able to see and target Australian infantry advancing along this road. (Author)

Cross from King George V at Buckingham Palace on 21st July 1917.

Howell returned to Australia and married a nurse, Sadie Yates. They lived in Coogee where Howell worked in the advertising department of Smith's Newspapers. By 1933 he was working for the *Brisbane Standard*.

Howell offered his services when World War Two broke out. He was appointed as a staff sergeant at the Headquarters of Eastern Command in Paddington on 14th October 1939 where he served until March 1941. Howell joined the US Army with the United States Sea Transport Service in August 1944 and participated in the liberation of Leyte from the Japanese.

Howell died at the Repatriation Hospital in Perth on 23rd December 1964 and was buried at Karrakatta Cemetery, Hollywood, Perth.

The Gordon Highlanders uniform was worn as a tribute to the soldiers who fought at Bullecourt in 1917 during the ANZAC Day Ceremony at Bullecourt on 25th April 2009. (Author)

NOTES

1. National Archives: WO 95/1655: 2nd Battalion Border Regiment War Diary.
2. *Over the Fence*, Sydney Shaw, Arthur H. Stockwell Ltd, Ilfracombe, Devon 1977.
3. National Archives: WO 95/1655: 8th Battalion Devonshire Regiment War Diary.
4. Major David Palithorpe account: Gordon Highlanders Museum.
5. Ibid.
6. Ibid.
7. Ibid.
8. *The Times*: 1917.
9. Official History of Australia in the War of 1914–1918, Volume 1: Charles Bean, Angus and Robertson Ltd 1922, p522.
10. *Over the Fence*.
11. Ibid.
12. National Archives: WO 95/4344: 9th Battalion AIF War Diary.
13. Major David Palithorpe account: Gordon Highlanders Museum.
14. Archives of the Keep Military Museum of Devonshire and Dorset: 2nd Lieutenant Charles Stewart Diary, May 1917.
15. All Hallows School Magazine, Honiton: Courtesy Roger Sandoe and John Moore.
16. Ibid.
17. Australian War Memorial: AWM 28/1/22/0006: Recommendation for Military Medal: Corporal George Howell.
18. *London Gazette*: Issue 30154: 26th June 1917.

CHAPTER 26

ASSAULT UPON THE RED PATCH: 9TH MAY 1917

During the evening of 7th/8th May, the 2nd Border Regiment and C and D Companies from the 8th Devonshire Regiment had relieved the 2nd Gordon Highlanders and the 9th Devonshire Regiment. The Border Regiment was holding the Green Line whilst the 8th Devonshires were secured along the Blue line. A and B Companies from the 8th Devonshires were held in reserve at the railway embankment and a quarry close to the theatre of operations. One Company from the 9th Devonshires remained in the Blue Line to the right of the 8th Devonshires to protect their right flank. The relief was carried out with few casualties.

The 9th Battalion AIF was relieved during the early hours of the morning on 8th May. One particular tragedy occurred when Private John Downs, a Scotsman, was killed by a shell. Corporal Cecil Cutteford later wrote:

> About 1 am on 8th May we were mobbing out, having been relieved by the 5th Battalion. Downs had discovered that he had picked up a rifle that did not belong to him. He went back to get his own rifle although I advised him not to do so. He has not been heard of since as far as I know, and as no trace of his body has been found I can only suppose that a shell must have exploded right on him.[1]

Soldiers from the Grenadier Regiment des Konig from the German Guards Division were holding the south-west corner of Bullecourt. The next British objective was to link with the Australians in OG 1 and OG 2 in the north-east of the village. The 8th Devonshires were to launch bombing attacks into the village; In particular they had to remove the German presence in the south-west sector, known as the 'Red Patch' or the 'Red Rectangle', as it was referred to in operational reports. It was called the Red Patch simply because it was marked in red on the map. The Red Patch was heavily defended and at its westernmost point was the large mound known as the Crucifix. This position was heavily fortified.

The drive to evict German forces from the Red Patch was scheduled to begin at 11 am on 8th May. C and D

Companies from the 8th Devonshires advanced north from the Blue Line and bombed German positions in the Red Patch.

With Captain Stanley Renton mortally wounded during the action on 5th May, 2nd Lieutenant C.J. Holdsworth led C Company. 2nd Lieutenant Girvan led parties from D Company west along Tower Trench. As these two companies advanced a creeping barrage was laid down upon the Red Patch from north to south and from east to west.

Bombing, rifle and Lewis Machine Gun sections swept along the Blue Line. Great care was taken to ensure that entrances to cellars were covered by sentries and communication trenches were blocked. Little resistance was encountered by Holdsworth and his Company as they advanced 150 yards and captured four dug-outs. They reached a point within 50 yards of the Bullecourt-Ecoust-St-Mein Road, where they were engaged by German machine guns and bombers. German snipers hidden in houses in the village picked off officers and NCOs. The 8th Devonshires' war diary:

> When the leading bombers came to within 50 yards of the BULLECOURT–ECOUST Road, they found it strongly held and were met with showers of egg bombs and Machine Gun fire. There was clearly an entrenched enemy strong point on the west bank of the road extending north and south from U.27.b.6.3. This was a very commanding position as our men had to advance uphill against a strong entrenched work. The enemy were holding this position in force, and as we advanced, strong supports were coming out. It is estimated that the garrison and supports to this post must have been at least 150 men.[2]

2nd Lieutenant Holdsworth was among those killed during this attack and his men from C Company were forced out of the range of the German bomb throwers. The 8th Battalion War Diary recorded that the soldiers from the Grenadier Regiment des Konig from the German Guards Division 'had fought exceedingly well and cleanly. They gave the impression that the village was tenaciously and efficiently held.'[3] The diary also commented upon one particular advantage the enemy enjoyed:

> The egg bomb is an invaluable asset to the enemy as he can out-range us with it. Till we are supplied with them, rifle grenades are essential. On the last day's operations, the turning point all the time was the supply or the lack of rifle grenades. The issue of our new egg bomb will be a great asset, as it is easier to handle than the rifle grenade.[4]

2nd Lieutenant Drew reorganised the remnants of C Company and launched a second attempt to dislodge the Germans from their strong point, but failed. The fighting subsided after two hours. 2nd Lieutenant F.W. Girvan led D Company in an advance along Tower Trench (the Blue Line) in a westerly direction. His party sustained heavy casualties from shell fire and was unable to launch any further counter attacks that day.

The brave men from the 8th Devonshires were not only battling against a determined enemy, the weather also hindered their efforts. The rain that had fallen the previous night had made the ground around the village very muddy. Persistent drizzle during the attack caused the ground to be slippery underfoot. 'There was little use of the Lewis guns. A considerable number of the guns were destroyed by direct hits from H.E. shells and many of the remainder became out of action owing to the mud.'[5]

The Germans were probably unaware that the Australians had extended their hold upon OG 2 because during that night a party of them stumbled into the Australian positions. The Diggers thought that the enemy was launching a counter attack and immediately fired S.O.S. flares to summon an artillery barrage. German artillery shelled the Australian positions throughout the night. The 8th Battalion AIF bore the brunt of the German onslaught. Sergeant Percy Lay,

an original from the 8th Battalion, was wounded at the beginning of the German counter attack but refused to leave his post. Lay helped the officers to hold. Private Donald Sinclair was a stretcher bearer working that evening and despite the enemy barrage risked his life to evacuate the wounded. On several occasions that night he ventured close to the German trenches and recovered wounded men from other units who had been lying near to the German position for up to six days. These men were brought to safety and provided valuable intelligence. Lieutenant Errey with 50 men from the 8th AIF Battalion secured 175 yards of the trench at a cost of five killed and 14 wounded.

After continuous vicious fighting, the fatigued Australian battalions east of Bullecourt were relieved by the 14th and 15th Brigades of the 5th Australian Division. During the night of 8th May, the 14th Brigade entered the line, followed by the 15th Brigade the next morning. They carried out the relief under heavy artillery fire. The 5th Division history:

> A continuous artillery battle raged along the whole front, but especially on the left, where the penetration of the Hindenburg defences rendered the position extremely sensitive. The enemy had lost no guns in his retirement from the Somme battle, and it is probable that his entire artillery from the old Somme battle, with, possibly, later additions to its strength, was now defending the Hindenburg line and concentrating particularly on the threatened sector near Bullecourt. Not only were our front lines pummelled day and night, but every approach to them, especially from Vaulx-Vraucourt through the well-named Death Valley to Noreuil and thence to the Railway Cutting, was swept with a fine impartiality by an almost constant stream of high explosive, shrapnel, and gas shells. Units going to and from the trenches invariably incurred casualties from this fire.[6]

German troops at the fortified position known as the Crucifix. Lieutenant Humphries from the 2nd/7th Battalion West Yorkshire Regiment described the site of the Crucifix as 'a mound with two entrances'. Many British soldiers paid with their lives to capture this position. (Author)

View from the Crucifix looking west. The British 62nd Division attacked on this front on 3rd May 1917. (Author)

A solitary German soldier sits amongst the ruins of the village of Bullecourt. In the background is the large mound, the Crucifix. (Author)

While the 5th Australian Division was relieving the line during the evening of 8th May, the Commanding Officer of the 8th Battalion Devonshire Regiment was ordered to repeat the attack the following day. A and B Companies from the 8th Devonshires entered the front line in order to relieve the remaining company of the 9th Devonshires who were holding onto the Blue Line. C Company was ordered to lead the assault for a second time. They had survived the bitter battle of the previous day, having lost their commanding officer, Captain Renton, and with no time to rest, or ease their strained nerves, they were expected to launch another attack upon the same positions. This time the enemy would be expecting them.

Since C Company had suffered heavy casualties the previous day, a platoon from B Company was assigned to C Company to provide additional support. At noon on 9th May C Company, led by 2nd Lieutenant Drew, advanced north west into the Red Patch as a platoon from A Company attacked German positions along the road running north west through the village to protect the right flank of C Company advancing west along Tower Trench. Two guns from the 20th Trench Mortar Battery fired a barrage along the Ecoust-St-Mein Road. German artillery immediately responded.

Drew sent his bombers into the assault first, followed closely by Lewis machine gunners and riflemen. 'The enemy clearly expected our attack.'[7] The only two officers from C Company became casualties before the remnants of the Company reached the Ecoust-St-Mein–Hendecourt Road. It was here that their advance was checked by the strong point that thwarted their attack on the 8th. Three parties of well supplied German bombing units were garrisoned at this strong point. They were ready and waiting for the Devonshires. Their defence was so strong that C Company was forced to withdraw. With no officers to lead a counter attack, it was left to Company Sergeant Major Heal to reorganise the remnants of C Company to launch a second attack at 12.30 that afternoon. They fought their way into the Red Patch, but they were unable to consolidate their positions. A Company could only advance 200 yards into Bullecourt, suffering heavy casualties, before they too were compelled to retire.

Lieutenant Marshall commanding a platoon from B Company in reserve assumed command. In preparation for the oncoming German advance, which drove through C Company, Marshall organised a defensive line either side of the trench at position U.22.a.2.2, supported by a Vickers machine gun. Marshall's men offered stout resistance. During the action, all Marshall's Lewis guns were knocked out of action and supplies of rifle bombs were exhausted. Despite this they were able to fight off the German attack with rifle fire until the three remaining platoons from B Company commanded by Lieutenant Drake arrived. 'The enemy sniping, as on previous day, was very heavy and accurate.'[8] Despite German shells pouring down and accurate snipers in operation, Lieutenant Drake led his men in small groups of twos and threes across open ground until he reached the sunken road that led into Bullecourt from the south east to reach Marshall's position at 1.15 pm.

Another party from the 9th Devonshire Regiment consisting of 50 men also brought up supplies of bombs and rifle grenades. When this support arrived, Marshall immediately organised a fresh attack. Marshall and his men bombed their way along the Blue Line until they reached the Ecoust-St-Mein Road. Marshall positioned bombers and Lewis Gunners along the bank of this road to protect both his flanks. Soldiers from the Border Regiment supported Marshall's left flank. The German defenders found themselves caught between Marshall's assault and a barrage of British artillery shells. These German infantrymen were forced into the open to head towards Ecoust-St-Mein where they were exposed to Lewis Machine gunners positioned on the railway embankment. Three columns of German bombers made a concentrated effort against Tower Trench at 4 pm. This last attempt to dislodge Marshall and his men failed. Marshall and his men had engaged with about 250 of the enemy. It was estimated that they caused 50% casualties. This significant toll came at a high price. The 8th Devonshire had lost five officers – Captain Renton, 2nd Lieutenant Lionel Cumming, 2nd Lieutenant K. Duncan, 2nd Lieutenant Charles Holdsworth, 2nd Lieutenant Gordon Hamilton Smith – with six officers wounded, Captain E.H. Littlewood, 2nd Lieutenants V.B. and F.C. Armstrong, E.D. Gregory, G.A. Drew and F.W. Pinkard. The battalion also lost 57 killed or missing and 184 wounded men.

The 9th Devonshire Regiment lost one officer, 2nd Lieutenant Montague Sandoe and 22 men killed. The battalion had six officers wounded – Captain Symes, Captain Reynolds, 2nd Lieutenants Dyson, Martin, Morse and Silk – and 94 men wounded. The 9th Devonshires were awarded two Military Crosses to Captain Fergusson and Captain Raffin and 10 Military Medals.

The 2nd Border Regiment supporting the Devonshires also suffered casualties on 9th May. A shell landed on the battalion headquarters wounding Major G. E. Beaty-Pownall and killing three other men. 2nd Lieutenant B. L. Cumpston was also wounded by this shell and later died of his wounds.

Fighting subsided over the next few days, which gave an opportunity for the 7th Division to relieve its tired 20th Brigade with the 91st Brigade. Before the 2nd Gordon Highlanders were withdrawn from the line, they were sent to hold trenches at Bullecourt for another day, much to the consternation of the soldiers who had already fought so hard. Major Palithorpe later wrote, 'Our hopes were dashed to the ground that we might have finished with Bullecourt as the battalion was ordered back again on the night of the 9th – a horrid feeling going back to exactly the same area.'[9]

Lieutenant W.N. Brown was a bombing officer belonging to the 2nd Gordon Highlanders and after surviving the action of 7th May, he was very reluctant to return:

Have just come out and had another splendid success. This is the second successful assault within a month. I never went through anything like it. We were under shell fire, 5.9s, for two days and only a 6ft bank to lie under; I have just got orders to go up again, Cheerful!!!!

Well I'm back again – the worst time I have ever had. However I am out all well so it is not so bad. The Germans are putting up a terrible fight ... I hope it will end soon. We have had enough.

The grass and trees are showing life now and the larks sing even up near the front line, while all over the downs you see the last year's crop making an attempt to come up. Everywhere the grass is covering up the broken houses and ruined trenches and the more terrible results of man's inhumanity are at least getting a veil.

You can look out when it is quiet and the scene is as peaceful as if it was at home, and in a few minutes it is a raging hell of black smoke, dust and indistinguishable things. The trees lie in every direction and this makes the landscape dull and uninteresting. The houses are gradually disappearing, the bricks on the roads, the ribs for firewood. So the villages are passing, Kultur has done its work.[10]

Although there was no attack at Bullecourt on 10th May, German machine gunners and artillery were still active. The only protection that the Gordon Highlanders had was to shelter behind the railway embankment. Answering the call of nature while on the line was a difficult and deadly process. Palithorpe:

Shell holes were of course our only latrines. Nobody ventured further out than 20 yards from the embankment and nobody spent more time over nature's demands than he could help. I noticed when I returned from my excursions that – I imagine in order to prevent an officer feeling conspicuous in these circumstances – the gentleman Jocks were always looking anywhere than in my direction.[11]

The 2nd Gordon Highlanders were relieved during the night of 10th May. As the battle for Bullecourt continued and Gough's Fifth Army's attempt to evict the German presence from the village notwithstanding, Field Marshal Haig was transferring resources from Bullecourt to Belgium; he had issued an order on 9th May to move most of the heavy artillery units from this sector to Flanders.

CORPORAL ERNEST JOHNS 7166 MM,
9TH BATTALION DEVONSHIRE REGIMENT

Ernest Edwin Johns was born on 27th October in Exeter. He worked as an errand boy until 1889, when he joined the Royal Navy aged 17 for twelve years service. He began as a Ship's Boy and served on many vessels. His record was one of good conduct and he attained the rank of Petty Officer. He married Mary Jane in 1900 and the first of his four children was born the following year. Johns left the Royal Navy during 1902 to become a carpenter and joiner.

In 1914 Johns enlisted to serve with the 3rd Devonshire Regiment, a training battalion. The Army did not take into consideration his previous service with the Royal Navy on enlistment and he joined as a private. Johns had developed strong leadership skills while serving with the Royal Navy and the Army soon recognised his abilities. By 1916 he was a Corporal and had been transferred to the 9th Devonshire Regiment. On 1st July 1916, during an attack upon Mansell Copse near Mametz, the battalion suffered heavy casualties, but Corporal Johns led a party into a German trench, capturing the position and taking prisoners. He was awarded the Military Medal. His citation stated:

> For outstanding bravery in the field. The Somme, Mametz, July 1st 1916, a bombing section under command of Sergeant Paddon [also awarded the MM] and Cpl Johns were outstanding in clearing a German trench defence system, taking many prisoners of war and saving many of the 9th Battalion soldiers' lives.[12]

During May 1917 Corporal Johns was again in action when the 9th Devonshire Regiment assaulted Bullecourt. When the war ended in 1918 Johns had attained the rank of Drill Sergeant. His service record reported that Corporal Johns was 'an excellent NCO, hardworking and reliable, performed his duties conscientiously.'[13] After demobilisation, Johns returned to his trade, working as a master carpenter with the Kings Asphalt Company. During 1935 he was the Foreman in charge of the construction of the Exe Suspension Bridge at Trews Weir.

When the Second World War began he was too old to serve; however he played an important 'peace-keeping' role in Wonford when USA soldiers stationed at Wyvern Barracks engaged in disputes with local men, which were often fuelled by alcohol. At the Heavitree and Wonford Service Men's Club and Wonford Inn 'Ern' Johns and his brother Alf Davey were hired as bouncers to keep the GIs under control. His grandson Gerald Foggin recalled 'There are men today in Wonford who still speak of him with respect and pleasure, recalling him with his pipe and his dog Johno'. Ernest Johns died before the Second World War ended and was buried at Heavitree Church.

LANCE CORPORAL WILLIAM IRISH 20088,
8TH BATTALION DEVONSHIRE REGIMENT

William George Irish was born in 1896. Before the war he lived in Silvertown, in the East End of London. According to family legend, he was under age to serve and tried to enlist, but failed. On 23rd August 1915, William Irish enlisted in a Woolwich recruitment office where he was not known. He gave his age as 19 years 150 days.

After completing his basic training William Irish married Lilian Beatrice May Morrison on 8th December 1915 at a register office in West Ham. He was sent to Exeter and joined the 8th Devonshire Regiment. Irish belonged to Number 10 Platoon, C Company. He was sent to France on 11th February 1916. Private Irish would see action during the first day of the Somme campaign when on 1st July 1916; the 8th Devonshire Regiment supported the 9th Devonshires and the 2nd Gordon Highlanders in an attack on Mansell Copse. As all three battalions advanced across No Man's Land, heavy casualties were sustained. B Company, 8th Devonshires left their trenches at 10.30 am and were held up in a small dip in the terrain near the Fricourt Road until 4.00 pm. The battalion continued to advance to capture deep German dug-outs in Danzig trench before proceeding towards Hidden Wood. They fought their way into Orchard Trench and achieved all their objectives. The battalion suffered 207 casualties. Private Irish was to find himself in the thick of action once again when the battalion formed part of the leading wave in the attack on Bazentin-le-Grand Wood on 14th July 1916. They crawled

Corporal Ernest John.

(Courtesy Gerald Foggin)

Private William Irish.

(Courtesy Alan Quirk)

Soldiers from the 8th Battalion Devonshire Regiment. Private William Irish (seated front row, left). (Courtesy Alan Quick)

into No Man's Land under the cover of a British artillery barrage and formed up 25 yards from the German lines. They left their starting position at 3.25 am and within a minute they had entered their first objective and in 20 minutes they had captured their second objective and were able to send patrols to consolidate the north-east sector of the wood. Irish was lucky to get through this second battle as the battalion suffered a further 171 casualties. The battalion took part in the assault on High Wood on 20th July 1916 and would replicate the successful tactics used at Bazentin-le-Grand Wood. 20 minutes prior to Zero Hour, scheduled for 3.25 am, the 8th Battalion crawled towards their designated start off positions in No Man's Land under the cover of a British barrage. Many casualties were inflicted upon the Devonshires owing to British shells falling short. At 3.25 am they gained a foothold in High Wood, but they were relieved later that day after sustaining 201 casualties.

Irish was promoted to Lance Corporal on 20th December 1916. While in France Lilian gave birth to a daughter who died aged 11 months. It is thought that William never saw his first-born. Lilian wrote a letter to William, dated 16th March 1917, informing him of the terrible news. Cause of death was bronchopneumonia.

He would see action again during May 1917 in the assault upon Bullecourt and at the Battle of Broodseinde Ridge, near Passchendaele on 4th October 1917, during the Third Ypres campaign.

William Irish, like many First World War veterans, spoke little about the horrors of the war; however, he did mention being wounded twice. His service record states that he was in England from 16th October 1917 until 31st March 1918. It is possible that Lance Corporal Irish was wounded at Broodseinde Ridge and was evacuated to England to recover. He was demoted back to private after failing to attend a tattoo on 3rd January 1918.

After recovering from his wounds he was sent back to France on 1st April 1918. As his original battalion was sent to the Italian Front in November 1917, he was given a new service number 34555 and attached to the Oxford and Buckinghamshire Light Infantry. Irish took part in fighting 11 days before the war ended, on 1st November 1918 his battalion attacked an enemy position at the St Hubert crossroads, west of Maresches. At 6.30 am they overwhelmed the German position capturing 550 prisoners and two tanks. He would remain in France until February 1919.

After the war William Irish returned to his job in the sugar refinery in Silvertown. Later he became a painter and decorator until his retirement.

Bill had three more daughters. One died aged 27 another died aged two; he was survived by his last daughter. William George Irish died in December 1971.

PRIVATE STANLEY WATSON 23706,
2ND BATTALION BORDER REGIMENT

Stanley Wilson was born in 1895 in the village of Ennerdale, in the Lake District. He was married to Adele from the Apple Tree Hotel in Workington, Cumberland. Private Stanley Watson was carrying an injured

Private Stanley Watson photographed at Llandudno 1916. (Courtesy Lynn & Betty Dixon)

Stanley is sitting on stretcher, second from left, 1916. (Courtesy Lynn & Betty Dixon)

comrade over his shoulder when he was shot in the back and killed by a German sniper at Bullecourt on 8th May 1917. Adele was informed of his death the following day, on her 22nd birthday. His remains were not recovered and his name is commemorated on the Arras Memorial.

NOTES

1. Australian War Memorial: AWM 1DRL428/00010: Australian Red Cross Missing File: Private John Downs.
2. National Archives: WO 95/1655: 8th Battalion, Devonshire Regiment War Diary.
3. Ibid.
4. Ibid.
5. Ibid.
6. *The Story of the Fifth Australian Division* by Captain A.D. Ellis MC.
7. National Archives: WO 95/1655: 8th Battalion Devonshire Regiment War Diary.
8. Ibid.
9. Major David Palithorpe account: Gordon Highlanders Museum.
10. Captain W.N. Brown papers: Gordon Highlanders Museum.
11. Major David Palithorpe account: Gordon Highlanders Museum.
12. Corporal Ernest Johns papers. (Courtesy Gerald Foggin.)
13. Ibid.

CHAPTER 27

FURTHER ATTEMPTS TO CAPTURE BULLECOURT: 12TH–13TH MAY 1917

On 12th May the 58th Battalion from the 5th Australian Division supported the British 7th Division as they launched another attack on Bullecourt. They had entered the line during the night of 9th May and for the next three days were subjected to heavy German bombardments. Among those killed was 2nd Lieutenant Simon Fraser, the subject of the Cobbers statue at Fromelles. He was killed by shell fire. The 58th Battalion was ordered to advance westwards in an effort to capture Hindenburg Line support trenches with intention of linking with the 91st Brigade, 7th Division, at the crossroads north east of Bullecourt. The 91st Brigade comprising the 2nd Queen's (Royal West Surrey) Regiment and 1st South Staffordshires were the two battalions ordered to lead the attack supported by two companies from the 21st Manchester Regiment who would follow and mop up. Their objectives were to occupy the village up to the Riencourt Road, then establish positions along the northern perimeter, from where scouting parties could venture north to investigate German strength in support trenches. The 22nd Manchester Regiment, the fourth battalion within the 91st Brigade, was held in reserve by the railway embankment.

On 10th May 1917, two days before the attack Lieutenant Colonel A. B. Beauman commanding officer of the 1st South Staffordshire Regiment issued the following message to all ranks:

> In a few days you will be called on to capture BULLECOURT. Owing to its great importance both to us and to the enemy, the village has already become historic and if we capture it we shall add undying glory to the Regiment's proud record. I do not anticipate an easy victory but I am confident that you will smash the enemy's resistance as you have done many times before.[1]

The 1st South Staffordshire Regiment would advance on the left flank while the 2nd Queen's (Royal West Surrey) Regiment commanded by Lieutenant Colonel Longbourne would assault on the right. At the same time, the 62nd Division would try to dislodge the German stranglehold on the Red Patch, south west of the village. Their objective was to capture the Crucifix. They were also ordered to establish contact with units from the 7th Division on their right flank. Zero Hour was scheduled for 3.40 am but the previous night's bombardment had caused many casualties. Two Lewis guns were buried by debris from the barrage with their teams either killed or wounded. Half an hour before Zero Hour two Stokes mortars and their crews was buried but rescued by Private McBride who dug them out.

The Australian battalions from the 5th Division were poised to play their part in assisting the British Divisions in this next assault. The 58th Battalion commanded by Lieutenant Colonel Charles Denehy was positioned in OG 1 on the right flank of the 2nd Queen's (Royal West Surrey) Regiment. The 58th Battalion also held the communication trench that led to OG 2 and held parts of OG 2. In between the trenches OG 1 and OG 2 was a heavily defended German concrete pillbox armed with machine guns. Lieutenant Rupert Moon's platoon from A Company was designated the task of assaulting and capturing this redoubt. Once Moon had achieved his objective, Captain Norman Pelton would lead B Company westwards along OG 2 into the German-held sector. The third objective was allotted to Lieutenant Samuel Topp from C Company who was ordered to capture the trench and dug-outs close to the crossroads, north east of Bullecourt.

The casualties sustained by the 58th Battalion were so severe that a company from the 59th Battalion needed to be brought up to reinforce it.

The British barrage began promptly at 3.40 am on 12th May. Once it lifted at 14 minutes after Zero Hour, four platoons from 58th Battalion attacked from OG 2. Lieutenant Rupert Moon led a party of 28 men and two Lewis machine guns from A Company, 58th Battalion in an attack upon the concrete German redoubt. They were ordered to lie in No Man's Land, wait for the barrage to cease, then rush the strong point. The German machine guns in the pillbox continued to fire at the oncoming Australians. Lieutenant Moon was wounded in the face while leading his platoon's charge.

Moon was aware of the consequences of failure to capture this enemy position. When he was first wounded he fell to the floor and was dazed. His men wavered and the assault was losing momentum. Moon encouraged his men to carry on, with 'Come on boys, don't let me down.' They did not, forcing the occupiers to escape into OG 2 to the north. The pillbox was captured within 20 minutes, which enabled Lieutenant Topps and C Company to advance towards the crossroads.

Moon watched these Germans in the pillbox head for OG 2 and decided to act. Moon, who must have suffered considerable pain from wounds already sustained, pursued them across open ground with a Lewis gun team who fired upon them. Moon was followed by carrying parties from the 60th Battalion who were bringing up bombs and ammunition to support the attack. Moon got another wound to his shoulder in the pursuit, but he did not stop.

Captain Norman Pelton had been killed at the beginning of the assault and Dawson assumed command of the three platoons from B Company attacking along OG 2. Despite Lieutenant Dawson peppering the German position in OG 2 with rifle grenade fire, the defenders quickly bought up reinforcements of bombers, 12 men, to repel B Company. Dawson's party was held up by this determined German resistance until Lieutenant Moon fired upon the position and orchestrated a breakthrough. Dawson was left to consolidate the trench and four bombing squads from the 60th Battalion were sent up to the trench as reinforcements.

Moon was determined to secure B and C Company's objectives. Accompanied by Lance Corporal Charles Free he led a bombing party west along OG 2. He ordered a Lewis gun team to climb out of OG 2 and position themselves in a shell hole, from where they were able to pour machine gun fire to their left and dislodge the enemy in OG 2. Within minutes the Germans withdrew west along OG 2 towards the crossroads. Moon followed them as they headed for a railway cutting. At one point Moon was alone and accounted for several of them as he fired his rifle. German bombers targeted Moon and he was forced to get back into OG 2. Lance Corporal Free fired at the lead German bomber to help Moon escape. Australian bombers got closer and were able to assist Moon in his attack upon the Germans in the cutting. Many Germans fell and Moon led his party into the cutting. German survivors sought shelter in dug-outs below the cutting. Moon had all the entrances into this dug-out covered by rifle fire and trapped them. At that point Moon's party numbered 30 and they waited for

Lieutenant Dawson to reinforce their numbers. Dawson secured the Germans in the dug-out as prisoners. 186 German prisoners were taken.

With wounds to his leg and foot Moon refused to leave the battlefield until the captured ground was secured. The process was made difficult by German snipers on a bank on the left side of the road. Moon ordered his men to dig in but he and Dawson realised that it was impossible to hold the ground during daylight so they made the decision to withdraw their men from the road temporarily. It was at this point that Moon was shot in the face by a sniper and his jaw was shattered. He was withdrawn from the battlefield. Moon was responsible for the capture of four machine guns and 186 German prisoners. For this action Moon received the Victoria Cross. Dawson was awarded the Military Cross. Lance Corporal Free received the Distinguished Conduct Medal.

While Moon and Dawson were fighting their way along OG 2, Lieutenant Topp led A Company towards the trench and dug-out system located north west of the crossroads. Their left flank was exposed to fire because the advance of the 2nd Queen's (Royal West Surrey) Regiment had been held up. Despite this setback they crossed between OG 1 and OG 2 and secured their objective assisted by Lieutenant Moon's party, capturing more prisoners.

The 58th Battalion did succeed on the left flank though at one stage they were pinned down by this fire and forced to take cover in nearby shell-holes. As Lieutenant Samuel Topp commanding C Company, stood out of a shell hole and pointed out something to Lieutenant J Syder, he was shot in the head by a sniper. Lieutenant Robertson was wounded. Lieutenant Robert Kidd who was advancing on the far left flank succeeded in establishing communication with the 2nd Queen's. The 58th Battalion had captured five machine

2nd Battalion (Queen's) Royal West Surrey Camp at Mory before Bullecourt in May. Gardner, Streeter, and Pinchbeck and Abel are the officers. (Courtesy Surrey History Centre)

Officers from A-Coy, 2nd Battalion Royal West Surrey Regiment: Lavers, Tidy, Chapman and Gardner. 2nd Lieutenant Theodore Chapman was aged 19 and a recipient of the Military Cross. Within days of this photo being taken, Chapman would be killed at Bullecourt. (Courtesy Surrey History Centre)

guns, three minenwerfer, two pineapple bomb throwing machines and 186 soldiers. On the battlefield lay approximately 150 dead Germans. Lieutenant Colonel Charles Denehy was awarded the DSO for his command of the 58th Battalion at Bullecourt. 'When in command of a defence which was continuously bombarded he was able, by his courage and fine example, to maintain the spirit of his men in spite of heavy losses.'[2]

The 2nd Queen's were ordered to capture the Brown Line from the crossroads to the road junction north of Bullecourt church. Soldiers from the 2nd Queen's were exhausted before they entered the battle. They had been in the line working as fatigue parties supporting other battalions. Drained, they were at a disadvantage before the battle began. Lieutenant R.L. Atkinson commanding B Company:

The Coy. was by no means fresh as the time spent in reserve May 7th–9th had involved a heavy fatigue for two platoons and frequent standing to. The trenches now occupied were enfiladed from the right and being a captured line were very much knocked about and full of unburied dead.[3]

As soon as the British barrage began at 3.40 am the 2nd Queen's (advanced behind a creeping barrage which moved at a rate of 100 yards every six minutes. Lieutenant R.L. Atkinson commanding B Company recalled that 'there was a tendency to go too quickly and run into our own barrage.'[4]

The 2nd Queen's fought their way into the village of Bullecourt to the church and tried to secure the buildings in the eastern sector. They were supported by four platoons from the 21st Manchesters and they secured the right flank of the 62nd Division's objective up to the church by 4.15 am.

No German resistance was encountered in the ruined houses and they quickly consolidated along the Brown Line with Lewis guns in position. They pushed forward patrols to the north of the captured road and linked up with a company from the 58th Battalion on their right.

On the 2nd Queen's left flank, the 1st South Staffordshires could not secure the Red Patch. The 1st South Staffordshires were commanded by Lieutenant Colonel Beauman. Having lost men in the starting position to German artillery, they were confronted by heavy German machine gun fire and snipers. They advanced to the left of the main road into Bullecourt but became disorganised. The battalion's right flank also sustained casualties from this fire, but managed to enter the village.

The attack carried out by the 2nd/6th and 2nd/7th Battalions from the West Yorkshire Regiment, 62nd

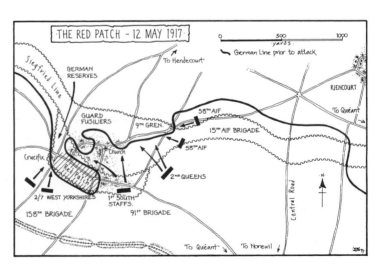

Red Patch operations 12th May 1917. (From *The Blood Tub* by Jonathan Walker, map copyright Spellmount)

Division, was reported to have failed at 4.45 am. A heavy German barrage upon the south-east sector of Bullecourt and concentrated machine gun and sniper fire at Zero Hour had caused many casualties. The South Staffordshires became scattered and those who survived were disorganised. Despite this major setback some parties did reach the north and north-western perimeters of the village to link up with the 2nd Queen's and consolidate positions by 7 am.

The German shelling severed lines of communication established by the 91st Brigade. As soon as a wire of communication was reconnected, it was cut by the German barrage. Brigadier Hanway Cumming commanding the 91st Brigade:

> Judging that the enemy's retaliation would be heavy and continuous, every means of communication was carefully thought out and organised by the Brigadier and his signal Staff. Relay posts for runners were established in the communication trench (the only one) from Longatte to the South-West corner of Bullecourt. Two telephone lines had also been laid by different routes to the combined Battalion Headquarters in the line. A 'power buzzer' set in duplicate was established, and this was supplemented by a field wireless apparatus. Every battalion was also supplied with carrier pigeons.[5]

Despite these contingencies as Cumming remembered:

> In spite of these preparations, communication broke down badly. The enemy very early in the proceedings put down a heavy high explosive and shrapnel barrage, which in a few minutes cut both telephone wires, smashed the power buzzer and the wireless apparatus, and in spite of heroic efforts on the part of all members of the signal section, the telephone lines remained practically useless for the rest of the day; as soon as they were renewed, they were cut again and again. All communication therefore devolved on the hard worked 'runner,' many of whom became casualties in their endeavours to get through. The pigeons were also a failure – most probably they refused to fly through the heavy barrage, or else became confused by it and lost their way or were killed.[6]

The right flank of the South Staffordshires had secured positions north and north west of the village and had established contact with the 2nd Queen's on their right flank. Lieutenant Colonel A. B. Beauman was organising the South Staffordshires for another attempt:

> By this time I was convinced that the RED PATCH was very strongly held and would require a fresh attack in strength to reduce it. I therefore asked for reinforcements and in the meantime collected two officers and 50 men from my reserve Company. With these I decided to launch an attack along both sides of the road with the objective of strengthening my position near the CRUCIFIX and if possible cutting off the retreat of the RED PATCH garrison by joining hands with the 62nd who were reported to have made progress near the CRUCIFIX.[7]

At that time Cumming was ignorant of the progress of the battle. He had no news at Brigade headquarters. His frustrations were doubled by irritating requests from his superiors at Division Headquarters. With all his runners being killed or wounded Cumming had to resort to sending one of his Staff officers to the South Staffordshires' Headquarters to assess the position.

The 182nd Brigade did enter the strong point at the Crucifix. Volunteers were sought to establish communication with the 2nd Queen's at the Crucifix from B Company 2nd/7th West Yorkshire Regiment. Rifleman James William Walker and Rifleman Herbert Hemsworth volunteered to try to link up with the contingent at the Crucifix that had been cut off and isolated by counter attacks. Both men had reached the first belt of barbed wire when they came under rifle fire. Hemsworth was shot dead. Walker could not continue. He returned to British lines and then made another attempt to get through the wire and reach the Crucifix. This time he was accompanied by Rifleman Holdsworth Spencer. The second attempt was again thwarted by German rifle fire, Spencer was killed and Walker made his way back. For his courageous attempt to reach the 2nd Queen's, Walker was awarded the Military Medal.

Air reconnaissance confirmed that the 2/7th West Yorkshires had reached the Crucifix, but were unable to consolidate the position and were forced to retire. The Crucifix would become a dangerous running sore for the British; they had control of the village except for this south-western sector. The Germans were tenaciously holding on to this salient and could reinforce it through a sunken road that passed through the Crucifix. This was a very unusual situation in that the British were cheek by jowl with the Germans in the Red Patch yet could not drive them out.

At 8 am the 1st Staffordshires launched another attack, but were met by strong German resistance in the Red Patch. Machine gunners killed one officer and made casualties of half the assault party. The survivors led by the one officer left were forced to dig in under fire.

Cumming's staff officer brought back news at 11 am, two hours after he had been sent to the South Staffordshires' headquarters. At midday three companies from the 22nd Manchesters were assigned to the 1st South Staffordshires to be deployed in a further attack, but sustained German fire from machine guns and shells made the movement of reinforcements into the village impossible. This new initiative was quickly aborted and the men from the 22nd Manchesters kept in reserve. Lieutenant Colonel Beauman got the men from the 22nd Manchesters in a place where they were sheltered from fire and decided that it was more prudent to launch the next attack at night. Cumming was anxious to see the position of the 2nd Queen's, 1st South Staffordshires and the 21st Manchesters with his own eyes. Accompanied by Brigade Major Captain Morshead he braved German shells and machine gun fire to visit each battalion headquarters. Cumming was satisfied with the progress of the 2nd Queen's, but was concerned about the other two battalions:

The 1st S. Staffordshire's and the 'mopping up' Battalion, the 21st Manchesters … although well established in the village, were much disorganised from the constant fighting in which they had been engaged among the ruined houses and derelict streets, than which nothing is more conducive to disorganisation and difficulties of control. Moreover the men were thoroughly exhausted by the heat and suffering from the want of water, which although supplies were adequate, was difficult to distribute owing to constant sniping which came from the enemy line on the West of the village.[8]

After seeing the situation for himself he made the decision to pull out the 1st South Staffordshires and the 21st Manchesters and replace them with the 22nd Manchesters. Cumming realised that it would be futile to continue the attack during daylight and suspended all operations for that day.

The 1st South Staffordshires lost two officers and 37 men killed, seven officers and 107 men wounded with 27 missing. The 2nd Queen's (Royal West Surrey) Regiment entered the battle with a battalion strength of 20 officers and 609 men. They left the battlefield with eight officers and 362 men.[9] Amongst those killed were Captain Theodore Victor Chapman MC and Second Lieutenant G.G. Smith.

Cumming telephoned Major-General Shoubridge at 7th Division Headquarters later that afternoon to appraise him of his plan to attack the following day from the east. He thought his brigade had done well to have gained a foothold within the village, but Shoubridge denounced the attack that day as a complete failure. Cumming was rebuked and ordered by Shoubridge that the battalions in place were not to be relieved and that he should continue the attack. Cumming had seen the situation with his own eyes and knew that his battalions in Bullecourt were not in a fit state to continue. He resisted Shoubridge's demands

to push forward the attack, much to consternation of the 7th Divisional Commander. Cumming tried to convince him that it was best to wait until the morning. Shoubridge was incensed that his orders should be questioned by a subordinate officer and terminated the phone call. Shoubridge was determined that his orders were not to be undermined and Cumming soon received a second telephone call ordering him to hand over command to Lieutenant-Colonel Norman, commander of the 21st Manchester Regiment. At 8.00 pm on 12th May Brigadier General Hanway R. Cumming relinquished command of the 91st Brigade. Half an hour later Shoubridge decided that another attack would be launched at 3.40 am the following morning.

During the evening 12th May, German attempts to remove the South Staffordshires from their positions near the Crucifix at Bullecourt through heavy bombing attacks were fiercely repelled by a party led by Lieutenant T.N. Woof. The Australian 5th Brigade was relieved by the 173rd Brigade from 58th Division. This Division had been newly established with recruits from London. Their entry into the line at Bullecourt was their first experience of battle. The relief did not pass without incident for the 58th Australian Battalion lost 11 officers and 234 men, while the 60th AIF Battalion suffered the loss of four officers and 105 other ranks. As the 2/3rd and 2/4th London Regiments moved forward they suffered 80 casualties.

Four companies from the 21st Manchester Regiment were withdrawn and replaced by the 2nd Royal Warwickshire Regiment, which was attached to the 91st Brigade for the attack on 13th May. They were to work together with the 22nd Battalion Manchester Regiment in the impending attack.

Max Pemberton wrote an account of the struggle for the village entitled 'How Bullecourt was Won', which featured in *War Illustrated* on 8th June 1917:

From the north, from the east, even from the east, the attacks upon them came. Snipers to the south found open trenches and enfiladed them with bullets. There were rushes of Germans perpetually: the grey waves appearing suddenly from the bowels of the earth and leaping to the attack with savage cries. It was 'Stand by' and again 'Stand by'. Their machine guns rattled like sticks upon a railing; their rifles were always in their hands. And when night came the whole heaven would be lit up with the blue-white light of the flaming star-shells and the whirlwind barrage would open and men would wait for dawn with eyes that had forgotten how to sleep. Yet this was the preliminary to the fierce fighting of Sunday May 13th by which Bullecourt was won for us.[10]

The next attack to drive the Germans from the Red Patch was attempted at 3.40 am with a simultaneous attack by the 2nd Royal Warwickshire from the south west and A and D companies from the 22nd Manchester Regiment from the north east. The 2nd /6th Duke of Wellington was ordered to attack the Crucifix at the same time. The weather conditions were appalling as thunderstorms and heavy rain descended.[11] They charged with bayonets fixed, but the effort was a complete disaster. It was difficult for the artillery to direct its barrage onto the salient with any accuracy. It was dark and when the barrage fell short it fell upon the 2nd Royal Warwickshires first, then the shells overshot the German position and fell upon the 22nd Manchesters, causing heavy casualties. Hardly any British shells found their target. 'The 2nd Battalion Royal Warwickshire Regt. advanced at 3.40 am under heavy hostile shelling but were unable to make any appreciable progress except on the extreme right where a small party worked round the wire and went forward into the middle of the village.'[12]

The 22nd Manchesters were unable to advance from their starting positions because of the British barrage which fell directly upon them. Chaos dominated the morning's proceedings. The Manchesters and the Warwickshires were so lost in the darkness that both units advanced past the German trenches:

> The two Companies of the 22nd Bn. Manchester Regt. attacking from the North were unable to advance at Zero Hour being held up by our own barrage which opened heavily on the road through the village instead of on the German front line trench. So soon as this barrage lifted the attacking companies pushed forward but were again held up by heavy machine gun fire from what appeared to be three strong points in the old front line trench. Several attempts were made against the centre strong point but all failed.[13]

When the barrage lifted the remnants of the 22nd Manchesters who charged over the destroyed village towards the Crucifix met heavy machine gun fire. The 22nd Manchester Regiment lost three officers killed and one wounded and 106 casualties amongst the other ranks. Among the casualties who died on that day were Captain Charles Duguid DSO and MC, Private William Kendall and Private Thomas Higson, all have no known graves, their bodies consumed in the cauldron of Bullecourt.

By 10 am the survivors from the 2nd Royal Warwickshire Regiment were withdrawn. Max Pemberton's account of the battle that morning provides an impression of ferocity amidst the ruins of the village:

> Dust-begrimed men with sweat upon their faces, they fought from the early hours as demons possessed. Here were things done and seen which shall not be surpassed in the story of the war. Men fought with men as animals in some ruined arena. You saw Germans upon one side of a shattered barn and British upon the other, and their grenades went over the wreck of the roof and men trod upon their own dead to get at the enemy. Every cellar was a possible refuge for the Boche and his machine-gun. And we must hunt amid the brick and the mortar, turn every stone, lift every beam that the bomb may go down and the dead be garnered.[14]

Max Pemberton continued his graphic and harrowing account of the battle on 13th May:

Battle for Bullecourt Village. A sniper's paradise. (*The Great War*, published 1918)

There was no village now, now any thought of church or market place or street that Bullecourt had marked upon its map – only this ruin and the blackened figures leaping from stone to stone of it and the bayonets flashing in the sunshine, and the cries going up of despair or of appeal as the steel went home and the life's blood gushed out. A fight to the bitter end, beyond all description horrible – yet for us a triumph beyond all expectation magnificent. Perhaps the climax of all this deadly business came in the cemetery, where the graves were opened and the dead flung out. Here, the Boche found in the vaults an emplacement for his machine-guns which could not have been bettered. And he fought to the very death amid the bodies and bones of those who had lived their humble lives in this once pretty village, and had known, perhaps, the greatness and the glory of France, and had believed that civilization would leave those white crosses standing until the end. So little did he know of the German, the corpses of those proud Foot Guards now lie amid the broken coffins and whose blackened faces send even strong men shuddering from this hallowed acre.[15]

Later the Germans launched a counter attack upon the Londoners who held the lines that the Australians had fought for, capturing four prisoners in the process.

The 1st South Staffordshires made yet more attempts to try to dislodge the Germans from the Crucifix. As they bombed along trenches their assaults were thwarted by persistent German machine gun fire from the south west sector. At 7.00 pm a composite unit was formed with men from the 21st Battalion Manchester Regiment who were placed under the command of officers from the 1st Battalion South Staffordshires. They made another brave effort to enter the Red Patch. Again, the German machine gun firepower overwhelmed them.

During the night of 13th May the 20th Manchesters and the 2nd Honourable Artillery Company from 22nd Brigade, together with the 1st Royal Welch Regiment, were ordered to take over the line at Bullecourt. The 2nd HAC was also ordered to relieve the 1st Battalion South Staffordshires. The battalion had been reduced to 250 men after their mauling on 4th May. Recognising that the attack carried out on the 13th May had been a complete shambles, Shoubridge reverted to attacking Bullecourt from the east. The 1st Royal Welch Fusiliers were ordered to clear the German presence.

By 11.10 pm on the night of the 13th B and D Companies from the 1st Battalion Royal Welch Fusiliers were guided by men from the 22nd Manchester Battalion into positions in the front line near to Red Patch, with A and C Companies entrenched along the sunken road.

Lieutenant Colonel Albert Lambert-Ward commanding the 2nd HAC was at the front line with Captain F.A. Garrett to appraise the situation and organise the relief. His Company had been told to wait for further orders at 8.40pm. They received the go ahead to proceed to the front line at 11.00 pm, by which time the communication trench was full of pioneers working on the trench, which impeded their progress. Captain Amoore and 10 men were wounded by shell fire as they moved forwards. The rest slowly reached their line and were in position by 12.30 am on 14th May. The Royal Welch Fusiliers were scheduled to attack at 2.30 am. With an attack being carried out imminently it was not safe for Lambert-Ward to take over the line because a heavy enemy bombardment was a certainty. Lambert-Ward made efforts to get the Royal Welch Regiment to postpone the time of the assault by an hour, while his men took command of the line. This could not be achieved and after consulting with Battalion commanders on the line he decided to withdraw the 2nd HAC back to Ecoust-St-Mein.

B and D Companies from the 1st Royal Welch Regiment attacked the Red Patch at 2.10 am. This attack faltered and the remnants of these companies were ordered to regroup and launch a second attack. This was launched at 4.00 am. Once again these units failed to break the German entrenched positioned in the Red Patch. However they did establish small pockets facing the Crucifix. A and C Company from the 1st Royal Welch Regiment launched a third attack while they were covered by B and D Company who bombarded German positions at the Crucifix and a point at U.27.b.40.40 with rifle grenades; still no victory. By 10 am the battalion had sustained many casualties and was in urgent need of bombs and small arms ammunition. They had practically surrounded the strong point at U.27.b.40.40. Their ammunition supplies were hastily replenished at 10.45 am. A and C Company were ordered to reorganise. At 2.30 pm C Company nearly succeeded in penetrating the German defences, but they were forced back owing to lack of bombs. Lieutenant Colonel Holmes was ordered to initiate another attack later that day on 14th May. Holmes protested the tired state of his men to staff officers at Brigade. He won the argument and the attack was cancelled.

During the afternoon of the 14th, the 2nd Honourable Artillery Company was ordered to relieve the South Staffordshires. Lambert-Ward made his reservations known to Colonel Norman. 'I pointed out to Colonel Norman that the strength of my Battalion was only 250 with 11 Lewis Guns, and it would not be advisable to take over that length of line with so few men.[16] He was nevertheless ordered to deploy his battalion. The 21st Battalion Manchester Regiment was holding the line around the Red Patch. The 2nd

HAC completed their relief by 2.45am on 15th May. At 4.15 am S.O.S. flares were fired from the direction of the Crucifix, west of Bullecourt. Major Wright sent a message confirming that the enemy had attacked a position held by an adjacent battalion. The remnants of the 2nd HAC held off this German counter attack. Captain Bower had sent a patrol into the Red Patch and reported that it 'was alive with enemy and that they had been unable to get anywhere near C Company.'[17]

C Company had been completely overwhelmed by this German assault. Captain John Pritchard had been killed and Captain C.R. McGowan had been severely wounded. Pritchard's remains were recovered and identified in 2009 at Bullecourt in a pasture adjacent to the Rue d'Arras where the Red Patch was situated. Papers and two pistols were found on his remains. He was wearing two watches, both stopped at 12.25. As a result of annihilating C Company, German forces had been able to drive a wedge into the village, placing them in a position to outflank B Company and push them back towards Battalion Headquarters. German forces had been so strong that they were able to get to within 30 yards from of Lambert-Ward's Battalion HQ.

At 4 pm the 22nd Infantry Brigade Commander ordered the 1st Royal Welch Regiment to stop all further attacks since the 20th Manchesters and the 2nd HAC would relieve the Queen's and South Staffordshires and the 21st Manchesters would relieve the 1st Royal Welch Regiment.

Minutes after sending this message to Lambert-Ward, Captain Bower was bearing the brunt of a German counter attack from the south west and he and his men were withdrawing. They were encountering heavy enemy shelling and machine gun fire. Amongst

Didier Guerle & Yves Fohlen. Didier Guerle found Captain Pritchard's remains in a pasture that he owns in Bullecourt. Yves Fohlen (right) is a battlefield guide and author. He has helped many families from Britain and Australia when they make pilgrimages to the battlefields of the Western Front in France. He is the archivist at the Jean & Denise Letaille Bullecourt Museum and he is affectionately known by Australian pilgrims as the 'Froggy Cobber'. (Author)

Location in Bullecourt where Captain Pritchard's remains were found in 2009. The darker patch between the two posts marks the position. He had been lying there for 92 years. It was here that the 2nd Battalion HAC fought so valiantly to capture the village. (Author)

the dead was Lieutenant Clifford Jack St Quintin. Major Wright placed 10 of his remaining men under the command of Lieutenant Montgomery, an officer from the Royal Welch Fusiliers and ordered him to carry out a bombing attack to beat the Germans back. Wright also ordered Captain Bower to drive towards the Church crossroads which he did without incurring many casualties, Later that morning Bower reached a mixed unit comprising soldiers from the HAC and 20th Manchesters on his right flank and a party of men from the 21st Manchesters on his left. The 2nd HAC was relieved later that day by 8th London Regiment. They were off the line by 3.15 am on 15th May.

B and D Companies from the 1st Royal Welch Fusiliers were relieved by the 21st Manchester Regiment. At 3.20 am A and C Companies received the bad news that they were not going to be relieved and were ordered to embark on a further attack supported by a platoon from the 21st Battalion, Manchester Regiment. The

Commanding officer of the 1st Royal Welch Fusiliers protested at Staff level at 91st Brigade that 'an attack there with tired troops was not feasible until the Crucifix had been taken'.[18] Before it could even be attempted, at 3.50 am German forces launched an attack of their own from point U.27.b.65.20 and from the Crucifix.

The 21st Manchester Regiment held onto their positions despite being outnumbered. 2nd Lieutenant S.R. Smith and his party found themselves surrounded. Their position became hopeless when their Lewis machine guns malfunctioned. With most of his party killed, Smith was severely wounded. He was captured with Private Higgins. Higgins found an opportunity to escape when he dropped several bombs amongst his captors. Other parties from the 21st Manchesters were unable to hold on and retired.

The Welch units holding posts in the western sector of Bullecourt were driven back as the German infantry advanced into the valley and got to within 250–300 yards of the Battalion Headquarters. Captain T. Bluck MC, 2nd Lieutenant H.A. Freeman and 2nd Lieutenant J.M. Davies MC gathered as many able-bodied men as possible from A and C Companies and organised a defensive position at the crossroads until a more substantial counter attack could be prepared. They held off the German attack until 4.15 am when a counter attack was launched, which pushed the German line back beyond the road that led from the Church to the crossroads. Contact was established with isolated units of the Welch battalion that had held their ground despite being encircled. Major Charles Kemp and 2nd Lieutenant Birbeck rallied men from the 21st Manchesters and assisted the Welch Fusiliers in their counter attack. Kemp was awarded the DSO for his efforts:

> For conspicuous gallantry, when in command of his battalion. After an enemy attack, when some disorganisation had set in, he rendered invaluable aid in collecting stragglers and leading them forward, under heavy fire in a counter-attack. His coolness and bravery enabled him to successfully reorganise the troops at his disposal.[19]

A and C Companies from the 1st Royal Welch Fusiliers were not relieved until later that night on the 15th/16th May, when their retired to Achiet-Le-Grand. The 1st Royal Welch Fusiliers lost many men. Captain the Reverend the Honourable Maurice Peel MC and Bar was killed, together with 2nd Lieutenants Lewis George Madley and R.P. Evans. 2nd Lieutenant Brocklebank had been wounded and would later die of wounds sustained weeks later on 17th June 1917. three officers were wounded, 14 men were killed, 49 wounded and 31 missing.

German soldiers at Bullecourt. (*Die Osterchlacht bei Arras II. Teil Zwisch*)

Of the 21st Manchesters, 2nd Lieutenants F. Walsh and Alfred Parkinson were killed. Lieutenant S.R. Smith was captured and 2nd Lieutenant S.W.J. Danziger died of his wounds. Six officers were wounded. 19 ranks were killed, 127 wounded and 21 missing.

The fighting at Bullecourt had reduced the entire 91st Brigade to the size of an understrength battalion and all that was left of the 2nd Honourable Artillery Company were four officers and 94 men.

THE REVEREND THE HONOURABLE MAURICE PEEL MC & BAR,
CHAPLAIN 4TH CLASS, ROYAL ARMY CHAPLAINS' DEPARTMENT

Maurice Peel was born in Hanover Square in 1873. He came from a distinguished political family. His father was Arthur Wellesley Peel, the First Viscount Peel and was a former Speaker of the House of Commons. His grandfather was Sir Robert Peel, Prime Minister and founder of the Metropolitan Police Force. Maurice Peel chose the church. On completing his education at the Oxford and after being ordained in 1899 he worked in the East End slums in Bethnal Green, London, where he helped the poor and the destitute. On his arrival he found the local churches and schools more or less empty. By the time that he left the East End church congregations and school attendances had increased.

Living amongst the squalor of the East End was not conducive to his health and Peel left London to become rector of Wrestlingworth in Bedfordshire. Peel would not forget the children he helped

Chaplain Maurice Peel. (Courtesy Nigel Maurice, Vice Chairman, Peel Society)

in the East End and would invite them to the country for holidays. He remained here for three years before becoming vicar of St Paul's Church in Beckenham. Peel was married in 1909. In 1914 Peel enlisted as a Chaplain and was assigned to the 7th Division.

Within six months of enlisting Peel had received the Military Cross gazetted on 18th February 1915. At Festubert during 15th May 1915 Peel wanted to 'go over the top' with the men from the 1st Battalion Royal Welch Fusiliers so that he could tend to the wounded and comfort the dying on the battlefield. It was not common practice for Army Chaplains to advance with the men during an assault. Peel requested permission from General Gough and permission was granted. Peel was carrying a walking stick and a Bible as he advanced with the first wave when he was shot several times by machine gun fire.

Peel was evacuated to England and to hospital. After recovering he left the Army on 15th October 1915. He was then appointed Vicar of Tamworth. Peel was greatly missed by the soldiers with whom he served in the 7th Division. With the men asking for him, Peel would return to the Army as a Chaplain in January 1917. He went back to the 1st Royal Welch Fusiliers. As soon as he had returned to the front line, he would distinguish himself once again. Wherever a shell fell Peel would go in that direction to tend to the wounded. Peel was awarded a bar to his Military Cross:

> For conspicuous gallantry and devotion to duty. He went out to the advanced patrols with two stretcher bearers and succeeded in bringing in several wounded men. Later, he worked for 36 hours in front of the captured position and rescued many wounded under very heavy fire.[20]

As the 1st Royal Welch Fusiliers fought on 14th May 1917, Peel was crawling amongst the rubble of the devastated village, clutching a Bible as he searched for the wounded and dead from his regiment. Offering prayers for the dead and tending to the wounds of the injured, Peel carried out his work under the scorching sun and the fire of machine guns. It was while he was carrying a wounded man near to what was left of Bullecourt church that he was shot in the abdomen by a German sniper and died of his wounds. His death was described as 'truly Christ-like, for he died to save'.[21]

His successor at St Paul's Church, Beckenham, the Reverend Gerald Sampson wrote a book about Peel as a tribute to him entitled A Hero Saint. The book contains a letter written by the Reverend Eric Milner-White, which describes the circumstances of Peel's death:

> Maurice (we all called him by his Christian name) was the greatest chaplain in France; none could

be greater. His own 'immortal' Division used to call him 'the bravest man in the Army'. He always accompanied his men into the line. Wherever a shell burst he at once ran towards it, lest any man had been hit and he might be of service. The men, of course, worshipped him ... When he came back to us in January he did not rest on the laurels gained so desperately on Festubert field. He nerved himself to greater efforts of mercy on the battlefield and went everywhere regardless of risks, wherever a wounded man lay. ... At dawn on the 15th, the second anniversary of Festubert, he got out of his trench to visit either a wounded man or an isolated post of men. On the day a sniper's bullet caught him in the chest; he fell unconscious and died very shortly, one Welch Fusilier officer crawling out and staying with him till the end.

> That same night one of the chaplains, McCalman, with great courage went up to B with a cross, hoping to bring in the body and bury it. Arrived within a few yards, he was not allowed to go further, the risk being too great.[22]

Chaplain Maurice Peel's remains were eventually recovered after the battle and his body was laid to rest in Quéant Road Cemetery.

2ND LIEUTENANT CLIFFORD ST QUINTIN,
2ND HONOURABLE ARTILLERY COMPANY

Clifford Jack St Quintin was born in Kew, London in 1887. He married Margaret Nicholson in Wandsworth in 1912. He was residing in Putney when war broke out. He joined the HAC on 14th March 1916 as a private and was given the service number 2705. In May 1916 he was assigned to the 3rd Battalion and on 11th August 1916 he was commissioned as a 2nd Lieutenant. He arrived on the Western Front on 7th May 1917 and joined the 2nd Battalion Honourable Artillery Company. 2nd Lieutenant Clifford St Quintin led an attempt with Captain Bower to drive German forces from Bullecourt village on 15th May 1917. It was during this assault that St Quintin was killed by a German sniper. He has no known grave and his name is commemorated on the Arras Memorial.

2nd Lieutenant Clifford St Quintin. (Courtesy Honourable Artillery Company Archives)

SERGEANT WILFRED JACKSON 4246
2ND BATTALION HONOURABLE ARTILLERY COMPANY

Wilfred Henry Jackson was born in 1895 in Lendal-In-Furness, Cumbria. John Jackson, his father was a blacksmith in Kirkby. Wilfred attended Queen Elizabeth Grammar School in Kirkby, Lonsdale. During the four years he spent there, Wilfred excelled in languages and mathematics. He was a keen sportsman and school football team captain. Wilfred played the violin and competed in competitions at the Winter Gardens in Morecombe. He studied to gain entry into the Civil Service and gained a position with the Inland Revenue. When war broke out in 1914, Wilfred was working as a clerk for the Admiralty. His role was considered as war work and he was under no obligation to enlist He nevertheless enlisted on 23rd August 1915 and was assigned to the 2nd Battalion, HAC. After completing his training at Tadworth training Camp in Surrey, he spent a year with the battalion on Home Service. Jackson impressed his superiors and on 30th September 1916 he was promoted to Lance Corporal. He left Southampton on 1st October 1916 arriving at Havre on the 3rd.

During his first days on the front line a German shell exploded near to him and he was buried under the earth. He was promoted to Corporal in February 1917 to Sergeant on 7th March. Jackson took part in the assault on Bullecourt on 3rd May 1917. The 2nd Honourable Artillery Company had been reduced to 250 men and Jackson was among those lucky few who survived that first assault. Despite sustaining many casualties the 2nd HAC relieved the 1st South Staffordshire Regiment during the early hours of 15th May. At 4.15 am they were attacked. Sergeant Wilfred Jackson was in command of a Lewis gun team and was killed. He has no known grave and his name is commemorated on the Arras Memorial.

Sergeant Wilfred Jackson. (Courtesy Queen Elizabeth's Grammar School, Kirkby)

PRIVATE HORACE BISHOP 9733
2ND HONOURABLE ARTILLERY COMPANY

Horace Reginald Bishop was born in Southampton in 1879 and later resided in Southsea, Portsmouth. Bishop joined the Honourable Artillery Company on 22nd December 1916. He was transferred to 2nd Company, 3rd Battalion on 27th December. He was sent to France on 18th March 1917. He joined No.4 Company, 2nd

Private Horace Bishop, pictured right with moustache. (Courtesy Honourable Artillery Company Archives)

Battalion. Bishop took part in the battle for Bullecourt village on 15th May 1917 where he was killed. He has no known grave and his name is commemorated on the Arras Memorial. Bishop is pictured right, with moustache.

LIEUTENANT CECIL PHILCOX MC,
1ST BATTALION SOUTH STAFFORDSHIRE REGIMENT

Cecil Ernest Philcox was born in Lambeth, London in 1895. He was educated at Dulwich College from 1909 to 1912. After completing his education he worked for a timber broker in the City of London. Philcox enlisted to join The Rangers, 12th Battalion London Regiment in September 1914. In February 1915 he transferred to the Inns of Court Officers Training Corps and five months later received a temporary commission with the South Staffordshire Regiment. During June 1916 Philcox was attached to the 1st Battalion South Staffordshire Regiment and sent to France. He first saw action on 1st July 1916 when he took part in the assault upon Mametz. Philcox was in action again within weeks when the 1st South Staffordshires attacked High Wood at 7.00 pm on 15th July. They succeeded in entering the wood, but a strong German counter barrage forced them to withdraw at 11.25 that evening. Woods were difficult positions to hold for the enemy artillery could easily target the position. They would endure trees unearthed and wood splinters as shells exploded. Philcox would be rewarded with a promotion to temporary Lieutenant for his work at High Wood. In November 1916 Philcox was appointed the battalion bombing officer.

Lieutenant Cecil Philcox. (By kind permission of the Governors of Dulwich College)

Philcox took part in the Battle of Bullecourt on 12th May 1917. During the battle, Philcox followed the advance with a telephone and all communication was passed to battalion headquarters through him.

After the battle the battalion was brought behind the lines to Achiet-le-Petit for rest. On 21st May 1917 Philcox was giving instruction in bombing. During a training exercise a Mills bomb exploded prematurely and shrapnel struck Philcox in the head. He died three days later. He was aged 21 and was buried in Achiet-le-Grand Communal Cemetery Extension. Philcox was awarded the Military Cross for conspicuous gallantry and devotion to duty. He did not live to see his award gazetted in the *London Gazette* on 1st June 1917.

PRIVATE HERBERT THOMAS 32669,
21ST BATTALION MANCHESTER REGIMENT

Herbert Austin Thomas was born in 1884. Known as Bert to his family he worked as a commercial traveller prior to the war. He was married and a father of two children when he enlisted in 1916. After completing basic training he was sent to France on 12th December 1916.

He was captured when the 21st Manchester Regiment supported the 2nd Queen's and 1st South Staffordshires at Bullecourt on 12th May 1917. Bert was listed as missing soon after. The Chaplain from the 21st Manchester Regiment wrote to his family saying that during 'a big battle between the 11th and 15th May 1917 … Bert is missing believed killed'. A member of Bert's family wrote:

> We have just received a letter from the chaplain of the 21st Manchester Regt saying that Bert is missing and believed to be killed. We are waiting for official news from the War Office. It seems that Bert was in a big battle which lasted from 11th-15th May and the chaplain's letter was dated 21st so that Bert had been missing for six days at the time the letter was written. We are all exceedingly upset over the suspense and are eagerly awaiting War Office news.[23]

For six months, his family believed that he had been killed. While his family was mourning his loss, Bert was sent to a camp at Gustrow Kriegsgef-Lager, Mecklenburg, where he was put to work building railways. While incarcerated, Bert wrote letters home to confirm that he was safe and well. It was not until November 1917 that his family began to receive his messages. Bert was later sent to a Prisoner of War camp at Gettorf, near Kiel, where he remained for the duration. As the war ended, Thomas and his fellow captives were liberated by German communist sailors who had mutinied against their commanders. In 1947 Bert received a letter from Franz Hoffman enquiring if he remembered his 'old guard from Gettorf':

> My Dear friend,
> After long time I look at the photos I got from my dear English prisoners at Gettorf and Berkenmoor in the year of 1918 and I ask me, if you remember your old guard Hoffmann, who has never forgotten you.
> You were younger than I and I hope you are still alive and well. I'm 73 years old and my force is disappearing, but I am always enjoyed to work little things in my electrical profession.
> Through all the hard years the kindness of God has saved me. My dear wife died in 1940 and now I am alone with my sister who is also a widow of the first war without children.
> It would be a great joy for me to hear from you. I remain with best wishes for a blessed Christmas (please read St John's gospel 3, 16 and 44) and a blessed new year, and with many greetings from all my heart
> > Your old friend
> > Franz Hoffmann'[24]

Bert never replied to Franz's letter. Receiving such a letter thirty years after the war may have been too much for him. Bert had moved on and had become the father of six children. Bert died in 1956.

PRIVATE JOSEPH LAMB 21202,
22ND BATTALION MANCHESTER REGIMENT

Joseph Lamb was born in 1896. Before the war he played football for Newton Heath and was a keen cricketer. His attestation papers on enlistment state that he was employed as a stoker. He enlisted on 7th January 1915 and joined the 22nd Manchester Regiment at the Free Trade Hall in Manchester. After completing basic training he was sent to France towards the end of 1915. On 1st July 1916 Lamb took part in the capture of Mametz. He continued to serve with the battalion through 1916 and in 1917. He took part in

Private Herbert Thomas.
(Courtesy Simon Lamb)

Private Joseph Lamb.
(Courtesy Simon Lamb)

the Battle of Bullecourt on 13th May 1917 and was wounded during the Battle of Broodseinde Ridge on 4th October when the his regiment attacked German positions south of Polygon Wood. Lamb's leg was amputated and he was fitted with an artificial one. He received the Silver War Badge and was discharged from the army as unfit for service. When he was convalescing back home he and fellow soldiers were ridiculed by the grocer's delivery boy, who taunted them saying the crippled soldiers couldn't catch him. Lamb stole the boy's bike. After the war, Lamb returned to the Electric Department Store at Manchester Corporation, where he had worked prior to the war. He died in 1943.

SERGEANT GEORGE BEARDSWORTH 16855,
22ND BATTALION MANCHESTER REGIMENT

George Beardsworth was born in Whittle-le-Woods, Lancashire in 1891. He was one of four sons and six daughters born to James and Annie. James moved his large family to Nelson, Lancashire. His family remembered him as 'a quiet, rather studious young man, who loved books'.[25] George worked with his father James and his brother John as a gardener before the outbreak of war. George enlisted to join the 22nd Manchester Regiment. He become a machine gun instructor and was promoted to Sergeant. Sergeant George Beardsworth was killed on 13th May while preparing to advance with C Company upon the Red Patch. All four Beardsworth boys joined up and served during the war; three returned home. Annie Beardsworth was devastated. Shelagh Cheeseman, his great niece, wrote: 'It is said that his mother was always singing and had a beautiful

voice, but after George was killed, she never sang again'.[26] George Beardsworth was aged 26 when he died. His body was never found and he has no known grave. His name is therefore commemorated on the Arras Memorial.

Sergeant George Beardsworth. (Courtesy Shelagh Cheeseman)

PRIVATE CHARLES KAY 28400, D COY,
22ND BATTALION MANCHESTER REGIMENT

Charles Kay was born in 1895 at Shaw, Oldham. He worked as a spinner in a local cotton factory prior to the war. Kay enlisted in December 1915 at Ladysmith Barracks, Ashton under Lyne. After completing his basic training he was sent to France and assigned to the

Lance Sergeant Charles Kay. (Courtesy Brian Kay)

22nd Manchester Regiment. He first experienced action at High Wood on 16th July 1916. His son Brian recalled: 'I once asked him how far he got into High Wood, he stretched out his arms and with a smile on his face said "that far".

On 24th April 1917 Kay was promoted to Lance Sergeant. At 3.30 am on 13th May 1917 he took part in the Battle of Bullecourt when the 22nd Manchesters tried to capture the Red Patch. On 27th July 1917 he was promoted to Sergeant. The 22nd Manchesters were redeployed to Flanders during the autumn of 1917. On 4th October Kay took part in the Battle of Broodseinde Ridge and was awarded the Military Medal for his role in that action. In November 1917 the 22nd Manchesters were sent to the Italian front where they remained for the duration. When the war ended he spent a few months in Egypt before returning home with the rank of Company Sergeant Major. He returned home to Shaw, where he married Mary Leadbetter in 1921. Kay worked on a farm owned by his father-in-law at Curbar, near Baslow in Derbyshire. He later moved to Compstall, a mill village near Stockport, where in 1925 he opened a news agency business.

During the Second World War Kay served as a Lieutenant with the 38th Cheshire's Home Guard at Compstall. Kay was an enthusiastic member of the platoon. When the platoon was issued with new cup grenades, he dashed 100 yards from the guardroom to his home and within ten minutes he had brought back an original 1916 manual for the weapon. Kay seldom spoke about his First World War experiences, but while he was serving with the Home Guard he did reveal some information to his son Brian: 'He appeared to have been a bomber when in the army and he mentioned how many thousands of mills bombs his mates armed ready for use, their fingers were blistered with constantly arming grenades'.

As a 2nd Lieutenant, Kay would have played a role in supervising the construction of defences in the village of

During World War Two Charles Kay served with the Home Guard. (Courtesy Brian Kay)

Compstall. Brian remembered: 'As a child of seven I could see a trench on the edge of the village heavily laced with barbed wire and one or two machine gun nests around the village (no machine guns)'. Brian recounted another story of his father in the Home Guard:

> Back about 1941 there was a parade in the next village, all four local villages had their platoons there, Dad was there, stood to attention in front of his lot, swagger stick under his arm when I walked on to the parade ground and asked could he buy me an ice cream.

Kay worked for 32 years as a postmaster until 1957 when he suffered a heart attack. He passed away later that year aged 62.

PRIVATE WILLIAM KENDALL 44291,
22ND BATTALION MANCHESTER REGIMENT

William Kendall was born in Tottenham, London in 1880. He worked as a painter prior to the war. He enlisted on 20th September 1914 at a recruiting office in Tottenham with the Royal West Kent Regiment. He was posted to depot where he trained with the 9th Battalion. Kendall was drafted to the 1st Royal West Kent Regiment on 25th May 1915 and sent to France. The 1st Battalion had distinguished itself in the action at Hill 60 during April and Kendall was assigned to the battalion as a replacement. When Kendall joined, the battalion was sent to hold the line near St Eloi. They were deployed on this front for two months and Kendall would experience aggressive German mortar and sniper fire. The battalion was deployed to Carnoy on the Somme sector in August

1915. The five months spent in the trenches at Carnoy were very quiet. On 7th March 1916 Kendall returned to England and was posted at the depot in Maidstone. Three months later Kendall was assigned to the 8th Royal West Kent Regiment and joined that battalion in France on 29th June 1916. The battalion was training in preparation for its role in the Battle of the Somme at Sandpit Camp, Meaulte, near to Albert. On the morning of 10th August the 8th Battalion was ordered to take over the line at Trones Wood. They 'were treated to quite a healthy bombardment on the way in'.[27]

Kendall would have had to dig frantically as deep as he could when the 8th Battalion reached positions east of Trones Wood, to construct a new line under shell fire. The 8th Battalion unit history described the situation on 11th August 1916:

> Such trenches as there were had only just been scratched out, and were mostly not more than a foot deep. From dusk to dawn work by the front companies was continuous. It was a case of digging for our lives, and at stand to in the morning every man had trench room nearly six feet deep. The positions were heavily shelled by the enemy in the morning, and our casualties would have been very heavy had it not been for the strenuous digging of the night before. As it was, very few were hit, and the experience was a very healthy object-lesson to all of us. The unfortunate village of Guillemont in front of us was practically gone. Our shelling was continuous. The Hun did no persistent shelling, but he gave us hurricane bombardments at intervals, which were most unpleasant.[28]

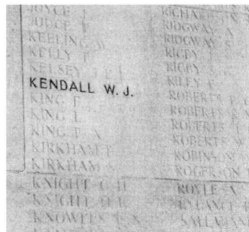

Private William Kendall's death plaque. Families of soldiers who were killed in action and have no known grave received such a plaque, which was known as a 'Dead Man's Penny'. The family of William Kendall has no photo of him so the only remembrance of this fallen soldier is this plaque and the inscription of his name on the Arras Memorial. (Author).

They spent two days in the line and were withdrawn to the rear. The 8th Battalion was sent back to hold the line at Trones Wood on 15th August. Although there was no direct contact with the enemy the battalion would sustain 152 casualties until they came out of the line on 18th August. At Trones Wood Kendall would have helped in recovering the wounded from the attack upon the village of Guillemont:

> Practically every shell-hole in front of us had a corpse or a wounded man in it. All night cries for 'water' were heard. We had large parties out every night, and every soldier in front of us who was not past human assistance was got back.[29]

After a brief period in reserve the 8th Battalion was sent to Delville Wood and Kendall would experience a tough time in trying to reach the front line during the evening of 30th August 1916. The last mile of this journey was carried out in pouring rain, under heavy shell fire and through deep mud, taking 11 hours to complete:

> In the evening we went up to Delville Wood. Will anyone who was with the Battalion ever forget that night? At Bernafay Wood we were to be met by guides, and from there to Inner Trench the distance was about a mile 'as the crow flies'. The men were excessively heavily laden. Each company carried three days' rations, 25 petrol tins of water, 25 boxes of bombs, 12 boxes of flares, 12 boxes of Very Lights, and some boxes of S.A.A. It had rained hard all day, and showed no signs of abating at night. The guides were picked up successfully at 9.30 pm, and the crawl across Caterpillar Valley and through the wood began. Nominally there was a communication trench leading all the way, but there was little or nothing of it left, and the guides could scarcely be expected to keep direction. Delville Wood was notorious for changing its shape and appearance every hour. Details of that terrible night's march are innumerable, and cannot be dwelt on here. Most of them can be recalled by those who were there, and they can be imagined when it is stated that the rain was continuous, the shelling of the wood heavy and incessant, and the mud knee-deep at least. Added to this it should be remembered that the Battalion had already marched ten miles during the day, and the men were loaded up like desert camels.[30]

They were in the front-line trenches at Delville Wood by 8.00 am. They had very little time to settle into their new position, because soon German artillery unleashed a hurricane barrage. This terrible ordeal in Delville Wood would be a precursor to what Kendall would experience at Bullecourt.

It was the day of the enemy's last and biggest attempt to retake the high ground from High Wood to Guillemont. We just had time to have our breakfast of sodden biscuits and cold bacon, when the shelling began, shortly after 8 am. It is not intended to paint lurid details of this shelling. Suffice it to say that Delville Wood went up in fire and smoke for five and a half hours. In Inner Trench was one deep dug-out. In this we kept five machine guns and crews of the 72nd M.G.C., also some of our Lewis guns and teams. The shelling round the dug-out was particularly heavy, but by the grace of God the enemy failed to demolish it. In Edge Trench cover was scanty and the shelling terrific. Most of the forward platoons of A Company were casualties before 10 am, and B Company on the left suffered very severely too.[31]

Kendall survived the bombardment and once it had subsided he and the remnants of the battalion fought off a German infantry assault:

> At 1.30 pm the shelling suddenly and very obviously lifted on to the south edge of the wood. Shelters and dug-outs were immediately cleared, machine guns and Lewis guns were got into position, and our depleted garrison disposed to meet an attack.
>
> Scouts crawled out in front to beyond the edge of the wood to watch a piece of dead ground there. On the right we were in fair order for meeting an attack. We had our machine guns and most of our Lewis guns intact, and quite a fair supply of ammunition. The enemy was some 600 yards away, and was bound to show himself clearly at 500 yards' range. On the left of our position was more difficult, the enemy was much closer, and there was a covered way of approach opposite the front of the Battalion on our left. The men were tremendously eager. After terrific shelling which numbs the senses while it lasts, the reaction often took this form. As the first of the attacking troops began to trickle into view it was difficult to hold our rifle fire down. We kept perfectly silent, however, and, encouraged by this, the enemy came forward in considerable numbers till he arrived at an intermediate jumping-off trench some 500 yards away. Here he collected for half an hour, and word was passed down our line that as soon as he debouched from these positions in force, every rifle, machine gun, and Lewis gun was to open fire. At about 2.30 pm the enemy came forward all along the front, at a slow trot. Immediately all along our line machine guns, Lewis guns, and rifles let fly at him. He was stopped dead within 50 yards of his trenches, while his men fell right and left. For a moment his line wavered, and the next his troops

were running back in a mad rush to their original positions, followed all the way by our fire.[32]

On 23rd January 1917 Kendall was transferred to the 22nd Battalion Manchester Regiment. On 10th March Kendall was incapacitated by diarrhoea and sent to a casualty clearing station for several days to recover. He was fortunate to have missed the battle for Bucquoy on 13th March where 150 men from the battalion were lost. Kendall rejoined the battalion on 17th March and within two weeks it was thrown into the attack upon Croisilles. Private William Kendall's luck would run out by the time he reached Bullecourt. At 3.40 am on 13th May 1917 he was killed as the 22nd Battalion Manchester Regiment launched a futile attack upon the Red Patch at Bullecourt. His body was missing and his name was commemorated on the Arras Memorial.

William Kendall's family has no photo of him. All they have is his death plaque, his name listed on the Arras Memorial and the knowledge that his remains possibly lie in a field south of the village of Bullecourt.

CORPORAL STANLEY VINCE 44510,
20TH and 22ND BATTALION MANCHESTER REGIMENT

Stanley Gilbert Gordon Vince was born in Monks Eleigh, Suffolk in 1895. Prior to the war, Stanley worked as a Clerk in the Packing Room of Henry Poole and Co, tailors in London's Savile Row. Working for a tailor, he was always immaculately dressed.

Stanley enlisted as a private in the Royal Fusiliers (City of London Regiment) on 11th January 1916. He arrived at Etaples in France on 29th June 1916. On 25th October he was transferred to the 20th Battalion Manchester Regiment to replace the heavy casualties suffered during the Somme campaign. At some point he was transferred to the 22nd Manchester Regiment. His service record indicates that he was serving in the field in May 1917, which means that there is a high probability that Vince took part in the battle for Bullecourt either on 4th May or 13th May 1917.

Clive Mabbutt, Stanley's grandson, said that he rarely spoke of the war to the family, but he did mention to his wife being involved in 'hand-to-hand fighting' and 'being buried alive by mud from an exploding shell'.

He served on the Italian front from 13th May 1918. Two years of war on the Western Front and on the Italian Front had severely affected his health, for while on the mountains in Italy Stanley Vince suffered a heart attack. On 30th November 1918 Vince was invalided out of the Army.

He returned to W.H. Poole to work and they paid him double pay. His employer was sent a message confirming that he was suffering from a 'Dilated Heart with Valvular Disease'. Despite suffering from heart

Stanley Vince in 1916, as a Royal Fusilier (*left*). There is a bullet hole in the photo. His grandson Clive was told that his younger brother Sydney, who served with Anson Battalion, Royal Naval Division, carried this photograph in a wallet in his breast pocket of his RNVR uniform. The hole is alleged to have been caused by a bullet that killed him during the battle at Varlet Farm, near Passchendaele on 26th October 1917. Sydney has no known grave and he is commemorated on the Tyne Cot Memorial. Stanley's other brother Alfonso Vince was killed at the Battle of Loos on 25th October 1915. He also has no known grave and his name is commemorated on the Loos Memorial. The photo on the *right* shows Stanley wearing the Manchester Regiment uniform. (Courtesy Clive Mabbutt)

problems, Stanley served as a Special Constable giving nine years unpaid service made up of 50 duties per year. In 1939 he received the Special Constabulary Long Service Medal with bar. When World War Two broke out it is believed that Stanley continued service as a Special Constable because at the end of the war he was awarded The Defence Medal.

From 1929 Stanley Vince owned the Post Office and General Stores in Monks Eleigh with his wife Lillian. In 1952 ill health and further heart problems arising from his World War One service forced him to retire and he moved to Plymouth with his wife and daughter, Doreen. Stanley Vince died in 1969 and was buried in St Budeaux Church, Plymouth.

PRIVATE WALTER CHATTERLEY MM 846,
C COMPANY, 2ND BATTALION ROYAL WARWICKSHIRE REGIMENT

Walter Chatterley was born in 1889 and was brought up in Birmingham. Walter was a regular soldier who

Private Walter Chatterley. (Courtesy Kenneth and Steve Chatterley)

enlisted on 27th September 1909. He was serving in Malta with the 2nd Royal Warwickshire Regiment when war broke out. The battalion was recalled home and arrived in England on 19th September and was assigned to the 22nd Brigade, 7th Division, which was assembling at Lyndhurst in the New Forest. The battalion sailed for France on 6th October, but Chatterley remained in England. Being a regular soldier he was retained to train new recruits to the battalion. Chatterley joined the 2nd Royal Warwickshire's when he arrived in France on 4th May 1915. He held the rank of Sergeant and first saw action at the Battle of Loos on 25th September 1915. It was while the battalion was attacking the German lines at Quarry Trench and the sap called Spurn Head that Walter's friend, Private Arthur Vickers, known as 'Titch', won the Victoria Cross. As they advanced towards the German positions under horrendous machine gun fire, they found that the wire was uncut. Vickers went ahead of his company and in full view of the enemy, used bolt-cutters to cut two gaps in the wire. He was awarded the Victoria Cross and would serve with Chatterley throughout the war.

Chatterley rarely spoke of his First World War experiences to his family. His son remembered that he first mentioned he had fought when he was looking through a copy of *War Illustrated* magazine.

Chatterley fought during the Somme campaign in 1916, taking part in the actions to seize Mametz during the afternoon of 1st July, the attack on Bazentin-le-Petit on 14th July and the assault upon Ginchy on 3rd September. During the following year, Chatterley would see action at Bullecourt in May 1917 and at the Third Ypres campaign towards the end of 1917. It was during the offensive to capture Passchendaele that Chatterley was awarded the Military Medal for 'bravery in the field' during the action at Reutel on 4th October 1917. The

Private Walter Chatterley and Private Arthur 'Titch' Vickers VC. (Courtesy Kenneth and Steve Chatterley)

2nd Royal Warwickshires fought a ferocious battle to capture the German held trenches and woods north of Reutel. Mud clogged the mechanisms of their rifles and they had to resort to the bayonet. The officers from the Battalion were cut down and the remnants were led by NCOs like Walter Chatterley. When Passchendaele ridge was captured the 2nd Royal Warwickshires were deployed to the Italian front on 24th November 1917. Chatterley would take part in some heavy fighting on the Piave. He would end the war serving in Italy.

He was demobbed in 1920 with the rank of Acting Sergeant Major. He had been wounded once. After leaving the Army he worked for Birmingham Corporation. During the Second World War, while digging an air raid shelter, he banged the shovel aggressively in front of his son, as memories of the Great War came back to him. Walter Chatterley died prematurely aged 53 in 1943 from an ulcer.

2ND LIEUTENANT SIMON FRASER,
58TH BATTALION AIF

Simon Fraser was born at Byaduk, Victoria, in 1877. He was the son of James and Mary and later worked as a farmer in Byaduk. He belonged to the Byaduk Rifle Club and served for 13 years with the Victorian Mounted Rifles.

He enlisted on 13th July 1915 aged 38. He was given the rank of private and service number 3101. On 26th November 1915 he boarded the troopship HMAT *Commonwealth* at Melbourne and sailed to Egypt. He held the rank of acting sergeant when he left Australia.

On 23rd February 1916 he was assigned to the 22rd Battalion. He was promoted to Sergeant four days later. On the 11th March he was transferred to the newly established 57th Battalion and trained at Tel-el-kebir. On 17th June Fraser and the battalion were heading for the Western Front boarding HMAT *Kalyan* at Alexandria. They arrived at Marseille on 24th June 1916. On 19th July Fraser took part in the Battle of Fromelles.

He was mentioned in dispatches in the *London Gazette* on 4th January 1917. The citation signed by Brigadier-General H.E. Elliott states:

This N.C.O. has done continuous good work in NO MAN'S LAND during the period 10th July to 20th July, while the battalion has been in the trenches near Sailly. He has shown splendid courage and resource on many occasions setting a very fine example of fearlessness to his

2nd Lieutenant Simon Fraser. (Courtesy Max & Maria Cameron)

Cobbers Memorial at Fromelles. (Author)

men. He was responsible for some very gallant work during the period 19th/23rd July in leading parties into NO MAN'S LAND and rescuing many wounded. His example has been of greatest value to his company.[33]

Fraser was mentioned in Sir Douglas Haig's dispatch on 13th November 1916 for his courage at Fromelles. Fraser's bravery would also be honoured 83 years later when a statue depicting him carrying a wounded comrade was unveiled on 5th July 1998 at Fromelles. An identical statue was unveiled on 20th July 2008 in Melbourne. The statue was sculpted by Peter Corlett and named 'Cobbers'. The statue bears the face of Fraser. He epitomises the many men who went out into No Man's Land at great risk to recover the wounded during the nights of the 20th to the 22nd July. Many soldiers looked for wounded friends. In a letter to his brother Peter, Simon Fraser recalled his actions at Fromelles. '... another man about 30 yards sang out, "Don't forget me, cobber." I went in and got four volunteers with stretchers and we got both men in safely.'[34] Although only 20% of Australians wore the slouched hat at Fromelles the sculpture's wounded Digger tightly holds onto the hat that represents Australia. Peter Corlett's statue originally did not have a personality attached to it, but when he heard of Sergeant Fraser's bravery he sculpted his features upon the memorial. He is depicted carrying a wounded colleague from the 60th Battalion.

By 26th November 1916, the horrors and stresses of life in the trenches of the Western Front was beginning to take their toll on Fraser's health. On 26th November 1916, suffering from exhaustion he was admitted to the 15th Australian Field Ambulance and spent several days in hospital. He left for England on 2nd December 1916 to begin officer training at Balliol College with the cadet Training Battalion. He continued his training at Trinity College, Cambridge.

On 30th March 1917 he was promoted to 2nd Lieutenant and posted to Infantry Reinforcements. On 26th April he was sent back to France. After passing through Etaples he was assigned to the 58th Battalion and joined them on the front line on 30th April 1917.

During the evening on 11th May 1917 while the 58th Battalion was preparing to raid German trenches east of Bullecourt 2nd Lieutenant Fraser was killed when a shell exploded on the parapet of the trench he was occupying. All that was left of him was his arm on the hand of which was a signet ring inscribed with the initials S.F., which allowed identification. Private Thomas Hewitt recalled Fraser's last moments:

> 2nd Lieutenant Fraser was blown to pieces on the 11th of May 1917 in the evening after dark in the Hindenburg Line to the right of Bullecourt. I saw one of his arms just afterwards but do not know what happened to the rest of him as a lot of had been thrown over the place, nor do I know whether he was afterwards found or buried.[35]

Private Ruston Stephenson, 58th Battalion:

> He was killed at Bullecourt by a shell which landed right on the parapet. It wounded quite a number of men, besides killing and burying some, amongst which was Lieut. Fraser. We tried to unearth him but could not an account of the barrage. We only found his arm which was identified by Lieut. Davies as belonging to him by a ring which was on one of his fingers.[36]

He was aged 40. Having no known grave his name is commemorated at the Australian National Memorial at Villers-Bretonneux.

LIEUTENANT RUPERT MOON VC,
58TH BATTALION AIF

Rupert Vance Moon was born in Bacchus Marsh, Victoria in 1892. He was educated at Kyneton Grammar School and completing his education, his father Arthur Moon who was a bank inspector found him a position where he worked as a bank clerk in the National Bank in Melbourne. He served with the 13th Light Horse and 8th Infantry Regiments before the war. Moon enlisted on 21st August 1914. He joined the 4th Light Horse Regiment and was given

Lieutenant Rupert Moon VC. (Australian War Memorial: AWM AO2592)

the rank Trumpeter and service number 153. After completing basic training he was sent to Egypt. He embarked aboard HMAT *Wiltshire* on 19th October 1914 from Melbourne. He arrived in Gallipoli in May 1915 where his unit served as dismounted infantry. He was promoted to Lance Corporal in November and a month later withdrew from the peninsula.

Moon was promoted to Sergeant on 3rd March 1916 while undergoing training in Egypt. He left Alexandria on 10th June 1916 and arrived in Marseille on 17th June. On 9th September 1916 he was transferred to the 58th Battalion and given a commission being promoted to 2nd Lieutenant. He was promoted to Lieutenant on 6th April 1917. Brigadier Pompey Elliott was not impressed by Moon's command abilities. Charles Bean described Moon as 'a slight, modest boy, whom his brigadier, General Elliott, had inclined to regard as too diffident for command.'[37] Lieutenant Moon would prove Elliott wrong and demonstrated his abilities as a courageous commander at Bullecourt. When the 58th Battalion tried to push forward along OG 1 and OG 2 Trenches Moon was engaged in a savage bomb fight as he fought to capture his objective, a German concrete position located between OG 1 and OG 2. In order for the 58th Battalion to achieve all its objectives it was imperative that this German position be captured. The position was held in strength and its German occupants offered determined resistance. During the fight Moon received a wound to his face, but he continued and successfully overwhelmed the position. He then led an attack upon

German positions in OG 2, which was holding up another company from the 58th Battalion. During this attack Moon received a wound to his shoulder which knocked him to the ground and dazed him. While he was in a state of disorientation the momentum of the attack wavered. Moon summoned enough energy to get to his feet and continue the assault on the trench encouraging his men with the words 'Come on, you'll not see me left boys.' His men rallied and followed him in the charge that broke the German resistance. He pursued fleeing Germans who were running to a dugout north of this trench. Sustaining a third wound to his foot he succeeded in overwhelming this position and capturing 184 prisoners and four machine guns. Blood and sweat was pouring from his face. As he and his men were consolidating the position he received a fourth wound when a bullet hit him in the face, fracturing his jaw. Moon was awarded the Victoria Cross for his valour and his citation published in the *London Gazette* on 14th June 1917 records:

> For most conspicuous bravery during an attack on an enemy strongpoint. ... it was only after [his] fourth and severe wound in the face that he consented to retire from the fight. His bravery was magnificent, and was largely instrumental in the successful issue against superior numbers, the safeguarding of the flank of the attack and the capture of many prisoners and machine-guns.[38]

Lieutenant Moon recovered from his wounds and rejoined his battalion on 10th June. On 3rd August 1917 he travelled to London where he attended the investiture ceremony where he received the Victoria Cross from King George V at Buckingham Palace. Moon was sent back to Australia in March 1918, but returned to Europe in May. He was promoted to Captain in February 1919 and returned home to Australia. He was demobilized on 4th October 1919. After serving five years in the AIF, Moon had to adapt to civilian life. He resumed his career in banking for a while, but then worked for an accountancy firm, Dennys Lascelles, based in Geelong. He would become the company's general manager between 1948 until 1959. Rupert Moon died on 28th February 1986.

NOTES

1. National Archives: WO 95/1670: 1st Battalion South Staffordshire Regiment War Diary: Lieutenant Colonel A.B. Beauman's address to the battalion: 10th May 1917.
2. *London Gazette*: Issue 30188: 17th July 1917.
3. National Archives: WO 95/1670: 2nd Battalion Queen's (Royal West Surrey) Regiment: Lieutenant

    R.L. Atkinson, CO B Company Report.
4. National Archives: WO 95/1670: 2nd Battalion Queen's (Royal West Surrey) Regiment: Lieutenant R.L. Atkinson, CO B Company Report.
5. *A Brigadier in France*, Hanway R. Cumming, Jonathan Cape 1922.
6. Ibid.

7. National Archives: WO 95/1670: 1st Battalion South Staffordshire Regiment War Diary: Lieutenant Colonel A.B. Beauman's report: 12th May 1917.
8. *A Brigadier in France*, Hanway R. Cumming, Jonathan Cape 1922.
9. National Archives: WO 95/1664: 2nd Battalion Queen's (Royal West Surrey) Regiment War Diary.
10. 'How the Bullecourt was Won', Max Pemberton, featured in The *War Illustrated*, 8th June 1917.
11. National Archives: WO 95/1670: 2nd Battalion Queen's (Royal West Surrey) Regiment: Lieutenant R.L. Atkinson, CO B Company Report.
12. National Archives: 91st Brigade War Diary: WO 95/1667.
13. National Archives: 91st Brigade War Diary: WO 95/1667.
14. 'How the Bullecourt was Won'.
15. Ibid.
16. National Archives: WO 95/1661: 22nd Brigade War Diary.
17. Ibid.
18. National Archives: WO 95/1661: 22nd Brigade War Dairy.
19. *London Gazette*: 18th July 1917.
20. *London Gazette*: 30023: 4th April 1917.
21. Sportsmen Parsons in Peace and War by Mrs. S.
Menzies, Hutchinson and Co. London.
22. A Hero Saint compiled by the Rev. Gerald Sampson.
23. Private Herbert Thomas papers, courtesy Simon Lamb.
24. Ibid.
25. Courtesy Shelagh Cheeseman, great niece.
26. Ibid.
27. *The History of the Eighth Battalion the Queen's Own Royal West Kent Regiment 1914–1919*, 1921.
28. Ibid.
29. Ibid.
30. Ibid.
31. Ibid.
32. Ibid.
33. *London Gazette* 29890: 4th January 1917.
34. *Don't Forget Me Cobber*, Robin S. Corfield: Published Corfield and Company 2000.
35. Australian War Memorial: AWM 1DRL428/00013: Australian Red Cross Missing File: 2nd Lieutenant Simon Fraser.
36. Ibid.
37. The Official History of Australia in the War of 1914–18, Volume IV, C.E.W. Bean, Angus and Robertson Ltd 1938.
38. *London Gazette*: Issue 30130: 14th June 1917.

CHAPTER 28

AUSTRALIANS AND LONDONERS HOLD THE LINE: 14TH–17TH MAY 1917

As the battle for Bullecourt continued into the third week of May 1917 General Otto von Moser and the soldiers under his command were being worn down. General Otto von Below was appointed German 6th Army Commander and he was anxious to drive British and Australian forces back and assert his authority in his new command. Suffering heavy casualties after launching successive counter attacks with very little impact, General Otto von Moser became despondent at losing so many high calibre storm troops. The German 3rd Guard Division had arrived in the Bullecourt sector during the second week of May. General von Moser wanted to initiate an attack using these fresh troops, but was restrained and told to wait until Germany artillery units had stockpiled enough shells to launch an effective and substantial preliminary artillery barrage.

As they waited for supplies of ammunition, General von Below orchestrated a carefully planned attempt to regain the Hindenburg Line. He deployed two battalions of the 91st Lehr Regiment, a training regiment, to drive out the British and Australian battalions holding the line and then the 91st Reserve Infantry Regiment would consolidate the recaptured ground. It was codenamed Operation Potsdam.

By 14th May 1917, the only Australians in the line were the 54th Battalion from the 5th Australian Division, holding positions to the right of the Central Road. The Battalion was commanded by Lieutenant Colonel Stephen Midgley DSO and was made up of men from New South Wales. They had a difficult time in reaching the line owing to the German barrage that day, but they had relieved the 23rd Battalion and were in control of the captured portions of the Hindenburg Line by 3 am.

The British 173rd Brigade commanded by Brigadier General B.C. Freyberg VC had relieved the Australian 15th Brigade commanded by 'Pompey' Elliott during the night of 12th/13th May. The 2nd/3rd London Regiment, The Royal Fusiliers, a unit with very little combat experience, continued the line to the left of the

Australian 54th Battalion, west of the Central Road. The battalion's commander was Lieutenant Colonel Percy William Beresford, who was affectionately known as 'the Reverend'. He had been the Assistant Priest at St Mary's Church in Westerham, Kent, prior to the war. It was unusual for a man of the cloth to take up arms and lead a battalion in battle. Beresford was regarded as 'the pocket Napoleon' because he was a small man; he was a strict disciplinarian who improved morale when he took command. His leadership would play an important role in ensuring that the British and Australian line held at Bullecourt.

Company commanders and intelligence officers with their platoon sergeants from the 2nd/4th London Regiment had been sent during the afternoon of 12th May to front-line trenches held by the 15th Australian Brigade to appraise the situation before the battalion arrived. Captain F. Clive Grimwade wrote:

> The air was oppressive with the heat of a premature burst of summer weather; the stench from hundreds of unburied bodies and the ominous silence of the guns prior to the attack which was to be renewed the following day caused the whole atmosphere to be heavy with the presage of hard fighting to come.[1]

60,000 high explosive shells were fired into British and Australian positions as German infantry units massed on the front line. Private Hubert Hobbs from the 2nd/3rd London Regiment entered the line under this heavy shelling:

> We had now left the long roads of poplars behind and were in the land of sunken roads. Now one or two shells were coming over. It was a nightmare and the stunted trees on the top of the banks looked ghastly – shell torn and twisted. Then it was into the trenches. Shells now came thick and fast. We progressed up the line in a succession of tumbles and falls – something like walking the plank.[2]

Trench Mortar Team at Bullecourt. (Australian War Memorial: AWM E00457)

Many casualties were incurred during the barrage. The 2nd/4th London Regiment entered the line with battalion strength of 418 men on the night of the 12th/13th May, but when they left the line days later they had lost 289 to artillery.[3] The 2nd/4th London Regiment tried to get settled into their positions west of the Central Road as the shells fell. Lieutenant Colonel W.A. Nunneley, at the time second in command of the 2nd/4th London Regiment, recorded that 'the men were magnificent in spite of the heavy shelling.'[4] Communication by power buzzer was severed by the barrage and reliance was placed upon battalion runners. Stretcher bearers were among the casualties and Australian stretcher bearers had to assist. Lieutenant Colonel W.A. Nunneley: 'Casualties in the 2/4th Regt. include 28 stretcher bearers, and

Australian stretcher bearers were brought up to make good this wastage. Their work earned the warm praise of the Londoners.'[5] During 14th May riflemen from the 2nd/4th London Regiment established contact with a wounded Australian soldier who had been lying in between the front and support trenches for four days while the German guns were shelling. He was found in a state of near unconsciousness, badly wounded and so desperate for nourishment he was licking the insides of an empty bully beef tin. After dusk the barrage subsided on the front line but was diverted to rear lines and villages, gas shells were zeroed on allied guns.

A German barrage at 1.20 am presaged the German attack. German parties tried to enter trenches held by the 2nd/4th London Regiment at 4.00 am. Twelve

Map of positions of the 2nd/4th Battalion London Regiment (Royal Fusiliers) at Bullecourt in May and June 1917. ('The War History of the 4th Battalion The London Regiment (Royal Fusiliers) 1914–1919' by Captain F. Clive Grimwade)

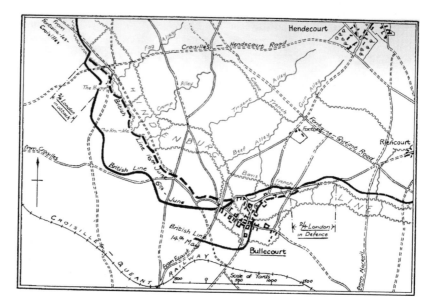

German parties armed with machine guns made a spirited attack upon C Company's sector. These patrols were sent to probe and test the defences before the major assault. C Company was commanded by Captain George Leake and these patrols were repelled. 2nd Lieutenant S.G. Askham saw Leake's reaction:

> We were inspecting the sentry posts and our attention was drawn to considerable movement near our front line. Without a moment's hesitation Capt. Leake leapt over the parapet and in a few seconds we heard revolver shots being fired. He had single-handed attacked a German machine-gun team who were on the point of establishing a post in a position overlooking the whole of our front line. He killed four of the team and the remainder were wounded by our rifle fire. Leake returned with three prisoners and their machine-gun, which he also secured ... Leake was a tower of strength to both officers and men in the Company and we all felt that he richly deserved the V.C., for which he was afterwards recommended.[6]

Lieutenant Colonel W.A. Nunneley recorded in the battalion war diary: 'about 4 am 12 bosche with a machine gun attacked C Coy; bosche all wiped out. Captain Leake shot two and captured machine gun, three bosche were taken prisoner but were killed by their own shell fire while going down our trenches.'[7]

Captain George Leake returned to his Company Headquarters, but was badly wounded when a shell struck the headquarters wounding Captain Long, 2nd in command of C Company and several other Company staff. Leake was placed on a stretcher and as he was being evacuated to an aid station a shell burst killed the two stretcher bearers. Leake was taken to hospital in Rouen. The former Headmaster of Taplow Church of England School in Buckinghamshire was recommended for a Victoria Cross by Lieutenant Colonel Dann for this action but received the Distinguished Service Order. Leake died of his wounds on 2nd June 1917 at Rouen and never lived to know that he had received this award. His citation recorded:

> For conspicuous gallantry and devotion to duty when in command of his company. He showed a splendid example of coolness, disregard of danger, and cheerfulness, and, although wounded, he remained at duty. It was largely owing to his influence that all ranks showed such a splendid spirit under the most intense hostile barrage which lasted for 14 hours.[8]

The 2nd/2nd London Regiment supported the 2nd/4th Battalion London Regiment. An unknown Captain from the 2nd/2nd Battalion later recalled the difficulties of bringing supplies to the front line under the savage German artillery bombardment:

> 'A' company's position was a thousand yards behind the front line trenches. At 2pm the enemy began to subject the whole area to an intense bombardment which lasted more than thirteen hours.
>
> In the middle of the bombardment (which was described by the G.O.C.-in-Chief as 'the most intense bombardment British troops had had to withstand'), No.3 platoon of 'A' company was ordered to proceed to the front line with bombs for the battalion holding it. The platoon consisted of 31 N.C.O.s and men and one officer.
>
> The only means of communication between the support and front lines was a trench of an average depth of two feet. Along this trench the platoon proceeded, carrying between them forty boxes of Mills bombs. Every few yards there were deep shell holes to cross; tangled telephone wires tripped the men; M.G. bullets swept across the trench, and heavy shells obtained direct hits frequently, while shrapnel burst overhead without cessation.
>
> A man was hit every few minutes; those nearest him rendered what aid was possible, unless he was already dead; his bombs were carried on by another.
>
> Of the thirty-one who started, twenty-one were killed or wounded; the remainder, having taken an hour and a half to cover the 1,000 yards, reached the front line with the forty boxes of bombs intact.
>
> They were ordered to remain, and thus found themselves assisting in repulsing an attack made by the 3rd Lehr Regiment of Prussian Guards, and two of the men succeeded in wounded and capturing the commanding officer of the attacking regiment.
>
> Of the ten N.C.O.s and men who were left, a lance-corporal was blown to pieces in the trench; the remainder stayed in the front line until they were relieved four days later.[9]

By the morning of the 15th, the 54th Battalion AIF held OG 2 east of the Central Road. The 2nd/4th London Regiment held OG 2 west of the Central Road and the 2nd/3rd London Regiment was on their left flank. The 20th Manchesters, 2nd Honourable Artillery Company and the Royal Welch Fusiliers were holding out amongst the ruins of Bullecourt.

On 15th May the German barrages intensified. This strengthening of the bombardment signalled the launch of the last German counter attack on this sector. The shelling began with mortar fire at 1.00 am aimed at levelling forward trenches and was intensified at 2.45 am by German heavy artillery and machine gun fire between Bullecourt and Riencourt. Lewis gun positions were buried or destroyed by shell fire and the reserve supply of Mills bombs was blown up.

2nd Lieutenant Charles Depinna from the 2nd/3rd London Regiment noted that the German artillery fire had lifted from his trench, so he ordered his men up from under cover. In his words: 'I visualised, when the bombardment ended after three days, that we were going to be attacked, and I was right. I got all my men out, lining the trench, waiting for the attack to start.'[10] The 54th Battalion war diary:

> During the early morning our front line and support trenches were subjected to a heavy bombardment from enemy artillery, also their minenwerfer and pineapple bombs. 'C' Company, at that time commanded by Captain A.G. Morris, came in for a severe gruelling, being in a part of the Hindenburg Line where the trenches were badly knocked about. 'B' Company, who were in support in the rear with two platoons on sunken road, fared even worse, and our casualties were unfortunately heavy.[11]

Company Sergeant Major Patrick Mealey was among those killed from B Company, 54th Battalion. He had previously earned the Military Medal for holding back German counter attacks at Fromelles on 19th July 1916. A piece of shrapnel pierced him near to his heart. As he lay dying he was giving instructions to a Sergeant on how to continue the defence. He also passed over personal possessions that he wanted sent to his wife.

Captain Alfred Morris, 54th Battalion, would win a bar to the Military Cross he had earned the previous year at Fromelles. As the shells poured down onto his

2nd Lieutenant D.J. Aron's Platoon & B Company, 2nd/3rd London Regiment in 1915. (Courtesy Hugh Hall)

position and the casualty list amongst his Company grew longer, he held on. His recommendation for the bar to his Military Cross:

> Captain Morris' position was in the most exposed position in that part of the line. The trenches were practically obliterated and the casualties many. Captain Morris, by his example of courage and devotion so inspired his men as to enable them to hold on to the position. In doing this Captain Morris was himself wounded and his Company so reduced in numbers as to only muster 17 after the attack had been repulsed.[12]

At 3.45 am Operation Potsdam was launched. German infantry from the II and III LIR leapt from their positions and headed towards the British lines. British mortars and machine guns opened fire. At 4.15 am Major Charles Stuart Lecky wrote the following message, but it was not received by Lieutenant Colonel Midgley until 6.45 am: 'Enemy is attacking all along the line. Situation at present is doubtful as our right company was wiped out previous to the attack.'[13]

Midgley would not have known that the German Lehr Regiment was descending en masse on the 54th Battalion's fragile position. Taking into account the severity of the German bombardment and having received this message two and half hours after it was written, Midgely immediately requested from 14th Brigade Headquarters reinforcements. As the morning progressed the Lehr Regiment had broken through on the 54th Battalion's right flank. Midgley received further desperate messages at 7.30 am from Captain Morris: 'Germans massing in trench on our right flank. Send up reinforcements immediately. We are expecting them over any minute. Get artillery barrage on at once.'[14]

2nd Lieutenant Charles Depinna from No.10 Platoon, C Company had found an uncompleted German dug-

out in his section and was able to send his men into this shelter to protect them from the shells. Private William Duhigh and Private Frank Dibley did not want to enter the claustrophobic underground confines of this dug-out and opted to stay above ground. A shell killed both of them.

Some Germans from the 91st Regiment (2nd Guard Reserve Division) managed to get into the trenches held by the 2nd/3rd London Regiment but they were soon repulsed. 2nd Lieutenant Charles Depinna:

> When they came over, we mowed them down like skittles, thank God. One sight I shall never forget was seeing about two or three men come over with flame throwers. I don't know what caught them alight, but evidently our fire was so terrific, it must have punctured something. These men were rolling around in No Man's Land covered in flames – the flames going about 12 to 15 feet in the air. Their bodies were alight and you may be surprised to know – and, looking back on it, it is not very pretty to say – but we laughed, naturally we laughed! Perhaps – we will be forgiven for laughing?[15]

Private Hubert Hobbs recorded in his diary his role on 15th May:

> I got up beside the Lewis gun chaps and lay on my face with rifle ready. Bullets whistled through the air with a continual 'sloh-e-or' and background shrapnel like the wind in telegraph wires. I enjoyed myself. I felt quite cold and callous and fired as if I was tapping a typewriter. We could see the field-grey uniforms gradually getting more definite in the morning half-light. Slowly they appeared to come, hesitating, stopping every now and then to take shelter. The thunder of our guns was terrific while sections of enemy trench seemed to vanish in smoke with objects too grim to describe, flung in mid-air – so accurate was our artillery fire that we could imagine nothing getting through. The battle continued for three hours. All we could do was fire and fetch new ammo as required. It was getting hot and sweltering and we had to go through a labyrinth of trenches blown to pieces, with a heavy box of 303 ammo. Anyone who has ever carried a box of 303 cartridges will realise what a game it is with a Lewis gun ammo over one shoulder, a rifle and all the other attachments.[16]

Living amongst rubble amongst the corpses of dead comrades and horses, fighting thirst and hunger in the heat, anxiously awaiting the next bombardment – that was the hell of the second battle of Bullecourt. Private Walter King from the 2nd / 2nd London Regiment described his feelings in a letter to his brother Alf written on 22nd May:

> It was real hell. Fritz put up a bombardment on our trenches that the boys will never forget. For thirty hours we laid in the bottom of the trenches awaiting our end. Here and there our trenches were going up and our boys blown to pieces. I lay there thinking of all at home, and with a wonderful spirit, and wondering if ever I should be spared to tell the tale. I could not have stuck it much longer. My nerves were beginning to give way. Officers and men were continually going out with shell shock. It was terrible and I shall never forget the ghastly sights of it all, and the stench of the dead was terrible. The consolation Boy, for which we have had great pride, is we held the line against it all. Fritz came over in massed formation and got a terrible thrashing, leaving the dead rows deep.[17]

With the increased intensity of the German barrage, the Australian guns responded. The Germans were targeting Australian batteries in the village of Noreuil. At 4.30 am Lieutenant Colonel Nunnerley reported that the 3rd Prussian Guard attacked trenches held by the 2nd/4th London Regiment and they were 'hopelessly beaten suffering tremendous casualties.'[18]

By 6.30 am a German party from the Lehr Regiment (3rd Guard Division) succeeded in capturing 150 yards of the front-line trenches held by the 54th AIF Battalion. The Australians requested support from the 2nd/3rd London Regiment to drive the Germans out. Lieutenant Donald McArthur had assumed control of the remnants of C Company, 54th Battalion when his commanding officer an all the NCOs became casualties. Commanding from the front trench he was in the thick of the battle.

"Something in the City"

58th London Division illustration. (The Bystander 1917)

Shell found near Digger Memorial during July 2001. The 2nd/4th London Regiment position in May 1917 was close to where the Digger Memorial stands. (Author)

In a dispatch to Midgley he reported that 'The Londons are helping me to hold the line.'[19] 2nd Lieutenant Charles Depinna was sent with a detachment from C Company to support the Australian lines:

> I was told that the Germans had penetrated the Australian trenches, and would we take over their line so that they could get rid of them — which, of course, I did instantly. I sent practically all my men into the Australian trenches and held the line, while they actually got out on to the parapet, and then killed all the Germans that had entered their trenches. We, in turn, held the front while this was being done.[20]

Depinna described the actions of Wilfred Hall and his Company:

> The moment his Lewis gun jammed, he mounted the parapet and started bombing the Germans in the open as if it was a football match, you might say, regardless of the danger to himself. [21]

The Lehr Regiment was dispersed by the accuracy of bomb throwing and precision shooting. 'The enemy losses were exceptionally severe and many dead were left in our trenches and in no-man's-land.'[22] Private Hobbs described the scene. 'Jerries were strewn over No Man's Land in hundreds. One man was shot dead as he was kneeling to take aim and remained in that position. Several continued to fire at this object thinking it was still alive.'[23]

The soldiers from the 54th Battalion appreciated the efforts of Deppina and the men from London. Although the German onslaught had been stopped, German artillery continued to fire. At 10 am a shell struck the regimental aid post near the sunken road where Captain Charles Leedham was tending to the wounded. The shell killed one of his medical team and wounded him. Leedham continued with his work.

Reinforcements from the 55th Battalion AIF arrived and were in position by 11 am. By then the 2nd/3rd London Regiment had lost one officer, 2nd Lieutenant Wilfred Hall, and 23 men killed. Captain Thompson the Medical Officer and 51 other ranks were wounded and eight were listed as missing.

Beresford was awarded the Distinguished Service Order. Captain George Harold Edwards, commanding C Company, 2nd/3rd London Regiment, was awarded the Military Cross. 'Owing to heavy casualties during a bombardment, he had continually to reorganise his unit. His personal example and ability as a leader had a splendid effect upon his men and enabled them to repulse a counter attack and hold on to their position.'[24]

The 54th Battalion war diary records 61 men killed and 201 wounded, including four officers, and 11 missing. It was a very bad day for the Lehr Infantry Regiment as well. Their casualties amounted to four officers and 75 other ranks killed; 298 wounded and 64 missing, a total of 441. The exhausted 7th Division had lost ground in Bullecourt but recaptured their positions. Many casualties were inflicted by the German bombardment that day with the 14th AIF Brigade losing 400 men and the 173rd Brigade losing 300.

Although British and Australian Battalions lost many men, they had resisted with great determination and defiance a well-planned German initiative to drive them out. Captured German prisoners expressed their surprise at the level of resistance they had encountered. The 54th Battalion War Diary observes that they had entered the battle confident of victory:

> The prisoners stated that our resistance was quite unexpected. They found themselves surrounded by our fire and were severely handled. The morale had been severely shaken, first because the Lehr Regiment, being a crack regiment, had not expected to be as severely handled; secondly the attack had been so carefully planned no one ever supposed it could be a failure and the casualties had been so extraordinarily large. The Regiment had lost 50 per cent of its effectiveness.[25]

After the failure of Operation Potsdam, *Generalleutnant* von Moser, commanding XIV Reserve Corps, told his superiors that any further attempts to recapture the Hindenburg Line trenches were futile, the cost in casualties was too high and recommended that the operation be abandoned. General von Below gave the order to withdraw from the Bullecourt sector. German engineers were sent in to destroy dug-outs and fortified positions in their possession during the evening of 16th May.

LIEUTENANT COLONEL PERCY BERESFORD, COMMANDING OFFICER
2ND/3RD (CITY OF LONDON) BATTALION, THE LONDON REGIMENT (ROYAL FUSILIERS)

Percy William Beresford was born in Brentford in 1875. After graduating from Oxford he worked for the family business. In 1902 Beresford moved to Westerham, Kent. Soon after, Percy decided to train for the priesthood. While training, Percy became actively involved in the community in Westerham and played a prominent role in establishing the Westerham and Chipstead Cadet Corps. 4th Bn. The Queen's Own Royal West Kent Regt. 1st Cadets, Kent, in 1904. Beresford cared for the well-being of the young men of the town and became an inspirational role model. He was ordained in 1905 in Rochester and appointed the curate of St Mary's Church, Westerham. Beresford also served as an officer in the Territorial Army. When war broke out he was called to serve with the London Regiment in 1914. He first served in Malta before being sent to France in 1915. Beresford took part in the Battle of Neuve Chapelle in March 1915 and was wounded.

After recovering Beresford was appointed commanding officer of the 2nd/3rd London Regiment, a unit which had very little combat experience. Beresford was affectionately known as 'the Reverend' by those under his command. In May 1917 Beresford led his battalion into the line at Bullecourt to the left of the Australian 54th Battalion, west of the Central Road. His leadership would play an important role in ensuring that the line held.

Beresford was awarded the Distinguished Service Order. His citation stated:

> For conspicuous gallantry and ability in command of his battalion during heavy enemy counter attacks. The skill with which he handled his reserves was of the utmost assistance to the division on his right and his determination enabled us to hold on to an impossible position. He repulsed three counter attacks and lost heavily in doing so.[26]

Beresford died of his wounds on 26th October 1917 during the Third Ypres campaign, aged 42. He was buried at Gwalia Cemetery, Belgium.

Lieutenant Colonel Percy Beresford. (Courtesy Jean & Denise Letaille Bullecourt Museum)

2ND LIEUTENANT HUGH WILFRED HALL,
2ND/3RD (CITY OF LONDON) BATTALION, THE LONDON REGIMENT (ROYAL FUSILIERS)

Hugh Wilfred Hall was born in 1894 in Durban, South Africa. Known by his family as Wilfred, he spent his early childhood on a farm in the Eastern Transvaal. He was sent to England for his education at Framlingham College, Suffolk. In 1908 he returned to South Africa to continue his education at Potchefstroom College. During the four years that he spent at Potchefstroom College Wilfred excelled at sports, including cricket and soccer.

In 1914 he enlisted to join the 1st Imperial Light Horse and served in German South West Africa during 1915. Wilfred was keen to serve on the Western Front, so during January 1916 he embarked aboard the *Walmer Castle*, bound for England. On 12th February Wilfred joined the Inns of Court Officers Training Corps, a unit established by London universities to prepare undergraduates for military service.

After completing four months training Wilfred Hall and Bob Lovemore were commissioned on 24th June 1916 into the 3rd Battalion, The London Regiment. After serving a few months with this unit, they were transferred to the 2nd/3rd Battalion, The London Regiment, a Territorial Force Battalion.

Wilfred would share command of a platoon with 2nd Lieutenant David Aron. Hall's desire to serve on the Western Front in France was to be fulfilled when the battalion received orders to deploy to France. Hall and the 2nd/3rd Battalion embarked aboard HMT *Viper* and HMT *Sidpar* on 22nd January 1917 from Southampton and sailed to Le Havre.

Hall belonged to B Company. They went into the line for the first time near Blaireville south west of Arras. They were assigned to the 1st/5th King's Own Yorkshire Light Infantry. Hall sustained a flesh wound to his hip on 4th February. Despite his wound he remained on the front line. During March the battalion followed the German withdrawal to the Hindenburg Line. During April and early May they were held in reserve at Achiet-le-Grand with battalions from the 173rd Brigade. On 11th May 1917 the 173rd Brigade was ordered to relieve the 15th Australian Brigade holding trenches east of Bullecourt. Around midday on 12th May Hall began the

2nd Lieutenant Hugh Wilfred Hall. (Courtesy Hugh Hall)

10-mile march towards the line. While they were being held being in reserve, they had been within earshot of the battle ensuing at Bullecourt April and May. They arrived at the village of Vaulx-Vraucourt before dusk, then waited for darkness to cover their advance to the front line. They were greeted by German shelling as they headed towards the trenches. Before reaching the front line the 2nd/3rd London Regiment sustained 80 casualties. 2nd Lieutenant Charles Depinna:

> We naturally knew that we were going to a very hot spot. Not only that, we were not very impressed by the fact that the Australians, whom we were relieving, came out shattered after their ordeal. I had never seen such a thing in my life before – I hope I never see it again – but many of them were crying as they were so shell-shocked. It was a dreadful sight to see these poor, battered, brave men come through in this terrible state.[27]

The defences were not completed and the soldiers from London did not have much cover to protect them from the German barrages. According to Walter Knight, a friend of Wilfred's, while the German shells were falling onto their positions Wilfred made great efforts to lift the morale of the men under his command.

At 3.45 am German infantry from the II and III LIR leapt from their positions and headed towards the British lines. British mortars and machine guns opened up. When the enemy came in sight Hall grabbed one of the Lewis machine guns, which had not been damaged by the German shell fire. He soon discovered that the gun was jammed. Unperturbed, he reached for a bag of hand grenades, mounted the parapet and began to throw them towards the advancing German infantry. Hall helped to counter this attack by holding off the advance until he was hit by a bullet which killed him. 2nd Lieutenant Charles Depinna, who was 2nd Lieutenant David Aron's cousin, and also a close friend of Wilfred's later reflected:

> He could throw a cricket ball twice as far as I could, and many of the bombs must absolutely have surprised the Germans. He must have killed quite a lot, but suddenly he was hit by a stray bullet. I always say it was not a sniper's bullet at all. Stray bullets were the most dangerous.[28]

Captain Henry Hay, commanding B Company, saw Wilfred Hall fall to the ground, and was able to speak a few words to him before he succumbed to his wound. 2nd Lieutenant Wilfred Hall was buried by Padre Whytehead the following day. His grave was marked by a small cross, but the position of this grave was later lost. His name was therefore commemorated on the Arras Memorial.

PRIVATE CHARLES HUNT 282622
2ND/4TH BATTALION LONDON REGIMENT ROYAL FUSILIERS

Charles Edward Hunt was born in Marylebone, London in 1882. He was one of three sons born to Charles and Annie Slate. Charles's father died in 1895 and Annie and her three sons moved to Spencer Street, Clerkenwell where they lived with William Hunt. William and Annie became close and they bore a daughter Lillian in 1896. Annie and her sons took the surname Hunt. Charles stepfather William was a regular soldier who had served in the Zulu War.

By 1901 Charles Hunt was working as a cabman and by 1911 as a painter. He enlisted in Whitehall in 1916. He was assigned to the 2nd /4th London Regiment, Royal Fusiliers. On 23rd January 1917 Private Charles Hunt and the battalion arrived in Havre, France. He was killed at Bullecourt on 14th May when German artillery bombarded the British-held sections of the Hindenburg Line. He has no known grave and his name is commemorated on the Arras Memorial. This was a terrible tragedy for his mother Annie. She was already grieving for the loss of her partner William, who enlisted in 1914 aged 54 and who after serving on the North Indian frontier in 1916, was discharged unfit for medical service on 10th May 1917 and died of TB on 11th May, three days before Charles was killed at Bullecourt. Months later her home was destroyed by a German Gotha bombing raid. Annie had lost her partner, her son and her home.

Private Charles Hunt.
(Courtesy David Lane)

Private Charles Hunt (marked x) with comrades from the 2nd/4th Battalion London Regiment who fought at Bullecourt in 1917. (Courtesy David Lane)

PRIVATE HUBERT HOBBS,
2ND/3RD (CITY OF LONDON) BATTALION, THE LONDON REGIMENT (ROYAL FUSILIERS)

Hubert Harold Hobbs was born in Margate in 1894. He was educated at Salmestone School in Margate. On completing his education he worked as a clerk/typist. He then worked for Leonard Hill Solicitors and spent sixteen months working for Leonard Roger Auctioneers in Cliftonville.

Hobbs was called up for active service on 21st January 1916 and joined the 2nd/3rd

Private Hubert Hobbs.
(Courtesy Jack Hobbs)

Battalion London Regiment. Hobbs saw action on the Somme, at Bullecourt and in the Ypres Salient. He was captured at St. Quentin in 1918 and was a POW for the duration. He was demobbed on 25th September 1919. The war did have a long-lasting effect. His son Jack recalled 'My mother used to say that he suffered nightmares in the early years of the marriage.'

After the war Hubert Hobbs was employed as a Civil Service clerical officer. He worked for The Stationary Office, the Department of Overseas Trade and then he transferred to the Board of Trade. Hubert Hobbs died of heart failure at his home in West Norwood on 29th May 1957 aged 63.

Number 1 Platoon, 2nd/3rd Battalion London Regiment. Private Hubert Hobbs is seated front row, third from left, wearing spectacles. (Courtesy Jack Hobbs)

NOTES

1. The War History of the 4th Battalion The London Regiment (Royal Fusiliers) 1914–1919, 1922.
2. Liddle Collection: Private Hubert Hobbs Diary.
3. *Reveille*, 29th May 1931, p10.
4. National Archives: WO 95/3001: 2nd/4th London Regiment War Diary.
5. *Reveille*, 29th May 1931, p10.
6. The War History of the 4th Battalion The London Regiment (Royal Fusiliers) 1914–1919, 1922.
7. National Archives: WO 95/3001: 2nd/4th Battalion London Regiment War Diary.
8. *London Gazette*: 26th July 1917.
9. The Best 500 Cockney War Stories.
10. 2nd Lieutenant Wilfred Hall papers: Courtesy Hugh Hall.
11. National Archives: WO 95/3629: 54th Battalion AIF War Diary.
12. Australian War Memorial: AWM28/1/273/0015: Captain Alfred Morris bar to MC recommendation.
13. National Archives: WO 95/3629: 54th Battalion AIF War Diary.
14. Ibid.

15. 2nd Lieutenant Wilfred Hall papers: Courtesy Hugh Hall.
16. Liddle Collection: Private Hubert Hobbs diary.
17. Imperial War Museum Department of Documents: IWM Ref: 89/7/1) Private Walter King, 2nd/2nd London Regiment Private King was killed in action on 16th June 1917).
18. National Archives: WO 95/3001: 2nd/4th Battalion London Regiment War Diary.
19. National Archives: WO 95/3629: 54th Battalion AIF War Diary.
20. 2nd Lieutenant Wilfred Hall papers: Courtesy Hugh Hall.
21. Ibid.
22. National Archives: 54th Battalion AIF War Diary.
23. Liddle Collection: Private Hubert Hobbs diary.
24. The *London Gazette*: Issue 30188: 17th July 1917.
25. National Archives: WO 95/3629: 54th Battalion AIF War Diary.
26. The *London Gazette*: Issue 30188: 17th July 1917.
27. 2nd Lieutenant Wilfred Hall papers: Courtesy Hugh Hall.
28. Ibid.

CHAPTER 29

THE POST OFFICE RIFLES ENTER THE CAULDRON

The 2/8th London Regiment, known as the Post Office Rifles, entered the line on the night of 15th/16th May 1917. This battalion had been raised in September 1914 from men working for the Post Office. The battalion trained during the first three years and supplied drafts to the 1st/8th London Battalion serving in France. The Post Office Rifles commanded by Lieutenant Colonel P.J. Preece, with Major E de Vesian second in command and Lieutenant H.W. Priestley as adjutant, sailed from Southampton for Havre, France aboard SS *Huntscraft* on 27th January 1917 and received training in the line in the Arras region. At Bullecourt they were ordered to attack the village and clear the German occupants together with the 2nd/5th London Rifle Brigade.

Private James Moddrel belonged to the 2nd/5th London Rifle Brigade. He was 18 years old and was batman to Lieutenant Herbert Wilkinson when he entered the line at Bullecourt:

We heard lots of stories from the men who had come out of the line as to the terrible nature of the fighting going on around the place. Bullecourt had been given the gruesome nickname 'The Blood Tub'. This was to be the battalion's first real battle in its history. We moved up from Mory to Ecoust – constant flashing and noise of the guns, the continuous moving to the side of the road to allow artillery wagons to go by, the difficulty of keeping up with one's own party in the growing darkness. At Ecoust, there were three odours mixed in the air, first the smell of cordite, second the several kinds of gas, third and the worst of all, the smell of dead horses and men. We were all going up to Bullecourt Avenue. It is impossible to give an adequate description of the piece of ground – there was only one place I ever saw in France that was worse. The ground was literally covered with dead ... At night the German Very lights served to keep us from going into the line. They also served another purpose, which was to show us that wherever we went, the ground was still covered with dead ... This No Man's Land was like the popular conception of a

battlefield, every inch of the place had been shelled and a good many inches were covered with things that had once been human bodies but which were now unrecognisable among the mud and litter. Once we had to stop when a shell burst and I looked down to find myself nearly treading on a poor fellow who had had his legs and the lower part of his body blown right away. At the time this did not affect me but I have many times remembered his white face and sightless eyes and wished fervently that I could forget them.[1]

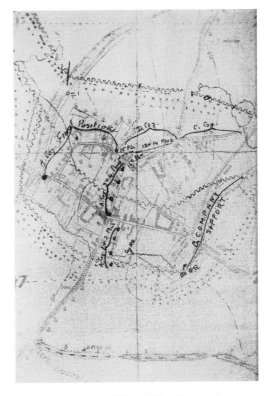

Position of the Post Office Rifles Companies during 15th/16th May. (National Archives: WO 95/3002 174th Brigade War Diary)

The 2nd/5th London Rifle Brigade had one day to get settled in their sector of the line. Private James Moddrel recalled that their section of the Hindenburg Line was full of German corpses that had to be cleared:

> We occupied a trench and a machine-gun team at once got their gun into position in case of a counter attack. We started to throw all the dead Bosch out of the trench. When we moved one particular fellow, we found he was very much alive. He objected to us touching him and finding his ruse, so he started to make trouble with a dagger.[2]

Moddrel's testimony also suggests that German soldiers had obtained the uniforms of British soldiers and had used them for deception purposes. 'We found in one German dug-out, bundles of British clothing and equipment and there us little doubt that some of it had been used for the purpose of dressing Bosch soldiers as British troops.'[3]

The gruesome discovery of a dead soldier in another dug-out may have been a reprisal inflicted by British soldiers for German troops dressing in their uniforms. Moddrel continued:

> In another dug-out, halfway down the stairs a German soldier had been fastened with his face to the wall by a semi-circular piece of iron, clamped tight to the wall on both sides. The iron was round his waist and his arms were inside so that he could not possibly move them. He had obviously committed some crime – this was his punishment. He was quite dead having a large wound in his head made with a chopper.[4]

Within twenty four hours of their deployment the Germans counter attacked and drove British units from their position to the west of the Longatte–Bullecourt Road. The line was now changed and the Post Office Rifles would take up their positions along the road from the crossroads to the rubble of Bullecourt Church. The unit history of the Post Office Rifles:

> In Bullecourt itself the situation was extraordinary. Parts of the village were in enemy hands, and parts occupied by British troops. The outpost positions changed almost hourly, and when the Battalion was sent up to relieve the remnants of H.A.C., Royal Welch Fusiliers, and two Battalions of the Manchester regiment, the situation was, to say the best of it, obscure. Here the Battalion had its first taste of real fighting, for within 48 hours of taking up this line it was ordered to make a concerted attack with the 2/5th (L.R.B.) and clear the village of the enemy.[5]

C and D Companies faced in a northerly direction along the Bullecourt-Reincourt Road, while A Company held positions south through the centre of the village towards the original Hindenburg Line to the south of the village. It was from this southerly point that the Germans had fortified themselves in the Red Patch. When the Post Office Rifles entered the line, they did not know the strength of the German forces south of Bullecourt. With the enemy within close proximity, there was a risk of getting lost and disorientated. It was easy to enter enemy trenches by mistake and there was the danger of being shot by friendly fire as soldiers moved around the ruins and trenches.

Rifleman Tom Crook was a runner for Number 13 Platoon and provided a very precise account of the dangers of entering enemy positions in error:

> I was the 13 Platoon runner and had to go back to Company HQ to get the rations. I used to leave the trench just as it was getting dark, between 10 pm and 11 pm. On my way I passed 14 Platoon, and in a small trench was the officer and a sgt. I am afraid I cannot remember their names. On one or two occasions they stopped me and told me to get in their trench until it was darker, and when the officer thought it was dark enough he let me go. A little further along the small path I took there was leaning against a bit of wall an Australian soldier with no arms or legs and I looked for him every time I went to HQ, and on my way back, as I didn't want to wander into Jerry's front line, which wasn't far away.
>
> When the rations were obtained, and I got back, the question arose who was going to take the rations to the Machine Gun Crew, in No Man's Land. After some discussion, it fell upon the Signaller, little Billy Bacon. Now he wasn't going to get lost so he went down the sunken road, unwinding the wire as he went along. The lads with the machine gun were very alert, and they heard Billy come down this sunken road and called 'Halt, who are you?' So Billy went up in the direction of the voices and so was able to deliver their rations. The machine gunners told Billy he was very lucky that they heard him as a little further down that sunken road was a German machine gun, and very fortunate that they hadn't fired it. So, whilst we were in that front trench Billy Bacon always delivered the rations to the machine gun crew, using his telephone wire for safety's sake.[6]

The men from the Post Office Rifles were in position by 4.35 am on 16th May. Their first day on the line at Bullecourt involved consolidating their positions and burying the dead. German artillery shelled their line continuously throughout the day. Captain W.E.C. Staplyton, commander of A Company, had become a casualty on that first day and was suffering from shell shock. At 11.00 pm all Company commanders from The Post Office Rifles were summoned to Battalion Headquarters to receive orders for a dawn attack to clear the enemy from the western sector.

Zero Hour was scheduled for 3.00 am on 17th May. The attack would be made in conjunction with one by the 2nd/5th London Rifle Brigade (174th Brigade). They were positioned along the railway embankment south west of Bullecourt and would drive their advance northwards as the Post Office Rifles attacked in a westerly direction. The first objective was to take the German trench south of the village between Ecoust-St-Mein and Bullecourt and the Ecoust-St-Mein–Longatte Roads. Their second objective was to reach the road that ran parallel northwards. As soon as the 2nd/5th London Rifle Brigade had reached this second objective, A Company, Post Office Rifles would advance north westwards through the village behind the 2nd/5th LBR and clear any German pockets of resistance. Since Captain Staplyton had become a casualty, 2nd Lieutenant Blanche was appointed Company Commander and would lead the support.

A two-minute heavy bombardment of German positions was launched before a direct onslaught upon the Red Patch, which was accomplished successfully, with the capture of five machine guns and 23 prisoners. Once these front-line trenches had been secured A Company leapfrogged over the 2/5th lines and clear the enemy from the ruins. By 3.30 am the Post Office Rifles were in control of Bullecourt. An anonymous stretcher bearer later recalled:

> It was a curious attack or rather advance for we met with very little opposition. A few shots were fired. I remember Mr Bland firing at an object which turned out to be a tree stump. Once we lost direction a bit and had to change it. We cleared the remainder of the village and our platoon went about 50–100 yards beyond and in the grey dawn dug a little protection from ourselves along some shell holes. Kerry and I were still together. He and I dug against the shelling I felt sure would be directed at us later on. Then we sat down to eat a little breakfast, a mess tin of tea and a tin of Macconachie – the last meal poor Kerry was ever to have. When we finished Kerry got up. A minute later he gave a cry and called to me. I crawled into the next shell hole and found him lying with several wounds. Apparently he had forgotten our exposed position for it was now daylight. He had been shot in the stomach and both arms.[7]

A Company had three officer casualties, one wounded and two with shell shock. 2nd Lieutenant Blanche also lost seven men killed, another three men died of

wounds, 45 were wounded and five were shell shocked.

The Post Office Rifles then set about consolidating their new positions despite the German snipers harassing them. The Germans were already planning to withdraw from the village and this was evident in the small number of prisoners captured. This small party of Germans was in the process of demolishing their dug-outs and command posts before they withdrew completely.

The Post Office Rifles fortified their positions during that day and established new posts. They held the line until 3.00 am on 19th May.

SERGEANT HERBERT MANSER 370495,
2ND/8TH BATTALION LONDON REGIMENT, (POST OFFICE RIFLES)

Herbert Edward Manser was born in Bermondsey, London in 1892. He served with the 2nd/8th London Regiment (Post Office Rifles) during the war and attained the rank of Sergeant. Manser was wounded at Bullecourt when the battalion captured the village on 17th May 1917 and died of his wounds at No.45 Casualty Clearing Station later that day. He was aged 24 and was buried in Achiet-le-Grand Communal Cemetery Extension.

Sergeant Herbert Manser.
(Author)

SERGEANT ALFRED KNIGHT 370995, VICTORIA CROSS,
2ND/8TH BATTALION LONDON REGIMENT, POST OFFICE RIFLES

Alfred Joseph Knight was born in Ladywood, Birmingham in 1888. He was educated at St Philip's Grammar School in Edgbaston, where he excelled at maths and was a keen sportsman. As a teenager he became the secretary of the cricket and football teams representing Little Oratory Roman Catholic Church. After completing his education in 1909 he was employed by the Post Office

Sergeant Alfred Knight VC.
(Courtesy Anne Walsh)

Knight with the Mayor of Birmingham at a civic reception on 17th November 1917. He is wearing the Victoria Cross. (Courtesy the Post Office Museum Archives)

Sergeant Knight charged this position alone, rushing through the falling shells from the British barrage and killed the machine gunner manning the position. On two occasions he charged though the British barrages that day. Knight remembered little of the action itself:

Looking back afterwards, it was all a bit of a blur, but I can remember being fascinated by the pattern made all the way around me in the mud by the German bullets. I hardly knew myself how it all happened! All I know is I was up to the waist in mud at one time. I couldn't tell whether I had a watch or not; but I found a new rig-out afterwards, so that was all right!

as a clerical assistant for the Engineering Department in the north Midlands. Knight moved to Nottingham when this department was relocated in 1912.

When the First World War began Alfred enlisted on 26th October 1914. His commanding officer granted Alfred special leave to allow him to marry Mabel Saunderson in 1915. They would raise three children together. In January 1917, the 2nd/8th Battalion London Regiment was sent to France. Knight would leave his wife Mabel and his three-month-old daughter named Marjorie. By the time the battalion experienced battle for the first time at Bullecourt in May Alfred Knight had reached the rank of Lance Sergeant. As the Post Office Rifles captured the village of Bullecourt on the 17th, Knight recovered wounded men from the battlefield under heavy fire. In recognition he was awarded a certificate and promoted to sergeant. The certificate read 'For gallant conduct, May 14th, 1817, at Bullecourt. Special congratulation of the general commanding officer, 58th London Division, Major General Fanshawe!

After Bullecourt, Knight returned home and was able to spend time with Mabel and Marjorie during June 1917. On returning to the Western Front his battalion had been transferred to the Ypres salient and would play a role in the Third Campaign, Haig's drive to break through and capture the submarine base at Bruges in an effort to stop the German submarine campaign. The submarines from the German Flanders Flotilla had a devastating impact upon the British merchant fleet and were responsible for sinking a third of all merchant ships during the war. Sergeant Alfred Knight took part in the Battle for Wurst Farm Ridge on 20th September 1917. This formed part of an advance upon Gravenstafel spur. On that day Knight would distinguish himself and become the only rifleman from the Post Office Rifles to receive the Victoria Cross. As the Post Office Rifles were advancing upon Wurst Farm Ridge, they were held up by a strongly defended German machine gun position.

This was his first act of heroism that day and he would show tremendous determination and courage in the events that soon followed. His citation appeared in the *London Gazette* on 8th November 1917:

Sjt. Knight did extraordinary good work, and showed exceptional bravery and initiative when his platoon was attacking an enemy strongpoint, and came under very heavy fire from an enemy machine gun. He rushed through our own barrage, bayoneted the enemy gunner, and captured the position single handed.

Later, twelve of the enemy with a machine gun were encountered in a shell hole. He again rushed forward by himself, bayoneted two and shot a third and caused the remainder to scatter.

Subsequently, during an attack upon a fortified farm, when entangled up to his waist in mud, and seeing a number of the enemy firing upon our troops, he immediately opened fire upon them without waiting to extricate himself from the mud, killing six of the enemy.

Again, noticing the company on his right flank being held up in their attack on another farm, Sjt Knight collected some men and took up a position on the flank of this farm, from where he brought a heavy fire to bear on the farm as a result of which the farm was captured.

All the platoon officers had become casualties before the first objective was reached, and this gallant N.C.O. took command of all the men of his own platoon and of the platoons without officers. His energy in consolidating and reorganisation was untiring.

His several single-handed actions showed exceptional bravery, and saved a great number of casualties in the company. They were performed under heavy machine gun fire, and rifle fire, and without regard to personal risk, and were the direct cause of the objectives being captured.[8]

Hubner Farm was the last farm and the unit Knight assisted in capturing this position was the 2nd/5th London Rifle Brigade, which attacked Bullecourt with the Post Office Rifles on the 17th. It was remarkable that Knight was unharmed:

> All my kit was shot away almost as soon as we were in it. Everything went, in fact. The bullets rattled on my steel helmet – there were several significant dents and one hole in it I found later – and part of a book was shot away in my pocket. A photograph-case and a cigarette-case probably saved my life from one bullet, which must have passed just under my arm-pit – quite close to enough to be comfortable.[9]

Sergeant Alfred Knight received the Victoria Cross from King George V at Buckingham Palace on 3rd January 1918. He was honoured as a civic reception by the people of Nottingham when he was presented with a silver tea service and a £100 war bond. His colleagues from the Post Office collected enough money to buy an inscribed marble clock. His courage was also commemorated at another civic reception in Birmingham, the city where he was born. Knight received a lot of attention from the press: one local Birmingham newspaper dubbed him 'the Jolly VC'[10] because of the way he jovially dismissed stories that 'he was a man from whom the bullets bounced'.[11]

Knight continued to serve with the 2nd/8th Battalion Post Office Rifles through to the end of the war. On 17th March 1919 he was commissioned as a Second Lieutenant.

After leaving the Army he returned to Nottingham and resumed his career with the Post Office. He left in 1920 and worked for the Ministry of Labour.

Knight was keen to serve his country a second time when World War Two broke out 9. He tried to enlist in the Army, but he was aged 51 and was considered too old for active service. Instead he joined the Observer Corps as a Captain. In 1947 he was sent by the Ministry of Labour to India in order to advise British troops about the demobilization process.

He was Senior Wages Inspector when he retired from the Ministry of Labour, Midland Section in 1951. On retirement he received the MBE. Knight would pursue his passion for cricket and would play the game into his sixties. Unable to settle into retirement he returned to work as a casual clerical officer at Handsworth Labour Exchange until a stroke forced him into permanent retirement.

Alfred Knight passed away at home in Birmingham on 4th December 1960 aged 72. He was buried in Oscott Catholic Cemetery. On 9th November 2006, 46 years after his death, a road was named Alfred Knight Way in Birmingham. The street name was unveiled by his granddaughter Anne Walsh (who held his Victoria Cross) and her cousin. Alfred Knight was a modest man. Anne recalled:

> I do know that he would never speak about his experiences to the family, even to his son, who was also in the army during the next war. He would always attend any event he was invited to as a VC which, my cousins and I feel, was to honour those of his comrades who did not make it back. He was certainly very quick to dismiss any praise directed at himself, preferring to redirect it to his comrades. As far as he was concerned, the VC was awarded for the gallantry of the whole battalion, not just one man.

SERGEANT ALFRED PICKLES 4488,
2ND/8TH BATTALION LONDON REGIMENT, POST OFFICE RIFLES

Alfred Pickles was born in Bradford in 1897. At 14 he was working as a Post Office messenger in Bradford. Pickles was underage to enlist when war broke out but he lied about his age and joined the Post Office Rifles. He served at Bullecourt during May 1917. He is pictured seated middle row left in the photo. With fellow sergeants from the 2nd/8th Post Office Rifles who fought at Bullecourt. After the war Pickles returned to Bradford and employment with the Post Office. He retired as a Head Postman in 1955. Alfred Pickles died in Lancaster on 4th October 1969.

Pickles seated left. (Courtesy Paul Baldock)

PRIVATE JAMES MODDREL 2082,
2ND/5TH BATTALION LONDON RIFLE BRIGADE

James Moddrel was born in 1898 in Upton Park, East London. He worked as a junior clerk for a shipping company before enlisting to join the 2nd/5th Battalion, London Rifle Brigade. Moddrel took part in the battle for Bullecourt. After demobilisation during 1919 he worked in various positions with a wood pulp importer and eventually became managing director. He would serve his country once again during the Second World War, with Z Battery (Anti-aircraft Rockets) stationed on Hampstead Heath. This branch of the Home Guard was one of the few Home Guard units to engage the enemy with direct fire. James Moddrel died on 30th July 1963 aged 65.

NOTES ....

1. Liddle Collection: Private James Moddrel's diary.
2. Ibid.
3. Ibid.
4. Ibid.
5. *History of the Post Office Rifles 8th Battalion City of London Regiment 1914–1918*, Gale and Polden Ltd, Wellington Works 1919.
6. IWM Museum Ref: Misc 2165: Rifleman Thomas Edward Crook, No.13 Platoon 2nd/8th Battalion London Regiment, The Post Office Rifles.
7. *Terriers in the Trenches*, Charles Messenger, Picton Publishing 1982, p73.
8. *London Gazette*: 30372 dated 6th November 1917.
9. *VCs of The First World War: Passchendaele*, Stephen Snelling Sutton Publishing 1998.
10. Ibid.
11. Ibid.

CHAPTER 30

RECOVERING THE WOUNDED: 18TH MAY 1917

As the Post Office Rifles consolidated their position the officers and men belonging to the 2/3rd Home Counties Field Ambulance (58th Division) launched an operation to recover the wounded who had been lying exposed to machine gun fire since 12th May. Captain W Maile from the 2/3rd Home Counties Field Ambulance recalled: 'Dozens of wounded were left out in No Man's Land, and as the Huns were only a few hundred yards away it was a tricky operation to get them out. Each division had tried to get the poor chaps in without success.'[1]

During the evening of 17th May Captain Maile was having mess when his commanding officer brought orders for he and Captain Cummings to take 100 stretcher bearers to Bullecourt to recover the wounded. They arrived during the night so that they could recover the wounded under the cover of darkness. Cummings would be dead by the end of the following day and before they ventured off to the front, Maile recalled:

> This was the first time I came across a clear case, to my mind, of Premonition. Cummings, who shared a tent with me at that time, and I went to collect a few necessary things. To my great surprise he knelt down and said his prayers. When I remarked 'I have never seen you do that before' he replied 'Well, you never know.'[2]

The plan was for Captain Maile and his party to meet guides at various intervals who would lead them to the front. Heavy shelling was taking place and all the guides were killed. Mailie had to fend for himself and find his own way. As they got close to the line Cummings and 20 bearers set up an aid post away from the front while Mailie and 80 men continued:

> It was pitch dark and I found the going very difficult owing to the trench being blocked in places. I stopped to investigate and found what we had been tumbling over was dead men!! So out we came and walked in the open – luckily with no casualties – in spite of the shelling.[3]

Mailie had reached the front by dawn on 18th May. As he was explaining the reason why they were late, to his great surprise, Brigadier-General Freiberg appeared from his bunk to meet him:

> A man got up from the wire bed on which had been and put on his tunic which had red tabs, I wondered what on earth he was doing up there. It was my first meeting with Frieberg!! He always used Battalion Head Quarters as his whenever there was a show on, not like most of the Brigadiers who had their H.Q. much further back.[4]

Captain W Maile served with the 2nd/3rd Field Ambulance during the Battle of Bullecourt. (Courtesy Tim Maile)

They discussed the options. Now that the dawn had broken, should they wait for nightfall, or risk the German bullets in order to get their wounded back to safety during the daylight hours? Freiberg asked them to try and recover the wounded during the day and he showed them the way to the front in person. 'So we moved in and found a first class shambles – No Man's Land littered with dead and wounded which the other Divisions had failed to get in. The first thing to do was to try and cope with this lot before further attacks'.[5]

Being sniped at by the enemy as they worked, they brought many men back to the British trenches at a cost of one officer 20 stretcher bearers:

Although by now it was daylight we decided we must have a go, which we did. By the grace of God we got them all in by crawling on our tummies and pulling them along the best way we could. When I got back to my relay post I found my friend, Captain Cummings, had had a direct hit on the shelter, and he and all the men with him were killed.[6]

Captain Cummings was buried in Mory Abbey Military Cemetery.

NOTES

1. IWM Department of Documents: IWM 7266/76/65/1: Captain W.C.D. Maile.
2. Ibid.
3. Ibid.
4. Ibid.
5. Ibid.
6. Ibid.

CHAPTER 31

THE 2ND/6TH BATTALION LONDON REGIMENT STRAIGHTEN THE LINE

The 2nd/6th London Regiment was the next unit from the 174th Brigade that would launch a further attack upon German positions holding Bovis Trench north of Bullecourt in an effort to straighten the British line. Lieutenant Commander A Foord had just taken over command of the battalion. He had previous belonged to the Manchester Regiment and was Brigade Major of the 173rd. His appointment was seen as an effort to strengthen the ties that bound this London battalion to other units within the division. The unit history describes the destruction that they encountered at Bullecourt:

> For six weeks now Bullecourt had been subjected to heavy bombardments by guns of all calibres ... Nothing remained but heaps of stones and piles of debris, and these, constantly shifting by the hourly bursting of thousands of shells were daily giving to Bullecourt the appearance of a wide plain of heaving desolation. Of all the buildings only the church could be identified, a white mound of crumbling stone, higher than the rest, marking the centre of the village. Over all hung perpetually a cloud of dust, and through it passed continually every missile that modern weapons could throw. One object alone remained almost intact. An isolated crucifix to the west of the village, partly sheltered by a sunken road, had so far escaped destruction.[1]

The information on the British position in Bullecourt provided to Foord was vague. Lieutenant Colonel J.E. Turner working on the staff of 58th (London) Division reported on 13th May that 'the situation in Bullecourt is at the present moment, somewhat obscure'.[2]

Soldiers from the 2nd/6th London Regiment got into their start off positions one hour before Zero Hour on 21st May. Each company was armed with 300 German egg grenades. Sergeant Grundy had led a party to lay down white tapes 200 yards in front of Bovis Trench. In the dark they had used compass bearings as they crawled over shell holes to 50 yards from the enemy trenches. German units were firing Very Lights into the sky illuminating the ground they were marking. Shells were also falling upon their positions.

The overall objective for the battalion was to capture Bovis Trench, but there were other subsidiary tasks. A Company was ordered to send one of its platoons to attack enemy positions along the Riencourt road and establish a Lewis gun position in the communication trench running northwards from Bovis Trench. A platoon from C Company was ordered to advance along the Crucifix–factory road and neutralise the dug-outs built into the banks to protect the left flank of the advance upon Bovis Trench. D Company was assigned the task of protecting the right flank in an advance along the Bullecourt–factory road. They had been told that once the British barrage moved forward, they would enter Bovis Trench with ease. Intelligence reports suggested that the trench was held by limited number of German personnel who would offer little resistance and could be easily overwhelmed.

At Zero Hour a four-minute hurricane bombardment was launched against known machine gun emplacements in Bovis Trench. As the shells fell A and B Companies 2nd/6th Battalion advanced with bombs and grenades. An anonymous member of Sergeant Grundy's party wrote that 'the men were heavily laden, so it was only possible to go slowly, and with great difficulty.[3]

Despite the British artillery barrage, German machine gunners fired upon these men as they slowly pushed forward. Shells had failed to knock out the machine gun posts. Casualties in the central advance fell as a result of their fire. Many officers were lost in the central push, which caused further confusion. The right and left flanks lost touch as a consequence of the central advance faltering.

As soon as the Londoners advanced German artillery also targeted the line of advance. Many fell within moments of leaving their start off position. As those that survived proceeded through the storm it was difficult for them to distinguish the point where the German barrage began and the British barrage ended. A combination of darkness and dust caused disorientation.

D Company advancing on the right flank was unable to distinguish Bovis Trench because of the number of shell holes in the vicinity. They lost direction and passed their objective, advancing 200 yards to the north of their objective. As they tried to consolidate their position they risked being surrounded. The company was forced to retire. 2nd Lieutenant Pickup was wounded, but carried on. He received a further wound on entering a trench. He was captured and had his compass and revolver taken from him. The two German guards holding him were shot by men from his own battalion. Pickup killed another man and crawled back to his own lines.

C Company advancing on the left flank was unable to reach Bovis Trench. A wounded Corporal from C Company recounted the disastrous attempt to protect the left flank:

> Every available man was 'roped in', and we seemed to be so hard put to it that even wounded men were sent back from the dressing station to take part in the attack. I remember one N.C.O., who was wounded by shrapnel in the leg during the afternoon – not badly of course – had to report back in the evening. We lost quite a lot of men getting through Bullecourt. Jerry was dropping 'whiz-bangs' quite frequently. We arrived on the tapes about two am. I remember the officers shaking hands just before the whistle went. We were told that the trench we had to take was only sparsely occupied, probably by a machine gun or two. As soon as the whistle went, however and we got under way, the most awful inferno broke out. Jerry simply swamped us with shell-fire, machine-gun fire and rifle fire. It seemed as though they knew all about this business. To me it seemed more like 600 yards than 200 yards, and afterwards, when discussing it with other prisoners, we were all agreed that the distance was wrong, as was the information that the trench was only partially held.[4]

Sergeant Garlick was the only person from C Company to get into Bovis trench on the left flank. He followed the artillery barrage and jumped into the trench just as the barrage lifted. As soon as he entered he was bombed from the rear and wounded. He managed to get into a nearby shell hole, 20 yards from the trench, where he laid low until 9 pm that evening. Unfortunately, the Germans launched an artillery barrage at 9.00 pm that night and he had to wait another two hours in the shell hole before he could make an attempt to return

to British lines. As he headed back he nearly crawled into a German listening post established in a shell hole in No Man's Land. He was challenged, but they did not fire upon him. He reached safety later that night. An unidentified Company Sergeant Major from the battalion confirmed that few men reached Bovis Trench:

> I don't think many actually reached the trench, most of our men at all events, seemed to have stopped in the shell holes about thirty yards away, and to have done more rifle firing than anything else. The casualties were so many that they were reduced to mere groups, and they retired as best they could during the darkness of the ensuing night.[5]

With many officers killed or wounded the attack became a complete shambles. Further problems were caused by a breakdown in communication when shell fire destroyed telephones and the men who were in charge of the pigeons became casualties. The attack launched by the 2nd/6th London Regiment was a terrible failure. Lieutenant Colonel A.J. Foord commanding the 2nd/6th London Regiment:

> The enemy apparently held the left strongly but retired from the right to a line of consolidated shell holes in rear and advancing again threatened to work round to the left flank of our right Coy who were digging in. Machine guns and well posted snipers caused heavy losses and the right, unable to hold their ground gradually withdrew to the original position on the road from U22 c 7520 to U22 c 3010, which had been taken over by a platoon of the 7th London when the attack began. Some portion remained out until night and apparently all but one became casualties in an attempt to rejoin the Battalion. Isolated men of the left Coy and of the left flanking platoon including wounded crawled back to our front line during the morning, the remainder stood their ground until the evening when the enemy attacked in strong force from both flanks and drove them back.[6]

It was a bitter fight; 111 men were initially reported as missing from the battalion. Lieutenant Colonel Foord:

> Of the 111 men reported missing, four have since reported and evidence points to the fact that the remainder were either killed or so severely wounded as to be unable to get back to our lines. Of 11 Officers who went over only three have returned, all of them wounded.[7]

Overall Lieutenant Colonel Foord lost 50% of his men, for the 2nd/6th London Regiment had lost 13 officers and 226 men who were killed, wounded or listed as missing. The battalion had been sacrificed to move the front a few more yards north of Bullecourt.

The British had straightened the line and had reached Bovis Trench, the sector of OG 2 that crossed along the northern perimeter of the village. After weeks of bloody fighting and sacrifices made by the Australian and British Divisions Bullecourt was finally under Allied control. The 7th Division was dizzy with exhaustion after 12 days of continuous fighting. By 17th May the second battle of Bullecourt reached a conclusion because both armies were too worn out to continue. There had been 6,000 German and 7,000 Australian casualties. The trenches captured would remain in Allied hands until March 1918, when they were lost during the Kaiser's Offensive.

The region was one huge graveyard. The smell at Bullecourt was putrid. Company Sergeant Major Lott from the 2nd/9th London Regiment wrote of the scene as he entered the line on 22nd May:

> I think the night 'B' Company first went into the line at Bullecourt was one of the worst we ever had. It was pitch dark and raining. The route up to the front was a mass of craters and shell holes and we were heavily laden too, being in Full Marching Order and carrying two days' rations, extra bombs, etc. All the way dead English and Germans were strewn about and the enemy was very active with his artillery ... Practically no trenches were left – just mud holes ... The stench in Bullecourt was terrible, was awful and I never will forget Capt. White going about with a large drum of creosol trying to improve matters, but with little success.[8]

RIFLEMAN LEON AUGUSTE PAGEOT 345001,
2ND/6TH LONDON REGIMENT (CITY OF LONDON RIFLES)

Leon Auguste Pageot was born in Dijon, France in 1891. In later years he moved to Paris where he trained as a jewellery designer. Pageot emigrated to London after successfully winning a competition to work in the English capital. It was here that he established a reputation as an acclaimed designer. He was responsible for designing the Royal Cipher for King George V on the familiar red British post boxes. Some of these ciphers can still be seen today.

Rifleman Leon Auguste Pageot. (Courtesy Henri Pageot)

Pageot's wife Louise bore him a daughter, Louise Amélie Gladys and son, Edmond Rène Henri. The Pageot family lived at 24 Gladsmuir Road, Highgate, in north London.

Leon Pageot enlisted to join the British Army in September 1916. He was ordered by The Central London Recruitment depot at Whitehall to report for duty at 10 am on 5th September 1916.

He was assigned to the City of London 5th. Regiment, (39th Platoon, B Company) as a Rifleman and began his basic training at Fovant Camp in Wiltshire. In one letter written within days of enlisting, Pageot asks his wife to send him his French/English dictionary:

> My dear Louise,
> I hope you are in the very best of health and also our Sonny and Girly without forgetting your Ma and Pa, sisters and brother. I was inoculated yesterday so you can guess I am not very strong but we have four days rest to get better, here is not so bad, it could be better but it is dearer, the food up to the present is decent but I cannot get used to their tea so I go without it. I am with a very nice lot of fellows that means a lot, we are in huts, the bed consist of three boards and a straw mattress and pillow, the first night I could not sleep. but last night I had a good rest, yesterday we have done a bit of drilling before our inoculation and this morning we have been for a four-mile walk round the country with our corporal, a nice fellow and after that we had a Kit inspection, and then our dinner, which consisted of Toad-in-the hole, cabbage and murphy and bread and butter pudding, which were very nice. Now dear Lou I am going to ask you for things which are of great importance for a soldier's life. I will be extremely pleased when you can forward them to me by post, the sooner the better. first of all some rags to clean my equipment, then two small towels for washing my face, a couple of old tooth brushes, some more handkerchiefs, a box to put my soap in. I should like to have a strap to sharpen my razor as we have got to shave every day and the razor gets

King George V Post Office Cruciform designed by Pageot for British post boxes. (Courtesy Henri Pageot)

out of order, and also my slippers and my old pair of boots as I will be glad to have a change, mine are rather heavy. Can you also send me three pairs of socks and an old cup to put my shaving water in, which is hot (I don't think) and also my dictionary French/English? You will find it in one of the drawers of my writing desk. I think that is all for the moment except that I will be pleased if you put them all in a wooden box and get me a padlock and two hinges. I had to buy the plates, mug, polishes, brush etc which were of first importance and you can guess that my pockets are not very deep but never mind, it is all in one lifetime. We had down here very nice weather, not a drop of rain, and it is quite a treat to get up at half past five in the morning.[9]

Within a week of writing this letter, his loving wife sent him the items he required. On 15th September 1916 he wrote:

Dear Louise
I have received your parcel, I am very pleased to have slippers and boots, also the razor strap, it is absolutely it! ... I would be pleased if you [could send] my bottle of Oxygen Water to rinse my mouth, if you have some tooth powder to spare send me some, if not I will buy some down here. – and some small cigarettes, you know the ones I mean, the very small ones I use to buy at Highgate ...

Last night I could not sleep through worrying about you and it is so cold down here now that I was shivering all the night long, well old girl I shall have to get used to it ... I have my boots on now and you can guess I am swanking with them on ... I hope you are alright by now, let me know if you get on, will you. I would be pleased if you write several times in the week, that will make me feel more happy. I also hope that our dear little children are quite alright, and also your mother and father, and your brother and sisters, so give them my best love and tell them I shan't forget to remember them to my mother as she always enquires about them. ...

With my best love and kisses from your affectionate husband.
Auguste
Thousands XXXXXXXX for you and Girlie and Sonny. Speak to them all for me so they don't forget their father XXXX
Auguste.[10]

By May 1917 Rifleman Pageot had been transferred to the 2nd/6th London Regiment (City of London Rifles). On 21st May 1917 Pageot was killed when his battalion was advancing on Bovis Trench. Rifleman Leon Auguste Pageot's remains were never found. He was one of the few Frenchman serving in the British Army listed as missing in the homeland he fought and died to liberate. His name is commemorated on the Arras Memorial. Louise Pageot received confirmation that her husband had died at Bullecourt from Lance Corporal Fox on 27th May:

Dear Mrs Pageot.
If you have not already heard the sad news, I am sorry to tell you your dear husband was killed in action on the 20/5/17. I am writing to tell you a parcel arrived for him, being unable to send it back I have shared it amongst the chaps of our platoon. I offer you my deepest sympathy and can assure you he did not suffer as he was killed outright. All his comrades sympathise with you in your great loss. Some day I hope to be able to tell you more about it as he was killed by my side. Hoping this will find you as well as can be expected under the sad circumstances, I remain yours respectfully,
E. FOX. L/Cp.
14 Platoon. D. Coy.[11]

At some point, Louise received official notification that her husband was missing in action, which meant an agony of waiting. Louise received definite confirmation that her husband had been killed at Bullecourt soon after from Lance Corporal Fox. Despite Fox's letter, Louise was in a state of denial. In a letter written in early 1918 to Madame Pageot, her mother-in-law in Paris, Louise was still hoping to hear that Auguste had been captured:

My Chere Mama
Just a few lines hoping that you and Henri are both quite well and that you received my last letter, I must tell you that I had a very quiet Christmas and New Year under the circumstances and I can tell you that I missed my Dear Auguste very much. I am still waiting to hear further news about him. I only wish that I could receive the news that he was taken prisoner, I cannot believe that he is gone. I am still living in hope that he is alive. I should very much like to send you a little present but I am afraid that you would not get it [here the words 'on account of the post' have been crossed out, perhaps because Louise was afraid to appear critical to the censors] so I think it would be better to wait until the war is over, I should not think that it will last much longer ...

With Best Love and Kisses
From My Dear Children Edmonde [sic] and Louise to their Dear Grandma and Uncle Henri and accept the same from Your Affectionate Daughter Louise Pageot.[12]

There is a photo of Louise Pageot wearing mourning dress that was taken in 1917. Her grandson Henri Pageot wrote:

> Louise looks numb with grief — a look which I think never entirely left her ... Louise had in fact already received the news that her husband was dead. She was obviously still willing reality to be untrue and the fact that she had indeed been 'living in hope' for so long implies that she was enduring a terrible period of a kind of suspended existence.[13]

As the months passed Louise began to come to terms with reality. In a letter to Henri, her brother in law in Paris she wrote:

> My Dear Henri
> I hope that you will excuse me not writing to you before, I am sure you must think me awfully unkind but I am sure you can understand how I feel after having the terrible news of my dear husband Auguste. I cannot believe it now that he is gone. I will be pleased when the War is over to know for sure. I am still waiting for his things to be returned to me, if I get some of his things I shall know then that he has been killed. I should very much like to have the news that he was taken prisoner of war. I am sure that you would also I would like to get hold of the beastly Boche that killed him. I am afraid that he would not stand a chance ...[14]

With so many fathers, sons and brothers lost, it was left to widows and mothers to pick up the pieces of shattered lives as they grieved. Edmond, who died in 2005, had always held his father in high esteem and his ashes were scattered at Bullecourt in order for him to rest closer to his father.

NOTES

1. *The Cast Iron Sixth*, Captain E.G. Godfrey MC, F.S. Stapleton, 1938.
2. National Archives: WO 95/3005: 2nd/6th Battalion London Regiment: War Diary.
3. Ibid.
4. Ibid.
5. Ibid.
6. National Archives: WO 95/3002: Lieutenant Colonel A.J. Foord, 2nd/6th Battalion London Regiment Report.
7. National Archives: WO 95/3002: Lieutenant Colonel A.J. Foord, 2nd/6th Battalion London Regiment Report.
8. *The History and Records of the Queen Victoria's Rifles 1792–1922*, Major Cuthbert Keeson, Constable & Company Limited 1923.
9. Letter from Rifleman Auguste Pageot to his wife Louise: 8th September 1916: Courtesy Henri Pageot.
10. Ibid.
11. Letter from Lance Corporal E. Fox to Louise Pageot: 27th May 1917: Courtesy Henri Pageot.
12. Letter from Louise Pageot to her mother-in-law Madame Pageot: January 1918: Courtesy Henri Pageot.
13. Courtesy Henri Pageot.
14. Letter from Louise Pageot to her brother-in-law Madame Pageot: January 1918: Courtesy Henri Pageot.

CHAPTER 32

ASSESSMENT OF THE SECOND BULLECOURT BATTLE

British units held Bullecourt from May 1917 until the Kaiser's Offensive launched in March 1918, when the village was recaptured. The heavy fighting subsided towards the end of May 1917 but British units who had played a prominent role during the battle remained on this front and took part in minor raids on German trenches throughout the summer of 1917.

After the battle men were left lying in No Man's Land for three days and nights, unable to help themselves and in fear of being captured by a German patrol. Padre Guy Vernon-Smith organised a party of 48 volunteers from the 2nd/8th Battalion London Regiment, the Post Office Rifles to go out into No Man's Land and recover these men.

Some historians have strongly attacked General Gough for Bullecourt. Gough was a cavalry officer from the Victorian era. He fought World War One with strategies that might have succeeded in the Boer War, but he could not adapt to fighting a modern industrial war, a mechanized war. He made mistakes in initiating disjointed attacks on narrow fronts; he was impulsive and lacked originality. After making mistakes in the ill-conceived plan to of 10th April, Gough made the same mistakes on the 11th.

Field Marshal Douglas Haig bears overall responsibility for the calamity at Bullecourt as the supreme commander of the British Expeditionary Force, it was Haig who allowed Gough to carry on despite repeated failure. Commanders such as Haig and Gough were under enormous pressure to achieve results, to overcome the stalemate of trench warfare, break through German lines and deliver a decisive victory to bring the war to an end. Nevertheless, it is difficult to comprehend how he could continue the Bullecourt offensive through May 1917 while planning a bigger offensive in Flanders for the summer. In Haig's Dispatch published in the *London Gazette* on 4th January 1918 gave some kind of answer:

A necessary part of the preparations for the Messines attack was the maintenance of activity on the Arras front, sufficient to keep the enemy

in doubt as to whether our offensive there would be proceeded with. I therefore directed the Armies concerned to continue active operations with such forces as were left to them.[1]

The human price for both battles was high. Many corpses of soldiers lay in the ruins of Bullecourt and the surrounding fields. Some of those poor men were killed a month earlier in the first battle and were in a state of decomposition. Some men were lying dead entangled in the dense wire entanglements. Some had been buried but unearthed during bombardments, while the remains of others were completely pulverised. The bodies could not be recovered for fear of being killed by German machine gunners and snipers. The unit history of The Post Office Rifles describes the devastating scene after two months of battle:

By this time Bullecourt and its surroundings had become a veritable charnel-house, dead bodies and dead mules were lying about in hundreds, and the place was so offensive that it was a question whether it could be retained. Parties were organised to clear up, and in a short space of time, in spite of every adverse condition, it was made tolerably healthy.[2]

Haig declared that the capture of Bullecourt was 'among the great achievements of the war'.[3] The Australian Official History states that 1st Anzac Corps lost 292 officers and 7,190 men. The 2nd Division AIF lost 173 officers and 3,725 men; the 1st Division sustained casualties of 80 officers and 2,261 men; and the 5th Division suffered losses of 39 officers and 1,204 men.[4]

The British V Corps had lost 300 officers and 6,500 men. The 62nd Division had sustained casualties of 143 officers and 3,284 men; the 7th Division had lost 128 officers and 2,554 men and the 58th Division suffered casualties of 39 officers and 680 men.[5]

Second Bullecourt was indeed a slaughter. Approximately 14,000 men were lost for an objective which had little impact in ending the war or altering the strategic position in favour of the allies.

The German army also suffered in its defence of Bullecourt. The 27th Division comprising Württemberg troops had lost 2,176 men.[6] The 3rd Guard Division had lost 1,146 and the Lehr Division lost nearly 2,000.

British cemeteries around the village contain few graves of those killed in the battles of Bullecourt. The majority of those interred in these cemeteries fell during 1918. Those Australian and British soldiers who fell earlier were mostly listed as missing and now lie in the fields. Throughout 1917 trench raids took place at Bullecourt where a static war ensued.

The way that Gough conducted the battle of Bullecourt caused the Australians to become extremely sceptical about British command. Their confidence was badly shaken, especially after the mistakes made during the first battle of 10th and 11th April. The 4th Australian Division was so badly mauled on the 11th that they were withdrawn from the line for several months so that the division could train replacements. The Australian Divisions was exhausted by their experiences in Gallipoli in 1915, during the Somme in 1916, the harsh winter of 1916/17 and by the debacle at Bullecourt. Generals Birdwood and White wanted Australian units relieved and despite making requests to General Haig, the men were kept on the line. Both Birdwood and White were concerned that if their troops were not given some respite, the issue would escalate into a national outcry at home and recruitment would be severely affected. They felt their concerns were not reaching the ears of Haig and his staff.

White was so frustrated by the situation that he threatened that if an Australian was not appointed to Haig's staff to represent the Australian Imperial Force, then he would never again support an Australian overseas expedition. After a serious debate about the condition of Australian troops and the future conduct of the war the 5th Division was given leave on 12th May. The 1st and 2nd Divisions were also given leave and rest.

Survivors of the 4th Division, however, who fought at Bullecourt on 11th April, were deployed north to Belgium where within weeks they would be taking part in the Messines offensive.

It is difficult to find anything positive about Bullecourt when so many men were sacrificed. There was nothing positive about it for the bereaved families who received telegrams in Britain and Australia informing them of the loss of fathers, sons and brothers. Yet Bullecourt did have positive results. German defence was based on confidence in the impregnability of the Hindenburg Line. The Australians had shaken this confidence during the first battle when their infantry advanced unsupported by artillery and tanks

and severely undermined it when they succeeded in recapturing and consolidating them during the second battle. When the Germans lost ground they were compelled to concentrate large numbers of reserve forces in the area. Heavy casualties were inflicted upon the Germans. The German divisions defending Bullecourt were being worn down by the attacks. Haig wrote the following message on 12th May 1917:

The capture of the Hindenburg Line east of Bullecourt, and the manner in which it has been held ... against such constant and desperate efforts to retake it, will rank high among the great deeds of the war and is helping very appreciably in wearing out the enemy. The fine initiative shown by all commanders down to the lowest is admirable.[7]

Haig would later write

To secure the footing gained by the Australians in the Hindenburg Line on 3rd May it was advisable that Bullecourt should be captured without loss of time. During the fortnight following our attack, fighting for the possession of this village went on unceasingly; while the Australian troops in the sector of the Hindenburg Line to the east beat off counter attack after counter attack. The defence of this 1,000 yards of double trench line, exposed to counter attack on every side, through two weeks of almost constant fighting, deserves to be remembered as a most gallant feat of arms.[8]

The lessons learnt from the Bullecourt battle did eventually play a role in the overall victory. Just as in the Second World War the success of the Normandy Landings on D-Day in 1944 might never have been achieved if the failure of Dieppe in 1942 had not shown the Allies how not to make an amphibious assault. The first battle of Bullecourt demonstrated to allied commanders how not to conduct a battle with modern technology. The failure of the tanks highlighted their weaknesses. It was Jacka's report that was studied by Major General Monash a year later, while he was preparing for his attack upon Le Hamel. Monash studied the errors made at Bullecourt and made sure that they would not be repeated. By reading about the tanks' failings he was able to use the tank effectively in conjunction with infantry, artillery and air support. Monash would capture objectives at Le Hamel using the resources of modern warfare on 4th July 1918.

Bullecourt was captured after six weeks of bitter fighting. Before the war Bullecourt was a village of just 396 inhabitants. When the village was captured by the

British 7th Division all the villagers had of course left and the houses had been reduced to rubble. The battle for Bullecourt could be deemed a victory, but the huge sacrifices made by the courageous soldiers from Britain and Australia would make the battle of Bullecourt, if not pyrrhic, then certainly a flawed victory.

NOTES ···

1. *London Gazette*: Issue 30462: 4th January 1918: Douglas Haig's Dispatch.
2. *History of the Post Office Rifles 8th Battalion City of London Regiment 1914–1918*, Gale and Polden Ltd, Wellington Works 1919.
3. Official History of the Australian Medical Services 1914–1918.
4. *History of the Great War Military Operations: France and Belgium 1917* by Cyril Falls: 1940: p479.
5. Ibid.
6. Official History of Australia in the War of 1914–1918, Volume 4, Charles Bean, Angus and Robertson Ltd 1938: p541.
7. Ibid.
8. *London Gazette*: Issue 30462: 4th January 1918: Douglas Haig's Dispatch.

PART FOUR

MEMORIALS AND CEMETERIES

CHAPTER 33

BULLECOURT TODAY

THE AUSTRALIAN DIGGER MEMORIAL

The Australian Digger Memorial is situated north east of Bullecourt on the road to Riencourt-les-Cagnicourt. At the entrance of the Australian Digger Memorial Park stands a commemorative plaque created by Dr Ross Bastiaan which shows in bronze the topographical features of the battlefield. The Australian Digger sculpture by Peter Corlett stands on a plinth situated between where OG 1 and OG 2 trenches were located, on land donated by Monsieur Jean Letaille, the former Mayor of Bullecourt. The Bullecourt Digger Memorial was dedicated on Anzac Day on 25th April 1992 in the 75th anniversary year of the battles. The memorial was unveiled on Anzac Day 25th April 1993 by Monsieur Jean Letaille and Mr Kim Jones, the Australian Ambassador to France. On the front side of the plinth a plaque contains the following dedication:

SACRED TO THE MEMORY OF THE 10,000 MEMBERS OF THE
AUSTRALIAN IMPERIAL FORCE WHO WERE KILLED AND
WOUNDED IN THE TWO BATTLES OF BULLECOURT, APRIL
TO MAY 1917, AND TO THE AUSTRALIAN DEAD AND THEIR
COMRADES IN ARMS WHO LIE HERE FOREVER IN THE SOIL OF
FRANCE

'LEST WE FORGET'

The reverse side of the plinth contains the following inscription:

THE BULLECOURT DIGGER IS THE WORK OF
AUSTRALIAN SCULPTOR PETER CORLETT AND
MERIDIAN SCULPTURE FOUNDRY OF MELBOURNE
AUSTRALIA. IT WAS COMMISSIONED BY THE OFFICE OF
AUSTRALIAN WAR GRAVES IN AUGUST 1992, FLOWN

TO THE UNITED KINGDOM BY THE ROYAL AUSTRALIAN
AIR FORCE AND PLACED ON THE AIF MEMORIAL
AT BULLECOURT BY THE COMMONWEALTH WAR
GRAVES COMMISSION (FRANCE OFFICE). IT WAS
UNVEILED ON ANZAC DAY 25 APRIL 1993 BY
HIS EXCELLENCY MR. KIM JONES AUSTRALIAN
AMBASSADOR TO FRANCE AND M. JEAN LETAILLE
MAYOR OF BULLECOURT. THE SCULPTURE PORTRAYS
AN AUSTRALIAN SOLDIER WEARING THE UNIFORM
AND EQUIPMENT CARRIED BY THE AIF AT THE BATTLES
OF BULLECOURT. WHILE THE SCULPTURE IS OTHERWISE
AUTHENTIC IN DETAIL THE FIGURE BEARS THE
COLOUR-PATCH INSIGNIA OF ALL FOUR AUSTRALIAN
INFANTRY DIVISIONS (FIRST, SECOND, FOURTH
AND FIFTH THAT WERE PRESENT AT EITHER FIRST

Signposts featuring an Australian Digger and a British Tommy welcome visitors to the village on the north and southern approaches to Bullecourt. (Author)

BULLECOURT 10–11 APRIL 1917 OR SECOND
BULLECOURT 3–17 MAY 1917 REFLECTING THE
CHARACTERISTICS FOR WHICH THE AUSTRALIAN
SOLDIER OF THE FIRST WORLD WAR WAS BEST
KNOWN, THE BULLECOURT DIGGER IS STURDY,
ARCADIAN, AUDACIOUS AND RESOLUTE.
IMPORTANTLY AS WELL THE SCULPTURE EXPRESSES
THE HOPE THAT THE DEEDS OF AUSTRALIANS AT
BULLECOURT IN APRIL/MAY 1917 WOULD BE OF
ENDURING RELEVANCE AND INSPIRATION TO THIS
AND FUTURE GENERATIONS

Australian Digger Memorial. (Author)

**Water Tower at Bullecourt commemorating the
90th anniversary of the Battle of Bullecourt.
(Author)**

**Australian Digger Memorial standing between
the Australian national flag and the French
Tricolor. The statue looks towards Hendecourt.
(Author)**

The memorial is informally known as the young
digger and not only represents the 'sturdy,
arcadian, audacious and resolute qualities of
the Australian soldier', but reflects the fact that
Australia was a young nation. The First World
War saw it enter the world stage. Regarded as
a colonial support force, the Australians would
transform into formidable storm troops who
would play an important role in winning the war.

AUSTRALIAN MEMORIAL CROSS

The Australian Memorial Cross stands 400 metres east from the Australian Digger Memorial and is dedicated to the 2,249 Australians who were listed as missing in action, their bodies never to be recovered. Erected in 1982 by Jean Letaille Jean Lacourt and André Coillot it is located in the position where OG 2 trench ran parallel with the Riencourt–Bullecourt Road. 'REMEMBER SOUVIENS TOI' is inscribed on the cross.

The plinth on which the Australian Cross stands also contains plaques commemorating those Australian soldiers who died nearby, including Major Percy Black, Lance Corporal William Charles Madden, 22nd Battalion AIF (Killed 3rd May 1917) and Private Stanley George Edwards, 15th Battalion from Rockhampton, Queensland and Lieutenant Wilfred Griffith Barlow 58th Battalion, killed near the railway line on 12th May 1917 the plaque dedicated on 25th May 2008 by his family. Private Edward Frederick Crowley from the 2nd/1st Battalion London Regiment is also commemorated by a plaque written in French. R.M. Gunn from the 4th AIF left a plaque commemorating the comrades he lost at Bullecourt with the dedication:

IN MEMORY
OF ALL MY MATES KILLED IN ACTION
LEST WE FORGET
RM GUNN 4TH AIF

The sister of Private Alfred King 2675 from the 58th Battalion erected a plaque to her fallen brother with the words:

The Australian Cross Memorial stands on the site of the German trenches of the Hindenburg Line. OG 1 Trench passed through this position and was dug towards where the tree stands in the Central Road. The line of trees on the horizon denote where the railway embankment was positioned from where Australian Infantry battalions advanced. (Author)

FROM YOUR LOVING SISTER GLADY
FROM PORT MELBOURNE
I WILL ALWAYS REMEMBER

Private Roland Fenton who died aged 22 on 3rd May 1917 is commemorated with a plaque. The entire 18th Battalion is also commemorated with a plaque with the inscription:

IN MEMORY
TO ALL THE OFFICERS AND MEN OF THE
18TH BATTALION FIRST AIF WHO SERVED AND FELL
ON THE BATTLEFIELDS OF FRANCE 1914–18
WE FOREVER REMEMBER THE DEBT WE OWE
LEST WE FORGET

Slouch Hat Memorial at Bullecourt. (Author)

Below: **Anzac Day at the Slouch Hat Memorial, Bullecourt on 27th April 2002. (Author)**

SLOUCH HAT MEMORIAL, BULLECOURT

The Slouch Hat Memorial is a felt hat that was bronzed and rests on a plinth located outside Bullecourt Church. It is the focal point of the Anzac Day commemoration in April when at least 2,000 Australian relatives and dignitaries attend each year. Remains of a caterpillar track from Tank 586, commanded by 2nd Lieutenant Harold Clarkson, lie adjacent to this memorial.

Tank Memorial at Bullecourt unveiled 17th April 2010. The memorial which is positioned outside Bullecourt Church, next to a piece of tank track that came from Tank 586 contains the following dedication: 'To the memory of the crews of the tanks of D Battalion HBMGC engaged at Bullecourt on 11th April and 3rd May 1917.'. (Courtesy Yves Fohlen)

The Crucifix at Bullecourt. (Author)

CHAPTER 34

CEMETERIES WHERE THE BULLECOURT FALLEN REST

There are 2,249 Australian and 1,875 British soldiers who died at Bullecourt who have no known graves. The numbers are hard to comprehend. How could so many men disappear off the face of the earth? 2/Lt Bob Stevenson, serving with 2nd/7th London Regiment of 174th Brigade wrote an explanation in his diary on 30th May: 'Dead lying about literally in thousands. Stench terrible. Useless burying as ground continually being churned up by shell fire.'

From Red Cross records we know many men were buried in graves on the battlefield that were lost during the persistent barrages. There is evidence to suggest that the Germans buried many of the Australian dead in haste together with their identity discs. Lance Corporal Frederick Peachey from the 15th Battalion had been captured on 11th April. After he escaped from Limburg Prisoner of War Camp in Germany to Holland in November 1917, Peachey provided the following testimony regarding his missing Platoon Commander 2nd Lieutenant James Proctor:

> The last time I saw him was about 15 minutes after the advance when it was still dark near the British side of the German wire. He was wounded lying on his side, I think wounded about the head or face because he had blood on his face. He was quite still and may have been dead then. After I was captured a friend said ... he had seen Mr. Proctor killed. He was my platoon commander and we went over close together but the smoke was very dense. The German's made us bury about 200 of our own dead in the afternoon without removing discs but I don't know if Lieut. Proctor was buried or not.[1]

Private Albert Tutt from the 48th Battalion had been listed as missing after 11th April. His remains were found on 3rd May 1917 by the 27th German Infantry Division. His body was identified by his identity disc and German records confirm that he was buried 100m west of Riencourt.

The soldiers who died at Bullecourt and who were lost, their existence extinguished without a trace,

were commemorated with their names inscribed on memorials. The Australian fallen were commemorated at the Australian National Memorial at Villers-Bretonneux. The names of the British missing were inscribed on the Arras Memorial at Faubourg D'Amiens Cemetery, Arras.

There are some Bullecourt soldiers who do have a grave bearing their name who rest in Commonwealth War Grave Cemeteries. Soldiers who were evacuated from the battlefield and who died of their wounds at Casualty Clearing Stations were buried in cemeteries close by.

AUSTRALIAN NATIONAL MEMORIAL, VILLERS-BRETONNEUX

The Australian National Memorial at the Villers-Bretonneux Military Cemetery commemorates the names of 10,770 Australian soldiers who were killed during the First World War on the Somme in 1916, during the Arras campaign in 1917, including Bullecourt, resisting the German spring offensive in 1918 and the advance to victory during the last months of the war in 1918. The memorial was inaugurated by King George VI in July 1938. The listed all have no known graves. The remains of the fallen at Bullecourt that were recovered

Australian National Memorial, Villers-Bretonneux.

but were unidentified were buried in a grave with the inscription 'Known unto God'.

Bereaved mothers, wives and children, tormented by their loss, who were notified that their sons, husbands and fathers were missing and that their remains were not recovered, were denied the opportunity to grieve in the customary way. Despite testimonies from cobbers providing visual confirmations of death on the battlefield, the fact that their loved ones' remains were not buried in a war cemetery gave the relatives false hope that they might be alive and return home. Private Robert Johnston who was wounded at Pozières in 1916, was one of those killed at Bullecourt with no known grave. He was a blacksmith, born in Beaufort, Victoria, Australia. He was killed while advancing with the 22nd Battalion AIF towards the German lines in the attack on 3rd May. His mother, Mary Jane Johnston, was still searching for her son's grave six years after he was killed. She wrote a letter to the officer in command of base records at Army Headquarters, Victoria barracks in Melbourne on 26th January. She received the following reply dated 5th February 1923:

Dear Madam,
In reply to your enquiry of the 26th January relative to the grave of your son, the late No. 3854 Private R. Johnston, 22nd Battalion. I very much regret to inform you no advice of its registration has been received to date and in the absence of the same, it must reluctantly concluded that the Graves Services have not succeeded in locating the soldier's last resting place.

Waiting for the recovery and identification of the actual remains, it is understood the authorities contemplate the erection of suitable memorials to the missing on which the full regimental particulars of the soldier and date of death will be inscribed.

Should your son's grave be located later, his remains would be exhumed and re-interred in the nearest Military Cemetery. A permanent headstone would be erected over the site and all expense in connection therewith, with the exception of the personal inscription, will be defrayed by the Government.[2]

Mary Jane Johnston's son's name is commemorated on the Australian National Memorial at Villers-Bretonneux.

Annie White, the wife of Private Edward White, continued to look for husband for twenty years after he had died in the wire at Bullecourt. White, who was aged 29, advanced with the 24th Battalion on 3rd May when he was killed. He was originally listed as missing soon after the battle and on 17th September his wife was sent the following testimony from Private J. Lyons.

I knew Private Ted White of the 24th Btn. C Co. 11th Plt. He was in my platoon and I saw his body lying in No Man's Land near the German wires at Bullecourt on the morning of the 3rd May 1917 about 6 am (daylight). I was a stretcher bearer, and as he was dead I did not do anything to him but left him lying where he fell. We took our objective and held it. I was wounded about 8 am and left. I was certain that it was E.C.V. White; we called him the Alphabet.[3]

Despite receiving this compelling evidence, Annie still had hope and was convinced that he was still alive. For the next ten years she placed 'Soldier's' Whereabouts' notices in the local newspapers in Melbourne requesting any soldiers with information about Edward White to contact her.

Annie White received official confirmation from AIF officials that he was killed on 12th April 1918. On 14th April 1922 she sent to the Army the epitaph which she wanted to be engraved on his tombstone:

TOO DEARLY LOVED EVER TO BE FORGOTTEN
BY HIS LOVING WIFE AND FAMILY[4]

These words could not be inscribed on his tombstone because his body was not recovered. The physical absence of her husband's remains and the fact that he was listed as missing gave her hope that there might exist a remote possibility that he was alive. Annie was sending photos of her husband to mental institutions in Australia in her futile search for him in the 1930s. For the remainder of her life there was no closure. Edward White's name is commemorated on the Australian National Memorial at Villers-Bretonneux.

To lose one family member was a tragedy, but some families had more than one name commemorated on the Australian National Memorial at Villers-Bretonneux. The Buckingham brothers from Ballarat, Victoria are among them. Both William Samuel and George were born and educated in Ballarat. They worked as miners in Western Australia and both were married and each had five children. They enlisted together in Perth on 28th March 1916. William was aged 43 and George was 39 when they enlisted. Their younger brother, Frank aged 18, also enlisted with them on the same day. They were all assigned to the 16th Battalion and arrived in England in November 1916. On Christmas Eve 1916 they sailed for France. All three brothers took part in the Bullecourt battle on 11th April 1917. Frank was the only brother to survive. A comrade saw William killed when a shell exploded on their position in the sunken road; the same shell killed nine men.

The memorial lists the Noy brothers who were both killed while advancing with the 48th Battalion

Privates William & George Buckingham were both killed at Bullecourt on 11th April 1917. They have no known graves and their names are listed on the Australian National Memorial at Villers-Bretonneux. *(Australia's Fighting Sons of the Empire)*

at Bullecourt on 11th April 1917. Ernest Noy, aged 23 and his younger brother Leslie were brought up in Brompton South Australia. Their mother was left with the uncertainty of not knowing the fate of her beloved sons until a year later, when she received the following letter dated 9th April 1918 from the Australian Army authorities:

Dear Madam,
We beg to acknowledge the receipt of your letter of the 5th ... with reference to your enquiry for – 3740 Pte. E.H. Noy: 48th Battalion AIF. 588 Pte. L.C. Noy: 48th Battalion AIF.

We much regret to inform you that they are now both officially reported killed in action on 11-4-17 having previously been reported missing on that date.

In spite of our continuous efforts to do so we have never been able to obtain any information concerning their fate and we are much afraid there is little hope of news being received now so long after the engagement which they fell. It happens unfortunately in only too many cases of men eventually reported killed in an attack that no definite news of them is ever obtained. It can only be assumed that they fell unnoticed in the turmoil and confusion of the moment and that their bodies were buried either by the earth thrown up through subsequent shelling or later by the enemy.[5]

This letter received a year after the Noy brothers were reported missing would give no comfort to their mother. Parents, wives and the children of those men who are listed on the Australian National War Memorial would be left with the same questions, how could their loved ones disappear off the face of the earth? Where were their remains?

The Touzel Brothers from Wagga Wagga, New South Wales are also commemorated on the memorial. Sergeant John Touzel and his brother Private Clifford Touzel both served with the 16th Battalion and were both killed at Bullecourt on 11th April. Sergeant John Touzel worked as a fireman on locomotives prior to the war. He had reached OG 1 Trench when he was hit. His last moments were witnessed by Private W.A. Sisley from the 4th Machine Gun Company:

I saw him jump out on to parapet to throw a bomb, when he was killed outright by M/G bullet, hit in forehead. I was alongside him at the time. His body was left lying on top of parapet. The trench we were in was afterwards taken by the enemy.[6]

Another witness saw him lying next to the body of Lance Corporal Wadeson. Private V.D. Fallon 4547 was also nearby to Sergeant Touzel:

We had taken the enemy's first line trench. Touzel was standing on the parapet firing his rifle at some Germans crawling away when he was killed outright by a machine gun bullet. He fell where he was standing on parapet. I was at the time in the trench about 10 yards away. We afterwards worked along the trench towards the village of Riencourt where we were taken prisoners of war. I only knew him in the battalion. Was a good soldier.[7]

The brothers Lieutenant Walter and 2nd Lieutenant Robert Whitehead from Cheltenham, Victoria, both belonged to D Company, 21st Battalion and were both killed at Bullecourt on 3rd May, both have no known graves. Walter had been wounded during the battle and was last seen heading back towards an advanced dressing station, but never reached it. His brother Robert received fatal wounds to both his legs from a shell. Unable to walk he was reported to have encouraged his men by saying 'Go on boys' before he died.

Private Harold and Walter Piercy were brothers serving in D Company, 23rd Battalion. They came from Auburn, Victoria. Harold was a plumber and Walter was a carpenter. When they enlisted on 25th March 1916 Harold was aged 26 and Walter was 20. When one of the brothers was wounded during the attack on 3rd May, the other brother stayed behind to attend to him when a shell killed them both.

Lieutenant Wilfred Barlow is also listed on the memorial. He was aged 30 when he was killed on 12th May 1917, while taking part in an attack on German positions. He was a teacher from Elsternwick, Victoria. After he had carried out his own orders he volunteered to take command of a leaderless platoon. In doing so he paid the ultimate price. Lieutenant Colonel Charles Denehy wrote home to his bereaved widow explaining the circumstances of his death:

> He was with us but a short time and we had just begun to know him properly and appreciate his fine qualities. He was my grenade officer, keen and capable of the work. He was with me a few minutes before his death. His own portion of the work had been done, but we were being very severely shelled and casualties were numerous. I lost many good men that 12th of May and as report after report was brought to me from different points of the line that this officer ... had been put out of action Lt. Barlow came to me and said 'I am not wounded at headquarters now sir, let me go and take one of the leaderless platoons.' I gave him permission to go and it was not 10 minutes before he was killed. His was the supreme sacrifice, putting aside all thought of personal danger so that he might serve his regiment in its bitter struggle. It was the spirit of men like him that won the day and gained for the 58th a splendid victory that will live in the history of the AIF.[8]

Private Andre Tolstoi, 15th Battalion, a Polish immigrant born in Warsaw (in Russia before the First World War) who died at Bullecourt is also commemorated on the memorial. He was a 42-year-old miner from Rockhampton, Queensland, when he joined the AIF on 6th January 1916. Lance Corporal Stapleton later recalled:

> Tolstoi was in B Company. He joined in Australia. He was well over 40 years of age and was married ... He had several wounds on his body which he had got in other wars ... On the 11th April 1917, we were attacking Bullecourt. We failed to hold our objective which we had taken and when we were retiring to our lines I came across Tolstoi in a shell hole: he was then wounded in the leg and bandaging it himself. We did not hold the ground where he was and I did not see him again – This was about 1.30 pm.[9]

Private Leonard Grisbrook saw Tolstoi killed by a shell in OG 2 Trench.

Many of those soldiers listed on the memorial were British subjects who had immigrated to Australia and joined the AIF during the First World War. Francis Joseph Bland was a Londoner who joined up in Oaklands, South Australia. It is intriguing that he served under the alias Francis Joseph Potter. He served with the AIF and joined the 16th Battalion as reinforcement on 2nd June 1915 on Gallipoli. Within two weeks he suffered shrapnel wounds to his jaw. A year later he received a gun shot wound to his shoulder on 7th August 1916 during the fight for Pozières. He was sent back to England and to St Lukes Hospital in Halifax to recover. He had been awarded the Meritorious Service Medal. He died at Bullecourt on 11th April 1917.

Lieutenant Frederick Dadson from the 14th Battalion was born in London and emigrated to Australia where he served with the Queensland Police Force. He was last seen with a pipe in his mouth when he was killed as he approached the enemy wire in No Man's Land at Bullecourt on 11th April. He was among the first killed during the battle. According to Captain McDermott he was buried, but the grave was lost to shell fire.

WE WILL REMEMBER THEM – SOLDIERS COMMEMORATED ON THE AUSTRALIAN MEMORIAL, VILLERS-BRETONNEUX

PRIVATE ERNEST BUSBY 3760,
22ND BATTALION AIF

William Ernest Busby was born 1889 in Carlton, Victoria. He worked as a driver prior to enlisting on

14th April 1915. Busby was 28 when he was killed at Bullecourt on 3rd May 1917. He has no known grave.

**Private Ernest Busby.
(Courtesy Marcia Holdsworth)**

PRIVATE WILLIAM ECCLESTONE 3456,
16TH BATTALION AIF

William Basil Ecclestone was born at Boyanup. Prior to the war he worked as a farmer. He enlisted at Bunbury in July 1915. Before beginning his basic training he

**Private William Ecclestone.
*(Australia's Fighting Sons of the Empire)***

married Ada Gallimore on 3rd August 1915. Two days later he began basic training. He left his pregnant wife three months later and set sail for Europe. Ada bore him a baby son he would never meet. Ecclestone saw action at Pozières with the 16th Battalion and was killed on 11th April 1917 at Bullecourt.

PRIVATE NELSON PAGE 6565,
16TH BATTALION AIF

Tree planted to honour Private James Paterson and plaque on the Avenue of Heroes at Roma. (Courtesy Ian Malcolm)

Born at Kingsdown Stratton, near Swindon in England in 1882, **Private Page** is an example of the many soldiers born in the British Isles who fought and died at Bullecourt while serving with the Australian Imperial Force. Prior to enlisting, he worked as a boiler maker in Youanmi, Western Australia. He enlisted on 13th April 1916. He was killed on 11th April 1917.

Private Nelson Page. (*Australia's Fighting Sons of the Empire*)

PRIVATE JAMES PATERSON 3889,
49TH BATTALION AIF

James Thomas Paterson was born on 23rd October 1887 at Fifteen Mile Creek, near Toowoomba, Queensland. He began his education at Wallumbilla School. After completing his education at school he would work as a farmer on his father's property, and subsequently acquired a farm property at Lucky Flat, Pickenjennie, just outside Wallumbilla. James was apparently an excellent shot, like many men from the bush and had served with the Roma Commonwealth Light Horse. He enlisted on 31st August 1915. While on he leave he married Elizabeth (Lizzie) Maud Cahill on 1st November 1915. Private Paterson was sent to Egypt where he was assigned to 49th Battalion. After further training in Egypt his battalion was sent to France, arriving in Marseille on 12th June 1916.

Private James Paterson, 49th Battalion AIF. (Courtesy Ian Malcolm)

While he was in France, Lizzie gave birth to their only child, Elizabeth Maud Paterson. Within two months Paterson would experience battle for the first time at Pozières where on 14th August 1916 he received a gun shot wound to his elbow. It is thought by the family that Paterson received this wound from a German sniper. He was evacuated to England where he recovered from his wounds. Military authorities had not informed Lizzie that he was wounded and recovering in England. She was distressed to first discover the news from a report in the local newspaper.

After recovering from his wounds he was sent back to France in December 1916. Paterson rejoined the 49th Battalion on 6th January 1917. The 49th Battalion supported the 13th Brigade during the attack on Noreuil, near Bullecourt, on 2nd April 1917. Three days later Private James Paterson was killed as the 49th Battalion captured the railway embankment. He was aged 28. Private James Paterson's name is commemorated on the Australian Memorial at Villers-Bretonneux. He was also listed on the Wallumbilla Roll of Honour. The town of Roma planted rows of bottle trees around 1924, one of which honours James Paterson. This distinctly Australian memorial is known as Roma and District's

Avenue of Heroes, commemorating all those from the district that died and a ceremony is held each Anzac Day. His name is written alongside those of his fallen 49th Battalion colleagues on the bronze plaques lining the central courtyard of the Australian War Memorial in Canberra.

PRIVATE STANLEY PETTIT 6078,
16TH BATTALION AIF

Stanley Edward Pettit was born in Gippsland, Victoria. He was educated in North Fremantle in Western Australia. He enlisted on 20th March 1916. Pettit sailed for England on 7th August 1916. He was killed by a shell at Bullecourt on 11th April 1917.

Private Stanley Pettit. (Australia's Fighting Sons of the Empire)

PRIVATE ERNEST GEORGE VINEY 2259,
48TH BATTALION AIF

Ernest George Viney was born in Edwardstown, South Australia in 1893. He was the son of James and Sarah Regina Viney. Before the war he lived and worked on a farm ten miles south of Loxton. George Viney enlisted on 2nd May 1916. After completing his basic training he left Australia aboard HMAT *Ballarat* on 12th August 1916 from Adelaide. Viney arrived in Plymouth on 30th September 1916. After spending six weeks with the 12th Training Battalion in England, he was sent to France. On 20th November 1916 he left Folkestone aboard SS *Victoria* bound for Boulogne. He joined the 48th Battalion on 4th December 1916. Private Viney was killed at Bullecourt on 11th April 1917.

Private Ernest Viney. (Courtesy Fearn Viney)

PRIVATE IAN WOOD 4011,
11TH BATTALION AIF

Ian John Wood was born in Lanarkshire, Scotland in 1894. The family emigrated to Australia and lived in Bunbury, Western Australia. Here he found employment as a fireman for WAGR. He was aged 21 when he enlisted on 20th August 1915. After completing basic training he embarked aboard RMS *Mongolia* at Fremantle and sailed for Egypt on 22nd November 1915. He joined the 11th Battalion AIF on 2nd March 1916. The battalion was sent to Marseille, France on 5th April. Wood was wounded during operations in Pozières on 22nd August 1916 and was admitted to a casualty clearing station with gun shot wounds to his back. He was evacuated to hospital at Etaples. After convalescing he rejoined the 11th Battalion towards the end of September 1916. He was later sent back to hospital for a short period suffering from influenza during November 1916. Private Ian Wood was killed in action at Bullecourt on 6th May 1917, aged 23.

Private Ian Wood. (Courtesy Wendy Johnson)

ARRAS MEMORIAL

British soldiers who fought at Bullecourt and who were listed as missing are commemorated on the Arras Memorial at Faubourg D'Amiens Cemetery. The memorial lists the names of 34,719 men from Britain, New Zealand and South Africa who died in the Arras sector of the Western Front from spring 1916 to 7th August 1918 and who have no known grave.

Many of the families of the men who are honoured on the Arras Memorial did not receive official confirmation that their fathers, sons and brothers had been killed until months after they perished. Soon after the Bullecourt battle, James and Esther Coleman from Stratford-upon-Avon had been informed that their son Lance Corporal William Coleman serving with the 2nd Royal Warwickshire Regiment was reported missing on 4th May 1917. During October 1917 they received official notification that he was either killed or died

The Arras
Memorial.
(Author)

Interior of the
Arras Memorial.
(Author)

of wounds on or shortly after that date. Their son was officially declared dead, but there was uncertainty about how he died. The local newspaper *The Herald* reported that Coleman had

> ... enlisted in January 1915 and after three months training in the south of France he had been in several engagements being wounded and gassed in the big push last July. During service with the Colours he had only seven days leave. At the time of enlistment he worked for Mr. Bullen at the Head Press Printing works.[10]

Analysing the Commonwealth War Graves Commission website the devastation which affected every community can be seen. Sometimes the loss for one family was multiplied. Private Frederick King was one of eight brothers who served in World War One. He served with the 9th Devonshire Regiment when he was killed aged 29 on 7th May 1917 at Bullecourt. Five of the eight brothers were killed during the war.

James and Samuel Ainsworth were brothers from Bolton who are listed on the Arras Memorial. James was aged 34 and Samuel was aged 28. Both brothers served with the 21st Manchester Regiment,

William and Mary Forshew, of 90, Swallow Lane, Golcar, Huddersfield, would lose two sons killed during the battle for Bullecourt. Both sons served in the 2nd/7th Duke of Wellington's Regiment. Thomas aged 22 was killed on 3rd May during the first day of the second Bullecourt battle. His younger brother Horace was a Corporal, aged 21 and he was killed when the battalion attacked on 14th May.

Captain Theodore Victor Chapman MC was aged 19 when he was killed on 12th May 1917 while attacking Bullecourt with the 2nd The Queen's (Royal West Surrey Regiment). Theodore has no known grave. His parents Theodore C. Chapman and Alice B. Chapman, from Bristol had lost two other sons; Gordon and Percival also fell.

Captain Maitland Lockhart Gordon from the 2nd Gordon Highlanders is also listed. Gordon was born on 27th September 1882 in Kensington, London, but his barrister father relocated the family to Toronto, Canada. After graduating as a civil engineer from McGill University, Montreal, Gordon studied at the Royal Military College, Kingston, Ontario. He enlisted to join the Canadian Militia in 1902. When war broke out he was sent to England as part of the Canadian Expeditionary Force. During the early part of the war he served with the 16th and 17th Battalions. During early 1915 he requested transfer to the 3rd Gordon Highlanders and later during the war he was assigned to the 2nd Battalion. In February 1915 his commission was approved and on 2nd April he was appointed as a Lieutenant. Gordon was wounded for the first time on 18th June 1915 when he sustained severe wounds to his left shoulder. He was evacuated and sent to a hospital in England. He returned to the Western Front and 11th March and was promoted to Captain. On 30th June 1916 Gordon received wounds to his head, legs and right arm and was sent to England to recover. Captain Gordon led the 2nd Gordon Highlanders into Tower Trench on 7th May 1917. He established contact with the Australians on his right flank and was killed in the village on the same day. He was aged 35.

The Arras Memorial also commemorates many of the tank crewmen from D Battalion Machine Gun Corps Heavy Branch. They include Lieutenant Eric William Money. Money was born in 1893 and enlisted in the Army Cyclist Corps on 4th March 1916. He later transferred to the Machine Gun Corps Heavy Branch. He commanded one of the tanks during the First Battle of Bullecourt on 11th April 1917. He brought his tank near to the German wire but was killed when the tank received a direct hit from a German shell. He was aged 25 when he died

Benjamin Bown was born to William and Rosella Bown in 1895 in Atherstone, Warwickshire. He initially enlisted to join the Oxford and Buckinghamshire Light

Infantry. He later transferred to the Machine Gun Corps then he went on to serve as tank crew with D Battalion Machine Gun Corps Heavy Branch. He was aged 22 when after he exited Tank 799 as flames engulfed it he was killed by enemy fire during the first Bullecourt battle on 11th April.

Private Harry Lord, another tank man is honoured at the Arras Memorial. Lord was born in Cleckheaton, Yorkshire in 1893. He was the son of Walter and Lavinia Lord of 19 Highfield Terrace. Harry Lord enlisted to join the Northumberland Fusiliers on 25th August 1915. He was aged 24 when he was killed on 11th April.

Although all these men have no known graves, they are not forgotten and they were not forgotten by their grieving families. The family of Private John Charles Thornton wrote poems about their loss, which were printed in the local newspapers on the anniversary of his death. Thornton who served with the 1st South Staffordshire Regiment was killed at Bullecourt on 13th May. In May 1918, a year after his death, his mother and sisters wrote the following verses:

> Sad and our hearts do wander
> To a grave so far away,
> Where they laid our dearest brother
> Just a year ago today.[11]

Thornton's family wrote another poem in his memory in the following year:

> Two years have passed since that sad day,
> When one we loved was called away
> God took him home, it was His will,
> But in our hearts he liveth still.
> God will link the broken chain
> Closer when we meet again'
> From his sisters, Phyllis, Nellie, and brother George[12]

Farmers at Bullecourt are finding skeletons today. The remains of Captain John Pritchard from the 2nd Honourable Artillery Company were recovered in a field where sheep now graze in 2009. John Pritchard joined the 1st Honourable Artillery Company as a Private on 1st March 1909. He went to France on 18th September 1914, weeks after the war began. By that time he had reached the rank of Sergeant. Pritchard was wounded on 26th November 1914 while on the Neuve Eglise front, but did not need to go to hospital. On 13th January 1915 he was commissioned as a 2nd Lieutenant. He was wounded a second time on 16th March 1915 and returned to England on 21st March. After recovering from his wounds he was transferred to the 2nd Battalion HAC. On 21st January 1916 he was promoted to Lieutenant and on 17th September 1916 he received a further promotion to temporary

Captain. He returned to France with the 2nd HAC on 1st October 1916. Captain John Pritchard was killed on 15th May 1917 at Bullecourt. His remains were recovered in 2009, together with two pistols and papers which helped to identify him. Pritchard and Private Christopher Elphick, who also belonged to the 2nd HAC and was killed on the same date, were buried in the presence of their families at HAC Cemetery on 23rd April 2013. Technically Pritchard's name can now be removed from the Arras Memorial, because he is no longer missing.

WE WILL REMEMBER THEM – SOLDIERS COMMEMORATED ON THE ARRAS MEMORIAL

PRIVATE JAMES MCLELLAND 238027
2ND/4TH BATTALION DUKE OF WELLINGTON'S (WEST RIDING REGIMENT)

Killed on 3rd May 1917.

Private James McLelland. *(Bradford Weekly Telegraph)*

PRIVATE NORMAN METCALFE 268341,
2ND/6TH DUKE OF WELLINGTON'S (WEST RIDING REGIMENT)

Norman Sutton Metcalfe was born in Gomersal in 1898. Metcalfe lived in Bingley before enlisting to join the West Riding Regiment. He was killed on 3rd May 1917.

Private Norman Metcalfe. *(Bradford Weekly Telegraph)*

PRIVATE ARTHUR FIELD 241392
2ND/6TH BATTALION WEST YORKSHIRE REGIMENT

Son of Thomas and Sarah Arm Field, of 122, Willowfield St., Princeville, Bradford. **Private Arthur Field** was killed on the 11th April 1917.

Private Arthur Field. *(Bradford Weekly Telegraph)*

PRIVATE CLARENCE DUFTON 242059,
2ND/6TH BATTALION WEST YORKSHIRE REGIMENT

Clarence Percival Dufton was born in North Bierley, Yorkshire in 1895. Clarence was living in Halifax when he enlisted to join the Army as a private in a Bradford recruiting office. He was assigned to the 2nd/6th Battalion West Yorkshire Regiment and was killed on 11th April 1917. Private Clarence Dufton was aged 22 when he died at Bullecourt.

Private Clarence Dufton.
(Courtesy Nick Walton)

LANCE CORPORAL WILLIAM BIGGIN 241027,
2ND/6TH BATTALION WEST YORKSHIRE REGIMENT

William Biggin was killed on 3rd May 1917.

Lance Corporal William Biggin. (Bradford Weekly Telegraph)

PRIVATE JAMES ELTOFT 241917,
2ND/6TH BATTALION WEST YORKSHIRE REGIMENT

James William Eltoft was born in 1886 in Great Horton, Bradford. He was killed on 11th April 1917.

Private J Eltoft. (Bradford Weekly Telegraph)

PRIVATE JOHN STOCKS 240956 'C' COY,
2ND/6TH BATTALION WEST YORKSHIRE REGIMENT

John Stocks was killed on 3rd May 1917.

Private John Stocks. (Bradford Weekly Telegraph)

PRIVATE DOUGLAS STOWELL 240970,
2ND/6TH BATTALION WEST YORKSHIRE REGIMENT

Douglas Howell Stowell was born in 1895 in Bradford. He was killed on 3rd May 1917.

Private Douglas Stowell.
(Bradford Weekly Telegraph)

PRIVATE ROBERT MCCULLEY 242460,
2ND/6TH BATTALION WEST YORKSHIRE REGIMENT

Robert McCulley killed on 3rd May 1917.

Private R McCulley. (Bradford Weekly Telegraph)

PRIVATE MAURICE RAISBECK 306618
2ND/7TH DUKE OF WELLINGTON'S (WEST RIDING REGIMENT)

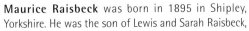

Maurice Raisbeck was born in 1895 in Shipley, Yorkshire. He was the son of Lewis and Sarah Raisbeck, of Greenroyd, Coach Rd., Baildon, Shipley, Yorks. He was killed on 3rd May 1917 aged 23.

Private Maurice Raisbeck.
(Bradford Weekly Telegraph)

PRIVATE FRED MORGAN 306520
2ND/7TH BATTALION DUKE OF WELLINGTON'S (WEST RIDING REGIMENT)

Fred Morgan was aged 24 when he was killed on 3rd May 1917.

Private Fred Morgan.
(Bradford Weekly Telegraph)

PRIVATE WALTER MACKINTOSH 201528,
2ND/5TH WEST YORKSHIRE REGIMENT

Walter Mackintosh was killed on 3rd May 1917.

Lance Corporal Walter Mackintosh. (*Harrogate Herald* 27th June 1917)

LANCE CORPORAL WALTER SMITH 201463,
2ND/5TH WEST YORKSHIRE REGIMENT

Walter Smith was killed on 3rd May 1917.

Lance Corporal Walter Smith. (*Harrogate Herald* 27th June 1917)

CORPORAL ARCHIE BAINES 201671,
2ND/5TH WEST YORKSHIRE REGIMENT

Archie Baines was killed on on 3rd May 1917.

Corporal Archie Baines. (*Harrogate Herald* 27th June 1917)

PRIVATE WILLIAM MORRELL 242235,
2ND/6TH WEST YORKSHIRE REGIMENT

William Morrell was killed on 3rd May 1917.

Private William Morrell. (*Harrogate Herald* 18th July 1917)

PRIVATE MAURICE WARD 202510,
2ND/4TH BATTALION YORK & LANCASTER REGIMENT

Maurice Ward was killed aged 22 on 3rd May 1917.

Private Maurice Ward. (*Sheffield Daily Telegraph*)

PRIVATE EDWARD CROWLEY 203483
2ND/1ST BATTALION LONDON REGIMENT

Born **Frederick Edward Crowley** in Haggerston, London in 1884. He became a carpenter and married Ellen Butler on 31st May 1909. They lived above a shop in Lillington Street, Westminster. It is probable that Crowley served in the Territorial Army prior to the war for the service number 4724 (3/10 London Regiment) is stated in his records. Crowley enlisted at a recruiting office in Whitehall in the 1st City of London Battalion (Royal Fusiliers). After completing his training in Warminster, Crowley and the battalion sailed for France on 20th January 1917. Crowley was killed on 17th May 1917.

Private Edward Crowley. (Jean & Denise Letaille Bullecourt Museum)

PRIVATE HAROLD COPE 242751,
2ND/5TH BATTALION KING'S OWN YORKSHIRE LIGHT INFANTRY

Harold Cope was killed in action at Bullecourt on 21st May 1917. He left a widow, Blanchard, and four children. On Friday 1st June 1917, the following article was published in the *Derby Mercury*:

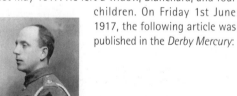

Private Harold Cope. (Courtesy Christopher Preston)

Derby Tradesman's Loss

Private Harold Cope, KOYLI, one of seven brothers serving with the forces and third son of Mr James Cope, Pork Butcher of Irongate, Derby, was, we regret to state, killed in action on May 21st. He was 35 years of age and married and like some of the other sons was, prior to the war, engaged in his father's extensive business. He was a man of marked ability and a wide circle of friends will bear his death with deep regret and will extend every sympathy to his widow and four young children. Mr Cope had nine sons, the two eldest of which remain at home and the other six still with the forces are:

Second Lieutenant Charles Cope – Liverpool Regiment

Driver James Cope – Army Service Corps

Private Wilfred Cope – Notts and Derby Regiment (In France)

Second Lieutenant George Cope – Machine Gun Corps (In France)

Corporal Rowland Cope – Notts and Derby Regiment

Gunner Frederick Cope – Royal Field Artillery (In France)[13]

NOREUIL AUSTRALIAN CEMETERY

Noreuil Australian Cemetery was established in April 1917 and is located south of the village of Noreuil. This region was where British and Australian artillery was positioned during April and May 1917. The area received heavy bombardment during the second battle of Bullecourt. The cemetery contains 182 Australian and 62 British graves; 28 graves contain unidentified soldiers and 82 graves were destroyed by German shell fire, including the graves of the Clayton brothers. Edward and William Clayton from Dover, Tasmania both joined the 52nd Battalion and died together on 12th April 1917. They are buried next to each other in Noreuil Australian Cemetery (Graves E5 (E. Clayton) and E6 (W. Clayton).

Major George Tostevin, although listed as belonging to the 1st Coy Machine Gun Company, was commanding the 3rd Coy MGC when he was killed on 5th May while on reconnaissance between Noreuil and Bullecourt by a shell. He came from Guernsey and emigrated to Tasmania where he worked as an engine driver. He initially belonged to the 12th Battalion but transferred to the 1st Machine Gun Company. Tostevin was brought to Noreuil dressing station, where he died from his wounds on 5th May 1917. He was buried in the presence of the men from his Company, who erected the Cross of St George over his grave. Tostevin was highly regarded by the men under his command. Private John Reid paid this tribute to him: 'He was one of the best. We couldn't have got a better if we had hunted the whole Division.'[14]

QUÉANT ROAD CEMETERY, BUISSY

Quéant was strongly fortified by the Germans who incorporated it into the Hindenburg Line defences. The village was held by the Germans until the 52nd, 57th and 63rd Divisions from the Third British Army took it on 2nd September 1918. Quéant Road Cemetery at Buissy was established by the 2nd and 5th Casualty Clearing Stations in October and November 1918, with 71 graves. After the war ended the cemetery was enlarged and remains from smaller cemeteries in the region were brought there. Many of those remains belonged to Australian and British soldiers who died at Bullecourt. 2,377 Commonwealth servicemen rest in Quéant Road Cemetery – there are 1,266 British, 997 Australian, 87 Canadian, two British West Indies, three German and one New Zealand graves.

Major Benjamin Leane who lies in the cemetery, was killed with 21 other men from the 48th Battalion when a German barrage descended upon Battalion Headquarters on 10th April 1917. He was the 2nd in

Noreuil Australian Cemetery. (Author)

Quéant Road Cemetery. (Author)

command of the Battalion. His brother Lieutenant Colonel Raymond Leane carried the remnants of his brother's body to a place near the railway embankment to bury him. Private John Martin:

> Major Leane was standing alongside looking after us. A whiz-bang hit him and blew him to pieces. The only thing we could find was his head and a leg. I was alongside of him when he was killed. Colonel Leane, the Major's brother, next day collected his remains and buried them in the sunken road by Bullecourt.[15]

After the war Major Leane's remains were brought to Quéant Road Cemetery. His epitaph reads:

HE DIED FOR THE GREATEST CAUSE IN HISTORY EVER
REMEMBERED

Private Gladstone Bannatyne, 13th Battalion had fought his way into OG 2 Trench on 11th April. They held onto the captured position for several hours, until they could hold out no longer. Instead of surrendering, Bannatyne chose to make a dash across the snow-covered No Man's Land, but was killed by machine gun fire. Private Alfred Neate saw Bannatyne's last moments, recalling:

> He got up on parados to get back when he was hit by machine gun bullets in arm – which was almost severed. He jumped back into trench. I don't know what became of him when we were taken prisoners. I think he must have bled to death as there was no one to attend to him.[16]

One of the remarkable stories associated with this cemetery is that of Sergeant Jack White, who was killed on 3rd May while advancing with the 22nd AIF Battalion. Listed as missing in action, his body lay undisturbed in the fields of Bullecourt until a local farmer discovered his remains while he was ploughing his field in December 1994. Among the possessions found upon him that confirmed his identity was a wallet and a lock of hair, which is assumed to have belonged to his wife Lillian. Sergeant White was given a proper burial in this cemetery in the presence of his family, local residents from Bullecourt and representatives from the Australian Embassy.

There are some Englishmen who were killed at Bullecourt while serving with the Australian Imperial Force. Lieutenant Archibald Taplin who was killed while serving with the 17th Battalion AIF at Bullecourt on 3rd May was born in Bristol, England. Taplin, who was a Gallipoli veteran, was seen lying dead in a crater near to the German wire.

Lance Corporal Arthur Emmins, who served with the 48th Battalion AIF was born in London. He was killed on the parapet of the German trenches at Bullecourt. Private A Wilson recalled:

> I was with him in the Hindenburg Line at Bullecourt and saw him hit first and wounded about and then about two minutes after a shell came and killed him instantly. I do not think that he was buried except the Germans buried him, as we had to retire and left the dead and a good many wounded in the trench. I was with him in the 10th Platoon for four months. He was a good pal.[17]

His epitaph reads:

NO GREATER LOVE, HATH NO MAN THAN THIS,
HE DIED TO SAVE OTHERS

Private Charlie Chalk, who rests in this cemetery, was born in Tichfield, Hampshire, England. He was killed on 3rd May 1917 while advancing with the 26th Battalion AIF. Sergeant John Dawson was another Englishman who died while fighting as an Australian soldier at Bullecourt. Dawson was a scouser born in Liverpool, England. He was killed on 3rd May while advancing with the 19th Battalion.

HAC CEMETERY ECOUST-ST MEIN

HAC Cemetery was established soon after the British 7th and Australian 4th Division had captured German positions from Doignies to Henin-sur-Cojeul on 2nd April 1917. The 7th Division was responsible for its creation when 27 soldiers from the 2nd HAC were buried there after the battle. A further 12 Australian gunners who were killed during the German counter attack at Lagnicourt on 15th April were buried in the cemetery. After the war remains from other smaller

HAC Cemetery. (Author)

cemeteries were exhumed and re-interred at HAC Cemetery. The cemetery contains the graves of 1,508 British, 162 Australian, 26 Canadian, four New Zealand and 145 unknown soldiers. It also contains 65 special memorials to soldiers buried in nearby cemeteries that were obliterated by shell fire and lost forever.

Many of the men buried at HAC Cemetery were killed during the Bullecourt battles. Private G.A. Culpan from the 2nd/4th Duke of Wellington's Regiment and Private F. Illingworth from the 2nd/7th West Yorkshire Regiment were killed during the first Bullecourt battle on 11th April and their remains were buried here.

Private Herbert Brown was born in Lower Tranmere, Birkenhead, England, but emigrated to Nungarin in Western Australia where he became a farmer. He enlisted to serve with the AIF on 23rd February 1916 and was assigned to the 16th Battalion as a reinforcement. He fought his way into the German trenches but was wounded. Unable to get back to the Railway Embankment he was captured by the Württemburgers. He was taken to a German dressing station, Wurt. Sanitate Komp 31, where he died from his wounds later that day. He was initially buried in Cagnicourt Cemetery but after the war his remains were transferred to HAC Cemetery.

Several Yorkshiremen who were killed on 3rd May are also buried in the cemetery. They include Lieutenant Gerald Brown from the 2nd/6th Battalion West Yorkshire Regiment who came from Leeds and was killed aged 21. Lieutenant Selwyn Upton 20th Battalion AIF was killed on 3rd May and is buried here.

2nd Lieutenant William Sandoe from the 9th Devonshire Regiment who was killed by shell fire near to the Railway Embankment on 8th May was brought here for burial. 2nd Lieutenant Charles Holdsworth from the 9th Devonshire's was also killed on the same date. Sergeant William Dadson from the 2nd Battalion Queens (Royal West Surrey) Regiment, aged 28 from Gravesend and Private William Kitchen from the 21st Battalion Manchester Regiment, aged 22 from Bradford lie here. 2nd Lieutenant Alfred Parkinson, 21st Manchesters who was killed on 12th May rests in this cemetery. His epitaph reads:

THERE IS A CORNER OF A FOREIGN FIELD SHALL BE
FOR EVER ENGLAND

Private William Dilley was killed by shell fire as he was advancing with the 22nd Battalion between OG 1 Trench and OG 2 Trench on 3rd May 1917.

VRAUCOURT COPSE CEMETERY

Vraucourt Copse Cemetery was built in September 1918 and was initially the resting place for 43 British soldiers

Vraucourt Copse Cemetery. (Author)

who were killed only weeks before the war ended. The cemetery was enlarged in 1928 when graves buried in the nearby Vaulx Advanced Dressing Station Cemetery were relocated there. The cemetery contains the graves of 65 British soldiers and 38 Australian soldiers, of which five are unknown, except for the fact they came from Australia.

Captain Norman Shierlaw MC was the medical officer for the 13th Battalion. Shierlaw received his Military Cross for tending to the wounded during the attack on Stormy Trench, near Geudecourt on 4th/5th February 1917. His award was posted in the *London Gazette* on 26th March 1917 stating that: 'He continually attended to the wounded for two days and nights under heavy fire.'[19] On 11th April 1917 Shierlaw had established a dressing station close to the railway embankment. While he was dressing the wound of a fellow officer he was mortally wounded by an HE shell. The explosion killed several other men including Sergeant Peter Kibble DCM. Kibble was an original member of the 13th Battalion and was wounded on Gallipoli on 3rd May 1915 and received the DCM for his bravery at Pozières in August 1916. Kibble was having his leg wound dressed when he was killed by the blast. Kibble was congratulating himself that he had received a Blighty wound. He was found still clutching his pipe in his hand. Shierlaw was tended at the dressing station, but did not regain consciousness and died from his wounds. The padre of the 13th Brigade buried him close to the railway cutting. After the war his remains were brought to Vraucourt Copse Cemetery.

2nd Lieutenant Richmond Howell-Price MC, 1st Battalion AIF who was killed on 3rd May at Bullecourt was buried here. His brother, Lieutenant Colonel O.G. Howell-Price had been killed the previous year at Flers. Another brother, Major Philip Howell-Price, would die at Broodseinde in October 1918. A fourth brother, Lieutenant John Howell-Price would be awarded the

DSC for the role he played aboard the submarine C3 at Zeebrugge during the raid on 23rd April 1918.

Private Robert Bamford 5984 19th Battalion may have been wounded on 3rd May and died of his wounds at Vraucourt Advanced Dressing Station. He was born in Wigan, England.

BAPAUME AUSTRALIAN CEMETERY

Bapaume Australian Cemetery was established in March 1917 when Australian units occupied the town as German forces were withdrawing to the Hindenburg Line. The cemetery, which stands amongst some allotments on the edge of a residential area in Bapaume, was created to accommodate burials from the nearby 3rd Australian Casualty Clearing Station and was in operation from March to June 1917 and then again during April and May 1918.

Among those resting within this small cemetery is Lieutenant Harry McKinley, who was an intelligence officer belonging to the 14th Battalion who worked as Jacka's assistant. McKinley had been awarded the Croix de Guerre for his work at Pozières in August 1916, where he supervised the digging of a 350-yard sap from Box Lane to OG 2 Trench, during the night and under heavy shell fire, which greatly assisted the assault upon Mouquet Farm. At Bullecourt, he was mortally wounded on 11th April by a shell while in the sunken road prior to the start of the assault. Jacka who was near to McKinley was thrown to the ground by the blast. McKinley was taken to the 13th Battalion Aid Post, then onto the 3rd Australian Casualty Station where he died from his wounds.

Private John Brown an original from the 16th Battalion was also mortally wounded at Bullecourt on 11th April. He suffered a fractured left leg and severe shell wounds and died on 12th April. He was buried at Bapaume Australian Cemetery.

Private William Stute, 46th Battalion, received a wound which penetrated his abdomen at Bullecourt on the 11th. He was anointed by the Chaplain before he died the following day.

GRÉVILLERS BRITISH CEMETERY

Grévillers British Cemetery contains the graves of 2,106 Commonwealth servicemen, of whom 189 are unidentified. Allied soldiers entered Grévillers on 14th March 1917 as German forces were withdrawing to the Hindenburg Line. During April and May 1917, the 3rd and 29th Australian Casualty Clearing Stations were established at Grévillers in order to accommodate the wounded brought in from the Bullecourt battlefield. Many of the wounded from Bullecourt died from their wounds at these casualty clearing stations and were buried. The cemetery was used by Allied forces until Grévillers was captured by German forces during the Kaiser's offensive in March 1918. The New Zealand Division recaptured Grévillers in August 1918 and the cemetery was used again, when the 34th, 49th and 56th Casualty Clearing Stations were set up there.

Among the Bullecourt wounded who died and were buried at Grévillers Cemetery was Captain Oscar Jones, 21st Battalion. Jones, who served as a policeman in Melbourne prior to the war, had been wounded in the attack on the German trenches on 3rd May. He sustained severe wounds to his thigh and both legs by shell fire just in front of OG 1 Trench. Stretcher bearers evacuated from Jones from the battlefield to a First Aid Post near to the sunken road, and then he was transferred to the 29th Australian Casualty Clearing Station. He died on the stretcher as soon as he arrived on 4th May.

Private Charles Kenny from the 19th Battalion received a gun shot wound to his chest on 3rd May. He was brought to the 3rd Casualty Clearing Station later

Bapaume Australian Cemetery. (Author)

Grévillers Cemetery. (Author)

Another view of Grévillers Cemetery. (Author)

that day and he was unconscious on arrival. Kenny, aged 26, never regained consciousness and died of his wounds. He lies in Grévillers British Cemetery where his epitaph reads:

HE DIED AS HE LIVED, NOBLY

Private Michael Meenan from the 24th Battalion received a bullet wound in the stomach on 3rd May. He was a jockey and former railway worker prior to the war. Meenan had reached OG 2 Trench when he was wounded. Despite his wounds he tried to get back to the safety of the Railway Embankment for his comrade, Private James McIntosh testified, 'On the way back I saw Meenan on the ground wounded. I saw him now and again crawling making his way gradually back to our lines.'[19] Somehow, Meenan got to the Railway Embankment where he was taken to the 3rd Casualty Clearing Station where he died on 4th May. He was buried on that same day by the Catholic Chaplain Cullen.

Private Fearnley Lock, 9th Devonshire Regiment, was wounded on 7th May and died of his wounds at Grévillers the following day. He was aged 19 and came from Buckfastleigh, Devonshire.

Private William Penwill, 9th Devonshire Regiment was also wounded on 7th May. He was brought to Grévillers where he died. He was aged 31 and the son of William and Maria Penwill, of Liswomey, Torquay; husband of Ellen Penwill, of Aberystwyth. His epitaph reads:

SAFE IN THE HOMELAND

Private Arthur Perman, a stretcher bearer for the 6th Field Ambulance, Australian Army Medical Corps, also rests within Grévillers Cemetery. He was bank clerk from Brighton, Victoria. He was severely wounded by shrapnel when he was carrying a wounded man by stretcher from the battlefield. Shrapnel had entered his chest and Perman was brought to the 3rd Australian Casualty Clearing Station near Grévillers on 6th May 1917. He died from his wounds on 8th May 1917.

Perman was highly respected by the men in his section. Private Dight recalled 'we were all very fond of him. He was old fashioned and very well liked. He was called the father of the Corps and the Dad of the section.'[20]

Private Roy Hart was a friend of Perman's and wrote a very moving letter to his family give details of his wounds, his death at the 3rd Australian Casualty Clearing Station and his burial at Grévillers Cemetery:

Dear Mr and Mrs Perman and family,

It is with a very sad heart that I sit down and write to you the letter of sympathy on account of Arthur's death. He was your son, and brother, and my pal, there was never a man that carried out the duties of each in a truer way, once again, I ask you to accept my deepest sympathy.

It may be very painful for you to read, especially as it will be long after you first receive word of Arthur's death, yet I feel it my duty to tell you all I know what led up to it, and how he spent his last few hours of life.

Arthur was wounded on the morning of the 6th May and was at the time carrying a wounded man with the other members of his squad (Pts Harris, Pery and Rose). A 5.9 H.E. shell burst some twenty yards behind them and a piece entered Arthur's chest from the right shoulder. His only words on being hit were, 'My poor Father, my poor Father'. He passed through our dressing station about 11.30 am and went straight on to the Casualty Clearing Station where he arrived about 1.30 pm. I went straight to the C.C.S. and got there in time to help remove his clothes and fix up his personal effects, prior to his being moved to a ward. He was suffering a good deal of pain at the time, so of course could speak very little, he however expressed a wish that I should write to you. I went down to the C.C.S. again in the evening about 7.30 he was suffering a lot and breathing was difficult, it was too early to say if he had a chance of recovery or not. I was down to see him again on the morning of the 7th and his condition was much the same. I was not able to visit Arthur again until the afternoon of the 8th. He saw me enter the ward and called me by name. He was propped up in bed by pillows, etc. and although looking worse, was decidedly more comfortable and breathing easier. Before leaving I had a long talk with Arthur's nurse, she told me that he could not possibly recover and would probably not live till the following morning, gangrene having set in, he was not, however suffering any pain, certain drugs having been administered to relieve both pain and breathing, she also assured me that everything possible under the circumstances had been done for Arthur's welfare, which fact I'm sure is quite true. I made another trip to the C.C.S. at 7 pm in the evening but only to learn that he had passed away about 5.30 pm. The nurse, at Arthur's desire will probably have written you ere this. At 2.15 pm on Wednesday, 9th May, a party of about 20 men from the Ambulance attended the burial service in a small cemetery close to the C.C.S. Arthur was held in high esteem by all in this Ambulance who knew him. I have known Arthur ever since the 6th Aust. Field Ambulance has been formed, we served on Gallipoli and here in France together and I can safely say that never has a braver, truer or finer life been given for his country's sake than Arthur's. We are having a nice, though plain wooden cross erected on the grave, in the course of a few days. Arthur's personal effects will be forwarded to you through A.I.F. Headquarters ... I enclose an unfinished letter of Arthur's which he wrote just prior to going up to the front line.

Trusting that I have done some small service for Arthur in writing you and that it will cause you far less pain to read than it was me to write. Believe me. A pal of Arthur's Roy W Hart, Pte. 3274.[21]

Lieutenant Eric Costin MM 4th Battalion AIF rests at Grévillers Cemetery. Costin served in Gallipoli during 1915 and was awarded the Military Medal for action at Pozières. He was buried twice by shell fire at Pozières and led a patrol that culminated in the capture of 100 German soldiers and a fully equipped dressing station, which was utilised by the Australians. At Bullecourt on 6th May Costin received a shrapnel wound to the abdomen. He was brought to No.3 Casualty Clearing Station on that same day, but died on 8th May. He was buried in this cemetery the following day by Chaplain C.T. Walters.

Private Frederick Hayward from the 8th Battalion was mortally wounded while holding the Hindenburg Line at Bullecourt on 8th May. Shrapnel from a shell blast lacerated his body causing multiple penetrations to his chest. Hayward, who was born in Asfordbury, Leicestershire, England, died on 9th May. His epitaph reads:

HE FOUGHT THE FIGHT, THE VICTORY WON,
AND ENTERED INTO REST

Private H. Shipp 24009, 2nd Queen's (Royal West Surrey Regiment) was mortally wounded at Bullecourt on 12th May and died at Grévillers the following day. He rests within this cemetery.

FAVREUIL BRITISH CEMETERY

Favreuil was captured by British forces during March 1917 and a cemetery was established in April 1917 and was used by the 62nd Division and Field Ambulances. The cemetery holds the graves of 399 Commonwealth soldiers including many soldiers who died from wounds sustained at Bullecourt. Private M Way had died from the effects of gas poisoning at the 13th Australian Field Ambulance on 11th April and was buried in this cemetery adjacent to the Main Dressing Station at Favreuil.

Most notable is Private Wilfred Walters from the 6th Field Ambulance. His service number was 992 and he was an original. Walters was a stretcher bearer who was mortally wounded when a shell exploded while he was bringing in a wounded man from the battlefield at Bullecourt on 3rd May. As he was been evacuated to a dressing station he died from the wounds sustained to his stomach. His father was a farrier sergeant in the same unit and buried his son at Favreuil. His epitaph reads:

OUR DEAR BOY
FAITHFUL, TRUE AND LOYAL
KILLED WHILE SAVING OTHERS

Favreuil British Cemetery. (Author)

ACHIET-LE-GRAND COMMUNAL CEMETERY

The 45th and 49th Casualty Clearing Stations were in operation at Achiet-le-Grand from April 1917. The allied railhead ended at Achiet Station and played an important role in transferring stretcher cases to Pozières and then onto hospitals in Rouen and at Wimereux. The communal cemetery and extension was used by Commonwealth medical units to bury soldiers who had

Achiet-Le-Grand Cemetery. (Author)

died from their wounds. 1,256 Commonwealth soldiers rest in this cemetery.

Lance Corporal William McCarty received gun shot wounds to the chest and abdomen on 11th April. He was brought to the 49th Casualty Clearing Station at Achiet-le-Grand the following day. McCarty succumbed to his wounds two days later and died at 11.45pm. He was buried in this cemetery on the following day. McCarty was a recipient of the MM and his epitaph reads:

THE PRICE OF PEACE

2nd Lieutenant Harold Grimshaw from the 21st Manchester Battalion is buried here. Harold Shrieves Grimshaw was a schoolteacher before the war. His wife Elsie came from Orono, Ontario in Canada. He enlisted to join the HAC on 28th January 1916. He was transferred to the Officer Training Corps on 7th September and was commissioned on 18th December. Assigned to the 21st Manchester Regiment he left England for the Western Front in France in December 1917. He suffered severe wounds while holding an outpost position near Bullecourt on 30th April. He was evacuated from the front line, but died of his wounds on 24th May. Harold Grimshaw was aged 27 when he died.

Lieutenant Cecil Philcox from the 1st Battalion South Staffordshire's and Sergeant Herbert Manser from the Post Office Rifles were buried here too. Private Albert Lindley who was among a party of ten men from the 2nd Honourable Artillery Company within the ruins of village who

2nd Lt Harold Shrieves Grimshaw. (The War Illustrated)

held onto captured positions for four nights and three days while surrounded by the enemy is also buried here. Lindley died of the wounds on 8th May 1917.

VAULX AUSTRALIAN FIELD AMBULANCE CEMETERY

Vaulx Australian Field Ambulance Cemetery was in operation from April 1917. It contains the graves of 52 Commonwealth soldiers and after the Germans recaptured the position in February 1918 the German forces used it to bury their own war dead. There are 61 German graves in the cemetery.

Private William Jarrett, from the 13th Battalion received devastating wounds to his right leg from a high explosive shell at Bullecourt on 11th April. He was brought to the Advanced Dressing Station at Vaulx, where his right leg was amputated. Jarrett died from his wounds on 12th April and was buried in this cemetery.

Several Australian medics were buried here. Private Jean Louis Michel Gallanty from the 7th Field Ambulance was killed while sleeping in a dug-out close to the front line at Bullecourt on 5th May 1917. He was dead when they recovered him. Gallanty was a dispensing chemist from Mackay and could speak fluent French. He was awarded the Military Medal for his work on Gallipoli.

Private Richard Sharp was wounded by shell fire while stretcher-bearing at Bullecourt while serving with the 3rd Field Ambulance. A piece of shell had penetrated his chest and he was taken to the Main Dressing Station at Vaulx where he died from his wound on 7th May. Sharp was recommended for a Military Medal for constructing a road to evacuate the wounded at Pozières on 19th August 1916 while under heavy enemy fire, but the decoration was not approved. Private N.G. Rondray 5596 wrote 'I knew Sharp well, he was a very gallant fellow whom we expected would get the MC.'[22]

Vaulx Field Ambulance Cemetery. (Author)

Private Eric Willis from the 7th Field Ambulance was reported to have received a machine gun bullet in the neck while carrying a wounded soldier from the battlefield at Bullecourt, close to the railway embankment at 11 am on 3rd May. Another soldier testified that he was hit by pieces of shell which entered his back and penetrated his abdomen. He remained conscious for half an hour after reaching the Main Dressing Station at Vaulx. During that time he was giving messages to be passed on to his loved ones. As his life ebbed away he was reported to have been calling for his mother. He passed away soon after arriving at the dressing station.

NOTES

1. Australian War Memorial: AWM 1DRL428/00029: Australian Red Cross Missing File: 2nd Lieutenant James Proctor.
2. Private Robert Johnston papers: Courtesy Teresa Prince.
3. Australian War Memorial: AWM 1DRL428/00037: Australian Red Cross Missing File: Private Edward White.
4. National Archives of Australia: Private Edward White's Service Record.
5. Australian War Memorial: AWM 1DRL428/00026: Australian Red Cross Missing File Private Ernest Noy.
6. Australian War Memorial: AWM 1DRL428/00035: Australian Red Cross Missing File Sergeant John Touzel.
7. Ibid.
8. Letter of Condolence from Lieutenant Colonel Charles Denehy to the widow of Lieutenant Wilfred Barlow: AWM Papers of Lt. W. Barlow, 58th Battalion AWM PR00030.
9. Australian War Memorial: AWM 1DRL428/00035: Australian Red Cross Missing File Private Andre Tolstoi.
10. Stratford-upon-Avon Herald, 5th October 1917.
11. Courtesy The Magic Attic Archives.
12. Ibid.
13. Derby Mercury, 1st June 1917.
14. Australian War Memorial: AWM 1DRL428/00035: Australian Red Cross File Major George Tostevin.
15. Australia War Memorial: AWM 1DRL/428/00021: Australian Red Cross Missing File: Major Benjamin Leane.
16. Australian War Memorial: AWM 1DRL/0428/00002: Australian Red Cross Missing File: Private Gladstone Bannatyne.
17. Australian War Memorial: AWM 1DRL/428/00011: Australian Red Cross Missing Files: Private Arthur Emmins.
18. The London Gazette: 26th March 1917.
19. Australian War Memorial: AWM 1DRL/428/00023 Australian Red Cross Missing File: Private Michael Meenan.
20. Australian War Memorial: AWM 1DRL428/00028: Australian Red Cross Missing File: Private Arthur Perman.
21. Ibid.
22. Australian War Memorial: AWM 1DRL428/0032: Australian Red Cross Missing File: Private Robert Sharp.

ORDER OF BATTLE AT BULLECOURT: FIFTH ARMY, APRIL–MAY 1917

FIFTH ARMY: GENERAL SIR HUBERT GOUGH

V Corps: Lieutenant-General Sir Edward Fanshawe

7TH DIVISION: MAJOR-GENERAL T.H. SHOUBRIDGE

20th Brigade: Brigadier-General H.C.R. Green
  2nd Battalion Borders Regiment
  2nd Battalion Gordon Highlanders Regiment
  8th Battalion Devonshire Regiment
  9th Battalion Devonshire Regiment

22nd Brigade: Brigadier-General J. McSteele
  2nd Battalion Royal Warwickshire Regiment
  1st Battalion Royal Welch Fusiliers.
  20th Battalion Manchester Regiment
  2nd Battalion Honourable Artillery Company

91st Brigade: Brigadier H.R. Cumming (Colonel W. Norman acting commander from 12th May 1917)
  2nd Battalion (Queen's) Royal West Surrey Regiment
  1st Battalion South Staffordshire Regiment
  21st Battalion Manchester Regiment
  22nd Battalion Manchester Regiment

58TH DIVISION (2ND/1ST LONDON) DIVISION: MAJOR-GENERAL H.D. FANSHAWE

173rd Brigade: Brigadier-General B.C. Freyberg VC
  2nd/1st Battalion London Regiment
  2nd/2nd Battalion London Regiment
  2nd/3rd Battalion London Regiment
  2nd/4th Battalion London Regiment
174th Brigade: Brigadier-General C.G. Higgins

  2nd/5th Battalion City of London (London Rifle Brigade)
  2nd/6th Battalion City of London (Rifles)
  2nd/7th Battalion City of London Regiment
  2nd/8th Battalion City of London (Post Office Rifles)

175th Brigade: Brigadier-General H.C. Jackson
  2nd/9th Battalion County of London (Queen Victoria Rifles)
  2nd/10th Battalion County of London (Hackney)
  2nd/11th Battalion County of London (Finsbury Rifles)
  2nd/12th County of London (The Rangers)

62ND (WEST RIDING) DIVISION: MAJOR-GENERAL W.P. BRAITHWAITE

185th Brigade: Brigadier-General V.W. de Falbe
  2nd/5th Battalion West Yorkshire Regiment
  2nd/6th Battalion West Yorkshire Regiment
  2nd/7th Battalion West Yorkshire Regiment
  2nd/8th Battalion West Yorkshire Regiment

186th Brigade: Brigadier-General F.F. Hill
  2nd/4th Battalion Duke of Wellington's Regiment
  2nd/5th Battalion Duke of Wellington's Regiment
  2nd/6th Battalion Duke of Wellington's Regiment
  2nd/7th Battalion Duke of Wellington's Regiment

187th Brigade: Brigadier-General R. Taylor
  2nd/4th Battalion King's Own Yorkshire Light Infantry
  2nd/5th Battalion King's Own Yorkshire Light Infantry
  2nd/4th Battalion York and Lancaster Regiment
  2nd/4th Battalion York and Lancaster Regiment

I ANZAC Corps: Lieutenant-General Sir William
Birdwood

Chief-of-Staff: Major-General C.B. White

1ST AUSTRALIAN DIVISION: MAJOR-GENERAL H.B. WALKER

1st (New South Wales) Brigade: Brigadier-General W.B. Leslie
1st Battalion
2nd Battalion
3rd Battalion
4th Battalion

2nd (Victoria) Brigade: Colonel (Temporary Brigadier-General) J. Heane
5th Battalion
6th Battalion
7th Battalion
8th Battalion

3rd Brigade: Brigadier-General H.G. Bennett
9th (Queensland) Battalion
10th (South Australia) Battalion
11th (Western Australia) Battalion
12th (South and Western Australia, Tasmania) Battalion

2ND AUSTRALIAN DIVISION: MAJOR-GENERAL N. SMYTH, VC

5th (New South Wales) Brigade: Brigadier-General R. Smith
17th Battalion
18th Battalion
19th Battalion
20th Battalion

6th (Victoria) Brigade: Brigadier-General J. Gellibrand
21st Battalion
22nd Battalion
23rd Battalion
24th Battalion

7th Brigade: Brigadier-General E.A. Wisdom
25th (Queensland) Battalion
26th (Queensland and Tasmania) Battalion

27th (South Australia) Battalion
28th (Western Australia) Battalion

4TH AUSTRALIAN DIVISION: MAJOR-GENERAL W. HOLMES

4th Brigade: Brigadier-General C.H. Brand
13th (New South Wales) Battalion
14th (Victoria) Battalion
15th (Queensland and Tasmania) Battalion
16th (South and Western Australia) Battalion

12th Brigade: Brigadier-General J.C. Robertson
45th (New South Wales) Battalion
46th (Victoria) Battalion
47th (Queensland and Tasmania) Battalion
48th (South and Western) Battalion

13th Brigade: Brigadier-General T.W. Glasgow
49th (Queensland) Battalion
50th (South Australia) Battalion
51st (Western Australia) Battalion
52nd (South and Western Australia, Tasmania) Battalion

5TH AUSTRALIAN DIVISION: MAJOR-GENERAL J.J.T. WHITE

8th Brigade: Brigadier-General E. Tivey
29th (Victoria) Battalion
30th (New South Wales) Battalion
31st (Queensland and Victoria) Battalion
32nd (South and Western Australia) Battalion

14th (New South Wales) Brigade: Brigadier-General C.J. Hobkirk
53rd Battalion
54th Battalion
55th Battalion
56th Battalion

15th (Victoria) Brigade: Brigadier-General H.E. Elliott
57th Battalion
58th Battalion
59th Battalion
60th Battalion

ORDER OF BATTLE AT BULLECOURT: GERMAN XIV RESERVE CORPS, APRIL–MAY 1917

XIV RESERVE CORPS: GENERAL VON MOSER

27TH (ROYAL WÜRTTEMBERG) DIVISION: MAJOR-GENERAL VON MAUR

53rd Brigade
  120th Grenadier Regiment
  123rd Grenadier Regiment
  124th Grenadier Regiment

DIVISIONS ATTACHED TO XIV RESERVES CORPS

3RD GUARD DIVISION: LIEUTENANT-GENERAL VON LINDEQUIST

6th Guard Brigade
  Guard Fusiliers
  Lehr Regiment
  9th Grenadier Regiment

2ND GUARD RESERVE DIVISION: MAJOR-GENERAL VON PETERSDORFF

38th Reserve Brigade
  15th Reserve Regiment
  77th Reserve Regiment
  91st Reserve Regiment

38TH DIVISION: LIEUTENANT-GENERAL SCHULTHEIS

83rd Brigade
  94th Regiment
  95th Regiment
  96th Regiment

4TH ERSATZ DIVISION: GENERAL-DER-KAVALLERIE VON WERDER

13th Ersatz Brigade
  360th Regiment
  361st Regiment
  362nd Regiment

207TH DIVISION: MAJOR-GENERAL SCHROETE

89th Reserve Brigade
  98th Reserve Regiment
  209th Reserve Regiment
  213th Reserve Regiment

BRITISH DIGGERS WHO DIED AT BULLECOURT, APRIL–MAY 1917

A significant number of British citizens were killed while serving with the AIF. The following appendix lists the British diggers who were killed at Bullecourt between 10th April to 15th May 1917.

BRITISH 'DIGGERS' WHO DIED AT FIRST BULLECOURT

NAME/RANK/SERVICE NO.	BATTALION	KILLED	AGE	PLACE OF BIRTH	BURIED/COMMEMORATED
Alexander, George Pte. 4728A	46th Battalion	11.04.17	25	Llanelly, Wales	Villers-Bretonneux Mem
Allan, Daniel Pte.5326	14th Battalion	11.04.17	27	Largs, Ayrshire, Scot.	Villers-Bretonneux Mem
Anderson, Thomas Pte. 4129	46th Battalion	11.04.17	28	Glasgow, Scotland	Villers-Bretonneux Mem
Archibald, John Pte. 5224	47th Battalion	11.04.17	19	Glasgow, Scotland	Quéant Road Cemetery
Beechey, Harold Pte 200	48th Battalion	10.04.17	26	Friesthorpe, Lincs.	Villers-Bretonneux Mem
Belcher, William Pte. 4733	15th Battalion	11.04.17	25	Reading, Berkshire	Villers-Bretonneux Mem
Bird, Henry, Pte. 1884	48th Battalion	14.04.17	25	Croydon	Charleroi Communal Cem
Bland, Francis Pte 1736	16th Battalion	11.04.17	U	London	Villers-Bretonneux Mem
(Bland served as Potter)					
Blencowe, Sydney Pte 2863	48th Battalion	11.04.17	28	Dulwich, London	Villers-Bretonneux Mem
Bourne, Henry Lnc Corp 1457	15th Battalion	11.04.17	23	Hanley	Villers-Bretonneux Mem
Brown, George, Pte 3688	46th Battalion	11.04.17	25	Kirkaldy, Scotland	Villers-Bretonneux Mem
Brown, Herbert, Pte 6482	16th Battalion	11.04.17	22	Birkenhead	H.A.C. Cemetery
Burn, Robert, Lnc Corp 3228	48th Battalion	11.04.17	29	Gateshead	Villers-Bretonneux Mem
Burnard, Harry, Pte 4578	16th Battalion	11.04.17	40	London	Quéant Road Cemetery
Buswell, George, Pte 4758	48th Battalion	11.04.17	29	Moulton, Northants	Villers-Bretonneux Mem
Campbell, William, Lnc Corp 5786	15th Battalion	11.04.17	31	Glasgow, Scotland	Villers-Bretonneux Mem
Campbell, William, Pte 2304	46th Battalion	11.04.17	30	Bradford, Yorkshire	Villers-Bretonneux Mem
Chantler, Charles, Pte 2643	48th Battalion	11.04.17	21	London	Villers-Bretonneux Mem
Chisnall, Fred, Pte 1821	46th Battalion	11.04.17	21	Timperley, Cheshire	Villers-Bretonneux Mem
Clark, Donald, Pte 6493	16th Battalion	11.04.17	21	Ayr, Scotland	Villers-Bretonneux Mem
Codrington-Forsyth, Guy, Lt	48th Battalion	11.04.17	23	London	Villers-Bretonneux Mem
Collier, George, Pte 5078	48th Battalion	11.04.17	33	Alnwick	Villers-Bretonneux Mem
Corlett, Walter, Pte 6229	16th Battalion	11.04.17	21	Isle of Man	Villers-Bretonneux Mem
Coulthard, Robert, Sgt 766	4th Coy MGC	12.04.17	27	Norwell, Notts.	Bapaume Australian Cem
Cross, George, Pte 1504	13th Battalion	11.04.17	28	Lambeth, London	Villers-Bretonneux Mem
Currie, Alexander, Pte 4851	51st Battalion	11.04.17	29	Castle Douglas, Scot.	Villers-Bretonneux Mem
Dadson, Frederick, Lt	14th Battalion	11.04.17	37	Maidstone, Kent	Villers-Bretonneux Mem
Douglas, Stanley, Pte 3454	16th Battalion	11.04.17	30	London	Villers-Bretonneux Mem
Duce, Eric, Pte 3451	16th Battalion	11.04.17	23	Sevenoaks, Kent	Villers-Bretonneux Mem
Emmins, Arthur, Lnc Corp 3044	48th Battalion	11.04.17	21	London	Quéant Road Cemetery
Fairley, James, Pte 6735	13th Battalion	11.04.17	19	Glasgow, Scotland	Villers-Bretonneux Mem

NAME/RANK/SERVICE NO.	BATTALION	KILLED	AGE	PLACE OF BIRTH	BURIED/COMMEMORATED
Ferrier, Thomas, Pte 1450	13th Battalion	11.04.17	38	Gosport, Hants	Villers-Bretonneux Mem
Galloway, John, Pte 775	13th Battalion	11.04.17	31	Bangor, Wales	Villers-Bretonneux Mem
Giffard, Percy, Pte 3494	14th Battalion	11.04.17	20	Newcastle	Villers-Bretonneux Mem
Goertz, Harold, Pte 1917	46th Battalion	11.04.17	44	Reading, Berkshire	Villers-Bretonneux Mem
Good, James, Pte 1746	15th Battalion	11.04.17	41	Glasgow	Villers-Bretonneux Mem
Goodchild, Paul Pte 6516	16th Battalion	11.04.17	22	Wokingham, England	Sauchy-Lestree Com Cem
Goodhand, Fred Pte 6270	16th Battalion	11.04.17	32	Kirton, England	Villers-Bretonneux Mem
Hamill, Andrew Lance Corp 5113	48th Battalion	14.04.17	19	Lanarkshire, Scotland	Grévillers British Cemetery
Harber, Alfred, Pte 2210	46th Battalion	11.04.17	22	London,	Villers-Bretonneux Mem
Hebenton, Thomas, Pte 4948	46th Battalion	11.04.17	33	Kirriemuir, Scotland	Quéant Road Cemetery
Hide, Cecil, Pte 3476	16th Battalion	11.04.17	28	Eastbourne, England	Villers-Bretonneux Mem
Hinds, Charles, Pte 2485	16th Battalion	11.04.17	25	Batheaston,	Villers-Bretonneux Mem
Howlett, John, Pte 6270	15th Battalion	11.04.17	42	Sheffield	Villers-Bretonneux Mem
Hunter, Charles, Pte 5110	13th Battalion	11.04.17	27	Bethnal Green, London	Villers-Bretonneux Mem
Irwin, Edwin, Pte 4222	14th Battalion	11.04.17	25	Belfast, Ireland	Villers-Bretonneux Mem
Jarrett, William, Pte 6062	13th Battalion	12.04.17	26	Betchcott	Vaulx Aust Field Amb Cem
Kamman, George, Pte 3128	16th Battalion	11.04.17	27	London	Villers-Bretonneux Mem
Kirkland, George, Lt	4th Coy MGC	13.04.17	27	Ireland	Hem-Lenglet Com Cem
Knox, Thomas, Pte 6548	13th Battalion	11.04.17	28	Leven, Scotland	Villers-Bretonneux Mem
Lawrie, Charles, Pte 5059	15th Battalion	11.04.17	19	Glasgow	Villers-Bretonneux Mem
Leaney, William, Pte 2693A	52nd Battalion	11.04.17	U	Harrietsham, Kent	Villers-Bretonneux Mem
Levett, Albert, Pte 2195	48th Battalion	13.04.17	22	Brighton	Cabarat-Rouge British Cem
Long, James, Pte 6303	14th Battalion	11.04.17	U	Clifton, Bristol	Villers-Bretonneux Mem
Lowe, Richard, Pte 5133	48th Battalion	11.04.17	30	St. Helens, England	Villers-Bretonneux Mem
Maclean, Peter, Pte 6304	16th Battalion	11.04.17	39	Lewis, Scotland	Villers-Bretonneux Mem
Main, Halero, Corporal 1611	50th Battalion	12.04.17	32	Glasgow, Scotland	St. Sever Cem Ext Rouen
March, Douglas, Pte 2720B	48th Battalion	11.04.17	30	Kensington, London	Villers-Bretonneux Mem
McArthur, Duncan Pte 5159	2nd Battalion	10.04.17	24	Elgin, Scotland	St. Sever Cem Ext Rouen
McCabe, James, Pte 2706	48th Battalion	11.04.17	28	Glasgow, Scotland	Villers-Bretonneux Mem
McCormick, James, Pte 6547	14th Battalion	11.04.17	40	Dublin, Ireland	Villers-Bretonneux Mem
McLean, Kenneth, Pte 5411	48th Battalion	11.04.17	37	Gooan, Scotland	Tilloy British Cemetery
Tilloy-Les-Moffleines					
Mesney, Valentine, Pte 2712	48th Battalion	11.04.17	29	Tottenham, London	Villers-Bretonneux Mem
Moody, James Sgt. 712	1st Bdg AFA	14.04.17	31	Dunbar, Scotland	Noreuil Australian Cem
Moppett, George, Pte 6835	13th Battalion	11.04.17	37	Brighton	Villers-Bretonneux Mem
Morgan, Robert, Sgt 3159	54th Battalion	12.04.17	21	London	St Sever Cemetery
Extension Rouen					
Nutley, Herbert, Pte 4258	13th Battalion	11.04.17	26	Alresford, Hants	Villers-Bretonneux Mem
Page, Alma, Pte 3117	48th Battalion	11.04.17	22	Leicester, England	Villers-Bretonneux Mem
Page, Nelson, Pte 6565	16th Battalion	11.04.17	U	Kingsdown Stratton	Villers-Bretonneux Mem
Palmer, James, Pte 4303	15th Battalion	13.04.17	28	Aberdeen, Scotland	Cabarat-Rouge British Cem
Pateman, Herbert, Pte 5724	14th Battalion	11.04.17	20	Hertford, England	Villers-Bretonneux Mem
Patterson, Ross, Pte 899	13th Battalion	11.04.17	32	Hutton, Scotland	Quéant Road Cemetery
Pollitt, Arthur, Pte 3917	51st Battalion	12.04.17	21	Manchester	Pozières British Cemetery
Rees, Edward, Pte 5416	16th Battalion	11.04.17	40	Treorchy, Wales	Villers-Bretonneux Mem
Reid, William, Pte 5730	14th Battalion	11.04.17	34	Glasgow, Scotland	Villers-Bretonneux Mem
Rice, Hubert, Pte 4211	1st Field Amb.	10.04.17	30	Holt	Bapaume Aust. Cem
Ronald, William, Pte 3122	48th Battalion	11.04.17	32	Greenock, Scotland	Villers-Bretonneux Mem
Rossington. George, Pte 640	15th Battalion	11.04.17	27	Manchester	Villers-Bretonneux Mem
Sands, Percy, Pte 2971	1st Battalion	11.04.17	32	Chichester	St. Sever Cem Ext Rouen
Scandrett, Robert, Pte 6106	13th Battalion	11.04.17	23	Ballynahinch, Ireland	Favreuil British Cemetery
Shadwick, John Lt	48th Battalion	11.04.17	25	Devon, England	Villers-Bretonneux Mem
Smith, Arthur, Pte 2489	48th Battalion	11.04.17	33	Croydon	Villers-Bretonneux Mem

NAME/RANK/SERVICE NO.	BATTALION	KILLED	AGE	PLACE OF BIRTH	BURIED/COMMEMORATED
Smith, Claude, Pte 382	14th Battalion	11.04.17	30	Kings Lynn	Villers-Bretonneux Mem
Smith, Stanley, Pte 6325	13th Battalion	11.04.17	29	London	Villers-Bretonneux Mem
Stenhouse, John, Pte 2448	47th Battalion	11.04.17	30	Dundee, Scotland	Villers-Bretonneux Mem
Strand, Walter, Pte 6575	16th Battalion	11.04.17	41	Womenswold, Kent	Villers-Bretonneux Mem
Thompson, James, Pte 6342	16th Battalion	11.04.17	31	Burnley	Villers-Bretonneux Mem
Thornley, James 2nd Lt	13th Battalion	11.04.17	41	Cleethorpes, Lincs.	Villers-Bretonneux Mem
Travis, William, Pte 5221	46th Battalion	11.04.17	42	Lancashire, England	Villers-Bretonneux Mem
Wilkinson, Sydney, Pte 461	31st Battalion	10.04.17	26	Burton-on-Trent	St. Sever Cem Ext Rouen
Wood, Henry, Pte 712	6th Machine Gun Corps	12.04.17	21	Dorking	Villers-Bretonneux Mem
Yates, John Corporal 215	15th Battalion	11.04.17	24	Brighton	Villers-Bretonneux Mem

BRITISH DIGGERS WHO DIED AT SECOND BULLECOURT

NAME/RANK/SERVICE NO.	BATTALION	KILLED	AGE	PLACE OF BIRTH	BURIED/COMMEMORATED
Allen, Frederick, Pte. 3978	22nd Battalion	03.05.17	27	Somerset	Villers Bretonneux Mem
Anthony, Charles, Pte. 1302	11th Battalion	06.05.17	27	Kilsyth, Scotland	Villers-Bretonneux Mem
Bamford, Robert, Pte. 5984	19th Battalion	05.05.17	U	Coppull	Vraucourt Copse Cemetery
Bartlett, James Corp. 1615	17th Battalion	03.05.17	25	Sheffield	Villers-Bretonneux Mem
Barton, William, Pte. 6035	23rd Battalion	03.05.17	24	Bolton	Villers-Bretonneux Mem
Beale, Leonard, Pte 5296	24th Battalion	03.05.17	22	Bristol	Villers-Bretonneux Mem
Bell, Sydney, Pte. 3306	2nd Pioneers	06.05.17	20	Greenwich, London	Villers-Bretonneux Mem
Bennett, Arthur, Pte. 5550	24th Battalion	07.05.17	33	London	Villers-Bretonneux Mem
Blake, Frederick, Pte. 6471	1st Battalion	05.05.17	37	Jersey, Channel Isles	Villers-Bretonneux Mem
Boyd, Stewart, Pte. 2225	5th Coy MGC	05.05.17	33	Lowestoft	Villers-Bretonneux Mem
Brannan, Ellis, Pte. 6708	10th Battalion	07.05.17	22	Manchester	Villers-Bretonneux Mem
Brookhouse, Robert, Pte. 2614	53rd Battalion	08.05.17	36	Liverpool	St Sever Cem. Ext. Rouen
Cameron, Arthur, Pte. 376	18th Battalion	03.05.17	23	Edinburgh, Scotland	Villers-Bretonneux Mem
Cameron, Ernest Pte. 3794	21st Battalion	03.05.17	35	Galashiels, Scotland	Villers-Bretonneux Mem
Campbell, James, Pte. 5310	24th Battalion	03.05.17	30	Troon, Scotland	Villers-Bretonneux Mem
Cant, James, 2nd Lt	19th Battalion	03.05.17	34	Workington	Villers-Bretonneux Mem
Chalk, Charlie, Pte. 4698	26th Battalion	03.05.17	27	Titchfield, Hants	Quéant Road Cemetery
Chatters, Reginald, Pte. 1326	9th Battalion	06.05.17	22	Sudbury	Villers-Bretonneux Mem
Clark, James, Pte. 4678	19th Battalion	03.05.17	27	Brockenhurst	Villers-Bretonneux Mem
Clewlow, Richard Pte. 2875A	20th Battalion	03.05.17	26	Hanley	Quéant Road Cemetery
Collins, Daniel, Pte. 4395	22nd Battalion	03.05.17	U	Briton Ferry, Wales	Villers-Bretonneux Mem
Cook, Albert, Pte. 5557	23rd Battalion	03.05.17	22	Manchester	Villers-Bretonneux Mem
Cozens, Oliver, Pte. 4089	20th Battalion	03.05.17	33	Butts	Villers-Bretonneux Mem
Coughlin, Vincent, Pte.4802	26th Battalion	03.05.17	36	Rathmullen, Ireland	Villers-Bretonneux Mem
Crank, Norman Pte. 819	19th Battalion	03.05.17	25	Manchester	Quéant Road Cemetery
Crocombe, Walter, Lnc Corp.711	3rd Battalion	05.05.17	27	Stogursey	Villers-Bretonneux Mem
Cullingford, Herbert, Pte 6136	24th Battalion	03.05.17	24	Yoxford	Villers-Bretonneux Mem
Davidson, William, Pte. 5001	22nd Battalion	03.05.17	23	Lilybank, Scotland	Villers-Bretonneux Mem
Daws, Robert, Lnc Corp. 412	18th Battalion	04.05.17	23	Croydon	Grévillers British Cemetery
Dawson, John, Sgt. 2132	19th Battalion	03.05.17	26	Liverpool	Quéant Road Cemetery
Dean, Leonard, Pte. 5810	17th Battalion	03.05.17	28	Edmonton, London	Villers-Bretonneux Mem
Dobson, Leonard, Sgt. 769	24th Battalion	03.05.17	26	Enfield	Villers-Bretonneux Mem
Down, Daniel, Corporal 1705	23rd Battalion	03.05.17	39	Sussex	Villers-Bretonneux Mem
Duffield, Harry, Lnce Corp. MM 4479	2nd Battalion	04.05.17	28	Macclesfield	Villers-Bretonneux Mem
Dunlop, Wilson, Pte. 5573	22nd Battalion	11.05.17	20	Auschin Lech, Scot.	Grévillers British Cemetery

NAME/RANK/SERVICE NO.	BATTALION	KILLED	AGE	PLACE OF BIRTH	BURIED/COMMEMORATED
Edwards, William, Pte. 4720	26th Battalion	03.05.17	28	Hammersmith, London	Villers-Bretonneux Mem
Elliott, George MM Pte. 5331	20th Battalion	03.05.17	40	London	Quéant Road Cemetery
Etheridge, Reginald, Pte. 4224	23rd Battalion	03.05.17	29	London	Villers-Bretonneux Mem
Forster, William, Lt.	21st Battalion	03.05.17	25	Scotland	Villers-Bretonneux Mem
Fryer, Frank, Pte. 6287	4th Battalion	05.05.17	22	Thornton Heath	Villers-Bretonneux Mem
Gee, Edward, Pte. 1193	19th Battalion	08.05.17	U	Hyde	Grévillers British Cemetery
Gilvear, Alexander, Lnc Corp. 4496	9th Battalion	07.05.17	22	Stirling, Scotland	Villers-Bretonneux Mem
Goring, Henry, Pte.4630	54th Battalion	15.05.17	24	London	Villers-Bretonneux Mem
Greene, Frank, Pte. 6501	11th Battalion	06.05.17	21	London	Villers-Bretonneux Mem
Haddon, Henry, Pte 14475	14th Fld Amb	04.05.17	22	Kettering	Quéant Road Cemetery
Hadfield, Joseph, Sgt. 817	27th Battalion	05.05.17	30	Manchester	Grévillers British Cemetery
Hammond, Alfred, Corp.3554	54th Battalion	15.05.17	24	London	Villers-Bretonneux Mem
Harrison, James, Pte. 31	21st Battalion	03.05.17	21	Hull	Villers-Bretonneux Mem
Harrison, Thomas, Lnc Corp 4414	6th Field Coy Eng	06.05.17	32	Walton-on-Thames	Villers-Bretonneux Mem
Harvey, Wilfred, Pte. 6280	2nd Battalion	05.05.17	37	Southampton	Grévillers British Cemetery
Hayward, Frederick, Pte.6528	8th Battalion	09.05.17	23	Asfordby, Leic.	Grévillers British Cemetery
Heady, Joseph, Pte. 6092	22nd Battalion	03.05.17	35	Forest Gate	Villers-Bretonneux Mem
Helme, Henry, Pte. 5358	21st Battalion	03.05.17	36	Lancashire	Villers-Bretonneux Mem
Hicks, William, Pte. 5590	20th Battalion	04.05.17	19	Isle of Man	Grévillers British Cemetery
Hill, Arthur, Pte. 384	18th Battalion	09.05.17	23	Lancashire	Grévillers British Cemetery
Hind, Walter, Pte. 6765	11th Battalion	06.05.17	33	Preston	Villers-Bretonneux Mem
Hodges, Alfred, Pte. 6517	11th Battalion	06.05.17	31	Stourbridge	Villers-Bretonneux Mem
Hollis, Harry, Pte. 5798	4th Battalion	08.05.17	32	London	Grévillers British Cemetery
Horn, Arthur, Lance Corp.5034	54th Battalion	15.05.17	25	Upton Park, London	Villers-Bretonneux Mem
Ingle, William, Corporal 4226	11th Battalion	06.05.17	30	London	Villers-Bretonneux Mem
Jackson, Joseph, Pte. 3390	11th Battalion	07.05.17	24	Fairfield, Lancs.	Villers-Bretonneux Mem
Johnson, Cecil, Pte. 6781	11th Battalion	09.05.17	23	Pelham, Herts.	Grévillers British Cemetery
Jones, Alan, Pte. 1970	9th Battalion	06.05.17	28	Rye	Villers-Bretonneux Mem
Keeling, George, Pte. 2695	55th Battalion	06.05.17	30	Staffordshire	St Sever Cem Ext Rouen
Kent, James, Pte. 3839	1st Battalion	05.05.17	30	Barnes	Villers-Bretonneux Mem
Kinloch, Stephen, Pte. 4168	18th Battalion	03.05.17	38	Glasgow, Scotland	Villers-Bretonneux Mem
Knuckey, James, Pte. 4716	20th Battalion	03.05.17	23	Cornwall	Warlencourt British Cem
Lardeaux, Stanley, Pte, 3821	3rd Battalion	05.05.17	19	Peckham, London	Villers-Bretonneux Mem
Latham, Thomas, Pte. 1055	2nd Battalion	04.05.17	43	Dover, Kent	Villers-Bretonneux Mem
Lee, Harold, Pte. 2174	20th Battalion	03.05.17	23	Chester	Villers-Bretonneux Mem
Leggett, Nathan, Pte. 5608	25th Battalion	03.05.17	24	Bacton, Suffolk	Villers-Bretonneux Mem
Lester, George, Pte.5819	18th Battalion	03.05.17	U	London	Villers-Bretonneux Mem
Lewes, Arthur, Pte. 2168	1st Battalion	06.05.17	36	Brightlingsea	Villers-Bretonneux Mem
Little, Robert, Pte. 4152	17th Battalion	03.05.17	36	Stranraer, Scotland	Villers-Bretonneux Mem
Lupson, George, Pte. 4856	2nd Field Amb	05.05.17	24	Greenwich, London	Villers-Bretonneux Mem
Maben, Henry, Pte 177	25th Battalion	08.05.17	29	Kingskerswell, Dev.	Villers-Bretonneux Mem
MacColl, Malcolm, Pte.5927	18th Battalon	03.05.17	46	Camberwell, London	Arras Rd Cem Roglincourt
MacQuibban, William, Pte. 6283	1st Battalion	05.05.17	25	Perth, Scotland	Villers-Bretonneux Mem
Macrow, James, Pte. 5890	28th Battalion	13.05.17	28	Rochdale	Etaples Military Cemetery
Martin, Francis, Pte. 5067	22nd Battalion	03.05.17	35	Bonhill, Scotland	Villers-Bretonneux Mem
Marshall, John, Pte. 3406	1st Battalion	07.05.17	U	Cuddes, Scotland	Grévillers British Cemetery
Masters, Reginald, Lnc. Corp 4523	2nd Battalion	04.05.17	21	Wellington	Villers-Bretonneux Mem
Maclean, John, Pte, 6119	1st Battalion	05.05.17	38	Glen Urquhart, Scotland	Villers-Bretonneux Mem
McCanch, Peter, Lnc. Corp.3086	56th Battalion	15.05.17	27	Workington	Villers-Bretonneux Mem

NAME/RANK/SERVICE NO.	BATTALION	KILLED	AGE	PLACE OF BIRTH	BURIED/COMMEMORATED
McGrorty, Hugh, Pte. 288	3rd Coy MGC	06.05.17	27	Jarrow	Villers-Bretonneux Mem
McGough, John, Pte. 5431	20th Battalion	03.05.17	32	Carlisle	Villers-Bretonneux Mem
McGuire, Percy, Pte. 166	25th Battalion	08.05.17	23	London	Villers-Bretonneux Mem
McIntosh, John, Pte. 5709	9th Battalion	06.05.17	31	Broxburn, Scotland	Villers-Bretonneux Mem
McMaster, James, Pte. 5867	20th Battalion	03.05.17	34	Boyne, Ireland	Villers-Bretonneux Mem
Miles, Percy, Pte. 6214	18th Battalion	03.05.17	26	Bishopstone	Villers-Bretonneux Mem
Millership, John, Pte. 5855	19th Battalion	03.05.17	31	Oldham	Villers-Bretonneux Mem
Money, Edward Pte. 5734	1st Battalion	05.05.17	38	Great Yarmouth	Villers-Bretonneux Mem
Mott, William, Pte 2421	18th Battalion	03.05.17	22	London	Bailleul Road East Cem
Moule, Cyril, Pte. 5379	25th Battalion	03.05.17	24	Cambridge	Villers-Bretonneux Mem
Newman, William, Pte. 2762A	17th Battalion	05.05.17	24	Northampton	Grévillers British Cemetery
Niven, James, Pte. 2075	23rd Battalion	03.05.17	33	Glasgow, Scotland	Villers-Bretonneux Mem
Noak, Arthur, Pte. 3893	22nd Battalion	03.05.17	25	Exeter	Villers-Bretonneux Mem
North, Arthur, Corporal 453	21st Battalion	03.05.17	27	Swindon	Villers-Bretonneux Mem
Osborne, Joseph, Pte.6554	3rd Battalion	06.05.17	31	Donegal	Villers-Bretonneux Mem
Ogier, George, Pte. 5444	12th Battalion	05.05.17	U	Guernsey, Channel Isl.	Quéant Road Cemetery
Oldfield, Thomas, Pte. 1245	23rd Battalion	03.05.17	25	Leeds	Villers-Bretonneux Mem
Oliver, Stanley, Pte. 2153	26th Battalion	03.05.17	20	Hatfield Peverel	Villers-Bretonneux Mem
Paul, James, Pte. 5745	2nd Battalion	04.05.17	25	St. Fergus, Scotland	Villers-Bretonneux Mem
Pedersen, Christian, Pte. 39A	9th Battalion	06.05.17	32	Liverpool	Villers-Bretonneux Mem
Pickering, Joseph, Pte. 3226	8th Battalion	08.05.17	27	Cockermouth	Villers-Bretonneux Mem
Piggott, John, Pte. 1563	21st Battalion	06.05.17	22	Wallington	Grévillers British Cemetery
Piper, Stanley, Pte. 5344	11th Battalion	05.05.17	23	Wolverhampton	Quéant Road Cemetery
Poll, Walter, Pte. 6567	11th Battalion	06.05.17	40	Liverpool	Quéant Road Cemetery
Pomroy, Oscar, Pte. 2187	1st Inf Bdg HQ	05.05.17	24	London	Villers-Bretonneux Mem
Porter, Alexander, Pte. 2950	58th Battalion	10.05.17	24	Lanarkshire, Scotland	Villers-Bretonneux Mem
Porter, Harry, Pte. 2472	27th Battalion	03.05.17	U	Bridgwater	Villers-Bretonneux Mem
Potter, Benjamin, Pte. 3665	18th Battalion	03.05.17	23	Hayes	Grévillers British Cemetery
Pratt, Ernest, Pte. 5389	18th Battalion	03.05.17	27	Cheltenham	Bailleul Road East Cem
Price, Henry, Pte 6305	19th Battalion	03.05.17	23	Tooting, London	Villers-Bretonneux Mem
Priest, Edward, Pte 4212	19th Battalion	03.05.17	22	England	Villers-Bretonneux Mem
Prior, Alfred, Pte. 6135	22nd Battalion	03.05.17	35	London	Villers-Bretonneux Mem
Robertson, Daniel, Pte. 4289	2nd Battalion	03.05.17	37	Glasgow, Scotland	Villers-Bretonneux Mem
Robinson, Philip, Pte. 6576	11th Battalion	06.05.17	40	Liverpool	Quéant Road Cemetery
Richards, Charlie, Pte. 5731	3rd Battalion	05.05.17	27	Cardiff, Wales	Villers-Bretonneux Mem
Russel, Michael, Pte. 5904	25th Battalion	03.05.17	35	Bexleyheath	Villers-Bretonneux Mem
Rutterford, William, Pte. 4520	24th Battalion	03.05.17	21	Woodcott	Villers-Bretonneux Mem
Sale, Charles, Pte. 1067	10th Battalion	06.05.17	31	Tunstall	Noreuil Australian Cem
Samuel, Alexander, Pte. 4214	17th Battalion	03.05.17	U	Airdrie, Scotland	Villers-Bretonneux Mem
Savage, James, Pte. 6306	1st Battalion	05.05.17	45	London	Quéant Road Cemetery
Sayer, Herbert, Pte. 2207	9th Battalion	07.05.17	25	London	Villers-Bretonneux Mem
Scammell, Sydney, Lt.	22nd Battalion	03.05.17	U	Bradford-on-Avon	Villers-Bretonneux Mem
Scarr, Frank, Lt	5th Fld Coy Engineers	06.05.17	37	Romford	Villers-Bretonneux Mem
Sellar, Frank, Pte. 1791	4th Battalion	07.05.17	22	Aberdeen, Scotland	Villers-Bretonneux Mem
Sharkey, John, Pte. 2350	1st Battalion	05.05.17	32	Belfast, Ireland	Villers-Bretonneux Mem
Shimmin, Samuel, Pte. 4592	2nd Battalion	05.05.17	25	Isle of Man	Grévillers British Cemetery
Simpson, Alexander, Pte 5413	26th Battalion	03.05.17	35	Glasgow	Villers-Bretonneux Mem
Simpson, Willoughby, Pte. 1082	1st Battalion	05.05.17	30	Redditch	Villers-Bretonneux Mem
Skelton, Walter, Pte. 6357	3rd Battalion	05.05.17	28	Epsom	Villers-Bretonneux Mem
Smith, Edwin, Pte. 6585	2nd Battalion	07.05.17	35	Alton	Vaulx Australian Field Ambulance Cemetery
Smith, Ernest, Pte. 2215	19th Battalion	03.05.17	27	Brixton, London	Villers-Bretonneux Mem

NAME/RANK/SERVICE NO.	BATTALION	KILLED	AGE	PLACE OF BIRTH	BURIED/COMMEMORATED
Smith, Francis, Pte. 5423	24th Battalion	03.05.17	29	Brixton, London	Quéant Road Cemetery
Smith, James. Pte. 6550	4th Battalion	07.05.17	36	Stirling, Scotland	Grévillers British Cemetery
Snow, John, Pte,2980A	20th Battalion	03.05.17	33	Oldham	Villers-Bretonneux Mem
Spowart, Archibald, Pte. 5636	19th Battalion	03.05.17	18	Newcastle-on-Tyne	Villers-Bretonneux Mem
Sproat, Thornton, Pte. 193	4th Battalion	06.05.17	33	Netherwitton	Villers-Bretonneux Mem
Stephen, William, Corp. 668	19th Battalion	03.05.17	29	Mardy, Wales	Villers-Bretonneux Mem
Stubbing, Rodney, Pte. 3488	1st Battalion	06.05.17	22	Dartford	Grévillers British Cemetery
Sturman, John, Pte. 6103	11th Battalion	06.05.17	43	Lewisham	Villers-Bretonneux Mem
Sutherland, Sinclair, Pte. 1412	11th Battalion	06.05.17	24	Inverness	Villers-Bretonneux Mem
Swain, John, Pte. 5742	3rd Battalion	05.05.17	23	Winshill	Villers-Bretonneux Mem
Taplin, Archibald Lt	17th Battalion	03.05.17	38	Bristol	Quéant Road Cemetery
Taylor, Ernest, Pte. 5434	24th Battalion	03.05.17	37	Birmingham	Quéant Road Cemetery
Tostevin, George, Major	3rd Coy MGC	05.05.17	25	Guernsey	Noreuil Aust. Cemetery
Turnbull, George, Pte. 289	24th Battalion	04.05.17	23	Chelsea, London	Quéant Road Cemetery
Turner, Edmund, Pte. 5423	22nd Battalion	03.05.17	38	Brighton	Villers-Bretonneux Mem
Vallance, Ernest, Pte. 5904	24th Battalion	03.05.17	31	Dorking	Villers-Bretonneux Mem
Wallis, Benjamin, Pte.6170	22nd Battalion	03.05.17	25	Penzance	Bailleul Road East Cem
Ward, William, Pte. 6133	23rd Battalion	03.05.17	26	Kent	Villers-Bretonneux Mem
Watson, Robert, Corporal 2490	3rd Battalion	05.05.17	28	Glasgow, Scotland	Villers-Bretonneux Mem
Whisker, Alexander, Pte 5439	17th Battalion	03.05.17	25	Crossgar, Ireland	Villers-Bretonneux Mem
Williams, Arthur, Pte 5671	20th Battalion	03.05.17	27	Hereford	Villers-Bretonneux Mem
Wood, Alfred, Pte. 6834	11th Battalion	06.05.17	34	Leeds	Villers-Bretonneux Mem
Wood, Ian, Pte.4011	11th Battalion	06.05.17	23	Lanarkshire, Scotland	Villers-Bretonneux Mem
Worsnip, James, Pte 4267	17th Battalion	03.05.17	38	Mossley	Villers-Bretonneux Mem
Worth, Robert, Pte. 2699	58th Battalion	11.05.17	37	Liverpool	Villers-Bretonneux Mem
Yorke, John MM Sgt. 195	3rd Battalion	04.05.17	24	York	Villers-Bretonneux Mem
Young, Robert, Pte. 1127	24th Battalion	03.05.17	U	Aberdeen, Scotland	Villers-Bretonneux Mem

APPENDIX 4

THE BULLECOURT MISSING

Source for appendices: Yves Fohlen Bullecourt Database: compiled from CWGC and AWM roll of Honour.
Approximately 10,000 Australian and 7,000 British soldiers were killed during the battles for Bullecourt; 2,249
Australian and 1,875 British soldiers who died at Bullecourt have no known graves. The remains of these men where
either pulverised to nothing at the time of death, or their graves were lost after the battle. Many of these men still
lie in the fields surrounding Bullecourt. Bullecourt is in effect a large graveyard.

NAMES LISTED ON AUSTRALIAN WAR MEMORIAL AT VILLERS-BRETONNEUX

DATE	MISSING SOLDIERS
11th April 1917	743
3rd May 1917	791
4th May 1917	74
5th May 1917	198
6th May 1917	99
7th May 1917	69
8th May 1917	24
9th May 1917	33
10th May 1917	20
11th May 1917	14
12th May 1917	70
13th May 1917	13
14th May 1917	5
15th May 1917	89
16th May 1917	4
17th May 1917	1
18th May 1917	2
Total	**2,249**

NAMES LISTED ON ARRAS MEMORIAL

DATE	MISSING SOLDIERS
11th April	54
3rd May	914
4th May	152
5th May	12
6th May	8
7th May	55
8th May	20
9th May	59
10th May	11
11th May	44
12th May	82
13th May	76
14th May	79
15th May	126
16th May	34
17th May	18
18th May	12
19th May	3
20th May	20
21st May	96
Total	**1,875**

APPENDIX 5

AIF SOLDIERS KILLED ON 11TH APRIL 1917 WHO HAVE NO KNOWN GRAVE AND ARE COMMEMORATED ON THE AUSTRALIAN NATIONAL MEMORIAL AT VILLERS-BRETONNEUX

NAME	RANK	NUMBER	UNIT	NAME	RANK	NUMBER	UNIT
Abbott, George	Private	6465	14th Bn	Barber, John	Private	2123A	48th Bn
Abrahams, Eric	Lnce Corp	5646	46th Bn	Barker, Oliver	Private	4447	52nd Bn
Adams, Harry	Lnce Corp	465	13th Bn	Barlow, James	Private	5032	47th Bn
Adams, William	Private	4746	16th Bn	Barnes, Frank	2nd Lieut		15th Bn
Ahradsen, Alexander	Sergeant	2778	13th Bn	Bartley, Patrick	Private	5035	47th Bn
Alexander, Charles	Private	5226	13th Bn	Bates, Benjamin	Private	1879	48th Bn
Alexander, George	Private	4728A	46th Bn	Bates, George	Private	1880	48th Bn
Allan, Daniel	Private	5326	14th Bn	Bates, Joseph	Private	5040	13th Bn
Allan, Harold Gladstone	Private	1714	13th Bn	Batters, Anthony	Private	2032	46th Bn
Allen, Harold	Private	1668A	48th Bn	Battersby, William	Private	6226	15th Bn
Allen, Leslie John	Private	5974	13th Bn	Baxter, Thomas	Private	2108	4th Light TMB
Amey, Percy	Private	1234	16th Bn				
Anderson, Charles	Private	2368	46th Bn	Baxter, Thomas	Private	5038	47th Bn
Anderson, Henry	Sergeant	1580	48th Bn	Beale, Herbert	Sergeant	299	46th Bn
Anderson, Oliver	Private	4129	13th Bn	Beattie, Roy	Private	6470	14th Bn
Anderson, Thomas	Private	4129	46th Bn	Beggs, Ferris	Private	2817	46th Bn
Andrews, Alfred	Private	6214	14th Bn	Beitzel, Frederick	Lnce Corp	3007	47th Bn
Andrews, Ernest	Private		54th Coy MGC	Belcher, William	Private	4733	15th Bn
				Bell, Gilbert	Lnce Corp	4735	46th Bn
Anslow, Ernest[1]	Private	4683	48th Bn	Bell, Sidney	Private	5654	46th Bn
Archer, Frank	Private	6457	14th Bn	Benham, Raymond	Private	2542	46th Bn
Armitage, Reginald	2nd Lieut		47th Bn	Benson, Francis	Corporal	1405	15th Bn
Artery, William	Private	2121	13th Bn	Bentley, Edward	Private	6478	16th Bn
Arthur, Algernon	Private	1200	13th Bn	Berg, Herbert	Driver	8027	14th Bn
Ashton, Clarence	Private	6460	13th Bn	Berry, Charles	Private	3417	16th Bn
Baker, George	Lnce Corp	3574	15th Bn	Berry, James	Private	4736	46th Bn
Baker, Reginald	Private	2561	13th Bn	Berry, Rupert	Sergeant	817	14th Bn
Baldry, Frederick	Private	4950	48th Bn	Bird, Percy	Private	5337	14th Bn
Baldwin, Amos	Private	2296A	48th Bn	Birthisel, William	Private	6472	14th Bn
Bandera, Thomas	Private	6219	13th Bn	Black, Percy DSO DCM	Major		16th Bn

NAME	RANK	NUMBER	UNIT	NAME	RANK	NUMBER	UNIT
Blackman, Arthur	Private	6480	14th Bn	Carson, Norman	Private	5350	14th Bn
Blake, Edward	Private	4137	14th Bn	Carter, Ernest	Private	6496	16th Bn
Blamey, Reginald	Sergeant	162	14th Bn	Castlesmith, Rupert	Private	118A	15th Bn
Bland, Francis	Private	1736	16th Bn	Catterson, Robert	Lnce Serg	3294	15th Bn
Bleakley, John	Private	6234	16th Bn	Cavanagh, Daniel	Lnce Corp	923	14th Bn
Blencowe, Sydney	Private	2863	16th Bn	Challis, George	Private	2165	46th Bn
Boddington, Frederick	Captain		46th Bn	Challis, Sydney	Private	5996	14th Bn
Bolger, Patrick	Private	5986	15th Bn	Chantler, Charles	Private	2643	48th Bn
Booth, Thomas	Private	2819	46th Bn	Chapman, Norman	Private	3285	13th Bn
Bott, Arthur	Lnce Corp	6225	14th Bn	Charles, Harry	Corporal	1691	16th Bn
Boucher, Albert	Private	2633	48th Bn	Chipper, Michael	Private	6243	16th Bn
Bourdon, Cyril	Private	5989	14th Bn	Chisnall, Fred	Private	1821	46th Bn
Bourne, Frederick	Sergeant	2336	13th Bn	Christian, Henry	Private	6237	15th Bn
Bourne, Henry	Lnce Corp	1457	15th Bn	Clapp, Joseph	Private	1650	48th Bn
Bowman, Archibald	Private	5343	14th Bn	Clapton, Frederick	Private	1311	47th Bn
Bradley, James	Private	4443	46th Bn	Clark, Donald	Private	6493	16th Bn
Brady, James (Alphonso)	Private	5340	16th Bn	Cleary, Arthur	Private	2461	48th Bn
Brannigan, James	Lnce Corp	1691	13th Bn	Cleary, John	Private	5067	14th Bn
Bratchford, Anthony	Private	1688	15th Bn	Clifford, Charles	Private	6003	14th Bn
Brauer, William	Lnce Corp	555	46th Bn	Clingan, Colin	Private	2163	46th Bn
Bray, William	Private	5647	15th Bn	Codrington-Forsyth, Guy	Lieut		48th Bn
Brealey, James	Private	5998	16th Bn	Coffey, Leslie	Private	5690	16th Bn
Brennan, Anthony	Private	6704	13th Bn	Coffey, William	Private	3712	46th Bn
Brodie, George	Private	6481	14th Bn	Cole, Ernest	Private	2351	15th Bn
Brown, George	Private	3688	46th Bn	Cole, George	Private	6967	13th Bn
Brown, John	Private	3012	49th Bn	Colebatch, Hector	C.S.M	2332	48th Bn
Bruce, Albert	Private	2639	48th Bn	Coleman, Patrick	Private	5350	4th Light TMB
Brunton, Andrew	Private	6483	16th Bn				
Brusnahan, Patrick	Sergeant	1124	16th Bn	Collier, George	Private	5078	48th Bn
Buchan, George	Sergeant	240	13th Bn	Coman, Walter	Private	6716	13th Bn
Buchanan, George	Private	2463	46th Bn	Compton, Walter	Lnce Corp	1039	6th Coy MGC
Buckingham, George	Private	6237	16th Bn				
Buckingham, William	Private	6238	16th Bn	Conlon, Thomas	Private	5789	13th Bn
Buckles, James[2]	Lnce Corp	2621	46th Bn	Conole, Walter	Lnce Corp	1925	14th Bn
Buckman, Norman	Lnce Corp	2054	14th Bn	Considine, Percy	Private	4475	46th Bn
Budge, William	Private	5053	46th Bn	Cook, Phillip	Corporal	4470	46th Bn
Budgen, William	Private	2391	47th Bn	Coombs, Kennion	Private	2314	48th Bn
Buls, August	Private	2454	46th Bn	Coombs, Norman	Private	2399	48th Bn
Bunter, William	Private	5993	15th Bn	Cooper, Albert	Corporal	3297	47th Bn
Burlace, Cyril	Private	3016	48th Bn	Cooper, John	Lnce Corp	3063	48th Bn
Burley, Thomas	Lnce Corp	2034	46th Bn	Cooper, Oliver	Private	5665	13th Bn
Burn, Robert	Lnce Corp	3228	48th Bn	Cooper, Sidney	Private	5667	13th Bn
Burne, Charles	Private	4742	15th Bn	Cooper, Sydney	Lnce Corp	5679	49th Bn
Burns, Daniel	Private	2573	13th Bn	Copeman, Arthur	Private	1680	46th Bn
Burns, Matthew	Private	5659	46th Bn	Corbett, Vincent	Private	2144	47th Bn
Burrows, Arthur	Lnce Corp	3247	14th Bn	Corlett, Walter	Private	6229	16th Bn
Burton, George	Private	2384A	46th Bn	Cormack, Stuart	Private	5997	13th Bn
Buswell, George	Private	4758	48th Bn	Cornish, Herbert	Private	1900	48th Bn
Cairns, Frank	Private	5065	46th Bn	Coughlin, James	Private	1844	46th Bn
Caithness, Charles	Private	2385	46th Bn	Coulter, Wilfred[3]	Lnce Corp	2464	4th Coy MGC
Campbell, William	Lnce Corp	5786	15th Bn				
Campbell, William	Private	2304	46th Bn	Counsel, Wilfred	Sergeant	1172	4th Coy MGC
Carroll, Sydney	Private	5686	16th Bn				

NAME	RANK	NUMBER	UNIT	NAME	RANK	NUMBER	UNIT
Courtney, William	Private	5061	13th Bn	Dwyer, Timothy	Lnce Corp	2171	46th Bn
Coverley, James	Private	5346	16th Bn	Dyer, Edward	Private	6255	16th Bn
Cowley, Henry	Private	5799	16th Bn	Eason, Thomas	Private	6502	14th Bn
Cox, Clarence	Corporal	3713	46th Bn	Ecclestone, William	Private	3456	16th Bn
Craig, David	Private	4163	14th Bn	Edwards, Stanley	Private	6009	15th Bn
Cramond, David	Private	3263	14th Bn	Edwards, Thomas	Private	3357	24th Bn
Crane, George	Lnce Corp	2810	4th Coy MGC	Eibel, Henry	2nd Lieut.		15th Bn
Crawford, Thomas	Private	2354	46th Bn	Emery, Hurtle	Corporal	2611A	4th Light TMB
Crellin, Walter	Private	5702	16th Bn	Evans, Arthur	Private	4269	16th Bn
Cremer, Edward	Sergeant	3021	46th Bn	Evans, Arthur	Sergeant	1483	15th Bn
Cross, George	Sergeant	1504	13th Bn	Evans, Clarence	Private	1911	48th Bn
Crouch, Charles	Private	2157	46th Bn	Evans, Ernest	Private	6508	16th Bn
Crowe, Roy	Lnce Corp	1998A	48th Bn	Evans, Robert	Private	3041	48th Bn
Cullen, Frank	Corporal	3029	13th Bn	Fahey, John	Private	6500	15th Bn
Cullen, Patrick	Private	6715	13th Bn	Fairley, James	Private	6735	13th Bn
Cullen, Thomas	Private	1700	13th Bn	Fairlie, Edward	Private	2167	52nd Bn
Cundy, William	Private	5680	48th Bn	Featherby, Arthur	Private	2409	46th Bn
Currie, Alexander[4]	Private	4851	51st Bn	Ferrier, Thomas	Private	1450	13th Bn
Cutter, Robert	Private	2407A	47th Bn	Field, William	Private	1865	15th Bn
Dadson, Frederick	Lieut		14th Bn	Finlayson, Charles	Private	4191	4th Coy MGC
Dahler, William	Private	280A	12th Coy MGC	Finn, George	Private	1151	15th Bn
Dalziell, Ernest	Private	2650	48th Bn	Firmin, Alfred	Private	1694	46th Bn
David, Thomas	Private	6486	15th Bn	Fitzgerald, John	Private	5582	15th Bn
Davies, Albert	Private	4480A	46th Bn	Fletcher, Basil	Captain		13th Bn
Davies, Harold	Private	4794	48th Bn	Fletcher, David	Private	3319	46th Bn
Davies, Tasman	Corporal	3117	12th Bde AFA	Fogarty, Frederick	Private	6262	15th Bn
				Foote, Alexander	Lnce Corp	227	46th Bn
Davis, Henry	Captain		46th Bn	Forrest, Andrew	Lnce Corp	136	15th Bn
Dawson, Charles	Private	2176	46th Bn	Forrest, Darcy	Private	6017	16th Bn
Deane, John	Lnce Corp	1905	48th Bn	Fowless, Archibald	Lnce Corp	2374	13th Bn
Denteith, Thomas	Private	6251	16th Bn	Fraher, Edward	Private	4490	14th Bn
Dickinson, James	Lnce Corp	1933	14th Bn	Fraser, George	Private	3195	46th Bn
Dickman, William	Private	2173	46th Bn	Fraser, Robert	Corporal	4274	12th Coy MGC
Divall, Burban	Private	5706	16th Bn	Fraser, William	Private	6017	15th Bn
Dixon, Harry	Private	1351	13th Bn	Frost, Patrick	Sergeant	2517	13th Bn
Dodgshun, Eric	Lnce Corp	1209	13th Bn	Fuhrman, Norman	Private	746	15th Bn
Dolan, Matthew	Private	2299	48th Bn	Fullagar, Thomas	Private	3763	13th Bn
Donald, Harold	Private	3932	15th Bn	Fulwood, William	Private	4275	48th Bn
Donovan, Christopher	Private	5085	48th Bn	Gaghin, John	Private	2528	46th Bn
Doolan, Eric	Private	1902	46th Bn	Gainger, Oliver	Private	2294	46th Bn
Douglas, Stanley	Private	3454	16th Bn	Gallagher, Albert	Private	1919	48th Bn
Doyle, Ernest	Private	2097	16th Bn	Galloway, John	Private	775	13th Bn
Doyle, William	Private	2649	48th Bn	Gamlen, Alban	Lnce Corp	1723	48th Bn
Drennan, David	Private	2149	48th Bn	Gammon, Alfred	Private	2655	46th Bn
Drew, William	Private	6624	16th Bn	Gange, John	Private	2195A	46th Bn
Duce, Eric	Private	3451	16th Bn	Garratt, Reginald	Lnce Corp	4812	14th Bn
Dudley, Alfred	Private	4178	14th Bn	Gathercole, William	Private	3750	46th Bn
Duff, William	Private	1705	14th Bn	Gebhardt, Ernest	Private	1921	48th Bn
Dunderdale, Reginald	Private	49	16th Bn	Geldard, Lancelot	Private	3473	4th Coy MGC
Durdin, William	Private	2151B	48th Bn				
Dusting, Harold	Private	4486	46th Bn				

NAME	RANK	NUMBER	UNIT	NAME	RANK	NUMBER	UNIT
Gent, Lionel	Private	6022	16th Bn	Higgs, Robert	Private	6030	14th Bn
Gibson, George	Private	2665	49th Bn	Hindmarsh, Edwin	Private	4806	15th Bn
Giffard, Percy	Private	3494	14th Bn	Hinds, Charles	Private	2485	16th Bn
Glasson, Thomas	Private	5722	16th Bn	Hobbs, Herbert	Private	2424	48th Bn
Glen, Archibald	Lnce Corp	590	14th Bn	Hodder, James	Private	5365	16th Bn
Glover, Henry	Private	4147	48th Bn	Holdsworth, Herbert	Private	2760	46th Bn
Glowrey, Lindsay	2nd Lieut.		16th Bn	Holland, Herbert	Private	1934	48th Bn
Goertz, Harold	Private	1917	46th Bn	Holley, Bertie	Private	3328	15th Bn
Golding, Hugh	Private	2066	13th Bn	Horne, Alfred	Private	5711	48th Bn
Good, James	Private	1746	15th Bn	Horsman, Henry	Sergeant	1046	16th Bn
Goodhand, Fred	Private	6270	16th Bn	Horton, Robert	Private	5115	47th Bn
Goodman, Francis	Private	4280	48th Bn	Howlett, John	Private	6270	15th Bn
Gowing, Archie	2nd Lieut.		13th Bn	Howley, Martin	Private	1746	16th Bn
Graf, Emil	Private	6269	14th Bn	Hull, William	Private	2479	46th Bn
Graham, George MM	Private	1728	4th Coy MGC	Hunt, George	Private	3807	13th Bn
				Hunter, Charles	Private	5110	13th Bn
Graham, Gordon	Private	1910	46th Bn	Hunter, Samuel	Private	6047	13th Bn
Granland, Herbert	Private	14555	46th Bn	Hurley, Joseph	Private	5696	15th Bn
Gray, Frederick	Private	2197	46th Bn	Hutton, Ernest	Private	3012	48th Bn
Green, Alfred	Private	2192	46th Bn	Inch, James	Private	2152	15th Bn
Green, Henry	Private	2198	46th Bn	Ingram, David	Private	1716	46th Bn
Green, Marshall	Private	5675	14th Bn	Ireland, William	Private	1937	48th Bn
Greene, Percival	Lnce Corp	5380	14th Bn	Irvine, John	Private	4223	14th Bn
Gregory, Arthur	Private	2276	48th Bn	Irwin, Edwin	Private	4222	14th Bn
Griffiths, Sydney	Private	6740	13th Bn	Isbel, William	Private	726	14th Bn
Grimbly, Alfred	Private	5690	13th Bn	Jacob, Llewellyn	Private	2491	16th Bn
Gross, Jack	Private	4205	14th Bn	Jacobs, Victor	Private	6046	16th Bn
Gullifer, Albert	Private	6741	13th Bn	Jacobson, Fritz	Private	6042	16th Bn
Gunst, Frederick	Private	5106	4th Light TMB	Jago, John	Private	6039	14th Bn
				James, William	Private	1679	48th Bn
Haase, Robert	Corporal	4955	46th Bn	Jamieson, Edward	Private	5744	13th Bn
Hamann, Clarence	Private	4825	46th Bn	Jecks, Alec	Private	4632	48th Bn
Hammerberg, Robert	Private	2604	14th Bn	Johnson, John	Private	7018	13th Bn
Hanrahan, Michael	Private	2562	16th Bn	Johnson, Wallie	Private	2444	47th Bn
Harber, Alfred	Private	2210	46th Bn	Johnston, John	Lnce Corp	5040	48th Bn
Hardie, Norman	Lnce Corp	5113	46th Bn	Johnston, Thomas	Private	605	14th Bn
Hardy, Robert	Private	2393	14th Bn	Johnstone, George	Private	4523	14th Bn
Harmening, Frederick	Private	5412	15th Bn	Jones, Claude	Private	1938A	46th Bn
Harris, Allan	Private	2426	46th Bn	Jones, Daniel	Private	2558	46th Bn
Harris, Frederick	Private	4214	14th Bn	Jones, George	Private	3803A	13th Bn
Hart, William	Corporal	2395	14th Bn	Jones, Raymond	Corporal	79	14th Bn
Hartnup, Bertie	Private	6272	16th Bn	Jones, Richard	Lnce Corp	2057	13th Bn
Harvey, George	Private	4512	15th Bn	Jones, Samuel	2nd Lieut.		48th Bn
Harvey, Lionel	Lnce Corp	1169	48th Bn	Jordan, Edward	Private	2393	13th Bn
Hatt, Claude	Private	2427	46th Bn	Joyce, John	Private	1418	15th Bn
Hayes, George	Private	2766	13th Bn	Joyce, Matthew	Private	3786	46th Bn
Hayne, Thomas	Private	949	46th Bn	Kamman, George	Private	3128	16th Bn
Healy, Jack	Lnce Corp	1665	47th Bn	Kannan, Alfred	Private	4234	14th Bn
Healy, John	Private	2673	48th Bn	Kelly, Cecil	2nd Lieut.		47th Bn
Heinke, Arthur	Private	1621	13th Bn	Kelly, Lewis	Private	2057	48th Bn
Henderson, George	Private	1319	16th Bn	Kemble, Walter	Private	6281	16th Bn
Heuschkel, John[5]	Private	4213	13th Bn	Kennedy, Victor	Private	5687	14th Bn
Hide, Cecil	Private	3476	16th Bn	Kibble, Peter	Sergeant	966	13th Bn

NAME	RANK	NUMBER	UNIT	NAME	RANK	NUMBER	UNIT
Kilby, Thomas	Private	4528	14th Bn	March, Douglas	Private	2720B	48th Bn
Kilpatrick, Arthur	Lnce Corp	4237	14th Bn	Mark, Edward	Corporal	1062	15th Bn
King, Leslie	Private	867	13th Bn	Markham, Andrew	Private	4247	14th Bn
King, Robert	Corporal	2770	46th Bn	Markham, Chester	Private	5727	13th Bn
Klintworth, Henry	Private	1946	48th Bn	Marshall, George	Private	1725	47th Bn
Knights, Edward	Private	330	4th Coy MGC	Marshall, Victor	Lnce Serg.	90	16th Bn
				Marshall, William	Private	2714	48th Bn
Knox, Thomas	Private	6548	13th Bn	Martin, Austin	Private	1355	46th Bn
Ladner, Edward	Private	4464	13th Bn	Martin, Daniel	Private	5149	16th Bn
Lahey, Henry	Corporal	3087A	48th Bn	Martin, Samuel	Private	2687	51st Bn
Laing, John Ord	Private	2284	46th Bn	Martin, Thomas	Private	3946	16th Bn
Lamb, Robert	Private	6077	13th Bn	Mason, Roy	Private	5057	13th Bn
Larkin, Thomas	Private	2672	13th Bn	Masters, Thomas	Private	3724	48th Bn
Laskie, Norman	Private	2706	46th Bn	Matheson, Dudley	Sergeant	1796	13th Bn
Lathby, Horace	Lnce Serg.	3859	11th Bn	Mavor, James	Private	4957	16th Bn
Laurie, Clarence	Private	2275	48th Bn	May, Leslie	Private	2622	16th Bn
Lawlor, John	Private	511	48th Bn	Mayell, Edward	Private	5728	48th Bn
Lawrence, James	Private	3059	46th Bn	Mayfield, Frank	Private	6218	15th Bn
Lawrie, Charles	Private	5059	15th Bn	Mayo, Ernest	Sergeant	1098	13th Bn
Le Brun, George	Lnce Corp	1970	14th Bn	McAlpine, James	Private	6068	16th Bn
Leaney, William	Private	2693A	52nd Bn	McCabe, James	Private	2706	48th Bn
Leslie, Francis	Captain		15th Bn	McCann, James	Private	5756	16th Bn
Lester, Albert	Private	4243	14th Bn	McCarthy, Henry	Private	5379	16th Bn
Lewis, Charles	Private	1298	16th Bn	McCarthy, Oscar	Private	6623	14th Bn
Lewis, Percy	Corporal	1166	14th Bn	McCormack, Thomas	Private	1601	47th Bn
Lewis, William	Private	2407	46th Bn	McCormick, James	Private	6547	14th Bn
Liddiard, Alfred	Lnce Corp	3825	46th Bn	McCurry, George	Private	3803	47th Bn
Lilley, Richard	Private	2738	14th Bn	McDonald, Alexander	Private	758	13th Bn
Lindon, William	Private	4529	46th Bn	McDonald, James	Lnce Corp	2186	14th Bn
Linter, Arthur	Private	6300	15th Bn	McDonald, Robert	Corporal	3082	46th Bn
Liston, Robert	Lnce Corp	5711	46th Bn	McDonald, Robert	Sergeant	3402	14th Bn
Litt, Oliver	Corporal	527	4th Coy MGC	McDougall, Archie	Corporal	3559	26th Bn
				McDougall, James	Private	6548	16th Bn
Lockwood, George	Private	1761	16th Bn	McDowell, William	Private	6540	16th Bn
Long, James	Private	6303	14th Bn	McEwan, Robert	Private	4553	46th Bn
Louden, Henry	Private	2698	48th Bn	McGan, James	Private	2560	46th Bn
Love, Percival	Lnce Corp	3327	46th Bn	McGeachin, Hugh	Private	3998	46th Bn
Love, Sydney	Private	4163	48th Bn	McGee, Bryan	Private	6782	13th Bn
Lovell, William	Private	2411	14th Bn	McGinley, Walter	Private	3191	15th Bn
Lowe, Richard	Private	5133	48th Bn	McGowan, William	Private	5710	14th Bn
Luke, James	Private	6048	14th Bn	McGrath, Patrick	Private	1820	46th Bn
Luxton, Robert	Lieut.		15th Bn	McGrath, Peter	Private	5760	16th Bn
Mackie, Thomas	Private	3410	13th Bn	McKellar, Duncan	Private	2800	46th Bn
Maclean, Peter	Private	6304	16th Bn	McKinnon, Alexander	Private	2705	48th Bn
MacMillan, Henry	Private	4264	46th Bn	McKissock, Alexander	Private	3396	14th Bn
Madden, William	Private	6388	15th Bn	McLachlan, William	Private	6059	14th Bn
Mahaffy, Kenneth	Private	2720	46th Bn	McLean, Eugene	Private	2239	46th Bn
Mahoney, Thomas	Private	5124	13th Bn	McLean, Kenneth	Private	5411	48th Bn
Mahony, Clement	Private	935A	48th Bn	McLellan, James	Private	1709	48th Bn
Main, William	Private	6057	16th Bn	McLelland, Arthur	Lnce Corp	1930	47th Bn
Manson, Alfred	Private	7088	15th Bn	McLeod, Peter	Private	5651	16th Bn
Manson, Henry	Lnce Corp.	4546	14th Bn	McLoughlin, Patrick	Private	4850	15th Bn
Manzie, George	Private	2722	46th Bn	McNamee, Kenneth MM	Private	4258	14th Bn

NAME	RANK	NUMBER	UNIT	NAME	RANK	NUMBER	UNIT
McNellee, Shadrac	Private	2689	13th Bn	Noy, Leslie	Private	588	48th Bn
McPherson, George	Private	6396	14th Bn	Nutley, Herbert	Private	4258	13th Bn
McRae, Alexander	Private	4560	46th Bn	Nuttall, Alexander	Private	3854	46th Bn
McRae, John	Lnce Serg.	3388	14th Bn	O'Brien, David	Private	2520	4th Light TMB
McWhinney, George	Sergeant	405	16th Bn	O'Brien, James	Lnce Corp	2467A	48th Bn
Meginess, Michael	Private	5745	16th Bn	O'Callaghan, John	Corporal	1832	46th Bn
Mehegan, William	Private	6317	14th Bn	O'Connell, Henry	Private	1971	46th Bn
Mell, Henry	Private	6770	13th Bn	O'Connor, Daniel	Private	6852	13th Bn
Menzies, David	Private	3415	14th Bn	O'Donnell, Michael	2nd Lieut.		14th Bn
Menzies, John	Private	5130	13th Bn	Officer, Geoffrey	Private	2003	4th Light TMB
Mesney, Valentine	Private	2712	48th Bn	Oliver, Norman	Private	754	15th Bn
Miatke, Frederick	Private	3729	48th Bn	Olsen, Marius	Private	4895	46th Bn
Milburn, William	Private	6295	16th Bn	Orr, Robert	Captain		14th Bn
Millar, Alexander	Corporal	4650	48th Bn	Orr, William	Sergeant	2923	14th Bn
Miller, Charles	Corporal	4255	14th Bn	Oxman, Alfred	Private	4684	48th Bn
Millett, Leslie	Lnce Corp	3430	46th Bn	Page, Alma	Private	3117	48th Bn
Mills, Fred	Private	6068	14th Bn	Page, Nelson	Private	6565	16th Bn
Mills, Herbert	Private	4539	46th Bn	Parker, Charles	Private	5426	14th Bn
Mitchell, John	Sergeant	3833	12th Coy MGC	Parker, Ernest	Private	2479	46th Bn
Molyneux, David	Private	4542	46th Bn	Parker, Fred	Private	3110	46th Bn
Monico, John	Private	1961	4th Bn	Parker, James	Private	4887	15th Bn
Moore, George	Private	1782	4th Coy MGC	Parsons, John	Private	6073	16th Bn
Moore, Hugh	Private	6781	13th Bn	Parsons, William	Private	5849	48th Bn
Moore, Kenton	Corporal	2578	52nd Bn	Pateman, Herbert	Private	5724	14th Bn
Moppett, George	Private	6835	13th Bn	Patterson, Oliver	Private	2470	48th Bn
Morehouse, Lindsay	Private	2466A	46th Bn	Payne, Mervyn	Private	5770	16th Bn
Morgan, Thomas	Lieut.		13th Bn	Perks, William	Private	339	4th Coy MGC
Morris, Charles	Private	3419	14th Bn	Peters, Roy	Private	1202	16th Bn
Morris, Edward	Private	6310	15th Bn	Petersen, Samuel	Private	4874	15th Bn
Mounce, Charles	Private	518	48th Bn	Peterson, Charles	Private	3116	46th Bn
Mullett, Leslie	2nd Lieut.		14th Bn	Pettit, Stanley	Private	6078	16th Bn
Mullins, John	Private	516	46th Bn	Phillips, George	Private	6338	14th Bn
Mullins, Thomas	Private	6309	15th Bn	Piukkula, Otto	Lnce Corp	2361	4th Light TMB
Mumby, Jhon	Private	6291	13th Bn	Pontin, Norman	Sergeant	3120	46th Bn
Munro, John	Private	757	15th Bn	Poore, William	Private	6097	13th Bn
Murphy, James	Private	3399	47th Bn	Porter, John	Lnce Corp	5425A	14th Bn
Murray, Horace	Private	6772	13th Bn	Postlethwaite, Claude	Corporal	1995	14th Bn
Murtagh, Michael	Private	5456	15th Bn	Potts, James	Private	6250	16th Bn
Myers, James	Private	2459	48th Bn	Price, John	Private	4639	47th Bn
Naylor, George	Private	3099	46th Bn	Price, John	Private	1980	46th Bn
Needham, George	Private	6072	14th Bn	Prior, Richard	Lnce Corp	427	16th Bn
Neighbour, James	Private	6073	14th Bn	Proctor, James	2nd Lieut.		15th Bn
Nelson, Arnold	Lnce Corp	5714	14th Bn	Punzell, John	Private	5571	15th Bn
Neville, Louis	Private	6074	14th Bn	Quinton, David	Private	5725	14th Bn
Neville, Malcolm	Private	2214	48th Bn	Radway, Joshua	Private	2078	16th Bn
Newbold, Walter	Private	6806	13th Bn	Read, Edgar	Private	5449	14th Bn
Niall, Alfred	Private	5740	13th Bn	Redmond, John	Private	3125	15th Bn
Nicolson, Donald	Sergeant	1732A	47th Bn	Rees, Edward	Private	5416	16th Bn
Noblet, Charles	Private	5737	13th Bn	Reid, William	Private	5730	14th Bn
Nottage, Reuben	Private	3059	16th Bn				
Noy, Ernest	Private	3740	48th Bn				

NAME	RANK	NUMBER	UNIT	NAME	RANK	NUMBER	UNIT
Reid, William	Private	608	16th Bn	Sleight, Thomas	Private	6090	15th Bn
Reynolds, Edward	Private	5182	16th Bn	Sloan, Joseph	Private	3911	46th Bn
Richards, Raymond	Lnce Corp	2368	48th Bn	Smedley, Stanley	Private	1863	15th Bn
Richardson, Forrest	Private	3429	15th Bn	Smith, Alfred	Private	293	4th Coy
Richardson, James	Private	6588	13th Bn				MGC
Richardson, Robert	Private	2226	13th Bn	Smith, Arthur	Private	2489	48th Bn
Ridge, Leslie	Sergeant	3469	14th Bn	Smith, Claude	Private	382	14th Bn
Riley, Ernest	Private	6591	13th Bn	Smith, James	Private	3433	4th Light
Riley, Thomas	Private	6091	14th Bn				TMB
Roach, Albert	Private	4596	14th Bn	Smith, Stanley	Private	6325	13th Bn
Roads, Harold	Lnce Corp	5753	46th Bn	Smith, Stewart	Private	4898	15th Bn
Roberts, Herbert	Private	1976	48th Bn	Sorensen, James	Private	2198	15th Bn
Rollins, Karl	Private	2538	46th Bn	Sowton, Claude	Private	3043	16th Bn
Ronald, William	Private	3122	48th Bn	Sparks, Robert	Lnce Corp	1861	16th Bn
Rooney, Charles	Sergeant	3896	46th Bn	Speck, John	Private	1938	48th Bn
Ross, Charles	Sergeant	3543	14th Bn	Spiers, Victor	Private	1956	47th Bn
Ross, Nathaniel MM	Private	2248	46th Bn	Spring, William	Private	5175	13th Bn
Ross, Percy	Private	6087	14th Bn	Spruce, Harold	Private	5424	16th Bn
Rossington, George	Private	640	15th Bn	Stanton, Frederick	Captain		14th Bn
Rouse, Alfred	Private	5415	16th Bn	Steele, Charles	Private	2026	14th Bn
Rowe, John	Private	574	46th Bn	Stenhouse, John	Private	2448	47th Bn
Rowley, Cornelius	Private	4303	46th Bn	Stephen, Harry	Private	6090	16th Bn
Rushton, Charles	Private	5450	45th Bn	Stephens, Stanley	Private	6320	13th Bn
Russell, George	Private	3990	48th Bn	Stewart, Harry	Private	2434	5th
Russell, Reginald	Private	5796	13th Bn				Pioneers
Russell, Walter	Private	4289	13th Bn	Stewart, Jack	Private	384	14th Bn
Rutherford, Gordon	Private	2286	47th Bn	Stewart, John	Private	5174	13th Bn
Rutherford, Hiram	Private	3885	46th Bn	Stewart, Victor	Private	5974	16th Bn
Rutherford, William	Lnce Corp	414A	46th Bn	Stewart, Walter	Private	1070	52nd Bn
Rutter, Charles	Private	6083	14th Bn	Stewart, William	Private	3444	15th Bn
Ryan, John	Private	2634	15th Bn	Storer, Herbert	Corporal	2434	14th Bn
Samson, David	Private	3548	16th Bn	Strand, Walter	Private	6575	16th Bn
Saunders, William	Private	6595	13th Bn	Stuart, Sydney	Lnce Corp	5187	13th Bn
Scanlon, James	Private	2250	47th Bn	Sutton, Alfred	Private	3829	13th Bn
Schultz, Ambrose	Sergeant	2007	14th Bn	Sutton, Arthur	Private	5428	16th Bn
Scott, Douglas	Private	3633	15th Bn	Swasbrick, James	Driver	135	13th Bn
Sebbens, Ernest	Private	7073	13th Bn	Sweeney, Cornelius	Private	1449	15th Bn
Shadwick, John	Lieut.		48th Bn	Sweeney, Garrett	Private	4346	46th Bn
Sharp, George	Sergeant	139	16th Bn	Sweeney, George	Private	6346	15th Bn
Shepherd, Horace	Private	2243	48th Bn	Thomas, Bertram	Private	6112	14th Bn
Shillabeer, Albert	Private	1731	48th Bn	Thomas, Herbert	Private	5190	4th Coy
Shirtley, William	Lieut.		13th Bn				MGC
Short, Cecil	Private	2404	4th Coy	Thomas, William	Lnce Corp	2253	48th Bn
			MGC	Thompson, George	Lnce Corp	2919	13th Bn
Short, John	Corporal	5790	16th Bn	Thompson, James	Private	6342	16th Bn
Shueard, William	Private	2492	48th Bn	Thompson, Stanley	2nd Lieut.		14th Bn
Sims, Francis	Private	2984	48th Bn	Thomson, Robert	Private	5740	14th Bn
Sims, Frederick	Private	2983	48th Bn	Thornley, James	2nd Lieut.		13th Bn
Singleton, Albert	Private	6839	13th Bn	Thornton, Harold	Private	215	13th Bn
Siviour, Norman	Private	1989	48th Bn	Thorp, Harold	Lnce Corp.	1334	16th Bn
Skinner, George	Private	4594	47th Bn	Ticklie, Albert MM	Lnce Corp.	4347	48th Bn
Slade, Harold	Corporal	638	16th Bn	Tilley, Ernest	Lnce Corp.	5770	13th Bn
Slater, Herbert	Private	2755	46th Bn	Tobin, Francis	Lnce Corp.	1891	46th Bn

NAME	RANK	NUMBER	UNIT	NAME	RANK	NUMBER	UNIT
Todd, Joseph	Private	2140	16th Bn	Watson, John	Private	2002	48th Bn
Tolstoi, Andre	Private	5760	15th Bn	Watson, William	Private	1791	46th Bn
Totten, Alfred	Private	6332	13th Bn	Westerbeck, Arthur	Private	1791A	46th Bn
Touzel, Clifford	Private	1790A	16th Bn	Weston, Robert	Private	1759	47th Bn
Touzel, John	Sergeant	1680	16th Bn	Wheeler, Thomas	Private	2263	48th Bn
Townsend, Harold	Private	6108	14th Bn	Whelan, Norman	Private	1707	14th Bn
Travis, William	Private	5221	46th Bn	Whitchurch, William	Private	1859	4th Coy MGC
Trenorden, William	Private	1044	16th Bn				
Trethowan, Harold	Lnce Serg.	3930	46th Bn	White, Frank	Corporal	1395	48th Bn
Try, Ernest	Private	6364	13th Bn	White, Frederick	Sergeant	3529	46th Bn
Tucker, Virgil	Captain		16th Bn	White, Gordon	Corporal	5455	16th Bn
Turner, Charles	Private	2499	48th Bn	White, Michael	Sergeant	3521	13th Bn
Turner, Herbert	Private	5331	16th Bn	Whitford, Richard	Private	2942	16th Bn
Turner, Leonard	Lnce Serg.	1571	46th Bn	Whitman, Ernest	Private	10333	46th Bn
Tutt, Albert	Private	2477A	48th Bn	Whittles, John	Sergeant	2012	46th Bn
Twigg, Arnold	Private	5461	14th Bn	Wiese, Reinhold	Private	2507	48th Bn
Twining, Percy	Private	2371	16th Bn	Willett, William	Private	6367	15th Bn
Urie, Archibald	Sergeant	2028	14th Bn	Williams, Francis	Private	2005	46th Bn
Urquhart, Finlay	Private	2423	15th Bn	Williams, Gordon	Lnce Corp.	2838	48th Bn
Viney, Ernest	Private	2259	48th Bn	Williams, John	Private	3963	46th Bn
Voumard, Henry	Private	2004	46th Bn	Williams, Thomas	Private	2514	47th Bn
Wachman, Robert	Corporal	4451	48th Bn	Williams, Walter	Private	3573	16th Bn
Wade, Ernest	Private	5476	14th Bn	Williamson, Alfred	Captain		14th Bn
Walker, Frank	2nd Lieut.		46th Bn	Wilson, Andrew	Private	3509	11th Bn
Walker, George	Private	4322	46th Bn	Wilson, Robert	Private	3537	14th Bn
Walker, George	Corporal	3977	13th Bn	Wilson, William	Private	2400	47th Bn
Wallis, David	Private	4338	14th Bn	Wise, Charles	Private	1874	16th Bn
Walsh, Frederick	Private	4936	16th Bn	Withers, Walter	Private	5767	15th Bn
Ward, Arthur	Private	2453A	48th Bn	Wood, Archibald	Private	1751	47th Bn
Warner, Francis	Private	6609	13th Bn	Worthington, Richard	Private	4334	46th Bn
Warner, Frederick	Sergeant	3893	47th Bn	Wright, Drury	Private	2510	48th Bn
Warren, Roy	Private	3973	4th Light TMB	Wright, Edwin	Lnce Corp.	2033A	48th Bn
				Yates, John	Corporal	215	15th Bn
Warren, Urban	Corporal	1385	48th Bn	Yells, Cyril	Private	216	15th Bn
Warwick, John	Lnce Corp.	6341	13th Bn	Yorke, Leo	Private	5468A	14th Bn
Watson, Herbert	Lieut.		48th Bn	Youdan, Thomas	Private	5788	13th Bn
Watson, John	Captain		15th Bn	Young, William	Lnce Corp.	2919	14th Bn

NOTES
1. Used alias 'Ernest Onslow'.
2. Used alias 'Morrow'.
3. Used alias 'Wilfred Lawrence Coulter'.
4. Used alias 'Alexander Manson'.
5. Used alias 'John Frederick Huskell', possibly to conceal his German name.

AIF SOLDIERS KILLED ON 3RD MAY 1917 WHO HAVE NO KNOWN GRAVE AND ARE COMMEMORATED ON THE AUSTRALIAN NATIONAL MEMORIAL AT VILLERS-BRETONNEUX

NAME	RANK	NUMBER	UNIT	NAME	RANK	NUMBER	UNIT
Abell, Frederick	Private	3810	17th Bn	Bamkin, Bert	Private	4975	23rd Bn
Adams, William	Private	4651	18th Bn	Banks, Arthur	Private	5941	19th Bn
Adamson, Arthur	Private	5307	22nd Bn	Barber, Samuel	Private	5791	24th Bn
Alderson, Charles	Private	2955A	20th Bn	Barker, William	Private	4977	22nd Bn
Allen, Frederick	Private	3978	22nd Bn	Barlow, Harold	Corporal	1880	18th Bn
Alliston, James	Sergeant	3753	23rd Bn	Barnden, Albert	Corporal	5787	23rd Bn
Amery, Alexander	Private	4974	22nd Bn	Barr, George	Private	5547	21st Bn
Anderson, Frederick	Private	4356	21st Bn	Barry, John	Private	482	18th Bn
Anderson, Garner	Private	6029	22nd Bn	Bartlett, James	Corporal	1615	17th Bn
Andrew, Percy	Corporal	5537	22nd Bn	Bartlett, Thomas	Private	3770	23rd Bn
Antonio, Arthur	Private	4267	23rd Bn	Barton, William	Private	6035	23rd Bn
Apps, David	Private	2858B	19th Bn	Bassett, Thomas	Private	1884	17th Bn
Archer, Henry	Corporal	262	26th Bn	Baxter, Harry	Gunner	10386	5th Bde AFA
Armstrong, Percy	Private	4059	22nd Bn				
Arndell, Leslie	Private	1568	19th Bn	Bayliss, Alfred	Gunner	10121	5th Bde AFA
Arnott, George	Corporal	1212	23rd Bn				
Arrowsmith, Alfred	Private	6027	24th Bn	Beale, Leonard	Private	5296	24th Bn
Ashton, John	Private	752	19th Bn	Beaton, Lance	Private	3019	8th Light TMB
Atfield, Herbert	Lnce Serg.	2551	18th Bn				
Attwood, Arthur	Private	5783	19th Bn	Beattie, Melville	Corporal	2129	21st Bn
Attwood, John	Private	4055	17th Bn	Beaumont, Walter	Lnce Corp.	3022	17th Bn
Austin, Hedley	Corporal	2106	19th Bn	Beck, Horace	Corporal	1091	4th Div AFA
Avard, David MC	2nd Lieut.		19th Bn				
Baggett, Arthur	Private	4659	17th Bn	Beddows, Arthur	Private	4060	17th Bn
Bailey, Frank[1]	Private	5554	22nd Bn	Bennett, Norman	Private	3770	17th Bn
Bailey, William	Private	3771	23rd Bn	Berlowitz, Joseph	Private	5787	22nd Bn
Bain, Edward	Private	5544	23rd Bn	Bermingham, Francis	Gunner	3230	4th Div TMB
Baker, Arthur	Lnce Corp.	111	22nd Bn				
Baldock, Harold	Private	4975	19th Bn	Bettles, Albert	Corporal	4979	23rd Bn
Bamford, Charles	Private	5558	28th Bn	Betts, Thomas	Private	6037	20th Bn

NAME	RANK	NUMBER	UNIT	NAME	RANK	NUMBER	UNIT
Bevan, David	Private	2570	23rd Bn	Campbell, William	Private	130	22nd Bn
Billings, James	Private	1896	28th Bn	Campion, Sydney	Private	4377	20th Bn
Binnie, William	Private	5558	21st Bn	Cant, James	2nd Lieut.		19th Bn
Bird, Charles	Private	3023	23rd Bn	Cantwell, Philip	Private	5116	21st Bn
Black, Hector	Private	5789	17th Bn	Carlsen, Sidney	Lnce Corp.	4082	19th Bn
Black, John	Private	5303	18th Bn	Carroll, Albert	Corporal	385	19th Bn
Black, William	Private	2591	17th Bn	Carroll, William	Private	4989	17th Bn
Blackwood, George	Private	5300	24th Bn	Carter, Claud	Private	5330	28th Bn
Blair, Robert	Private	4981	24th Bn	Catton, James	Private	5716	22nd Bn
Blencowe, Sidney	Private	5553	23rd Bn	Caudry, William	Private	5447	22nd Bn
Bloore, Alfred	Private	4369	22nd Bn	Chamberlain, Stanley	Private	1325	24th Bn
Boak, Alexander	Lnce Corp	2340	24th Bn	Channon, Percy	Private	4176	21st Bn
Bond, Sydney	Corporal	2336	20th Bn	Chapman, James	Corporal	3808	18th Bn
Bosustow, William	Private	4375	22nd Bn	Chapman, William	Private	1070	23rd Bn
Bourke, Cornelius	Private	4092	25th Bn	Charlton, Robert	Sergeant	4685	21st Bn
Bourke, Francis	Private	1665	17th Bn	Chatley, Norman	Lnce Corp.	3798	22nd Bn
Bown, Alfred	Private	1890	27th Bn	Cheriton, James	Private	6047	19th Bn
Bowyer, Herbert	Private	4985	22nd Bn	Chestnut, William	Private	5175	18th Bn
Boyce, Arthur	Private	5790	19th Bn	Chick, Gordon	Sergeant	1901	17th Bn
Boysen, Charles	Lnce Corp.	810	20th Bn	Childs, George	Corporal	2038	17th Bn
Boyton, Gordon	Private	2865	17th Bn	Christey, John	Private	6056	22nd Bn
Bren, John	Private	4988	22nd Bn	Clark, George	Private	5825	28th Bn
Brennan, Grattan	Private	6204	18th Bn	Clark, James	Private	4678	19th Bn
Brennan, Patrick	Private	5119	24th Bn	Clark, Walter	Private	2134	6th Coy
Brennan, William	Private	1885A	21st Bn				MGC
Brent, John	Private	4982	21st Bn	Clarke, Julius	Private	1593A	19th Bn
Brickley, William	Private	5785	18th Bn	Cleary, Leo	Lnce Corp.	4077	22nd Bn
Briggs, Frank	Private	3762	17th Bn	Cockshell, Sydney	Gunner	2004	4th Div
Bright, Stanley	Private	4535	23rd Bn				TMB
Britcher, Herbert	Private	5539	20th Bn	Cogan, George	Private	5562	26th Bn
Brooks, Alfred	Private	5792	21st Bn	Cohen, Lewis	Private	3780	24th Bn
Brown, Charles	Private	2868	18th Bn	Cole, Allen	Private	3821	18th Bn
Brown, William	Private	6040	17th Bn	Cole, George	Private	4568	26th Bn
Browning, Walter	Private	4383	22nd Bn	Collins, Daniel	Private	4395	22nd Bn
Buckle, Arthur	Private	4370	19th Bn	Collins, Daniel	Private	5971	23rd Bn
Bugge, Ernest	Private	5544	22nd Bn	Collins, Ernest	Private	2881	19th Bn
Burke, Thomas	Private	6038	17th Bn	Collins, Francis MM	Private	4391	20th Bn
Burke, William	Private	5802	24th Bn	Collins, Norman	Private	6065	27th Bn
Burns, John	Corporal	2030	24th Bn	Collis, Sidney	Private	5307	18th Bn
Busby, Ernest	Private	3760	22nd Bn	Commons, Hugh	Private	177	17th Bn
Bushnie, David	Private	4074	22nd Bn	Conlon, John	Private	1787	59th Bn
Butcher, Leonard	Private	3056	28th Bn	Connor, Charles	Private	5555	17th Bn
Byfield, Reginald	Lnce Corp.	3777	18th Bn	Cook, Albert	Private	5557	23rd Bn
Byrnes, John	Private	4686	26th Bn	Corbett, Harold	Sergeant	6876	19th Bn
Byron, Charles	Private	6032	18th Bn	Cordingly, Arthur	Private	3799	23rd Bn
Callaway, Norman	Private	5794	19th Bn	Corrigan, Alfred	Private	5565	21st Bn
Cameron, Arthur	Private	376	18th Bn	Cotter, Guy	Sergeant	4999	23rd Bn
Cameron, Ernest	Private	3794	21st Bn	Coughlin, Vincent	Private	4802	26th Bn
Cameron, James	Private	4116	26th Bn	Cowell, Charles	Private	5880	22nd Bn
Campbell, George	Private	3008A	19th Bn	Cox, Edward	Private	181	17th Bn
Campbell, James	Private	5310	24th Bn	Cozens, Oliver	Private	4089	20th Bn
Campbell, James	Gunner	4454	4th Div	Crane, Edmund	Private	5330	22nd Bn
			TMB	Crawford, Frederick	Private	5331	22nd Bn

NAME	RANK	NUMBER	UNIT	NAME	RANK	NUMBER	UNIT
Cree, Joseph	Lnce Corp.	4080	23rd Bn	Driscoll, James	Private	1797	24th Bn
Creighton, Albert	Private	5323	24th Bn	Drummond, Morris	Lieut.		18th Bn
Creswick, William	Private	5324	24th Bn	Duane, Joseph	Private	5126	23rd Bn
Crewe, William	Private	5686	17th Bn	Dunkley, Clement	Private	5781	22nd Bn
Crittenden, Reginald	Private	2883B	19th Bn	Dunn, Francis MC	Captain		23rd Bn
Crocker, Frederick	Sergeant	368	17th Bn	Dunn, William	Lnce Corp.	2359	17th Bn
Cromack, Charles	Private	5159	18th Bn	Dwyer, Pat	Gunner	1178	4th Div TMB
Crossland, Sydney	Private	5428	19th Bn				
Crow, John	Private	15249	25th Bn	Dyer, Herbert	Lnce Corp.	149	22nd Bn
Crowle, Albert MM	Private	128	21st Bn	Easton, Douglas	Private	3835	18th Bn
Crowley, Henry	Private	1104	19th Bn	Eckersley, Frederick	Sergeant	2047A	18th Bn
Cruickshank, Thomas	Private	5570	28th Bn	Eckford, Alan	Private	4407	24th Bn
Crump, Clarence	Private	4404	22nd Bn	Edwards, William	Private	4720	26th Bn
Cullingford, Herbert	Private	6136	24th Bn	Elliott, Plunkett	Private	5580	26th Bn
Cullingham, Henry	Corporal	405	5th Light TMB	Ellis, Ambrose	Private	4108	19th Bn
				Ellis, Reginald	Private	1479	18th Bn
Culmsee, Robert	Private	3788	22nd Bn	Ellis-Hall, Arthur	Private	1670A	21st Bn
Currie, Robert	Private	2885B	19th Bn	England, Walter	Private	6043	21st Bn
Curtiss, Edward	Lnce Serg.	3060	20th Bn	Ennis, William	Private	2352	21st Bn
Curvey, Archibald	Lnce Corp.	4675	20th Bn	Etheridge, Reginald	Private	4224	23rd Bn
Dale, Benjamin	Private	833	19th Bn	Evans, Charles	Sergeant	3836	18th Bn
Dalitz, Carl	Private	277	6th Coy MGC	Ewen, Ernest	Private	6052	24th Bn
				Farquharson, Walter	Sergeant	1689	19th Bn
Dare, Francis	Private	1897	18th Bn	Fenton, Roland	Private	5022	18th Bn
Davidson, Robert	Corporal	1815	24th Bn	Fernandez, Edwin	Private	6466	19th Bn
Davidson, William	Private	5001	22nd Bn	Filmer, Walter	2nd Lieut.		22nd Bn
Davies, Arthur	Private	5576	22nd Bn	Finney, Robert	Private	5588	26th Bn
Davies, Clive	Lieut.		19th Bn	Fisher, Fred	Private	5587	26th Bn
Davis, Octavius	Private	2177A	22nd Bn	Fitzgerald, John	Private	3810	21st Bn
Davis, Richard	Private	4010	23rd Bn	Fitzpatrick, William	Corporal	109	24th Bn
Daw, Arthur	Gunner	20933	12th AFA	Fitzsimmons, Peter	Private	4310	24th Bn
Daws, James	Private	3809	23rd Bn	Flack, James	Private	5570	17th Bn
Dawson, Edward	Private	2474	17th Bn	Fleming, Norman	Private	4397	23rd Bn
De Vere, Edward	Private	2099	20th Bn	Flett, Arthur	Private	2655	21st Bn
Dean, Alfred	Private	5328	24th Bn	Flett, John	Private	5815	19th Bn
Dean, Leonard	Private	5810	17th Bn	Flindell, Frank	Corporal	1620	8th Light TMB
Deans, Frederick	Corporal	5539	28th Bn				
Deering, Ralph	Lnce Corp.	4724	28th Bn	Forster, Charles	Private	1026	22nd Bn
De-la-Hunty, Richard	Private	5124	26th Bn	Forster, Walter	Private	5144	24th Bn
Denmead, Allan	Private	3017B	19th Bn	Forster, William	Lieut.		21st Bn
Dennett, Cecil	Private	2033	22nd Bn	Foss, Henry	2nd Lieut.		28th Bn
Denton-Fethers, Percival	Lieut.		24th Bn	Fossey, George	Lnce Corp.	2631	24th Bn
Desmond, Robert	Lieut.		6th Coy MGC	Franklin, Charles	Private	344	6th Coy MGC
Devereux, Alex	Private	1684	19th Bn	Fraser, Finlay	2nd Lieut.		5th Coy MGC
Dickinson, George	Private	5843	28th Bn				
Dickson, James	Private	5337	23rd Bn	Fraser, Hubert	Lieut.		22nd Bn
Ditton, James	Private	6072	22nd Bn	Freeman, David	Private	5098A	22nd Bn
Dobinson, Arthur	Corporal	4686	24th Bn	Freyne, James	Private	5600	21st Bn
Dobson, Leonard	Sergeant	769	24th Bn	Fristrom, Oscar	Corporal	6190	26th Bn
Doney, Herbert	Private	3826	22nd Bn	Fry, Thomas	Private	5584	22nd Bn
Dougherty, William	Private	3802	21st Bn	Fuller, George	Private	5582	26th Bn
Down, Daniel	Corporal	1705	23rd Bn	Gardiner, Silas	Private	4437	28th Bn

NAME	RANK	NUMBER	UNIT	NAME	RANK	NUMBER	UNIT
Gardiner, Thomas	Private	5015	28th Bn	Harrison, Charles	Corporal	630	24th Bn
Garnett, Henry	Private	4429	20th Bn	Harrison, James	Private	31	21st Bn
Garton, Samuel	Private	5341	20th Bn	Hart, John O'Beirne	Private	3847	23rd Bn
Gartrell, Roy	Private	4430	18th Bn	Hartnett, John	Gunner	17183	5th Bdg AFA
Gascoyne, Archibald	Private	155	22nd Bn				
Gaston, David	Lnce Corp.	1709	28th Bn	Harvey, Francis	Gunner	12193	2nd Div TMB
German, John	Private	2668	6th Coy MGC				
				Harwood, Harold	Private	1542	21st Bn
Gibson, Douglas	Private	5586	20th Bn	Haskew, Herbert	Gunner	28966	2nd Div TMB
Gilchrist, Walter	Captain	6th	Coy Field Eng				
				Hassett, John	Private	5886	22nd Bn
Gilliatt, Tom	Lnce Corp	3845	19th Bn	Hauenstein, Charles	Private	4710	23rd Bn
Gilligan, Patrick	Private	3232	17th Bn	Hayden, John	Private	5347	24th Bn
Gleaves, John	Private	2403	19th Bn	Hayes, Denis	Private	2680	18th Bn
Glover, Edwin	Lnce Corp.	2166	19th Bn	Hayes, John	Private	4142	18th Bn
Godding, Clarence	Private	5342	19th Bn	Heady, Joseph	Private	6092	22nd Bn
Gooda, Alfred	Private	1220	17th Bn	Healey, Harry	Private	3825	2nd Pioneers
Goode, Norman	Private	6061	24th Bn				
Gore, Graham	Private	5956	18th Bn	Healey, Robert	Lnce Serg.	3853	18th Bn
Gosper, Clarence	Private	6025	19th Bn	Heathcote, Albert	Corporal	734	3rd Bn
Graham, Samuel	Private	2895	17th Bn	Hedrick, Norman	Private	5704	18th Bn
Grant, James	Private	4703	23rd Bn	Hegarty, Percy	Private	2193	2nd Pioneers
Green, Edward	Private	4436	18th Bn				
Green, George	Private	5359	18th Bn	Helme, Henry	Private	5358	21st Bn
Green, Henry	Private	4427	21st Bn	Hewitt, William	Private	1675	2nd Pioneers
Greenaway, Arthur	Corporal	4429	21st Bn				
Griffin, James	2nd Lieut.		22nd Bn	Hickson, Alfred	Private	5834	25th Bn
Griffiths, Herbert	Private	5885	22nd Bn	Hill, George	Private	4120	22nd Bn
Griffiths, John	Private	4756	18th Bn	Hillier, Henry	Private	5375	28th Bn
Gunn, Duncan	Private	5020	22nd Bn	Hilsly, Cecil	Private	5966	23rd Bn
Hagan, Charles	Private	5342	21st Bn	Hind, Joseph	Private	3143	28th Bn
Haggis, John	Private	2660	8th Coy MGC	Hodgman, Douglas	Private	1104	26th Bn
				Hogarth, Eric	Captain		22nd Bn
Haig, Robert	Private	1806	24th Bn	Holland, Thomas	Private	5600	22nd Bn
Hair, Alexander	Sapper	7228	5th Field Coy Eng.	Holt, Edgar	Private	5684	19th Bn
				Horan, Michael	Private	2662	18th Bn
Hales, Jack	Lnce Corp.	390	2nd Pioneers	Houston, Colin	2nd Lieut.		17th Bn
				Howat, George	Private	4578	22nd Bn
Hall, Hugh	Private	2161	23rd Bn	Howells, Frank	Private	526	8th Light TMB
Hamilton, John	Lnce Corp.	6195	18th Bn				
Hamilton, Thomas	Private	5834	17th Bn	Howes, Alfred	Private	1946	23rd Bn
Hancock, Charles	Private	6266	19th Bn	Hughes, Albert	Private	5985	23rd Bn
Hansen, Bert	Private	6130	25th Bn	Hughes, Llewellyn	Private	5801	18th Bn
Harding, Ernest	Private	238	17th Bn	Hughes, Richard	Sergeant	5296	22nd Bn
Harding, William	Private	5350	26th Bn	Hunt, Leslie	Private	5597	22nd Bn
Harley, James	Private	2130	3rd Bn	Hunter, David	Sergeant	1912	22nd Bn
Harrington, Henry	Private	5608	22nd Bn	Hunter, Gordon	Gunner	4625	4th Heavy TMB
Harris, Ernest	Lnce Corp.	4721	22nd Bn				
Harris, George	Private	4408	23rd Bn				
Harris, John	Private	5039	18th Bn	Hunter, Horace	Lnce Corp.	2333	8th Light TMB
Harris, John	Lieut.		24th Bn				
Harris, Walter	Private	1917B	19th Bn	Huntley, Charles	Private	5587	17th Bn
Harrison, Arthur	Lnce Corp.	1732	22nd Bn	Hurley, John	Lnce Corp.	5931	22nd Bn

NAME	RANK	NUMBER	UNIT	NAME	RANK	NUMBER	UNIT
Hustler, Thomas	Private	534A	8th Light TMB	Leslie, Charles	Lnce Serg.	1226	19th Bn
				Lester, George	Private	5819	18th Bn
Inglis, Thomas	Private	5842	20th Bn	Lilly, Evan	Corporal	901	21st Bn
Isteed, Sydney	Private	4709	21st Bn	Lincoln, James	Private	5153	24th Bn
Jackson, William	Private	4758	18th Bn	Lindsay, Francis	Lnce Corp.	221	24th Bn
James, William	Private	4475	25th Bn	Litchfield, Vincent	Private	5946	24th Bn
Jenkins, Alexander	Private	497A	18th Bn	Little, Robert	Private	4152	17th Bn
Jenner, James	Gunner	1867	4th Heavy TMB	Littlewood, Edward	Lnce Corp.	4139	24th Bn
				Livermore, Henry	Private	2410	18th Bn
Jennings, Arthur	Private	4759	18th Bn	Lodge, Arthur	Gunner	4532	4th Heavy TMB
Jennings, John	Lieut.		21st Bn				
Jenson, Rasmus	Private	4455	17th Bn	Lohman, David	Private	908	24th Bn
Johansen, Henrick	Lnce Corp.	4728	22nd Bn	Lonergan, Thomas	Private	6095	19th Bn
Johnson, Herbert	Private	5453	21st Bn	Louttit, Roy MC	RSM	588	23rd Bn
Johnson, Walter	Private	1957	28th Bn	Lowe, Harry	Private	4742	22nd Bn
Johnston, Herbert	Lnce Corp.	5459	24th Bn	Luscombe, Sidney	Private	2172	19th Bn
Johnston, Robert	Private	3854	22nd Bn	Lynch, Peter	Private	6097	19th Bn
Jolly, Robert	Corporal	591	17th Bn	Lyte, Henry	Private	5050	22nd Bn
Jones, Albert	Private	4147	21st Bn	Mabbitt, Bertram	Private	4159	22nd Bn
Jones, James	Private	6104	27th Bn	Macartney, Temple	Private	5852	23rd Bn
Jones, Wynn	Private	5363	17th Bn	Macbeth, Hedley	Private	4802	24th Bn
Jonston, Harry	Private	4448	24th Bn	Macdonald, Jack	Corporal	3901	23rd Bn
Julin, John	Private	100	26th Bn	Macleod, Murdock	Sergeant	2738	18th Bn
Kelsey, John	Private	5589	19th Bn	Madden, William	Lnce Corp.	5379	22nd Bn
Kemp, Frederick	Lnce Corp	2405	17th Bn	Magee, Stephen	Private	2360	21st Bn
Kemp, George	Private	6113	18th Bn	Maher, Dudley	Private	5598	19th Bn
Kerford, Michael	Private	6274A	27th Bn	Maine, Leonard	Corporal	3869	22nd Bn
Kerr, Andrew	Private	2926A	20th Bn	Mallett, Albert	Private	5050	24th Bn
Kesby, Lewis	Gunner	30929	X/2A TMB	Maloney, John	Lnce Corp.	740	19th Bn
				Maltby, George	Private	5382	17th Bn
Kiddle, John	Sergeant	4291	19th Bn	Manallack, Thomas	Private	5375	24th Bn
Kierulf, Harry	Lnce Corp.	3862	22nd Bn	Manzie, Percy	Private	5623	24th Bn
King, William	Private	5616	24th Bn	Marr, Arthur	Private	3369	15th Light TMB
Kinloch, Stephen	Private	4168	18th Bn				
Kinnane, Martin	Private	2401	24th Bn				
Kinsey, Henry	Private	416	22nd Bn	Marriott, Arthur	Private	2484	8th Light TMB
Kinsman, Harley	2nd Lieut.		23rd Bn				
Kirkby, Sidney	Private	6080	23rd Bn	Marshall, Peter	Private	5895	22nd Bn
Kirkwood, William	Lieut.		19th Bn	Martin, Claude	Private	2474	22nd Bn
Knox, John	Lnce Corp.	2165	19th Bn	Martin, Francis	Private	5067	22nd Bn
Kroll, John	Private	2923B	19th Bn	Martin, Leslie	Private	6142	20th Bn
Lafranchi, Peter	Private	5377	22nd Bn	Martin, Stanley	Corporal	4488	22nd Bn
Landers, Harold	Private	6116	22nd Bn	Marzol, Luke	Private	5626	18th Bn
Lang, Horace MM	Corporal	903	24th Bn	Mason, Frederick	2nd Lieut.		19th Bn
Langdon, Lewis	Gunner	2717	4th Div TMB	Maxey, Percy	Lnce Serg.	273	19th Bn
				Maxfield, Gordon	Captain		24th Bn
Lanyon, Robert	2nd Lieut.		28th Bn	Maxwell, Henry	Private	5364	18th Bn
Leathart, Arthur	Private	2927B	19th Bn	McAlister, Patrick	Private	6095	23rd Bn
Lee, Harold	Private	2174	20th Bn	McAuliffe, Joseph	Private	4486	17th Bn
Lee, Jack	Private	4135	24th Bn	McCarthy, Francis	Private	4743	19th Bn
Lee, Roy	Sergeant	4454	26th Bn	McConaghy, Frederick	Lnce Corp.	5060	23rd Bn
Leggett, Nathan	Private	5608	25th Bn	McCormack, John	Private	5896	28th Bn

NAME	RANK	NUMBER	UNIT	NAME	RANK	NUMBER	UNIT
McCowan, Norman,	Private	5301	22nd Bn	Mortimer, Ralph	Gunner	2003	4th Div TMB
McCoy, Louis	Private	5380	20th Bn				
McCully, William	Private	4486	19th Bn	Morton, James	Private	2000	22nd Bn
McCurran, Francis	Private	5643	24th Bn	Moss, Joel	Bombardier	814	4th Div TMB
McDermid, Hume	Lnce Corp.	2859	17th Bn				
McDiarmid, John	Lieut.		17th Bn	Moule, Cyril	Private	5379	25th Bn
McDonald, Donald	Corporal	4183	21st Bn	Murdoch, William	Private	5379	17th Bn
McDonald, Wilfred	Gunner	4858	4th Div TMB	Murphy, Stanley	Private	5385	24th Bn
				Murray, John	Private	6174	18th Bn
McEwan, Daniel	Private	4487	19th Bn	Murray, Thomas	Private	216	22nd Bn
McGolrick, Thomas	Private	4200	18th Bn	Nalder, Gordon	Lieut.		17th Bn
McGough, John	Private	5431	20th Bn	Naughton, Charles	Private	5674	19th Bn
McIlveen, Francis	Private	5930	19th Bn	Neal, William	Private	5861	19th Bn
McKay, Robert	Private	2887	20th Bn	Neilson, Robert	Private	5726	26th Bn
McLean, John	Corporal	5935	18th Bn	Nichols, Arthur	Private	5860	23rd Bn
McLoskey, Roy	Private	5879	24th Bn	Nichols, David	Private	6126	28th Bn
McMann, John	Private	4502	18th Bn	Niven, James	Private	2075	23rd Bn
McMaster, James	Private	5867	20th Bn	Nixon, William	Private	6551	3rd Bn
McNair, Arthur	Private	5474	19th Bn	Noak, Arthur	Private	3893	22nd Bn
Meldrum, William	Private	5476	4th Div TMB	Noble, Robert MM	2nd Corporal	3436	6th Field Coy Eng
Merritt, Frederick	Private	4491	22nd Bn	Nolan, Charles	Private	5066	19th Bn
Michael, Robert	Lnce Corp.	1965	18th Bn	Norris, Gilbert	Private	1425	19th Bn
Michell, Sidney	Gunner	2719A	4th Div TMB	North, Arthur	Corporal	453	21st Bn
				Northey, Francis	Private	4178	22nd Bn
Miles, Percy	Private	6214	18th Bn	Norton, Thomas	Private	2964A	18th Bn
Miller, Charles	Private	4492	22nd Bn	Oakley, Thomas	Private	4182	22nd Bn
Millership, John	Private	5855	19th Bn	Oakman, Reuben	Private	5391	17th Bn
Millin, Frederick	Private	5821	18th Bn	O'Gorman, John	Corporal	345	6th Field Coy Eng
Mills, George	Lnce Corp.	4164	21st Bn				
Millward, Edgar	Corporal	578	24th Bn	O'Grady, John	Private	5611	19th Bn
Miskell, Michael	Lnce Corp.	2206	19th Bn	Oldfield, Thomas	Private	1245	23rd Bn
Mitchell, James	Private	2207	19th Bn	Olive, George	Bombardier	2091	4th Div TMB
Mitchell, James	Private	5632	22nd Bn				
Mitchell, John	Private	4465	24th Bn	Oliver, Stanley	Private	2153	26th Bn
Mitchell, Joseph	Corporal	1967	21st Bn	O'Loughlin, Michael	Private	4161	23rd Bn
Mitchell, William	Gunner	2222	4th Div TMB	Olsen, Henry Victor	Private	5651	22nd Bn
				O'Neill, William	Private	2959	19th Bn
Mitchell, William	Private	4141	23rd Bn	O'Reilly, John	Lnce Corp.	5296	28th Bn
Mitchener, Charles	Gunner	2636	4th Div TMB	O'Reilly, Peter	Lieut.		10th Bde AFA
Molloy, Robert	Private	2937	19th Bn	Orr, Vincent	CSM	424	23rd Bn
Moodie, George	Private	1972	21st Bn	Osmond, Leslie	Private	5613	19th Bn
Mooney, John	Private	5623	18th Bn	Osmond, Robert	Private	5649	18th Bn
Mooney, John	Private	4751	22nd Bn	Padroth, Robert	Private	3587	19th Bn
Moore, Harold	Gunner	2050	4th Div TMB	Page, George	Private	2970A	20th Bn
				Pallant, John	Private	2434	23rd Bn
Moore, Thomas	Private	5383	17th Bn	Palling, Aubrey	Lieut.		6th Coy MGC
Moran, James	Private	5376	17th Bn				
Morfee, William	Private	5630	22nd Bn	Palmer, William	Private	5439	21st Bn
Moriarty, Harry	Private	2941B	19th Bn	Palmes, Bryan	Private	4798	25th Bn
Morrish, Henry	Private	4472	26th Bn	Pantlin, William	Private	2967A	20th Bn
Morrison, Charles	Private	431	22nd Bn	Parker, James	Private	5901	22nd Bn

NAME	RANK	NUMBER	UNIT	NAME	RANK	NUMBER	UNIT
Parker, Oswald	Private	2956	19th Bn	Regan, Reginald	Private	6132	17th Bn
Parkes, Joseph	Gunner	2348	4th Div TMB	Reid, David	Private	642	19th Bn
				Reid, Denis	Lnce Corp.	5083	20th Bn
Parsons, Albert	Gunner	1643	4th Div TMB	Reid, John	Gunner	3481	4th Div TMB
Pascall, Albert	Gunner	3442	4th Div TMB	Reidy, Michael	Gunner	1608A	4th Div TMB
Paxin, George	Private	4749	24th Bn	Rennie, James	Private	5959	24th Bn
Pearce, William	Private	5069	23rd Bn	Renshaw, Horace	Corporal	4194	22nd Bn
Penn, Louis	Private	6132	22nd Bn	Rentoul, Dougal MC	Lieut.		2nd Div Sig Coy Eng
Perry, Eric	Private	5734	26th Bn				
Perry, Henry	Private	6164	21st Bn				
Perry, Herbert	Private	5077	23rd Bn	Reynolds, Donald	Private	2359	22nd Bn
Perry, Robert	Private	930	24th Bn	Rhynehart, Harold	2nd Lieut.		24th Bn
Petch, Arthur	CSM	584	24th Bn	Rickard, Everett	Private	5906	22nd Bn
Peters, Frederick	Private	6101	23rd Bn	Ricks, Joseph	Private	1990	18th Bn
Petersen, Carl	Private	5654	22nd Bn	Riley, Charles	Corporal	4760	23rd Bn
Peterson, James	Corporal	1724	22nd Bn	Ritchie, Frederick	Private	4476	23rd Bn
Philip, Harold	Private	2433	23rd Bn	Roberts, Alfred	Private	5081	23rd Bn
Phillips, Alfred	Private	5885	20th Bn	Roberts, James	Private	5871	18th Bn
Phillips, Walter	Private	2769	22nd Bn	Robertson, David	Sergeant	2442	10th Bde AFA
Phillips, William	Corporal	3910	23rd Bn				
Piercy, Harold	Private	5427	23rd Bn	Robie, Alexander	Private	5406	22nd Bn
Piercy, Walter	Private	5428	23rd Bn	Robins, Henry	Private	5407	22nd Bn
Piper, Charles	Private	5885	17th Bn	Robinson, Alfred	Private	4210	25th Bn
Plant, John	Lnce Corp.	5069	21st Bn	Robinson, James	Private	5081	24th Bn
Plummer, John	Corporal	4789	28th Bn	Robinson, John	Private	1269	23rd Bn
Porter, Harry	Private	2472	27th Bn	Robinson, Sydney	Lnce Corp.	3230	22nd Bn
Porter, William	Lieut.		18th Bn	Robinson, William	Private	5082	23rd Bn
Postlethwaite, Leonard	Private	5429	23rd Bn	Robson, George	Private	5889	17th Bn
Powell, Frederick	Gunner	2011	4th Div TMB	Rolls, James	Lnce Corp.	3625	24th Bn
				Rooney, George	Private	6107	21st Bn
Prett, Harold	Private	2963	19th Bn	Rosenwax, Charles	Private	2236	19th Bn
Price, Henry	Private	6305	19th Bn	Rosewarne, Henry	Private	4040	24th Bn
Price, Thomas	Private	4017	23rd Bn	Ross, James	Private	4234	18th Bn
Priddle, Claude	Private	2748	24th Bn	Rudder, Reginald	Private	5401	17th Bn
Pridmore, Henry	Private	5962	23rd Bn	Rudkin, William	Lnce Corp.	2439	17th Bn
Priest, Edward	Private	4212	19th Bn	Runting, Alfred	Private	1763	24th Bn
Prior, Alfred	Private	6135	22nd Bn	Russel, Michael	Private	5904	25th Bn
Prior, Leslie	Private	5071	23rd Bn	Russell, Claude DCM	Sergeant	5087	23rd Bn
Pritchard, Richard	Private	2961	19th Bn	Russell, Robert	Private	5916A	28th Bn
Pritchard, Walter	Private	4778	22nd Bn	Russell, Sidney	Private	5749	25th Bn
Prosser, Thomas	Private	2964B	19th Bn	Rutter, Thomas	Private	5396	20th Bn
Quinn, Jack	Private	5658	18th Bn	Rutterford, William	Private	4520	24th Bn
Quinn, Michael	Private	2754	23rd Bn	Ryan, Albert	Lnce Corp.	409	17th Bn
Rait, Samuel	Private	6169	17th Bn	Ryan, Thomas	Private	5681	23rd Bn
Ramsey, Frederick	Private	5891	17th Bn	Samuel, Alexander	Private	4214	17th Bn
Rands, Albert	Private	683	22nd Bn	Sandison, John	Private	5665	18th Bn
Ravell, Thomas	Private	34	19th Bn	Sawley, Harold	Private	5438	23rd Bn
Rawson, Harry	Sergeant	1178	21st Bn	Scammell, Sidney	Lieut.		22nd Bn
Raymond, Henry	Private	5390	19th Bn	Scanlan, Hugh	Private	1257	18th Bn
Read, Ernest	Private	6129	19th Bn	Schollar, Ernest	Private	5403	25th Bn
Rees, Joseph	Sergeant	3914	21st Bn	Schulze, Hermann	Lnce Corp.	3245	22nd Bn

NAME	RANK	NUMBER	UNIT	NAME	RANK	NUMBER	UNIT
Scott, Harry	Private	5645	25th Bn	Sutherland, Donald	Private	4820	19th Bn
Scott, Percy	Private	2410	22nd Bn	Sutton, Ernest	Sergeant	1108	22nd Bn
Scott, Vivian	Private	4538	2nd Pioneers	Swalwell, Robert	Private	5901	24th Bn
				Swaney, Vincent	Lnce Corp.	3924	22nd Bn
Seeuwen, Cornelius	Private	5955	23rd Bn	Swift, Robert	Corporal	3941	22nd Bn
Sewell, Calliss	Corporal	2790	19th Bn	Tate, George	Private	1292	18th Bn
Shanks, George	Private	5091	22nd Bn	Taylor, Henry	Private	519	21st Bn
Shaw, Edward	Lieut.		20th Bn	Taylor, Percy	Sergeant	1551A	24th Bn
Sheehan, John MM	Private	3930	17th Bn	Taylor, Robert	Lnce Corp.	3976	21st Bn
Shields, Hubert	Private	1612	22nd Bn	Taylor, Thomas	Private	3933	17th Bn
Sibley, Walter	Private	5676	19th Bn	Taylor, William	Private	3952	22nd Bn
Sim, John	Private	1274	19th Bn	Teichelmann, Neville	Lnce Corp.	2440	22nd Bn
Simmons, Jack MM	Private	2455	23rd Bn	Telfer, John	Private	5450	23rd Bn
Simons, Joseph	Private	5911	21st Bn	Thompson, Michael	Private	6191	23rd Bn
Simpson, Adam	Lnce Corp.	1586	24th Bn	Tidd, George	Private	5893	23rd Bn
Simpson, Alexander	Private	5413	26th Bn	Toulmin, John	Private	4510	23rd Bn
Simpson, Henry	Lnce Corp.	1965	23rd Bn	Tout, Leonard	Private	5677	24th Bn
Simpson, Samuel	Private	1656	19th Bn	Townsend, Bennett	Private	5096	17th Bn
Skiller, Charles	Private	4188	23rd Bn	Train, Joseph	Private	5670	18th Bn
Slater, Joseph	Captain		22nd Bn	Tranter, Harold	Private	5649	17th Bn
Smallmon, Donald	Private	6132	21st Bn	Trask, Joseph	Private	4537	21st Bn
Smart, Alfred	Private	5638	17th Bn	Travers, Ambrose	Private	5745	3rd Bn
Smith, Albert	Private	3938	23rd Bn	Travers, Antonio	Private	5892	19th Bn
Smith, Ernest	Private	2215	19th Bn	Treglown, Albert	Private	5420	22nd Bn
Smith, Ernest	Private	5691	21st Bn	Tregoning, William	Private	5305	22nd Bn
Smith, Ernest	Private	5953	23rd Bn	Trewick, Roger	Private	2723	2nd Pioneers
Smith, Francis	Private	6051	21st Bn				
Smith, Fred	Private	2003A	18th Bn	Trigg, Thomas	Lnce Corp.	2425	22nd Bn
Smith, Howard	Gunner	2709A	4th TMB AFA	Tripcony, Albert	Private	5655	25th Bn
				Tripcony, Benjamin	Private	5453	23rd Bn
Smith, John	Private	6142	19th Bn	Tucker, Edward	Private	5709	21st Bn
Smith, Wilson	Private	6148	23rd Bn	Tucker, Robert	Private	3927	21st Bn
Smithers, William	Private	6151	18th Bn	Turner, Edmund	Private	5423	22nd Bn
Smythe, Herbert	Corporal	1175	3rd Bn	Tuttleby, Alfred	Private	5423	21st Bn
Snee, John	Private	5425	24th Bn	Tuxford, Reginald	Sergeant	5096	21st Bn
Snodgrass, Cosby	Private	4519	26th Bn	Underwood, John	Private	6164	22nd Bn
Snow, John	Private	2980A	20th Bn	Upton, Leslie	Private	5437	24th Bn
Somers, Maurice	Private	5718	22nd Bn	Vallance, Ernest	Private	5904	24th Bn
Spence, John	Private	5933	19th Bn	Van Den Berg, Abraham	Sergeant	667	18th Bn
Spowart, Archibald	Private	5636	19th Bn	Waghorn, John	Corporal	335	18th Bn
Stead, Bertram	Private	5469	18th Bn	Waight, Cyrus	Private	3007A	20th Bn
Stephen, William	Corporal	668	19th Bn	Wakefield, Algernon	Private	6171	19th Bn
Stephens, Alfred	Private	5029	19th Bn	Wallace, Walter	Private	3617	18th Bn
Stephens, John	Private	4783	26th Bn	Walthall, William	Private	2268A	25th Bn
Stevens, Ernest	Private	4527	21st Bn	Waltho, William	Private	4785	24th Bn
Stewart, Alex	Private	4204	24th Bn	Wann, Robert	Private	3682	18th Bn
Stokeld, George	Private	3598	18th Bn	Ward, William	Private	5898	18th Bn
Street, Francis	Private	5887	18th Bn	Ward, William	Private	6133	23rd Bn
Streeter, Samuel	Private	4237	25th Bn	Wates, Cecil	Private	2994B	20th Bn
Stringfellow, George	Private	5411	25th Bn	Watkins, John	Private	2429	21st Bn
Stuntz, John	Private	5407	17th Bn	Watson, Ernest	Private	3299	25th Bn
Sullivan, Frederick	Lnce Corp.	4251	19th Bn	Watson, Leslie	Private	5697	23rd Bn
Sullivan, Martin	Private	4236	17th Bn	Watt, Frederick	Private	3686	18th Bn

NAME	RANK	NUMBER	UNIT	NAME	RANK	NUMBER	UNIT
Watt, Reginald	Lnce Corp.	5446	28th Bn	Williams, Hector	Lnce Corp.	3973A	20th Bn
Waugh, John	Private	5908	20th Bn	Williams, John	Private	5911	20th Bn
Wealand, Nels	Private	3958	22nd Bn	Williams, Norman	Private	5431	17th Bn
Webb, Wilfred	Private	1922A	28th Bn	Wills, Leslie	Private	2996B	19th Bn
Welch, Edgar	Lnce Corp.	5833	22nd Bn	Wilson, David	Private	5107	22nd Bn
Wells, Edward	Private	5455	18th Bn	Wilson, Frederick	Private	3996	22nd Bn
Wemyss, George	Corporal	1986	23rd Bn	Wilson, John	Private	6597	3rd Bn
West, Joseph	Private	4801	22nd Bn	Wilson, Ronald	Private	1137	21st Bn
Whimpey, William	Private	2013	23rd Bn	Winnell, Charles	Private	5110	22nd Bn
Whisker, Alexander	Private	5439	17th Bn	Winsor, Arthur	Private	4569	22nd Bn
Whitaker, James	Private	5917	17th Bn	Wood, John	Corporal	3156	26th Bn
Whitchurch, David	Private	4275	21st Bn	Woodgate, Harold	Private	5704	26th Bn
White, Edward	Private	4792	24th Bn	Woods, Alexander	Private	5692	22nd Bn
White, Robert	Private	5165	24th Bn	Wooldridge, John	Private	4567	18th Bn
Whitehead, Robert	2nd Lieut.		21st Bn	Woolfe, Neil	Private	6182	17th Bn
Whitehead, Walter	Lieut.		21st Bn	Worsnip, James	Private	4267	17th Bn
Whitelaw, Robert	Sergeant	1003	21st Bn	Worth, Hector	Private	6155	17th Bn
Whiteley, Richard	Private	5928	17th Bn	Wyatt, William	Corporal	3148	5th Field Coy Eng
Whitlock, Ernest	Private	6153	21st Bn				
Wiedemann, Oscar	Private	493	22nd Bn	Wyles, James	Private	5905	23rd Bn
Wiesner, William	Private	6160	18th Bn	Wylie, Hector	Private	5960	22nd Bn
Wilkes, William	Private	4924	25th Bn	Yates, Ernest	Private	5414	27th Bn
Wilkinson, Harry	Private	2995B	20th Bn	Young, Frederick	Private	5043	19th Bn
Willcox, Raymond	Private	5712	21st Bn	Young, George	Private	5937	28th Bn
Williams, Arthur	Private	5671	20th Bn	Young, Herbert	Private	547	24th Bn
Williams, Arthur	Private	3694	25th Bn	Young, Robert	Private	1127	24th Bn
Williams, Benjamin	Private	6172	22nd Bn	Young, Walter MM	Private	2290	26th Bn
Williams, David	Private	5666	17th Bn				

NOTES

1. Served under alias Frank Earnest Bailey.

BRITISH SOLDIERS KILLED ON 11TH APRIL 1917 WHO HAVE NO KNOWN GRAVE AND ARE COMMEMORATED ON THE ARRAS MEMORIAL

NAME	RANK	NUMBER	UNIT
Atkinson, John	Private	242421	2nd/6th West Yorks
Badland, John	Private	242046	2nd/6th West Yorks
Baines, William	Private	266310	2nd/7th West Yorks
Baldwinson, John	Private	242422	2nd/6th West Yorks
Bamford, John	Private	36743	49th Field Ambulance
Barrett, Charles	Private	76375	D HMGB MGC (Tanks)
Bendig, William	Private	242021	2nd/6th West Yorks
Bown, Benjamin	Private	206100	D HMGB MGC (Tanks)
Brown, Miles	Private	242043	2nd/6th West Yorks
Bywater, Leonard	Private	242406	2nd/6th West Yorks
Clarkson, Harold	2nd Lieut.		D HMGB MGC (Tanks)
Collins, Harry	Private	242132	2nd/6th West Yorks
Court, Edward	Lnce Corp.	242024	2nd/6th West Yorks
Crawford, John	Sergeant	266160	2nd/7th West Yorks
Crowther, Frank	Private	241446	2nd/6th West Yorks
Davies, Harold	2nd Lieut.		D HMGB MGC (Tanks)
Dewhurst, Herbert	Private	241095	2nd/6th West Yorks
Drummond, Angus	Private	75921	D HMGB MGC (Tanks)
Dufton, Clarence	Private	242059	2nd/6th West Yorks
Eltoft, James	Private	241957	2nd/6th West Yorks
Evans, George	Private	241985	2nd/6th West Yorks
Field, Arthur	Private	241392	2nd/6th West Yorks
Foulds Edgar	Private	241176	2nd/6th West Yorks
George, Walter	Private	67888	212th Company MGC
Haigh, Robert	Private	241142	2nd/6th West Yorks
Hall, Arthur	Private	242017	2nd/6th West Yorks
Halliday, Fred	Private	235165	2nd/7th West Yorks
Harness, Frederick	Private	76278	D HB MGC (Tanks)
Hind, James	Private	242269	2nd/6th West Yorks
Hirst, Benjamin	Private	240734	2nd/6th West Yorks
Horn, George	Private	241161	2nd/6th West Yorks
Killingbeck, Joshua	Private	35833	49th Field Ambulance

NAME	RANK	NUMBER	UNIT	NAME	RANK	NUMBER	UNIT
Leat, Henry	Private	206131	D HB MGC (Tanks)	Pattison, John	Private	241872	2nd/6th West Yorks
Lord, Harry	Private	76782	D HB MGC (Tanks)	Potter, George	Private	266979	2nd/7th West Yorks
Lumley, Robert	Private	267255	2nd/7th West Yorks	Robertson, Kenneth	Private	206101	D HB MGC (Tanks)
Mitchell, James	Private	241403	2nd/6th West Yorks	Robson, James	Private	241804	2nd/6th West Yorks
Money, Eric	Lieut.		D HB MGC (Tanks)	Sharkey, William	Private	241979	2nd/6th West Yorks
Moody, Charles	Lnce Corp	242049	2nd/6th West Yorks	Sharp, James	Lnce Serg.	241916	2nd/6th West Yorks
Murgatroyd, Herbert	Private	242350	2nd/6th West Yorks	Shoesmith, James	Private	241253	2nd/6th West Yorks
Murray, Robert	Private	75336	D HB MGC (Tanks)	Smithies, Arthur	Private	235174	2nd/7th West Yorks
Newton, Alfred	Private	241063	2nd/6th West Yorks	Swears, Hugh	Lieut.		D HB MGC (Tanks)
Nicholson, Harold	Private	306276	2nd/8th West Yorks	Wright, William	Private	240877	2nd/6th West Yorks
Palmer, John	Private	206110	D HB MGC (Tanks)				

NOTE

DHB MGC (Tanks) relates to D Battalion Heavy Branch Machine Gun Corps (Tanks).

APPENDIX 8

BRITISH SOLDIERS KILLED 3RD–21ST MAY 1917 WHO HAVE NO KNOWN GRAVE AND ARE COMMEMORATED ON THE ARRAS MEMORIAL

SOLDIERS KILLED 3RD MAY 1917

NAME	RANK	NUMBER	BATTALION	NAME	RANK	NUMBER	BATTALION
Abbott, Phillip	Private	7457	2nd HAC	Arnold, Albert	Private	6503	2nd HAC
Abbott, Harold	Private	200557	2nd/5th WY	Arnold, Richard	Private	242164	2nd/5th
Abbott, Reginald	Private	204268	2nd/4th Y&L				KOYLI
Abson, William	Private	202472	2nd/4th Y&L	Ashforth, Charles	Private	202238	2nd/4th
Ackroyd, George	Private	242079	2nd/6th WY				DOW
Adcock, Percy	Private	204212	2nd/4th Y&L	Ashton, Thomas	Private	242107	2nd/5th
Adlington, William	Corporal	241308	2nd/5th Y&L				KOYLI
Alderson, Naylor	Private	241021	2nd/5th	Ashworth, John	Private	240817	2nd/6th WY
			DOW	Athorn, George	Private	265947	2nd/6th
Alker, Edward	Private	241960	2nd/5th Y&L				DOW
Allen, Frank	Private	241785	2nd/5th	Atkins, James	Private	267101	2nd/6th
			DOW				DOW
Allen, James	Private	241962	2nd/5th	Ayling Thomas	Private	7684	2nd HAC
			DOW	Aylwin, Ernest	Private	65473	208th Coy
Allsopp, Arthur	Private	240280	2nd/5th				MGC
			DOW	Ayrton, Henry	Sergeant	266192	2nd/6th
Ambler, William	Private	242152	2nd/6th WY				DOW
Anderson, Harry	Private	241918	2nd/5th Y&L	Backhouse, Ernest	Private	202207	2nd/4th
Anderson, Walter	Private	242770	2nd/5th				KOYLI
			DOW	Bacon, Harry	Private	24809	1st RWF
Ansell, Joseph	Private	204376	2nd/4th Y&L	Bailey, Leonard	Private	9846	2nd HAC
Anthony, Arthur	Private	241422	2nd/5th	Bailey, John	Private	241254	2nd/5th Y&L
			KOYLI	Bailey, Walter	Private	241879	2nd/5th
Appleyard, Fred	Private	305138	2nd/8th WY				DOW
Archer, Ben	Sergeant	305185	2nd/8th WY	Baines, Archies	Lnce Corp.	201671	2nd/5th WY
Armistead, Dick	Private	241717	2nd/5th	Baker, George	Gunner	12998	38th HB RGA
			DOW	Baker, Reginald	Private	202646	2nd/4th Y&L
Armitage, Harry	Private	241006	2nd/5th	Bamford, Samuel	Private	242808	2nd/5th
			DOW				DOW
Armitage, Lawrence	Private	201532	2nd/4th	Bamforth, George	Private	241783	2nd/5th
			KOYLI				DOW
Armstrong, Alfred	Private	201531	2nd/4th Y&L	Banks, George	Private	242100	2nd/6th WY

NAME	RANK	NUMBER	BATTALION	NAME	RANK	NUMBER	BATTALION
Bannister, Harold	Private	241954	2nd/6th WY	Biltcliffe, Percy	Lnce Corp.	305486	2nd/7th DOW
Barker, Francis	Private	265684	2nd/6th DOW	Binks, Harold	Lnce Corp.	201207	2nd/4th Y&L
Barker, Robert	Private	265297	2nd/6th DOW	Birtles, John	Private	242754	2nd/5th KOYLI
Barrett, Douglas	Private	65465	208th Coy MGC	Blackburn, Thomas	Lnce Corp.	305921	2nd/8th WY
Barrett, Frederick	Private	308129	2nd/7th DOW	Blackburn, William	Private	306987	2nd/8th WY
Barrow, William	Private	241751	2nd/5th DOW	Blackburn, William	Private	241846	2nd/5th DOW
Bartle, Frederick	Private	306527	2nd/7th DOW	Blake, Frederick	Private	6792	2nd HAC
Bates, Reginald	Lnce Corp	202231	2nd/4th DOW	Blakey, Frank	Private	200940	2nd/4th DOW
Batty, Joseph	Private	241823	2nd/5th DOW	Bloomer, Albert	Private	202021	2nd/4th DOW
Battye, W	Private	241773	2nd/5th DOW	Bockett, Harold	2nd Lieut.		2nd HAC
Battye, Dan	Private	241696	2nd/5th DOW	Bond, Henry	Private	63224	8th FA
Baul, Ernest	Private	202050	2nd/5th WY	Boothroyd, Percy	Private	241924	2nd/5th DOW
Baxter, Harry	Private	267644	2nd/7th DOW	Bower, Herbert	Private	241834	2nd/6th WY
Bayliss, Arthur	Corporal	201187	2nd/4th Y&L	Bowes, Frederick	Private	242725	2nd/5th Y&L
Beard, Herbert	Private	241724	2nd/5th DOW	Bowness, William	Private	240708	2nd/5th DOW
Beaumont, Albert	Private	306870	2nd/7th DOW	Bracken, Thomas	Private	241600	2nd/5th DOW
Beaumont, Lewis	Private	242023	2nd/5th DOW	Bradbury, Edgar	Private	202594	2nd/4th Y&L
Beecham, George	Private	241644	2nd/5th DOW	Brady, James	Private	326051	2nd/8th WY
Beever, Charles	Private	267173	2nd/6th DOW	Bramall, Ernest	Lnce Corp.	241904	2nd/5th Y&L
Bellamy, Joseph	Lnce Serg.	201107	2nd/4th Y&L	Bratley, Martin	Private	202006	2nd/5th WY
Benstead, George	Lnce Corp.	202680	2nd/4th Y&L	Brayfield, Arthur	Sergeant	3544	2nd HAC
Bent, Charles	Private	240311	2nd/5th Y&L	Brearley, Ewart	Lnce Corp.	306894	2nd/7th DOW
Bentley, Charlie	Private	235048	2nd/4th DOW	Brearton, William	Private	240898	2nd/6th WY
Bentley, Irvin	Private	241708	2nd/5th DOW	Breeze, William	Private	306958	2nd/7th DOW
Berry, Fred	Private	306556	2nd/7th DOW	Bridge, Arthur	Private	265177	2nd/6th DOW
Bett, Harry	Private	242239	2nd/6th WY	Bridgman, Richard	Private	242773	2nd/5th KOYLI
Bex, Phillip	Private	9848	2nd HAC	Briggs, Ambrose	Private	266449	2nd/6th Bn DOW
Biddles, Joseph	Private	306600	2nd/7th DOW	Briggs, Henry	Lnce Corp.	306574	2nd/7th DOW
Biggin, William	Lnce Corp.	241027	2nd/6th WY	Broadbent, John	Private	202061	2nd/4th Bn DOW
Bilbrough, George	Private	242423	2nd/6th WY	Broadbent, Stanley	Private	241859	2nd/5th Bn DOW
Bilbrough, Percy	Private	21094	2nd/5th KOYLI	Brook, Arthur	Private	241793	2nd/5th DOW
Bill, John	Private	305383	2nd/7th DOW	Brook, Cyril	Private	241146	2nd/6th WY
				Brook, Harry	Sergeant	240082	2nd/5th DOW
				Brook, Harry	Private	241200	2nd/6th DOW

NAME	RANK	NUMBER	BATTALION	NAME	RANK	NUMBER	BATTALION
Brook, John	Corporal	240758	2nd/6th WY	Cawthra, Walter	Private	241035	2nd/6th WY
Brook, Norman	Private	267682	2nd/6th DOW	Chadbund, John	Private	241106	2nd/5th Y&L
Brookes, William	Private	202022	2nd/4th DOW	Chapman, Ernest	Sergeant	201311	2nd/4th DOW
Brotherton, Ben	Private	267167	2nd/6th DOW	Chapman, George	Sergeant	267467	2nd/6th WY
Broughton, Ernest	Private	240209	2nd/6th WY	Chapman, John	Lnce Corp.	266305	2nd/6th DOW
Brown, Frank	Private	306572	2nd/7th DOW	Chapman, Walter	Lnce Corp.	240535	2nd/5th KOYLI
Brown, George	Sergeant	200963	2nd/5th WY	Chapman. William	Private	201192	2nd/4th Y&L
Brown, John	Private	306496	2nd/7th DOW	Charlesworth, James	Private	242380	2nd/6th WY
Brown, Jonathan	Private	241958	2nd/5th Y&L	Cheetham, Arthur	Private	241940	2nd/5th DOW
Brown, Thomas	Private	21020	2nd/4th DOW	Clark, Samuel	Private	201990	2nd/5th WY
Brown, William	Private	201728	2nd/5th WY	Clarke, James	Private	242031	2nd/6th WY
Brown, William	Private	204421	2nd/4th DOW	Clayton, John	Private	306813	2nd/7th DOW
Brown, William	Private	13347	2nd/5th KOYLI	Clayton, Oswald	Private	206156	D HB MGC
Brunt, Frederick	Sergeant	240706	2nd/5th DOW	Clempson, Walter	Lnce Serg.	241393	2nd/5th KOYLI
Bruster, John	Private	6821	2nd HAC	Clinton, Joseph	Private	241591	2nd/5th Y&L
Buckeridge, Ernest	Private	9945	2nd HAC	Coleman, Frederick	Private	242798	2nd/5th DOW
Bull, Harry	Private	240575	2nd/5th DOW	Colley, John	Private	9823	2nd HAC
Bulmer, John	Private	200941	2nd/4th DOW	Conlon, Joseph	Private	306742	2nd/8th WY
Burdett, Albert	Private	242828	2nd/5th KOYLI	Cook, Ben Private		241899	2nd/5th Y&L
Burke, Patrick	Private	306134	2nd/8th WY	Cookson, James	Private	267150	2nd/6th DOW
Burstall, Bernard	Private	240124	2nd/6th WY	Cotton, Charles	Private	202501	2nd/4th DOW
Butler, Henry	Sergeant	45213	208th Coy MGC	Couldwell, Arthur	Private	201204	2nd/4th Y&L
Butler, Sam	Private	10160	2nd/4th DOW	Couling, Frank	Private	9715	2nd HAC
Byron, Jesse	Private	306754	2nd/7th DOW	Coulton, David	Private	306722	2nd/7th DOW
Calder, Montague	Private	9041	2nd HAC	Coupland Robert	Private	241649	2nd/5th DOW
Calladine, Ernest	Private	241347	2nd/5th Y&L	Court, Ernest	Private	9358	2nd HAC
Calvert, John	Private	240820	2nd/5th DOW	Cowley, Herbert	Private	242161	2nd/5th KOYLI
Campbell, Norman	Captain		189th Sp Bde RE	Cox, Joseph	Private	241812	2nd/5th Y&L
Capstick, Harry	Private	267088	2nd/6th DOW	Cox, Norman	Private	201303	2nd/4th DOW
Carter, Herbert	Lnce Sgt	201310	2nd/4th DOW	Crabtree, Angus	Private	263031	2nd/5th DOW
Cassidy, William	Private	240791	2nd/5th DOW	Crabtree, Percy	Lnce Serg.	240534	2nd/6th DOW
Caudle, Cedric	2nd Lieut.		2nd HAC	Cramp, James	Private	242147	2nd/5th KOYLI
				Crawford, Alexander	Private	9889	2nd HAC
				Crawford, Reginald	Private	5761	2nd HAC
				Crawshaw, Winfield	Private	201198	2nd/4th Y&L
				Craythorne, John	Private	242155	2nd/5th KOYLI

NAME	RANK	NUMBER	BATTALION	NAME	RANK	NUMBER	BATTALION
Creaton, Harry	Lnce Corp.	241598	2nd/5th DOW	Driver, Frank	Lnce Corp.	201154	2nd/5th WY
				Driver, John	Lnce Corp.	242008	2nd/5th KOYLI
Crisp, Herbert	Lnce Corp	202503	2nd/4th Y&L				
Criswick, Jack	Private	5058	2nd HAC	Duffy, Charles	Lnce Serg.	241410	2nd/6th WY
Crossland, Ernest	Private	241944	2nd/5th Y&L	Dufton, Norman	Private	240800	2nd/6th WY
Crossland, Norman	Private	241666	2nd/5th Y&L	Dunkley, George	Private	242095	2nd/5th KOYLI
Crossley, Norris	Sergeant	305856	2nd/7th DOW	Dunn, Arthur	Sergeant	6961	2nd HAC
Crowther, Hubert	Corporal	241797	2nd/5th DOW	Durkin, John	Corporal	240216	2nd/5th DOW
Crowther, John	Private	241784	2nd/5th Y&L	Dyson, Ewart	Private	202105	2nd/4th DOW
Cryer, Cecil	Lnce Corp.	7178	2nd HAC	Dyson, Leonard	Private	201625	2nd/4th DOW
Cunnane, Thomas	Private	202599	2nd/4th Y&L				
Curtois, Harry	Private	241709	2nd/5th DOW	Dyson, Tom	Private	241896	2nd/5th DOW
Daley, John	Private	305919	2nd/7th DOW	Dyson, Walter	Private	307001	2nd/8th WY
Dalton, Michael	Lnce Corp.	240509	2nd/5th KOYLI	Earnshaw, Harold	Private	241542	2nd/5th DOW
Davies, Gilbert	Private	7190	2nd HAC	Eastwood, Frederick	Private	240715	2nd/5th DOW
Davies, Walter	Private	201369	2nd/4th KOYLI	Edwards, Arthur	Private	7367	2nd HAC
Davison, Sam	Private	200878	2nd/5th KOYLI	Edwards, Albert	Private	201607	2nd/4th Y&L
				Elliot, Joseph	Private	241185	2nd/5th DOW
Davison, Wilfred	Private	202270	2nd/4th KOYLI	Elliott, Dan	Lnce Corp.	200988	2nd/4th Y&L
Day, Arthur	Private	202565	2nd/4th DOW	Elliott, William	Lnce Corp.	241754	2nd/5th KOYLI
Deighton, Herbert	Private	203508	2nd/5th WY	Ellis, Evelyn	2nd Lieut.		2nd HAC
Denton, John	Private	242076	2nd/5th KOYLI	Ellis, HarryPrivate		241547	2nd/5th DOW
Dewhirst, George	Private	240678	2nd/5th DOW	Ellison, Herbert	Private	242447	2nd/6th WY
Dickson, Malcolm	Private	6959	2nd HAC	Elvidge, Percy	Private	306510	2nd/7th DOW
Dixon, Albert	Private	201940	2nd/5th WY	Etchells, Joseph	Private	202598	2nd/4th Y&L
Dixon, George	Private	242428	2nd/6th WY	Evans, Richard	Lnce Serg.	6818	2nd HAC
Dodds, Douglas	Private	7080	2nd HAC	Evans, George	Private	241252	2nd/5th KOYLI
Donnellan, William	Private	240649	2nd/5th DOW	Exley, Alfred	Private	265789	2nd/6th DOW
Dore, Howard	Private	200941	2nd/4th Y&L	Fagan, William	Private	241724	2nd/5th KOYLI
Dorran, Harry	Private	242145	2nd/6th WY				
Dowden, John	Private	9786	2nd HAC	Fairbank, William	Private	306338	2nd/7th DOW
Downing, William	Private	202778	2nd/4th Y&L				
Drake, Willie	Private	202395	2nd/4th DOW	Farrar, Raymond	Private	241944	2nd/6th WY
Dransfield, Edwin	Private	242184	2nd/5th KOYLI	Farrington, Oswald	Private	241977	2nd/5th KOYLI
Dransfield, Joshua	Private	242338	2nd/6th KOYLI	Faulkingham. John	Private	24318	2nd/5th KOYLI
Drew, Ernest	Sergeant	201239	2nd/4th Y&L	Featherstone, Alfred	Private	241633	2nd/5th Y&L
Driscoll, Daniel	Private	230952	2nd/2nd London	Fedden, Raymond	2nd Lieut.		2nd HAC
				Fellows, William	Private	242388	2nd/6th WY

NAME	RANK	NUMBER	BATTALION
Ferriday, Frank	Sergeant	241296	2nd/5th Y&L
Field, Jonathan	Private	202348	2nd/4th KOYLI
Fielding, Willie	Lnce Corp.	201135	2nd/4th DOW
Finch, William	Rifleman	452952	2nd/11th London
Firth, Harry	Private	242051	2nd/6th WY
Firth, Harry	Private	240930	2nd/6th WY
Fisher, Allott	Private	20534	2nd/5th DOW
Fisher, George	Corporal	206161	D HB MGC
Fisher, Hobson	Private	241040	2nd/5th DOW
Fisher, John	Private	242398	2nd/6th WY
Fitz-John, Arthur	Lnce Corp.	242801	2nd/5th DOW
Flanagan, Edward	Private	201717	2nd/5th WY
Flanagan, Thomas	Corporal	200654	2nd/5th WY
Fletcher, Walter	Private	306504	2nd/7th DOW
Forrest, Henry	Private	267045	2nd/6th DOW
Forshew, Thomas	Private	306364	2nd/7th DOW
Foster, Milford	Private	240254	2nd/6th WY
Foulger, Marlton	Private	29049	2nd/6th DOW
Fowler, Joseph	Private	308107	2nd/7th DOW
France, Bernard	Private	242376	2nd/6th WY
Franklin, Isaac	Private	201882	2nd/5th WY
French, William	Private	200772	2nd/5th WY
Frost, Maurice	Private	200858	2nd/4th Y&L
Furness, Herbert	Private	235064	2nd/4th DOW
Furness, Joseph	Private	306183	2nd/8th WY
Gamble, Davis	Private	268625	2nd/6th DOW
Gander-Dower, L F	2nd Lieut.		2nd HAC
Garside, Thomas	Private	241814	2nd/5th DOW
Garthwaite, Edgar	Private	241966	2nd/6th WY
Garthwaite, James	Private	300059	2nd/6th WY
Gatward, William	Lnce Corp.	7549	2nd HAC
Gee, Ronald	Sergeant	265026	2nd/6th DOW
Gentry, Frank	Private	7360	2nd HAC
Gilbert, John	Private	306344	2nd/7th DOW
Gill, James	Private	241216	2nd/5th KOYLI
Ginever, John	Private	204399	2nd/4th Y&L
Gledhill, Robert	Lnce Corp.	241894	2nd/5th DOW
Godber, Harold	Private	306948	2nd/7th DOW
Goddard, Brandon	Lnce Corp.	241934	2nd/5th DOW
Goddard, James	Lnce Corp.	40488	20th Manchester
Goddard, John	Private	202590	2nd/4th Y&L
Goldsbrough. Horace	Private	241905	2nd/5th DOW
Goldthorpe, Walter	Private	242155	2nd/6th WY
Goodair, Morris	Private	201281	2nd/4th KOYLI
Goodall, William	Private	268390	2nd/6th DOW
Goode, Frederick	Private	202015	2nd/4th DOW
Gordon, John	Private	9825	2nd HAC
Gornall, Edward	Private	266380	2nd/6th DOW
Goundry, Oliver	Sergeant	20099	2nd/5th WY
Graham, Bertie	Private	267029	2nd/6th DOW
Graham, Ernest	Private	201505	2nd/5th WY
Graham, Harry	Private	266939	2nd/6th DOW
Graham, Lincoln	Private	265815	2nd/6th DOW
Grant, Fred	Private	241955	2nd/5th DOW
Grant, John	Private	306651	2nd/8th WY
Gray, Albert	Lnce Corp.	3919	2nd HAC
Gray, Harry	Private	200794	2nd/4th DOW
Gray, James	Lnce Corp.	305899	2nd/7th DOW
Gray, William	Private	15346	2nd/5th DOW
Grayson, Charles	Private	242233	2nd/6th DOW
Grayson, William	Private	241778	2nd/5th Y&L
Greaves, John	Private	241577	2nd/5th DOW
Green, Alfred	Lnce Corp.	242076	2nd/6th WY
Green, Arthur	Private	241782	2nd/5th DOW
Greenwood, Albert	Private	202551	2nd/4th DOW
Greenwood, David	Private	201282	2nd/4th DOW
Greenwood, Harry	Private	306877	2nd/7th DOW

NAME	RANK	NUMBER	BATTALION
Greenwood, James	Private	268342	2nd/6th DOW
Greenwood, Joe	Private	202348	2nd/4th DOW
Greenwood, John	Private	202514	2nd/4th DOW
Greenwood, Joseph	Private	306624	2nd/7th DOW
Greenwood, Harry	Private	240948	2nd/6th WY
Grieves, Joseph	Private	242695	2nd/5th Y&L
Griffiths, Joseph	Lnce Corp.	30027	2nd/4th DOW
Grocott, Frederick	Private	9200	2nd HAC
Groundwell, George	Private	200175	2nd/5th KOYLI
Gunn, Harold	Private	241601	2nd/5th DOW
Hackett, Alexander	Private	10703	2nd/7th DOW
Hague, Willie	Private	241005	2nd/5th DOW
Haigh, Edgar	Private	202338	2nd/4th DOW
Haigh Joe	Private	240133	2nd/5th DOW
Haigh, John	Private	267178	2nd/6th DOW
Haigh, Willie	Private	241833	2nd/5th DOW
Haime, Leonard	Private	7553	2nd HAC
Hale, Horace	Private	241943	2nd/5th DOW
Haley, Frank	Corporal	30662	2nd/7th DOW
Hall, Charles	Private	235254	2nd/8th WY
Hall, Frank	Private	242781	2nd/5th DOW
Hall, George	Private	202317	2nd/4th DOW
Hall, Robert	Lnce Corp.	241747	2nd/5th KOYLI
Hall, Walter	Private	66521	208th Coy MGC
Hall, William	Private	242103	2nd/6th WY
Hallat, Randolph	Private	201663	2nd/4th Y&L
Halstead, Walter	Private	201414	2nd/4th DOW
Hambrey, Ernest	Sergeant	24118	2nd/5th DOW
Hamer, Thomas	Private	240673	2nd/5th DOW
Hammond, Ernest MC	2nd Lieut.		2nd HAC
Hampshire, Lewis	Private	241893	2nd/5th DOW
Hanford, Arthur	Private	5013	2nd HAC
Hanson, Colin	Private	241556	2nd/5th DOW
Hanson, Ernest	Private	240565	2nd/5th DOW
Hardingham, Frederick	Private	9055	2nd HAC
Hardy, Charles	Lnce Corp	240841	2nd/5th Y&L
Hardy, Herbert	Corporal	240288	2nd/5th DOW
Harewood, Thomas	Private	86330	212th Coy MGC
Harewood, Willie	Private	306744	2nd/7th DOW
Hargreaves, Sylvester	Private	241017	2nd/5th DOW
Harker, George	Private	242668	2nd/5th Y&L
Harper, Harry	Private	202364	2nd/4th KOYLI
Harper, Sydney	Lnce Serg.	240810	2nd/5th Y&L
Harpin, Henri	Private	240317	2nd/5th DOW
Harrington, Bernard	Private	242101	2nd/6th WY
Harris, Roland	Private	201676	2nd/4th Y&L
Harrison, Frank	Private	241068	2nd/5th DOW
Harrison, William	Private	201868	2nd/5th WY
Hart, George	Lnce Corp	3/1682	2nd/4th KOYLI
Hartley, John	Private	202407	2nd/4th Y&L
Hartley, Percy	Private	201266	2nd/4th DOW
Hartshorn, Thomas	Private	241170	2nd/5th Y&L
Haugh, John	Private	53912	27th FA
Hawksworth, Fred	Private	241752	2nd/5th Y&L
Haxby, Charles	Private	204263	2nd/4th Y&L
Heald, Edgar	Drummer	306235	2nd/7th DOW
Heaton, William	2nd Lieut.		2nd/5th DOW
Hebden, Arthur	Corporal	266047	2nd/6th DOW
Hedgecock, John	Private	9921	2nd HAC
Heggie, Frederick	Private	4456	2nd HAC
Hellawell, Ernest	Private	241930	2nd/5th DOW
Henshaw, Sidney	Private	204273	2nd/4th Y&L
Herbert, Charles	Private	24227	2nd/6th WY
Herbert, Fred	Private	241120	2nd/5th DOW
Heryet, Cyril	Lnce Corp.	6648	2nd HAC
Hetherington, William	Private	242776	2nd/5th Y&L
Hewkin, Edwin	Private	202388	2nd/4th Y&L
Hewson, Archibald	Private	201982	2nd/5th WY

NAME	RANK	NUMBER	BATTALION	NAME	RANK	NUMBER	BATTALION
Hey, Lawrence	Lnce Corp.	306910	2nd/7th DOW	Howcroft, John	Sergeant	241026	2nd/5th Y&L
Hibberd, George	Private	242045	2nd/5th KOYLI	Howland, Richard	Private	240852	2nd/6th WY
				Howson, Tom	Private	202459	2nd/4th Y&L
Hibberson, George	Private	201205	2nd/4th Y&L	Hubbard, Malcolm	Private	9008	2nd HAC
Higgins, Walter	Private	202377	2nd/4th Y&L	Hughes, Alexander	Private	242783	2nd/5th Y&L
Hill, Ernest	Private	241593	2nd/5th DOW	Hughes, Thomas	Private	201632	2nd/4th DOW
Hill, Frank	Private	238021	2nd/4th DOW	Hunt, James	Lnce Corp.	86415	208th Coy MGC
Hill, Willie	Private	240998	2nd/6th WY	Hurrell, Walter	Private	202337	2nd/4th DOW
Hill, William	Private	7559	2nd HAC				
Hiller, Harry	Private	242480	2nd/6th WY	Ibbotson, Joseph	Private	231966	2nd/5th DOW
Hinchcliffe, Allan	Private	235069	2nd/4th DOW	Ince, Frank	Corporal	240767	2nd/5th Y&L
Hinchcliffe, George	Private	202436	2nd/4th Y&L	Jackson, Bibe	Private	201793	2nd/4th KOYLI
Hind, Herbert	Private	200952	2nd/4th DOW	Jackson, Herbert	Private	241594	2nd/5th DOW
Hirst, Harold	Private	241784	2nd/5th DOW	Jackson, Lawrence	Private	201124	2nd/5th WY
Hirst, James	Private	201397	2nd/4th DOW	Jacques, Ralph	Private	241949	2nd/5th KOYLI
Hobson, Albert	Private	241961	2nd/6th WY	Jeaffreson, Ronald	Lnce Corp.	5019	2nd HAC
Hodgson, John	Private	201861	2nd/4th DOW	Jenkins, George	2nd Lieutenant		2nd/5th Y&L
				Jennings, George	Private	240894	2nd/6th WY
Hodgson, Norman	Private	241865	2nd/6th WY	Jepson, Percy	Private	241954	2nd/5th DOW
Hodgson, William	Private	202468	2nd/4th DOW	Jepson, William	Private	241124	2nd/5th Y&L
Holdsworth, George	Private	240560	2nd/6th WY	Johnson, Herbert	Private	242092	2nd/6th WY
Hollingworth, John	Private	240837	2nd/5th DOW	Johnson, Thomas	Private	241745	2nd/5th DOW
Holmes, Harry	Drummer	241538	2nd/5th DOW	Johnson, Walter	Private	300069	2nd/6th DOW
Holmes, Norman	Private	202570	2nd/4th Y&L	Johnson, William	Private	241561	2nd/5th Y&L
Holmes, Percy	Private	242321	2nd/6th WY	Johnson, William	Lnce Serg.	200947	2nd/4th Y&L
Holroyd, Clifford	2nd Lieut.		2nd/6th DOW	Jones, George	Private	238022	2nd/4th DOW
Holroyd, Harry	Private	241655	2nd/5th DOW	Jones, William	Private	263060	2nd/5th KOYLI
Holroyd, William	Private	202071	2nd/4th DOW	Joplin, Walter	Private	242055	2nd/5th KOYLI
Horner, Harry	Private	201678	2nd/5th WY	Judd, George	Private	201951	2nd/5th WY
Horner, James	CSM	200013	2nd/5th WY	Judge, Leopold	2nd Lieut.		110th TM Bty
Horsfall, Frank	Private	241651	2nd/5th DOW	Judson, Harold	Private	201556	2nd/5th WY
Horsfield, Stanley	Corporal	241536	2nd/5th DOW	Kaye, Harry	Private	240266	2nd/5th DOW
Houghland, Thomas	Corporal	241201	2nd/5th DOW	Kaye, Joseph	Private	266224	2nd/6th DOW
				Kelly, Thomas	Private	201638	2nd/4th Y&L
Hounslow, Leo	Private	202325	2nd/4th Y&L	Kendle, Arthur	Private	241134	2nd/5th Y&L
Houseman, Clare	Lnce Corp.	240111	2nd/5th DOW	Kenworthy, John	Private	241779	2nd/5th DOW
Howard, Harold	Drummer	240287	2nd/5th Y&L	Kershaw, Arthur	Private	240720	2nd/5th DOW

NAME	RANK	NUMBER	BATTALION	NAME	RANK	NUMBER	BATTALION
Kershaw, Arthur	Private	306500	2nd/7th DOW	Lloyd, Thomas	Private	31596	DOW 1st RWF
Key, Arthur	Private	265954	2nd/6th DOW	Loader, George	Private	240235	2nd/5th DOW
Kighley, Levi	Private	22820	2nd/6th DOW	Lockerbie, Andrew	Private	9618	2nd HAC
Kilburn, Wilfred	Private	241586	2nd/5th DOW	Lockwood, Arthur	Private	241780	2nd/5th KOYLI
Kimpton, Frederick	Private	306137	2nd/7th DOW	Lockwood, Ernest	Private	241798	2nd/5th Y&L
Kingsley, John	Private	306711	2nd/8th WY	Lockwood, Herbert	Sergeant	241178	2nd/5th Y&L
Kirby, Charles	Lnce Corp.	241256	2nd/5th Y&L	Lockwood, John	Lnce Corp.	241381	2nd/5th DOW
Kirby, John	Private	242378	2nd/6th WY	Lodge, Charles	Private	204279	2nd/4th Y&L
Kirby, Wilfred	Private	202601	2nd/4th Y&L	Lodge, Harold	Lnce Corp.	241083	2nd/5th DOW
Kirk, John	Private	202025	2nd/5th WY	Lodge, William	Private	240233	2nd/5th DOW
Kirwin, John	Private	242217	2nd/6th WY	Long, David	Sergeant	265822	2nd/6th DOW
Knapp, James	Gunner	290331	38th Heavy Bty RGA	Lovell, Hedley	Private	267672	2nd/6th DOW
Knapton, Albert	Private	241739	2nd/5th DOW	Lowery, Thomas	Private	242768	2nd/5th DOW
Knoll, Edmund	Private	201594	2nd/4th Y&L	Lowry, William	Private	241639	2nd/5th Y&L
Kramer, Arthur	Private	241582	2nd/5th DOW	Lucas, John	Private	308103	2nd/7th DOW
Lamb, Alexander	Private	242790	2nd/5th DOW	Lumb, Willie	Private	306851	2nd/7th DOW
Lambert, Herbert	Private	266907	2nd/6th DOW	Lund, Arthur	Private	267201	2nd/6th DOW
Land, Fred,	Private	306675	2nd/7th DOW	Lund, Ernest	Private	265956	2nd/6th DOW
Lang, Mark	Sergeant	306176	2nd/8th WY	Lupton, Joseph	Private	266102	2nd/6th DOW
Langton, Harold	Private	306933	2nd/7th DOW	Lyon, Edgar	Private	202243	2nd/4th KOYLI
Law, Walter	Private	241367	2nd/6th WY	Mackintosh, Walter	Private	204528	2nd/5th WY
Law, Walter	Lnce Corp.	266171	2nd/7th WY	Mackman, Arthur	Private	240929	2nd/5th DOW
Lawrance, William	Corporal	242033	2nd/6th WY	Madeley, Charles	Private	241821	2nd/5th Y&L
Lazenby, William	Private	201896	2nd/5th WY	Mahr, Augustine	Private	9932	2nd HAC
Leadbetter, Frederick	Private	240780	2nd/5th KOYLI	Mansley, Stephen	Private	305953	2nd/7th DOW
Lee, Thomas	Private	7054	2nd HAC	Marks, Wolfe	Private	242775	2nd/5th Y&L
Lee, Sidney	Private	265985	2nd/6th DOW	Marriott, Joseph	Private	241543	2nd/5th DOW
Levell, Charles	Private	242801	2nd/5th Y&L	Marsden, John	Private	241953	2nd/5th Y&L
Levitt, Charles	Private	241089	2nd/5th KOYLI	Marsh, John	Lnce Corp.	241957	2nd/5th DOW
Lewis, Ben	Private	267247	2nd/7th WY	Marshall, Joseph	Lnce Corp.	240785	2nd/5th DOW
Lewis, Willie	Private	241519	2nd/5th DOW	Marshall, Thomas	Private	201187	2nd/5th WY
Linacre, William	Private	241787	2nd/5th KOYLI	Marshall, Walter	Private	266359	2nd/6th DOW
Lindley, John	Private	202477	2nd/4th Y&L				
Lindsay, Albert	Private	202016	2nd/5th KOYLI				
Littlewood, Frank	Private	241936	2nd/5th				

NAME	RANK	NUMBER	BATTALION	NAME	RANK	NUMBER	BATTALION
Marson, Claud	Private	240279	2nd/5th Y&L	Mitchell, Herbert	Private	242015	2nd/6th WY
Martin, Frank	Private	201556	2nd/4th DOW	Mitchell, Lewis	Private	268345	2nd/6th DOW
Martin, Samuel	Private	306692	2nd/7th DOW	Mitchell, Stanley	Private	240842	2nd/5th Y&L
Mason, John	Private	202403	2nd/4th Y&L	Mitchell, William	Corporal	265085	2nd/6th DOW
Mathers, Sydney	Private	263025	2nd.5th DOW	Moffat, William	Private	6966	2nd HAC
Matson, John	Private	202317	2nd/4th Y&L	Montford, Alfred	2nd Lieut.		208th Coy MGC
Matthews, Frederick	Private	241318	2nd/6th WY	Moreland, Thomas	Private	266900	2nd/6th DOW
Matthews, James	Private	201059	2nd/4th KOYLI	Morgan, Fred	Private	306520	2nd/7th DOW
Maudsley, Herbert	Sergeant	265693	2nd/6th DOW	Morgan, James	Lnce Corp.	240572	2nd/5th DOW
Mawson, Joe	Private	267183	2nd/6th DOW	Morley, James	Private	242087	2nd/5th KOYLI
May, Robert	Private	241888	2nd/6th WY	Morrell, William	Private	242235	2nd/6th WY
Mazza, Joseph	Lnce Serg.	305895	2nd/8th WY	Morris, Ernest	Private	9303	2nd HAC
McCoull, William	Lieut.		D HB MGC	Mortimer, Dennis	Lnce Corp.	64454	231st Coy MGC
McCulley, Robert	Private	262460	2nd/6th WY				
McHale, John	Private	241856	2nd/5th Y&L	Morton, James	Private	9862	2nd HAC
McHugh, John	Private	201469	2nd/4th DOW	Moseley, James	Private	202626	2nd/4th Y&L
McHugh, Stephen	Private	307592	2nd/7th DOW	Mosley, Arnold	Lnce Corp.	241890	2nd/5th DOW
McKeown, Francis	Private	242234	2nd/6th WY	Mosley, James	Private	267094	2nd/6th DOW
McLelland, James	Private	238027	2nd/4th DOW	Mowatt, John	Private	67404	212th Coy MGC
Medley, Arthur	Private	200586	2nd/5th WY	Moxon, David	Private	241863	2nd/5th DOW
Medley, Walter	Private	267241	2nd/7th WY				
Meggett, Walter	Private	241925	2nd/5th Y&L	Moysey, Lionel	Private	6755	2nd HAC
Mellers, Joseph	Lnce Serg.	241059	2nd/5th KOYLI	Murgatroyd, John	Private	201154	2nd/4th DOW
Mellor, Arthur	Private	241610	2nd/5th DOW	Myers, Edwin	Private	242385	2nd/6th WY
Mellor, George	Private	18178	2nd/6th DOW	Naylor, Gilbert	Private	306652	2nd/7th DOW
Mellows, John	Private	18302	2nd/4th KOYLI	Neale, Charles	Private	306752	2nd/7th DOW
Metcalfe, George	Private	266960	2nd/6th DOW	Ness, Douglas	Private	241765	2nd/5th DOW
Metcalfe, Norman	Private	268341	2nd/6th DOW	Newns, Charles	Sergeant	265925	2nd/6th DOW
Middleton, George	Private	242115	2nd/5th KOYLI	Nicholson, Herbert	Lnce Corp.	235084	2nd/5th DOW
Midgley, Herbert	Private	241604	2nd/5th DOW	Nicholson, John	Private	267105	2nd/6th DOW
Miller, Arthur	Private	201346	2nd/5th WY	Nimmo, Frederick	Private	307593	2nd/7th DOW
Milner, Walter	Private	241968	2nd/5th KOYLI	Noble, William	Private	308090	2nd/7th DOW
Milnes, Herbert	Private	241825	2nd/5th DOW	Normington, Frank	Private	241453	2nd/6th WY

NAME	RANK	NUMBER	BATTALION	NAME	RANK	NUMBER	BATTALION
North, Charles	Private	241864	2nd/6th WY	Piggott, Herbert	Private	241720	2nd/5th DOW
Oakes, John	Private	308135	2nd/7th DOW	Pilley, Frank	Private	241058	2nd/5th Y&L
Oakes, Selwyn	Private	200194	2nd/4th DOW	Pilling, Nathaniel	Private	266828	2nd/6th DOW
O'Brien, Charles	Private	235194	2nd/5th KOYLI	Pilsworth, William	Private	241721	2nd/5th DOW
O'Brien, Joseph	Sergeant	240944	2nd/5th DOW	Pinkney, Thomas	Sergeant	240818	2nd/5th DOW
Oddy, Edgar	Private	202555	2nd/4th DOW	Pinkney, Walter	Private	242792	2nd/5th DOW
Oldreive, Reginald	Private	9194	2nd HAC	Pipe, William	Private	9764	2nd HAC
Oldroyd, Horace	Private	235086	2nd/5th DOW	Platt, George	Sergeant	240291	2nd/5th KOYLI
O'Hanlon, Edward	Lnce Corp.	241747	2nd/5th DOW	Platts, Ernest	Private	202380	2nd/4th Y&L
Ormondroyd, Sharpe	Private	267233	2nd/6th DOW	Pleasants, Stanley	Private	306592	2nd/7th DOW
Orr, Herbert	Lnce Serg.	305971	2nd/7th DOW	Plews, Thomas	Private	306972	2nd/7th DOW
Palmer, Bertie	Private	65652	208th MGC	Pole, Wilfred	Private	265331	2nd/6th DOW
Palmer, Joseph	Private	242810	2nd/5th KOYLI	Pollard, Archie	Private	202623	2nd/4th Y&L
Pape, William	Private	242137	2nd/6th WY	Pollard, John	Private	242241	2nd/6th WY
Park, George	Private	241825	2nd/5th Y&L	Porter, Arthur	Private	9878	2nd HAC
Parker, Charles	Private	241234	2nd/6th WY	Poulson Edward	Private	241777	2nd/5th DOW
Parker, Richard	Private	241946	2nd/5th DOW	Prest, Robert	Private	201062	2nd/5th WY
Parkinson, Ernest	Lnce Corp.	307613	2nd/7th DOW	Preston, Arthur	Private	240913	2nd/5th Y&L
Parkinson, Harry	Private	19156	2nd/5th KOYLI	Price, Daniel	Private	241091	2nd/5th KOYLI
Parr, John	Private	241074	2nd/5th DOW	Price, Louis	Private	306925	2nd/8th WY
Parry, Percy	Private	9724	2nd HAC	Prosser, William	Private	241284	2nd/6th WY
Patchett, James	Private	300074	2nd/6th DOW	Proverbs, Stuart	Private	7499	2nd HAC
Pearson, Pelham	Private	201722	2nd/5th WY	Pugh, George	Lnce Serg.	7707	2nd HAC
Pearson, Robert	Private	266682	2nd/6th DOW	Quinlan, Joseph	Private	241547	2nd/5th Y&L
Peet, Telford	Private	203952	2nd/4th KOYLI	Quinn, John	Private	240684	2nd/5th Y&L
Perkins, Frank	Private	81941	213th Coy MGC	Raisbeck, Maurice	Private	306618	2nd/7th DOW
Petty, George	Private	242020	2nd/6th WY	Ralph, Harry	Private	265425	2nd/6th DOW
Petty, William	Private	266446	2nd/6th DOW	Rathmell, Leslie	Private	265224	2nd/7th WY
Pickering, Alfred	Private	201658	2nd/4th Y&L	Rawlinson, Frank	Private	242454	2nd/6th WY
Pickering, George	Private	241197	2nd/5th Y&L	Ray, Ernest	Private	19267	2nd/5th KOYLI
Pickles, Jack	Private	265890	2nd/6th DOW	Read, Tom	Private	266952	2nd/6th DOW
Pickthall, William	Private	240750	2nd/6th WY	Reason, Harold	Lnce Corp.	201730	2nd/5th WY
				Reaston, William	Private	201769	2nd/5th WY
				Redfearn, Frank	Private	235209	2nd/7th WY
				Redman, Lewis	Private	307609	2nd/7th DOW
				Redshaw, James	Private	201693	2nd/5th WY

NAME	RANK	NUMBER	BATTALION	NAME	RANK	NUMBER	BATTALION
Reeder, Leonard	Private	204261	2nd/5th Y&L	Satchwell, Frank	Captain		2nd HAC
Rees, John	Private	235090	2nd/5th DOW	Scoltock, William	Private	241653	2nd/5th KOYLI
Rhodes, Sam	Corporal	241076	2nd/6th WY	Seamark, Harry	Private	9728	2nd HAC
Richardson, Fred	Private	202981	2nd/5th KOYLI	Seddon Norman	Private	241412	2nd/5th KOYLI
Richardson, William	Private	242244	2nd/6th WY	Selby, Donovan	Lnce Corp.	3632	2nd HAC
Richmond, Fred	Corporal	201301	2nd/5th WY	Seymour, William	Private	9170	2nd HAC
Riley, Harry	Sergeant	200953	2nd/4th DOW	Seymour, James	Private	201897	2nd/5th WY
				Sharp, Sam	Private	242127	2nd/6th WY
Riley, Willie	Sergeant	201312	2nd/4th DOW	Sharpe, John	Private	241285	2nd/5th KOYLI
Ripley, Thomas	Private	240851	2nd/6th WY	Shaw, Edwin	Private	242797	2nd/5th DOW
Roberts, Arthur	Private	268370	2nd/6th DOW	Shaw, Ernest	Private	242016	2nd/5th DOW
Roberts, Willie	Private	240631	2nd/5th DOW	Shaw, Fred	Private	268364	2nd/6th DOW
Robertson, Noel	Private	7303	2nd HAC	Shaw, Harold	Sergeant	241117	2nd/6th WY
Robertson, Charlie	Sergeant	201523	2nd/4th DOW	Shaw, Thomas	Private	305925	2nd/8th WY
Robinson, Edward	Private	306878	2nd/7th DOW	Shearer, David	Corporal	202005	2nd/4th DOW
Robinson, George	Private	242461	2nd/6th WY	Shearsmith, Sydney	Private	241634	2nd/5th DOW
Robinson, Thomas	Private	242741	2nd/5th Y&L				
Robinson, William	Sergeant	201528	2nd/4th DOW	Sheen, Edward	Private	204258	2nd/4th Y&L
				Shepherd Ernest	Private	206102	D HB MGC
Rodgers, Charles	Private	242161	2nd/6th WY	Sheppard, Duncan	Private	9254	2nd HAC
Roebuck, Frank	Private	241645	2nd/5th DOW	Sherwin, Alfred	Private	267050	2nd/6th DOW
Roebuck, Oliver	Private	203745	2nd/5th KOYLI	Shindler, Cecil	Private	235095	2nd/5th DOW
Rogers, Frederick	Private	9908	2nd HAC	Short, Frank	Corporal	201575	2nd/4th Y&L
Rogers, John	Private	308098	2nd/7th DOW	Simmonite, William	Private	201276	2nd/5th WY
				Simonite, James	Lnce Corp.	201137	2nd/4th Y&L
Rotheray, Percy	Sergeant	240860	2nd/6th WY	Simpkin, Travers	Private	9866	2nd HAC
Rothwell, John	Private	241780	2nd/5th DOW	Simpson, Alfred	Private	241259	2nd/5th KOYLI
Rowe, Herbert	Private	241661	2nd/5th DOW	Simpson, Victor	Private	7362	2nd HAC
				Simpson, Harry	Private	241995	2nd/6th WY
Ruddy, James	Private	201171	2nd/4th DOW	Simpson, Timothy	Private	20007	2nd/6th DOW
Rush, Laurence	Private	201475	2nd/5th WY	Singleton, Clarence	Private	306140	2nd/7th DOW
Ryalls, William	Private	202474	2nd/4th Y&L				
Rylance, Ernest	Private	240733	2nd/5th DOW	Size, Harry	Private	242058	2nd/6th WY
				Skeldon, Thomas	Private	306050	2nd/7th DOW
Saddington, William	Private	306959	2nd/7th DOW	Slater, Herbert	Private	202446	2nd/4th KOYLI
Salter, Harold	Private	9880	2nd HAC	Smallpage, Percy	Private	242285	2nd/6th WY
Sanderson, Arthur	Lnce Serg.	201236	2nd/4th Y&L	Smith, Albert	Sergeant	265075	2nd/6th DOW
Sanderson, Walter	Private	202564	2nd/4th Y&L				
Sandford, Fred	Private	241540	2nd/5th DOW	Smith, Albert	Private	266141	2nd/6th DOW

NAME	RANK	NUMBER	BATTALION	NAME	RANK	NUMBER	BATTALION
Smith, Arthur	Private	21207	2nd/5th KOYLI	Swindells, George	Private	241083	2nd/5th Y&L
Smith, Charles	Private	202332	2nd/4th Y&L	Sykes, Ernest	Private	240730	2nd/5th DOW
Smith, Edwin	Private	266041	2nd/6th DOW	Sykes, France	Corporal	305462	2nd/7th DOW
Smith, Edwin	Private	268646	2nd/7th WY	Sykes, Harold	Private	201971	2nd/4th KOYLI
Smith, Francis	Private	76210	D HB MGC				
Smith, Henry	Private	242213	2nd/5th KOYLI	Sykes, John	Lnce Corp.	306629	2nd/7th DOW
Smith, James	Private	267216	2nd/6th DOW	Sykes, Stanley	Sergeant	240672	2nd/5th DOW
Smith, John	Private	266752	2nd/6th DOW	Sykes, Walter	Private	241919	2nd/5th DOW
Smith, John	Private	235106	2nd/6th WY	Talbot, Gordon	Private	267083	2nd/6th DOW
Smith, Joseph	Private	268432	2nd/7th DOW	Tate, Wilfred	Private	241613	2nd/5th DOW
Smith, Joseph	Private	65502	208th Coy MGC	Taylor, Albert	Private	241622	2nd/5th Y&L
Smith, Leonard	Private	242282	2nd/5th WY	Taylor, Albert	Private	241987	2nd/5th DOW
Smith, Mark	Private	202147	2nd/5th WY				
Smith, Samuel	Private	306550	2nd/7th DOW	Taylor, Willie	Corporal	240758	2nd/5th Y&L
				Thackeray, Frank	Private	202375	2nd/4th Y&L
Smith, Walter	Lnce Corp.	201463	2nd/5th WY	Thomas, George MM	Private	75068	D HB MGC
Smith, William	Private	202129	2nd/4th DOW	Thompson, Frank	Private	306602	2nd/7th DOW
Smith, William	Private	203033	2nd/4th Y&L	Thompson Fred	Private	26856	2nd/5th KOYLI
Smith, Willis	Corporal	241000	2nd/4th Y&L				
Southwell, George	Corporal	201581	2nd/4th Y&L	Thompson, John	Private	241281	2nd/5th Y&L
Southwell, William	Private	202557	2nd/4th DOW	Thompson, Joshua	Corporal	241359	2nd/5th KOYLI
Spedding, William	Private	265402	2nd/6th DOW	Thompson, Robert	Lnce Corp.	241131	2nd/6th WY
				Thompson William	Private	241298	2nd/6th WY
Speight, John	Private	241851	2nd/6th WY	Thomson, John	Private	206123	D HB MGC
Spencer, Bernard	Private	241864	2nd/5th Y&L	Thornton, Stanley	Private	4857	2nd HAC
Spencer, Stanley	Captain		2nd/5th Y&L	Thornton, Herbert	Private	241533	2nd/5th DOW
Staley, John	Private	241885	2nd/5th Y&L				
Stanley, Wright	Private	267139	2nd/6th DOW	Thornton, Samuel	Private	235100	2nd/5th DOW
Starkey, William	Private	202688	2nd/4th Y&L	Thornton, William	Private	305928	2nd/8th WY
Stead, Sidney	Private	307751	2nd/8th WY	Thorpe, Albert	Private	241803	2nd/5th Y&L
Stevenson, George	Corporal	201590	2nd/4th Y&L	Thresh, Walter	Private	240969	2nd/6th WY
Stockdale, Joseph	Private	240952	2nd/5th DOW	Tidswell, Harry	Private	306895	2nd/7th DOW
Stocks, John	Private	240956	2nd/6th WY	Tindall, James	Lnce Corp.	241621	2nd/5th DOW
Stockton, Benjamin	Private	201249	2nd/4th DOW				
				Tinker, Percy	Private	242008	2nd/5th DOW
Stoker, Thomas	Private	242691	2nd/5th Y&L				
Stowell, Douglas	Private	240970	2nd/6th WY	Tinsley, John	Private	24113	2nd/5th KOYLI
Summers, Robert	Private	4922	2nd HAC				
Sunderland, Edgar	Private	306917	2nd/7th DOW	Tomlinson, Albert	Private	240951	2nd/6th WY
				Tomlinson, Fred	Private	242158	2nd/6th WY
Sutton, Percy	Lnce Corp.	242815	2nd/5th KOYLI	Topham, George	Private	204374	2nd/4th Y&L

NAME	RANK	NUMBER	BATTALION	NAME	RANK	NUMBER	BATTALION
Townend, Lewis	Private	242009	2nd/5th DOW	Watkin, John	Private	240814	2nd/5th Y&L
				Watkins, Cecil	Private	5554	2nd HAC
Train, Walter	Private	242288	2nd/6th WY	Watkinson, Walter	Corporal	201196	2nd/4th Y&L
Turnbull, John	Private	242753	2nd/5th Y&L	Watson, Albert	Private	242822	2nd/5th KOYLI
Turner, Charles	Private	202339	2nd/4th DOW	Watson, John	Private	235104	2nd/5th DOW
Turner, Ernest	Private	241641	2nd/5th DOW	Watson, Norman	Private	241574	2nd/5th DOW
Turner, John	Private	267821	2nd/7th DOW	Watson, Thomas	Private	9856	2nd HAC
Turner, Tom	Private	242821	2nd/5th KOYLI	Watson, Thomas	Private	266181	2nd/6th DOW
Twivy, George	Lnce Corp/	241321	2nd/6th WY	Watson, William	Lieut. Col.		2nd/5th KOYLI
Tyrer, Fred Private		267085	2nd/6th DOW	Watson, William	Private	202420	2nd/4th Y&L
Veal, Frederick	Private	268381	2nd/6th DOW	Wear, Frank	Private	241690	2nd/5th DOW
Vickers, James	Private	241734	2nd/5th DOW	Webster, Charles	Private	241743	2nd/5th DOW
Wadsworth, James	Lnce Corp.	11300	2nd/5th KOYLI	Webster, Harry	Private	240142	2nd/5th DOW
Wainwright, Sampson Private		202661	2nd/4th Y&L	Welch, Frank	Private	352698	2nd/7th London
Walker, Lionel	Lnce Corp.	7097	2nd HAC				
Walker, Frank	Private	241231	2nd/5th Y&L	Wells, Fred	Private	241896	2nd/6th WY
Walker, James	Private	241150	2nd/5th KOYLI	Wells, Gilbert	Private	202574	2nd/4th DOW
Walker, John	Private	201270	2nd/4th DOW	Wesley, Ronald	Sergeant	200755	2nd/4th Y&L
				Westerby, Joseph	Private	241711	2nd/5th DOW
Walker, John	Sergeant	240480	2nd/5th KOYLI	Westwood, William	Corporal	241454	2nd/5th KOYLI
Walker, Robert	Private	268667	2nd/6th DOW	Whear, Ralph	Private	9897	2nd HAC
Walker, Robert	Sergeant	265035	2nd/6th DOW	Wheelhouse, Norman Private		240160	2nd/5th DOW
Walker, Tom	Private	266474	2nd/6th DOW	Whitaker, Sydney	Private	201989	2nd/5th WY
				White, Arthur	Private	241773	2nd/5th Y&L
Wallbridge, William	Gunner	89338	C Bty, 46th Bdg RFA	White, Charles	Private	7293	2nd HAC
				White, Donner	Private	242248	2nd/6th WY
Walsh, Martin	2nd Lieut.		2nd/4th KOYLI	White, Harry	Private	241686	2nd/5th DOW
Walter, Fred	Private	241684	2nd/5th DOW	White, Harry	Private	305224	2nd/8th WY
				Whiteside, Thomas	Private	40628	1st South Staffs
Walton, Frank	Private	240152	2nd/6th WY				
Walton, John	Sergeant	265399	2nd/6th DOW	Whitworth, Frank	Private	306034	2nd/7th DOW
Ward, Fred	Private	60381	MGC	Whitworth, Harry	Private	202246	2nd/5th KOYLI
Ward, John	Private	307026	2nd/8th WY				
Ward, Maurice	Private	202510	2nd/4th Y&L	Wigley, Ernest	Private	202327	2nd/4th Y&L
Wardle, Joseph	Corporal	53319	206th Coy MGC	Wilcock, Willie	Private	240989	2nd/5th DOW
Warrington, Benjamin Private		306820	2nd/7th DOW	Wilds, Frank	Private	240522	2nd/5th DOW
Warrington, Frank	Private	201579	2nd/4th Y&L	Wiles, Sidney	Private	9832	2nd HAC

NAME	RANK	NUMBER	BATTALION
Wilkin, Fred	Private	242293	2nd/6th WY
Wilkins, Albert	Private	238004	2nd/4th KOYLI
Wilkinson, Charlie	Private	306667	2nd/7th DOW
Wilkinson, Joseph	Corporal	241673	2nd/5th DOW
Wilkinson, William	Private	241618	2nd/5th DOW
Willey, James	Lnce Corp/	201776	2nd/8th WY
Williams, Henry	Private	201611	2nd/4th Y&L
Wilson, Albert	Private	4272	2nd HAC
Wilson, Ernest	Private	202016	2nd/4th DOW
Wilson, Freeman	Private	235103	2nd/5th DOW
Wilson, Harold	Private	265721	2nd/6th DOW
Wilson, Harry	Private	267049	2nd/6th DOW
Wilson, Henry	Private	241849	2nd/5th Y&L
Wilson, John	Private	242291	2nd/6th WY
Wilson, Patrick	Private	66301	208th Coy MGC
Wilson, Percy	Private	G/21254	2nd Queen's

NAME	RANK	NUMBER	BATTALION
Winpenny, Arthur	Private	306777	2nd/7th DOW
Winterburn, William	Corporal	265798	2nd/6th DOW
Wise, Harold	Private	6848	2nd HAC
Wood, Andrew	Private	242718	2nd/5th DOW
Wood, Cecil	Private	7651	2nd HAC
Woodhead, Frank	Private	241520	2nd/5th DOW
Woollard, George	Private	306952	2nd/8th WY
Wormald, Harry	Sergeant	240369	2nd/6th WY
Wortley, John	Private	204411	2nd/4th DOW
Wortley, William	Private	201373	2nd/5th WY
Wray, Harry	Private	201650	2nd/4th DOW
Wright, Benjamin	Private	9795	2nd HAC
Wright, Thomas	Lnce Corp.	201504	2nd/4th Y&L
Yeadon, Horace	Private	22787	2nd/5th DOW
Yeadon, Hugh	Private	265799	2nd/6th DOW
Yeadon, Walter	Private	240774	2nd/8th WY
Young, Ernest	Private	201194	2nd/4th DOW

SOLDIERS KILLED 4TH MAY 1917

NAME	RANK	NUMBER	BATTALION
Aird, William	Private	6494	1st RWF
Aldred, Alfred	Private	11282	2nd Royal Warwick's
Andrews, Thomas	Private	23631	2nd Royal Warwick's
Andrews, William	Private	23687	2nd Royal Warwick's
Atkins, Ernest	Private	609	2nd Royal Warwick's
Bakewell, Albert	Private	16687	2nd Royal Warwick's
Balls, Samuel	Private	27108	2nd Royal Warwick's
Barker, Richard	Private	26983	2nd Royal Warwick's
Bayliss, Eden	Private	9623	1st RWF
Beswick, William	Private	17344	2nd Royal Warwick's
Bidgood, William	Private	23676	2nd Royal Warwick's

NAME	RANK	NUMBER	BATTALION
Bolver, Leonard	Private	40393	20th Manchester
Bott, George	Private	15286	2nd Royal Warwick's
Bowen, William	Corporal	15589	2nd Royal Warwick's
Bowker, Edwin	Corporal	8482	1st RWF
Brazendale, Alfred	Private	53772	1st RWF
Bryan, Joseph	Private	40202	20th Manchester
Buckwright, George	Corporal	17029	20th Manchester
Burrell, Frederick	2nd Lieut.		2nd Royal Warwick's
Bye, John	Private	27268	2nd Royal Warwick's
Chadwick, William	Private	40285	20th Manchester
Chambers, Frank	Private	27102	2nd Royal Warwick's

NAME	RANK	NUMBER	BATTALION	NAME	RANK	NUMBER	BATTALION
Child, George	Private	23632	2nd Royal Warwick's	Griffiths, Thomas	Private	53821	1st RWF
Chinery, George	Private	271257	2nd Royal Warwick's	Guest, Harry	Private	3320	2nd Royal Warwick's
Clay, Percy	Private	27052	2nd Royal Warwick's	Hammond, George	Private	20669	2nd Royal Warwick's
Clemmetsen, Stanley	Private	7140	2nd HAC	Hannibal, Frederick	Private	1145	2nd Royal Warwick's
Coleman, William	Private	10515	2nd Royal Warwick's	Harris, Fred	Private	29987	2nd Royal Warwick's
Coles, George	Private	23698	2nd Royal Warwick's	Harris, Stephen	Private	88552	42nd FA
Collins, Hugh	Private	28078	20th Manchester	Healey, William	Private	40062	20th Manchester
Collins, John	Private	63596	1st RWF	Heatherington, Eric	2nd Lieut.		2nd Royal Warwick's
Connell, Frank	Private	4661	2nd Royal Warwick's	Henderson, John	Private	53909	1st RWF
Conquest, William	Private	18430	20th Manchester	Heywood, Samuel	Lnce Corp.	21754	2nd Royal Warwick's
Cooper, Harry	Private	26993	2nd Royal Warwick's	Hiam, Charles	Private	7849	2nd Royal Warwick's
Crawford, Arthur	Private	27085	2nd Royal Warwick's	Hickman, Frederick	Lnce Corp.	4866	2nd Royal Warwick's
Croft, Thomas	Private	54162	1st RWF	Hill, Albert	Private	17924	20th Manchester
Crowder, William	Private	53774	1st RWF	Hills, Vincent	Private	21440	213th Coy MGC
Davies, David	Private	53958	1st RWF				
Davies, Idris	Private	16477	1st RWF	Hirst, Frederick	Private	26900	20th Manchester
Dodd, William	Private	27081	1st RWF	Holden, Harold	Private	31399	20th Manchester
Downes, Frank	Private	19364	2nd Royal Warwick's	Holden, James	Private	40222	20th Manchester
Durrans, Arthur	Private	306585	2nd/7th DOW	Horton, Frederick	Private	9808	2nd Royal Warwick's
Earl, Thomas	Private	23641	2nd Royal Warwick's	Hunt, Joseph	Private	4919	1st RWF
Edwards, David	Private	53959	1st RWF	Jackson, Albert	Corporal	1737	2nd Royal Warwick's
Ellis, Clifford	Private	23643	2nd Royal Warwick's	Jackson, Leonard	Private	27047	2nd Royal Warwick's
Ellis, William	Private	23624	2nd Royal Warwick's	Jacobs, Jesse	Private	9612	2nd Royal Warwick's
Fawdry, Alfred	2nd Lieut.		2nd Royal Warwick's	James. George	Lnce Serg.	11528	2nd Royal Warwick's
Felton, William	Private	2969	2nd Royal Warwick's	James, Harry	Corporal	1731	2nd Royal Warwick's
Foulkes, Thomas	Private	53613	1st RWF	Johnson, Walter	Private	27054	2nd Royal Warwick's
German, Ernest	Private	23652	2nd Royal Warwick's	Johnson, William	Private	15355	2nd Royal Warwick's
Gough, Albert	Private	29928	2nd Royal Warwick's	Jones, Daniel	2nd Lieut.		1st RWF
Greaves, James	Private	16/1772	2nd Royal Warwick's	Jones, James	Private	53715	1st RWF
Green, Arthur	Corporal	16/1765	2nd Royal Warwick's	Kerans, Ernest	Private	26178	1sr RWF
Greenway, Vincent	Private	4397	2nd Royal Warwick's	Knight, Joseph	Private	178	2nd Royal Warwick's

NAME	RANK	NUMBER	BATTALION	NAME	RANK	NUMBER	BATTALION
Lamboll, Frederick	Private	18702	2nd Royal Warwick's	Rigby, Archibald	Private	10852	1st RWF
Lane, Harry	Private	27092	2nd Royal Warwick's	Ring, Norman	Lieut.		2nd Royal Warwick's
Lee, George	Private	23615	2nd Royal Warwick's	Roberts, Henry	Private	23707	2nd Royal Warwick's
Lewis, Arthur	Lieut.		1st RWF	Rodwell, Frederick	Lnce Corp.	29939	2nd Royal Warwick's
Lewis, John	Private	40641	1st RWF	Rowley, Arthur	Private	18032	2nd Royal Warwick's
Livesey, Herbert	Private	53830	1st RWF				
Lloyd, Robert	Private	53916	1st RWF	Rushton, John	Private	10456	2nd Royal Warwick's
Lockett, Albert	Private	44503	20th Manchester	Sandall, Harry	Private	27173	2nd Royal Warwick's
Markland, James	Sergeant	40381	20th Manchester	Scriven, Arthur	Private	7944	2nd Royal Warwick's
Medley, John	Lnce Corp.	27032	2nd Royal Warwick's	Sharp, John	Private	26980	2nd Royal Warwick's
Meech, Reginald	Private	15/1352	2nd Royal Warwick's	Sharratt, Joseph	Lnce Corp.	1716	2nd Royal Warwick's
Needham, Fred	Private	27057	2nd Royal Warwick's	Shortall, John	Private	42956	22nd Coy MGC
Newnham, William	Private	27146	2nd Royal Warwick's	Shufflebotham, Edward	Lnce Corp.	1645	2nd Royal Warwick's
Nicholson, George	Corporal	27147	2nd Royal Warwick's	Simpson, Samuel	Private	27096	2nd Royal Warwick's
Nightingale, Fred	Private	40236	20th Manchester	Sitch, Albert	Lnce Corp.	1420	2nd Royal Warwick's
Norton, James	Private	267071	2nd/7th WY	Southam, Ernest	Private	17984	2nd Royal Warwick's
Padbury, Samuel	Private	21915	2nd Royal Warwick's	Spofford, Charles	Private	11531	2nd Royal Warwick's
Parker, John	Gunner	34784	A Bty, 93rd Bdg RFA	Starling, George	Private	23605	2nd Royal Warwick's
Parkinson, William	Private	39953	21st Manchester	Steadman, Bertram	Private	3497	2nd Royal Warwick's
Patterson, William	Corporal	17456	20th Manchester	Stevens, Thomas	Private	26968	2nd Royal Warwick's
Payne, William	Private	19336	2nd Royal Warwick's	Stubbs, William	Private	4700	2nd Royal Warwick's
Peake, Joseph	Private	14941	20th Manchester	Syrett, Alfred	2nd Lieut.		1st RWF
Perkins, George	Private	14453	2nd Royal Warwick's	Taylor, George	Private	22092	2nd Royal Warwick's
Pickering, Walter	Sergeant	34877	1st RWF	Thomas, David	2nd Lieut.		1st RWF
Pilling, George MM	Corporal	23811	1st RWF	Trinder, Walter	Private	30056	2nd Royal Warwick's
Pooley, Bert	Private	27242	2nd Royal Warwick's	Vear, Henry	Private	27073	2nd Royal Warwick's
Prescott, Albert	Private	10518	2nd Royal Warwick's	Walden, William	Sergeant	23393	1st RWF
Randall, Charles	Private	23665	2nd Royal Warwick's	Walker, Robert	Private	1582	2nd Royal Warwick's
Randell, Walter	Private	27160	2nd Royal Warwick's	Ward, James	Private	27021	2nd Royal Warwick's
Rawlings, Bernard	Private	19483	2nd Royal Warwick's				

NAME	RANK	NUMBER	BATTALION	NAME	RANK	NUMBER	BATTALION
Waters, George	Private	11623	2nd Royal Warwick's	Wilkinson, Frederick	Private	52670	1st RWF
Watts, Frank	Private	22093	2nd Royal Warwick's	Williams, Alfred	Private	53981	1st RWF
				Williams, John	Private	53801	1st RWF
Webb, William	Private	18112	2nd Royal Warwick's	Williams, Thomas	Private	45157	1st RWF
				Wilson, George,	Lnce Corp.	2216	20th Manchester
Welbourn, Jacob	Private	27213	2nd Royal Warwick's	Winrow, Robert	Private	53800	1st RWF
				Wood, Cecil	Corporal	10466	2nd Royal Warwick's

SOLDIERS KILLED 5TH MAY 1917

NAME	RANK	NUMBER	BATTALION	NAME	RANK	NUMBER	BATTALION
Appleyard, Joseph	Private	240671	2nd/5th KOYLI	Roberts, Evan	Private	53732	1st RWF
				Roberts, John	Private	11480	1st RWF
Blackburn, Arnold	Private	201244	2nd/4th Y&L	Shipman, Rigney	Private	38107	21st Manchester
Burt, Edwin	Private	17681	8th Devonshire				
				Simpson, William	Gunner	2503	56th Bty 34th Bde RFA
Davies, Thomas	Lnce Corp.	19215	1st RWF				
Holdroyd, Percy	2nd Lieut.		2nd/5th KOYLI	Smalley, Herbert	Private	203937	2nd/4th KOYLI
Jackson, Richard	Private	241596	2nd/5th KOYLI	Smith, Edward	Private	203884	2nd/5th KOYLI
Lee, John	Private	266758	1st RWF				
Randall, George MM&Bar	Sergeant	52903	56th Bty 34th Bde RFA				

SOLDIERS KILLED 6TH MAY 1917

NAME	RANK	NUMBER	BATTALION	NAME	RANK	NUMBER	BATTALION
Archer, Albert	Private	15769	9th Devonshire	Knowles, Thomas	Private	16627	9th Devonshire
Biles, William	Private	548215	513th Field Coy RE	Murrin, Frederick	Private	20172	9th Devonshire
Field, Walter	Private	3/6879	8th Devonshire	Wood, Walter	Private	28512	8th Devonshire
Grimes, George	Private	25666	9th Devonshire	Wooldridge, William	Private	28753	8th Devonshire

SOLDIERS KILLED 7TH MAY 1917

NAME	RANK	NUMBER	BATTALION	NAME	RANK	NUMBER	BATTALION
Andrews, George	Private	241647	2nd/5th Y&L	Beer, William	Private	25046	9th Devonshire
Anley, George	Private	946	2nd GH				
Barbour, William	Private	S/43001	2nd GH	Bigwood, F	Private	33707	9th Devonshire

NAME	RANK	NUMBER	BATTALION
Black, Edward	Private	33708	9th Devonshire
Booth, Larrett	Private	240649	2nd/5th Y&L
Bridger, John	Private	20977	9th Devonshire
Brimblecombe, Ernest	Private	16943	8th Devonshire
Brodie, William	Lnce Corp.	S/40106	2nd GH
Burness, David	Private	3/6489	2nd GH
Burt, Charles	Sergeant	7771	9th Devonshire
Cameron, Duncan	Private	238043	2nd GH
Duffy, Philip	Private	S/12307	2nd GH
Edmondson, Arthur	Private	S/9903	2nd GH
Fanning, Peter	Private	14660	9th Devonshire
Ferguson, Donald	Captain		2nd GH
Flynn, Frank	Private	306523	2nd/7th DOW
Gilbert, James	Private	6932	2nd GH
Gordon, Maitland	Captain		2nd GH
Griffiths, David	Lnce Corp.	33430	8th Devonshire
Hemmingway, Leonard	Private	15537	9th Devonshire
Henderson, Robert	Private	S/7011	2nd GH
Hogg, Archibald	Private	S/9424	2nd GH
Isaac, Mark	Private	26970	9th Devonshire
Johnstone, James	Lnce Corp.	S/9654	2nd GH
Kennedy, Robert	Private	S/43541	2nd GH
King, Frederick	Private	16282	8th Devonshire
Knight, Woodman	Private	47623	8th Devonshire
Laverance, William	Private	S/7404	2nd GH
Lee, Mortimore	Private	25931	9th Devonshire

NAME	RANK	NUMBER	BATTALION
Lyall, John	Private	S/40025	2nd GH
McAssey, Michael	Private	43240	9th Devonshire
McDonald, Allan	Corporal	S/11928	2nd GH
McKenzie, Donald	Private	S/17446	2nd GH
McPherson, Alexander	Private	S/3383	2nd GH
Mears, Thomas	Private	30191	9th Devonshire
Mills, William	Private	26502	9th Devonshire
Morrish, William	Private	33373	8th Devonshire
Nugent, Charles	Sergeant	S/8807	2nd GH
Orr, Alexander	Private	S/4446	2nd GH
Ray, Frank	Private	58052	8th Devonshire
Rock, William	Lnce Corp.	18244	20th Coy MGC
Roud, Albert	Private	33462	8th Devonshire
Scott, James	Private	S/43124	2nd GH
Shirra, Henry	Private	S/40606	2nd GH
Sneddon, William	Private	S/15457	2nd GH
Spacagna, Vicenzo	Private	30034	9th Devonshire
Spiller, Tola	Private	14062	9th Devonshire
Stallabrass, Harry	Private	9994	9th Devonshire
Towns, Robert	Private	S/43010	2nd GH
Webster, John	Private	S/2577	2nd GH
Western, William	Private	472308	2nd/12th London
Williams, Arthur	Private	20396	9th Devonshire
Wilson, John	Private	S/11588	2nd GH

SOLDIERS KILLED 8TH MAY 1917

NAME	RANK	NUMBER	BATTALION
Aburrow, Henry	Private	33411	8th Devonshire
Britton, Frank	Private	50323	9th Devonshire
Connell, William	Sergeant	33385	2nd Border
Dewar, Thomas	Sergeant	33089	2nd Border
Durrant, William	Sergeant	7923	8th Devonshire

NAME	RANK	NUMBER	BATTALION
Glover, Stanley	Private	42666	9th Devonshire
Haiden, Trew	Corporal	1301	9th Devonshire
Hurford, Jacob	Private	15877	8th Devonshire
Manning, Ernest	Corporal	9605	8th Devonshire

NAME	RANK	NUMBER	BATTALION	NAME	RANK	NUMBER	BATTALION
Mewett, Frank	Private	55536	197th Coy MGC	Southard, Reginald	Lnce Corp.	30630	8th Devonshire
Pointon, Llewellyn	Sergeant	7317	2nd Border	Watson, Stanley	Private	23706	2nd Border
Rowe, Hubert	Private	50346	9th Devonshire	Wellington, William	Private	15747	9th Devonshire
Selley, Sidney	Corporal	30444	8th Devonshire	Wigley, Richard	Private	30697	8th Devonshire
Smith, Sam	Private	27023	2nd Border	Wood, William	Lnce Corp.	27118	2nd Border

SOLDIERS KILLED 9TH MAY 1917

NAME	RANK	NUMBER	BATTALION	NAME	RANK	NUMBER	BATTALION
Andrews, Reginald	Private	26499	8th Devonshire	Hannaford, Willam	Lnce Corp.	3/5109	8th Devonshire
Balsom, Frederick	Corporal	9086	8th Devonshire	Harris, John	Private	10829	2nd Border
				Hilton, Peter	Private	30244	2nd Border
Beale, Harry	Lnce Corp.	28604	8th Devonshire	Hocking, George	Private	30590	8th Devonshire
Beesley, Howard	Private	49007	8th Devonshire	Keegan, Thomas	Private	5504	2nd Border
				Kingdon, Frederick	Private	45622	8th Devonshire
Braddon, Fred	Private	28489	8th Devonshire	Le Ruez, Francis	Lnce Corp.	30691	8th Devonshire
Burrows, John	Private	30626	8th Devonshire	Lowery, George	Private	6764	2nd Border
Bush, Arthur	Private	30681	8th Devonshire	Madden, Daniel	Private	20952	2nd Border
Cann, Albert	Private	15405	8th Devonshire	Maddern, Willie	Private	33377	8th Devonshire
Clatworthy, Frederick	Lnce Corp.	30497	8th Devonshire	Maher, Sydney	Sergeant	18255	20th Coy MGC
Counter, William	Private	38057	8th Devonshire	Manning, George	Private	50330	9th Devonshire
Crabb, William	Private	45610	8th Devonshire	Martin, Charles	Lnce Corp.	10981	8th Devonshire
Crook, Frederick	Private	10627	8th Devonshire	Maskew, John	Private	26533	2nd Border
Crowle, Lyman	Private	33274	8th Devonshire	Massey, Reginald	Private	33498	8th Devonshire
Cumming, Lionel	2nd Lieut.		8th Devonshire	Morrish, Fred	Private	28777	8th Devonshire
Curtis, Henry	Private	33085	2nd Border	Parish, George	Private	24627	8th Devonshire
Davis, William	Corporal	16140	8th Devonshire	Parkin, William	Private	30673	8th Devonshire
Discombe, William	Private	24897	8th Devonshire	Patey, Ambrose	Private	14989	8th Devonshire
Dyer, Albert	Private	45673	8th Devonshire	Pearce, Claude	Lnce Corp.	45699	8th Devonshire
Foster, William	Private	10082	8th Devonshire	Peers, William	Private	27283	2nd Border
				Perry, Tracey	Private	27572	8th Devonshire
George, Wilfred	Private	45678	8th Devonshire	Reeves, Henry	Private	30682	8th Devonshire

NAME	RANK	NUMBER	BATTALION	NAME	RANK	NUMBER	BATTALION
Reynolds, Percy	Private	45702	8th Devonshire	Stamford, Joseph	Corporal	11671	8th Devonshire
Roach, Douglas	Private	11116	8th Devonshire	Sturt, Arthur	Private	57528	20th Coy MGC
Roberts, Stanley	Private	45703	8th Devonshire	Took, Wilford	Private	38096	8th Devonshire
Rousell, Percy	Private	30719	8th Devonshire	Trathen, James	Private	33406	8th Devonshire
Schofield, Thomas	Private	16020	8th Devonshire	Watkins, Charles	Corporal	8271	8th Devonshire
Scutts, John	Lnce Corp.	33398	8th Devonshire	Wilson, Charles	2nd Lieut.		2nd GH
Smith, Gordon	2nd Lieut.		8th Devonshire	Wood, John	Private	30726	8th Devonshire
Snell, Fred	Private	33312	8th Devonshire	Yelland, William	Private	20357	8th Devonshire

SOLDIERS KILLED 10TH MAY 1917

NAME	RANK	NUMBER	BATTALION	NAME	RANK	NUMBER	BATTALION
Barwick, William	Private	470858	528th Field Coy RE	Potter, Frederick	Private	22544	2nd Border
				Quinn, Hubert	Private	18216	2nd Border
Burns, Joseph	Private	S/9711	2nd GH	Reid, Donald	Private	S/40615	2nd GH
Garratt, Arthur	Private	32499	1st South Staffs	Townend, William	Private	49541	20th Manchester
Gibbins, William	Sapper	470517	528th Field Coy RE	Williamson, William	Private	8982	2nd Border
				Wolstenholme, Thomas	Private	30291	2nd Border
McLeod, William	Private	S/40581	2nd GH				

SOLDIERS KILLED 11TH MAY 1917

NAME	RANK	NUMBER	BATTALION	NAME	RANK	NUMBER	BATTALION
Ainsworth, James	Private	49553	21st Manchester	Earnshaw, William	Private	33889	21st Manchester
Ainsworth, Samuel	Private	49571	21st Manchester	Fitzsimmons, Thomas	Private	9461	21st Manchester
Barber, Thomas	Private	40633	21st Manchester	Graham, Thomas	Sapper	470559	528th Field Coy RE
Brooks, Alfred	Private	232448	2nd/2nd London	Haines, Thomas	Private	265244	2nd/7th WY
				Harris, Henry	Private	G/21378	2nd Queen's
Brown, Arthur	Private	49550	21st Manchester	Hartley, Abraham	Private	49569	21st Manchester
Claughan, Thomas	Gunner	56535	131st Heavy Bty RGA	Hayes, William	Private	49560	21st Manchester
Davies, Edwin	Private	30250	21st Manchester	Heasman, Charles	Corporal	G/40230	2nd Queen's
				Henman, Francis	Private	202485	2nd/1st London
Day, Frederick	Private	26817	20th Manchester				
Dunn, Frederick	Private	G/22317	2nd Queen's	Herriott, Vernon	Private	G/21408	2nd Queen's

NAME	RANK	NUMBER	BATTALION	NAME	RANK	NUMBER	BATTALION
Howson, George	Private	49579	21st Manchester	Taylor, James	Private	49946	21st Manchester
Lakey, Albert	Private	G/21231	2nd Queen's	Tew, Arthur	Private	32359	1st South Staffs
Ling, John	Private	G/21388	2nd Queen's				
Little, Arthur	Private	L/11028	2nd Queen's	Thwaites, John	Lnce Serg.	43528	21st Manchester
Mansell, Sidney	Private	201301	2nd/1st London	Tibbalds, Joseph	Lnce Corp.	G/40246	2nd Queen's
March, Thomas	Private	S/6485	2nd Queen's	Turner, James	Private	11021	21st Manchester
Philpot, Charles	Private	36742	21st Manchester	Turner, Leonard	Private	36746	21st Manchester
Pilling, James	Private	49944	21st Manchester	Wadsworth, Sam	Lnce Corp.	35629	21st Manchester
Rainford, William	Private	43497	21st Manchester	Warburton, Harry	Private	202636	21st Manchester
Ray, Henry	Corporal	40196	21st Manchester	Westcombe, Herbert	Private	38455	21st Manchester
Singleton, Robert	Private	37423	21st Manchester	Whitrod, Jack	Private	282403	2nd/4th London
Stackhouse, George	Private	31580	1st South Staffs	Wright, Edwin	Lnce Corp.	7608	21st Manchester
Sumner, Albert	Private	G/12983	2nd Queen's				
Tasker, John	Private	40661	21st Manchester				

SOLDIERS KILLED 12TH MAY 1917

NAME	RANK	NUMBER	BATTALION	NAME	RANK	NUMBER	BATTALION
Alker, William	Private	49588	21st Manchester	Daniels, Henry	Private	231241	2nd/2nd London
Barwick, Ernest	Private	266490	2nd/7th WY	Denholm, William	Private	66789	212th Coy MGC
Bowerman, Herbert	Private	G/37600	2nd Queen's				
Broadly, James	Private	265808	2nd/7th WY	Duxbury, Robert	Private	235186	2nd/7th WY
Brown, Percy	Lnce Corp.	13017	1st South Staffs	Eaton, George	Lnce Corp.	L/9700	2nd Queen's
				Fletcher, Joseph	Corporal	7978	1st South Staffs
Burkin, William	Private	G/5367	2nd Queen's				
Burn, Ernest	Private	266082	2nd/7th WY	Gilbank, Charles	Private	267183	2nd/7th WY
Burton, Percy	Captain		2nd/4th London	Gill, William	Private	235189	2nd/7th WY
				Goodall, David	Private	16677	1st South Staffs
Callander, John	Private	67863	212th Coy MGC	Griffiths, John	Private	G/22697	2nd Queen's
Chambers, John	Private	17304	1st South Staffs	Grigg, William	Lnce Corp.	232260	2nd/2nd London
Chapman, Theodore	Captain		2nd Queens's	Hall, Alfred	Private	21932	1st South Staffs
Cleveley, Alfred MM	Sergeant	9627	1st South Staffs	Harrison, James	Private	40092	1st South Staffs
Collins, Harry	Private	266145	2nd/7th WY				
Connell, Joseph	Private	43257	1st South Staffs	Hemsworth, Herbert	Private	265264	2nd/7th DOW
Cooney, Albert	Lieut.		291st Bde RFA	Henson, Percy	Private	43249	1st South Staffs

NAME	RANK	NUMBER	BATTALION	NAME	RANK	NUMBER	BATTALION
Hiley, Tom	Private	266936	2nd/7th WY	Poole, Edward	Private	31214	1st South Staffs
Ingram, Ernest	Private	19661	1st South Staffs	Puttock, George	Private	G/39244	2nd Queen's
Jarvis, William	Private	L/10617	2nd Queen's	Radford, Ernest	Lnce Corp.	32655	1st South Staffs
Jones, James	Private	6502	1st South Staffs	Richardson, Adam	Private	31765	1st South Staffs
Kettlewell, George	Private	267001	2nd/7th WY	Richardson Edward	Private	L/11381	2nd Queen's
Lathe, William	Private	16419	1st South Staffs	Riley, Harry	Private	266147	2nd/7th WY
Leaver, Samuel	Sergeant	19178	21st Manchester	Robinson, Shirley	Private	32660	1st South Staffs
Lee, James	Private	266431	2nd/7th WY	Rowland, Thomas	Private	267190	2nd/7th WY
Lockley, George	Private	13102	1st South Staffs	Rubery, William	Private	16876	1st South Staffs
Macey, Frederick	Private	G/21280	2nd Queen's	Rutherford, Abraham	Private	267050	2nd/7th WY
Macmillan, Frederick	Private	233839	2nd/2nd London	Sanford, John	Private	24108	1st South Staffs
				Sharman, Joseph	Private	23105	1st South Staffs
Marshall, William	Private	23073	1st South Staffs	Sharp, William	Private	24383	1st South Staffs
				Shepherd, Irvine	Private	268568	2nd/7th WY
Maxtone, Benjamin	Private	83168	212th Coy MGC	Smith, Godfrey	2nd Lieut.		2nd Queen's
Mearis, Francis	Private	266271	2nd/7th WY	Smith, William	Private	8909	1st South Staffs
Metcalfe, John	Private	266329	2nd/7th WY				
Miller, Norman	Private	265655	2nd/7th WY	Spencer, Holdsworth	Private	268696	2nd/7th WY
Morris, Thomas	Private	18126	1st South Staffs	Stenner, Richard	Private	233836	2nd/2nd London
Moss, Edmund	Private	G/22341	2nd Queen's	Stone, Henry	Gunner	13588	49th Bty 40th Bde RFA
Munton, Frederick	Private	266473	2nd/7thWY				
Payne, William	Private	19782	1st South Staffs	Stubbs, Albert	Private	20063	1st South Staffs
Pearce, Arthur	Private	32468	1st South Staffs	Vass, Arthur	Lnce Corp.	G/24773	2nd Queen's
Penketh, Alfred	2nd Lieut.		1st South Staffs	Vaughan, Harry	Private	18946	1st South Staffs
Phillips, Albert	Private	G/22466	2nd Queen's	Welch, William	Private	49561	21st Manchester
Pilling, Joe	Private	235192	2nd/7th WY	Wilson, Richard	Sergeant	9005	1st South Staffs
Pinnock, Harry	Lnce Corp.	32538	1st South Staffs	Woodmass, W	Private	267642	2nd/7th WY
Pirie, Francis	Private	283383	2nd/4th London	Yeomans, Frank	Private	31870	1st South Staffs
Pitt, Albert	Private	32651	1st South Staffs				

SOLDIERS KILLED 13TH MAY 1917

NAME	RANK	NUMBER	BATTALION	NAME	RANK	NUMBER	BATTALION
Addison, Herbert	Private	1686	2nd Royal Warwick's	Balcombe, Richard	Private	23556	2nd Royal Warwick's
Bagnall, Charles	Lnce Corp.	17443	1st South Staffs	Barker, Theodore	2nd Lieut.		22nd Manchester

NAME	RANK	NUMBER	BATTALION	NAME	RANK	NUMBER	BATTALION
Barratt, Harold	Lnce Corp.	15/1542	2nd Royal Warwick's	Franks, Arthur	Private	252473	2nd/3rd London
Bates, James	Private	40760	22nd Manchester	Gordon, Israel	Private	283397	2nd/4th London
Bayford, Lewis	Private	G/21346	2nd Queen's	Handley, Joseph	Private	39987	22nd Manchester
Beck, John	Private	31025	1st South Staffs	Heath, Charles	Private	9973	2nd Royal Warwick's
Booker, Joseph	Private	39411	22nd Manchester	Higson, Thomas	Private	47929	22nd Manchester
Bookless, Charles	Private	204276	2nd/1st London	Hillman, Albert	Private	2980	2nd Royal Warwick's
Bowles, Samuel	Private	21777	22nd Manchester	Hirst, Harry	Private	265978	2nd/7th WY
Bradford, Ernest	Private	23684	2nd Royal Warwick's	Holloway, Walter	Private	12932	2nd Queen's
Brett, John	Private	40693	22nd Manchester	Howard, Percy	Private	G/22327	2nd Queen's
				Howarth, James	Gunner	117372 V	31st T.M. Bty RFA
Bryan, Thomas	Private	16316	22nd Manchester	Jackson, Thomas	Lnce Corp.	32617	1st Bn South Staffs
Bunting, George	Private	266315	2nd/7th WY	Jolley, George	Private	231234	2nd/2nd/ London
Carpenter, Thomas	Private	282308	2nd/4th London				
Coleman, Timothy	Private	40042	1st South Staffs	Judge, Thomas	Private	25957	22nd Manchester
Collard, Edward	Private	G/24742	2nd Queen's	Kendall, William	Private	44291	22nd Manchester
Conroy, Frederick	Private	S/43517	2nd GH	Lands, Charles	Private	281709	2nd/4th London
Crown, Frederick	Private	G/22702	2nd Queen's				
Daley, Edward	Private	45202	22nd Manchester	Maloney, Austin	Private	49251	22nd Manchester
Deakin, Harold	Private	18903	2nd Royal Warwick's	Martin, Frederick	Private	20107	22nd Manchester
Derbyshire, Thomas	Lnce Corp.	40047	1st South Staffs	Martindale, Thomas	Private	47644	22nd Manchester
Drake, Walter	Private	26994	2nd Royal Warwick's	Matravers, Thomas	Private	G/39293	2nd Queen's
				Milton, William MM	Corporal	L/10036	2nd Queen's
Duguid, Charles DSO MC	Captain		22nd Manchester	Moore, George	Private	10001	1st South Staffs
Ellis, William	Private	G/5469	2nd Queen's	Myers, J Harry	Private	276003	22nd Manchester
Evans, John	Private	32597	1st South Staffs	Ostler, Arthur	Private	23575	2nd Royal Warwick's
Everett, Edward	Private	200049	2nd/3rd London	Pitcher, Walter	Private	252889	2nd/3rd London
Fallowfield, William	Private	32598	1st South Staffs	Povah, William	Private	16314	22nd Manchester
Fernley, Richard	Private	21654	22nd Manchester	Powis, Charles	Private	3327	2nd Royal Warwick's
Finch, William	Private	49592	21st Manchester	Robinson, Frank MC	Lieut.		22nd Manchester
Foster, Robert	Private	32735	22nd Manchester	Rolfe, Herbert	Private	252323	2nd/3rd London
Francis, Henry	Driver	70191 V	31st T.M. Bty RFA	Shepherd, Arthur	Private	27179	2nd Royal Warwick's

NAME	RANK	NUMBER	BATTALION	NAME	RANK	NUMBER	BATTALION
Steadman, William	Lnce Corp.	282216	2nd/4th London	Trump, Raymond	Private	510413	58th Div. Signal Coy RE
Sykes, George	Private	61647	206th Coy MGC	Wallace, Henry	Private	1023	2nd Royal Warwick's
Teagle, John	Private	282352	2nd/4th London	Watson, William	Private	282330	2nd/4th London
Teare, James	Private	30038	2nd Royal Warwick's	Weiner, Philip	Private	283399	2nd/4th London
Thornton, John	Private	40082	1st South Staffs	Wingfield, Albert	Lnce Corp.	709	2nd Royal Warwick's
Toogood, Frederick	Private	510523	58th Div. Signal Coy RE	Witton, Hyla	Private	18983	1st South Staffs
Townsend, Arthur	Private	G/21335	2nd Queen's	Young, James	Private	34967	91st Coy MGC

SOLDIERS KILLED 14TH MAY 1917

NAME	RANK	NUMBER	BATTALION	NAME	RANK	NUMBER	BATTALION
Abbotts, Frank	Private	308122	2nd/7th DOW	Doel, James	Sergeant	231729	2nd/2nd London
Adams, Wilfred	2nd Lieut.	212th	Coy MGC	Dowling, John	Private	9866	1st RWF
Appleyard, Laurence	Private	232462	2nd/2nd London	Dunn, George	Private	282233	2nd/4th London
Barker, John	Private	40210	20th Manchester	Enderby, Harry	Private	268433	2nd/7th DOW
Bentley, George	Lnce Corp.	282660	2nd/4th London	Felstead, Arthur	Private	24386	1st South Staffs
Birchall, Richard	Lnce Corp.	53771	1st RWF	Foley, Leonard	Private	268402	2nd/7th DOW
Blacker, William	Private	282592	2nd/4th London	Forshew, Horace	Corporal	305235	2nd/7th DOW
Brads, Herbert	Private	200384	2nd/1st London	Franklin, George	Sergeant	281518	2nd/4th London
Brook, Amon	Private	306795	2nd/7th DOW	Gadd, Horace	Private	282718	2nd/4th London
Champion, Percy	Private	203546	2nd/1st London	Hamburg, Nathan	Private	283366	2nd/4th London
Chapman, George	Private	232625	2nd/2nd London	Hamer, Edward	Private	282470	2nd/4th London
Chapman, Horace	Private	86482	212th Coy MGC	Hidden, Frederick	Lnce Serg.	231748	2nd/4th London
Chenery, Edwin	Private	203478	2nd/1st London	Hopcroft, Arthur	Sergeant	281346	2nd/4th London
Clarke, Leonard	Private	202672	2nd/1st London	Horton, Richard	Private	233827	2nd/2nd London
Conway, Arthur	Private	282222	2nd/4th London	Hunt, Charles	Private	282622	2nd/4th London
Cooper, Bertram	Private	231675	2nd/2nd London	Hurst, James	Private	267245	1st RWF
Copeland, James	Private	232501	2nd/2nd London	Kiddy, John	Private	305913	2nd/7th DOW

NAME	RANK	NUMBER	BATTALION	NAME	RANK	NUMBER	BATTALION
Lear, Arthur	Private	232466	2nd/2nd London	Punter, Joseph	Private	283413	2nd/4th London
Lockley, William	Private	8899	1st RWF	Reed, John	Private	G/21093	2nd Queen's
Lord, Thomas	Private	63306	1st RWF	Robins, Percy	Sergeant	282154	2nd/4th London
Madley, Lewis	2nd Lieut.		1st RWF				
Markham, Jack	Corporal	23025	1st South Staffs	Rollison, George	Private	307031	2nd/7th DOW
Marshall, William	Private	232654	2nd/2nd London	Rose, Stanley	Lnce Corp.	43617	1st RWF
				Rosenbaum, Solomon	Private	203115	2nd/4th London
McClary, Arthur	Private	282564	2nd/4th London	Shepherd, Arthur	Private	280940	2nd/4th London
Metcalfe, Reginald	Lnce Serg.	205254	2nd/7th DOW	Sims, Francis	Private	26748	1st RWF
Miller, Arthur	Private	282431	2nd/4th London	Stoaling, Thomas	2nd Lieut.		2nd/4th London
Morgan, Robert	Private	53802	1st RWF	Stroud, Horace	Private	S/6995	2nd Queen's
Mortimer, Ernest	Private	306635	2nd/7th DOW	Taylor, John	Private	5277	1st RWF
				Thompson, William	Private	282372	2nd/4th London
Needham, Samuel	Private	53918	1st RWF				
Olsen, John	Private	53791	1st RWF	Thorogood, Benjamin	Private	65637	206th Coy MGC
Palmer, Frank	Private	231544	2nd/2nd London	Van Lockem, Noah	Private	202630	2nd/1st London
Parker, Henry	Private	282562	2nd/4th London	Vincent, Thomas	Private	202843	2nd/1st London
Parkes, Charles	Private	27033	2nd Royal Warwick's	Wallis, Reginald	Private	233632	2nd/2nd London
Parry, John	Private	53672	1st RWF	Ward, Edwin	Private	30668	2nd/7th DOW
Pilkington, Thomas	Private	54150	1st RWF				
Pitty, Thomas	Private	283426	2nd/4th London	Ward, Robert	Private	56651	1st RWF
				Wheatley, Richmond	Private	52216	1st RWF
Powell, Edward	Private	55715	1st RWF	Whitbread, William DCM MM CSM		10677	1st RWF
Pratt, Ernest	2nd Lieut.		2nd/4th London				
Pugh, Roger	Private	55073	1st RWF	Zeiler, Maurice	Lnce Corp.	29566	1st RWF

SOLDIERS KILLED 15TH MAY 1917

NAME	RANK	NUMBER	BATTALION	NAME	RANK	NUMBER	BATTALION
Anslow, James	Private	252505	2nd/3rd London	Bealey, A	Lnce Corp.	510388	58th Signal Coy RE
Baker, Arthur	Private	202334	2nd/3rd London	Beams, William	Private	282228	2nd/4th London
Baker, George	Private	252727	2nd/3rd London	Beck, Aubrey	2nd Lieut.		2nd HAC
Baker, Henry	Private	252739	2nd/3rd London	Beckett, William	Private	283841	2nd/4th London
Barbieri, Joseph	Private	282649	2nd/4th London	Bishop, Horace	Private	9733	2nd HAC
				Bizat, Louis	Private	283885	2nd/4th London
Barton, Charles	Private	231313	2nd/2nd London	Bloom, Jack	Private	282011	2nd/4th London

NAME	RANK	NUMBER	BATTALION	NAME	RANK	NUMBER	BATTALION
Botting, Henry	Private	252764	2nd/3rd London	Grant, William	Private	233818	2nd/2nd London
Bow, Percy	Private	232583	2nd/2nd London	Gunn, Albert	Private	9662	2nd HAC
Bremer, Henry	Private	233888	2nd/2nd London	Hall, Hugh	2nd Lieut.		2nd/3rd London
Brown, Benjamin	Private	252758	2nd/3rd London	Harsant, Frank	Private	7477	2nd HAC
				Hart, Ernest	Private	9231	2nd HAC
Brown, Charles	Private	252431	2nd/3rd London	Hasler, Lancelot	Private	283867	2nd/4th London
Brown, George	Private	19746	21st Manchester	Heath, William	Lnce Corp.	232613	2nd/2nd London
Buckley, Edward	Private	232470	2nd /2nd London	Hood, George DCM	Corporal	36003	1st RWF
Bushell, George	Private	252807	2nd/3rd London	Hood, Percy	Private	233723	2nd/2nd London
Carter, Alexander	Private	232581	2nd/2nd London	Huff, Adolf	Private	65525	206th Coy MGC
Chalk, Henry	Private	252393	2nd/3rd London	Hunt, Herbert	Private	9644	2nd HAC
				Jackson, Wilfred	Sergeant	4246	2nd HAC
Clay, Robert	Private	252511	2nd/3rd London	James, Herbert	Private	252398	2nd/3rd London
Copps, Harry	Private	7282	2nd HAC	Jenkins, George	Private	9247	2nd HAC
Corne, Charles	Private	282342	2nd/4th London	Johnson, Rowland	Private	9496	2nd HAC
				Jones, Edward	Private	36798	1st RWF
Cornish, James	Private	7657	2nd HAC	Kelsey, Joseph	Private	283341	2nd/4th London
Crompton, Charles	Private	9708	2nd HAC	Keyes, Charles	Private	266979	1st RWF
Cutting, Charles	Private	4943	2nd HAC	King, Frank	Private	9057	2nd HAC
Dawson, Alfred	Private	252524	2nd/3rd London	Kingston, William	Private	251212	2nd/3rd London
Dibley, Frank	Private	252270	2nd/3rd London	Lambourn, Ernest	Private	232611	2nd/2nd London
Double, Henry	Private	9627	2nd HAC	Laming, William	Private	9789	2nd HAC
Driscoll, Denis	Private	283240	2nd/3rd London	Le Gros, Claude	Private	6980	2nd HAC
				Lee, Harry	Private	232369	2nd/2nd London
Duhigh, William	Private	252520	2nd/3rd London	Lever, Harry	Private	281522	2nd/4th London
Elphick, Christopher	Private	7379	2nd HAC	Lillie, Charles	Private	56632	1st RWF
Exall, Sydney	Private	282329	2nd/4th London	Lipsham, Alfred	Private	231652	2nd/2nd London
Faldo, Henry	Private	252708	2nd/3rd London	Lufkin, Charles	Private	9248	2nd HAC
				Matthews, Frederick	Private	252518	2nd/3rd London
Farrow, Percy	Corporal	5227	2nd HAC				
Forrest, Ernest	Lnce Corp.	6855	2nd HAC	McCormack, Frederick	Private	282368	2nd/4th London
Franklin, Cyril	Corporal	5520	2nd HAC				
Fraser, George	2nd Lieut.		2nd HAC	Meech, Ernest	Private	9801	2nd HAC
Friend, Edward	Private	7465	2nd HAC	Monroe, Arthur	Private	9225	2nd HAC
Garrad, Herbert	Private	6744	2nd HAC	Morrell, William	Private	6967	2nd HAC
Gilbert, Ernest	Private	232451	2nd/2nd London	Mosford, Albert	Private	29867	21st Manchester
Goldstone, Mark	Private	232500	2nd/2nd London	Mycock, Alfred	Private	18671	21st Manchester

NAME	RANK	NUMBER	BATTALION	NAME	RANK	NUMBER	BATTALION
Osborne, William	Private	18674	21st Manchester	Sheehy, John	Private	232287	2nd/2nd London
Painter, Charles	Sergeant	281508	2nd/4th London	Sheppard, Herbert	Private	282700	2nd/4th London
Park, Edward	Private	252417	2nd/3rd London	Simpson, Percy	Private	233872	2nd/2nd London
Pawsey, Frederick	Private	281466	2nd/4th London	Smith, Arthur	Private	9778	2nd HAC
Peace, Frank	Private	282445	2nd/4th London	Smith, William	Private	252499	2nd/3rd London
Pearman, William	Private	232440	2nd/2nd London	Spears, Eric	Private	9819	2nd HAC
				Springfield, Roland	Private	9820	2nd HAC
Peel, Edward	Private	4968	2nd HAC	St. Quintin, Clifford	Lieut.		2nd HAC
Potter, William	Lnce Corp.	201926	2nd/4th London	Steggal, William	Private	203526	2nd/2nd London
Poynton, William	Private	53727	1st RWF	Sullivan, Richard	Private	5733	1st RWF
Price, Norman	Private	9831	2nd HAC	Taylor, Robert	Private	7149	2nd HAC
Pritchard, John	Captain		2nd HAC	Thomas, Harold	Private	9909	2nd HAC
Pulleyn, Herbert	Private	6953	2nd HAC	Thomas, George	Private	231168	2nd/2nd London
Radley, Henry	Private	232536	2nd/2nd London	Thompson, Joseph	Sergeant	4756	1st RWF
				Tilley, Thomas	Private	40336	20th Manchester
Rainbird, Edward	Private	252814	2nd/3rd London	Toop, Edwin	Private	251043	2nd/3rd London
Ringer, Arthur	Private	283326	2nd/4th London	Wale, Sydney	Sergeant	321085	2nd/6th London
Ritter, Henry	Private	283402	2nd/4th London	Watkins, George	Private	56650	1st RWF
Rogers, Leon	Private	281450	2nd/4th London	Whitbread, William	Private	28201	2nd/4th London
Rossa, Thomas	Private	282712	2nd/4th London	Whiting, Edward	Private	9466	2nd HAC
Sanson, Arthur	Private	281365	2nd/4th London	Williams, Sydney	Private	252715	2nd/3rd London
Schofield, Leonard	Private	40364	20th Manchester	Wincles, Alfred	Private	282336	2nd/4th London
Shaw, John	Private	38702	21st Manchester	Wood, Eric	Private	202439	2nd/4th London
Shead, Henry	Private	253594	2nd/3rd London	Woodger, Noel	Sergeant	3644	2nd HAC

SOLDIERS KILLED 16TH MAY 1917

NAME	RANK	NUMBER	BATTALION	NAME	RANK	NUMBER	BATTALION
Baker, Edward	Private	282279	2nd/4th London	Coaker, Albert	Sergeant	O/3053	Royal Army Service Corps
Barrow, Ernest	Private	252768	2nd/3rd London	Curtis, John	Private	282476	2nd/4th London
Brider, Percy	Private	252875	2nd/3rd London	Godding, Ernest	Private	252689	2nd/3rd London
Chapkoski, Sydney	Corporal	251374	2nd/3rd London	Goldspring, Sidney	Private	252481	2nd/3rd London

NAME	RANK	NUMBER	BATTALION	NAME	RANK	NUMBER	BATTALION
Jones, Herbert	Private	300824	2nd/5th London	Simper, Joseph	Private	252823	2nd/3rd London
Lane, Frank	2nd Lieut.		2nd/1st London	Sizer, Sidney	Private	252734	2nd/3rd London
Lawler, Daniel	Private	252366	2nd/3rd London	Stubbs, John	Private	O/2300	RAOC
Lawrence, Robert	Private	282293	2nd/4th London	Symons, William	Private	252316	2nd/3rd London
Lewis, John	Private	282501	2nd/4th London	Taylor, George	Private	301743	2nd/5th London
Litchfield, Henry	Private	253372	2nd/3rd London	Theobald, Bertie	Private	282208	2nd/4th London
O'Brien, Robert	Private	252776	2nd/3rd London	Tyler, William	Private	281567	2nd/4th London
Peek, Donald	Private	251553	2nd/3rd London	Ware, Joseph	Private	252506	2nd/3rd London
Preston, George	Private	O/7017	RAOC	Waters, Richard	Private	202040	2nd/3rd London
Rickard, Thomas	Private	O/4071	RAOC	Williams, William	Private	252529	2nd/3rd London
Roper, Thomas	Rifleman	302275	2nd/5th London	Willis, Harold	Lnce Serg.	251089	2nd/3rd London
Rushman, William	Private	283831	2nd/5th London	Withey, Albert	Lnce Corp	282423	2nd/4th London
Selby, Arthur	Lnce Corp.	282493	2nd/4th London	Worley, Herbert	Sergeant	281215	2nd/4th London

SOLDIERS KILLED 17TH MAY 1917

NAME	RANK	NUMBER	BATTALION	NAME	RANK	NUMBER	BATTALION
Champion, Arthur	Private	231505	2nd/2nd London	Purton, William	Private	251243	2nd/3rd London
Crowley, Edward	Private	203483	2nd/1st London	Robins, Nathaniel	Private	252778	2nd/3rd London
Dowton, James	Private	204375	2nd/1st London	Rough, Christopher	Private	252794	2nd/3rd London
Fone, Arthur	Private	203967	2nd/1st London	Settree, James	Rifleman	372509	2nd/8th London
Herring, Arthur	Private	252670	2nd/3rd London	Spear, Mark	Private	202776	2nd/1st London
Hunt, George	Private	252763	2nd/3rd London	Spencer, George	Private	252441	2nd/3rd London
Kerry, Richard	Rifleman	373129	2nd/8th London	White, George	Corporal	252388	2nd/3rd London
Parrett, Percy	Rifleman	302427	2nd/5th London	Winter, Percy	Private	252629	2nd/3rd London

SOLDIERS KILLED 18TH MAY 1917

NAME	RANK	NUMBER	BATTALION	NAME	RANK	NUMBER	BATTALION
Brothers, Fred	Sergeant	200493	2nd/1st London	Chapman, Walter	Rifleman	301457	2nd/5th London

NAME	RANK	NUMBER	BATTALION	NAME	RANK	NUMBER	BATTALION
Goodchild, William	Rifleman	302463	2nd/5th London	Parsons, John	Private	22696	1st South Staffs
Harris, Alfred	Rifleman	374062	2nd/8th London	Ringrose, Raymond	Rifleman	372542	2nd/8th London
Horley, William	Private	204483	2nd/1st London	Scholefield, Arthur	2nd Lieut.		2nd/5th London
Jones, Albert	Private	204421	2nd/1st London	Sheppard, Bertram	Corporal	300387	2nd/5th London
Nelki, Albert	Rifleman	300980	2nd/5th London	Sims, Edward	Rifleman	302254	2nd/5th London

SOLDIERS KILLED 19TH MAY 1917

NAME	RANK	NUMBER	BATTALION	NAME	RANK	NUMBER	BATTALION
Goldstein, Frederick	Private	281362	2nd/4th London	Scutt, Powell	Rifleman	303860	2nd/5th London
Rayner, Harry	Rifleman	320229	2nd/6th London				

SOLDIERS KILLED 20TH MAY 1917

NAME	RANK	NUMBER	BATTALION	NAME	RANK	NUMBER	BATTALION
Baker, W	Private	202611	2nd/1st London	Garland, John	Private	353431	2nd/7th London
Child, William	Private	202795	2nd/1st London	Hughes, Alfred	Private	202610	2nd/1st London
Coulson, George	Bombardier	810578	232nd Bde RFA	Kellow, Reginald	Private	200361	2nd/1st London
Cropley, Robert	Private	13255	198th Coy MGC	King, Leonard	Rifleman	321872	2nd/6th London
Crump, Ernest	Private	202609	2nd/1st London	Lloyd, George	Rifleman	321902	2nd/6th London
Elsom, Thomas	Private	202580	2nd/1st London	Nixon, Thomas	Gunner	129122	D Bty 46th Bde RFA
Fordy, Frank	Private	232502	2nd/2nd London	Platt. Harry	Private	203589	2nd/1st London
French, William	Private	203488	2nd/1st London	Stone, William	Private	204587	2nd/1st London
Frith, Charles	Corporal	43588	198th Coy MGC	Whittlesey, William	Rifleman	321942	2nd/6th London

SOLDIERS KILLED 21ST MAY 1917

NAME	RANK	NUMBER	BATTALION	NAME	RANK	NUMBER	BATTALION
Alderton, Thomas	Rifleman	323694	2nd/6th London	Ambrose, Albert	Rifleman	320725	2nd/6th London

NAME	RANK	NUMBER	BATTALION
Bailey, Harry	Rifleman	345007	2nd/6th London
Bain, Archibald	Rifleman	321720	2nd/6th London
Bannister, Frederick	Corporal	450508	2nd/11th London
Barker, Frank	Rifleman	321689	2nd/6th London
Barnett, Morris	Rifleman	452180	2nd/11th London
Bence, Richard	Rifleman	321556	2nd/6th London
Bindoff, Philip	Rifleman	321854	2nd/6th London
Binns, John	Rifleman	323507	2nd/6th London
Bint, Philip	Private	352263	2nd/7th London
Brightley, Edward	Private	352595	2nd/7th London
Brown, Alfred	Private	352166	2nd/7th London
Carpenter, Ernest	Rifleman	323619	2nd/6th London
Chaplin, William	Rifleman	321888	2nd/6th London
Childs, William	Rifleman	323577	2nd/6th London
Coldicott, Hubert	2nd Lieut.		2nd/6th London
Collett, John	Rifleman	323979	2nd/6th London
Cook, Frederick	Rifleman	322257	2nd/6th London
Cope, Harold	Private	242751	2nd/6th KOYLI
Cotton, Harold	Rifleman	322279	2nd/6th London
Cousins, Frank	Rifleman	321985	2nd/6th London
Cue, Frederick	Rifleman	323624	2nd/6th London
Cutler, Roland	Private	241954	2nd/5th KOYLI
Darvell, John	Rifleman	322182	2nd/6th London
Dorsett, Alfred	Private	352290	2nd/7th London
Drake, Edward	Rifleman	322540	2nd/6th London
Ead, William	Private	204462	2nd/1st London
Eckford. Henry	Drummer	202201	2nd/1st London
Edward, Herbert	Sergeant	320803	2nd/6th London
Ehrenberg, Joseph	Rifleman	322404	2nd/6th London
Emery, Ernest	Rifleman	321981	2nd/6th London
England, Albert	Rifleman	322436	2nd/6th London
Evans, Charles	Rifleman	321852	2nd/6th London
Farnes, William	Rifleman	322492	2nd/6th London
Fisher, James	Private	323702	2nd/6th London
Gardner, Percy	Rifleman	322297	2nd/6th London
German, George	Sergeant	321058	2nd/6th London
Goldacre, George	Rifleman	322569	2nd/6th London
Golding, Frank	2nd Lieut.		2nd/1st London
Gray, Victor	Sergeant	320790	2nd/6th London
Grimes, Alexander	Rifleman	320955	2nd/6th London
Gunning, Sidney	Rifleman	322430	2nd/6th London
Halnon, Arthur	Rifleman	323975	2nd/6th London
Hartley, William	Captain		2nd/6th London
Hayworth, Charles	Rifleman	5305	2nd/6th London
Herbert, Reginald	Lieut.		2nd/11th London
Higlett, Henry	Rifleman	322876	2nd/6th London
Hunter, Samuel	Rifleman	322294	2nd/6th London
Jarvis, Walter	Rifleman	322301	2nd/6th London
Juler, Frederick	Rifleman	321546	2nd/6th London
Lewcock, William	Rifleman	320950	2nd/6th London
Macey, Walter	Sergeant	320654	2nd/6th London
Martin, Frederick	Rifleman	322382	2nd/6th London

NAME	RANK	NUMBER	BATTALION	NAME	RANK	NUMBER	BATTALION
Massey, Charles	Rifleman	321966	2nd/6th London	Smith, Charles	Rifleman	323599	2nd/6th London
Matthews, Sidney	Lnce Corp.	320626	2nd/6th London	Smith, Frederick	Rifleman	320224	2nd/6th London
Montandon, Edward	Rifleman	322411	2nd/6th London	Spink, Christopher	Rifleman	322425	2nd/5th London
Murray, Patrick	Rifleman	323525	2nd/6th London	Spriggs, William	Rifleman	322295	2nd/6th London
Oman, Daniel	Lnce Corp.	351114	2nd/7th London	Stables, Ernest	Private	58419	198th Coy MGC
Pageot, Leon	Rifleman	345001	2nd/6th London	Talbott, Herberte	Rifleman	320194	2nd/6th London
Partridge, Allen	Rifleman	322322	2nd/6th London	Tarran, James	Corporal	320744	2nd/6th London
Patterson, George	Rifleman	321750	2nd/6th London	Taylor, William	Rifleman	322406	2nd/6th London
Pead, Frank	Rifleman	322392	2nd/6th London	Thompson, Robert	Rifleman	321761	2nd/6th London
Plummer, Alfred	Rifleman	323790	2nd/6th London	Tinsley, Edward	Sergeant	43900	198th Coy MGC
Postle, Arthur	Rifleman	322417	2nd/6th London	Tunmer, William	Rifleman	321730	2nd/6th London
Potter, Harold	Corporal	320700	2nd/6th London	Twyford, Frank	Rifleman	321460	2nd/6th London
Rees, Alfred	Private	452785	2nd/11th London	Warne, Henry	Private	321117	2nd/6th London
Richards, Frederick	Rifleman	345011	2nd/6th London	Wells, William	Rifleman	322489	2nd/6th London
Rowland, John	Rifleman	320141	2nd/6th London	Williams, Albert	Rifleman	322282	2nd/6th London
Ruse, Charles	Rifleman	320861	2nd/6th London	Williams, James	Rifleman	322280	2nd/6th London
See, Charles	Rifleman	452890	2nd/11th London	Wiltshire, Huse	Lnce Corp	322429	2nd/6th London
Singer, Walter	Rifleman	321660	2nd/6th London	Wraith, Percy	Rifleman	323601	2nd/6th London
Smith, Archibald	Rifleman	320411	2nd/6th London	Young, Charles	Rifleman	323403	2nd/6th London

ABBREVIATIONS

Bty – Battery
Border – Border Regiment
Devonshire – Devonshire Regiment
HAC – Honourable Artillery Company
DOW – Duke of Wellington Regiment
FA – Field Ambulance
GH – Gordon Highlanders
HB MGC – Heavy Branch Machine Gun Corps (Tanks)
HB RGA – Heavy Battery Royal Garrison Artillery

KOYLI – Kings Own Yorkshire Light Infantry
Lnce Corp. – Lance Corporal
Lnce Serg. – Lance Sergeant
London – London Regiment
MGC – Machine Gun Corps
Manchester – Manchester Regiment
Queen's – Queen's Royal West Surrey Regiment
RAOC – Royal Army Ordnance Corps
RE – Royal Engineers

RFA – Royal Field Artillery
RGA – Royal garrison Artillery
RWR – Royal Welch Fusiliers
Royal Warwick's – Royal Warwick'shires
South Staffs – South Staffordshire
SP BDE RE – Special Brigade Royal Engineers
WY – West Yorkshire Regiment
Y&L – York and Lancaster Regiment

Source for appendices: Yves Fohlen Bullecourt Database: compiled from CWGC and AWM roll of Honour

BIBLIOGRAPHY

PUBLISHED SOURCES

A Brigadier in France, Hanway R. Cumming, Jonathan Cape 1922

A Company of Tanks, Major W.H.L. Watson, William Blackwood and Sons, Edinburgh and London 1920

Balnarring to Bullecourt: A Tribute to a Soldier, Kevin Davies, 2008

Bullecourt: Arras: Battleground Europe, Graham Keech, Pen and Sword 1999

'Conceal, Create, Confuse': Deception as a British Battlefield Tactic in the First World War, Martin Davies, Spellmount, 2009

Die Osterlacht bie Arras: Riechsarchive, Berlin 1929

Die Württemberger im Weltkrieg, Otto von Moser, 1927

Don't Forget Me Cobber, Robin S. Corfield, Corfield and Company 2000

Douglas Haig and the First World War, J.P. Harris, Cambridge University Press 2008

Forward Undeterred, History of 23rd Battalion, Ron Austin

Haig's Generals, Ian Beckett and Steven Corvi, Pen and Sword 2006

History of the Great War Military Operations: France and Belgium 1917, Cyril Falls, 1940

History of the Post Office Rifles 8th Battalion City of London Regiment 1914–1918, Gale and Polden Ltd, Wellington Works 1919

History of The Queen's Royal Regiment, Colonel H.C. Wylly, Gale and Polden Ltd

'How the Bullecourt was Won', Max Pemberton, in *The War Illustrated*, 8th June 1917

In Good Company, An Account of the 6th Machine Gun Company AIF 1915–19, Lieutenant William Carne, Melbourne 1937

Massacre on the Marne: The Life and Death of the 2nd/5th Battalion West Yorkshire Regiment in the Great War, Fraser Skirrow, Pen and Sword 2007

Military Operations, France and Belgium 1917, Captain Cyril Falls, Macmillan 1940

Official History of the Australian Army Medical Services, 1914–1918: The Western Front, 1940

Official History of Australia in the War of 1914–18, Volume 1, Charles Bean, Angus and Robertson 1922

Official History of Australia in the War of 1914–18, Volume 4, Charles Bean, Angus and Robertson 1938

Pereginations of an Australian Prisoner of War, the Experiences of an Australian Soldier in Germany and Bolshevik Russia, Private T.E. Taylor, 1932

'Playing a Man's Game', Captain Percy Toft MC in the *Queensland Digger* 2nd December 1935

Post Office Rifles, 8th Battalion City of London Regiment 1914–1918, Gale and Poledon 1919

Soldering On, General Sir Hubert Gough, Arthur Baker, London, 1954

Storm of Steel, Ernst Junger, Zimmerman and Zimmerman, New York, 1985

The Blood Tub: General Gough and The Battle of Bullecourt 1917, Jonathan Walker, Spellmount, 1998

The Cast Iron Sixth: A History of the Sixth Battalion, London Regiment (The City of London Rifles), Captain E. Godfrey, MC, F.S. Stapleton 1938

The Devonshire Regiment 1914–1918, C.T. Atkinson, Eland Brothers, Exeter 1926

The History and Records of the Queen Victoria's Rifles 1792–1922, Major Cuthbert Keeson, Constable, 1923

The Honourable Artillery Company Journal, Volume 1, 1923

The Honourable Artillery Company Journal, Volume 37, 1960

The Honourable Artillery Company 1914–1919, Major G. Goold Walker, Seeley, Service and Co. Ltd

The Seventh Division 1914–1918, C.T. Atkinson, 1926

Jacka's Mob, Edgar Rule, Angus and Robertson Limited 1933

Jacka VC, Australia's Finest Soldier, Ian Grant, Sun Books 1990

Over the Fence, Sydney Shaw, Arthur H. Stockwell Ltd, Ilfracombe, Devon 1977

Sportsmen Parsons in Peace and War, Mrs. S. Menzies, Hutchinson and Co. London

Tank Warfare, F. Mitchell MC, Thomas Nelson and Sons Ltd 1933

Terriers in the Trenches, Charles Messenger, Picton Publishing 1982

The Cast Iron Sixth, Captain E.G. Godfrey MC, F.S. Stapleton 1938

'The Fighting Thirteenth' The History of the Thirteenth Battalion by T.A. White, Tyrells Limited Sydney 1924

The Old Sixteenth, Captain C. Longmore, the History Committee of the 16th Battalion Association, 1929

The Story of the Fifth Australian Division, Captain A.D. Ellis MC

The Tank Corps, Major Clough Williams-Ellis MC and A. Williams-Ellis, 1919

The Tank Corps Honours and Awards: 1916–1919, Midland Medals, Birmingham 1982

The Tanks By Colonel E.D. Swinton CB, DSO Royal Engineers, George H. Doran Company, New York 1918

The Tanks at Flers, T. Pidgeon, Fairmile Books 1995

The Devonshire Regiment 1914–1918, C.T. Atkinson, Elland Brothers, Exeter 1926

The History of the Kings Own Yorkshire. Light Infantry, H.C. Wylly 1926

The History of the Eighth Battalion the Queen's Own Royal West Kent Regiment 1914–1919, 1921

The Story of the 62nd (West Riding Division) 1014–1918, Everard Wyrall, John Lane, London

'Three Weeks on Gallipoli', Harry Murray in *Reveille*, 1st April 1939

The War History of the 4th Battalion The London Regiment (Royal Fusiliers) 1914–1919, Captain F. Clive Grimwade, 1922

To the Last Ridge, W.H. Downing, H.H. Champion Australasian Author's Agency 1920

VCs of The First World War: Passchendaele, Stephen Snelling, Sutton Publishing 1998

UNPUBLISHED SOURCES

'A Hero Saint', compiled by Reverend Gerald Sampson

Lance Corporal Edwin Bull papers. (Courtesy Ross Moon)

Private Harry Catterson's papers. (Courtesy Noeleen Ridgway)

Private Francis Ellison Dare papers. (Courtesy Scott Wilson)

Company Quartermaster Alfred Guppy papers, courtesy (Russell Williams)

2nd Lieutenant Wilfred Hall papers: Courtesy Hugh Hall

'Pedigree of the Jeaffreson Family with Notes and Memoirs', Marie Therese Jeaffreson 1922. (Courtesy Saint Mary Magdalene Church, Enfield)

Corporal Ernest Johns papers. (Courtesy Gerald Foggin)

Private Robert Johnston papers. (Courtesy Teresa Prince)

Private Joseph Kennedy's diary. (Courtesy Ron Wilson)

Private Herbert Thomas papers,. (Courtesy Simon Lamb)

Private William Layburn's papers. (Courtesy Wilf Layburn)

Private Charles Malthouse papers. (Courtesy Joan Coatman)

Rifleman Auguste Pageot papers. (Courtesy Henri Pageot)

Private Leslie Pezet's diary. (Courtesy Ken Pezet)

Corporal Bert Smythe papers. (Courtesy Jacqui Kennedy)

Private Jack Stewart papers. (Courtesy of Lesley Desborough)

Sam Wadeson papers. (Courtesy John Wadeson)

Corporal Ivor William's diary. (Courtesy Hugh Williams)

Private Henry Wood papers. (Courtesy Dave Cooper and Eileen Ring)

'World War 1 Experiences of my Grandfather'. (Courtesy Gordon Wills)

NEWSPAPERS AND JOURNALS

All Hallows School Magazine, Honiton

Derby Mercury: 1st June 1917

Hamilton Spectator: 1917

Harrogate Herald: 20 June 1917

Harrogate Herald: 4 July 1917

Harrogate Herald: 12 December 1917
Harrogate Herald: 29 January 1919
London Gazette: 23 July 1915
London Gazette: 25 July 1916
London Gazette: 14 November 1916
London Gazette: 4 January 1917
London Gazette: 10 March 1917
London Gazette: 26 March 1917
London Gazette: 4 April 1917
London Gazette: 25 May 1917
London Gazette: 26 May 1917
London Gazette: 14 June 1917
London Gazette: 15 June 1917
London Gazette: 26 June 1917
London Gazette: 17 July 1917
London Gazette: 24 July 1917
London Gazette: 16 August 1917
London Gazette: 14 August 1917
London Gazette: 25 August 1917
London Gazette: 6 November 1917
London Gazette: 4 January 1918
London Gazette: 13 September 1918
Oban Times: 16 March 1918
Reveille: 30 April 1931: Lance Corporal Bert Knowles testimony
Reveille: 29 May 1931
Reveille: 1 April 1933: Sergeant Douglas Blackburn's testimony
Reveille: 1 April 1933: Lieutenant William Boland MC (and Bar) testimony
Reveille: 1 April 1933: Lieutenant Colonel Howard Denham's testimony
Reveille: 1 April 1933: Captain David Dunworth MC testimony
Reveille: 1 April 1933: Lieutenant Colonel Raymond Leane's testimony
Reveille: 1 April 1933: Captain Harry Murray's testimony
Reveille: 1 April 1933: Major Alban George Moyes MC testimony
Reveille: 1 September 1933
Reveille: 1 January 1934
Reveille: 1 May 1935: Sergeant Max McDowall's testimony
Reveille: 1 June 1935: Captain N.G. Inlay MC testimony
Reveille: February 1938: R.C. Winn's testimony
Royal Tank Corps Journal
Stratford-upon-Avon Herald: 5 October 1917
The Times: 1917
The War Illustrated: 8 June 1917

AUSTRALIAN WAR MEMORIAL

AWM 1DRL/428/00002: Australian Red Cross Missing File: Private Gladstone Bannatyne
AWM 1DRL428/00002: Australian Red Cross Missing File: Lance Corporal Harold Beechey
AWM 1DRL/428/009: Australian Red Cross Missing File: 2nd Lieutenant James Proctor
AWM 1DRL/428/00004: Australian Red Cross Missing Files: Private Edward Bentley
AWM 1DRL/0428/00002: Australian Red Cross Missing File: 2nd Lieutenant Frank Barnes
AWM 1DRL/428/00004: Australian Red Cross Missing File Private William Birthisel
AWM 1DRL/428/00004: Australian Red Cross Missing File: Captain Frank Boddington
AWM 1DRL/428/00006: Australian Red Cross Missing File: Lance Sergeant Harry Catterson
AWM 1DRL/428/00007: Australian Red Cross Missing File: Sergeant Gordon Chick
AWM 1DRL428/00009: AWM: Red Cross Missing File: Lance Corporal Archibald Curvey

AWM 1DRL/428/00009: Australian Red Cross File Private Ellison Dare
AWM 1DRL/428/00009: Australian Red Cross Missing File: Private Hubert Demasson
AWM 1DRL428/00010: Australian Red Cross Missing File: Private William Doyle
AWM 1DRL428/00010: Australian Red Cross Missing File: Private John Downs
AWM 1DRL428/00010: Australian Red Cross File: Captain Frank Dunn
AWM 1DRL/428/00011: Australian Red Cross Missing Files: Private Arthur Emmins
AWM 1DRL/428/00013: Australian Red Cross Missing File: Private George Fraser
AWM 1DRL428/00013: Australian Red Cross Missing File: 2nd Lieutenant Simon Fraser
AWM 1DRL428/00015: Australian Red Cross Missing File: Sergeant Alfred Guppy
AWM28/1/273/0015: Captain Alfred Morris bar to MC recommendation
AWM 1DRL428/00016: Australian Red Cross Missing File: Private Joe Heady
AWM 1DRL428/00017: Australian Red Cross Missing File: Captain Eric Hogarth
AWM 1DRL428/00018: Australian Red Cross File: Private Claude Jones
AWM 1DRL428/00020: Australian Red Cross File: Private John Laing
AWM 1DRL428/00021: Australian Red Cross File Lance Corporal William Layburn
AWM 1DRL428/00021: Australian Red Cross Missing File Lieutenant Benno Lehmann
AWM 1DRL/428/00021: Australian Red Cross Missing File: Major Benjamin Leane
AWM 1DRL428/00027: Australian Red Cross Missing File: Private Henry Olsen
AWM 1DRL/428/00023: Australian Red Cross Missing File: Captain Gordon Maxfield
AWM 1DRL/428/00023: Australian Red Cross Missing File: Private Michael Meenhan
AWM 1DRL/428/000023: Australian Red Cross Missing File: Private Joseph Miller
AWM 1DRL428/00024: Australian Red Cross Missing File: Private Frederick Morley
AWM 1DRL428/00024: Australian Red Cross Missing File: Private Arthur Morris
AWM 1DRL428/00026: Australian Red Cross Missing File Private Ernest Noy
AWM 1DRL428/00027: Australian Red Cross Missing Files: Private Alfred Oxman
AWM 1DRL1:428/00027: Australian Red Cross Missing: Private James Paul
AWM 1DRL428/00028: Australian Red Cross Missing File: Private Arthur Perman
AWM 1DRL428/00029: Australian Red Cross Missing File: 2nd Lieutenant James Proctor
AWM 1DRL428/00030: Australian Red Cross Missing File: Private Charles Rosenwax
AWM 1DRL428/00032: Australian Red Cross Missing File: Private Albert Shillabeer
AWM 1DRL428/0032: Australian Red Cross Missing File: Private Robert Sharp
AWM 1DRL428/00032: Australian Red Cross Missing File Captain Joseph Slater
AWM 1DRL/428/00034: Australian Red Cross Missing File: Private James Swasbrick
AWM 1DRL428/00035: Australian Red Cross Missing File Private Andre Tolstoi
AWM 1DRL428/00035: Australian Red Cross Missing File Sergeant John Touzel
AWM 1DRL428/00035: Australian Red Cross File Major George Tostevin
AWM 1DRL428/00036: Australian Red Cross Missing File: Lance Corporal Samuel Wadeson
AWM 1DRL428/00037: Australian Red Cross Missing File: Private Edward White
AWM 1DRL428/00039: Australian Red Cross Missing File: Private Arthur Zowe
AWM 2DRL/0268: Sergeant William Charles Groves Papers
AWM 28/1/24P1/0055: Lance Corporal Alonzo Hudson DCM recommendation
AWM 28//1/24P2/0071: Lieutenant Benno Lehmann's MC recommendation
AWM 28/1/87/0084: Captain Jack Lloyd MC recommendation
AWM 28/1/1/87/0267: Chaplain Francis Durnford MC recommendation
AWM 28/1/69/0071: Captain Frank Dunn MC recommendation
AWM 28/1/86/0032. Private Albert John McMahon, Private Ernest Elliott, Private Thomas Bourke and Private Sydney
Bond DCM recommendation
AWM 28/1/95P2/0018: Private William Layburn MM recommendation
AWM 28/1/95P2/0039: Captain Jack Lloyd bar to MC recommendation
AWM 28/1/95P2/0041: Lieutenant Viv Smythe bar to MC recommendation
AWM 28/1/128/0092: Private Maurice Bercovitch MM recommendation
AWM 28/1/183P1/0014: Sergeant Peter Kibble DCM recommendation
AWM 28/1/183P/0085: Lance Corporal John Williamson MM recommendation
AWM 28/1/198/0004: Captain Harry Murray Bar to DSO recommendation
AWM 28/1/198/0018: Sergeant Alfred Guppy MM recommendation

AWM 28/1/198/0057: Private George Gilson MM recommendation
AWM 28/1/198/0082: Private Percy Larratt, MM recommendation
AWM 28/198/1/0085: Lance Corporal George Ball MM recommendation
AWM 28/1/198/0085: Sergeant Henry Choules recommendation
AWM 28/1/198/0086: Private Leonard Rzeszkowski MM recommendation
AWM 28/1/198/0090: Private William Affleck, MM recommendation
AWM 28/1/198/0094: Privates Elliott Buswell, Rowland Taylor and Patrick Fox, MM recommendation
AWM 28/1/198/0095: Private Thomas Caldwell: MM recommendation
AWM 28/1/198/0132: Sergeant Robert Rafferty, MM recommendation
AWM28/1/198/0133: Corporal Tom Loxton, MM recommendation
AWM 28/1/246/0070: Sgt. Douglas Blackburn's MM recommendation
AWM 28/1/255P1/0030: Captain Alfred Morris MC recommendation
AWM PR00030: Letter of Condolence from Lieutenant Colonel Charles Denehy to the widow of Lieutenant Wilfred Barlow, 58th Battalion. Chapter 15
AWM 28/1/22/0006: Corporal George Howell MM recommendation
AWM 28/2/78/0004: Distinguished Service Order Recommendation: Lieutenant Harold Wanliss
AWM 28/2/308/0040: Captain Albert Jacka MC recommendation
AWM 28/2/308/0057: Captain Albert Jacka MC recommendation
AWM PR00030: Papers of Lt. W. Barlow, 58th Battalion
AWM PR83/018 Private George Edward King

GORDON HIGHLANDERS MUSEUM

Captain W.N. Brown papers
Major David Palithorpe account

IMPERIAL WAR MUSEUM DEPARTMENT OF DOCUMENTS

IWM Ref: Misc 2165: Anonymous Rifleman from the Post Office Rifles account
IWM Ref: 79/25/1: Private W.G. Bishop 2nd / 1st London Regiment
IWM Con Shelf: Private Oswald Blows IWM Con Shelf
IWM 6/5/17: Private Arthur Burke, 20th Battalion Manchester Regiment
IWM Ref: Misc 2165: Rifleman Thomas Edward Crook, No.13 Platoon 2nd/8th Battalion London Regiment, The Post Office Rifles
IWM Docs Fourth Army papers: Proposals for attack on 15th September 1916
IWM REF 7376 76/169/1: Magnus McIntyre Hood
IWM Ref: 89/7/1: Private Walter King 8519, 13th Platoon, 19th Company 2nd / 2nd London Regiment
IWM Ref: 12281: Brigadier T.S. Louch 51st Battalion
IWM Ref: 7266 / 76/65/1: Captain W.C.D. Maile testimony

IMPERIAL WAR MUSEUM DEPARTMENT OF SOUND

IWM Ref: 494: Lieutenant Ralph Cooney
IWM: Ref: MISC 95(1457) Private Willie Greaves, 2nd/ 6th Battalion West Yorkshire Regiment: Letter 25th July 1981
IWM Ref: 7029: Corporal Ernie Hayward MM, D Battalion Machine Gun Corps Heavy Branch
IWM Ref: IWM 9488: Private William Parry-Morris, 2nd Battalion Honourable Artillery Company
IWM Reference: 4260: A. Wilson

JEAN AND DENISE LETAILLE BULLECOURT MUSEUM

Private Montague Calder Papers

KEEP MILITARY MUSEUM OF DEVONSHIRE AND DORSET

2nd Lieutenant Charles Stewart Diary

NATIONAL ARCHIVES

WO 95/97: 1st Brigade Tank Corps Headquarters
WO 95/1047: Lieutenant General Julien Byng's report on the actions of the tank on 15th September 1916
WO 95/1047 Major General R.E. Turner's report on the actions of the tank on 15th September 1916
WO 95/1047: Captain A. Ingliss Report of Operations of the Tanks of No.1 Section 'C' Company' H.S.M.G.C
WO 95/1047: Lieutenant F.W. Bluemel report
WO 95/ 1655: 2nd Battalion Border Regiment War Diary
WO 95/1655: 8th Battalion Devonshire Regiment War Diary
WO 95/1661: 22nd Infantry Brigade War Diary
WO 95/1664: 2nd Battalion Queen's (Royal West Surrey) Regiment War Diary
WO 95/1664: 2nd Battalion Royal Warwickshire Regiment War Diary
WO 95/1665: 1st Battalion Royal Welch Fusiliers War Diary
WO 95/1667: 91st Infantry Brigade War Diary
WO 95/1670: 2nd Battalion Queen's (Royal West Surrey) Regiment War Diary: Lt R.L. Atkinson, CO B Coy Report
WO 95/1670: 1st Battalion South Staffordshire Regiment War Diary: Lieutenant Colonel A.B. Beauman's report: 12th May 1917
WO 95/3001: 2nd/4th Battalion London Regiment War Diary
WO 95/3002: 174th Brigade War Diary
WO 95/3002: Major A.J. Ford, 2nd/6th Battalion London Regiment Report
WO 95/3005: 2nd/6th Battalion London Regiment: War Diary
WO 95/3006: 2nd / 8th London Regiment (The Post Office Rifles) War Diary
WO 95/3079: 185th Brigade War Diary
WO 95/3082: 2nd/6th Battalion West Yorkshire Regiment War Diary
WO 95/3082: 2nd/7th Battalion West Yorkshire Regiment War Diary
WO 95/3084: 186th Brigade War Diary
WO 95/3087: 2nd/6th Battalion Duke of Wellington Regiment War Diary
WO 95/3088: 187th Brigade War Diary
WO 95/3217: 1st AIF Battalion War Diary
WO 95/3343: 28th Battalion War Diary
WO095/3443 HQ: Branches and Services General Staff, 4th Australian Division Nov 1916–June 1917 Appendix 39 by Major General Holmes
WO 95/3322: 6th Brigade War Diary
WO 95/3491: 13th Battalion AIF War Diary
WO 95/3494: 14th Battalion AIF War Diary
WO 95/3498: 15th Battalion AIF War Diary
WO 95/3499: 16th Battalion AIF War Diary
WO 95/3506: 12th Brigade War Diary
WO 95/3510: 46th Battalion AIF War Diary
WO 95/3514: 48th Battalion AIF War Diary
WO 95/3629: 54th Battalion AIF War Diary
WO 95/4344: 9th Battalion AIF War Diary
WO 158/137: Haig to Nivelle 12th April 1917
WO/161/99/194: Private John Lee 4534, 14th Battalion AIF: POW Report
WO 161/100/93: Private Thomas Ensor 2207, 16th Battalion AIF: POW Report
WO/161/100/494: Sergeant Percy Fleming 2835, 15th Battalion AIF: POW Report
WO/161/100/479: Private Claude Benson, 16th Battalion AIF, Prisoner of War Report
WO 161/96/28: Captain John Mott, 48th Battalion AIF: Prisoner of War Report
WO 161/100/250: Private Alfred Lister, 2nd/6th Battalion West Yorkshire Regiment POW Report
WO 95/3079 185th Brigade War Diary

NATIONAL ARCHIVES OF AUSTRALIA

Private William Campbell service record
Sergeant Gordon Chick service record
Private Hubert Demasson servicer
Private Alexander Gloster service record
Sergeant Alfred Guppy service record
Private John Laing service record
Brigadier John Lloyd service record
Private Joseph Miller service record
Private Frederick Morley service record
Private Jack Stewart service record
Private Thomas Taylor service record
Captain Percy Toft service record
Corporal Stan Richards service record
Lieutenant Harold Wanliss service record
Private Edward White service record

LIDDLE COLLECTION: UNIVERSITY OF LEEDS

Lance Corporal Hugh Orr interview: Liddle Collection: Reference Tape 239
Private James Moddrel Diary
Private Hubert Hobbs Diary

TANK MUSEUM

Records of D Battalion Heavy Branch Machine Gun Corps

INDEX

416

INDEX

The History Press
The destination for history
www·thehistorypress·co·uk